S0-BXO-892

A HISTORICAL AND ECONOMIC GEOGRAPHY OF OTTOMAN GREECE

WITHDRAWN
UTSA LIBRARIES

HESPERIA SUPPLEMENTS

1* S. Dow, *Prytaneis: A Study of the Inscriptions Honoring the Athenian Councillors* (1937)
2* R. S. Young, *Late Geometric Graves and a Seventh-Century Well in the Agora* (1939)
3* G. P. Stevens, *The Setting of the Periclean Parthenon* (1940)
4* H. A. Thompson, *The Tholos of Athens and Its Predecessors* (1940)
5* W. B. Dinsmoor, *Observations on the Hephaisteion* (1941)
6* J. H. Oliver, *The Sacred Gerusia* (1941)
7* G. R. Davidson and D. B. Thompson, *Small Objects from the Pnyx:* I (1943)
8* *Commemorative Studies in Honor of Theodore Leslie Shear* (1949)
9* J. V. A. Fine, *Horoi: Studies in Mortgage, Real Security, and Land Tenure in Ancient Athens* (1951)
10* L. Talcott, B. Philippaki, G. R. Edwards, and V. R. Grace, *Small Objects from the Pnyx:* II (1956)
11* J. R. McCredie, *Fortified Military Camps in Attica* (1966)
12* D. J. Geagan, *The Athenian Constitution after Sulla* (1967)
13 J. H. Oliver, *Marcus Aurelius: Aspects of Civic and Cultural Policy in the East* (1970)
14 J. S. Traill, *The Political Organization of Attica* (1975)
15* S. V. Tracy, *The Lettering of an Athenian Mason* (1975)
16 M. K. Langdon, *A Sanctuary of Zeus on Mount Hymettos* (1976)
17 T. L. Shear Jr., *Kallias of Sphettos and the Revolt of Athens in 268 B.C.* (1978)
18* L. V. Watrous, *Lasithi: A History of Settlement on a Highland Plain in Crete* (1982)
19* *Studies in Attic Epigraphy, History, and Topography Presented to Eugene Vanderpool* (1982)
20* *Studies in Athenian Architecture, Sculpture, and Topography Presented to Homer A. Thompson* (1982)
21 J. E. Coleman, *Excavations at Pylos in Elis* (1986)
22 E. J. Walters, *Attic Grave Reliefs That Represent Women in the Dress of Isis* (1988)
23 C. Grandjouan, *Hellenistic Relief Molds from the Athenian Agora* (1989)
24* J. S. Soles, *The Prepalatial Cemeteries at Mochlos and Gournia and the House Tombs of Bronze Age Crete* (1992)
25 S. I. Rotroff and J. H. Oakley, *Debris from a Public Dining Place in the Athenian Agora* (1992)
26 I. S. Mark, *The Sanctuary of Athena Nike in Athens: Architectural Stages and Chronology* (1993)
27 N. A. Winter, ed., *Proceedings of the International Conference on Greek Architectural Terracottas of the Classical and Hellenistic Periods, December 12–15, 1991* (1994)
28 D. A. Amyx and P. Lawrence, *Studies in Archaic Corinthian Vase Painting* (1996)
29 R. S. Stroud, *The Athenian Grain-Tax Law of 374/3 B.C.* (1998)
30 J. W. Shaw, A. Van de Moortel, P. M. Day, and V. Kilikoglou, *A LM IA Ceramic Kiln in South-Central Crete: Function and Pottery Production* (2001)
31 J. K. Papadopoulos, *Ceramicus Redivivus: The Early Iron Age Potters' Field in the Area of the Classical Athenian Agora* (2003)
32 J. Wiseman and K. Zachos, eds., *Landscape Archaeology in Southern Epirus, Greece* I (2003)
33 A. P. Chapin, ed., *ΧΑΡΙΣ: Essays in Honor of Sara A. Immerwahr* (2004)

* *Out of print*

Hesperia Supplement 34

A HISTORICAL AND ECONOMIC GEOGRAPHY OF OTTOMAN GREECE

The Southwestern Morea in the 18th Century

FARIBA ZARINEBAF, JOHN BENNET, AND JACK L. DAVIS

WITH CONTRIBUTIONS BY
EVI GOROGIANNI, DEBORAH K. HARLAN,
MACHIEL KIEL, PIERRE A. MACKAY,
JOHN WALLRODT, AND AARON D. WOLPERT

The American School of Classical Studies at Athens
2005

Copyright © 2005
The American School of
Classical Studies at Athens

All rights reserved.

To order, contact:
(in North America)
The David Brown Book Company
www.davidbrownbookco.com
Tel. 800-791-9354

(outside North America)
Oxbow Books
www.oxbowbooks.com
Tel. +44 (0) 1865-241-249

Out-of-print *Hesperia* supplements
may be purchased from:
    Royal Swets & Zeitlinger
    Swets Backsets Service
    P.O. Box 810
    2160 SZ Lisse
    The Netherlands
    E-mail: backsets@nl.swets.com

Cover illustration: **View of Anavarin-i cedid and the bay of Navarino, ca. 1829.**
M. M. Puillon de Boblaye and T. Virlet, *Expédition scientifique de Morée: Section des sciences physiques* 5. *Atlas* (Paris 1835) pl. VII

Library of Congress Cataloging-in-Publication Data

A historical and economic geography of Ottoman Greece : the southwestern Morea
    in the 18th century / Fariba Zarinebaf, John Bennet, and Jack L. Davis ; with
    contributions by Evi Gorogianni . . . [et al.].
       p.   cm.—(Hesperia Supplement ; 34)
    Includes bibliographical references and index.
    ISBN 0-87661-534-5 (alk. paper)
    1. Pylos (Greece)—Historical geography. 2. Pylos (Greece)—Economic
conditions—18th century. I. Title: Southwestern Morea in the 18th century.
II. Zarinebaf, F. (Fariba), 1959– III. Hesperia (Princeton, N.J.). Supplement ; 34.

DF951.P85H57 2005
330.9495′22—dc22   2005048185

Library
University of Texas
at San Antonio

Dedicated to our Turkish and Greek students in hope of promoting a better understanding of a shared history and common humanity.

The authors also dedicate this volume to Halil İnalcık, and to the memory of Nionios Androutsakis, William A. McDonald, and Peter Topping.

CONTENTS

ILLUSTRATIONS

All illustrations are also on the CD-ROM, most in color.

TABLES

PREFACE AND ACKNOWLEDGMENTS

This book represents a first attempt by its three authors to compose a social and economic history of the Morea (the Greek Peloponnese) in the 15th through 18th centuries that extensively incorporates information drawn from Turkish sources. It also includes a translation and detailed analysis of an Ottoman cadastral survey of A.D. 1716, *Tapu Tahrir* 880 (TT880), that included the small part of the Morea that, in the early 1990s, was the focus of multidisciplinary archaeological, geological, and historical research supported by the Pylos Regional Archaeological Project (PRAP).[1]

Zarinebaf, an Ottomanist, traveled twice (in 1995 and 1997) to Istanbul on behalf of PRAP. Her research in the Başbakanlık Archives (the prime minister's archives in Istanbul) had two objectives: to provide documentation for the overview that is here presented as Chapter 1, and to collect information sufficiently detailed to permit Bennet and Davis to compose, with her guidance, a human geography specifically for the Pylos area. Most of PRAP's study area belonged to the Ottoman *kaza* (judicial district) of Anavarin (i.e., Greek Navarino, the area around modern Pylos), though small parts belonged to the adjacent districts of Andrusa (to the east) and Arkadiye (to the north). At the center of Anavarin was the fortress of Anavarin-i cedid (Neokastro or Niokastro in Greek), today still well preserved at the southern outskirts of the modern town of Pylos.[2]

In the Başbakanlık Archives (BBA), Zarinebaf's goal in 1995 was to identify in a general way texts that were most pertinent. This research was by no means exhaustive and sought only to identify relevant registers that were already catalogued by the archivists.[3] The documents described below were considered.

---

1. This cadastral survey had never previously been the target of a detailed scholarly examination when we began our research. Coincidentally, while this volume was in production, there appeared in print a valuable discussion of the social and economic organization of the city of Kyparissia (Ottoman Arka-diye) in 1716, as it is reflected in the text of TT880 (Parveva 2003). This paper forms a useful complement to our volume. Parveva is continuing research with case studies of other settlements in the district of Arkadiye.

2. See Bennet, Davis, and Zarine-baf-Shahr 2000, pp. 352–357, and Appendix III below, regarding the history of this settlement.

3. We found no *mufassal* registers for the 17th-century Morea immediately prior to the Venetian conquest of 1685, although M. Kiel (pers. comm.) has informed us that one exists.

I. *Tapu tahrir*s (TT). These are surveys of land grants (*timar*s, *zeᶜamet*s, and *hass*es), including both *mufassal* (detailed) *defter*s (cadastral surveys) and *icmal* (summary) *defter*s (lists of land grants given to military staff and members of the bureaucracy). For the Morea, the earliest *tapu tahrir defter* dates to the reign of Mehmed II (15th century) and the latest to the 18th century (A.H. 1138/A.D. 1725).[4] There are approximately 24 *tapu tahrir defter*s for the Morea in the Başbakanlık Archives.[5] Sixteen are of special interest and were examined in detail, though not all of them contain information specific to Anavarin:

1. TT10 (Mehmed II; second half of the 15th century). *Maliye* (Finance Bureau). 191 pp. *Mufassal defter.* Includes the districts *(nahiye)* of Korintos (Corinth), Klavrita (Kalavrita), Londar (Leondari), and Arkadiye (Arkadia).[6]

2. TT80 (Selim I; early 16th century [1512–1520]). *Maliye.* 1,241 pp. *Mufassal defter.* The most detailed *mufassal defter* for the Morea as a whole.

3. TT367 (Sultan Süleyman I, *kanuni;* mid-16th century [1520–1566]).[7] *Dahiliyye* (Internal Affairs Bureau). 453 pp. *İcmal defter* of Karlı-eli (Aitolia), Eğriboz (Euboia), Modon (Methoni), Tirhala (Trikala), Yanya (Ioannina), Ohri (Ohrid), and Elbasan (in central Albania). Contains the tax regulations *(kanunname)* of the Morea.[8]

4. TT446 (mid-16th century).[9] *Maliye.* 759 pp. *Mufassal defter* of Korintos (Corinth), Anabolu (Nafplion), Arhos (Argos), Karitena (Karitaina), and Modon (Methoni).

5. TT509 (A.H. 979/A.D. 1571). *Maliye.* 291 pp. *Timar. İcmal defter* of Modon (Methoni), Holomiç (Hlemoutsi), Korintos (Corinth), Kalamata, Arhos (Argos), Klavrita (Kalavrita), Karitena (Karitaina), Balye Badre (Patras), and Arkadiye (Arkadia).

6. TT565 (Selim II; A.H. 979/A.D. 1571). 88 pp. *İcmal defter* of Mezistre (Mystras).

7. TT605 (A.H. 991/A.D. 1583). *Maliye.* 551 pp. *Mufassal defter* of Arhos (Argos), Karitena (Karitaina), Poliçe (Tripolitsa), Koron (Koroni), and Korintos (Corinth).

8. TT607 (A.H. 991/A.D. 1583). *Maliye.* 614 pp. *Mufassal defter* of the Morea. Includes Balye Badre (Patras), Arkadiye (Arkadia), Klavrita (Kalavrita), Korintos (Corinth), and Holomiç (Hlemoutsi).[10]

---

4. On the conversion of Islamic dates to the Christian calendar, see Freeman-Grenville 1995. We here give the Christian year in which the first day of the Islamic year fell.

5. For a description of the 16th-century *defter*s relevant to the Morea, see Alexander 1998, pp. 217–222.

6. Alexander 1978; Beldiceanu and Beldiceanu-Steinherr 1980, 1986. See Beldiceanu and Beldiceanu-Steinherr

1986 for a study of parts of this document relevant to the region of Corinth. Corinth is variously spelled in Ottoman *defter*s (Pitcher 1972, p. 158). Beldiceanu and Beldiceanu-Steinherr (1980, p. 20) suggest a date of 1461 for the document.

7. Alexander (1998, p. 219) suggests a date of ca. 1528.

8. See Barkan 1943, pp. 326–332; Alexander 1985a, pp. 187–196, 363–

374 (English translation); and Balta 1993, pp. 39–46 (Greek translation).

9. Alexander (1998, pp. 219–220) discusses the date of this document and attributes it to the reign of Süleyman I (1520–1566).

10. This document also contains a *kanunname:* Alexander 1985a, pp. 196–197, 374–375; Balta 1993, pp. 47–48.

9. TT777 (A.H. 1022/A.D. 1613). *Maliye. Askeriye* (Military Affairs). List of gunpowder-makers *(barutçiyan)* and musket-sellers *(kundakçıyan)* of the fortresses of the Morea, Eğriboz (Euboia), and Karlı-eli (Aitolia).

10. TT796 (A.H. 1076/A.D. 1665). *Maliye.* 36 pp. *Mukataʿa* (tax-farm) of the fortress of Kordos (Corinth) and its suburb *(varış).*

11. TT876 (A.H. 1127/A.D. 1715). *Maliye.*

12. TT878 (A.H. 1127/A.D. 1715). *Maliye.* 97 pp. *Mufassal defter.*

13. TT880 (A.H. 1128/A.D. 1716). *Maliye.* 101 pp. *Mufassal defter* of Arkadiye (Arkadia) and Anavarin (Navarino).[11] This *defter* is the most detailed register for Anavarin.

14. TT881 (A.H. 1128/A.D. 1715). 712 pp. *Timar. Ruzname* (grants from *timar*s) for Anabolu (Nafplion), Anavarin (Navarino), Kordos (Corinth), and Modon (Methoni).[12]

15. TT884 (A.H. 1128/A.D. 1715). *Maliye.* 504 pp. Record of the takeover of Venetian and local property. Lists of landholdings in the Morea, including new Muslim as well as old Christian and Venetian owners of urban property. Venetian possessions that were in Ottoman hands prior to 1685 are especially noted. There is less detail than in TT880, a document that it probably summarized.

16. TT890 (A.H. 1131/A.D. 1718). *Askeriye.* 110 pp. Fortresses of Anabolu (Nafplion), Koron (Koroni), and Baliye Badre (Patras).

II. *Ahkam* (imperial orders), *şikayet* (imperial orders), and *mühimme* (important affairs) *defter*s.[13] These are copies of imperial orders to provincial officials and address political, administrative, financial, and military matters, usually issued in response to complaints from local officials and imperial subjects *(reaya).* The *ahkam defter*s that contain references to the Morea in the 18th and 19th centuries include:

*Mora Ahkam Defter*s
vol. 1 (1716–1729), 258 pp.
vol. 2 (1717–1750), 221 pp.
vol. 3 (1742–1746), 290 pp.
vol. 4 (1742–1749), 296 pp.
vol. 5 (1749–1753), 152 pp.
vol. 6 (1753–1768), 350 pp.
vol. 7 (1758–1762), 364 pp.
vol. 8 (1762–1765), 374 pp.
vol. 9 (1765–1775), 374 pp.
vol. 10 (1775–1797), 144 pp.
vol. 11 (1775–1779), 396 pp.

11. There is a second manuscript of TT880 in Ankara, but the Istanbul version appears to be the original. M. Kiel (pers. comm., 2002) has examined both manuscripts and writes that "the Istanbul version is the basis for the Ankara version. The Istanbul register is far too well written to be a simple hurried copy. The Ankara version (Tapu ve Kadastro Genel Müdürlüğü 15) must have been a copy made to present to the sultan and is adorned with miniatures (vegetative ornaments) and thick gilded frames."

12. TT881 and TT884 must date to A.D. 1716.

13. *Şikayet defter*s pertain to imperial orders issued in response to petitions by the *reaya*, in contrast to the *ahkam defter*s, which are responses to petitions by provincial officials and the military.

vol. 12 (1775–1797), 144 pp.
vol. 13 (1783–1785), 120 pp.
vol. 14 (1785–1794), 330 pp.
vol. 15 (1794–1795), 130 pp.
vol. 16 (1795–1799), 304 pp.
vol. 17 (1801–1806), 302 pp.
vol. 18 (1806–1809), 216 pp.
vol. 19 (1809–1814), 260 pp.
vol. 20 (1814–1819), 198 pp.
vol. 21 (1819–1840), 138 pp.

The *mühimme, ahkam,* and *şikayet defter*s cover the entire Ottoman empire from the mid-16th century to the end of the 18th century. They contain scattered references to the Morea and are an especially significant source for the study of relationships between center and periphery and for insights regarding local problems. Because there are hundreds of volumes, they have not yet been examined in detail for information relevant to the area of Anavarin, but selected cases recorded in them are discussed in Chapter 1. In addition to the preceding sources, reference is made in a few instances to information drawn from financial records of the office of the head accountant (*Baş Muhasebe defter*s), and of the Topkapı Palace *(Cevdet Saray)*.

Soon after Zarinebaf's return to the United States in the fall of 1995, we discovered the extraordinary toponymic richness of TT880 and realized its particular historical significance. Its text had been prepared immediately following the Ottoman reconquest of the Morea in 1715. Venice abandoned Anavarin-i cedid on August 10, the conquest of the Morea was completed when Manafşe (Monemvasia) surrendered on September 7, and TT880 was already registered in Istanbul on January 15, 1716.[14] In many instances, the locations even of individual fields are noted.[15]

By the summer of 1997, a translation of those parts of TT880 that included the district of Anavarin had been prepared, and Bennet and Davis traveled to Pylos to gather evidence that would permit toponyms to be located more securely.[16] It soon became clear to them that several parts of the PRAP study area had lain outside the *kaza* of Anavarin in 1716. The modern towns of Hora and Gargaliani were in the *kaza* of Arkadiye (centered on modern Kyparissia, formerly called Arkadia), while the village of Maryeli[17] and its immediate vicinity belonged to the *kaza* of Andrusa.

Zarinebaf made a second study trip to Istanbul in the late summer and early fall of 1997. Her principal goal on that occasion was to gather

14. Such alacrity may not have been unusual. On Crete it is clear that a cadastral survey was carried out between A.H. 1080/A.D. 1669–1670 (the conquest) and A.H. 1084/A.D. 1673–1674, as TT825 attests. The grand vizier, Köprülü Fazil Ahmed Pasha, the conqueror of Crete, left the island in the spring of 1670, and

Greene (2000, p. 23 and n. 38) has suggested that the survey had been conducted under his supervision before his departure.

15. We thought that the information about settlement and land use recorded in TT880 could profitably be contrasted with similar information for the years A.D. 1688–1715 being col-

lected in Venice on behalf of PRAP by Siriol Davies. See this volume, passim, and Davies 2004.

16. Their methods are described in Chapter 3.

17. See Lee 2001 with regard to the modern history and material culture of this village.

information about the Ottoman town of Ğarğalian (Gargaliani) and the three villages that today form the town of Hora (Likudise [Ligoudista], Abdul Kadir Ağa [Tsifliki], and Kavalari [Kavalaria]). By the time of the Greek Revolution in 1821, these villages constituted a single center called Hores.[18] It is our intention to publish elsewhere a commentary on those parts of TT880 that describe Likudise, Abdul Kadir Ağa, Kavalari, and Ğarğalian.

Also in 1997, Zarinebaf examined tax-farming registers (*mukataᶜa defter*s) for parts of the 18th century (DBŞM 1750, 2055, 3998). These records list annual revenues for various types of tax-farms (such as the sheep tax, tax on olive oil, the head tax *[cizye]* from villages, and customs dues) by district, with the name of the tax-farmer *(mültezim)* indicated. Most tax-farmers in Anavarin were Janissary *ağa*s, that is, members of garrisons stationed in the Morea.

ACKNOWLEDGMENTS

It is our pleasure to express our appreciation to those who have helped us in this project. First and foremost, we are grateful to the administration and staff of the Başbakanlık Archives in Istanbul, for their generosity in permitting Zarinebaf to study the Ottoman documents discussed in this volume, and for giving her continuing access to the Ottoman archives. Zarinebaf appreciates help received from the American Research Institute in Turkey (ARIT), whose facilities she enjoyed while in Istanbul. She thanks Professor Halil İnalcık, who taught her how to question the traditional historiography of the Ottoman empire through critical study of sources in the central archives as well as local documentation. She also thanks Anthony Greenwood, director of ARIT in Istanbul, Ariel Salzmann of Queens University, Richard Beal of the Oriental Institute of the University of Chicago, and Joann Scurlock of Elmhurst College, for their endorsement of this project and for suggestions and comments that have helped guide the research. Finally, she thanks the Regenstein Library at the University of Chicago, the Center for Middle Eastern Studies at the University of Chicago, the Department of History of Northwestern University, and her family for their continuing support.

Bennet and Davis appreciate the assistance of the many residents of Messenia who were subjected to barrages of questions during visits to their villages and fields in 1997 and 1998, but who answered with patience and kindness, particularly Andreas Hrysovolis and Panayiotis Papahrysanthakis of Lefki (Mouzousta), and Thanasis P. Koulafetis of Romanou. They acknowledge the help they received from Papa-Fotis, Yiannis and Vicki Markopoulos, and the Matsakas family of Hora, who gladly shared their knowledge of their community and its geography with them.

They are also grateful for the company of their PRAP colleague, Sharon Stocker, who tolerated their sometimes excessive enthusiasm for this project, while trying to make headway in her own research. Her support, and that of Debi Harlan, who accompanied them in Messenia in 1998, has been critical to the success of our enterprise in Greece, in the United Kingdom, and in the United States. Harlan, who has managed records for PRAP

18. See, e.g., the atlas of the Expédition scientifique de Morée, where the villages are individually named, but are collectively labeled "Khoraes" (*Atlas*, pl. III.3). The Expédition scientifique, founded in 1828 through an act of the French government, conducted an archaeological, botanical, entomological, epigraphical, geological, and zoological survey of the Morea from 1829 to 1831. See Bourguet, Lepetit, Nordman, and Sinarellis 1998; Bourguet, Nordman, Panayotopoulos, and Sinarellis 1999; and Peytier 1971. Presumably the plural "Hores" was used instead of the singular "Hora" because the settlement consisted of more than a single village.

since the inception of the project, devised especially for us a computerized database that has facilitated manipulation of all data included in the Ottoman documents.

Rosemary Robertson transformed our crude computer-generated maps into the works of art that grace this book. Bill Alexander and Paul Halstead helped to conduct interviews in Messenia. Bennet and Davis also thank Phoebe Acheson, Evi Gorogianni, and Aaron D. Wolpert, who have ably served the project as research assistants in Cincinnati. In Oxford, we thank Bob Wilkins and Ian Cartwright of the Photographic Department of the Institute of Archaeology. Bennet also thanks the School of Archaeology of Oxford University, the Faculty of Classics of Oxford University, and Keble College for their support of his research.

Hamish Forbes of the University of Nottingham read most of our manuscript in draft and rescued us from many pitfalls in interpreting the agricultural data recorded in TT880. Malcolm Wagstaff and Pamela Catling shared with us their knowledge of Ottoman Greece, while Thurstan Robinson freely offered his expertise in matters concerning the integration of archaeological data and Ottoman texts. Jennifer Moody and Dick Grove supplied us with recent bibliography regarding climate change in the southern Aegean. Sharon Gerstel helped us obtain obscure publications. Siriol Davies has been a constant source of encouragement and support. The staff of the Lloyd Library and Museum in Cincinnati, notably Mary Lee Schmidt, has been especially helpful to us. David Hernandez assisted in the translation of Spanish sources, Hüseyin Öztürk in checking modern Turkish references. Our research would not have been possible without the resources of the Burnam Classics Library of the University of Cincinnati and the enthusiasm of its staff, in particular Jean Wellington, Jacquie Riley, Michael Braunlin, and David Ball. Michael Fitzgerald, our senior editor in the Publications Office of the American School of Classical Studies at Athens, worked miracles with our text, after it was initially edited by Sherry Wert. Sarah George Figueira deserves thanks for typesetting and layout; Carol Stein, Timothy Wardell, and Sara Lerner for help with proofreading; and last, but not least, Kay Banning, for preparing the index.

Finally, we all gladly acknowledge financial support from the National Endowment for the Humanities and from the Semple Fund of the Department of Classics at the University of Cincinnati, which also awarded a Margot Tytus Visiting Scholar fellowship to Bennet in the spring of 2001.

Fariba Zarinebaf
John Bennet
Jack L. Davis

TRANSLITERATION AND PRONUNCIATION

TRANSLITERATION OF MODERN GREEK

For other than common English forms, we have generally used the following scheme for the transliteration of modern Greek into roman letters:

Greek	roman	Greek	roman
α	a	υ	y
β	v	φ	f
γ	g (before a, o, u)	χ	h
	y (before i, e)	ψ	ps
δ	d	ω	o
ε	e	αι	ai
ζ	z	ει	ei
η	i	οι	i (final)
θ	th		oi (medial)
ι	i	αυ	af, av
κ	k	ευ	ef, ev
λ	l	ου	ou
μ	m	μπ	mb (medial)
ν	n		b (initial)
ξ	x	γγ	ng, g
ο	o	γκ	ng
π	p	τσ	ts
ρ	r	ντ	nd (medial)
σ, ς	s		d (initial)
τ	t	τζ	tz

PRONUNCIATION OF TURKISH

Modern Turkish uses an adapted form of the Latin alphabet, with the following exceptions or special characters:

Consonants

c   *j* (as in "Jack")
ç   *ch* (as in "church")
ğ   lengthens preceding vowel:
     dağ = "daa"; also used to
     represent Greek "gamma"
ş   *sh* (as in "sheep")

Vowels

â   long *a* (as in "bar")
ı, I   neutral vowel (as in second
     syllable of "women")
i, İ   short *i* (as in "dig") or
     long *i* (as in "machine"),
     depending on context
î   long *i* (as in "machine")
ö   as *ö* in German
ü   as *ü* in German, or French *u*,
     as in "lune"

TRANSLITERATION OF TURKISH

For other than common English forms (e.g., pasha, Istanbul), we have generally followed Sir James W. Redhouse's *Turkish and English Lexicon, New Edition,* Beirut 1987, for the English transliteration of Ottoman words, with occasional reference to the 1890 edition.

In this book, the plural forms of Turkish words or phrases are usually represented by the simple addition of -s or -es to the singular form.

GLOSSARY OF TERMS

The following terms are Ottoman Turkish unless noted otherwise.

acemi oğlan	boy conscript
adet-i ağnam	sheep tax
adım	pace
ağa	title given to persons employed on a military post
ağnam	sheep (pl.)
ahkam	imperial orders
akçe	Ottoman silver coin
alaybey	group commander in the army
alef	fodder
amelmande	disabled/incapable of work
arşun/arşın	the masonry *arşun*, equivalent to 0.758 meters; same as the *zira'* (q.v.)
arusane	marriage tax
askeri	of the military class, with complete tax exemption
Askeriye	Military Affairs Office
asma	vine trellis
asyab	water mill (see Chap. 2, n. 17)
asyab-i revğan	oil press
ᶜavariz	extraordinary dues and services to meet emergency expenses
avlu	courtyard
ayak	a measure of 1 foot
ayan	local notables
ayrancı	a maker of *ayran*, a chilled yogurt and water drink
ayva	quince
azeb	an unmarried young man; an auxiliary footman; a fighting man in the navy
babucı	shoemaker
bacaluşka-top	large heavy siege gun
bac-i bazaar	market dues
bac-i himr	tax on alcoholic drinks
bac-i siyah	transit dues
badem	almond

bad-i hava ve cürmü cinayet	crime tax from fines
bağ	vineyard, garden
bağçe	orchard
bakla	broad bean
barutçiyan	gunpowder manufacturers
Başbakanlık Arşivi	Prime Minister's Archives
başhane	market dues on head of sheep
bedel-i üşür	tithe in cash
bedeliye-yi işkenciyan	cash payment in substitution for service by irregular troops
berat	imperial certificate
bey	the title of a military commander of a *sancak* (q.v.)
beyaz olunmuşdur	certified copy
beylerbey	governor-general
beytülmal	public treasury; the branch of the public treasury concerned with the division of inheritances
bidᶜat	innovation; may refer to a tax that is an innovation
bive	widow
borgo (Venetian)	suburb of a town, usually located outside the walls of a fortress; same as Ottoman *varış* (q.v.)
boyacı	dyer or painter
bölük	military detachment, squadron, or company
bustan	kitchen garden
büyük	big
casale (Venetian)	hamlet
cerahor	one of a class of workmen employed in the repair of fortresses
ceviz	walnut
cizye	Islamic poll tax imposed on a non-Muslim household
çarşı	market
çavdar	rye
çavuş	sergeant; guard; herald
çayır	meadow
çift	a unit of arable land; the amount of land that could be plowed by one pair of oxen in an agricultural season
çift-hane system	fiscal unit based on a farm given to a peasant family to work by a pair of oxen to meet the family and tax demands
çiftlik	land workable by a peasant family using a pair of oxen; a big farm under the control of an absentee landlord; a plantation-like farm; a village
çift resmi	tax assessed on a Muslim peasant family, parallel to the *ispence* (q.v.) tax levied on non-Muslims
çuka/çuha	(broad) cloth; the island of Kythera

çuval	sack; unit of weight equivalent to two standard Ottoman *kantar*s (q.v.) of approximately 56.5 kilograms, or approximately 113 kilograms
Dahiliyye	Internal Affairs Bureau
dalyan/talyan	fishery
dar al-ḥarb	the abode of war; i.e., non-Muslim lands added to the Ottoman empire by conquest
defter	tax register
defterdar	accountant
delalbaşılık	headship of brokers
demet	bundle or sheaf
deng	one-half of a horse-load
der uhde	undertake
deştbani	tax on wastelands
devşirme	levy of Christian peasant boys for service in the army and the palace
dib	root
direht	tree, in TT880; the more common term was *seçer*
dirhem	a standard unit of weight, equal to 3.207 grams
divân	council
divânı kırması	Ottoman scribal shorthand script
divar	wall
dizdar	fortress commander
dönüm	measurement of surface area for land, equivalent to 919.3 square meters; TT71 (A.D. 1716), the *kanunname* (q.v.) that established the survey that resulted in the *mufassal defter* (q.v.) TT880, defines a *dönüm* as equivalent to 40 *hatve*s (q.v.) in length and width
elaiona (Greek)	olive harvest
ell	English measure, sometimes used to translate Turkish *arşun/arşın*
emin	a superintendent; an agent
emrud	pear
erzen	millet
fermân	imperial edict
fiddan	saplings
fuçı	barrel
gögül	cocoon
hamam	bathhouse
han	guest house
handak	ditch; channel
hane	tax unit based on a household
harab	in ruin
harbi	pertaining to war
haremlik	residence of the women and family

haric az defter   outside the register

hasil   total revenue

hass (has)   private holding; a prebend belonging to the sultan,
                           grand vizier, or another member of the elite with a
                           yearly income of over 100,000 *akçe*s (q.v.)

hassa çiftlik   private farm of a *sipahi* (q.v.) who holds a *timar* (q.v.)

hass-i hümayun   the imperial domain

hass-i mir-liva   revenues belonging to the district commander

hass-i mirmiran   prebend of a pasha of the second class, who governs
                           a province

hatib   preacher

hatve   step; equivalent to the *zira᾽* (q.v.) of 0.758 meters
                           used in TT880 (see also *dönüm*)

havale   sent

hınta   wheat

hınzır   pig (pl. *hinazir*)

hisar   fortress

hisar pece   curtain wall

hisse   share

hüküm   imperial order

icmal defter   summary tax-survey register, as opposed to a
                           mufassal defter (q.v.)

içhisar   the inner keep of a fortress; donjon

ifraz olunmamişdur   (has) not been set aside

ihtisab   market dues

ihtisabiyye   dues of the chief inspector of the market

ihzariyye   tax; expenses of a citation or summons

ikbal   concubine; the sultan's favorite female slave

iltizam   revenue contract

imam   prayer leader

imece   work done for the community by the whole
                           community

incir   fig

ipekhane   workshop for silk production

iskele   port

ispence   head tax paid by a non-Muslim to the holder of a
                           timar (q.v.)

Kaba   the Kaaba at Mecca

kadastro   cadastral survey

kadı   Muslim judge

kadıasker   military judge

kadı sicil   Islamic court record

kahveci   coffee-seller

kâkül   curl

kaldırım   paved road; *kalderimi* in Greek

kale   fortress

kalemiyye   extraordinary dues

kaltaban   pimp; mean or dishonest person

kantar   scales; Ottoman weight standard = 56.5 kilograms

kantariye	scales tax
kanun	imperial law
kanunname	imperial law code
kapan	scales
kapıkulu	imperial guard
kapucı	palace doorkeeper; gatekeeper
kapudan	captain in the Ottoman army
kapudanlık	subdistrict assigned to a captain in the Ottoman navy
kapudan pasha	Ottoman naval commander
karış	tax assessed when must is put in the cask
karye	village
katib	clerk, scribe, or secretary
kaza	a district under the jurisdiction of a judge
kebe	felt
kerhane	a place of work, a workshop, or a factory
ketan	flax
kethüda	steward; the head of a guild, a social and military group
kılıç	registered *timar* unit; sword
kışla	winter pasture or winter residence
kile (Istanbul standard)	capacity measure, equivalent to 16 *vukiyye*s (q.v.) of barley (20.48 kilograms) or 22 *vukiyye*s of wheat (28.16 kilograms)
kiraz	cherry
kirbas	cheap cotton or linen
kirjali	a Slavic form of the Turkish *kiracı*, "tenant"
kolumborna/ kolomborna	long-range gun used on land and at sea
konak	mansion
koruçuluk	guard
kul	a slave; a tax-paying subject of the state; the sultan's servants and soldiery at the Porte
kule	tower
kundakçı	musket-seller
kuruş	Ottoman currency of account, equal to 120 *akçe*s (q.v.) in the 18th century
kuvare	beehive; pannier
küçük	small
küp	(earthenware) jar
kürekçi	oarsman or rower
lağar	skinny
levend	privateer who joined the Ottoman navy; irregular soldier
lidre	standard of weight measurement for silk and cotton, normally equivalent to 100–120 *dirhem*s (q.v.) = 320.7–384.84 grams, but in TT880 explicitly defined as equal to 133 *dirhem*s (426.53 grams)
liman	harbor
limun	lemon
liva	a district and administrative unit

mahalle	a neighborhood within a town
mahkeme	Islamic court
mahsul	crop or yield of an agricultural product
malikane	life-term tax-farm
malikaneci	holder of a *malikane* (q.v.)
Maliye	Finance Bureau
*maliyeden müdevver defter*s	records of the Finance Bureau
mangır	bronze coin
mawat	dead and marginal land usually reclaimed by the state
mazraᶜa	a large farm with no permanent settlement; deserted land or village cultivated by a nearby village
medrese	Islamic college
mekteb	primary Qurᶜan (Koran) school
mengene	press
mercimek	lentils
mescid	small mosque
metohi (Greek)	land owned by a monastery
mevacib	income, salary
mevkuf	given in trust for a pious use; held in abeyance
mevzi	place
meyve	fruits
miranlık	governorship of a province
mîrî	belonging to the ruler or state
mir-liva	district governor
mirmiran	see *hass-i mirmiran*
mizan	scales or balance
muaccele	lump-sum first payment of a tax contractor
mufassal defter	detailed tax-survey register
muhafız	guard
muharir	registrar
muhassıl	tax collector appointed by the governor
muhassıllık	office of the tax collector
muhtesib	market inspector
mukabele	reciprocation
mukabeleci	official who collates documents
mukataᶜa	contract; tax-farm contract
mustahfızân	garrison soldiers of a fortress
mutesellim	deputy lieutenant-governor and collector of taxes
mücerred	unmarried man; household headed by a bachelor
müfettiş	inspector
müfti	Muslim priest or expounder of the law; member of the *ulema* (q.v.) in charge of issuing religious rulings (*fetvas*)
mühimme defter	register of important affairs
mülk	private property
mültezim	tax-farmer
mütenevveᶜe	various
nahiye	administrative district
nar	pomegranate

narh	officially fixed price
nazır	inspector or superintendent
nefer	individual person
nemazgah	prayer hall
nohud	chick-pea
nöbet	term of duty in the military
ocaklık	expenditures for the provisioning of fortresses
oda	Janissary barracks
oka	pre-metric Greek unit of weight (pl. *okades*) equivalent to the Ottoman *okka,* or 1.28 kilograms
okka	see *vukiyye*
orman	forest
ortakçıyan	sharecroppers
otlak	pasture
palamud	acorn
para	Ottoman coin, equivalent to 3 *akçe*s (q.v.); 40 *para*s = 1 *kuruş* (q.v.)
para di bo (Venetian)	unit of measure of surface area of arable land
peksimet	hard biscuit
penbe	cotton
qibla	precise direction toward the Kaaba in Mecca
reale (Venetian)	dollar-size silver coin employed by Venice in the Levant as a currency of account (pl. *reali*), equivalent to 120 *akçe*s (q.v.) ca. A.D. 1700
reaya	productive groups (peasants, merchants, artisans) subject to taxes, in contrast to *askeri* (q.v.) (military), who were tax-exempt
reaya çiftlik	farm over which *reaya* (q.v.) held usufruct
resm	tax
resm-i bennak	tax on a married peasant who holds very little land
resm-i çift	land tax
resm-i dönüm	tax assessed on the surface area of cultivated land
resm-i mücerred	bachelor tax
revğan	olive oil
ruzname	day-book of financial affairs
*sab*ᶜ	one-seventh
salariye	type of agricultural tax
saliyane	yearly stipend; yearly operation
sancak	provincial division
sancakbey	district governor
saray	mansion or palace
sarınc	cistern
sebet	basket (e.g., beehive)
sebzevat	vegetables
seguolatio (Venetian)	*çiftlik* (q.v.)

sekban	mercenary unit, armed with muskets and under the command of a Janissary officer
selamlık	male quarters of Ottoman house
selariye	extraordinary agricultural tax
sérail (French)	mansion or palace, from the Ottoman *saray* (q.v.)
serasker	military commander-in-chief
serhane	slaughterhouse
shariᶜa	Islamic law administered by the *kadı* (q.v.)
shiᶜi	the Shi'ite sect of Islam
sısam	sesame
sicil	register; judicial register
simsarlik	brokerage fee
sipahi	member of the cavalry
sirvat	vegetable patch
siyakat	Ottoman archival script
soğancı	onion-seller
stremma (Greek)	a modern metric unit of area measure (pl. *stremmata*) employed in Greece for the measurement of land and equaling 1,000 square meters; of variable size in Ottoman and Venetian times
su handak	channel of an aqueduct
su kemerler	arches of an aqueduct
sürgün	forceful transfer of populations
şaᶜir	barley
şatirvan	water tank
şeyh	head of a religious order; head preacher or teacher
şıre	must (grape juice)
şikayet	petition submitted by the *reaya* (q.v.) and officials to the members of the imperial council in Istanbul
şikayet defter	register of *şikayet* (q.v.) petitions
tabya	bastion of a fortress
tağdir veset	mountain land of medium quality
tahrir	registration; Ottoman system of surveying land, population, and sources of revenue
tahrirci	an official charged with compiling a written survey of a province
tamam-i sal	in operation all year
tapu	land deed
tapu tahrir	cadastral survey
tapu-yi zemin	tax on land deeds
tarla	a field of arable land
tasarruf	in possession of
taşlık	rocky place
temessük	bill acknowledging a claim or debt
tercüman	interpreter (dragoman)
tercümanlık	office of the interpreter (dragoman)
*tereke defter*s	records of the estates of the deceased

timar	prebend in the form of state taxes in return for regular military service, conventionally less than 20,000 *akçe*s (q.v.) in value
topçu	cannoneer
tulum	granulous curd
turunc	Seville orange
tut	mulberry
tüfenkçi	musket-seller
ulema	members of a Muslim religious hierarchy
usta	"master"; rank in a guild, the military, or other context
üşür	tithe (not always one-tenth; one-seventh in TT880)
üsür-i gönül	cocoon tithe
üsür-i muᶜadil	mulberry leaves tithe
vakf	Islamic charitable foundation and an endowed property normally exempt from state taxes
valı	governor-general of a province
varış	outer castle; suburb
vilayet	province
voyvoda	Slavic title for a prince; a military agent appointed by a governor for the purpose of tax collection
vukiyye	a measurement of weight used with grains and other commodities, equivalent to 1.28 kilograms; same as an *okka*
yabani	wild; uncultivated
yalı	waterside residence
yavru	piglets
yayabaşı	head of the foot soldiers of a province
yazlık	summer pasture for herders
yevmiye	daily cash and food stipends given to Janissaries
*yoklama defter*s	Janissary rolls
[y]ulaf	oats
yük	load of goods, varying in weight according to product and part of the Ottoman empire
zabit	officer; commissioner
zaim	district local subcommander holding a land grant, or *zeᶜamet* (q.v.)
zappada (Venetian)	unit of surface area based on work time
zeᶜamet	a large prebend usually ranging from 20,000 to 100,000 *akçe*s (q.v.) given to a commander or high *sipahi* (q.v.) officer
zengin	rich
zeytun	olives
zimmi	non-Muslim subjects
ziraᵓ	see *arşun/arşın*

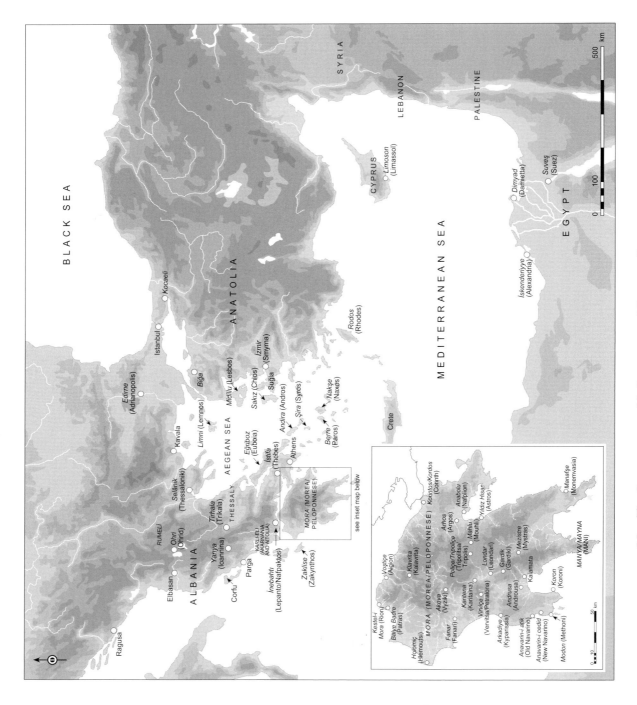

Map. The Ottoman eastern Mediterranean and Ottoman Greece. R. J. Robertson

BLACK SEA

SYRIA

LEBANON

PALESTINE

CYPRUS

Limoson
(Limassol)

ANATOLIA

Dimyad
(Damietta)

Suveş
(Suez)

Iskenderiyye
(Alexandria)

E G Y P T

MEDITERRANEAN SEA

Istanbul

Edirne
(Adrianopolis)

Kocaeli

Biga

Midillu (Lesbos)

Sakiz (Chios)

Suğla (Smyrna)

Izmir

Rodos
(Rhodes)

Andira (Andros)

Sira (Syrós)

Nakşe
(Naxós)

Berre
(Paros)

Kavala

Limni (Lemnos)

AEGEAN SEA

Eğriboz
(Euboia)

Istifa
(Thebes)

Athens

Crete

Selânik
(Thessaloniki)

RUMELI

Tirhala
(Trikala)

THESSALY

Ohri
(Ohrid)

ALBANIA

Elbasan

Yanya
(Ioannina)

Parga

Corfu

Inebahtı
(Lepanto/Nafpaktos)

KARLI-ELI
(AKARNANIA
AND AITOLIA)

MORA (MOREA/
PELOPONNESE)

Zaklise
(Zakynthos)

see inset map below

Ragusa

0   100   500 km

see inset map below

MORA (MOREA/PELOPONNESE)

Kestel-i
Mora (Rion)

Balye Badre
(Patras)

Hotomiç
(Helmoúts)

Fanar
(Fanari)

Akova
(Vyziki)

Vostiçe
(Aigion)

Klavrita
(Kalavrita)

Karitena
(Karitaina)

Polige/Tripoliçe
(Tripolitsai
Tripolis)

Vinviçe
(Vervitsa/Petraiona)

Arkadiye
(Kyparissia)

Anavarin-i atik
(Old Navarino)

Anavarin-i cedid
(New Navarino)

Modon (Methoni)

Koron (Koroni)

Andrusa
(Androusa)

Gardik
(Gardiki)

Kalamata

Londar
(Leondari)

Mahtu
(Mouni)

Arhos
(Argos)

Korinŋos/Kordos
(Corinth)

Anabolu
(Nafplion)

Yıldız Hisar
(Astros)

Mezistre
(Mystras)

MANYA/MAYNA
(MANI)

Manafşe
(Monemvasia)

0   10   50 km

OTTOMAN STUDIES AND ARCHAEOLOGY IN GREECE

by Fariba Zarinebaf, Jack L. Davis, and John Bennet

A Historical and Economic Geography of Ottoman Greece represents the fruits of a partnership between an Ottomanist, Fariba Zarinebaf, and two archaeologists, John Bennet and Jack L. Davis, who are both engaged in regional studies in Greece. The value of this collaboration should be clear to archaeologists, since the new information contained in this volume sheds light on a little-known period of the past and demonstrates the enormous contribution that a study of documents in the Ottoman archives can make to the reconstruction of local histories of settlement, land use, and toponymy. At the same time, this example from Greece offers Ottomanists a case study that can be employed, in comparison with others focused elsewhere in the Ottoman empire, to examine regional variation in social structure, demography, forms of property, and the commercialization of agriculture. The conclusions are also obviously relevant to ongoing controversies in Ottoman studies, such as the so-called *çiftlik* debate.

THE STATE OF MEDIEVAL AND EARLY MODERN ARCHAEOLOGY IN GREECE

Once they are dated, the pottery and other commonplace objects that are found in abundance in the Greek landscape generally allow archaeologists to determine where people lived, worked, and moved within a landscape. However, the sequence and range of pottery types and styles produced and consumed in post-Byzantine Greece are, at present, poorly understood. If it is true, as Haralambos Bakirtzis, a leading Greek ceramic expert, could write just a little over a decade ago, that "Byzantine pottery is a relatively unknown chapter of Byzantine Archaeology,"[1] this statement is all the more accurate for the post-Byzantine period. Though others have now joined Bakirtzis in amplifying our knowledge of Byzantine and contemporary Frankish wares—so much so that a substantial list can be added to his bibliography—studies of Ottoman and other modern wares are still few and far between, and our knowledge of the coarser and more plain types that were, after all, most plentiful in everyday use remains sparse.[2]

1. Bakirtzis 1989, pp. 11, 128.
2. Important exceptions include Hahn 1997; and Vroom 1998, 2003; see also Vionis 2001; Shelton 2004.

Even now, these artifacts are systematically understudied, probably for two reasons. First, there is still a tendency to ignore relics from periods of Ottoman domination because they represent an unwelcome reminder of Greece's colonial (and eastern) past. Many scholars consider the Ottoman past to be of little interest when set next to the glories of ancient Greece, Rome, and Byzantium.[3] Second, there is a more general belief that post-Byzantine Greek history is most effectively explored through documentary sources—in contrast to the "classical" past, which, while rich in texts (literary, historical, and epigraphical), is not so well known that study of its material culture can be ignored. Besides, there is a long tradition, beginning with Johann Joachim Winckelmann, of studying what might be termed the "high" material culture of classical antiquity. But in the more recent past, particularly in periods where there are "Western" historical accounts and documentary records of events in Greek lands, what could material culture contribute?

The answer, as always, lies in the questions. Undoubtedly, study of the material culture of medieval and early modern Greek rural settlement will not directly answer a question such as "Why did the battle of Lepanto occur?" But if one's goal is to study "history from below,"[4] then archaeology (and, perhaps, oral tradition) can help. More relevant to the present study, however, is the way an examination of material evidence can be used to develop a systematic and detailed understanding of the nature and distribution of settlement and land use, which can then be linked to documentary information about the ways in which the landscape and its inhabitants were exploited. The equation also operates in reverse: detailed study of documentary evidence can help with the interpretation of the social and political aspects of distributions of material culture within a landscape.

Only a relatively small fraction of those archived written records that are potentially of the most use to archaeologists actively studying late medieval and early modern Greece is yet available in accessible published format. Regional studies projects preceding ours attempted to uncover new information relevant to the reconstruction of patterns of modern settlement and land use by commissioning special historical studies of the regions they examined. These investigations were successful, but limited in scope, as relatively few resources were invested in support of the research. The Minnesota Messenia Expedition took the lead, as in so many other aspects of regional studies in Greek archaeology. Peter Topping, a professional historian of medieval and early modern Greece, was enlisted to write a political, economic, and social history of Messenia, one that was in part based on new data gathered in the course of his own investigations in the archives of Venice.[5] Topping undertook to perform similar services for the Southern Argolid Project, as did Halil İnalcık for the Phokis-Doris Archaeological Project in central Greece.[6]

Even in those instances where detailed documentary evidence has been published, rarely have there been attempts to integrate these written testimonia with the evidence of material culture in a way that might produce a more detailed or more nuanced view of the past than would be possible using either category of data by itself. For example, although Venetian

3. As noted in Herzfeld 1991, pp. 56–58; more generally, Baram and Carroll 2000.

4. See, e.g., Baram and Carroll 2000, pp. 33–35.

5. Topping 1972. On the Minnesota Messenia Expedition as a whole, see McDonald and Rapp 1972.

6. Topping 2000; İnalcık 1991b.

records provided a full picture of settlement in their region between 1686 and 1715, and a complete 14th-century Frankish census for at least one village (Kremmydia) had been published,[7] the archaeologists of the Minnesota Messenia Expedition did not integrate this information with their archaeological study, the focus of which was the Bronze Age. Topping's own discussion of landholding under Frankish, Ottoman, and Venetian domination is similarly detached from any discussion of specific archaeological discoveries and from programs of archaeological investigation organized by William A. McDonald and Richard Hope Simpson. In the southern Argolid also, the full archaeological potential of detailed Venetian cadastral maps[8] is still to be realized. No published study has yet attempted to relate the information contained in these documents to artifact distributions, although such research is planned;[9] it is clear that parts of the Venetian agricultural system remain fossilized in contemporary field divisions and arteries of communication.[10]

Ideally, regional archaeological projects will benefit most from the availability of written sources that contain ample information about past settlement and land use in enough detail to make it possible to locate accurately the settlements, fields, and other agricultural installations described. This will clearly be the most direct way in which archaeologists will be able to relate the evidence contained in such texts to the spatially variable artifact distributions recorded.

THE PYLOS REGIONAL ARCHAEOLOGICAL PROJECT AND OTTOMAN STUDIES

Even though a number of historians have made use of Western documentary sources in studying the Frankish and Venetian periods in Greece, and a substantial quantity has been published in collections, until recently the enormous potential of the archives in Istanbul and Ankara for understanding the nature of Ottoman domination (in the 15th through 19th/20th centuries) has gone largely unrecognized. Many Ottoman historians, on the other hand, considered the story of the territories that today constitute the nation-state of Greece to be peripheral to that of the massive Ottoman empire as a whole and therefore paid little attention to these areas.[11]

In the past two decades, the tide has started to turn. Regional histories rooted in Ottoman documents are being written by scholars based in Greece.[12] Other Ottomanists have also begun to mine Ottoman archives for information relevant to Greece, sometimes as emissaries of archaeological projects.[13] It is clear that these archives are a substantial source of information pertaining to virtually all parts of the modern nation-state.

In the 1990s Bennet and Davis had, with other colleagues, organized regional archaeological studies (1991–1995) in southwestern Greece, in the province of Messenia, in the district that was known as Pylos in antiquity.[14] Fieldwork sponsored by the Pylos Regional Archaeological Project (PRAP) involved the careful collection of surface archaeological remains

7. Longnon and Topping 1969, pp. 73–76; see also Gerstel 1998b.

8. See Topping 1976.

9. Jameson, Runnels, and van Andel 1994, p. 131, n. 56; Forbes 2000b.

10. Badekas 1988, p. 44, figs. 7, 8.

11. On these issues see, e.g., Greene 2000, pp. 3–6.

12. See, e.g., Alexander 1985a, 1985b, 1998; Balta 1989, 1992, 1993, 1997, 1999, 2004.

13. E.g., see Beldiceanu and Beldiceanu-Steinherr 1980, 1986; Kiel 1992a, 1997; Kiel and Sauerwein 1994; Lowry 2002; Greene 1996, 2000.

14. Davis et al. 1997; Zangger et al. 1997; Davis 1998.

of all periods in an area of several dozen square kilometers, through the implementation of techniques that have collectively come to be known as intensive surface survey. Their objective was to use this purely archaeological evidence, in conjunction, where possible, with textual records, to examine the complex interrelations between humans and the landscapes of Messenia in all periods of the past, including the more recent. They hoped that they would ultimately find themselves in a position to compare these interrelations at various times in the past in order to define the long-term patterns that have existed in the same region under a variety of political and economic systems, both those that developed internally and those that were externally imposed.

Their own project was not unusual in casting a broad net over the past and defining such ambitious goals. Regional archaeological expeditions that focus on the recovery of remains of only a single period of the past are rare in Greece today. The term "diachronic" has come to be chanted as a mantra so commonplace that it may be assumed, if it is not expressed. Nearly all archaeological surveys aim to collect material remains of all periods of the past and at least claim to devote equal effort to their analysis.

Already at the start of PRAP it was clear to them, on the basis of their own past experiences in organizing similar archaeological research projects in other parts of Greece, that contrary to the expectations of a nonarchaeologist, their goal of reconstructing patterns of settlement and land use might prove more difficult to achieve for the later medieval and early modern periods than for the classical period (i.e., Greek and Roman times), or even for the prehistoric Late Bronze Age (17th century B.C. to ca. 1200 B.C.). For reasons already discussed, they imagined that they would need to take extraordinary measures with reference to the study of these periods to ensure that they would be able to achieve their objectives of producing a truly diachronic history of the Pylos area from the time that it was first settled (by the Middle Paleolithic, as it now seems) to the present day, with regard to both the study of artifacts of these periods and the examination of documents from relevant archives.

From an archaeological perspective, they had before them as models the published work of projects similar to their own that have, in fact, paid a great deal of attention to modern material remains. Notable in this regard is the Southern Argolid Exploration Project, which has recently published an entire volume containing archaeological, ethnoarchaeological, anthropological, historical, and ethnohistorical examinations of their study area from the 18th to the 21st centuries.[15] The Methana archaeological survey has examined a comparable range of topics within the compass of the overall publication of its archaeological results,[16] and similar work is emerging in the context of other projects.[17]

15. Sutton 2000.
16. Mee and Forbes 1997; see also Forbes 2000a.
17. See, e.g., Brumfield 2000 and, more generally, for an examination specifically of changing physical landscapes from antiquity to the present, Rackham and Moody 1996. See also Cooper 2002, which is concerned specifically with documenting medieval and modern village architecture in the northwest Peloponnese.

OUR COLLABORATION

In order to gather documentary evidence, we needed to bring new members to the PRAP team. Susan E. Alcock, co-director within PRAP for historical studies, therefore enlisted the help of two historians: Siriol Davies, an expert on Venetian Greece, particularly the Morea (Peloponnese), and Fariba Zarinebaf, an Ottoman historian and coauthor of this volume.[18]

Zarinebaf traveled twice to Istanbul on behalf of PRAP.[19] Her expeditions have provided us with a rich documentary record for the Ottoman occupation of the Morea. Among other things, these texts have yielded a wealth of information about the older Ottoman land-management system in which rights to exploit agricultural resources were assigned to cavalrymen (*sipahi*s) as benefices known as *timar*s. These individuals were consequently obligated to provide military service to the state. The texts also contain valuable information concerning a newer system in which rights to collect income from particular lands were sold at auction as tax-farms, and about the process of transition between the two systems that occurred in the 18th century.

The first translations of these documents by Zarinebaf brought with them difficulties of comprehension, and it soon became obvious that their interpretation would not be straightforward. For example, we were astounded and initially baffled by the staggering amount of toponymic information contained in them. Although some of the toponyms recorded by Ottoman administrators remain in everyday use and were easily recoverable, and others were recorded on old maps, many had not survived in official governmental usage of the later 20th century and consequently could not be found on contemporary maps. These were highly localized names of the sort likely to be familiar only to farmers who still cultivate fields in a specific area. In almost all instances, the transliteration (or, at times, translation) of Greek names into Turkish written in the Ottoman script made it still more difficult to determine the location of a place.

The toponymy of the documents needed to be deciphered if they were to be of any practical use to archaeologists, since only in this way would it be possible to reconstruct a map of settlement and land use that might be compared to artifact distributions. This much seemed clear. What was less obvious at the time was that the documents had the potential to provide substantial information relevant to the economic and social history of the region, if close attention was paid to spatial differences in the status of the settlements recorded and in the nature of agricultural production. Historians have tended to be concerned with population and production levels within larger regions of the Ottoman empire, but we have found that such a macroscopic perspective runs the risk of failing to observe microregional variations that can be highly indicative of significant economic and social changes within the larger region.[20]

In part because of the difficulty of locating toponyms, a particularly close working relationship has developed between Bennet, Davis, and Zarinebaf over a decade. Duties have been distributed as follows. Zarinebaf, of course, has been responsible for the translation of documents and for their interpretation as they reflect the policies of the central, regional, and

18. For a full report on Davies's work, see Davies 2004. We thank her for making the results of her research available to us in advance of publication. We were in part encouraged to form partnerships between historians and archaeologists because of the successes of the Cambridge-Bradford Boiotia Expedition, which had made extensive use, through the expertise of Machiel Kiel, of Ottoman-period documentary evidence: e.g., Kiel 1997; Bintliff 1999. It is encouraging that other regional archaeological projects are now also investing substantial resources in the study of the Ottoman period. See, e.g., Doorn 1989; Nixon, Price, and Moody 1998; Forsén and Karavieri 2003; Armstrong 2002.

19. See pp. xv–xix. Trips to Istanbul were supported by grants from the National Endowment for the Humanities to the Pylos Regional Archaeological Project.

20. See also Bennet, Davis, and Zarinebaf-Shahr 2000.

local Ottoman bureaucracy. Bennet and Davis have contributed their expertise in Greek archaeology and linguistics. They have mapped toponyms
in the documents, and, since both have had a long-standing interest in the
agrarian history of Ottoman Greece, they have been able to orient the
team's work amidst relevant historical studies published in the modern
Greek language.

THE GOALS OF THIS VOLUME

We should frankly admit that our purposes in writing this book, although
complementary, differ according to our professional interests. Zarinebaf,
as a historian, has written a general social and economic history for the
Ottoman Morea, within which the specific trajectory of the Pylos area
may be understood and may be related to broader problems of general
interest to all Ottomanists. For this endeavor she has drawn on hundreds
of documents, nearly all of which she has examined in the original. Her
overview provides a context within which any specific Ottoman document
can be considered in greater detail. In addition, Zarinebaf's conclusions
will be invaluable to members of PRAP as, in accordance with that project's
objectives, they turn in the future to the composition of a diachronic social
and economic history of the area.

It was decided that the centerpiece of this volume would be the publication and analysis of pages 78–101 of an Ottoman tax register, *Tapu
Tahrir* 880 (TT880), dated early in A.D. 1716 (A.H. 1128) and held in the
Başbakanlık Archives in Istanbul. Our study of these pages constitutes the
most complete examination of a late Ottoman *tahrir* published to date.
Pages 78–101 record the first complete cadastral survey *(mufassal defter)* of
the district *(kaza)* of Anavarin (Navarino), an area within which most of
the region explored by PRAP fell, compiled by Ottoman administrators
after the expulsion of the Venetians from the Peloponnese only months
earlier. Data from Venetian censuses and other documents for the period
1685–1715 provided a solid toponymic baseline, giving us a general idea
of the settlement pattern that we might expect to find in the Ottoman
document.[21] Finally, because of its very detailed nature, including catalogues of buildings and their contents as well as people, we were convinced
that information drawn from TT880 would facilitate the design of any future fieldwork that might focus specifically on the detailed archaeological
investigation of those settlements occupied in Ottoman times.

Although Bennet and Davis are both archaeologists, and although we
trust that the publication of this volume will in the long run substantially
improve our knowledge of the archaeology of early modern Greece, the
actual archaeological analysis contained in it is limited. It is not our purpose in publishing this particular book to demonstrate comprehensively
how textual and archaeological sources can be employed to illuminate each
other. We do provide several specific examples of how the information in
TT880 might be integrated with artifactual data collected by PRAP, but it
would have been inappropriate in this volume to have advanced that venture further. First, PRAP's program of archaeological fieldwork (completed

21. The pioneering efforts of Sauerwein (1969) were especially useful to us.

in 1995) was designed without specific reference to the Ottoman settlement pattern. As a consequence, the majority of the places recorded in TT880 have not yet been targets of archaeological investigation. Second, in part for the reasons mentioned earlier, the chronology of the archaeological data that have been collected by PRAP is coarse, usually making it impossible to date individual artifacts to periods shorter than a century or more. It thus makes little sense to analyze the archaeological data in the light of a single document composed at a very specific point in time. In our view, a much better strategy will be to study PRAP's archaeological data comprehensively at a later date, in the light not only of TT880 but also of other Ottoman documents and the rich Venetian sources now published by Davies.[22]

THE ORGANIZATION OF THIS VOLUME

The organization of this volume reflects closely the goals that we have outlined above. Some parts of it contain translations of primary sources (e.g., Chap. 2 and App. I). Others analyze and explain the content of the translated Ottoman documents, or provide a general historical context for understanding them. In Chapter 1, Zarinebaf presents her first tentative social and economic history of the Morea, from its initial conquest by the Ottomans in the 15th century until the Greek Revolution of 1821, employing data extracted from the documents she examined in Istanbul and from other primary and secondary sources. It is, to the best of our knowledge, the first time that anyone has attempted to write such a history based principally on Ottoman, rather than Greek and Venetian, sources. Chapter 1 also serves to provide a general context in which TT880 must be understood. Zarinebaf's interest in and knowledge of the 18th century, in particular, is rooted in her dissertation, which examined another frontier region of the Ottoman empire, Azerbaijan, and in her forthcoming examination of the social history of Istanbul in the 18th century.[23]

In Chapter 2, we publish a translation of the part of TT880 that describes the district of Anavarin. The introduction to Chapter 2 also includes a translation and discussion of the imperial law code *(kanunname)* that mandated the collection of the information contained in this *mufassal defter*. Chapter 3 consists entirely of an analysis of the toponymy of the part of TT880 translated in Chapter 2. We review all the evidence we were able to collect pertaining to the location of each of the taxable units recorded in TT880, whether *çiftlik*s (quasi-commercial farms), villages (*karye*s), or deserted lands that were capable of supporting settlement (*mazra'a*s). This painstaking analysis has allowed us to compose a nearly complete map of settlement and land use in the district of Anavarin at the beginning of the 18th century. The construction of the map allows us in Chapter 4 to discuss in detail the agricultural system that operated in the district of Anavarin in 1716 and to consider population density, land use, and settlement within the district and their spatial distribution. We think that we have succeeded in establishing how much can be learned by examining microregional variability in settlement and land use within a

22. Davies 2004.
23. Zarinebaf-Shahr 1991 and Zarinebaf in press. The themes that she considers in Chapter 1 provide for the first time a view of processes at work in the Morea that were also more globally in operation in the Ottoman empire as a whole (see, e.g., Adanır 1998).

relatively small area of the Ottoman empire. Chapter 5 summarizes our conclusions and their significance for historians and archaeologists alike.

Several appendixes offer additional data or commentary on the information presented in the body of the book. Appendix I presents, in translation by Pierre MacKay, sections of Evliya Çelebi's *Seyahatname (Book of Travels)* that describe the condition in the 17th century of the forts of Anavarin-i atik (Old Navarino) and Anavarin-i cedid (New Navarino). Appendixes II (by Aaron Wolpert) and III (by Bennet, Davis, and Deborah Harlan) examine in detail the text of TT880 as it pertains to these establishments. In both cases, the substantial standing remains of the forts are discussed, as well as relevant travelers' accounts and Venetian and Greek documentary sources. Appendix IV by Machiel Kiel complements Appendix III by examining for the first time the construction history of Anavarin-i cedid as it is revealed in contemporary Ottoman documents.

Several concordances and a glossary will, we hope, assist users in finding names of people and places that are recorded in the text of TT880 translated in Chapter 2, and in understanding technical Ottoman, Venetian, and Greek vocabulary. Concordance I includes a complete list of the names of taxpayers (i.e., non-Muslims). Concordance II contains Muslim names. Concordance III lists toponyms, and Concordance IV is an index of the principal properties in TT880 so that the relevant passages can be located easily in the CD-ROM facsimile of TT880, pages 78–101, prepared by John Wallrodt and Davis, that accompanies this book. This CD also contains copies of photographs published in this volume, prepared by Evi Gorogianni, that may be enlarged for closer inspection. Many of these are in color, whereas illustrations in the book are in black and white only.

We are confident that Ottomanists, Balkan historians, and archaeologists will benefit from this volume and that our collaboration will make significant contributions to all of these fields. It was a challenge to communicate among the three of us across the gulfs between two very different disciplines with varied methodologies and histories of scholarship, but we hope that the fruits of this undertaking will open the door for more interdisciplinary and regional projects that address Ottoman and Balkan studies. The products of our collaborative efforts have far exceeded the expectations we had when we began the research that resulted in this publication.

Soldiers into Tax-Farmers and *Reaya* into Sharecroppers: The Ottoman Morea in the Early Modern Period

by Fariba Zarinebaf

The history of Ottoman Greece has traditionally received very little attention from Ottomanists, mainly owing to historiographical divisions in Ottoman studies based on current national borders; other non-Turkish provinces of the empire have been similarly ignored.[1] Such divisions in Ottoman studies have limited the kinds of questions and problems that can be posed by historians of the nation-state of Greece. The Ottoman period in Balkan history has generally been regarded pejoratively as the time of the "Turkish yoke," a period that lasted for four to five centuries and resulted in the decline of local economies and cultures. The attention of Balkan historians has consequently been focused on "proto-nationalist" resistance to growing Turkish oppression, and the "inevitable" demise of the Ottoman empire and rise of Balkan nation-states in the 19th and 20th centuries. Noticeably lacking have been comparative studies of or debates about variation in the structure of Turkish rule across time and space, transformations in its nature, or causes of its disintegration.

In recent years, however, it has become clear that Ottoman archives offer scholars an opportunity to examine the internal dynamics of Turkish rule in the Balkans, using vast and largely untapped collections of documents that cover some four hundred years.[2] Systematic study of these sources can undoubtedly help both to formulate and to address questions concerning the state of the Morea while it was under Ottoman rule,

1. The history of the 18th-century Ottoman Morea has, however, been much explored by Greek and Western scholars employing primary sources drawn from the archives of Venice and of the major mercantile powers. Sakellariou's examination (1939) of the so-called Second Turkish Occupation laid the essential foundations on which more recent scholarship has built. Kremmydas's study (1972) of the external economy of the Morea, based on French archival sources, remains indispensible. For a standard Greek perspective based mostly on selective secondary sources, see Vacalopoulos 1967. For a more balanced approach incorporating some Turkish archival material, see Alexander 1985a, 1985b; and Dimitriades 1986. For Western scholarship based on secondary sources, see Jelavich 1983.

2. For an important collaborative study of late medieval and early modern Greece by Byzantinists and Ottomanists, see Bryer and Lowry 1986. Balta (1989, 1992) has utilized the central Turkish archives for her studies of parts of central Greece and the island of Euboia (Eğriboz) during the early Ottoman period. Other relevant studies include Beldiceanu and Beldiceanu-Steinherr 1986 (for Corinth); Balta 1997, 1999, 2004; Lowry 1992; Mazower 2004. For critiques of the historiography of Ottoman Greece, see Kiel 1992a, 1997; McGowan 1981. McGowan's work is also based on Ottoman sources and sheds a great deal of light on the patterns of economic transformation in the Balkans and Morea during the 17th and 18th centuries.

particularly during the 18th century, when the economy and society of the empire entered a crucial transitional phase that radically altered the way in which provinces such as the Morea were administered.

At the conclusion of this chapter I discuss this transitional period and consider especially what can be deduced from the text of TT880 about changes that were occurring in the early 18th century in the nature of Ottoman administration in the district of Anavarin. But first I provide some of the extensive background that is necessary for the full comprehension of this complex topic. There follows, therefore, a consideration of the effects that the Ottoman conquest of the 15th century A.D. had on Greece, and particularly on its demographic health. I next discuss the structure of the classical system of administration imposed by the Ottomans on the Morea after the conquest of the 15th century, including the quasi-feudal Ottoman *timar* system, in which benefices of land were granted to warriors who had participated in the conquest of a new territory. I then describe how large-scale tax-farming, managed centrally from Istanbul, replaced the *timar* system. I explicate the factors that were promoting the emergence of quasi-commercial farms (*çiftlik*s) in many parts of the Ottoman empire in the 18th century. Finally, I examine the impact of these developments on the society of the Morea and the conditions of the peasantry.

POST-CONQUEST DEMOGRAPHIC TRENDS

There is an ongoing debate between Byzantinists, historians of modern Greece, and Ottomanist historians with regard to the impact that Ottoman conquest and rule had on Greece.[3] While scholars like Speros Vryonis, Apostolos Vacalopoulos, and Peter Topping have emphasized immediate negative effects of war and conquest on Byzantine lands (i.e., population loss, economic and cultural decline), others, such as Halil İnalcık, Heath Lowry, and Machiel Kiel, have observed that there was substantial continuity in social and economic institutions between the Byzantine and early Ottoman periods, and that there was recovery from the effects of war, even prosperity, during the 16th century.[4] This difference of opinion derives in part from the nature of the sources (Byzantine, Venetian, or Ottoman) and the periodization chosen for emphasis by each group of scholars. A close examination of the nature of the Ottoman conquest and rule will shed light on social and economic changes.

Mehmed II (1451–1481) conquered the Byzantine state of the Morea when a civil war broke out in 1459 between two despots, Thomas Palaiologos and his brother Demetrios.[5] Thomas rebelled against his brother, forcing the Ottomans to intervene. According to Babinger, this internal conflict and subsequent Albanian ravages and violence against the local Greek population caused great distress in southern parts of the Morea. Moreover, Ottoman punitive expeditions in the north resulted in great losses in 1459 to the local populations of Patras and Corinth, among other places in the Morea.

Thomas continued his defiance with the aid of a small papal contingent (300 men) during the governorship of Turhanoğlu Ömer Bey in mid-1459.[6] The Ottoman army, under the command of Hamza Bey, governor

3. For the best exposition of this debate, see Bryer and Lowry 1986.

4. For examples of the former, see Vryonis 1986; Vacalopoulos 1967; Topping 1972, p. 70. For examples of the latter, see İnalcık 1997; Lowry 1986; Kiel 1992a. See also notes 2 and 11 here, and İnalcık and Murphey 1978.

5. Babinger 1978, pp. 161–162. The Morea at that time consisted of a Byzantine despotate and various Venetian holdings (see Zakythinos 1953).

6. According to the Ottoman historian Tursun Beg [Bey], Demetrios surrendered after hiding in the fortress of Mezistre (Mystras) and received robes of honor from Mehmed II. He was granted a salary and was sent to Edirne (Adrianopolis). All of the Morea then accepted Ottoman rule except for several fortresses, among which were Hulomuc, our Holomiç (Hlemoutsi), Salmenik (the location is uncertain; a "Selmenico" is mentioned by S. Magno in Hopf 1873, p. 205), Gardik (Gardiki), Yıldız Hisar or "Star Fortress" (Astros), Mahlu (Mouhli), Levendar, our Londar (Leondari). Later, all of these fortresses were either

taken by force or surrendered peacefully. The populations of those taken by
force were put to the sword or taken
into slavery. Their monasteries and
churches were converted into mosques.
The inhabitants of the Morea were
made subject to religious and customary taxes. *Sancakbey*s, *kadı*s, and garrison commanders were appointed.
Abundant booty was taken by soldiers
and every tent had a slave market (İnal-
cık and Murphey 1978, p. 44; Tursun
Bey [b. 1426] served Mehmed II as a
finance secretary and surveyor, and
accompanied the grand vizier, Mahmud
Pasha, on many campaigns, including
those in Serbia, Morea, Bosnia, and
Albania).

7. Babinger 1978, pp. 165–166,
173–176.

8. Venice retained Nafplion and
Monemvasia until 1540.

9. Müneccimbaşı [1974], pp. 408–
411; on the fortress of Anavarin-i atik,
see Appendix II of this volume.

10. Müneccimbaşı ([1974], p. 411)
reports 3,000 Christians killed, but
Western sources differ on this point;
see Appendix II, pp. 233–234. For the
construction of the fortress, see Appendix IV. Selânikî Mustafa Efendi (1989,
p. 96) reports that the fortress was built
in 1574 with the help and direct
involvement of Kılıç Ali Pasha. Evliya
Çelebi wrongly dates the building of
Anavarin-i cedid to 1569 and the reign
of Murad III (1574–1595); see Appendix I. See also Appendix III.

of Thessaly, imposed a crushing defeat on the Italians. Thomas agreed to
pay 3,000 gold pieces as tribute and to evacuate his troops from the Peloponnese. The following spring, Mehmed II decided to lead a second expedition. This he did, in March 1460, with the help of Zaganos Pasha,
his commander and the newly appointed governor of Thessaly and the
Morea, in order to remove both Demetrios and Thomas permanently and
pacify the Peloponnese. This expedition was highly successful and left in
the hands of Venice only the fortresses of Koron (Koroni), Modon (Methoni), Anavarin (Navarino), Anabolu (Nafplion), and Manafşe (Monemvasia).
Thomas fled with his family to Messenia with the help of Venetians, ending up in Corfu in July 1462.[7]

Venice briefly occupied much of the Morea during the Ottoman-
Venetian wars of 1463–1479, but ultimately, between 1499 and 1503, an
Ottoman army, numbering 46,000 men and led by Sultan Bayezid II (1481–
1512), expelled Venice from most of the peninsula.[8] Yakub Pasha occupied
the fortress of Modon in August 1500. Ali Pasha and Kapudan Davud
Pasha subsequently attacked the fortress of Anavarin-i atik (which had
originally been built by the Frankish Saint Omer family in the 13th century) by land and sea.[9] By the time Ali Pasha took the fortress, the residents of Anavarin had already fled to Venice. Koron submitted peacefully,
and Ali Pasha became the governor of the Morea.

Venice reoccupied Anavarin with the aid of some local Greeks only a
few months later, in 1501. Bayezid ordered Ali Pasha and Kemal Reis, the
commander of the Ottoman navy, to attack, and Ottoman forces retook
the fortress and killed 3,000 Christians. Much later, between 1573 and
1577, in response to a continuing Western threat from the sea, the fortress
of Anavarin-i cedid was built inside the sheltered Bay of Anavarin.[10]

Most scholars would agree that the wars of conquest by Venice and
the Ottoman empire in general had a negative effect on the society and
economy of conquered territories. The Morea was taken forcibly by
Mehmed II and Bayezid II. Ottoman chronicles attest a loss of population
at the hands of Ottoman forces and the flight of many residents to Europe.
But the chronicles are silent concerning the nature of the post-conquest
period, which largely remains to be explored through the investigation of
unpublished archival sources.

Fortunately, Ottoman archives have lately become increasingly accessible, resulting in significant discoveries relevant to the history of Ottoman Greece. The best source for the study of demographic patterns and
economic trends in the Morea are *mufassal defter*s (detailed tax registers),
which are available for times from the post-conquest period until 1725.
They may contain detailed information about the number of Muslim
and non-Muslim tax-paying households (specifying if the head of the
household is a single or married man, or a widow), agricultural and urban
revenues, and official prices (*narh*s) in villages and towns throughout the
Ottoman empire. A *mufassal defter* (or *tapu tahrir*) was usually prepared
immediately after the conquest of a new territory, once central control had
been established. In principle, the registers were then updated for tax purposes every 30 to 40 years.

The study of a series of tax registers for a given district or province over
a period of time can yield important conclusions concerning population

trends, social developments, economic activities, and fiscal policies.[11] If combined with other sources, such as *maliyeden müdevver defter*s (records of the Finance Bureau), *mühimme defter*s (registers of important affairs), *ahkam defter*s (registers of imperial orders), *şikayet defter*s (registers of petitions), and *kadı sicil*s (Islamic court records), it is possible to describe in some detail interactions between the state government and local societies and to identify changes that occurred in the structures of both the central Ottoman institutions and those in the provinces.

The first detailed tax register for the Morea was prepared in 1461, immediately after the conquest by Mehmed II. A second followed during the reign of Selim I (1512–1520).[12] The content of these *defter*s was the subject of a preliminary study by Nicoară Beldiceanu and Irene Beldiceanu-Steinherr.[13] Based on these cadastral sources, they have shown that the population of the Morea increased from 20,000 to about 30,000 households between 1461 and 1488 (a 50% increase) and that more than 30 percent of this population was of Albanian origin. Turks represented only about 15 percent of the total population of the Morea in 1461.[14] State taxes on cereals (wheat) constituted about 45 percent of all those levied on agricultural production, followed by taxes on viticulture (about 35%) and on silk cocoons (about 6%).[15] Beldiceanu and Beldiceanu-Steinherr concluded that the fiscal burden on the peasantry during early Ottoman rule was lighter than it had been under either the Venetian or the Byzantine feudal systems.

Lowry's study of the island of Limnos during the first decades of Ottoman rule produced similar conclusions. He has demonstrated that since the island was conceded peacefully by Venice to Mehmed II in 1458, neither its administrative structure nor its ethnic constitution changed significantly. Limnos was ruled from 1460 to 1464 by Demetrios Palaiologos, as an Ottoman vassal, in exchange for a tribute of 3,000 gold coins.[16] Lowry has also shown that out of a total of 281 military men who received *timar*s in 1489, 261 were local Christians.[17] The island retained its Greek and Christian character; the number of priests increased from 4 in 1489 to 23 in 1519.[18] Moreover, the seven Athonite monasteries on the island retained their vast properties (fiefs, vineyards, and pastures) despite an initial flight of the monks in 1489.[19] At first, the population of the island fell by 50 percent (6,000 to 3,000) in 1470, but it had returned to former levels by 1519.[20]

11. İnalcık 1997, pp. 132–139. For an excellent example of interdisciplinary study of Palestine and parts of Syria based on *tapu tahrir*s, see Hütteroth and Abdulfattah 1977; figures and maps in their work describe the religious composition of the population of districts (fig. 4), the distribution of nomadic tribes (fig. 5), the location of the *timar*s and *zeʿamet*s (fig. 11), and the division of revenues (map 2). For similar studies, see Gö-

yünç and Hütteroth 1997 (on Diyarbakır); Kiel and Sauerwein 1994 (Eastern Lokris, Greece); and Lowry 2002 (Limnos).

12. TT10, 191 pp.; TT80, 1,241 pp.; see pp. xv–xix.

13. Beldiceanu and Beldiceanu-Steinherr 1980.

14. Beldiceanu and Beldiceanu-Steinherr 1980, p. 48.

15. Beldiceanu and Beldiceanu-Steinherr 1980, p. 30, table VII. Taxes

on olive-oil production represented less than 0.5 percent of the total revenue of the Morea in 1461.

16. Lowry 1986, p. 235. This was the same Demetrios Palaiologos who had been removed as despot of the Morea by Mehmed II in 1461.

17. Lowry 1986, p. 238.

18. Lowry 1986, p. 250.

19. Lowry 1986, p. 252.

20. Lowry 1986, pp. 255–256. See also Topping 1986, pp. 225–232.

TABLE 1.1. TAX-PAYING HOUSEHOLDS (*HANE*S) IN *TİMAR* AND *HASS* VILLAGES IN THE DISTRICT OF MODON, 1512–1583

Settlement	1512–1520	1520–1566	1583
Forts	2	2	1
Towns	2	2	2
Mazraʿas (timar)	21	14	17
Villages	32	35	36 (1 *çiftlik*)
*Çiftlik*s		1	
*Hane*s			
Muslims	80 (13 single)	83 (19 single)	
Christians	564 (72 single)	523 (92 single)	
Widows	9 (Christian)	10	
Jews	27 (5 single)	26 (5 single)	
Gypsies	22	20	
Total *hane*s	702	662	

Sources: TT80 *(mufassal)*, pp. 13–21; TT367 *(icmal)*, p. 132; TT607, p. 1.

Demographic developments in central Greece during the first century of Ottoman rule paralleled those in the Morea and on Limnos. Kiel's studies of Boiotia based on 15th- and 16th-century tax registers have shown that the population of the towns and villages in his sample quadrupled between 1461 and 1570. This represents a remarkable demographic expansion, one that appears to have been accompanied by economic growth and a general level of prosperity.[21] As in Limnos, there was a revival of religious life: new monasteries were built in the 16th century throughout the region.

The population of southwestern Messenia, including the district of Modon, seems to have remained stable after the Ottoman conquest. Table 1.1 indicates the number of urban and rural settlements and tax-paying households (Muslim and non-Muslim *hane*s) in the district of Modon from 1512 to 1583, when the area of Anavarin (including the fortress) belonged to the district of Modon. In the reign of Selim I (1512–1520), the fortress of old Anavarin (a *hass*, or private holding) had 31 households (8 Muslim and 23 Christian; Table 1.2), while the district of Modon, including Anavarin-i atik, had 80 Muslim, 564 Christian, 27 Jewish, and 22 Gypsy tax-paying households (plus 9 widows, for a total of 702 *hane*s).[22] In the time of the Süleymanic census (1520–1566), the population of the district of Modon appears to have remained steady with 662 households.[23] At the same time, the much larger district of Koron also remained at approximately the same size, with 980 tax-paying households (35 Muslim and 945 non-Muslim) in 1512 and 1,061 households in 1566.[24]

The demographic and economic decline attributed by Topping to Ottoman government of the Morea appears to be limited to the initial phase of conquest and the second half of the 17th century.[25] Conditions of Ottoman rule were not uniformly hostile to the rural peasantry. In fact, the evidence reviewed above suggests that in the 16th century, economic stability and a fairly even tax burden served to discourage flight of the peasantry to the towns from the countryside, as was also the case in Anatolia at

21. Kiel 1992a, 1997.

22. TT80, p. 15.

23. TT367, p. 132.

24. TT367, pp. 128, 136. TT367, an *icmal defter*, may have been based on the earlier TT80, a *mufassal defter*, explaining in part the similarities in the statistics contained in the two documents. I have not located a *mufassal defter* for the period 1520–1566. Consequently, it is important to note that any conclusions drawn from the data in TT367 may be based on partial surveys.

25. Kiel (1999, pp. 196) notes that Topping was wrong in assuming that the population of the Morea did not expand in the 16th century, and that, to the contrary, it more than doubled, and in some places trebled, after 1520. Topping (1972, 1976) emphasizes the transfer of Kızılbaş Turkmen from Anatolia to Modon and Koron by Bayezid II in the late 15th and early 16th centuries. These are possibly represented in the cadastral survey for 1512–1520 (TT80), where 64 Muslim households were recorded in the town of Modon (see Table 1.2). See also Gerstel 1998a, p. 227, and below in this chapter.

TABLE 1.2. TAX-PAYING HOUSEHOLDS (*HANE*S) IN THE TOWNS OF MODON AND ANAVARİN-İ ATİK, 1512–1566

Modon (Town)	1512–1520	1520–1566
Muslim	64 (13 singles)	64
Christian	133 (12 singles and widows)	130
Jewish	27 (5 single)	33
Gypsy	17	19
Total	241	246
Anavarin-i atik	*1512–1520*	*1520–1566*
Muslim	8	8
Christian	23	21
Total	31	29

Sources: TT80, pp. 13–21 (1512–1520); TT367, pp. 128, 132 (1520–1566).

this time. Social and economic stability in the Morea lasted until the economic crisis of the late 16th and the 17th centuries.[26] The Candian war of 1645–1669 and the Holy League war of 1685–1699 (with the Habsburg empire, Russia, Poland, and Venice) followed.

In the meantime, the ethnic and religious constitution of the district of Anavarin did not change greatly during the 16th century. In the reign of Selim I, the majority (five of eight) of Muslim *reaya* in the old fortress of Anavarin seem to have been converts to Islam, with names such as "Hızır son of Abdullah."[27] The enslavement of captives of war was practiced by the Ottomans and their enemies alike well into the 18th century. The ransoming of these individuals offered an important source of revenue to officials in the Ottoman frontier provinces. Those who were not ransomed had the option of converting to Islam to gain their freedom. In addition, when the Ottomans conquered an area controlled by Venice, previously Venetian subjects might convert to Islam in order to retain privileges or to move up the social scale. Abdullah ("slave of God") was a surname usually given to manumitted Christian slaves and converts. The larger Muslim community in Modon during the 16th century was more diverse and included few converts who carried the epithet Abdullah (only 8 of 64 *hane*s).

To finance its war efforts, the Ottoman state relied heavily on revenues from the *cizye* (poll tax) collected directly by the central treasury. Therefore, it generally did not support forced conversion of the non-Muslim *reaya*. The social pressure to convert must have been considerable, however, in areas where the majority of the population was Muslim. Furthermore, an increase in the amount of the *cizye* must also have indirectly encouraged conversion in the second half of the 16th century. An imperial order issued to the *kadı* of the districts of Manafşe and Modon on 19 *Zilkade* 978/March 1570 stated that there were illegal attempts by tax-farmers to collect *cizye* from converts who were *timar*-holders and who had been serving in the Ottoman army for fifteen years.[28] From this report it is clear that local Christians converted to Islam to enter the ranks of the military to avoid the payment of taxes. But it is also obvious that tax collectors and tax-farmers resented the tax-exempt privileges of the converts.

26. Conditions in Anatolia were similarly disturbed during the second half of the 16th century by the great economic and monetary crisis that occurred in the Ottoman empire at that time, and by the Celali rebellions (see below). For further discussion of demographic change specifically in the district of Anavarin, see Chapter 4.

27. TT80, p. 20.

28. Başbakanlık Archives 1996, p. 208: 439.

Topping has underlined a change in the ethnic makeup of the Morea through the transfer of the heretic Kızılbaş Turkmen to Modon and Koron.[29] The tax register TT80 records, however, only 64 Turkish/Muslim households in Modon, 33 in Koron, and 8 in Anavarin-i atik during the reign of Selim I (1512–1520).[30] Such a limited Muslim presence in the fortresses of Anavarin and Modon does not represent a radical change in the ethnic and religious makeup of the population, since the vast majority (90%) of the rural inhabitants remained Christian. The few Muslim/Turkish inhabitants who were scattered in the countryside were probably Ottoman *sipahi*s (cavalrymen) of Christian background who held *timar*s in the villages and resided there.

Evidence other than population statistics also supports a picture of economic stability in the 16th century. The number of uncultivated and abandoned units of agricultural land (*mazraʿa*s) dropped by 30 percent between the time of the cadaster of Selim I and that of Süleyman, while the number of villages increased slightly. The Ottoman state encouraged the cultivation of abandoned and empty land *(mawat)* so that it could collect taxes on it. In the case of the district of Modon, it is likely, as elsewhere, that those *mazraʿa*s were attached to neighboring villages or *çiftlik*s and had been brought under cultivation in response to an increase in the peasant population during the second half of the 16th century.

Since *tapu tahrir*s for the district of Modon have not yet been found for the 17th century, any demographic history for this period must rely largely on nonarchival sources. Existing evidence suggests, however, that there was no sharp decrease in the population in Modon before the conclusion of the wars with Venice and with the Holy League in the last quarter of the century. The decline in the Morea must have occurred somewhat later than in central Greece, for which Kiel has described a sharp demographic decline from 1570 to 1688, followed by a slow recovery from the 18th to the early 19th centuries. This 17th-century demographic decline may have been part of a general Ottoman pattern that has been attributed to a steep rise (200%) in prices caused by the flow of cheap American silver into the Ottoman empire, and by budget deficits, fiscal impositions, peasant flight, brigandage, and warfare.[31]

29. Topping 1972, p. 70. The Kızılbaş were the *shiʿi* followers of the Safavid dynasty in Iran who participated in a major uprising known as the Shah Kulu rebellion in 1511–1512; see Zarinebaf-Shahr 1997.
30. TT80, pp. 13–14, 20–21.
31. See Kiel 1997, tables VI–IX. See also İnalcık 1972; Cook 1972; Akdağ 1995; Barkey 1994; Pamuk 2000, pp. 131–148. Kiel has argued that peasant flight was not singly responsible for this demographic decline, asserting instead that, when under economic pressure, peasants reduced family size by delaying marriage. This thesis is not supported, however, with data

describing household size and marriage patterns in Greece. Relevant information can be found in the *tereke* registers (estates of deceased) assembled by the *kadı*, since they record numbers of surviving children and heirs. Kiel's hypothesis could be tested by examining changes in the percentage of single men (*mücerred*s) in a given population pool over time.

A recent article by Balta (2004) that appeared too late to be integrated fully into the analyses in this book discusses the content of a poll-tax register for the Morea that was assembled in 1645 (*Maliyeden Müdevver defter* [MM] 561), on the eve of the Cretan war. As

obtained by Balta, a photocopy of this register contains no information concerning Anavarin or Manya (Mani). According to her interpretation of this photocopy (2004, pp. 61–62), the population of the Morea remained more or less the same during the last half of the 17th century: there were 37,000 *zimmi* (non-Muslim) taxpayers recorded in 1645 and 38,000 families recorded in the 1700 Venetian census. But it is important to note that MM561 includes only *zimmi* and that the photocopy excludes Anavarin and Manya. The total population of the Morea in 1645 must, therefore, have been considerably greater than 37,000 families.

The demographic stability of Anavarin and Modon in the 17th century may be atypical for the Morea as a whole during that period. According to McGowan, the Ottoman-Holy League wars were significant causes of the loss of more than half of the population of the Morea already in 1685.[32] He has also considered climatic change as a factor in the increased aridity of the Morea, famine, and an increased frequency of epidemics such as typhus that contributed to the 17th-century demographic decline.[33] Based on head-tax figures drawn from the *cizye* records, he further concluded that population loss continued, resulting in a decrease of 13 percent for the Morea between 1700 and 1815.[34] This demographic pattern was not universal in the Balkans; a remarkable growth took place in the northwestern Bosnia-Serbia (208%) and the northeastern Dobrudja and lower Danube zones (35%) during the 18th century.[35] Nor does it seem to have been the case in all parts of the Morea, since it is clear that population in Anavarin remained stable during the 18th century.[36]

The most detailed account of the district of Anavarin in the 17th century is that of Evliya Çelebi in his *Sehayatname,* or *Book of Travels.* Evliya visited the fortresses of Anavarin-i atik and Anavarin-i cedid, Modon, and Koron at the end of the Ottoman-Venetian wars of the 17th century, around 1669, and he did not suggest that there had occurred a demographic or economic decline in the area by his day. According to him, Anavarin was then part of the *kaza* of Modon and was administered by a *voyvoda* who was based in Modon in the 16th and 17th centuries.[37] He counted 85 small masonry houses, 5 shops, and 1 mosque in Anavarin-i atik. These numbers are quite close to the number of houses recorded in the cadaster of 1512–1520, although his figures must always be regarded with caution.[38]

32. McGowan 1981, p. 91. The first Venetian governor of the Morea estimated that the population of the peninsula had been 200,000, of which only 86,468 remained in his day (Corner 1691 [1885–1889]). Venetian estimates of the total population of the Morea are not, however, entirely without problems; see Forsén and Karavieri 2003.

33. There is some reason to be skeptical of several of these explanations. In northern and central Europe, the so-called Little Ice Age was a cold period that lasted approximately three hundred years. The coldest decades were the 1590s and 1690s (Grove 1988, 1990; Grove and Conterio 1995; Grove and Rackham 2001, pp. 130–140). In Crete, it was a time of violent fluctuations in weather (Rackham and Moody 1996, pp. 39–41). See also Faroqhi 1999, pp. 83–86, regarding climatic explanations for the Celali rebellions in the 16th and early 17th centuries in Anatolia. But the long duration of this weather cycle makes it difficult to hold it responsible specifically for a decrease in population that occurred only in the 17th century. (A. T. Grove writes [pers. comm.]: "The influence of climate on population, we are inclined to think, is mainly through extreme events, especially droughts and floods and their effects on food supplies and the occurrence of famine.") Likewise, epidemics of the plague were a frequent problem in the Aegean, one that was not limited to the 17th century (e.g., Koukkou 1984, pp. 165–168; Davis 1991, pp. 152–153; Kostis 1995). Indeed, of the nearly 60 known attestations of the plague in the Greek peninsula in the 17th century prior to 1687, only a single outbreak in the Morea is recorded: in 1617 (from Patras to Parga and Zakynthos). In contrast, between 1685 and 1715, under the Venetian occupation, frequent outbreaks are recorded: in 1687, 1688, 1698, 1699, 1700, and 1701 (Kostis 1995, pp. 363–373, 375–379, 386–400). There is no specific reference to an outbreak of the plague in the area of Anavarin.

34. See McGowan 1981, pp. 88, 91; also Bennet, Davis, and Zarinebaf-Shahr 2000, pp. 376–377.

35. McGowan 1981, pp. 85–94.

36. See Chapter 4.

37. See Appendix I. The *kaza* of Anavarin became independent only after the Ottoman reconquest in 1716. According to MM561, the poll-tax register dated to 1645 recently studied by Balta (2004; see n. 31 above), the Morea at that time was divided into at least 9 provinces (*vilayet*s) and 23 districts (*kaza*s).

38. See also Appendix II, where evidence for the history of settlement in the fortress of Anavarin-i atik after Evliya's day is discussed.

Evliya also counted 33 inhabited (Muslim?) houses in the inner fortress and 600 Muslim houses, 2 mosques, 2 schools (a *mekteb* and a *medrese*), and 85 shops in the outer castle of Anavarin-i cedid. He recorded 200 Greek houses (two-story masonry structures roofed with tile) and gardens, 1 inn, 1 mosque, 15 shops, and many orchards and olive groves in the outer suburb (*varış*) of Anavarin-i cedid. If we accept his figures, the number of both Muslim and Greek residents had increased sixfold between the mid-16th century and the third quarter of the 17th century.

The fortress of Anavarin-i cedid was a center of both military and civilian settlement during Evliya Çelebi's visit. The fortress was also the site of Ottoman religious building activity, consisting of a small religious endowment (*vakf*) established by Ferhad Ağa, an Ottoman military commander. There were two Islamic schools and certainly also a *kadi*'s court (see Chap. 2), although Evliya does not mention it.[39] It is clear from his account, read together with that in TT880, that the Turks and Greeks lived in separate communities that were physically divided by the walls of the fortress. The Greeks, nevertheless, owned and operated small businesses, shops, and a workshop in the suburb outside the fortress, providing basic services and necessities for the Turkish settlers. Very few Turks lived in the villages outside the fortress, although many owned property throughout the district. There appears to have been an ethnic and religious segregation in the settlement of towns and villages.

The Ottoman conquest of Crete in 1669 undermined the Venetian position in the Mediterranean and the Aegean. But this victory was short-lived, since the Holy League imposed a crushing defeat on the Turkish army that resulted in a first series of Ottoman territorial losses in Europe and the Balkans (Hungary, Slovenia, the Morea) in 1685.[40] The treaty of Karlowitz formally granted control of the Morea to Venice in 1699. The long Ottoman-Venetian struggles for Crete and the Ottoman-Holy League wars, which lasted for almost three decades, resulted in economic devastation in the frontier areas and a major economic and political crisis for the Ottoman state. Detailed Venetian cadastral surveys from this period for the area of Anavarin unfortunately have not survived, but reports of Venetian administrators and censuses are extant.[41]

The forts of Anavarin were in a bad state of repair, and there was widespread depopulation in the Morea by 1700. The Venetian authorities consequently encouraged people from central Greece, the Aegean (most notably Chios), and the Ionian islands to settle there.[42] The population of the Venetian territory of Anavarin in 1700 was 1,801 souls (445 families).[43] The suburb (*borgo*) of Anavarin had 30 families, and the fortress 29 families. The towns of Ligudista/Likudise (83 families) and Cavallaria/Kavalari (62 families) were the largest in the district.[44]

The products of the district of Anavarin during Venetian rule were primarily wheat, wine, and oil, along with some cheese, wool, silk, kermes (red dye), wax, and honey. The fishery in Anavarin-i atik had the highest yield as a tax-farm in the territory.[45] Much of the agricultural land was abandoned at this time, or was undercultivated. The Venetians, like their Ottoman predecessors, farmed out to private individuals and groups the collection of taxes for the tithe on wheat, barley, and oil, as well as on wine, fisheries, silk, pasturage, beehives, pigs, soap, hostelries, playing

39. The presence of a *kadi*'s court would indicate that there once existed Islamic court records for this district, perhaps destroyed during the later Venetian and French occupations of the fortress (regarding these occupations, see App. III). These records would have shed great light on civilian life and on social and economic developments in the community had they survived the great upheavals in the region.

40. With regard to the struggles that led to the capture of the Morea by Venice, see Stouraiti 2001 and Marasso and Stouraiti 2001, with the copious bibliography there included.

41. Davies 2004, p. 69.

42. Davies 2004, p. 62.

43. Panayiotopoulos 1987, p. 262; see also Table 4.1 in this volume, and discussion in Chapter 4.

44. Panayiotopoulos 1987, p. 262.

45. Davies 2004, p. 78, and p. 79, table 2; see also Chapter 4 below.

cards, and slaughterhouses. The auction figure for the tithe in 1701 was highest, as one might expect, in the largest settlements and towns, namely Cavallaria/Kavalari (810 *reali*), Ligudista/Likudise (700 *reali*), and Gargaliano/Ğarğalian 480 *reali*).[46] The village of Lesaga/Elyas Ağa had the lowest auction figure for its tithe (4 *reali*). The Venetians also initially farmed out the tithe from monasteries to private individuals.[47] Auctions were held at Cavallaria for some of its surrounding villages, probably mainly in the territory of Anavarin. Most of the surplus cereals, olive oil, wine, wool, kermes, and silk were exported only to Venice.[48] In addition, the Venetians, like the Ottomans, might impose corvée (for construction and to provide transportation and lodging for soldiers) on the villagers.[49] In keeping with previous Ottoman policy, the Venetians appointed village guards to provide local security, and to prevent the banditry that had been a problem for the Ottoman authorities as well.[50]

The Venetian occupation lasted only three decades. Ottoman forces numbering 110,364 men under the command of Grand Vizier Damad Ali Pasha defeated the Venetians and regained the Morea in September 1715, thanks to their superior numbers (15,000 more men) and better firepower. Anavarin was taken peacefully, but the retreating Venetian army set fire to the fortress when the army of Ali Pasha approached on August 10, 1715.[51] According to Benjamin Brue, the French imperial agent who accompanied the army of Ali Pasha to the Morea, the Venetians generally inflicted considerable damage to property as they fled Ottoman troops.[52]

The Greek community in Koron switched its allegiance to the Ottomans in defiance of their former Latin overlords.[53] Damad Ali Pasha offered safe passage to the Venetian *provveditore* and to Greek inhabitants who remained faithful to Venice, if they submitted to the Ottoman forces peacefully. He ordered his troops to refrain from further violence and offered to escort the remaining Venetian forces to Corfu. The Janissaries, however, ignored his orders by enslaving the Venetians and taking booty. Discipline in the Ottoman army continued to be a problem, and by the time Ali Pasha reached Modon, the Ottoman forces had been reduced to 10,000 men owing to widespread desertion among the rank and file of the Ottoman troops.[54]

On account of his great familiarity with the Morea and his previous service, Aydındlı Mehmed Ağa was appointed the military governor *(alaybey)* of the peninsula.[55] Muhsinzade Abdullah Efendi, the former (pre-1685) chief accountant *(defterdar)* of the Morea, replaced Kara Mustafa Pasha, the former governor of Diyarbekır, and Damad Ali Pasha as the military commander of the Morea. *Sipahi* Mehmed Efendi became the *defterdar* of the province. The district governors *(sancakbeys)* were Cebecibaşi Mustafa Ağa, Kethüda Halil Ağa, İbrahim Ağa (Ağa of Turkmen), and Çavuşbaşi Şatır Ali Ağa.[56]

The Ottoman-Venetian war of 1715 appears to have resulted in further population decline in the region and in substantial destruction to property. The exchange of fire between the Venetian defenders and the Ottoman troops caused considerable damage to the fortresses of Koron and Modon. The Venetians themselves were responsible for destroying large parts of the two fortresses of Anavarin. TT880, the Ottoman cadastral

46. Davies 2004, p. 81, table 3. The *reale* was a silver coin the size of a dollar coin employed by Venice in the Levant only as a currency of account; see Tucci 1979; also Paolucci 1990, p. 90.

47. Davies 2004, p. 84, n. 123. On Venetian tax-farming in the Morea in general, see Davies 1994.

48. Davies 2004, p. 63.

49. Davies 2004, p. 63. The corvée was converted into a cash fee in 1704.

50. Davies 2004, p. 75.

51. Brue 1870, pp. 41–42, 66–67. See also Uzunçarşılı 1956, pp. 104–107.

52. Brue 1870, pp. 41–42.

53. Brue 1870, pp. 14–19.

54. Brue 1870, pp. 37, 42.

55. Raşid 1930, vol. 4, p. 155.

56. Raşid 1930, vol. 4, p. 184.

survey undertaken after the reconquest of 1715, describes ruined walls and houses in the two fortresses of Anavarin.[57] Much of the countryside appears to have been underutilized while under Venetian control.[58]

According to the Ottoman cadastral survey in TT880, the community of Anavarin-i cedid had 29 Greek houses in the *varış* (the suburb that lay outside the main gate of the fortress).[59] Perhaps as many as 160 Muslim houses inside the walls of the fortress had been damaged and partly burned by the Venetians during the Ottoman takeover in August 1715. The number of Greek residents in Anavarin-i cedid had dropped considerably between 1669 (if Evliya Çelebi's figures can be trusted) and 1700.[60] Fully one-third of the properties registered in the district of Anavarin in 1716 were described as uninhabited *mazra*ᶜ*as* and were attached to revenue-producing *çiftlik*s to be cultivated by their sharecroppers. Many lands and gardens, described as belonging to the Muslims prior to the Venetian takeover in 1685, remained to be returned to former owners. TT880 often explicitly states that fields were not being cultivated to the extent that they had been under the Ottomans prior to 1685. It is clear that two major wars between the Ottoman empire and Venice within a span of 30 years had done substantial physical damage to human life and property and had undermined the economic health of the region.

The Ottoman policy after the conquest was to nurture the economic well-being of the Morea and to encourage the local population, both Greek and Turkish, to return to their lands. The restoration of the *timar* system was a priority for the Ottoman government because of the strategic importance of the Morea, the area's economic value as a producer of grain, and the need to provide a strong defense in the southern Morea and gain the loyalty of the local population. Therefore, an imperial order issued immediately after the conquest requested that those who had fled during the Venetian occupation come back to the Morea with their families to their homes and take possession of their property. Ottoman officials were commanded to respect this order and to restore the property of the local Greeks and Turks.[61] In the Morea as a whole, 1,400 "sword" *(kılıç) timar*s and *ze*ᶜ*amet*s were granted from the state lands *(mîrî)* to members of the Ottoman cavalry *(sipahi*s).[62] The Janissaries received daily cash and food stipends *(yevmiye).* Also, the island of Euboea (Eğriboz) was incorporated into the province *(liva)* of the Morea to help augment the revenue base.[63]

57. See Chapter 2 of this volume for the relevant text, and Appendixes II and III for discussions of the condition of these fortresses when they were retaken by the Ottoman forces.

58. There were over 2,000 villages in the Morea in the 18th century according to Uzunçarşılı (1956, p. 107). This number is rather greater than the 1,498 settlements recorded, probably in 1711, by the Venetians as inhabited (Panayiotopoulos 1987, app. V). The total number recorded in 1700 was approximately

the same, 1,484 (Panayiotopoulos 1987, app. IV).

59. See Appendix III.

60. The population then appears to have remained more or less the same (about 30 households) until 1716. See also Chapter 4 and Appendix III.

61. Raşid 1930, vol. 4, pp. 154–155. It appears from this order that, at the time of the Venetian conquest, the flight of Muslims and Greeks and their settlement in Istanbul had resulted in underpopulation in the Morea and

losses to the local tax base. Other imperial orders in this same volume refer to the reconversion of churches to mosques, and to their restoration and upkeep. Another imperial order attempted to prevent holders of *timar*s from oppressing the *reaya* in Modon in August 1715. Several who had taken property and wives from *reaya* were executed by Damad Ali Pasha (Raşid 1930, vol. 4, p. 114).

62. Raşid 1930, vol. 4, pp. 154–155.

63. Raşid 1930, vol. 4, p. 186.

Despite the central government's desire to restore stability and economic well-being to the Morea, however, once away from the gaze of Istanbul, provincial officials satisfied their own greed. The Morea also became a source of reliable income for many Istanbul-based tax-farmers who had close ties to the ruling dynasty and to officials in the central government. Channels of communication between subjects and their ruler remained open, and complaints of the *reaya* about official abuse received some redress in Istanbul.[64]

THE OTTOMAN ARMY

The strategic importance of the southern Morea and the location of the Morea on the western frontier of the Ottoman empire required the maintenance of a large military presence in its major fortresses, namely Anavarin (Navarino), Modon (Methoni), Koron (Koroni), Arkadiye (Kyparissia), Kordos (Corinth), Holomiç (Hlemoutsi), Anabolu (Nafplion), and Manafşe (Monemvasia). It is clear that these contingents were strengthened at times when external threats to security increased.

In the period 1512–1520, there were 121 troops at the fortress of Anavarin-i atik. In response to a growing Venetian menace, however, the Süleymanic census (1520–1566) shows a fivefold increase in the Ottoman military presence in the fortress, to 643 troops. In addition to 295 Janissaries and 326 *sipahi*s, there were 2 fortress commanders (*dizdar*s), 16 artillerymen (*topçu*s), 2 Janissary *ağa*s, 1 preacher *(hatib),* and 1 prayer leader *(imam).*[65] By 1613 troops had been transferred to Anavarin-i cedid; the number of *timar*-holding *sipahi*s had dropped to 315 and the number of Janissaries to 37. It is likely, however, that there was a large troop increase at Anavarin during the Ottoman-Venetian wars over the island of Crete (1645–1669). According to Evliya Çelebi, Ottoman troops at Modon numbered 924 (200 Janissaries, 700 garrison personnel, 24 *ağa*s) in 1669.[66] It is clear from his account that the fortresses of both Anavarin-i atik and Anavarin-i cedid were garrisoned, but the number of troops is not specified.

According to the *Tarih-i Raşid,* the official history of the Ottoman empire from 1703 to 1730 written by Raşid, 1,400 sword (*kılıç*) *timar* and *ze°amet* grants were set up in the Morea after the conquest in 1715. A year later, in 1716, the number of troops at Anavarin-i cedid dropped to only 64 *sipahi*s, fewer than there were at the beginning of the 16th century at Anavarin-i atik. These *sipahi*s received *timar*s of 1,500–2,000 *akçe*s in *çiftlik*s such as Büyük Pisaski, İklina, Rudiye, Zaimzade, Ali Hoca, Pile, Kukunare, Rustem Ağa, Huri, Hasan Ağa, Avarniçe, and Kurd Ali Ağa.[67] The commander of the fort *(dizdar),* Mehmed Ağa, held the largest grant of all (10,000 *akçe*s) in the *çiftlik*s of Ali Hoca, Rustem Ağa, and Aşağı Katu in 1716.[68] The total amount of *timar* revenues granted to the *sipahi*s in Anavarin was 10,500 in 1716, a substantially smaller sum than the *timar* revenues of 62,222 *akçe*s for the district of Modon in 1520–1566 (Table 1.3). It is also significantly less than the sum of 21,173 *akçe*s that had been allocated as *timar*s and *ze°amet*s in 1512–1520, especially when it is considered that the silver content and value of the *akçe* had been hugely reduced in the intervening period.[69]

64. The best source for studying these petitions are the 200 volumes of *şikayet defter*s located in the Başbakanlık Archives in Istanbul.

65. TT80, pp. 1009–1068; TT367, p. 132.

66. For Evliya Çelebi's account on Anavarin, see Appendix I. We thank Pierre MacKay also for sharing with us his unpublished English translation of Evliya's description of Modon. See also Loupis 1999a, pp. 57–69, for a recent Greek translation of sections of his work relevant to Anavarin and Modon; and Kahraman, Dağlı, and Dankoff 2003, pp. 140–162, for the Morea.

67. Income from individual *timar*s was shared among several individuals.

68. TT881, pp. 158–288. He did not hold these *çiftlik*s alone.

69. Pamuk 2000, app. 2.

SOLDIERS INTO TAX-FARMERS

TABLE 1.3. DISTRIBUTION OF REVENUE FROM THE
DISTRICT OF MODON (INCLUDING ANAVARİN),
1520–1566

Expense	Amount (Akçes)
Imperial hass (hass-i hümayun)	310,666
Governor (hass-i mir-liva)	4,000
Military (timar and zeʿamet)	62,222
Vakf	15,430
Total	392,318

Source: TT367, pp. 131–132.

Janissaries were on cash payrolls (mevacibs) and were listed on registers (yoklama defters) separate from the sipahis. Entry into the Janissary corps depended traditionally on the customary devşirme collections from the Balkans, in which Christian boys were levied from the rural population and taken to Istanbul, where they converted to Islam and were trained in warfare. In the second half of the 16th century, recruitment from the reaya of Anatolia, the Caucasus, and Albania began to replace this system, and the use of Albanian irregulars (levends) increased considerably in the Morea during the 18th century. The latter received payment during the campaign season (March to September), but often roamed the countryside once the wars were over. Many turned to armed banditry and preyed on the peasants, whose options were limited to joining in the robbery or leaving the land and migrating to towns and cities.

THE CLASSICAL OTTOMAN MILITARY-ADMINISTRATIVE STRUCTURE

As a non-Muslim territory, the Morea belonged to the abode of war (dar al-harb), and its land became imperial domain (hass) or eminent domain and subject to state control (mîrî) after its conquest by Mehmed II. The original division of the Morea is unclear, but with the exception of the later conquests of Koron (Koroni) and Modon (Methoni) in 1500 and Manafşe (Monemvasia) and Anabolu (Nafplion) in 1540, it seems to have included, as districts (kazas), Arkadiye, Balye Badre (Patras), Londar (Leondari), Kalavrita, Korintos (Corinth), Voştiçe (Aigion), Holomiç (Hlemoutsi), Akova (Vyziki), Arhos (Argos), Mezistre (Mystras), and Karitena, each under the separate jurisdiction of an Islamic judge (kadı). The divisions were subject to change through time. By 1640 they included Balye Badre, Kalavrita, Korintos, Holomiç, Arhos, Anabolu, Andrusa (Androusa), Arkadiye, Londar, Fanar (Fanari), Tripoliçe (Tripolis), Karitena, Mezistre, Kalamata, Anavarin (Navarino), Modon, and Koron.[70]

The Morea was administered by a governor (sancakbey), a district judge (kadı), and a provincial accounts officer (defterdar), who were appointed by Istanbul to independent jurisdictions. One important duty of these provincial officials was to protect the mîrî status of land and prevent its conversion into freehold (mülk) orchards, or into religious and charitable endowments (vakfs). They neglected their duties frequently, however, and

70. As noted in notes 31 and 37 above, MM561 indicates that there were 23 districts in 1645, not including Anavarin and Manya (Mani). The number of districts had increased to 27 by 1786 (McGowan 1981, p. 118; see also Birken 1976, pp. 61–64). Anavarin, although a separate kaza from the 15th century, was administered as part of the district of Modon until the 18th century. In 1716 its revenues were recorded independently in TT880.

often abused the trust of their offices as economic conditions deteriorated during the 17th century. The *kadı* and *defterdar* first resided in the provincial center of Koron (then Tripoliçe in the 17th and 18th centuries) and were directly responsible to Istanbul. They were meant to act as a check on the authority of both the governor and *timar*-holders (*sipahi*s). Both the *kadı* and the *defterdar* held temporary postings and could be dismissed from office if reports of abuse and corruption were received by Istanbul. Their salaries were originally paid in cash, like those of other officials, but high inflation rates and the devaluation of Ottoman currency sharply decreased the real value of their remuneration. In response, some connived to receive *timar*s or to win tax-farms with the help of family members and professional colleagues in Istanbul, although this practice was contrary to the imperial law code *(kanunname)* and conflicts of interest resulted that could threaten the system of administrative checks and balances in the provinces.

The *defterdar* drew up tax registers with the help of a small staff and sent a copy of them to the finance department in Istanbul. He, together with the *kadı*, was also responsible for reporting to Istanbul any changes in the tax status of the *reaya,* and for overseeing the collection of taxes by the *sipahi*s and state agents (*emin*s or *kethüda*s). The finance department in Istanbul received reports and petitions from the *kadı* and *defterdar,* sometimes forwarded on behalf of the *reaya,* and might redistribute grants of revenue or revise rates of taxation in response to their recommendations.

The *kadı* administered the Islamic law *(shariᶜa)* and the imperial law *(kanun).* In this capacity he adjudicated lawsuits and officially registered all types of transactions conducted both by the *reaya* and by Ottoman officials, such as marriages, divorces, loans, purchases, and sales, for example. He also operated as an intermediary between the *reaya* and the central government and was supposed to report abuses and violations of the *shariᶜa* and *kanun* by the *sipahi*s or the governor. But during periods of administrative decentralization, *kadı*s and *defterdar*s regularly colluded with governors and tax-farmers to the disadvantage of the *reaya.* Indeed, many petitions by the *reaya* during the 17th century concerned the imposition of illegal dues by the *kadı*s themselves.

Most of the arable land in the Ottoman empire (90%) was *mîrî* and therefore subject to the imperial law code *(kanunname),* which was in turn based on both Islamic and local practices.[71] As for the Ottoman empire in general, most of the districts of Modon and Anavarin belonged to the imperial domain. Only urban residential units, commercial property, and orchards remained the private property *(mülk)* of their owners. Much commercial property in the Morea was, however, converted into *vakf*s to protect it against confiscation by the government and the imposition of high rates of taxation, though at least some state taxes were collected from all religious foundations. Muslim *vakf*s in the Morea were limited in number and were farmed out to local Ottoman elite. Some Christian religious properties were converted into Muslim *vakf*s, but most were not and retained the special tax status they had enjoyed prior to the Ottoman conquest. The tax-farming of such Christian religious property in the Morea by the Istanbul-based Greek Orthodox patriarchate was widespread.

The Morea's transition from the tributary status it had held under Demetrios and Thomas Palaiologos to total annexation by Mehmed II

71. İnalcık 1997, pp. 97, 105.

resulted in the imposition of a tighter political and fiscal control by the
central Ottoman government in the late 15th and 16th centuries. The
Morea became a significant source of income for imperial officials and for
the cavalry of the Ottoman empire (*sipahi*s). Ottoman naval commanders
(*kapudan pasha*s) and viziers, who served as governors (*sancakbey*s), would
have received large benefices (*hasse*s) of 100,000 *akçe*s or more from the
revenues of the Morea. The Ottoman cavalry and members of the administrative class received smaller revenue grants (*timar*s and *zeᶜamet*s) of 1,000–
100,000 *akçe*s for a period of one to two years.[72] Competition for such
prebends became more intense in the late 16th and 17th centuries, when
growth in the number of *timar*s did not keep pace with an increase in the
size of the Ottoman army, and when Ottoman borders started to shrink
after the loss of Azerbaijan to the Safavids in 1610. During the 17th century, the practice of granting tax-farms (the *mukataᶜa* system) expanded to
compensate for the insufficiency in the number of *timar*s available.

The *timar* system was very different from landholding systems that
had previously existed in the Byzantine empire and Europe.[73] The holder
of a *timar* or *zeᶜamet* did not own the land but received only the right to
collect taxes from the land and the peasants for a relatively short period of
time. The result was a system in which the state, the *sipahi*s, and the peasants all held simultaneous rights over the land.[74]

The *sipahi*s of the Ottoman empire generally resided in villages and
were responsible for collecting taxes from their *timar*s and maintaining security in the countryside. A *sipahi* was required to serve in military campaigns and to provide at least one fully armed horseman for each 1,000 *akçe*s
in the valuation of his prebend. A *sipahi* lost his *timar* if he did not serve
more than seven years in the army. He could also lose his *timar* upon dismissal from the army on charges of corruption. In addition to the *timar*
assigned by the state, a *sipahi* also received one *çift* of land (60–150 *dönüm*s =
5.5–13.8 ha) and a vineyard or orchard as support for himself and his family.

Under the *timar* system during the classical period of the Ottoman
empire, a peasant also might hold a *çift* of arable land and an orchard to
support his family. This land could not be fragmented upon his death, and
he could not sell, transfer, or transform the status of the land without the
permission of the *timar*-holder. He enjoyed hereditary usufruct *(tasarruf)*
rights to the land and was given land deeds (*tapu*s) that he could pass on to
his children and heirs. During the classical period, the state also prevented
the *timar*-holder from taking away the usufruct rights of the peasants
through the consolidation of land and its conversion into private estates
(mülk) or religious foundations (*vakf*s).[75]

The great tax registers and cadastral surveys of the classical period
were prepared with this principle in mind: to protect small independent
peasant households organized according to the *çift-hane* system from tax
abuses by *sipahi*s. A peasant was encouraged to remain on the land under
the protection of the state and the *sipahi,* and although the principle of
serfdom did not exist in the Ottoman empire, peasants generally could not
themselves decide to leave the land and thus avoid payment of tithes to
the *sipahi.* The Ottoman system contained checks to inhibit the development of permanent provincial bases of power. Sometimes, several *sipahi*s
held *timar*s in a single village to prevent the monopoly of power by one

72. İnalcık 1997, pp. 139–142.
73. İnalcık 1997, pp. 114–116.
74. İnalcık 1973, p. 110.
75. İnalcık 1997, pp. 110–117.

sipahi. Moreover, in order to prevent the development of feudalism, large prebends (in the form of a *hass*) that were granted to governors and other high officials usually were constituted by the intentional grouping together of individual properties that were scattered all over a region. Disturbances in the countryside could nonetheless bring about a considerable displacement of the peasant population that might result in the consolidation of land and the formation of elite estates. For example, in Anatolia, the great Celali uprisings of the late 16th and early 17th centuries encouraged the flight of peasants into towns and cities. This action in turn led to the takeover and consolidation of peasant land by the *sipahi*s who remained behind, with the *timar*-holders themselves becoming the agents that transformed these abandoned peasant farms into private estates (*çiftlik*s).

This trend spread to western Anatolia and the Balkans, whereas the *çift-hane* system survived in the rest of Anatolia and Syria.[76] Though the state and the *çiftlik* owners eventually reached some sort of accommodation, the peasants had the most to lose from transformations of this sort, because they could lose their land entirely. With the spread of commercial agriculture and *çiftlik* farming, the peasants were changed from tenants of small family-run farms into sharecroppers who worked the *çiftlik*s of the *sipahi*s and the local notables *(ayan)*. It is clear from the fact that some of the *çiftlik* names listed in TT880 appear already in Venetian census documents of the late 17th century (e.g., Osman Ağa, Rustem Ağa, Ali Hoca) that there were private *çiftlik*s in the Morea during the second half of the 17th century. Their formation reflected an increased commercialization of agriculture, but the extent of this commercialization and its timing have not been studied in detail. Suffice it to say that the continuing needs of Venice for its peasant-surplus production of grains, olive oil, sheep, silk, and wines had a great deal to do with its political ambitions to control the Morea.

Under the classical system, all peasants paid taxes either to the state or directly to a *sipahi*, if income from his holdings constituted part of a *timar* or *zeʿamet* grant. Among other dues, peasants paid a tithe *(üşür)* of one-eighth that was assessed on each crop, on gardens and orchards, must, flax, olive trees, and silk. A sheep tax *(adet-i ağnam)* of 1 *akçe* was exacted for every 2 sheep or pigs. Two *akçe*s were levied from each *dönüm* (919.3 m²) of arable land. There was a sales tax of 1 *akçe* for every 4 sheep and 1 *akçe* for every 2 goats. Fines from crimes *(bad-i hava ve cürmü cinayet)* were also paid.[77]

Muslim peasants were liable for a head tax known as *çift resmi* ("yoke tax") of 22 *akçe*s. Non-Muslim *reaya* paid a head tax known as *ispence* in place of providing corvée.[78] The amount of *ispence* exacted from Christian non-Muslim male heads of households had increased from 20 to 25 *akçe*s between 1480 and 1512.[79] In general it remained the same (25 *akçe*s) for Christians in the Morea and the Aegean islands until the 18th century.[80] Widows (*bive*s) were taxed at a lower rate of 6 *akçe*s. Non-Muslims also paid a poll tax *(cizye)*. The *cizye* in the mid-16th century was 1 gold coin (regarded as being equivalent to 40–60 *akçe*s). With the devaluation of the Ottoman *akçe*, the tax rose to 140 *akçe*s in the 17th century. The *cizye* was initially collected directly by the agents of the central state and was later farmed out by the central treasury to private individuals. According to İnalcık, in 1580 the average annual tax burden on every household

76. Tabak 1991, p. 137.

77. TT367, pp. 110–113; see also Alexander 1985a, pp. 187–197.

78. İnalcık 1959, pp. 602–608; Alexander 1985a, pp. 418–422. İnalcık has traced the origins of the *ispence* tax to Albania after the Ottoman conquest in 1471. Alexander believes that while the Ottoman jurists tried to define the *ispence* as the same as a *çift resmi* but imposed on non-Muslims, in reality they were "separate but parallel systems of personal taxation." According to İnalcık (1959, pp. 584–588), the amount of *çift resmi* varied from 22 to 50 *akçe*s in the Ottoman empire from 1455 to 1576. Corvée was an illegal imposition, often or only imposed in cases of emergency (e.g., for the construction of fortresses or for other military needs; see App. IV).

79. TT10, p. 115; TT80, p. 20. See Alexander 1985a, pp. 414–426, and Balta 1989, pp. 18–19. The amount of *ispence* collected from Jews was higher: e.g., in 1716 it was five times higher (125 *akçe*s) than the amount assessed on Christian households in the Morea (İnalcık 1959, p. 603).

80. TT446 (Süleyman Kanuni; mid-16th century), pp. 675–676; TT607 (Murad III; 1583); İnalcık 1959, p. 603.

in the Ottoman empire amounted to 250 *akçe*s.[81] The imposition of additional taxes, collectively known as extraordinary dues *(ᶜavariz),* became normal in the 17th century and greatly increased the tax burden on peasant households.

Archival sources allow the distribution of revenue, both urban and agricultural, to be described in considerable detail for the districts of Modon and Anavarin in the 16th century. Revenues from *vakf*s constituted a much smaller proportion (15,430 *akçe*s, or 3.9%) of total revenue of 392,318 *akçe*s than those that were *hass-i hümayun* (the imperial domain, 310,666 *akçe*s) or that were granted as prebends (Table 1.3). These taxes were farmed out, and a certain Ali Pasha established a *vakf* in Anavarin-i atik during the reign of Süleyman Kanuni (1520–1566) from annual *mukataᶜa* revenues of 15,430 *akçe*s from a bathhouse *(hamam),* a slaughterhouse, a butcher, and two houses.[82] The income from these *vakf*s helped support mosques, *hamam*s, and shrines in Modon. Military and administrative prebends (*timar*s and *zeᶜamet*s) constituted the second most important category of revenues (62,222 *akçe*s, or 15.9% of the total; Table 1.3), and initially the holders of these grants directly collected income from them, including the tithes on agricultural produce, which were paid in cash or in kind.

Urban taxes were usually *hass-i hümayun,* the imperial domain. Those that belonged to the state *(miri)* and were reserved for the imperial domain in the districts of Modon and Anavarin included customs dues, transit dues, market dues *(ihtisab),* and taxes on slaughterhouses and fisheries. *Hass-i hümayun* taxes represented the largest proportion (310,666 *akçe*s, or 79%) of taxes during the 16th century (Table 1.3) and were originally collected by imperial agents sent from Istanbul. By the 17th century, urban taxes were being farmed out to viziers, the *sipahi*s, the Janissaries, and the provincial elite as *mukataᶜa*s. These in turn subcontracted the collection of the taxes, an efficient way of collecting urban and commercial taxes as well as royal revenues, since the *sipahi*s could be called away to serve on campaigns.

According to the *kanunname,* or imperial tax code, of the Morea issued during the reign of Süleyman (1520–1566), the imperial *(hass-i hümayun)* tax on the fisheries (*talyan*s) consisted of half of the fish that were caught. Transit dues were assessed on goods that passed through towns at a rate of 2 *akçe*s per load *(yük).* The customs tax to be imposed on exports in the ports of the Morea was 2 percent on goods traded by Muslim merchants, 4 percent for merchants from Ragusa (Dubrovnik) and for local non-Muslims *(zimmi),* and 5 percent for non-Ottoman abode of war *(harbi)* merchants. The *sipahi*s were also required to pay customs dues when they engaged in trade. The customs tax on goods imported by sea varied from 2 *akçe*s per *arşun* (Turkish *ell* or yard, 0.76 m) of wool, 12 *akçe*s for every Arab slave, 1 *akçe* per sack *(çuval)* of flour or wheat, and 15 *akçe*s per barrel *(fuçı)* of wine imported.[83] Woolen textiles from England, slaves from North Africa (probably also referred to as Arab slaves), and wine and flour from Venice made up the bulk of imports to Anavarin.

Part of the income from the agricultural hinterlands of Modon and Anavarin was reserved for the central treasury and part was granted as military and administrative prebends in the form of *timar*s and *zeᶜamet*s. In the time of Süleyman, villages and fortresses in these districts were

81. İnalcık 1972, p. 349.
82. TT367, p. 131.
83. Alexander 1985a, pp. 187–197. On the length of the *arşun* employed for cloth, see İnalcık 1997, p. xxxvii.

TABLE 1.4. DISTRIBUTION OF SETTLEMENTS AND TAXABLE HEADS OF HOUSEHOLD IN THE DISTRICT OF MODON (INCLUDING ANAVARİN), 1520–1566

Settlement	Hass-i Hümayun	Parts of Timar or Zeᶜamet Grants
Fortress	2	0
Village	8	27 (8 in Anavarin)
Mazraᶜa	1	13
Muslim mahalles	2	0
Christian mahalles	2	0
Muslim hanes	74 (19 mücerreds)	9
Christian hanes	221 (28 mücerreds)	302 (40 mücerreds)
Widow hanes	6	4
Gypsy hanes	20	0
Jewish hanes	26	0

Source: TT367, p. 128.

distributed as shown in Table 1.4. Only 8 villages were *hass-i hümayun,* belonging to the imperial domain; the majority (27) were *timar*s or *zeᶜamet*s.

Table 1.5 lists average rural revenues from the town of Anavarin-i atik and its two *mazraᶜa*s (Pile and Vavalari) for the years 1512–1520, their total cash values, and local prices. The prices reflect the market values for these crops when the tithe was sold in the towns of Anavarin and Modon after the fortresses were provisioned.[84] Most of the taxes in Table 1.5 were *hass-i hümayun* and therefore were collected by the central treasury. The best sources of rural revenue in Anavarin were, in descending order, the tithe of must, wheat, acorns, barley, and olive trees. Sheep were not taxed by the head but indirectly, by taxing pastures (*otlak*s) at the sum of 100 *akçe*s. According to the *kanunname* of the Morea issued during the reign of Suleyman, a pasture tax of 25 *akçe*s was assessed for every 300 sheep. A pasture tax of 100 *akçe*s therefore implies the existence of 1,200 sheep. Most of the vineyards belonged to the Janissaries as private property *(mülk)* and provided relatively little public revenue. The taxes on the fishery and public weighing scales made up the best source of urban revenue in Anavarin.

The taxes in Table 1.5 do not include those from eight villages that were components of *timar*s or *zeᶜamet*s. The additional income from these dependencies of Anavarin amounted to 21,173 *akçe*s, bringing the total annual revenue for Anavarin to 50,259 *akçe*s.[85] In the early 16th century, the revenues of these eight villages were granted as *timar*s and *zeᶜamet*s for one to two years to 121 cavalrymen in the fortress of Anavarin-i atik.

By the 18th century, with the growing commercialization of agriculture, revenues from the sheep tax *(adet-i ağnam),* olive oil, and tithes on grains had became important tax-farms that were purchased by the members of the Ottoman bureaucracy (viziers, *voyvoda*s), the Janissary corps (*ağa*s), and other Muslim notables. Nonetheless, the *timar* system remained in use in the Morea in 1716, as will be seen below, and there were attempts to reform and restore it in ways that were responsive to significant changes in the composition and size of the Ottoman army that had occurred during the 17th century.

84. It is worth noting that these prices are substantially lower than in the early 18th century, at the time when TT880 was composed. The price of wheat had in 1716 risen to 50 *akçe*s per *kile,* that of barley to 30 *akçe*s/*kile,* and fodder to 20 *akçe*s/*kile.* There was as much as a 233 percent increase in the price of wheat from the early 16th century to the 18th century. The actual increase in the cost of grain appears to have been considerable, even discounting the substantial inflation of the *akçe* that occurred during this same period (see Pamuk 2000, pp. 161–171).

85. In contrast to Anavarin, the total annual revenue from the larger town of Modon and its 12 *mazraᶜa*s was 103,880 *akçe*s for the years 1512–1520.

TABLE 1.5. AVERAGE RURAL REVENUES FROM THE TOWN OF ANAVARİ-İ ATİK AND ITS *MAZRA^CA*S PİLE AND VAVALARİ, 1512–1520

Taxable Item	Amount in Kind	Cash Value (Akçes)	Value/Unit* (Akçes)
Head tax *(ispence)*	23 *hane*s	575	25/*hane*
Wheat	243 *kile*s	3,645	15/*kile*
Barley	230 *kile*s	1,840	8/*kile*
Fodder	14 *kile*s	56	4/*kile*
Fava beans	2 *kile*s	30	15/*kile*
Acorns	—	2,500	—
Chickpeas	5 *kile*s	75	15/*kile*
Lentils	2 *kile*s	30	15/*kile*
Millet	9 *kile*s	135	15/*kile*
Flax	48 *vukiyye*s (possibly *demet*s)	144	3/*kile*
Beehives	—	125	—
Orchards	—	107	—
Olive trees	2,853	1,000	0.35/tree
Gardens/vineyards	—	150	—
Mills	3 (2 working)	120	60/mill
Summer pasture *(yazlık)*	—	400	—
Pasture *(otlak)*	—	100	—
Meadow *(çayır)*	450 *dönüm*s	1,800	4/*dönüm*
Grass/hay	—	12	—
Fishery *(talyan)*	—	4,000	—
Port *(iskele)*	—	560	—
Slaughterhouse	—	300	—
Scales *(kapan)*	—	1,000	—
Market tax *(ihtisab)*	—	600	—
Oil press	1 in ruin	—	—
Flour mills	1 in ruin	—	—
Gardens of men	303 *dönüm*s	1,232	4/*dönüm*
Tile workshops	2 (1 working)	20	—
Onions	—	158	—
Guard *(koruçuluk)*	—	500	—
Karış	—	350	—
? (illegible)	—	150	—
Fines and bride tax	—	365	—
Mazra^ca	Vavalari	—	—
Mazra^ca	Pile	992	—
Kidney beans	1 *kile*	15	15/*kile*
Must *(şıre)*	775 *vukiyye*s (possibly *deng*s, = ½ a horse-load)	6,000	8/*vukiyye*
Total	—	29,086	—

Source: TT80, pp. 20–21.

*Amount for which the tithe was sold in the towns of Anavarin and Modon after the fortresses were provisioned.

THE TIME OF TROUBLES AND THE DECLINE OF THE *TİMAR* SYSTEM

The institution of the *timar* was the backbone of the Ottoman fiscal and administrative structure in Anatolia, Syria, and the Balkans during the classical period.[86] The system began to decline, however, during the last decades of the 16th century owing to population pressure, monetary crises, the Celali uprisings of 1580–1610 in Anatolia, and a revolution in military technology that continued well into the 17th century.[87] Developments in the Morea paralleled those in the empire as a whole, and in the second quarter of the 17th century the Morea was changed from a *timar* to a yearly-stipend *(saliyane)* province, with a fiscal status like that of Egypt and the Aegean islands.[88]

As a *saliyane* province, the Morea was one of 22 islands and coastal territories administered by the kapudan pasha (chief naval commander of the Ottoman empire) in the mid-17th century.[89] Its revenues were collected by the kapudan pasha or his acting tax-farmer as fixed amounts *(saliyane)* and were remitted to the central treasury after the military and administrative expenses of the territory were paid. It is not clear how long the *saliyane* system continued in the Morea, but, as we have already seen, the state made an attempt to restore the *timar* system immediately after the reconquest of the Morea in 1715.

This experiment in reviving the classical *timar* system proved to be unrealistic in the face of the transformation of the military organization and the constant need of the central treasury to raise cash revenue more efficiently. It was also short-lived.[90] In place of the *timar* system, the institution of tax-farming, which had existed in urban contexts since the classical period, spread to the countryside with increasing vigor. Provincial offices were also placed on auction and leased to bidders with significant economic resources and with political influence in Istanbul. Sometimes the same person or members of the same household held both fiscal tax-farms and auctioned provincial offices, a situation that provided provincial Janissary households and local notables *(ayan)* with the opportunity to build strong bases of power.[91]

86. İnalcık 1973, pp. 104–118; 1997, pp. 103–118.

87. İnalcık 1997, pp. 22–25; Akdağ 1995; İnalcık 1980; Murphey 1999.

88. Darling 1996, p. 27.

89. These *kapudanlık*s in A.H. 1040/ A.D. 1630 were Rodos (Rhodes, Greece), Mora (the Morea), Sakız (Chios, Greece), İnebahtı (Lepanto, modern Naupaktos, Greece), Andira (Andros, Greece), Suğla (the area of Çesme, east of Chios), Mezistre (Mystras, Lakonia, Greece), Karlı-eli (Akarnania and Aitolia, Greece), Eğriboz (Euboia), Nakşe ve Berre (Naxos and Paros), Midillu (Lesbos), Kocaeli (district of İzmid on the Sea of Marmara), Biğa (near the Dardanelles),

Limni (Lemnos, Greece), İskenderiyye (Alexandria, Egypt), Dimyad (Damietta, Egypt), Suveş (Suez), Kestel-i Mora (Rion), Anabolu (Nafplion, Argolida, Greece), Kavala (Kavala, Thrace, Greece), Tuzla (Tuzla in the Troad near Assos, or one of several others on the Sea of Marmara?), and Limoson (Limassol, Cyprus). See İnalcık and Zarinebaf, in press; cf. Birken 1976, pp. 101–108; Mostras 1995, p. 162; Stojkov 1970.

90. Greene (2000, pp. 22–35, esp. pp. 33–35), however, notes an apparently similar situation on the island of Crete, acquired by the Ottomans for the first time in 1669/1670, whereby a similar *mufassal defter* (TT825) was

first drawn up, followed by an *icmal defter* (TT801) showing the assignment of *timar*s to military personnel. Although a few key figures received much revenue from their *timar*s, the majority were given small shares. By the early 18th century, most of the tax revenue had been reassigned to the central treasury *(hass-i hümayun)*: Greene 2000, pp. 34–35.

91. The Azm household in Damascus, the Jalilis in Mosul, Ahmed Pasha al-Jezzar in Palestine, Kara Osmanoğlu in İzmir, Muridzade Haci Mehmed Ağa in Edremit, and Panayotis Benakis in Kalamata are examples of powerful local officeholders, tax-farmers, and *ayan* in the 18th century.

The expansion of the tax-farming system did not, however, necessarily bring about political decentralization and a "refeudalization" of the Ottoman economy. The state was always in a position to retract the tax-farms and to auction them to new bidders drawn from palace favorites and members of the Istanbul-based military and bureaucracy. The estates of powerful tax-farmers were, in fact, often confiscated by the state.[92] But it cannot be denied that there were important social ramifications of the expansion of tax-farming. Peasant indebtedness rose, and resulting social tensions provoked widespread rebellion and banditry in the countryside. Meanwhile, the local notables *(ayan)* resisted the attempts of the central government to undermine their power.

The expansion of private estates (*çiftlik*s) held by former *sipahi*s and *timar*-holders was another outcome of this process. Rural tax-farming and the privatization of revenue collection undermined the centralized checks and balances that ideally should have operated in the *timar* system to ensure stability, fiscal continuity, and permanent attachment of peasants to a *timar*.[93] When adequate response to complaints was not offered by the central government, peasants rose in revolt, creating cycles of rural disturbance that were similar to better-known examples that occurred in England during the same period.[94] The turmoils in the Ottoman empire were also responses to the modernization and commercialization of agriculture, but they reflected processes with decidedly local features.

The greater part of the Ottoman military had been supported by prebends. This source of income was now threatened by the consolidation of rural lands at the hands of tax-farmers and *çiftlik* owners who were drawn from the Ottoman military-bureaucratic elite and, to a lesser extent, from local notables. While there is very little published research that sheds light on the magnitude of this transformation outside Anatolia or that clarifies when and where it occurred, it is clear from dozens of imperial orders (*hüküm*s, *fermân*s) issued from Istanbul, in response to petitions by *reaya* to the imperial council and to reports by local administrators, that similar processes were under way in the Morea.[95]

In the Morea, as in Anatolia, the consolidation of land into private hands first took place during the second half of the 16th century, when local *sipahi*s and governors (*sancakbey*s) constructed estates from former *timar*s and from land abandoned by overtaxed peasants. During this period, demands for revenue imposed by the central government led to the creation of the new suite of taxes known as *ʿavariz*. Such taxes had traditionally been collected in support of specific military campaigns, but their collection became regularized in the 17th century and was greatly abused by the local *sipahi*s, local district judges, and governors. The following examples, drawn from the *mühimme defter*s (registers of important affairs), show in graphic detail how *timar*s in the Morea were appropriated by powerful military and bureaucratic figures. They thus shed light on the social and political crisis that the Morea faced already in the late 16th and the 17th centuries, a century prior to the compilation of TT880.

The district of Mezistre and the region of Mani were home to the most violent and long-lasting peasant rebellions in the Morea. These parts of Lakonia were wracked by cycles of violence from the second half of the 16th century to the early 19th.[96] The *sipahi*s and Janissaries became

92. On the confiscation of the estate of a powerful notable officeholder in western Anatolia, see Faroqhi 1991.

93. İnalcık 1977.

94. Cf. Charlesworth 1983.

95. Each region of the Ottoman empire was affected differently depending on its strategic importance and economic well-being. It is therefore impossible to generalize from one part of the empire to another. For the Balkans, see Gandev 1960 and McGowan 1981. For Anatolia, see İnalcık 1991a; Veinstein 1991; Faroqhi 1991; Nagata 1976.

96. Alexander 1985b. Alexander has not utilized the *mühimme defter*s for this period and relies mostly on local Greek sources and European accounts. Whereas he provides a description of brigandage by some Greeks and Turks, he does not analyze the causes of brigandage and economic and social changes in the Morea in the light of changes in other parts of the Ottoman empire. It is also worth noting that banditry in the Morea had a much older history (Wright 1999, pp. 284–292).

leaders of violent and criminal activities. Many had become wealthy landowners and accumulated great fortunes from illegally possessed land, banditry, and smuggling. Local peasants paid the price for the rupture in rural
law and order.

An imperial order dating to 7 *Ramadan* 975/April 1568 was sent to
the *kadı* of Modon describing a complaint of the agent *(kethüda)* of the
fortress of Manafşe (Monemvasia) against Ali Bey, the district governor
(sancakbey) of Mezistre, for illegally taking 28,000 *kuruş*es from the residents and for forcefully transferring the *timar*s of *sipahi*s to his own men.
He had also forced 60 *reaya* to work for him for 40 days and had illegally
taken 43,000 *akçe*s from them. The imperial order demanded, upon the
arrival of the herald *(çavuş)* who bore the order to Modon, an investigation and a report based on the *timar defter*s.[97]

In *Muharrem* 976/June 1568, a second contradictory imperial order
sent to Ali Bey, the provincial governor *(sancakbey)* of Mezistre who had
been the object of the earlier petition, repeated his own complaint against
Mehmed, the commander *(dizdar)* of the fortress of Manafşe. Mehmed
had removed the *timar*s of Ali Bey's men without an imperial certificate
(berat) and had taken more than 1,000 *akçe*s from them illegally. The petition also alleged that Mehmed had colluded with rebels Kara Memi and
Hasan Levend to raid merchants from Istanbul, and that they had killed
four soldiers and Muslim and non-Muslim *reaya*. Mehmed's activities were
reported to have caused peasants in the area to flee such unchecked oppression. The imperial council noted that it had already ordered an investigation into the affairs of Mehmed but had received no response. It again
demanded a careful and proper investigation and report.[98]

From the contradictory information contained in the two preceding
imperial orders that were issued, within three months of each other, to the
governor of Mezistre and to the *kadı* of Modon, it is clear that a struggle
over *timar*s had evolved into outright rebellion and banditry by the members of the Ottoman military and the Greek *reaya* as early as 1568. Nor
was this the first such rebellion in the southern Morea. An earlier report
submitted by the governor of Mezistre to the imperial council on 20 *Cemaziyülevvel* 975/November 1567 had warned about a rebellion by Greeks in
Mani and their contacts with some Spanish ships. An imperial order issued in response to this report mandated that the forts of Modon, Koron,
and Anavarin be strengthened.[99] The rebellion continued until January
1568. The governor *(bey)* of Mezistre was ordered to collect taxes according to the *kanun* and to carry out an investigation with the help of an
imperial herald, Mustafa Çavuş.[100]

The evidence that the *sipahi*s were engaged in contraband trade with
Venice and Spain is substantial, as is the evidence for their involvement in
banditry. The Ottoman state had placed a ban on the export of wheat that
was not lifted until the 18th century. But it is clear that the ban was regularly violated in frontier areas. A report by the *sancakbey* of the Morea to
the imperial council in *Safer* 975/August 1567 informed it of the illegal
sale of wheat and sheep to the Venetians by the *sipahi*s Nazir and Lutfi.[101]

From another imperial order, issued to the *kadı* of Modon and inspector *(müfettiş)* of the Morea on 10 *Receb* 975/January 1568, we learn that

97. MD7, no. 975.
98. MD7, no. 1477.
99. MD7, no. 459.
100. MD7, no. 631.
101. MD7, no. 120.

this same Lutfi owned a large *çiftlik* (70–80 *çift*s) on the coast and engaged in banditry with his 40 Arab slaves. He had several hundred cows, sheep, and goats and collected revenue from his *timar*s. He joined the pirates of the "infidels" in ravaging the countryside. And he conducted criminal activities against his fellow *sipahi*s. According to the report of the *bey* and *kadı* of Balye Badre, Lutfi, together with his slave Yusuf, had broken into the house of the *sipahi* Tur Ali and had kidnapped his wife. Yusuf had previously accused Tur Ali in the Islamic court *(mahkeme)* of marrying without proper permission and had threatened that he would be killed were he to remain in the village. Lutfi and Yusuf also broke into the house of Mustafa, son of Ahmed Bey, and kidnapped and raped his wife. They returned her pregnant after six months, and she gave birth to a daughter who was one year old at the time of this petition. The wife was brought into the court, where she claimed that Yusuf had raped her and was the father of her illegitimate daughter.[102]

In the following century the violence continued. A letter by the *kadı* of Tripoliçe to the imperial council in *Rebiyülevvel* 1056/April 1646 reported the banditry of a certain Yahya and his 30 to 40 followers who broke into the quarters of the *cizye*-collector Halil and robbed him of 6,000 *kuruş*es.[103] An imperial order from the middle of A.H. 1085/A.D. 1675, issued to the provincial governor of the Morea and to the *kadı* of Tripoliçe, relayed complaints of peasants against a certain Mehmed Kaplan and a certain Abdullah for breaking and entering, illegal impositions, and murder.[104]

Monetary crises also contributed to the downfall of the traditional *timar* system, particularly when the Ottoman-Venetian wars of 1645–1669 disrupted trade and precipitated a fall in state revenues in the southern Morea. In *Zilhicce* 1056/December 1648, a report sent to Istanbul by the governor of the Morea, Vizier Yusuf Pasha, related that salaries of Janissaries in various fortresses, including Anavarin, Modon, and Koron, were in arrears. He complained that the tax collector had imposed on the *ağa*s extraordinary dues *(kalemiyye)* that amounted to 50–60 *kuruş*es per man, and that he had demanded woolen textiles imported from England. According to the imperial order issued to the *kadı* of the Morea in reply, because of the war against Venice, revenues of the ports (*iskele*s) and harbors in the Morea had fallen, and it was these that normally supported the expenditures of the fortresses.[105]

During such times of economic distress, the Ottoman military was asked not only to accept long delays in the payment of their salaries, but even to pay special taxes. In a petition, Mehmed Topçu, the commander of artillery in the fortress of Anavarin-i cedid, complained in mid-*Muharrem* 1086/March 1675 about the failure of the head of artillery, Topçubaşi Ali, to pay his salary for the last eight years![106] Moreover, an increase in the number of men in military service during the Candian war resulted in a stiff competition over *timar* grants. A high inflation rate (100–200%) in the 17th and 18th centuries undermined the real value of those taxes that were collected in cash from the *timar*s. The tax registers prepared in the previous century did not adjust the tithe level to the current rate of inflation. There was a tendency by the *sipahi*s to collect all the taxes in kind.

102. MD7, no. 692.
103. Tulum 1993, p. 113.
104. Majer 1984, folio 28a.
105. Tulum 1993, pp. 411–412.
106. Majer 1984, folio 76b.

The local market prices did not correspond to prices in major cities and ports. Moreover, to overcome the loss of revenue due to hyperinflation and a reduction in the profitability of their *timar*s, the *sipahi*s and agents of the central state began imposing higher rates and a variety of *ᶜavariz* taxes on the peasants.

The number of petitions presented by the *reaya* to the imperial council regarding illegal impositions by the *sipahi*s and *kadı*s increased greatly during the second half of the 17th century. The living conditions of the local inhabitants of the Morea worsened during military campaigns in this period, and under these circumstances it is hardly a surprise that the Ottoman government could not anticipate the loyalty of the Greek *reaya* during the Holy League war of 1685–1699. In a petition dating from mid-*Zilkade* 1085/January 1675, the peasants of a village complained about illegal dues (70–80 *kuruş*es per person), demands for corvée, and an exaction of four to five *kile*s of barley and wheat per person imposed by Hasan Sipahi.[107] In a petition at the end of *Şevval* 1085/December 1674, residents of a village in the district of Karitena—Hasan, Ali, and two men named Osman—refused to pay extraordinary *(ᶜavariz)* dues, claiming descent from Janissaries, although they could not document this.[108]

After the Ottoman reconquest of the Morea in 1715, administrative problems resumed. The situation in the Morea deteriorated only two months later, when local inhabitants rebelled in November 1715, prior to the registration of TT880 in January 1716. The author of *Tarih-i Raşid* does not describe the causes and nature of this rebellion, although it must have sounded an alarm in Istanbul as Osman Pasha, former governor of Tirhala (Trikala), was sent to the Morea as military governor to suppress it. He was promoted to the position of vizier with one horsetail after his great success in dealing with the rebels.[109] After the Morea was quieted, the oppressive policies of Ottoman high officials continued to harm the *reaya*.

THE INSTITUTION OF TAX-FARMING AND THE PRIVATIZATION OF REVENUE COLLECTION

The *iltizam* (tax-farming) system lay at the foundation of economic and social changes in the Ottoman empire. The institution of tax-farming, like the *timar* system, predated the Ottoman empire and existed in other Islamic states (medieval Egypt, the Seljuk empire, Mughal India).[110] Tax-farming had always been a significant source of income for the Ottoman state. According to İnalcık, in 1528 tax-farms (*mukataᶜa*s) made up 30 percent of state revenues in the Ottoman empire.[111] Barkan estimated that tax-farms in the European provinces in 1527–1528 constituted about 23 percent of state revenues and in Egypt amounted to 80 percent of the total revenue.[112] It is, in fact, likely that, already in the 16th century, as much as one-half of all public revenue in the Ottoman empire was being farmed out to viziers, *timar*-holders, and a few private individuals for a limited time period (one–two years). The central state and its *timar*-holders gradu-

107. Majer 1984, folio 19a.
108. Majer 1984, folio 7a.
109. Raşid 1930, vol. 4, pp. 312–313.
110. Çizakça n.d.; Darling 1996, pp. 119–160.
111. İnalcık 1997, p. 64.
112. Barkan 1953, pp. 259–329.

ally lost the right to collect taxes as tax-farms increased in number. Çizakça has summarized the basic principles of Ottoman tax-farming:

> As in Medieval Egypt and Mughal India, in the Ottoman empire also, the *iltizam* [tax-farm] was basically considered as a system of revenue collection in the economy. The Ottoman *mültezim* [tax collector], like his counterpart in Medieval Egypt, was also essentially a risk taker, an entrepreneur, who was delegated the right to collect taxes from a *mukataʿa* (tax source) by the state. This delegation occurred in a competitive bidding where the highest bidder obtained the right to collect the taxes from a *mukataʿa*. The *mültezim* hoped to collect more revenue than his total cost (the auction price paid plus operational expenses). In that case he enjoyed a profit; otherwise he suffered a loss. The risks were also similar; as in the earlier Islamic states, a *mültezim* not able to pay to the state the promised amount determined in the auction, risked confiscation or imprisonment.[113]

Theoretically, there was open competition for the most lucrative tax-farms between Muslim and non-Muslim bidders of all social and ethnic backgrounds, sometimes in partnership with each other. But in practice, Istanbul-based tax-farmers usually appointed agents (*emins*) to collect their *mukataʿa* revenues for them in the provinces. It should be kept in mind that the state never intended to lose control of these revenues, as it auctioned them to new bidders every one to two years. Moreover, if the tax-farmer failed to pay the agreed-upon installments to the central treasury, the state could confiscate the tax-farm before the term expired. This led short-term tax-farmers to overexploit the tax sources and practice extortion. They made every attempt to increase their margin of profit (20–50% per annum) at the expense of the local *reaya*. They also relied on financiers and bankers for a ready supply of cash at high interest rates (20–50% per annum) to bid for new tax-farms. Moneylenders and Istanbul-based bankers sometimes invested directly in the most lucrative tax-farms, such as the collection of customs dues in major urban centers. It appears, therefore, that this system proved to be more oppressive for the taxpayers and potentially more corrupt than the *timar* system. Life-term tax-farms (*malikane*s) were established in 1695, on the assumption that holders of *malikane*s would have a long-term interest in preserving the stability of their investment by protecting the sources of their revenues.

Only certain members of the Ottoman bureaucracy, high military officials, Istanbul-based bankers and merchants, and members of the Ottoman dynasty with strong ties to the palace and the administration were in a financial and social position to win the most profitable life-term *(malikane)* tax-farms all over the empire. Long-term tax-farms were briefly retracted in 1715 because, like short-term tax-farms, they had negative consequences for the *reaya*. They were restored again by Grand Vizier Nevşehirli Damad İbrahim Pasha in 1718. But, according to Genç, the number of *malikane* tax-farms continued to increase (by 209%, from 220 to 680) between 1715 and the end of the 18th century. The increase in revenue produced by

113. Çizakça 1980, p. 147.

TABLE 1.6. LIFETIME *(MALİKANE)* TAX-FARMS *(MUKATAᶜAS)* IN THE MOREA, 1731

Malikane	Amount (Kuruşes)	Tax-farmer
Ispence of Monastery of . . . in Karitena	2,909.5 (1,754.5 *hass-i hümayun* + 1,155.0 *hass-i mirmiran*)	Mustafa Ağa, imperial . . .
Cizye of Kondra in Kordos	720.0	Süleyman Efendi, *emin*
Delalbaşılık of *mukataᶜas* of the Morea	500.0	Mehmed Ağa, imperial Janissary
Miranlık of the *muhassıl* of the Morea	200.0	Alexandri, imperial dragoman
Tercümanlık of the Morea	200.0	—

Source: DBŞM 1750, p. 11.

malikane tax-farms amounted to 88 percent in the 18th century.[114] In this system, the holder of the tax-farm *(malikaneci)* had to make two payments to the central fisc, a large lump-sum amount *(muaccele)* determined by auction, and an annual amount fixed by the government.[115] The minimum *muaccele* at which bidding began was fixed by the state as the estimated annual return multiplied by 2 to 10 times. The subcontracting of the most lucrative sources of revenue by Muslim *voyvodas*, *mutesellims*, and *ağas*, as well as Christian tax-farmers, became a normal practice in the provinces during the 18th century.

In the Morea, unlike in the Syrian provinces, a limited number of tax-farms were *malikanes* (Table 1.6). The institution of short-term tax-farming expanded considerably in the Morea by the end of the 18th century. The tax-farms of the tithes, the sheep tax, and the olive-oil tax were the most lucrative in the Morea. They were all farmed out to members of the Ottoman dynasty, governors of the Morea, and the Muslim members of the Ottoman military-administrative class in the Morea. The tax-farmers invested in *mukataᶜas* with the highest expected profitability. They were not interested in enhancing the productivity of the land.[116] This system contributed substantially to the accumulation of capital in the private sector by generating massive profits and forcing the entrepreneurs to form partnerships.[117] It gave rise to enormous economic dislocation and social tensions.

Moreover, the Ottoman state faced an immense problem in the late 17th and the 18th centuries, precipitated by the loss of provincial revenue just as it was in desperate need of financing its many wars. Since the *sipahi* cavalry that had been supported by the *timar* system had become an increasingly insignificant component in the military, the state found it more feasible to raise cash that could be used to hire new types of troops for the army by auctioning tax-farms as sources of revenue to the highest bidders.

When Ottoman governors also became provincial tax-farmers, as happened in the 18th century, there was vast potential for corruption and abuse of power. The imperial council was, however, responsive to petitions from the *reaya*. Complaints about abuses committed by Ahmed Pasha, governor and tax collector *(muhassıl)* of the Morea, resulted in his dismissal in 1723, and more generally in response to complaints by overtaxed *reaya*, the two positions were sometimes separated to prevent further oppression. According to the author of *Tarih-i Raşid*, in 1723 Hasan Pasha,

114. Genç 1975, p. 245. For a more recent and thorough analysis of the *malikane mukataᶜa* system, see Salzmann 1995.
115. Salzmann 1993, pp. 400–402.
116. Çizakça n.d., p. 17.
117. Çizakça n.d., p. 30.

TABLE 1.7. URBAN TAX-FARMS (*MUKATAᶜA*S) IN THE DISTRICT OF ANAVARİN, 1716

Source	Amount (Akçes/Year)
İskele (port) of Anavarin	4,500
Horse market, public scale *(kantar)*, transit dues *(bac-i siyah)*	2,500
Fishing on the coast	1,000
Candle workshop of Anavarin	500
Market *(ihtisab), ihzariyye, kile, kantar* of Anavarin	2,000
Fishery *(talyan)* across from old Anavarin	24,000
Slaughterhouse *(serhane)*	500
Total	35,000

Source: TT884, pp. 493–494.

the former governor of Ohrid, became the military governor of the Morea, while Hasan Ağa, the former tax collector *(muhassıl)* of Sakız (Chios), became the *muhassıl* of the Morea.[118] But, despite centralized efforts of the state, Ottoman governors and military elite continued to acquire large estates *(çiftliks)* and to amass great fortunes as tax-farmers *(muhassıls)* during the second half of the 18th century.

Table 1.7 lists annual urban revenues from tax-farms in the district of Anavarin in 1716. The names of the tax-farmers are not provided, so it is possible that these were imperial tax-farms *(hass-i hümayun)* or tax-farms farmed out to the vizier and governor of the Morea *(hass-i mir-liva)*.

According to Table 1.7, the tax-farm of the fishery *(talyan)* across from Anavarin-i atik (in the area that today is known as the Osmanaga Lagoon) yielded the highest revenue. Coastal fishing was also taxed but produced a smaller income. The customs dues from the port *(iskele)* of Anavarin constituted the second most important tax-farm in the district of Anavarin in 1716. Comparison of these revenues with those from other centers sheds light on the relative significance of the revenues of Anavarin compared to those of the Morea as a whole. Revenues from the fishery at Anavarin, for example, were much lower than those from fisheries in the districts of Holomiç (Hlemoutsi) (300,000 *akçes*) and Karitena (108,000 *akçes*) but represented a significant source of income that was nonexistent in Arkadiye and Modon. The *mukataᶜa* revenue of the customs dues from the port of Anavarin was much lower than that from the districts of Balye Badre (30,000 *akçes*), Holomiç (18,000 *akçes*), and Arkadiye (15,000 *akçes*).[119] As might be expected, external trade in Modon was more important than at Anavarin, and this circumstance is reflected in a *mukataᶜa* revenue of 20,000 *akçes* (compared to 4,500 *akçes* for Anavarin) for the customs dues of its ports.

As discussed above, in 1716 the Ottoman state made an attempt to restore the *timar* system in the Morea, owing to the strategic importance of this region and the need to maintain a high degree of military readiness. But the plan was soon abandoned, in part because a high rate of desertion in the military made a revival of the prebend system an undependable means of managing rural revenue.

118. Raşid 1930, vol. 4, pp. 117–118.

119. DBŞM 1750.

TABLE 1.8. RURAL TAX-FARMS (*MUKATAᶜA*S) AND TAX-FARMERS IN THE MOREA, 1731

Kaza	Amount (Kuruşes/Year)	Tax-farmer	Origin
Kalamata and dependencies	3,600	Musa Ağa	Janissary
Andrusa and dependencies	2,250	Musa Ağa	Janissary
Londar and dependencies	770	Kurdoğlu Mehmed Ağa	Janissary
Karitena, Fanar, and dependencies	550	Arnavud Mustafa Ağa	Janissary (Albanian)
Koron and dependencies	2,900	Al-Hac Ömer Hoca and Al-Hac Süleyman Ağa	*Müfti* and military
Mezistre and dependencies	8,950	Al-Hac Yusuf Ağa and Al-Hac Abdulkadir Ağa	*Voyvoda* (Mezistre) and Janissary
Manafşe and dependencies	530	Hüseyn Ağa	Janissary *(azeb)*
Arkadiye and dependencies	1,600	Ali Ağa son of Hüseynzade	*Voyvoda* of Arkadiye
Anavarin and dependencies	850	Şeyhi al-Hac Hüseyn Bey	*Ulema*
Anabolu and dependencies	2,600	Al-Hac Hüseyn Ağa	*Dizdar* (Anabolu)
Imperial *hass*es and *çiftlik*s	450	Al-Hac Hüseyn Ağa	*Dizdar*
Miri monasteries and dependencies	330	Al-Hac Hüseyn Ağa	*Dizdar*
Modon and dependencies	1,130	Şeyhi al-Hac Hüseyn Bey	*Ulema*
Kordos and dependencies	1,400	Al-Hac Ali Ağa	Janissary
Tripoliçe and dependencies	1,540	Al-Hac Mehmed Efendi and Mustafa Ağa Halife	Bureaucracy and *Mukabeleci* of Morea
Klavrita and dependencies	1,300	İsmaᶜil Ağa	*Voyvoda* of Klavrita
Total	28,054[*]		

Source: DBŞM 1750, pp. 6–7.
[*]30,750 minus 2,696 *hass-i mirmiran* of the Morea.

The conversion of *timar* villages in the district of Anavarin to *çiftlik*s had already been under way before the Venetian takeover in 1686, as will be discussed further below. These *çiftlik*s, and eventually, as can be seen in Table 1.8, all sources of revenue, including former *timar*s, came to be auctioned off to members of the Ottoman central and provincial military and bureaucracy, and also to female members (princesses and concubines) of the Ottoman household.

As can be seen from the data included in Tables 1.6, 1.8, and 1.9, 8 of the 19 tax-farmers in the Morea in 1731 were members of the Ottoman military, and more than half were administrative staff. These individuals included 3 *voyvoda*s, 1 *bey*, 1 *şeyh,* 12 *ağa*s, 1 *müfti,* and a bureaucrat. All the tax-farmers in the Morea during this period were Muslims. In 1731 some members of the Muslim religious elite (e.g., the *müfti* and *kadıasker* of Rumeli, Al-Hac Mehmed Efendi) were important tax-farmers.[120] Local Christian notables are absent from these tax-farm registers. They may have been subcontractors to Muslim tax-farmers.

Some tax-farmers held farms for former *timar*s as well as for tithes and the sheep tax. Al-Hac Yusuf Ağa, the *voyvoda* of Mezistre, and Al-Hac Abdulkadir Ağa held the largest total of tax-farms (13,763 *kuruşes*), consisting of the *mukataᶜa*s of the sheep tax *(adet-i ağnam)* of the districts of Mezistre, Manafşe, and two other districts (4,813 *kuruşes*) and of the tithe in the district of Mezistre (8,950 *kuruşes*). By himself, Al-Hac Yusuf Ağa also held the *mukataᶜa* of 20 former *timar*s in Mezistre, a sum that amounted

120. Al-Hac Mehmed Efendi, who is listed in Tables 1.8 and 1.9 as a tax-farmer at Tripoliçe, was both a *müfti* and a *kadıasker* (administrator).

TABLE 1.9. TAX-FARMS (*MUKATAᶜA*S) OF THE SHEEP TAX (*KURUŞ*ES/YEAR) IN THE MOREA, 1731

Kaza	Amount (Kuruşes/Year)	Tax-farmer	Origin
Kalamata and Andrusa	550	Musa Ağa	Janissary
Londar	1,250	Kurdoğlu Mehmed Ağa	Janissary
Karitena and Fanar	2,600	Arnavud Mustafa Ağa	Janissary (Albanian)
Mezistre, Manafşe, Aya Monove, . . . , Barduniye?	4,813	Al-Hac Yusuf Ağa and Al-Hac Abdulkadir Ağa	*Voyvoda* of Mezistre
Arkadiye	1,080	Ali Ağa son of Hüseynzade	*Voyvoda* of Arkadiye
Modon, Koron, Anavarin	2,200	Şeyhi al-Hac Hüseyn Bey	*Ulema*
Anabolu	2,070	Al-Hac Hüseyn Ağa	*Dizdar*
Kordos	2,850	Al-Hac Ali Ağa	Janissary
Tripoliçe	1,917	Al-Hac Mehmed Efendi and Mustafa Ağa Halife	Bureaucracy and *Mukabeleci* of Morea
Klavrita	1,300	İsmaᶜil Ağa	*Voyvoda* of Klavrita
Total	20,630		

Source: DBŞM 1750, p. 7.

to 300 *kuruş*es annually.[121] Arnavud Mustafa Ağa held the *mukataᶜa*s for the tithe and sheep tax of the districts of Karitena and Fanar, and for 100 former *timar* villages in the Morea that amounted to 1,020 *kuruş*es annually.[122] Other tax-farmers, such as Şeyhi al-Hac Hüseyn Bey, held the *mukataᶜa*s for the tithe and sheep tax for several districts (the tithe of Anavarin and Modon and the sheep tax of Anavarin, Modon, and Koron), a combined sum that amounted to 4,180 *kuruş*es annually. Still others held smaller tax-farms within their own districts. For example, İsmaᶜil Ağa, the *voyvoda* of Klavrita, held the tax-farms in his district for tithes and for the sheep tax, while the *müfti* of Koron held the tax-farm of Koron together with Al-Hac Süleyman Ağa.[123]

Already toward the middle of the 18th century, it is clear that olive oil was an important surplus crop, but most revenues from its export and sale were used to cover military expenditures *(ocaklık)* in fortresses in the Morea and elsewhere, namely Kordos, Manafşe, Modon, Anavarin, Anabolu, and İnebahtı. The *mukataᶜa* for olive oil was valued at 7,500–8,100 *kuruş*es in 1736–1747. It was at first farmed out to the grand vizier (who held nine shares, or *hisse*s), but then most of the olive-oil revenues were allotted to the *ocaklık* of the fortresses. In 1747, after the deduction of *ocaklık* dues, only 51.5 *kuruş*es out of a total revenue of 8,048.5 *kuruş*es remained as profit in the hands of Hotmanzade and Musa Ağa, notables *(ayan)* in the Morea who had contracted for this tax-farm.[124]

In addition, women of the palace also began to participate in increasing numbers in bidding for short-term tax-farms and *malikane*s in Istanbul, Anatolia, the Morea, and Egypt, a development that in general reflected the growing public visibility of palace women and Ottoman princesses during the 18th century.[125] Mamluk women also played a prominent role as tax-farmers (13% in 1797) in Egypt at this time.[126] Female tax-farmers there inherited their tax-farms (*iltizam*s) from their fathers or husbands or received them as gifts from their masters. By the second half of the 18th century, the number of *çiftlik* estates in the Morea had further increased,

121. DBŞM 1750, p. 10.
122. DBŞM 1750, p. 10.
123. DBŞM 1750, p. 10.
124. DBŞM 2055, pp. 2–3.
125. Zarinebaf-Shahr 1998, 2000.
126. Cuno 1992, pp. 39–41.

TABLE 1.10. TAX-FARMS (*MUKATA^CA*S) IN THE MOREA, 1769

Source	Amount (Kuruşes/Year)	Tax-farmer	Origin
Muhasıllık of the Morea	14,118.0	Mehmed Emin?	Bureaucracy
Olive oil in the Morea and dependencies	2,261.0	Ali Ağa, Mahmud Efendi, Abdullah Ağa, Hüseyn Ağa	Military-administrative
Kordos and dependencies	2,635.0	Ahmed Ağa, Hababe Hanım, Ahmed Ağa, Mehmed Bey, Ahmed Bey	*Muhassıl* of the Morea? Palace women, military
Klavrita and dependencies	1,444.0	Seyyid Mehmed Ağa, Al-Hac Süleyman Efendi	Military, bureaucracy
Manafşe and dependencies	1,565.0	Seyyid Ali Bey	*Ulema*
Anavarin and dependencies	807.0	Ebubekir Efendi, Ahmed Efendi, Ahmed Ağa	Bureaucracy
Balye Badre and dependencies	6,435.0	İbrahim Pasha	Vizier
Cizye of Astayos and dependencies	1,868.0	İbrahim Ağa	Imperial commander
Tripoliçe and dependencies	5,274.0	Hababe Hanım, Ahmed Ağa	Palace women (Mahmud I's *ikbal* [favorite])
Modon, Koron, and dependencies	565.0	Ahmed Ağa, Hüseyn Ağa	*Muhassıl* of the Morea?
Anabolu and dependencies	477.0	Mehmed Pasha	Vizier, *valı* of the Morea
Karitna and dependencies	1,859.0	Seyyid Mehmed Tahir Ağa, Abdulvehab Efendi, Abdurrahman Ağa	Military, bureaucracy
Andrusa and dependencies	2,320.0	Rukiye Hanım, Muhsinzade Mehmed Pasha	Daughter of vizier, *Muhafız* of the Morea
Mezistre and dependencies	1,963.0	Al-Hac İbrahim Efendi	*Kadıasker* of Rumeli
Kalamata and dependencies	6,494.0	Mehmed Emin, Mehmed Halife, Hafise Hanım, Aye Hanım, Emine Hanım, Hadice Hanım, Süleyman Ağa, Ali Ağa	*Muhassıl* of the Morea, palace women, military
İskele of Holomiç and dependencies	8,504.0	Mustafa Ağa, Ahmed Ağa, Hüseyn Ağa	Military
Cizye of ?	250.0	Al-Hac İbrahim Efendi	*Kadıasker* of Rumeli
Public scale *(mizan)* of silk?	1,062.0	Ahmed Ağa Ahmed Ağa, Selim Ağa, Ahmed Pasha, Nu^cman Efendi, Ebubekir Efendi, Ahmed Ağa	Military, bureaucracy
Cizye of Mezistre	58.5	Atif Hüseyn Efendi	Bureaucracy
Resm-i dönüm in the Morea	915.0	Ahmed Ağa	Military
Tithe on wheat and barley in the Morea	2,019.0	Mehmed Ağa	Military
Cizye of Arkadiye and dependencies	1,771.5	Al-Hac Süleyman Efendi	Bureaucracy
Cizye of . . . Yani and dependencies	250.0	Mustafa, Ahmed, Hasan	—
Ayo Yori in Kordos	61.0	—	—

Source: DBŞM 3998, pp. 2–3.

and commercial agriculture had expanded. The nature of tax-farming at that time reflected these changes.

These developments in tax-farming in the Ottoman empire as a whole can be recognized in data specifically from the Morea. For example, if the data in Table 1.10 (dating to 1769) are compared with those in Tables 1.8 and 1.9, notable differences can be discerned. Administrative positions were farmed out to Ottoman officials and subjects in the 18th century. By

1769, the office of tax collector *(muhassıl)* of the Morea had become the largest tax-farm (14,118 *kuruş*es). It was followed by the tax-farm for customs of the port of Holomiç (8,504 *kuruş*es), the tithe of Kalamata (6,494 *kuruş*), and the tithe of Balye Badre (6,435 *kuruş*es). Between 1731 and 1769, the revenues from rural tax-farms seem substantially to have increased for several districts in the Morea: Kordos by 88 percent, Manafşe by 195 percent, and Tripoliçe by 242 percent. In contrast, the rural tax-farm revenue from Anavarin and its dependencies appears to have decreased slightly, from 850 *kuruş*es in 1731 to 807 *kuruş*es in 1769, while those from Modon and Koron appear to have fallen dramatically.[127]

There is now a clear link between the holders of the highest administrative offices and the holders of the most lucrative tax-farms. Among approximately 44 tax-farmers active in the Morea in 1769, Vizier İbrahim Pasha, Vizier Ali Pasha (governor of the Morea), Muhsinzade Mehmed Pasha (commander of the Morea), Mehmed Emin (tax collector of the Morea), and Al-Hac İbrahim Efendi (former *kadıasker* of Rumeli) held the highest provincial offices and tax-farms.[128] In addition, the tendency for revenues of a given tax-farm district to be held in shares, or *hisse*s (e.g., shares of one-quarter or one-half), became stronger during the second half of the 18th century.

Short-term tax-farms auctioned to members of the provincial government, Janissary *ağa*s, and Ottoman princesses remained the dominant forms of revenue collection in the Morea, and during the 18th century these revenues also met the needs of local fortresses in the form of *ocaklık* (see above). But life-term tax-farms became increasingly common in the latter decades of the 18th century and in the early 19th century.

Minor provincial administrative offices (dragoman, *miranlık*, and broker of *mukataᶜa*s) were auctioned as *malikane*s to Greek notables, bureaucrats, and the imperial guard or *kapıkulu* *(ağa*s). Women now played prominent roles as tax-farmers. Six women, whose backgrounds we cannot determine, held shares in the tax-farms of Kordos, Tripoliçe, Andrusa, and Kalamata. They were not Ottoman princesses, but they may have been significant women of the palace, similar to Rukiye Hanım, the daughter of the vizier, and Hababe Hanım, the favorite concubine *(ikbal)* of Mahmud I (1730–1754). In addition, Ottoman princesses held many *malikane*s in the Morea and in the Aegean islands during the second half of the 18th century. Beyhan Sultan (1765–1824), the daughter of Mustafa III (1757–1774), was the favorite sister of Selim III (1789–1807) and received many *mukataᶜa*s from him and from her uncle Abdulhamid I (1774–1789). She was a wealthy Ottoman princess, owned two palaces on the Bosphorus (Beşiktaş, Arnavut Köy), and had a fountain built in her name in the Kuru Çeşme neighborhood of Istanbul.[129] Beyhan received *malikane*s in the districts of Andrusa, Kalamata, Fanar, Karitena, and Londar in 1802. In 1796 she appointed Nuᶜman Ağa, the *voyvoda* of these districts, to act as her agent *(kethüda)* to collect the *cizye* and *ᶜavariz* dues from her *çiftlik*s.[130] In 1802 she appointed Al-Hac Hasan Ağa as her *kethüda* when Hüseyn Ağa, a former *voyvoda*, was too oppressive.[131] She also appears to have received the *malikane* of the islands of Andros and Syros in 1789.[132] The rise of commercial *çiftlik*s also coincided with the expansion of tax-farming in the Morea.

127. Inflation of the *kuruş* can account only for a fraction of the increases; see Issawi 1980, p. 329; Pamuk 2000, pp. 161–171. The *kuruş* dropped from 14.9 g to 10.9 g of silver in this period. The records used to compile the figures presented in Tables 1.8 and 1.10 does not, however, represent a complete record of the total number of tax-farms in each district—see following note.

128. Vizier Ali Pasha does not appear in the document summarized in Table 1.10.

129. Uluçay 1980, pp. 102–104.

130. *Cevdet Saray* 1243, 1605.

131. *Cevdet Saray* 1396; see also Artan 1993.

132. Davis 1991, p. 157; Polemis 1981, p. 87. The *malikane* was granted to the "sister of Selim III."

THE EVIDENCE FROM ANAVARİN IN THE CONTEXT OF THE SO-CALLED *ÇİFTLİK* DEBATE

There is an ongoing debate between Balkan historians (Gandev, Stoianovich) and Ottomanists (İnalcık, Veinstein, McGowan, and Faroqhi) concerning the origins, location, size, and nature of private *çiftlik*s in the Ottoman empire.[133] Stoianovich tried to distinguish between the *reaya çiftlik* and the *hassa çiftlik*. He argued that, because of peasant indebtedness and because of the flight of peasants during war, famine, and plague, *hassa çiftlik*s, the private farms of *timar*-holding *sipahi*s, increased in size and number at the expense of *reaya çiftlik*s, where usufruct was held by the *reaya*.[134] According to Stoianovich and Gandev, Busch-Zantner's description describes well the physical characteristics of a typical *çiftlik* in Bulgaria:

> While preserving several variations, the *çiftlik* comprises a manor formed by two adjoining several-storied buildings, the *selamlik* or abode of the lord or his agent and *haremlik* or residence of the women. Subsidiary structures on the site of the manor are the male and female servants' quarters, the stalls for the animals, a bakery, and a smithy. At some distance from this structural complex are the low pitiful clay huts of the peasant, perched on piles and covered with a cone- or pyramid-shaped roof of straw. Frequently the manorial complex is separated from the dwellings of the peasants and protected against the incursions of unfriendly lords and *kirjali*s by a stone wall enclosure having a tower and observation post at each corner.[135]

In general, Balkan Marxist historians such as Stoianovich and Gandev chose to emphasize the role that external commerce played in promoting the development of large quasi-private and commercial *çiftlik*s (120–300 ha) in Bulgaria and elsewhere in the Balkans along arteries of trade and communication. They argued that the creation of these estates resulted in a peripheralization of the Ottoman economy, a change in relations of production, and a "second serfdom."[136] They locate the beginning of this transformation in the first decades of the 17th century.[137]

İnalcık, on the other hand, believes that quasi-private and commercial *çiftlik*s were originally formed from marginal and empty lands *(mawat)* that had always been in existence in all parts of the empire, with the full legal agreement of the state and the judicial authorities. The state allowed private, urban-based individuals and local *sipahi*s to bring these lands into cultivation as freehold or charitable *(vakf)* properties. After the deaths of their owners, they would become state property *(miri)* and could be assigned as *timar*s. Veinstein agrees with İnalcık and has furthermore emphasized that the state was always in a position to intervene, should it wish to do so, on behalf of dispossessed and overtaxed peasants by confiscating semiprivate estates and reestablishing their status as *miri* land. Both İnalcık and Veinstein contend that the formation of quasi-private *çiftlik*s did not necessarily alter radically the traditional small-peasant production unit (the *çift–hane*). Rather, they argue, this system continued to exist in many *çiftlik*s while sharecropping and wage labor spread to others.

133. İnalcık 1991a; Veinstein 1991, pp. 35–53.

134. Stoianovich 1953, p. 398.

135. Stoianovich 1953, p. 402, citing Busch-Zantner 1938, p. 107; cf. Gandev 1960.

136. Stoianovich 1953, pp. 402–403.

137. Stoianovich 1953, pp. 401–402.

Moreover, Veinstein is critical of the emphasis placed by Marxist historians on external trade as the principal cause for the development of commercial agriculture in the Ottoman empire. He believes instead that causes internal to the empire, such as transformations in the nature of the military, increased state expenditures, expansion of the tax-farming system, the Celali uprisings, and the growth of local commerce, may have played a more important role.[138] Veinstein argues that the big *çiftlik*s in Bulgaria and Anatolia described by Gandev and Nagata[139] were exceptions rather than the rule. Both Veinstein and McGowan believe that the average *çiftlik* in southern Europe and Anatolia was a small (25–50 ha) farm.[140] Veinstein, McGowan, and İnalcık argue that agricultural production in most *çiftlik*s was diversified and included cereals, orchards, and livestock. Owing to a shortage of labor, cattle breeding became a widespread activity in many *çiftlik*s of Anatolia and the Balkans as well. Production was not devoted exclusively to cash crops like cotton and tobacco.[141] This was also true in Anavarin, where the main surplus crops were olive oil, wine, and some grains at the start of the 18th century.[142]

There is evidence from the Morea, as early as the 16th century, that does support the notion that the existence of possibilities for external trade provided an economic motivation for the formation of private *çiftlik*s. The following example, drawn from imperial orders to local authorities in the Morea, clarifies one specific circumstance in which private *çiftlik*s in the Morea were being formed. The evidence suggests that *çiftlik*s were being formed legally and with the awareness of the state. Moreover, the state also appears to have been ready to intervene to protect its own interests.

An order to the *bey* of the Morea dating from 29 *Zilkade* 978/March 1570 commanded him to prevent local inhabitants of the Morea, other than *sipahi*s and men of the fortresses of the Morea, from acquiring *çiftlik*s close to the sea. The *bey* was ordered immediately to disband those *çiftlik*s that were not owned by *sipahi*s.[143] Another order issued several months later to the *bey* of the Morea (6 *Safer* 979/June 1571) reinforced the previous order and demanded the destruction of those *çiftlik*s that distributed or exported grain by sea and that engaged in contraband trade at Balye Badre. The *bey* of the Morea reported that he had attempted to destroy *çiftlik*s on the coast but had discovered that they belonged to a certain Osman Bey, to a certain Toyfun Bey, and to other notables. Nonetheless, the imperial order sought that these *çiftlik*s of district local subcommanders (*zaim*s) and local notables be disbanded and placed a ban on the export of grains by sea.[144]

From the contents of these two imperial orders, it is clear that the conversion of *timar*s into private *çiftlik*s by the *sipahi*s and local notables was a serious concern to the central Ottoman government as early as 1570. In part, the possibility of contraband trade in wheat and sheep with Venice and Spain seems to have encouraged the *çiftlik*s' creation. I have already cited the example of the *sipahi* Lutfi, who owned a large *çiftlik* on the coast that was devoted to breeding cattle. He used slave labor (Arab slaves) and was exporting wheat and sheep to Venice in 1567. Further research in the Turkish archives is needed to determine the extent to which the state was successful in preventing the spread of such large *çiftlik*s in the 17th century.

138. Veinstein 1991, pp. 48–50.
139. Gandev 1960; Nagata 1976.
140. Veinstein 1991, p. 48; McGowan 1981, pp. 72, 171. Most of the *çiftlik*s listed in TT880 fall within this size range: see below, Chapter 4.
141. İnalcık 1991a, pp. 32–33; Veinstein 1991, p. 48.
142. See Chapter 4.
143. MD12, no. 272.
144. MD12, no. 647.

But the *çiftlik*s that existed in 1716 in the district of Anavarin are far different from those discussed above, and points raised by İnalcık, McGowan, and Veinstein are in general applicable. The evidence from Anavarin (examined in greater detail in the following section of this chapter and in Chap. 4 of this volume) suggests that *çiftlik*s there in the 18th century were neither large nor specialized in agricultural production nor dependent on wage (or slave) labor. McGowan has shown that in Manastir during the 18th century, sharecropping rather than wage labor was the norm in a *çiftlik*, where the mean number of adult males was 3.5.[145] This was the case also in Anavarin, where sharecropping was the dominant form of peasant labor in the *çiftlik*s in 1716. The number of male sharecroppers resident in 26 inhabited *çiftlik*s ranged from 2 to 32, with an average of 5.4 individuals.[146]

Many *çiftlik*s had existed in the district of Anavarin prior to 1686. It is clearly stated in the heading for these *çiftlik*s that they had been *timar*s originally, but we do not know how long prior to 1686 the conversion from timars into *çiftlik*s occurred, or the specific conditions under which the *çiftlik*s were formed. As in Anatolia and the Balkans, such small quasi-private *çiftlik*s probably came into being as the result of a variety of factors: war, peasant flight, peasant indebtedness, and banditry. Such conditions provided opportunities for urban-based tax-farmers, local notables, and powerful military figures to take possession of both state land and peasant land and to consolidate their private holdings (*hasse*s). The desertion and population loss during the Ottoman-Venetian wars of the late 17th century and in 1715 would have offered further opportunities for the formation of additional *çiftlik*s in the later 18th century, since some villages were left empty and the Ottoman military forces previously stationed in Anavarin had been killed or fled after their defeat at the hands of Venice in 1686.

Probably in 1716 the state made an attempt to convert some of these private *çiftlik*s to state property *(miri)* and, as has already been mentioned, a near-contemporary document (TT881) indicates that some *çiftlik* villages (and *karye*s) were granted as *timar*s to 64 *sipahi*s.[147] It can be assumed that the original Muslim owners of the *çiftlik*s that were converted to *timar* were no longer resident in the Morea, for whatever reason, and that they or their descendants had not returned following the Ottoman reconquest. We have no evidence for how long this reinstituted *timar* system coexisted side by side with the private *çiftlik*s in the district of Anavarin, although the assignment of these as *timar*s must logically have occurred after the compilation TT880, since otherwise they would have been listed there as *timar*s. Presumably TT880 was first compiled in anticipation of the return of landowners;[148] then, when they did not return, the *çiftlik*s were assigned as *timar*s.

Economic, social, and political factors, however, continued to encourage the formation of private estates as opposed to the maintenance of the *timar* system. In the first place, in the post-conquest period there was more land without an owner, due to the abandonment of many fields, vineyards, orchards, and olive groves by Venetians or local Greeks who had fled or were killed. It would not have been a realistic expectation that the *timar* system by itself could have operated to bring all of this land under produc-

145. McGowan 1981, pp. 164–165.
146. Eight *çiftlik*s were not settled at all, and their status may later have been converted to that of *mazra'a*.
147. TT881, pp. 158–288. Their *miri* status is also indicated in TT880; see Chapters 2, 4.
148. See the 1716 *kanunname*, Chapter 2.

tion again. As we have already seen, the number of *timar*-holding *sipahi*s in Anavarin had declined from 315 in 1613 to 64 in 1716.[149] This reduction in numbers in part reflected the whole process of decline in the *timar* system and the traditional military organization that had already started in the late 16th century.

The recruitment of armed irregulars (*levend*s, *sekban*s) drawn from the *reaya* in place of the regular *sipahi*s became normal in the 17th and 18th centuries. But these troops were not properly trained, lacked discipline, and were not loyal to the system. There was a high desertion rate among the irregulars. They were primarily interested in booty and quick economic gain. Moreover, the state did not commit itself to support irregular units after the campaign season concluded, and many turned to banditry in order to make a living. In the face of the growing insecurity in the countryside that followed, the few remaining *timar*-holders found it increasingly difficult to collect the tithe and the *cizye* in a timely manner, thus encouraging further expansion of tax-farming. In addition, the recruitment of peasantry into the army often resulted in the abandonment of their fields and a concomitant loss of state revenues.

THE *ÇİFTLİK*S OF THE DISTRICT OF ANAVARİN IN 1716

The amount of arable land (*tarla*s) belonging to *çiftlik*s in the district of Anavarin in 1716 (as recorded in TT880) ranged from 10 *dönüm*s (0.9 ha at Has) to 1,500 *dönüm*s (138 ha at Osman Ağa), although in the majority of cases it fell within the 25–50 hectare range.[150] Sharecropping by a small number of Greek peasants (an average of 5.4) was the predominant form of agricultural labor in the *çiftlik*s, while tenant farming continued to exist in the villages (*karye*s), where the farmers were tenants of the state or of *sipahi*s. Many sharecroppers themselves were in possession of arable land that ranged in extent from half a *çift* to two *çift*s (see Chap. 4), although they would not have held a legal title *(tapu)* to it, and it would thus not have been inheritable; they owned sheep, pigs, and beehives as well. They paid state taxes on the produce of their own land (a tithe of one-seventh), and they paid to the owner of the *çiftlik* a portion of the produce from the lands that belonged to the *çiftlik*. The landlord probably owned the means of production (e.g., plows and oxen) and might also control trees, vineyards, a manor house, and storage buildings. Agricultural production appears to have been diversified and included the cultivation of cereals (wheat, barley, oats, and millet), the cultivation of a small amount of cotton, the production of olive oil, the husbandry of livestock, viticulture, and the manufacture of silk.[151] There is no evidence that maize was grown. Half of the olive oil was exported.

There were marked differences between *çiftlik*s and village settlements in the district of Anavarin. The villages (*karye*s) tended to be situated at higher elevations, whereas *çiftlik*s were more often at lower elevations near the coast, suggestive of their involvement in the export of agricultural surplus from the practice of diversified agriculture. A *çiftlik* was typically named

149. TT777, pp. 20–22; TT881, pp. 158–288.

150. These calculations assume that the figures given for arable land attached to each *çiftlik* do *not* include fallow land: see Chapter 4.

151. TT880 does not record any silk as being taxed in 1716, although a silk workshop at Osman Ağa is described.

after its original owner, usually an *ağa*. Types of settlements and their characteristics are discussed in greater detail in Chapter 4.

The *çiftlik* of Osman Ağa or Büyük Pisaski (entry 15 in Chap. 2) is the largest and most complex of the private *çiftlik*s in Anavarin. It had a large walled vineyard *(bağ)* of 300 *dönüm*s, a mulberry orchard of 95 *dönüm*s with 1,500 mulberry trees, and 1,000 olive trees, plus another 903 trees elsewhere on the property. It had 27 almond trees, 35 pear trees, 40 peach trees, and 55 fig trees. There was a silk workshop *(ipekhane),* the only one in the district that is recorded. In addition, a large two-story manorial house *(saray)* contained 8 upper rooms and 12 lower rooms, a kitchen with 2 ovens, a basement with 15 large earthenware jars, and a courtyard with a gate. It had an associated guest house *(han)* and 2 additional wooden structures, each with 2 rooms, probably for the storage of grain. Ten other houses were probably the residences of 12 sharecroppers and their families, and may have been owned by them. In at least some instances it is clear that sharecroppers owned houses (see Chap. 4). The Greek sharecroppers who lived on this *çiftlik* themselves owned 7.5 *çift*s of arable land and 40 sheep. They did not own orchards.

In contrast to the *çiftlik* of Osman Ağa, the *karye* of Virviçe (entry 49 in Chap. 2) had been a *timar* prior to 1685. It had 47 Greek tenant *reaya* who controlled 13.5 *çift*s of arable land, 46 *dönüm*s of vineyards, 343 sheep, 11 mulberry trees, 27 olive trees, 3 water mills, and 27 houses. The traditional *çift-hane* system operated in this village, whereby the *reaya* held the usufruct to the land and paid the tithe (of one-seventh) to a *sipahi,* or to the state if not assigned to a *sipahi.* Like the *çiftlik* of Osman Ağa, the village of Virviçe was engaged in diversified subsistence agricultural production that included cereals, animal husbandry, the cultivation of a few olives and a little cotton (60 *lidre*s; 25.5 kg), and the production of wine, probably for export (although this purpose is not specified in TT880).

For the most part, in 1716, there was not much difference in the economies of *karye*s like Virviçe and that of *çiftlik*s, in that small-scale diversified agriculture was the norm, from which some surplus was exported.[152] Only the *çiftlik*s of Osman Ağa and Has stand out as exceptional, in that vines, olives, and silk appear to have been produced there far in excess of the needs of the sharecroppers. But this situation may have changed later in the 18th century if the district of Anavarin followed the trend, established in other parts of the Ottoman empire, toward the establishment of more and larger *çiftlik*s oriented toward the production of cash crops (e.g., olive oil, wine, cotton, and wool) for regional and international trade. But we are not yet in a position to reconstruct the history of the district of Anavarin during the final century of Ottoman rule in any detail. Nor do we know whether villages such as Virviçe ever became *çiftlik*s. However, some properties that had been *çiftlik*s prior to 1686 were still being granted to *sipahi*s as *timar*s in the middle of the 18th century, as is clear from the following example.

At the end of *Muharrem* 1158/February 1745, Mustafa ibn Şeyh Ahmed, the *kethüda* of the fortress of Anavarin, complained to the imperial council that the *reaya* of the *çiftlik* of Alafine had refused to pay the tithe, including a tithe of one-tenth on olive trees, and other legal dues, owing to

152. Cf. McGrew 1985, pp. 30–31, regarding the small scale of *çiftlik*s in southern Greece.

interference by local notables.[153] He claimed a *timar* of 5,000 *akçe*s in this *çiftlik*. After examination of the *mufassal* and *icmal defter*s, it was confirmed that this *çiftlik*, a dependency of Anavarin with three *reaya*, and its tithe of one-seventh and its *ispence*, constituted his registered *timar*. An order was issued to the tax collector *(muhassıl)* and vizier of Anavarin to help him collect the taxes from his *timar*.[154]

It is also clear that processes were at work in the Morea in the later 18th century that were leading to the gradual impoverishment of the peasants and the loss of their rights. The *reaya* were often subject to the abuses of tax collectors.[155] Attempts by the *sipahi*s and *çiftlik* owners to extract higher taxes put the *reaya* into greater debt. At the beginning of *Receb* 1132/May 1720, the peasants of a village in the district of Mezistre petitioned that they were unable to pay additional taxes charged illegally by the local tax collectors. They claimed that they had abandoned their village because of such extortion.[156] In another petition made at the end of *Receb* 1132/May 1720, peasants in the district of Mezistre complained that the *sipahi*s were collecting illegal dues on the sheep tax.[157]

Christian *reaya* were not the only ones subject to abuse from corrupt Ottoman officials. Muslim peasants might go into debt to pay *ʿavariz* (extraordinary) taxes. At the beginning of *Muharrem* 1161/January 1748, Ahmed and Halil, residents of Anavarin, petitioned the imperial council in Istanbul, complaining that they had in A.H. 1158/A.D. 1745 placed the goods of Ahmed's sister and Halil's mother as a surety for a loan of 1,500 *kuruş*es taken from Mahmud, a Janissary and scribe, almost certainly borrowed to pay *ʿavariz* taxes. Ahmed and Halil asserted that they had paid the debt in full but that Mahmud refused to give back the surety. An order was issued by the imperial council to the *kadı* of Anavarin for the purpose of helping them obtain their full rights.[158]

These and numerous other petitions submitted by the *reaya* to the central government show that the burden of extraordinary taxes had increased considerably during the 18th century. Rebellion and banditry by impoverished peasants were particularly prevalent in the district of Mezistre. The scribe Salih reported to the imperial council, in mid-*Zilkade* 1136/ July 1724, that two Greek *reaya* (both named Yorgi) from Koron had joined Kapudanoğlu Andon and others in a rebellion and that they were engaging in banditry against innocent *reaya*.[159]

By the last decades of the 18th century, *ʿavariz* taxes had come to constitute the most important source of state revenue from the Morea, and the numerous petitions submitted by the *reaya* to the central government show clearly that the burden of extraordinary taxes had increased considerably. Rebellions of the sort that these impositions provoked worsened further the budgetary problems of the Ottoman empire. Especially devastating was a major rebellion in Manya (Mani) in 1770–1774, which further disrupted the collection of *mukataʿa* and *timar* revenues.

According to an imperial order issued in response to a petition from the *kadı* of the district of Mezistre that was copied into the register from which the data in Table 1.11 are drawn, the conditions of *timar-* and *zeʿamet-*holders were desperate already in 1770 owing to the rebellion in Mani/ Manya (which was under the jurisdiction of Mezistre). The imperial order

153. MD4, p. 134:3.
154. MD4, p. 134:3.
155. MD4, p. 242:3.
156. ŞD83, p. 299:1.
157. ŞD83, p. 358:3.
158. MD4, p. 242:3.
159. ŞD102, p. 12:2.

TABLE 1.11. REVENUES IN THE MOREA, 1771–1772

Revenue	Amount (Kuruşes)
Muhasıllık	31,000.0
Bedeliye-yi işkenciyan (cash substitute of irregular troops in lieu of service)	21,699.5
Poll tax *(cizye)*	220,648.0
*Çiftlik*s and land of runaway infidels	8,156.0
Sale of wheat (30,000 *kile*s)	58,750.0
Cizye installment (1 month)	61,242.0
Muhasıllık and *miranlık* dues	9,294.0
ʿAvariz dues	46,767.5
Total	457,557.0

Source: DBŞM 4175/A, p. 4.

demanded the full payment by the *sipahi*s of all substitute dues *(bedeliye-yi işkenciyan)*.[160] It indicates that 21,699.5 *kuruşes* of the total tithe could not be collected. Expenditures amounted to 563,925.5 *kuruşes*, resulting in a budget deficit of 106,368.5 *kuruşes*.

In response to a previous petition from the *kadı* of Mezistre, the governor of the Morea, Vizier Osman Pasha, had himself undertaken *(der uhde)* the collection of the tithe and sent *(havale)* 14,000 *kuruşes* to Istanbul in A.H. 1184/A.D. 1770. Moreover, the revenues and property (8,156 *kuruşes* in value) of those *reaya* who had been murdered or had fled from Anavarin, Modon, Kalamata, Koron, and other districts to Venice were confiscated by Vizier Osman Pasha.[161] The *kadı* of Mezistre now demanded a reduction of 50 percent in taxes.

At that time, the Ottoman state was involved in a conflict with Catherine II (the Great) of Russia, and hostilities spread to the Morea in 1770. With encouragement from her generals, the Orlov brothers, a major rebellion erupted in Mani and enveloped Anavarin (see App. III) and other areas of the Morea. As a result, Russian forces gained an important military foothold in the Aegean area. Ottoman budgetary problems worsened as the collection of *mukataʿa* and *timar* revenues (tithes) were disrupted, and these troubles ultimately set the stage for the disastrous loss of the Crimea in 1785, a catastrophe that gave Russia access to the Black Sea and to the Bosphorus.

Ottoman administrators themselves were very much aware of the problems that lay at the root of rebellion and were concerned to correct them. Moralı Süleyman Penah Efendi, the *defterdar* (accountant) of the Morea, in a long report entitled (in translation) "The Collection of Penah Efendi and the History of the Rebellion in the Morea," outlined the causes of the rebellion of 1770.[162] Penah Efendi was in the Morea when the revolt took place. He described Russian intrigues in 1769, and also provided a brief description of the tragic massacre in 1770, at the hands of some 20,000 Maniote rebels and their Russian collaborators, of thousands of Turkish civilians in the villages and towns of Balye Badre, Arkadiye, Karitena, Kalamata, Andrusa, Koron, Anavarin, and Tripoliçe.[163]

Penah Efendi blamed the participation of the Maniote peasants in the rebellion on their poor living conditions and on their oppression by

160. DBŞM 4175/A, p. 11.

161. DBŞM 4175/A.

162. Moralı Süleyman Penah Efendi 1942–1943. Penah Efendi wrote his account in 1785 in Istanbul, shortly before dying of the plague. I have used the Turkish version published in Türk Tarih Vesikları. His full manuscript has also been published in Greek by Sarris (1993), who also discusses other Ottoman sources for the rebellion in the Morea (pp. 14–15).

163. Uzunçarşılı 1956, pp. 394–400, 434–435.

local notables, corrupt Ottoman officials, and profit-driven tax-farmers. His report not only details the causes of Greek discontent but also calls for reform, including the restoration of central control; the establishment of justice, law, and order; and increased military discipline among Albanian irregulars and mercenaries. He reports that Albanian troops, in staunching the rebellion, had acted with so much ferocity that their behavior had side-tracked economic recovery and created a deep-seated ethnic and religious polarization between Greeks and Turks. Penah Efendi's report did not do much to improve the situation in the Morea, where local tensions ultimately set the stage for the Greek Revolution of 1821.

CHAPTER 2

Translations of Two Ottoman Documents Describing the State of the Morea and Anavarin in 1716

by Fariba Zarinebaf

This chapter contains translations of two documents that are critical to an understanding the condition of the Pylos area in 1716, following the Venetian withdrawal in September 1715 (see Chap. 1). The first is the *kanunname* (imperial law code) that established the general legal framework within which Ottoman officials administered the Morea. The second is a cadastral survey of the entire *kaza* of Anavarin, contained in pages 78–101 of TT880, a *mufassal defter*. As already mentioned in the Introduction to this volume, we decided that a translation and analysis of the cadastral survey would be included in our first major published work regarding the Ottoman Morea. We selected TT880 for translation because of its extraordinary level of detail and because of its importance for the history of the 18th-century Morea.[1]

THE *KANUNNAME* OF THE MOREA, 1716 (TK71): AN ABBREVIATED TRANSLATION

The *kanunname* for the province *(vilayet)* of the Morea in 1716, included in *Tapu Kadastro* (TK) 71 in Ankara (which I have not seen), was published more than half a century ago by Barkan.[2] An English translation of those parts of it that are most relevant to the interpretation of the text of TT880 follows.[3] This document, like other Ottoman *kanunname*s, comprises a collection of legal rulings and was not intended to give guidance in all circumstances, particularly where Islamic law *(shariᶜa)* was applicable.

1. A facsimile of pp. 78–101 of TT880 is reproduced on the CD-ROM that accompanies this volume. We understand TT880 to be the original on which a copy in Ankara (Tapu ve Kadastro Genel Müdürlüğü [TKGM] 15) is based (see p. xvii, n. 11). In the future we intend to discuss additional parts of TT880, in particular registers for those villages in Arkadiye that fall within the PRAP study area. We have also compared TT880 to contemporary documents (e.g., TT881) and to earlier

registers for the Morea. See pp. xv–xix and Chapter 1 for a discussion of these sources.

2. The *kanunname* was contained in a register separate from TT880 and other cadastral surveys. We translate Barkan's transcription of this text (Barkan 1943, pp. 326–332) and have not examined the original document in Ankara (TKGM, TK71). Barkan does not publish a facsimile of it. Paragraphs are numbered as in Barkan (who includes no paragraph 4). Paragraphs are

not numbered in the original text, and Barkan has also added his own punctuation and diacritical marks. TK71 was based on an older (1583) *kanunname* for the Morea in TT607, pp. 2–6. For a partial transcription and English translation of this and other earlier *kanunname*s of the Morea, see Alexander 1985a, pp. 178–197, 354–375.

3. See Balta 1993, pp. 49–58, for a Greek translation of the entirety of TK71.

1. This rich province, like Rumeli, is a *mîrî* (state) land. Since its conquest, the land found in the possession of the *reaya* has been rendered to them. The rest of the land has been claimed by the *beytülmal* (public treasury). But as long as the *reaya* cultivate the land, set up vineyards and orchards, and plant trees, and as long as they pay the tithe and the land tax and other dues and do not delay in paying taxes, no one should interfere in their rights. Their sons should take over after the death of the *reaya*. If they do not leave sons behind, their daughters and sisters can receive the *tapu* (land deed). If they do not survive, outsiders can cultivate the land and receive the *tapu* in return for certain fees. If they do not cultivate the land for three years, they will lose their rights to the land. They cannot claim any rights in addition to the above-mentioned rights. They can not sell, buy, give up as a gift, or set up *mülk* (private property) or *vakf*s (religious endowments). They can only transfer their rights to someone else with the permission of the *sipahi* and in return for a fee of some *akçe*s. Then the *sipahi* would give that person a *tapu* that is valid. These are the current rules now effective in Rumeli.

2. The conditions of *çift* and *çiftlik:* 60 *akçe*s should be collected from one *çift* of land in the possession of Muslim *reaya,* 30 *akçe*s from a half-*çift* in the possession of Muslim *reaya*, 12 *akçe*s from landless and married *reaya* as *resm-i bennak* (married peasant tax), and 6 *akçe*s from landless single *reaya*. Those who have less than a half-*çift* of land should pay 1 *akçe* per 3 *dönüm*s of high-quality land, 1 *akçe* per 5 *dönüm*s of medium-quality land, and 1 *akçe* per 10 *dönüm*s of low-quality land as *resm-i dönüm* (land tax). If one of the *reaya* loses his *çiftlik* owing to poverty, he is not liable for taxes.

3. If one of the *reaya* is registered as *amelmande* (disabled/incapable of work) in the *defter*, no taxes should be collected from him. The land of non-Muslim *reaya* who are incapable of working because of old age should be cultivated by their sons, who should pay the tithes and taxes. The incapable registered *reaya* should not pay the *ispence* (head tax) and dues.

5. The following taxes as *resm-i dönüm* (land tax) should be collected, according to its quality, from land of the Muslim *reaya* that is in excess of 1 *çift*, in accordance with custom. In the *çiftlik*s of the *kaza*s of Anabolu (Nafplion), Kordos (Corinth), Arhos (Argos), Kunye (?), Tesi (?), Lafuz (?), and Gastun (Gastouni): one *çift* of high-quality land equals 80 *dönüm*s, one *çift* of medium-quality land equals 100–120 *dönüm*s, and one *çift* of low quality equals 150 *dönüm*s.[4]

A *dönüm* is equal to 40 *hatve*s (steps) in length and width in accordance with the current measurements.[5] In the *çiftlik*s of the *kaza*s of Mezistre (Mystras), Manafşe (Monemvasia), Koron (Koroni), and Modon (Methoni), 50 *dönüm*s are equal

4. Balta (1993, p. 50) reads "Karitena" for Barkan's "Kunye," and "Renesi" and "Lakonia" for Barkan's "Tesi" and "Lafuz."

5. İnalcık (1982, p. 123) discusses this formula, a general definition repeated in *kanunname*s of the 16th century.

to 1 *çift*. In Çakunye (Tsakonia), 20–30 *dönüm*s are equal to 1 *çift*. The *çift*s of *kaza*s are different in their condition. And in every *kaza*, 60 *akçe*s *(çift akçesi)* are collected from 1 *çift* of land.

6. On *ispence* (head tax). In accordance with the *tahrir* of Mismari-zade in A.D. 1583, all non-Muslims should pay 25 *akçe*s in current value.[6] In accordance with the old *defter*, all those who are married and single, those who possess land and those who do not, should pay this head tax. But from the Jews and from them alone should be collected 125 *akçe*s in *ispence*. The *resm-i çift* (land tax), *resm-i bennak* (married peasant tax), *resm-i mücerred* (bachelor tax), and *ispence* should be collected in the month of March.

7. On *hassa* (prebend) *çiftlik*s and *mîrî* land. If someone sets up vineyards on *hassa çiftlik*s, after paying the land taxes (*resm-i dönüm*s), one-quarter of the revenue belongs to the owner of the land. But all the *çiftlik*s in this rich province used to belong to Muslims, and now their owners are appearing. The land should be given to them in accordance with the Islamic law *(shariᶜa)*. But if they do not appear, the land should not be registered as *hassa* but as *mîrî* and should be registered as "held in escrow" *(mevkuf)*. If vineyards, orchards, and olive roots are set up and planted, the taxes and tithe should be paid to the commissioner *(zabit)*. One-quarter of the revenue belongs to the *mîrî*. But if the original owner appears and proves ownership, it should be given to him according to the *shariᶜa*, and therefore he would collect one-quarter of the revenue after they pay the tithe and the dues. The cultivating *reaya* should pay one-fifth of the revenue as rent after paying the tithe (one-seventh) to the landowner, whether the land is *mîrî* or belongs to Muslims. But if the oxen, seeds, and other tools belong to the landowner, the rest of the revenue after the payment of the dues can be divided/shared with the *reaya*.

8. On the *çiftlik*s of the Muslims. Any number of *çiftlik*s belonging to Muslims that exist in a *karye* should be given to them in accordance with the *shariᶜa*. They should pay the taxes according to above-mentioned high-, medium-, and low-quality definitions, and not any more than that. Any land around these villages, whether cultivable or not, and whether used as pasture for sheep or not, is rendered to the *reaya*, who should cultivate it and pay the dues and tithe to the owner of the land. The *çiftlik* owners have no rights over them.

Provisions in other passages of the document may be summarized, rather than translated literally, and it is clear that the collection of taxes on a broad range of products is envisioned.

On sheep raised by Muslims, members of the military, and non-Muslims in the villages of the district, taxes of one *akçe* per head should be

6. The *kanunname* of 1583 is contained in TT607. See also Balta 1993, pp. 47–48; Alexander 1985a, pp. 196–197, 374–375.

collected, whether they own few or many sheep. Taxes on sheep and goats should be collected in May, after their wool is sheared.

The tithe on cereals (wheat, barley, and rye), fodder, and beans, as for millet, chick-peas, broad beans, and lentils, was to be one-eighth of the revenue for Muslims as tithes and *salariye* (an extraordinary agricultural tax) and one-seventh of the revenue for non-Muslims. From lentils, broad beans, cotton, sesame seed, flax, carob, walnuts and fruits, vegetables, beehives, chestnuts, and red dye, a tithe of one-tenth was to be collected from Muslims and non-Muslims. On the other hand, the tithe in cash (*bedel-i üşür)* assessed on vineyards amounted to 12 *akçe*s per *dönüm* for Muslims and 24 *akçe*s per *dönüm* for non-Muslims. Moreover, the old tithes on must and *fuçı*s (barrels), *karış*,[7] and *bac-i himr* (the tax on alcoholic drinks) were abolished. In the old register, the tithe on dried grapes (currants) had been set as 2 *çuval*s (sacks) per 15 sacks. This was not the case in 1716, and the *bedel-i üşür* (tithe in cash) was 100 *akçe*s per *dönüm* (of vineyard?) from Muslims and non-Muslims.

The *reaya* should pay to the owner of the land a tithe of one-third of the acorns they collect from land that is not their own.[8] But if it is land belonging to the *reaya*, one-tenth should be collected.

The tax on mills was 120 *akçe*s on those that ran throughout the year, 60 *akçe*s on those that ran only for 6 months, and 30 *akçe*s on those that ran for 3 months. The tax on an oil press was 50 *akçe*s; on a silk press, 50 *akçe*s; on lime kilns, 60 *akçe*s; and on brick, glass, and lime ovens, 30 *akçe*s.

The marriage tax on virgin Muslim women was 60 *akçe*s and on non-virgin Muslim women, 30 *akçe*s. It was 120 and 60 *akçe*s on virgin and non-virgin non-Muslim women, respectively. If the virgin (woman) got married, the tax belonged to the owner of the *reaya*, but if the non-virgin (woman) got married, the tax should be collected by the owner of the land. Soldiers and guards and local military men were to pay their marriage tax to the *mir-liva* (district governor).

On every beehive, 5 *akçe*s was to be collected as a tithe in cash when the beehive was full during the fall season and ready to be harvested.

In the old register, the tax on olive oil was registered as the tithe. But because its collection had been difficult and harsh for the *reaya*, the tithe was to be collected only from the olives.

The tax on silk that has been wound on a wheel was *üşür* (a tithe of one-tenth), and on non-wound silk was *üşür-i gönül* (a cocoon tithe). In those villages where no silk was being produced and the mulberry tree leaves were being sold instead, a tithe known as *üşür-i muᶜadil* was to be collected.[9] The tax on the silk scale, known as *simsarlik* (brokerage fee), was 3 *akçe*s per 1 *lidre* of thin silk and 2 *akçe*s for thick silk, to be collected from both Muslim and non-Muslim seller and buyer after they paid the tithe on silk to the landowner. If it was difficult to collect it from the buyer, the whole tax was to be collected from the seller, who could charge the buyer accordingly. The customs tax was to be collected in the *iskele* (port) henceforth. The customs tax on the *dar al-harb*[10] was 5 percent; on others, 4 percent. One *lidre* of silk was equivalent to 133 *dirhem*s. The *simsarlik* was to be collected in August.

7. On this tax, see Balta 1989, pp. 21–22 and table 2.4. Balta writes: "Le resm-i *kariş* est le droit que le timariote touche quand le moût est mis dans les tonneaux."

8. Acorns (*velandia* [βελανίδια]) of *Quercus aegilops* were a significant export crop in many parts of Greece (see Chap. 4).

9. The amount of tithe is not specified here.

10. The "abode of war," technically those Christian nations not incorporated within the Ottoman empire by conquest or treaty.

The tax on *talyan*s (fisheries) amounted to one-half of the fish that were caught. But if the fish were caught outside the fishery by casting a net, only one-fourth were to be collected as *mîrî* tax. If the fishery did not pay the tax, all the fish were to be confiscated by the state.

The *kantariye* (scales) tax on honey, oil, and other related items is 1 *akçe* to be collected from the buyer and seller each. The *ihtisab* (market tax) on woolen textiles imported from outside the province of the Morea is 2 *akçe*s per *arşun,* and 2 *akçe*s per *arşun* on *kebe* (felt) and *kirbas* (cheap cotton or linen) and similar fabrics, to be collected by the *muhtesib* (market inspector). The official price on food items would be set up by the *kadı,* and the market inspector would collect 2 *akçe*s from each kind of food item. From *tulum* (granulous curd) cheese, 1 *akçe.* If a butcher from outside the Morea slaughters sheep and cows, 2 *akçe*s will be paid as *kantariye* (scales) tax. On dried fish and other things from the sea, 2 *akçe*s per *kantar* should be paid.[11] On olive oil and milk, 2 *akçe*s per measure will be paid at the time of inspection by the *muhtesib.* If these items should be sold below the *narh* (official price), a fine will be imposed. The bakers should pay 2 *akçe*s as their monthly dues. For every animal that transports vegetables to the market, 1 *mangır* (bronze coin) should be collected. Those who sell wheat and barley should pay 1 *akçe* per 8 *kile*s as sales tax. On cotton, a tax of 1 *akçe* per 1½ *vukiyye*s is collected at the time of sale in the market. On flax and hemp, 1 *akçe* per 2 *vukiyye*s is collected.

The uninhabited land aside from that cultivated and in the possession of Muslim and non-Muslim *reaya* in a village is part of that village. Even if the uninhabited land receives another name later, it is still not to be considered a nonregistered village, but rather a dependency of the first village.[12] Its tithes and taxes are paid to the commissioner of the first village.

In a village, the *tapu* tax for a house and high-quality land is 60 *akçe*s, for medium-quality land 40 *akçe*s, and for low-quality land 20 *akçe*s. If a peasant leaves his village and the land remains empty, a landowner can take possession of it in exchange for a *tapu* from the peasant. The villagers can leave some land fallow for their oxen and cattle. That land should not be cultivated. The *deştbani* (tax on wasteland) and *bad-i hava* are one tax. This tax is a fine to be collected when someone's horse, mule, or ox enters arable fields. After the damage has been estimated, for every flock, 5 blows and a fine of 5 *akçe*s should be charged. Likewise, 4 *akçe*s for a cow, 1 *akçe* for a calf, 1 *akçe* for a sheep, and 1 blow per 2 sheep should be charged. The marriage tax, fines from crimes, and taxes on the *tapu*s of houses and lands and from those who come from outside to winter, and tobacco tax, and *deştbani*s are all called *bad-i hava* taxes.

If a peasant at the time of the survey is registered in a certain village and then leaves that village owing to lack of land, he should be returned to the original village according to the former *kanun.* If he is not registered in a certain village, he should not be prevented from leaving it after the passing of one year.

11. A *kantar* was a standard Ottoman measure equivalent to 44 *okka*s.

12. The expression used for this type of village is *haric az defter,* literally "outside the register." In some situations this expression may mean "tax-exempt," but not in this instance, as is clear from the context.

THE CADASTRAL SURVEY OF THE DISTRICT OF ANAVARİN CONTAINED IN *TAPU TAHRİR* 880

The remainder of this chapter comprises a complete translation of the cadastral survey of the district of Anavarin. This text is very much the centerpiece of this book. In Chapters 1 and 4 we discuss how provisions in the preceding *kanunname* help in its interpretation. In Chapter 1, Zarinebaf has already drawn on the information in TT880 and has integrated it with data collected from a wide variety of other Ottoman sources in order to describe how Ottoman provincial administration functioned in the Morea and how it was transformed in the 18th century. In Chapter 3, Bennet and Davis consider the toponyms mentioned in the survey, particularly the names of *karye*s (villages), *çiftlik*s, and *mazra'a*s (Fig. 2.1). Where were these places located?[13] In Chapter 4 the three authors jointly analyze the content of the document in great detail, in an attempt to write a human geography for the *kaza* of Anavarin ca. 1700.

TT880 is written on paper and measures 0.30 m wide × 0.45 m tall, each page of text being approximately 0.15 m wide. It was written in the *siyakat* script. Pages 1–77 of the document deal with the *kaza* of Arkadiye, those translated here (pp. 78–101), with the *kaza* of Anavarin, including Anavarin-i atik and Anavarin-i cedid. A codicil (p. 101) describes the purpose of the cadaster (to record "property of Muslims or Venetians or . . . of the *reaya*, including villages (*karye*s), *çiftlik*s, *mazra'a*s, vineyards, and trees") and the process of its registration in Istanbul. As might be anticipated from the codicil, most of the document appears to be the work of a single scribe, who seems to have recorded the observations of a team of surveyors: "And all of this was registered with the hand of your servant, Seyyid Mehmed Hatemi."

Forty-seven separate subheadings within the cadaster for Anavarin mark each *karye, çiftlik,* or *mazra'a*. Two others record at length property in the fortress *(kale)* of Anavarin-i cedid and in its suburb *(varış),* and the remains of the fortress of Anavarin-i atik. The entries marked by each such heading are recorded in a similar format. A heading consists of the status (*karye, çiftlik, kale,* or *mazra'a*) and its name; the final letter of the status extends across the page as a straight line. The physical setting (e.g., on a plain or in the mountains) of the property may be described above the line, and each *karye, çiftlik,* and *mazra'a* is also explicitly said to be a dependency of the *kaza* of Anavarin. The status of the property prior to the Venetian conquest of 1685 (e.g., a *timar*) may be recorded below the line.[14] After the heading there typically follows a catalogue of property belonging to the state (sometimes field boundaries are indicated), a list of the *reaya* (on *çiftlik*s called *ortakçıyan* [sharecroppers]) who are resident in the place, and a description of their personal property (e.g., sheep, fruit trees,

---

13. Discussion provides full justification for the locations mapped on fig. 12 of Bennet, Davis, and Zarinebaf-Shahr 2000, with some minor adjustments where necessary. With regard to the terms *karye* and *çiftlik*, we note that *karye* designated only a village, whereas *çiftlik* could be applied to a village, or to a unit of arable land, or to a large farm or plantation-like farm. See also Chapter 1.

14. In the translation that follows, information contained in the heading of each entry is presented in the lines of the translated heading. The numbers assigned to each individual entry, to each one of the *reaya*, and to individual properties in Anavarin-i cedid (no. 35) were inserted by us to facilitate reference to individual items later in this volume, particularly in Chapters 3, 4.

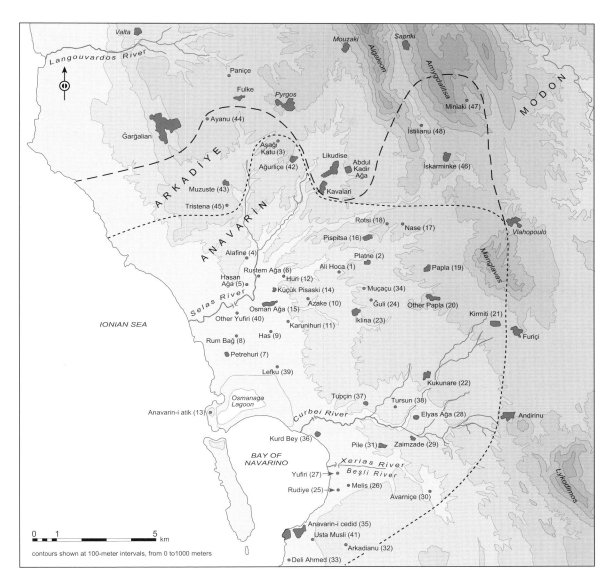

Figure 2.1. Settlements in the administrative district of Anavarin, with place-names as they appear in TT880. Settlements between the dotted and dashed lines were reassigned to Arkadiye after 1716. Some modern place-names are included (in italics) for reference.
R. J. Robertson, after Bennet, Davis, and Zarinebaf-Shahr 2000, fig. 12

house). Taxes that have been or that could be assessed on the property or activities of the *reaya* are noted; in a few instances, we are also given information about the productivity of the land and the market price of particular crops. Finally the boundaries of the village, *çiftlik,* or *mazraʿa* are recorded as a series of toponyms, written diagonally and sloping upward from right to left.

Annotations to the entries were added to the text, possibly by someone other than Seyyid Mehmed Hatemi. Each individual entry in the *defter* is specified as a certified copy *(beyaz olunmuşdur)* in the hand of the annotator, and most, but not all, are indicated as *mîrî* (property of the state) by the letter "m" written once or twice above the heading line; sometimes the word *mîrî* is also spelled out in full. A fraction (see Chap. 4) was written above each heading, also in the hand of this annotator, and other information was sometimes added in the left and right margins of the page and in the margin above the heading.

Figure 2.1 is a map of the settlements in the district of Anavarin, using the place-names as they appear in TT880.

A TRANSLATION OF THE CADASTRAL SURVEY OF ANAVARİN (1716)

[TT880, p. 78]

KAZA OF ANAVARİN

2/500[15]
1. ÇİFTLİK OF ALİ HOCA
Mirî. Formerly a timar. Plain.[16] A dependency of Anavarin.

2 houses; 1 oil press (*asyab-i revğan*);[17] 1 vineyard; 1 *tarla* (field).
A 2-floor house with 1 room on the top floor, a barn on the lower
    floor: L. 15 × W. 11 × H. 8.[18]
Attached to 1 side is a house with 2 rooms: L. 28 × W. 16.
    1 large barrel *(fuçı)* and 2 large earthenware jars *(küp).*
1 oil press: L. 22 × W. 8.
Another room attached to the oil press: L. 12 × W. 9.

1 vineyard (bağ)[19] *of 32* dönüm*s*
9 fig trees; 5 mulberry trees; 15 pear trees; 2 lemon trees; 1 orange
    tree; 6 almond trees

400 roots *(dib)* of olives

*Tarla*s of 300 *dönüm*s

Knowledgeable informants responded that only 6 pairs of oxen are
    needed to plow the land. Since the times when it passed from
    Muslim into Frankish hands, 100 *kile*s[20] of seeds have been sown
    with only 6 pairs of oxen.

Sharecroppers (Ortakçıyan):
1. Mihali son of Curci
    1 *çift* of land;[21] 80 sheep; 2 pigs; 5 beehives
2. Adamir son of Tanaş
    1 *çift* of land
3. Tuduri son of İstiratni
    ½ *çift* of land; 40 sheep
4. Yani his son

15. The formula written here as a fraction literally reads "of *y* (total) *çift*s, *x* *çift*s"; i.e., in this case, "of 500 *çift*s, 2 *çift*s."

16. The Turkish phrase is not entirely clear, but it appears to read *uvve dir*, "it is a plain," logical since other entries are described as "mountain."

17. The word *asyab*, strictly "water mill," is used throughout for mills and presses. Here, however, the word for "olive oil" *(revğan)* is added.

Elsewhere in this translation, "mill" is used for *asyab* alone and "oil press" for *asyab-i revğan*.

18. All measurements are assumed to use the *zira³*, equivalent to 0.758 m. Only in entry 13 (Anavarin-i atik) is the unit of measurement explicitly said to be the *zira³*.

19. Throughout the document, we understand the word *bağ* to refer to "vineyard." The word *bağce* refers to "orchard."

20. *Kile* is the standard volumetric measure employed for grain; in all instances where the value of the *kile* is specified, it is the Istanbul standard. We assume it also to be the case where the scribe is not explicit.

21. The land here measured is arable land planted in grain. A *çift* is the amount of land that could be plowed by one pair of oxen in an agricultural season.

Revenue (hasil): one-seventh *(sabᶜ)* of the grain[22]
Head tax[23] *(ispence):* 4 persons *(nefer)*
Wheat *(hınta):* 2½ *çift*s of land[24]
Barley *(şaᶜir):* [empty]
Fodder *(alef).*[25] [empty]
Millet *(erzen):* [empty]
Broad beans *(bakla):* [empty]
Lentils *(mercimek):* [empty]
Tithe *(üşür)* of flax *(ketan):* 10 *vukiyye*s[26]
Tithe of olives *(zeytun):* 400 roots
Tax *(resm)* on vineyards: 32 *dönüm*s
Tithe of beehives *(kuvare):* 5 beehives
Tithe of figs *(incir):* 9 trees *(direht)*
Tax on mulberries *(tut):* 5 trees
Tithe of pears *(emrud):* 15 trees
Tithe of lemons *(limun):* 3 trees
Tithe of various *(mütenevveᶜe)* fruits *(meyve):* 50 trees
Tithe of cotton *(penbe):* 50 *lidre*s. Every *lidre* is 133 *dirhem*s.[27]
Tithe of kitchen gardens *(bustan):* [empty]
Sheep tax *(adet-i ağnam):* 120 head
Tax on oil presses: 1 press
Tax on wastelands *(deştbani):* [empty]
Tax on land deeds *(tapu-yi zemin):* [empty]
Marriage tax *(arusane):* [empty]
Innovative tax *(bidᶜat)* on pigs *(hinazir)* and piglets *(yavru):* 2 head
Crime tax from fines *(bad-i hava ve cürmü cinayat):* [empty]

The total tithes have not been set apart.[28]

The inhabitants of this village gave the following information concerning the productivity of arable land.

On one çift *of land:*
6 *kile*s of seeds produce 24 *kile*s of wheat.
6 *kile*s of seeds produce 30 *kile*s of barley.
5 *kile*s of seeds produce 30 *kile*s of fodder.
1 *kile* of seeds produces 8 *kile*s of millet.

22. On Crete, the tithe was originally recorded as one-fifth but was changed to one-seventh in 1675–1676 (Greene 2000, p. 23, n. 38).

23. A head tax was levied on non-Muslim males who depended on agriculture for their livelihood (see Chap. 1 and the *kanunname* translated above, paragraph 6).

24. The revenue figure for wheat is invariably calculated as the sum of the arable land *(çift)* in possession of the individual *reaya* who are resident at that location.

25. The scribe has written *alef* in all cases, meaning "fodder." We suspect, however, that because the item appears among grains, and because figures are given below for the product in terms of seed-to-yield ratios, that "oats" *([y]ulaf)* is the commodity meant.

26. The *vukiyye* is the standard Ottoman *okka*, a measure of weight equivalent to approximately 1.28 kg.

27. Annotation giving equivalence is written diagonally to the left side of this entry.

28. The Ottoman treasury usually collected the tithe, because it was an Islamic tax and its collection was justified by Islamic law. Other taxes were either extraordinary taxes imposed during times of war or local taxes gathered by local lords (e.g., *çiftlik* holders). Here and elsewhere in TT880, the tithe has, however, "not been set aside *(ifraz olunmamış-dur)* for the central treasury," according to İnalcık, and the fact that no cash total is given indicates furthermore that the treasury was not collecting it in 1716, perhaps to encourage economic recovery. I thank H. İnalcık for discussing the interpretation of this phrase with me.

Prices:
Medium-quality wheat
    1 *kile* sells for 50 *akçe*s.
Barley
    1 *kile* sells for 30 *akçe*s.
Fodder
    1 *kile* sells for 20 *akçe*s.
Millet
    1 *kile* sells for 25 *akçe*s.

1 vineyard of 1 *dönüm* produces 250 *vukiyye*s of medium-quality
    grapes, and these sell for 250 *akçe*s.

When we asked about the productivity of olive orchards, we were
    told that 1 olive tree produces 30 *vukiyye*s of medium-quality
    olives. 15 *vukiyye*s of olives will be exported for the year, and
    15 *vukiyye*s of olives produce 2 *vukiyye*s of oil. 1 *vukiyye* of mid-
    quality oil sells for 10 *akçe*s.

1 *lidre* of medium-quality cotton costs only 10 *akçe*s, and 1 *tarla* of
    1 house produces only 10 *lidre*s of cotton.

This *çiftlik* is bounded by Çurukdun, Klurun, Vidizmadun,
    Mavriliçne, and Evluyol.

3/400
2. ÇİFTLİK OF PLATNE
Miri. Formerly a *timar.* Mountain *(tağdir);* medium-quality *(veset)* land.
A dependency of Anavarin. Near Yetince.

House: 1 room on the lower floor. L. 12 × W. 7.

Vineyard of 7 *dönüm*s

Orchard (bağce) *of 2* dönüm*s*
20 fig trees; 25 mulberry trees; 15 pear trees; 6 lemon and orange
    trees; 5 almond trees; 30 various fruit trees; 10 cherry trees;
    5 walnut trees; 15 pomegranate trees; ~~25 mulberry trees~~[29]

50 roots of olives

*Tarla*s of 120 *dönüm*s

*Tarla*s require only 50 *kile*s of seeds that can be sown with 4 pairs
    of oxen. Under both the Muslims and the Franks, the *tarla*s
    were plowed with 4 pairs of oxen.

[TT880, p. 79]

Sharecroppers:
1. Dimu son of Kuste
    1 *çift* of land; 30 sheep; 1 pig
2. Nikula son of Kuste
    2 *çift*s of land; 100 sheep; 7 pigs

29. The phrase is struck through in
the original text.

3. Panayud son of Aksanu
   25 sheep; 8 pigs

Revenue: one-seventh of the grain
Head tax: 3 persons
Wheat: 3 *çift*s of land
Barley: [empty]
Fodder: [empty]
Millet: [empty]
Broad beans: [empty]
Lentils: [empty]
Tithe of walnuts *(ceviz):* 5 trees
Tithe of olives: 50 roots
Tithe of figs: 20 trees
Tithe of pears: 15 trees
Tax on mulberries: 25[30] trees
Tithe of lemons: 6 trees
Tithe of cherries *(kiraz):* 10 trees
Tithe of pomegranates *(nar):* 15 trees
Tithe of various fruits: 30 trees
Tax on vineyards equal to tithe *(üşür):* 15 *dönüm*s
Tithe of kitchen gardens: [empty]
Sheep tax: 155 head
Tax on wastelands: [empty]
Tax on land deeds: [empty]
Marriage tax: [empty]
Innovative tax on pigs and piglets: 16 head
Crime tax from fines: [empty]

The total tithes have not been set apart.

The yields of this *çiftlik* have been registered together with, and have been computed based on, those of Ali Hoca.

This *çiftlik* is bounded by Paliumlu, Mizin, Çuruvne, Ali Hoca, and Pisitse.

2/500
3. MAZRAᶜA OF AŞAĞI KATU
Mirî. A dependency of Anavarin. Near Ğarğalian in Arkadiye.

*Tarla*s of 80 *dönüm*s

The *reaya* of the village of Ğarğalian in Arkadiye have taken over this.

The *tarla*s in this *çiftlik* require only 40 *kile*s of seeds to be sown by 2 pairs of oxen.

Revenue: one-seventh of the grain

This *çiftlik* is bounded by Karadimu, Hiristududrile, the Orman Mountains, and Dirastu.

30. Written above the entries for lemons and cherries.

2/500
4. *ÇİFTLİK* of Alafİne
Mirî. Formerly a *timar.* A dependency of Anavarin.

1 house, 2 rooms on the lower level. L. 21 × W. 12.
2 more lower rooms attached, in ruin. L. 18 × W. 10.
1 mill, in ruin *(harab).*
1 felt *(kebe)*[31] mill, in ruin.
1 oil press: L. 25 × W. 13.

1 vineyard of 1 *dönüm*

Orchard of 4 dönüms
24 lemon trees; 27 orange trees; 40 pomegranate trees; 18 fig trees;
   50 various fruit trees

462 roots of olives

12 roots of olives in Likuvun

*Tarla*s of 120 *dönüm*s

*Tarla*s in Pilalutaluni: 10 *dönüm*s, bounded by Hasan Ağa *tarla*
   and a big *(büyük)* valley with a stream
Tarla next to the big bridge: 5 *dönüm*s bounded by Rustem Ağa
   tarla and Purnari
Tarla next to Has *çiftlik:* 10 *dönüm*s bounded by the place *(mevzi)*
   Putme and an olive orchard belonging to Has
Tarla next to Rum Bağlari: 8 *dönüm*s bounded by the sea and the
   public road

The *çiftlik* requires only the 10 pairs of oxen that were used under
   both the Muslims and the Franks. They are sufficient for this
   land.

Sharecroppers:
1. Nikula son of Sakirli
   1 *çift* land; 60 sheep
2. Luke son of Panayud
   1 *çift* land
3. Puliduru son of Yorğu
   50 sheep

Revenue: one-seventh of the grain
Head tax: 3 persons
Wheat: 2 *çift*s of land
Barley: [empty]
Fodder: [empty]
Millet: [empty]
Rye *(çavdar):* [empty]
Lentils: [empty]
Tax on vineyards: 1 *dönüm*
Tithe of olives: 474 roots
Tithe of lemons: 24 trees

31. Probably a mill using water to
compact fibers for the manufacture
of coarse cloth (Greek *nerotrivi* [νερο-
τριβή]).

Tithe of oranges *(turunc):* 27 trees
Tithe of pomegranates: 40 trees
Tithe of figs: 18 trees
Tithe of various fruits: 50 trees
Tithe of kitchen gardens: [empty]
Tithe of flax: 5 *vukiyye*s
Sheep tax: 110 head
Tax on mills: 1 mill, in ruin, another felt mill, also in ruin
Tax on oil presses: 1 press

[TT880, p. 80]

Tax on wastelands: [empty]
Tax on land deeds: [empty]
Marriage tax: [empty]
Crime tax from fines: [empty]

The total tithes have not been set apart.

The accounting of the yield of this *çiftlik* (olives, vineyards, and other crops) has been based on that of Ali Hoca, and it is attached to it.[32]

This *çiftlik* is bounded by Diyuli, Diyuli Yariye, Balinmiyuz, a valley with a stream, Küçük Bisacki, and İstelidsire.

4/500
5. *ÇIFTLİK* OF HASAN AĞA
Mirî. Formerly a *timar.* Plain. A dependency of Anavarin.

A tower, 1 room on top and a storeroom on the bottom.
   L. 12 × W. 9.
1 room on the bottom. L. 11 × W. 7.
Another lower room attached to it. L. 10 × W. 6.
A courtyard in front. L. 15 × W. 12.
1 oil press; 1 oil press, in ruin; 1 mill, in ruin; 395 roots of olives;
   4 walnut trees; 3 lemon trees.

6 pairs of oxen were used when the *çiftlik* was in good condition.
   Now only 3 pairs suffice.

*Tarla*s of 160 *dönüm*s cultivated

Sharecroppers:
1. Yorğu son of Katlu
   1 *çift* land; 1 pig
2. His brother Kostantin
3. His brother Yani
4. Yani son of Andiria
   1 *çift* land; 1 pig
5. İstimad son of İstimad
   1 pig

32. I.e., figures given for Ali Hoca should be used to compute yields for this *çiftlik.*

6. Futni son of Anuştaş
   1 *çift* of land
7. Yani son of Tanaş
   10 sheep; 2 pigs
8. His brother Nikula
9. Yorğu son of Nikula

Revenue: one-seventh of the grain
Head tax: 9 persons
Wheat: 3 *çift*s
Barley: [empty]
Fodder: [empty]
Millet: [empty]
Broad beans: [empty]
Tithe of walnuts: 4 trees
Tithe of lemons: 3 trees
Tithe of olives: 395 roots
Tithe of kitchen gardens: [empty]
Tithe of flax: 15 *vukiyye*s
Sheep tax: 10 head
Tax on mills: 1 mill in ruin
Tax on oil presses: 1 press
Tax on wastelands: [empty]
Tax on land deeds: [empty]
Marriage tax: [empty]
Innovative tax on pigs: 5 head
Crime tax from fines: [empty]

The total tithes have not been set apart.

This *çiftlik* is bounded by the great valley with the river, Bey Konaki,
   Rustem Ağa *çiftlik,* and the sea.

4/500

6. *ÇİFTLİK* OF RUSTEM AĞA
Miri. Formerly a *timar.* Plain. A dependency of Anavarin.

Tower: 1 top room, 1 lower room, a storeroom at the bottom.
   L. 23 × W. 7 × H. 20.
Another room on the bottom. L. 18 × W. 14.
Another room on the bottom. L. 12 × W. 9.
Oil press. L. 16 × W. 8.
2 mills, under the same roof, 1 in operation all year *(tamam-i sal)*
   and 1 in ruin.
Another lower room attached to an oil press. L. 13 × W. 9.

Olives: 465 roots

Vineyard: 10 *dönüm*s

Orchard of 2 dönüm*s*
21 lemon and orange trees; 5 fig trees; 3 walnut trees; 6 fruit trees;
   9 mulberry trees; 100 various fruit trees

Sharecroppers:
1. Lamiru son of Yorğu
   1 *çift* of land
2. Dimitri son of İstatni
3. Tanaş son of İlya
4. Dimitri son of Yani
   1 *çift* of land; 50 sheep
5. His brother Aluviz
6. His brother Lamiru
7. Yorğu son of İstatni
   2 pigs

Revenue: one-seventh of the grain
Head tax: 7 persons
Wheat: 2 *çift*s of land
Barley: [empty]
Fodder: [empty]
Millet: [empty]
Broad beans: [empty]
Tithe of walnuts: 3 trees
Tax on vineyards: 10 *dönüm*s
Tithe of olives: 465 roots
Tithe of figs: 5 trees
Tithe of lemons and oranges: 21 trees
Tithe of quinces *(ayva):* 6 trees

[TT880, p. 81]

Tax on mulberries: 9 trees
Various fruit trees: 100 trees
Sheep tax: 50 head
Tax on mills: 2 mills, in operation all year[33]
Tax on oil presses: 1 press
Tithe of kitchen gardens and vegetable patches *(sirvat):*
   [empty]
Tax on wastelands: [empty]
Marriage tax: [empty]
Tax on land deeds: [empty]
Innovative tax on pigs and piglets: [empty]
Crime tax from fines: [empty]

The total tithes have not been set apart.

This *çiftlik* used to require 10 pairs of oxen for plowing when
   under Muslim rule. Now some parts are uncultivated, and the
   çiftlik only requires 6 pairs of oxen.

The attached *tarla*s will be listed below.

Attached tarla*s of 100* dönüm*s:*
Tarla in Narincir next to Huri and Bisaci: 4 *dönüm*s
Tarla in Famirlerun next to an old vineyard and the big valley:
   5 *dönüm*s

33. Despite the annotation above, in lines 6–7 below the entry heading, two operational mills are noted here.

Tarla in Tirankambu next to Alafine and the mountains: 4 *dönüm*s
Tarla in Aliğulivad next to Alafine and a rocky place *(taşlık):*
    9 *dönüm*s
Tarla in Arkudis next to Huri and Bisaci: 8 *dönüm*s
Tarla in Akşirulakad next to Osman Ağa *tarla*s: 8 *dönüm*s
Tarla in Makrikirak and Osman Ağa *tarla*: 9 *dönüm*s
Tarla in Vilandia next to the valley and Bisacki: 10 *dönüm*s
Tarla in Kuri next to the valley and the road: 7 *dönüm*s
Tarla in Rumenu next to Alafine and the sea: 8 *dönüm*s
Tarla in Rumike next to Osman Ağa *tarla*s and Has: 10 *dönüm*s

This *çiftlik* is bounded by Hasan Ağa, Huri, Alafine, and Osman
    Ağa *çiftlik*s.

The productivity of this *çiftlik* according to the inhabitants is as
    follows.

1 *çift* of land produces:
Wheat: 6 *kile*s of seeds produce 36 *kile*s.
Barley: 7 *kile*s of seeds produce 49 *kile*s.
Fodder: 5 *kile*s of seeds produce 30 *kile*s.
Millet: 1 *kile* of seeds produces 8 *kile*s.

Prices for medium-quality products:
1 *kile* of wheat sells for 40 *akçe*s.
1 *kile* of barley sells for 30 *akçe*s.
1 *kile* of fodder sells for 20 *akçe*s.
1 *kile* of millet sells for 25 *akçe*s.

Vineyard: 1 *dönüm* produces 300 *vukiyye*s of medium-quality
    grapes. 1 *vukiyye* of grapes sells for 1 *akçe*.

The *çiftlik*s of Alafine, Hasan Ağa, and Rustem Ağa are attached
    and share the same taxes and *tarla*s. 1 root of olive produces
    60 *vukiyye*s of olives; 30 *vukiyye*s are exported. 30 *vukiyye*s of
    olives produce 4 *vukiyye*s of oil that sell for 10 *akçe*s per *vukiyye*.
    This *çiftlik* also produces cotton. 1 *tarla* of 1 house produces
    15 *lidre*s of cotton. 1 medium-quality *lidre* of cotton is
    10 *akçe*s. Every *lidre* is 133 *dirhem*s.

2/500. It is being cultivated by the *reaya* of Hasan Ağa *çiftlik*.
7. MAZRA*ᶜ*A OF PETREHURİ
Miri. It is being cultivated. A dependency of Anavarin.

*Tarla*s: 200 *dönüm*s

Vineyard: 4 *dönüm*s

It was cultivated by the Frank, Hunduruz, and needs only 4 pairs
    of oxen.

Revenue: one-seventh of the grain

This *çiftlik* is bounded by İsbilia, the road, İstuputamu, the sea, and Has.

The yields of Petrehuri and Rum Bağ are counted as one.[34]

34. Written vertically as a notation
along the left margin.

[illegible][35]

8. *MAZRAᶜA* KNOWN AS RUM BAĞ. ANOTHER NAME IS LEFKU.

Dependency of Anavarin. It is not being cultivated.

Tarla: 50 *dönüm*s
Cultivated with 1 pair of oxen

Revenue: one-seventh of the grain

The revenues of Rum Bağ and Petrehuri are combined.

This is bounded by Rustem Ağa, the sea, Has, İstuputamu, and the mountains.

[TT880, p. 82]

2/500

9. *ÇİFTLİK* KNOWN AS HAS

Mîrî. Formerly a *timar*. Plain. A dependency of Anavarin.

Lower rooms: 2, in ruin. L. 22 × W. 10.
Olive press: 1, in ruin.

Olive yield *(mahsul):* 1,500 roots[36]
Wild/uncultivated *(yabani)* olives: 500 roots

Vineyard: 100 *dönüm*s

Orchard of 5 dönüms
39 pomegranate trees; 40 mulberry trees; 14 vine trellises;[37]
13 fig trees; 12 lemon trees; 20 apple trees; 5 pear trees;
6 quince trees

This *çiftlik* has a *tarla* that is 10 *dönüm*s in size and is cultivated with 1 pair of oxen.

Revenue: one-seventh of the grain
Wheat: [empty]
Barley: [empty]
Fodder: [empty]
Tithe of figs: [empty]
Tithe of apples: [empty]
Tithe of lemons: [empty]
Tithe of pears: [empty]
Tithe of quinces: [empty]
Tax on mulberries: [empty]
Tithe of olives: [empty]
Tax on vineyards: [empty]
Tax on oil presses: [empty]
Tax on wastelands: [empty]
Marriage tax: [empty]
Tax on land deeds: [empty]
Crime tax from fines: [empty]

35. The annotation here appears to be in the same hand and is in the same location as the fractions that appear at other entries. Yet it does not appear to include a fraction and is not sufficiently distinct to be legible.

36. These seem to be trees that bear fruit, as opposed to the wild olives.

37. The word appears to be *asma*, "vine trellis."

The total tithes have not been set apart.

This *çiftlik* is bounded by Kaniruni, Ağirlia, Kati Usta Baruli/
Baruvli, the boundary of Petrehur, and the public road.

3/500
10. *Çiftlik* of Azake
Mirî. Formerly a *timar.* Plain. A dependency of Anavarin. It should be
registered with the *çiftlik* of Muçaçu.

Top of tower; below it, a storeroom: H. 15 × L. 12 × W. 8.

Orchard of 1½ dönüm*s*
33 fig trees; 5 almond trees; 2 mulberry trees; 5 *dönüm*s of vineyard,
in ruin

166 roots of olives

The *tarla*s located here are only 80 *dönüm*s in size, and can be
plowed with 2 pairs of oxen.

Revenue: one-seventh of the grain
Wheat: [empty]
Barley: [empty]
Millet: [empty]
Fodder: [empty]
Broad beans: [empty]
Tithe of figs: [empty]
Tithe of almonds: [empty]
Tax on mulberries: [empty]
Tax on vineyards: [empty]
Tithe of olives: [empty]
Tax on wastelands: [empty]
Tax on land deeds: [empty]
Marriage tax: [empty]
Crime tax from fines: [empty]

Total tithes[38]

This *çiftlik* is bounded by Küçük Bisaci, Huri, Ali Hoca, the road,
and Osman Ağa.

2/500
11. *Mazra*c*a* of Karunihuri
Mirî. A dependency of Anavarin.

Tarla: 350 *dönüm*s
The *tarla*s can be plowed with 6 pairs of oxen.

Revenue: one-seventh of the grain

The *çiftlik* is bounded by Osman Ağa *çiftlik*, Seri Putamu, Ayu
Yurki, İstinayurki, and Likuvuni.

The revenues of this *çiftlik* and the *çiftlik* of Huri should be combined.[39]

38. The scribe has here written only
"total tithes" and does not explicitly
say that the tithes have not been "set
apart."
39. Written vertically as a notation
along the right margin.

2/500

12. ÇİFTLİK OF HURİ

Mîrî. Formerly a *timar.* A dependency of Anavarin.

Tower, in ruin: L. 11 × W. 9.
Top room, in ruin: L. 15 × W. 9.
Oil press: 1, in ruin.
Lower rooms, attached, 3: L. 35 × W. 20.

Orchard of 2 dönüm*s*
22 pomegranate trees; 19 fig trees; 6 almond trees; 11 lemon and
    orange trees; 3 vine trellises; 7 pear trees

Vineyard: 12 *dönüm*s, in ruin

Tarla in İstilake: 2 *dönüm*s bounded by the valley with a stream and
    Beruli
Tarla in İstirancuz: 5 *dönüm*s attached on one side to this *çiftlik*
Tarla in İstukufru: 10 *dönüm*s bounded by Bisaci and Has

Sharecroppers:
1. Nikula son of [illegible]
    1 *çift* of land; 30 sheep
2. İstimatlu son of Nikula
    1 *çift* of land; 50 sheep; 1 pig

210 roots of olives[40]

[TT880, p. 83]

Tarla in Usta Vilanide: 10 *dönüm*s bounded by Osman Ağa and
    Ser Putamu
Tarla in Ustu Hirisari/Stohroyasari: 20 *dönüm*s bounded by Hasan
    Ağa *tarla* and the road
Tarla in Ustu Lanita: 15 *dönüm*s bounded by Osman Ağa *tarla* on
    both sides
Tarla in İstru Lanka: 10 *dönüm*s bounded by Seri Putamu and the
    big valley
Another *tarla* in İstru Lanka: 9 *dönüm*s bounded by Karunihuri
    and Osman Ağa *tarla*s
Tarla in Antadiz: 3 *dönüm*s bounded by Lezake and the road going
    to Ali Hoca

The *tarla*s of this *çiftlik* are 85 *dönüm*s in size and can be plowed
    by 3 pairs of oxen.

Revenue: one-seventh of the grain
Head tax: 2 persons
Wheat: 2 *çift*s of land
Barley: [empty]
Fodder: [empty]
Millet: [empty]
Broad beans: [empty]
Sheep tax: 80 head[41]
Tithe of figs: 19 trees

40. This constitutes a separate entry;
it is not listed under *Sharecroppers.*

41. Inserted between lines 1 and 2
of the *Revenue* list, toward the left side
of the page.

Tithe of pomegranates: 22 trees
Tithe of almonds: 6 trees
Tithe of lemons and oranges: 11 trees
Tithe of pears: 7 trees
Tax on vineyards: 12 *dönüm*s
Tithe of olives: 210 roots
Tax on oil presses: 1 press
Tax on wastelands: [empty]
Marriage tax: [empty]
Tax on land deeds: [empty]
Crime tax from fines: [empty]

The total tithes have not been set apart.

6/500
13. *KALE* OF ANAVARİN-İ ATİK
A dependency of Anavarin.

> *A Description of the Outer Fortress*
> The walls on the side of the gate: 165 *zira*ʾs, 30 *zira*ʾs of these
>   in ruin.
> The right side: 132 *zira*ʾs.
> The left side: 157 *zira*ʾs.
> The bastion *(tabya)* above the gate, in ruin on one side: L. 15 ×
>   W. 12.
> The bastion on the left corner of the gate: L. 9 × W. 8.
> The bastion in the right corner of the gate, half-ruined: L. 8 × W. 8.
> Inside the walls of the fort, houses with ruined roofs, but walls in
>   good shape: 26 houses.
> Mosque, ruined on top but in satisfactory condition inside the walls:
>   L. 23 × W. 17.
> A harem in front of it: L. 17 × W. 5.
> Water cistern: L. 18 × W. 11.

> *A Description of the Inner Fortress*
> The walls next to the gate: 105 *zira*ʾs, of which 30 are in ruin.
> The left wall: 175 *zira*ʾs.
> The right wall: 84 *zira*ʾs.
> The west wall: 90 *zira*ʾs.
> The bastion on top of the gate, in ruin.
> 2 bastions attached to the left of the gate, in ruin.
> The bastion at the left corner of the wall: L. 11 × W. 7, in ruin.
> A cistern: L. 11 × W. 9.
> Another cistern: L. 8 × W. 8.
> Half-ruined houses inside the walls: 6.
> A church in good shape: L. 12 × W. 8.
> A guardpost to the left of the gate: L. 5 × W. 5.

The *çiftlik* of Budran near the old fortress of Anavarin is tilled by
    the people living in the fortress *(hisar)*.

*Tarla*s: 500 *dönüm*s

Meadows: 60 *dönüm*s

The summer pasture *(yazlık)* of Büyük Göl: W. 300 × L. 300 [empty]
The [*reaya* of the] village of Kilursarin, which is close to it, used to cut it.

The monthly revenues of the *talyan* across from the fortress are farmed out *(mukataᶜa)* for 20 *kuruş*es per month, producing 240 *kuruş*es in one year.[42]

And across from the fortress there is an island that pays taxes.[43] This number of animals passes through it: [empty]

[TT880, p. 84]

Revenue: one-seventh of the grain
Wheat: [empty]
Barley: [empty]
Fodder: [empty]
Millet: [empty]
Broad beans: [empty]
Chick peas: [empty]
Lentils: [empty]
Tithe of cotton: [empty]
Revenues from the fisheries: [empty]
Winter pasture: [empty]
Pastures across from Anavarin-i atik: [empty]
Taxes for the summer pasture: [empty]
Meadow *(çayır)* tax: [empty]
Tax on wastelands: [empty]
Tax on land deeds: [empty]

The total tithes have not been set apart.

The Budran *çiftlik* of this fortress is 500 *dönüm*s in size and requires only 10 pairs of oxen. 1 pair of oxen can sow 10 *kile*s of seeds. 1 *kile* of wheat yields 4 kiles; 1 *kile* of barley yields 5 *kile*s; 1 *kile* of fodder yields 5 *kile*s; and 1 *kile* of millet yields 10 *kile*s.

8/500

14. ÇIFTLİK OF KÜÇÜK PISASKİ
Miri. Plain. A dependency of Anavarin.

3 attached lower rooms: L. 35 × W. 12, 3 large earthenware jars inside.
3 big barrels.
Oil press: L. 22 × W. 11.
2 large earthenware jars inside.

42. *Talyan* here and in entry 36 is equivalent to the Turkish word *dalyan* and clearly refers to the fisheries in the lagoon east of Anavarin-i atik. The value of revenue from this source is somewhat greater than the 24,000 *akçe*s recorded in the listing of urban tax farms in the district of Anavarin in 1716 (see Table 1.7); 240 *kuruş*es were equal to 28,800 *akçe*s (see Pamuk 2000, p. 160, for exchange equivalences).

43. This island clearly is Sphakteria.

Olives: 1,000 roots

Lower room: L. 9 × W. 7.

Vineyards: 35 *dönüm*s

Orchard of 1 dönüm
9 fig trees; 3 almond trees; 5 pear trees; 2 mulberry trees

Tarla in the vicinity of Karunihuri: 40 *dönüm*s bounded by the
    fortress of Ustu İklina and Akşilukirayi
Tarla in Pulatnu: 30 *dönüm*s bounded by the public road and
    Osman Ağa *tarla*
Tarla in Ustu Buruvalu: 30 *dönüm*s, bounded by Osman Ağa *tarla*
    and Seri Putamu
Tarla in İstinintambu: 25 *dönüm*s, bounded by Yufir and Kirunkur
Tarla in İstefani Rumi: 8 *dönüm*s bounded by Vlanidiye and Has
Tarla in Ustu Huvacar: 20 *dönüm*s bounded by the road by İspitse
Tarla in İstilake: 25 *dönüm*s, bounded by Rustem Ağa and Osman
    Ağa *tarla*s
Tarla across from this *çiftlik*: 5 *dönüm*s

The orchard in the valley across from this *çiftlik*: 2 *dönüm*s

8 pairs of oxen are sufficient to plow this *çiftlik* and its *tarla*s.

Sharecroppers:
1. Tanaş son of Yuriyan
    1 *çift* of land; 50 sheep
2. Petru his son
3. Dimitri son of Yani
    1 *çift* of land; 1 pig
4. Nikula his brother
5. Hiristufilu son of Hiristufilu
    ½ *çift* of land; 15 sheep; 1 pig
6. Yani son of Anuştaş
    1 *çift* of land; 20 sheep
7. Kutnu his son
8. Yanağu son of Manu
9. Mihali son of Çakuye
    1 *çift* of land; 1 pig
10. Lamiru son of Kostantin
11. Yani son of Yani
    1 *çift* of land
12. Dimitri son of Kutnu
    ½ *çift* of land
13. Aluvizunlu son of Yurğake

All these *reaya* have a house each.

Revenue: one-seventh of the grain
Head tax: 13 persons
Wheat: 6 *çift*s

Barley: [empty]
Millet: [empty]
Broad beans: [empty]
Lentils: [empty]
Tithe of flax: 25 *vukiyye*s
Tithe of olives: 1,000 roots
Tax on vineyards: 35 *dönüm*s
Tithe of figs: 9 trees
Tithe of almonds: 3 trees
Tithe of pears: 5 trees
Sheep tax: 85 head
Innovative tax on pigs and piglets: 3 head

[TT880, p. 85]

Tax on mulberries: 3 trees
Tithe of kitchen gardens: [empty]
Tithe of beehives: 10 beehives
Tax on wastelands: [empty]
Tax on land deeds: [empty]
Marriage tax: [empty]
Crime tax from fines: [empty]

The total tithes have not been set apart.

8/500

15. *ÇİFTLİK* OF OSMAN AĞA OR BÜYÜK PİSASKİ
Miri. Plain. A dependency of Anavarin.

A big house with 8 attached upper rooms.
3 storerooms below.
A courtyard in front of the stable. L. 45 × W. 40.
A plot of vacant land. L. 38 × W. 25 × H. 17.
3 attached lower rooms in the courtyard: L. 27 × W. 16.
3 attached lower rooms inside the mansion: L. 25 × W. 10.
   15 big earthenware jars inside.
4 attached lower rooms to the right of the gate: L. 25 × W. 10.
2 lower rooms across from the gate: L. 20 × W. 12.
A wooden kitchen inside the courtyard: L. 18 × W. 11. 2 ovens
   inside.
Inside the outer courtyard, 2 attached lower rooms to the south:[44]
   L. 16 × W. 9.
8 masonry houses inside the outer courtyard, ruined on top. L. 26 ×
   W. 14.
A courtyard across from it: L. 30 × W. 25.
Oil presses: 2.
2 attached masonry buildings: L. 25 × W. 12. A masonry building
   next to it. L. 13 × W. 9.
A *han*-like building of masonry with a roof: L. 38 × W. 20.

44. Literally, "toward the *Kaba.*"

Attached on 1 side, a wooden structure with 2 lower rooms:
    L. 38 × W. 12.
On the other side, a second wooden structure with 2 lower rooms
    attached: L. 38 × W. 12.
A courtyard across from it with 4 standing walls: L. 4 × W. 4.
A vineyard with standing walls across from the *çiftlik:* vineyard of
    300 *dönüm*s.

1,000 roots of olives
600 mulberry trees
27 almond trees
35 pear trees
40 peach trees
55 fig trees
Total: 157[45]

A mulberry orchard of 95 *dönüm*s with 1,500 mulberry trees across
    from the same *çiftlik*

A silk workshop *(ipekhane)* with 3 lower rooms across from the gate:
    L. 35 × W. 18

Olives in the vicinity of the above-mentioned *çiftlik:* 903 roots

*Tarla*s in Tavarne, a place in the same *çiftlik:* 1,500 *dönüm*s
30 pairs of oxen are sufficient.

1 mansion *(saray)*[46]
10 houses
1 *han*

Sharecroppers:
1. Andiria son of Yanağu
2. İlya Panvilu son of Yani
    1 *çift* of land; 40 sheep
3. Yani his son
4. Tanaş his son
5. Yurki son of Yani
    1 *çift* of land
6. Kostantin son of Kalenuri
    1 *çift*
7. İstimatlu son of Yorğu
    1 *çift*
8. Anduni Bulinmirun son of Bulinmirun
    1 *çift*
9. Tanaş son of İstanu/İstatu
    ½ *çift* of land
10. Nikula son of Dimitri
    1 *çift* of land; 15 sheep
11. Yani son of İstifani
    1 *çift* of land
12. Yorğu Yurikan son of Yurikan

45. This total does not include the olive roots and mulberry trees noted just above.

46. This and the following two entries appear to summarize the information above.

Revenue: one-seventh of the grain
Head tax: 12 persons
Wheat: 7½ *çift*s
Barley: [empty]
Fodder: [empty]
Broad beans: [empty]
Millet: [empty]
Rye: [empty]
Tithe of flax: 40 *vukiyye*s
Tax on vineyards: 300 *dönüm*s
Tithe of olives: 1,903 roots[47]
Tithe of figs: 55 trees
Tithe of almonds: 27 trees
Tithe of pears: 35 trees
Tithe of peaches: 40 trees
Tithe of beehives: 10 beehives
Tithe of kitchen gardens and vegetables *(sebzevat):* [empty]
Tithe of cotton: 100 *lidre*s, 133 *dirhem*s per *lidre*[48]
Tithe of cocoons *(gögül):* [empty] *lidre*
Tax on mulberries: 2,100 saplings *(fiddan)*
Sheep tax: 55 head
Tax on presses *(mengene):* 3 presses[49]
Tax on oil presses: 2 presses
Tax on wastelands: [empty]
Marriage tax: [empty]
Tax on land deeds: [empty]
Crime tax from fines: [empty]

The total tithes have not been set apart.

This *çiftlik* is bounded by Budran, Seri Putamu, Vlanidiye, and Azake.

[TT880, p. 86]

9/400

16. ÇİFTLİK OF PİSPİTSA

Miri. Mountain; medium-quality land. It was a *timar* before. A dependency of Anavarin.

The top room, ruined on top, but the walls are in satisfactory condition: L. 15 × W. 9 × H. 7.

Olives: 350 roots
Figs: 20 trees
Almonds: 6 trees
Mulberries: 25 trees
Lemons and oranges: 5 trees
Pears: 10 trees
Walnuts: 25 trees

47. The figure was crossed out twice: first written "1,903," then "993," and finally changed back to "1,903."

48. Equivalence written diagonally to the left as an annotation.

49. Entry written above the sheep tax entry.

Pomegranates: 6 trees
Apples: 2 trees
Peaches: 4 trees

The *tarla*s of this *çiftlik* require only 12 pairs of oxen.

Sharecroppers:
1. Yani son of Dimu
     1 *çift* of land; 25 sheep; 1 pig
2. Yorğu son of Panayud
     1 *çift* of land; 100 sheep
3. Dimu his brother
4. Yani his brother
5. İstimatlu son of Tanaş
     1 *çift* of land; 30 sheep; 4 pigs
6. Kutnu son of Dimitri
     1 *çift* of land; 10 sheep
7. Yorğu son of Panayud
     1 *çift* of land; 10 sheep
8. Tanaş son of Dimu
     1 *çift* of land; 50 sheep
9. İlya son of Dimu
     1 *çift* of land; 30 sheep
10. Lamiru son of Panayud
     1 *çift* of land; 50 sheep
11. Yuri Nikula son of Kostantin
     1 *çift* of land; 50 sheep
12. Yani his son

Revenue: one-seventh of the grain
Head tax: 12 persons
Wheat: 9 *çift*s
Barley: [empty]
Fodder: [empty]
Millet: [empty]
Broad beans: [empty]
Rye: [empty]
Sheep tax: 245 sheep
Innovative tax on pigs and piglets: 5 head[50]
Tithe of flax: 20 *vukiyye*s
Tithe of beehives: 16 beehives
Tithe of olives: 350 roots
Tithe of figs: 20 trees
Tithe of almonds: 6 trees
Tithe of lemons: 5 trees
Tax on mulberries: 25 trees
Tithe of pears: 10 trees
Tithe of walnuts: 25 trees
Tithe of pomegranates: 6 trees
Tithe of apples: 2 trees
Tithe of peaches: 4 trees

50. The entries for sheep and pig taxes are inserted between lines 1 and 2 of the *Revenue* list, at the left side.

Tax on wastelands: [empty]
Marriage tax: [empty]
Tax on land deeds: [empty]
Crime tax from fines: [empty]

The total tithes have not been set apart.

This *çiftlik* is bounded by the Putamu Valley, the valley across from Platne, Munadundiyeri, and İskilukranes.

2/400
17. *MAZRAᶜA* OF NASE, OR *ÇİFTLİK* OF MEMİ AĞA
Mirî. A dependency of Anavarin.

Olives: 53 roots
Figs: 2 trees
Almonds: 1 tree

The *tarla*s of this *mazraᶜa* require only 2 pairs of oxen.

Revenue: one-seventh of the grain and other taxes

The total tithes have not been set apart.

Within the boundaries of Pispitsa

2/500
18. *MAZRAᶜA* OF ROTSİ, OR *ÇİFTLİK* OF DENMUSARİN
Mirî. A dependency of Anavarin.

The *tarla*s of this *mazraᶜa* used to be plowed by 2 pairs of oxen.
2 pairs of oxen are sufficient.

Revenue: one-seventh of the grain and other taxes

The total tithes have not been set apart.

In the vicinity of Pispitsa

The revenues of this *mazraᶜa* and the *mazraᶜa* of Nase should be combined. It is in the mountains.[51]

5/400
19. *ÇİFTLİK* ~~KNOWN AS~~ OF PAPLA OR *ÇİFTLİK* OF MUSTAFA AĞA
Mirî. Formerly a *timar.* A dependency of Anavarin.

1 room on the lower floor: L. 11 × W. 7.
Upper room with a barn underneath: L. 15 × W. 8.
Attached upper room with a barn underneath: L. 13 × W. 8.
Attached lower room: L. 9 × W. 6.
Storeroom: L. 7 × W. 6.
Lower room: L. 11 × W. 7.
Lower room: L. 8 × W. 6.
Courtyard across from it: L. 25 × W. 20.

51. Written vertically along the right margin, spanning entries 17 and 18; literally, the phrase reads "It is mountain."

Figs: 15 trees
Pears: 6 trees
Mulberries: 6 trees
Almonds: 3 trees
Apples: 3 trees
Olives: 143 roots
Vineyards: 25 *dönüm*s

The *tarla*s of this *çiftlik* require 5 pairs of oxen. It cannot take more.
    1 pair of oxen can plow 12 *kile*s of seeds.

The revenues of this *çiftlik* should be combined with those of the
    other Papla since they are attached. Mountain; medium-quality
    (land).[52]

[TT880, p. 87]

Sharecroppers:
1. İlya Mirevala son of Yani
    1 *çift* of land; 50 sheep; 1 pig
2. İstatni his son
3. Yanağu Velahuvirle son of Yorğu
    1 *çift* of land; 100 sheep
4. Yorğu son of Yani
5. Bulinmirun son of Anuştaş
    1 *çift* of land; 30 sheep; 1 pig
6. Yani his son
7. İstimatlu son of Miryan
    ½ *çift* of land; 50 sheep; 2 pigs
8. Pindazi son of Yani
    50 sheep
9. İstabişnu/İskabişnu son of Miryan
    ½ *çift* of land; 50 sheep; 2 pigs
10. Tanaş his son

Revenue: one-seventh of the grain
Head tax: 10 persons
Wheat: 4 *çift*s
Barley: [empty]
Millet: [empty]
Broad beans: [empty]
Lentils: [empty]
Sheep tax: 330 head
Innovative tax on pigs and piglets: 6 head[53]
Tithe of cotton: 30 *vukiyye*s
Tithe of beehives: 22 beehives
Tithe of olives: 139 roots
Tax on vineyards: 25 *dönüm*s
Tithe of figs: 15 trees
Tithe of pears: 7 trees
Tithe of almonds: 3 trees

52. Written vertically in the right margin.
53. The entries for sheep and pig are inserted between lines 1 and 2 of the *Revenue* list, at the left margin.

Tithe of apples: 4 trees
Tithe of kitchen gardens: [empty]
Tax on mulberries: 6 trees
Tax on wastelands: [empty]
Marriage tax: [empty]
Tax on land deeds: [empty]
Crime tax from fines: [empty]

The total tithes have not been set apart.

This *çiftlik* is bounded by Yalelulunuryu, Martilaf, Luteru, and Buhalu. This *çiftlik* is within these boundaries.

4/500
20. OTHER *ÇİFTLİK* OF PAPLA OR *ÇİFTLİK* OF AĞAKU
Mîrî. Formerly a *timar*. Plain. A dependency of Anavarin.

Lower room: L. 12 × W. 6.

30 olive roots
5 fig trees
5 pear trees
4 lemon trees
2 mulberry trees
3 orange trees

The *tarla*s of this *çiftlik* require only 5 pairs of oxen. *Tarla:* 350 *dönüm*s

Revenue: one-seventh of the grain and other taxes

The total tithes have not been set apart.

The *çiftlik* is bounded by İsta Platakia, Çupurulake, Kestusedile, Pulatnu, and Papla.

It is attached to above-mentioned Papla.

3/400. Mountain; medium-quality (land). It is cultivated by the *reaya* of the *karye* of Furiçi in Modon.
21. *MAZRA^CA* OF KİRMİTİ, ALSO KNOWN AS SEFER HOCA *ÇİFTLİK*
Mîrî. Formerly a *timar*. A dependency of Anavarin.

Figs: 12 trees
Pears: 25 trees
Olives: 2 roots

*Tarla*s: 170 *dönüm*s
The *tarla*s require 3 pairs of oxen. 1 pair of oxen can plow 10 Istanbul *kile*s of wheat.

Revenue: one-seventh of the grain and other taxes

The total tithes have not been set apart.

The *mazraʿa* is bounded by Serukambu, Usku Kunuri, Ustunu
   Rake, Likuri, and Furiçi (Modon). This *mazraʿa* is within these
   boundaries.

3/400. Mountain; medium-quality (land).
22. ÇİFTLİK OF KUKUNARE, ALSO KNOWN AS MUSLİHUDDİN EFENDİ ÇİFTLİK
Mirî. Formerly a *timar.* A dependency of Anavarin.

1 lower room: L. 9 × W. 7.
1 lower room: L. 13 × W. 8.
1 lower room: L. 13 × W. 10.

Olives: 50 roots
Figs: 25 trees
Pears: 30 trees
Mulberries: 12 trees
Walnuts: 6 trees

*Tarla*s: 550 *dönüm*s
The *tarla*s require only 10 pairs of oxen. Some areas are
   uncultivated.

[TT880, p. 88]

Sharecroppers:
1. Yani son of Andirğu
     çift of land; 2 pigs
2. Lamiru son of Kostantin
     1 *çift* of land; 30 sheep; 2 pigs
3. Yanağu son of Dimitri
     2 pigs

Revenue: one-seventh of the grain
Head tax: 3 persons
Wheat: 2 *çift*s
Barley: [empty]
Millet: [empty]
Fodder: [empty]
Broad beans: [empty]
Tithe of cotton: 15 *vukiyye*s
Tithe of olives: 50 roots
Tithe of beehives: 5 beehives
Tithe of figs: 25 trees
Tithe of pears: 30 trees
Tithe of walnuts: 6 trees
Tax on mulberries: 12 trees
Sheep tax: 30 head
Innovative tax on pigs and piglets: 6 head
Tax on wastelands: [empty]

Tax on land deeds: [empty]
Marriage tax: [empty]
Crime tax from fines: [empty]

The total tithes have not been set apart.

This *çiftlik* is bounded by the Likurni Mountains, Yalihur/Palihur, Rumiani valley, and Usti Kineta.

7/400

23. *ÇİFTLİK* OF İKLİNA, ALSO KNOWN AS KURD AĞA ÇİFTLİK

Mirî. A dependency of Anavarin.

2 rooms on the top floor, with a stable below: L. 20 × W. 9 × H. 7. The courtyard in front: L. 25 × W. 20.
2 attached rooms on the top floor with a stable below: L. 21 × W. 9 × H. 7.
1 attached top-floor room: L. 12 × W. 8. The courtyard in front with standing walls: L. 55 × W. 45.
Another room below: L. 20 × W. 12.
Another room on top: L. 12 × W. 9 × H. 7.
A *hamam* in ruin next to it: L. 19 × W. 9.
The courtyard in front: L. 20 × W. 16.
Attached room below: L. 11 × W. 8.
Oil press: L. 25 × W. 11.
2 rooms on top floor with a stable below: L. 19 × W. 9 × H. 7.

Vineyard: 40 *dönüm*s
Walnuts: 4 trees
Figs: 35 trees
Mulberries: 40 trees
Almonds: 15 trees
Pears: 35 trees
Pomegranates: 15 trees
Olives: 400 roots
Lemons and oranges: 18 trees

The *tarla*s of this *çiftlik* require only 6 pairs of oxen.

Sharecroppers:
1. Papa Yurğu son of Mihali
2. Hurini son of Vasil
    1 *çift* of land
3. Yani son of Mavurudi
    1 *çift* of land; 25 sheep
4. Hiristufilu son of Anuştaş
    1 *çift* of land; 40 sheep; 1 pig
5. Yorğu son of Kanlu
    ½ *çift* of land; 25 sheep
6. Lamiru son of Dimitri
    1 *çift* of land; 70 sheep

7. İlya son of Tuduri
   200 sheep; 10 pigs
8. Kostantin son of Nikula
   ½ *çift* of land; 25 sheep
9. Yorğu son of Tuduri
   ½ *çift* of land; 50 sheep; 1 pig
10. Tirandafilu son of Tuduri
    ½ *çift* of land; 25 sheep; 1 pig
11. Hiristu son of Tuduri
    1 *çift* of land; 20 sheep; 1 pig
12. Yorğu son of Panayud
    50 sheep
13. Kuste son of Dimitri
    1 pig
14. Yani son of Anuştaş
    25 sheep
15. Hilestu Avran son of Yilin
    5 beehives

Revenue: one-seventh of the grain
Head tax: 15 persons
Wheat: 7 *çift*s
Barley: [empty]
Fodder: [empty]
Millet: [empty]
Broad beans: [empty]
Lentils: [empty]
Tithe of flax: 25 *vukiyye*s
Tithe of beehives: 25 beehives
Tithe of olives: 400 roots
Tax on vineyards: 40 *dönüm*s
Tithe of walnuts: 4 trees

[TT880, p. 89]

Sheep tax: 555 head
Innovative tax on pigs and piglets: 15 head[54]
Tithe of figs: 35 trees
Tithe of almonds: 15 trees
Tax on mulberries: 40 trees
Tithe of pears: 35 trees
Tithe of pomegranates: 15 trees
Tax on oil presses: 1 press
Tithe of cotton: 60 *lidre*s
Tax on wastelands: [empty]
Marriage tax: [empty]
Tax on land deeds: [empty]
Crime tax from fines: [empty]

The total tithes have not been set apart.

When asked about the productivity of this *çiftlik*, the following
    estimates were given:[55]

54. The entries for sheep and pig taxes are inserted at the right margin between lines 2 and 3 of the *Revenue* list. At the bottom of pp. 88 and 93 of TT880 (see CD-ROM), there is a row of six symbols that perhaps signify "continued on next page."

55. See above, under Ali Hoca (1) and Rustem Ağa (6). The formula used there when information is presented in a similar format, "Prices for medium-quality products," appears to be omitted here.

1 çift of land produces:
Wheat: 6 *kile*s of seeds produce 30 *kile*s.
Barley: 6 *kile*s of seeds produce 36 *kile*s.
Fodder: 5 *kile*s of seeds produce 30 *kile*s.
Millet: 1 *kile* of seeds produces 15 *kile*s.

1 *kile* of wheat sells for 50 *akçe*s.
1 *kile* of barley sells for 30 *akçe*s.
1 *kile* of fodder sells for 20 *akçe*s.
1 *kile* of millet sells for 20 *akçe*s.

The local people said that the *kile* is based on the Istanbul *kile*. The earth is medium in quality. They said that 1 root of medium-quality olive produces only 30 *vukiyye*s of olives. 15 *vukiyye*s of these are exported, 10 *vukiyye*s are expected for the year, and 15 *vukiyye*s produce 2 *vukiyye*s of oil. 1 *vukiyye* of medium-quality oil is 10 *akçe*s in price. The *tarla* of 1 household would normally produce 8 *lidre*s of cotton. A *lidre* of medium-quality cotton sells for 3 *para*s. 1 *dönüm* of vineyard produces 200 *vukiyye*s of grapes. And 1 *vukiyye* of grapes costs only 1 *akçe*. Silk also used to be produced in this *çiftlik*, but they have not made silk for a few years.

This *çiftlik* is bounded by Balyamilu, Ustane Yuri, Muğanbali, and Hamulus.

This *çiftlik* and the *mazra'a* of Ğuli should be combined. It is in a plain and is medium-quality land.[56]

1/500
24. *MAZRA'A* OF ĞULİ KNOWN AS MEHMED AĞA ÇİFTLİK
Miri. A dependency of Anavarin.

*Tarla*s: 40 *dönüm*s
1 pair of oxen is sufficient. Some of the land is uncultivated.

Within the borders of İklina

Olives: 50 roots
Mulberries: 4 trees
Lemons: 3 trees
Almonds: 5 trees
Figs: 5 trees
Vineyards: 7 *dönüm*s
Various other trees: 30 trees

Revenue: one-seventh of the grain and other taxes
Within the boundaries of İklina, and the *reaya* of İklina will take possession of it.

The total tithes have not been set apart.

This *mazra'a* is bounded by İklina, Usulu Tirak, Kifuri, and Pilatnu. It is within these boundaries and in the possession of İklina.

56. Written vertically in the right margin; the first part of the sentence literally reads "It is plain."

2/500. Known as [illegible]. Close to Anavarin-i cedid.
25. MAZRA⁽ᶜ⁾A OF RUDİYE, ALSO KNOWN AS KURD ALİ AĞA ÇİFTLİK
Miri. A dependency of Anavarin.

> Tower, in ruin: L. 11 × W. 9
>
> The *tarla*s only require 2 pairs of oxen. 1 pair of oxen can sow 15 *kile*s of seeds.
> *Tarla*s: 75 *dönüm*s
>
> *Revenue:* one-seventh of the grain
>
> The *mazra⁽ᶜ⁾a* is in the possession of ~~Osman Ağa *çiftlik*~~ the *reaya* of the *varış* of Anavarin-i cedid.
>
> The total tithes have not been set apart.
>
> It is bounded by Muğle, the public road, İstisile, and the sea.
>
> The revenues of the *mazra⁽ᶜ⁾a*s of Melis and Rudiye should be combined. It is in a plain.[57]

2/500. Known as [illegible]. Close to Anavarin-i cedid.
26. MAZRA⁽ᶜ⁾A OF MELİS, ALSO KNOWN AS DERVİŞ KETHÜDA ÇİFTLİK
Miri. A dependency of Anavarin.

> The *tarla*s require only 2 pairs of oxen: 80 *dönüm*s.
>
> *Revenue:* one-seventh of the grain and other taxes
> In the possession of Pile
>
> The total tithes have not been set apart.
>
> It is bounded by Zurbe, Kumariçe, Ustu Birniçe, Ustu Ayvarniçe/ Ayurniçe, and İstalulid.

3/500. Should be registered with Kurd Ağa Bey Çiftlik.
27. MAZRA⁽ᶜ⁾A OF YUFİRİ, ALSO KNOWN AS BEŞLİ
Miri. Plain. A dependency of Anavarin.

> The *tarla*s require only 2 pairs of oxen: 80 *dönüm*s.
>
> *Revenue:* one-seventh of the grain and other taxes
>
> The *mazra⁽ᶜ⁾a* is bounded by İsbili, İstaluniye, Ustu Namu, the sea, and the public road. It is in the possession of Kurd Bey *çiftlik*.

[TT880, p. 90]

6/400. It is medium-quality (land). It is mountainous.
28. ÇİFTLİK OF ELYAS AĞA
Miri. Formerly a *timar.* In the possession of Kufurci. A dependency of Anavarin.

> The *tarla*s require only 6 pairs of oxen; some of the land is uncultivated and contains the following fruit trees:

57. Written vertically in the left margin alongside the entry for Rudiye; the second sentence literally reads "It is plain."

Lemons: 8 trees
Oranges: 3 trees
Figs: 22 trees
Mulberries: 11 trees
Pomegranates: 29 trees
Walnuts: 5 trees
Olives: 1 root

1 mill, in ruin. Full year *(saliyane)*, when in operation

Revenue: one-seventh of the grain
Wheat: [empty]
Barley: [empty]
Fodder: [empty]
Millet: [empty]
Rye: [empty]
Tithe of figs: 22 trees
Tithe of lemons: 8 trees
Tithe of oranges: 2 trees
Tithe of pomegranates: 29 trees
Tithe of walnuts: 5 trees
Tithe of olives: 1 root
Tax on mulberries: 11 trees
Tax on mills: 1 mill, in ruin
Tax on wastelands: [empty]
Tax on land deeds: [empty]
Crime tax from fines: [empty][58]

The total tithes have not been set apart.

Bounded by Andirinu *çiftlik*, the valley with the stream, Paliamilu, and Tursun Valley. This *çiftlik* is within these boundaries.

10.5/400
29. *ÇİFTLİK* OF ZAİMZADE
Mirî. Formerly a *timar.* It is middle quality. Plain. Dependency of Anavarin.

Two upper rooms and a stable below: L. 16 × W. 9 × H. 7.
An attached room on the lower floor: L. 12 × W. 10.
Another room on the lower floor: L. 12 × W. 7.
Another attached room on the lower floor: L. 13 × W. 7. The courtyard in front: L. 9 × W. 7.
Another room on the lower floor: L. 12 × W. 9. 6 vine trellises in front.
Another room on the lower floor: L. 7 × W. 5.
Another room on the lower floor: L. 8 × W. 6.

Figs: 12 trees
Almonds: 9 trees
Mulberries: 6 trees

The *tarla*s require 8 pairs of oxen.

58. Understandably, there is no entry for the marriage tax, even a blank entry, in the case of depopulated *çiftlik*s.

Sharecroppers:
1. Yani son of Panayud
    1 *çift* of land; 60 sheep; 2 pigs
2. Tuduri his son
3. Minuli his son
4. Lamiru son of Zahir
    1 *çift* of land; 70 sheep; 1 pig; 42 beehives
5. Nikula his son
6. Yorğu son of Anuştaş
    1 *çift* of land; 22 beehives; 2 pigs
7. Panayud son of Şideri
    ½ *çift* of land; 10 sheep
8. İlya his son
9. Tirandafilu son of Şideri
    1 *çift* of land; 15 sheep; 1 pig
10. Kilayuri son of Nikula
    1 *çift* of land; 50 sheep; 1 pig
11. Kilayuri son of Nikula[59]
12. Lamiru his son
13. Kutnu/Kuntu his son
14. Yanağu son of Hiristufilu
    1 *çift* of land; 50 sheep
15. Andruti/Andruni son of Yurğake
    1 *çift* of land; 30 sheep
16. Nikula his son
17. Pindazi son of Andruti/Andruni
    1 *çift;* 25 sheep; 1 pig
18. Yanağu son of Yorğu
    1 *çift* of land; 50 sheep
19. Yani son of Nekin
20. Lamiru son of Nikula
    1 *çift* of land in the *karye* of Kurd Bey
21. Yurğake his son
    In the *karye* of Kurd Bey
22. The goods in the possession of the wives of Kundilu and
    Anaştasni, the sons of Zahire
    70 sheep; 4 pigs

Revenue: one-seventh of the grain
Head tax: 21 persons
Wheat: 10½ *çift*s
Barley: [empty]
Fodder: [empty]
Millet: [empty]
Rye: [empty]
Sheep tax: 430 head[60]
Lentils: [empty]
Tithe of cotton: 30 *lidre*s
Tithe of beehives: 62 beehives
Tithe of figs: 12 trees
Tithe of almonds: 9 trees

59. It is possible that the name is repeated as a heading for the sons who follow. The *ispence* total is, however, 21. The list adds up only to 20, without Kilayuri being counted twice.

60. The entry is written in the left margin between lines 1 and 2 of the *Revenue* list.

Tithe of apples: 2 trees
Tithe of vine trellises: 6 plants
Tax on wastelands: [empty]
Tax on marriage: [empty]
Tax on land deeds: [empty]
Innovative tax on pigs and piglets: 12 head
Crime tax from fines: [empty]

The total tithes have not been set apart.

This *çiftlik* is bounded by Mankariarike, Demus, Ayu Nikula, and İstinkayu.

The revenues should be combined with those of Avarniçe.[61]

[TT880, p. 91]

2/500

30. *MAZRAᶜA* OF AVARNİÇE, OR *ÇİFTLİK* OF HACİ HASAN

Mîrî. In the possession of Pispitse/Pisitse. A dependency of Anavarin.

The *tarla*s of this *mazraᶜa* require only 2 pairs of oxen: 80 *dönüm*s.

Revenue: one-seventh of the grain and other taxes

It is bounded by Uste Yufiri, Ustune Yurki, Murafia, and Çuçurine.

6/500

31. *ÇİFTLİK* OF PİLE

Mîrî. Plain. A dependency of Anavarin.

Tower: top room L. 14 × H. 15 × W. 11; lower room L. 9 × W. 7.
Lower room: L. 9 × W. 7.
4 attached lower rooms: L. 25 × W. 9.
Lower room on the other side: L. 10 × W. 7.
4 attached lower rooms: L. 28 × W. 10.
5 attached lower rooms: L. 38 × W. 13.
3 attached lower rooms: L. 22 × W. 8.
2 attached lower rooms: L. 18 × W. 9.

Olives: 139 roots
Figs: 25 trees
Almonds: 5 trees
Mulberries: 4 trees
Pears: 2 trees
Vineyards: 20 *dönüm*s

The *tarla*s of this *çiftlik* require only 6 pairs of oxen: 250 *dönüm*s.

Sharecroppers:
1. İlya son of Panayud
   ½ *çift* of land
2. Abdi son of Nikula
   1 *çift* of land; 50 sheep

61. Written vertically at the right margin.

3. Lazuru son of Andiria
   50 sheep
4. Hiristufilu son of Nikula
   1 *çift* of land; 10 sheep; 1 pig
5. Yani his brother
6. Nikula son of Yorğu
7. Dimitri son of Virku
   50 sheep
8. Kostantin son of Yorğu
   ½ *çift* of land in the *karye* of Kurd Bey
9. Zahiri son of İstimad
   ½ *çift* of land in the *karye* of Kurd Bey
10. Tanaş son of Vavalari
11. Panayud son of Manialu
12. Yorğu son of Yanani
13. Yanağu son of Yorğu

Revenue: one-seventh of the grain
Head tax: 13 persons
Wheat: 3½ *çift*s
Barley: [empty]
Millet: [empty]
Fodder: [empty]
Broad beans: [empty]
Lentils: [empty]
Lentils:[62] [empty]
Rye: [empty]
Tithe of olives: 139 roots
Tithe of flax: 40 *vukiyye*s
Tax on vineyards: 20 *dönüm*s
Tithe of sesame *(sısam):* 20 *lidre*s
Tithe of cotton: 100 *lidre*s
Sheep tax: 160 head
Tithe of beehives: 15 beehives
Tithe of figs: 25 trees
Tithe of almonds: 5 trees
Tithe of pears: 2 trees
Tax on mulberries: 4 trees
Tax on wastelands: [empty]
Tax on land deeds: [empty]
Tax on marriage: [empty]
Crime tax from fines: [empty]

The total tithes have not been set apart.

Yield: with 1 pair of oxen, 12 Istanbul *kile*s of seeds of wheat can be
   planted. 1 *kile* of seeds of wheat yields 7 *kile*s of medium-quality
   wheat.

Tirukalyun, Ustna Nikula, Tursun Valley, Beşli, and Yufiri. This
çiftlik is within these boundaries.

62. The word "lentils" is written here again, but is misspelled.

2/500
32. *MAZRA^cA* OF ARKADİANU OR THE MÜFTİ ÇİFTLİK
Mîrî. Cultivated by the *reaya* of the *varış*. A dependency of Anavarin-i cedid.

> The *tarla*s of this *mazra^ca* require only 2 pairs of oxen: 80 *dönüm*s.

> *Revenue:* one-seventh of the grain

> This *mazra^ca* is close to Anavarin. It is bounded by the mountains, the public road, Viğle/Vifle, the sea, and the road that goes to Mesinmure/Mesihure. In the possession of Mesinmure/Mesihure.

> This *mazra^ca* of Arkadianu and Deli Ahmed are attached. Plain.[63]

2/500
33. *MAZRA^cA* DELİ AHMED ÇİFTLİK
Mîrî. Cultivated by the *reaya* of Anavarin-i cedid. A dependency of Anavarin.

> The *tarla*s of this *mazra^ca* require only 2 pairs of oxen: 90 *dönüm*s.

> *Revenue:* one-seventh of the grain

> This *mazra^ca* is close to Anavarin. The big road going to Modon, the valley with the stream, the mountains, the old wall, and the boundaries of Arkadiyanu. This *mazra^ca* is within these boundaries and is in the possession of the *varış*.

[TT880, p. 92]

4/500. Should be listed with the *çiftlik* of Azake.
34. *ÇİFTLİK* OF MUÇAÇU OR MUSLİHUDDİN ÇİFTLİK
Mîrî. Plain. A dependency of Anavarin.

> The *tarla*s of this *çiftlik* require only 9 pairs of oxen, but it has turned into a forest and wilderness, now requiring therefore only 4 pairs of oxen: 150 *dönüm*s.

> 1 pair of oxen can sow 12 Istanbul *kile*s of seeds; each *kile* (of seeds) yields 5 medium-quality *kile*s.

> Olives: 70 roots
> Figs: 9 trees
> Almonds: 3 trees
> Mulberries: 5 trees

> *Revenue:* one-seventh of the grain

> The *çiftlik* is bounded by Kifuri, Lezake, Ali Hoca, Putamu Valley, and Osman Ağa. In the possession of Küçük Bisaci.

63. Written at the left margin, alongside entries 32 and 33.

12/500
35. *KALE* OF ANAVARİN-İ CEDİD
Dependency of the aforementioned.[64]

1. The house of Haci Hasanoğlu Mustafa Çelebi,[65] in the fort in front of the gate of the fort, in ruin: L. 37 × W. 16.

2. The house of Usta Muslioğlu, in ruin: L. 22 × W. 12. Attached orchard, L. 20 × W. 15, with 1 lemon tree and 1 fig tree. The Janissary barracks *(oda)* on the one side, and the house of Haci Hasanoğlu on the other side.

3. The house of a certain Deli İsmail, in ruin: L. 12 × W. 10. Attached orchard: L. 29 × W. 10, with 2 lemon trees. The house of Usta Muslioğlu on one side, and the wall of the fortress *(hisar)* on the other.

4. The house of Dumbul Mustafa, in ruin: L. 29 × W. 11. Attached orchard, L. 15 × W. 12, with 3 lemon trees and 1 fig tree. The house of Deli İsmail on one side, and the fortress wall on the other.

5. The house of the Muslim Koca Firuz, in ruin: L. 19 × W. 10, with 1 lemon tree. The Harbor *(liman)* Gate on the one side and the house of Dumbul Mustafa on the other.

6. The house of Küçük İdris Ağa, in ruin: L. 23 × W. 12. The big street on the one side and the Harbor Gate on the other.

7. The house of Sakin Hoca, in ruin: L. 12 × W. 10. The big street on the one side and the house of Küçük İdris Ağa on the other.

8. The house of Haci Hasanoğlu Mustafa, in ruin: L. 25 × W. 23; in front of it, an orchard, L. 16 × W. 15; on the other side, a court-yard *(avlu),* L. 6 × W. 6; on one side of the house, a date tree, and on the other, the Harbor Gate.

9. The house of Dustoğlu Mustafa Çavuş, in ruin: L. 35 × W. 30, with 1 lemon tree. The big street on the one side and the Harbor Gate on the other.

10. The house of Bekir Hoca, in ruin: L. 27 × W. 18, with 2 lemon trees, 1 pomegranate tree, and 1 mulberry tree. The house of Mustafa Çavuş on the one side and the wall *(divar)* of the fort on the other.

11. Another house of Hasan Çavuş, in ruin: L. 40 × W. 15. The street on the one side and the house of Bekir Çavuş on the other.

12. In front of the gate of the workshop *(kerhane),*[66] the vacant land with ruined houses: L. 120 × W. 100. The gate of the workshop on the one side, the house of Hasan Çavuş and the wall of the fortress on the other.

64. Each individual entry in the *kale* is annotated with the letter "m" as an abbreviation for *miri.*

65. The last name is given first. One might also translate here and in similar cases, "Mustafa, the son of Hasan Kethüda."

66. *Kerhane* is a Persian word that in an Ottoman context meant literally "a place of work, workshop, or factory."

13. To the right of the door of the workshop, an area of ruined houses: L. 56 × W. 50. The door of the workshop on the one side and the big road on the other.

14. House of Ömer Ağa, the cousin of Osman Ağa, in ruin: L. 32 × W. 19. The house of Halil Ağa on the one side and the gate of the workshop on the other.

15. House of Halil Ağa, in ruin: L. 24 × W. 20. The big road on the one side and the house of Kadir Ağa on the other.

16. House of Abdulkadir Ağa, in ruin: L. 34 × W. 26. The house of Halil Ağa on the one side and the house of Osman Ağa on the other.

17. House of Osman Ağa, in ruin: L. 18 × W. 18. The house of Halil Ağa on the one side and the house of Kadir Ağa on the other.

18. House of Küçük Hüseyin Hoca, in ruin: L. 27 × W. 19. 1 olive root, 1 lemon tree, and 1 peach tree. The house of Osman Ağa on the one side and the big road on the other.

19. House of Çaçe Hatun, in ruin: L. 18 × W. 12. 2 lemon trees and 4 peach trees. The house of Hüseyin Hoca on the one side and the house of Haci Bey on the other.

20. *Selamlık* of Haci Bey, in ruin: L. 17 x W. 12. The house of Kadir Ağa on the one side and the house of İdris Ağa on the other.

[TT880, p. 93]

21. House of the *dizdar* Ağa, in ruin: L. 25 × W. 23. The street on the one side and the house of Osman Ağa on the other.

22. Attached to the *selamlık* of Haci Bey, the house of a Muslim, in ruin: L. 23 × W. 12. The Harbor Gate on the one hand and the house of Haci Bey on the other.

23. House of Küçük İdris Ağa, in ruin: L. 28 × W. 16. The big road on the one side and the house of Kadir Ağa on the other.

24. Harem houses of Haci Bey, in ruin: L. 40 × W. 28. Has an orchard: L. 15 × W. 12. 2 lemon trees, 1 peach tree. The house of the şeyh on the one side and the big street on the other.

25. House of Şeyh Muvali, in ruin: L. 35 × W. 28. The *hamam* on the one side and the harem of Haci Bey on the other.

26. House of Kurd Ali Ağazade Mehmed Ağa, in ruin: L. 23 × W. 17. 2 orange trees. The big road on the one side and the house of Kadir Ağa on the other.

27. House of a Muslim attached to it, in ruin: L. 17 × W. 10. The big road on the one side and the house of Kurd Ali Ağazade on the other.

28. *Beylik Hamam:* L. 18 × W. 12. The house of Şeyh Muvali on the one side and the house of Kurd Ali Ağazade on the other.

29. House of Kuparmazoğlu Mustafa Ağa, in ruin: L. 27½ × W. 26. The road on the one side and the house of Mehmed Ağa on the other.

30. House of Abdürrahman Ağa, in ruin: L. 20 × W. 20. The house of Halil Ağa on the one side and the house of Mehmed Ağa on the other.

31. House of a Muslim attached to it, in ruin: L. 14 × W. 12. The big road on the one side and the house of Kadir Ağa on the other.

32. House of the brother of Abdürrahman Ağa, in ruin: L. 19 × W. 15. 1 orange tree, 1 pomegranate tree, and 1 lemon tree. The big road on the one side and the fortress on the other.

33. House of the *ayrancı* (yogurt-drink maker) Receb and the house of a Muslim attached to it, in ruin: L. 35 × W. 24. 1 orange tree, 1 pomegranate tree, 2 lemon trees. The road on the one side and the wall of the fortress on the other.

34. House of a Muslim attached to it, in ruin: L. 17 × W. 15. The big road on the one side and the house of Receb on the other.

35. Another house of a Muslim attached to it, in ruin: L. 17 × W. 15. The house of Ataullah Efendi on the one side and the big road on the other.

36. House of Ataullah Efendi, in ruin: L. 25 × W. 19. 2 lemon trees and 1 orange tree. The road on the one side and the house of Hüseyin Ağa on the other.

37. House of Hüseyin Ağa, in ruin: L. 15 × W. 15. The house of Ataullah Efendi on the one side and the big road on the other.

38. House of a Muslim, in ruin: L. 17 × W. 15. The road on the one side and the wall of the fortress on the other.

39. House of Haci Alioğlu, in ruin: L. 33 × W. 25. The wall of the fortress on the one side and the road on the other.

40. House of a Muslim attached to it, in ruin: L. 15 × W. 12. The house of Hasan Kethüdaoğlu on the one side and the house of Mustafa Ağa on the other.

41. House of Ali Ağa, in ruin: L. 18 × W. 14. The house of Haci-oğlu on the one side and that of his brother on the other.

42. House of Hasan Kethüdaoğlu Mustafa, in ruin: L. 25 × W. 18. 3 lemon trees, 1 orange tree, and 1 fig tree. The house of Mustafa Çelebi on the one side and the road on the other.

43. Musli Çelebizade Büyük İdris Ağa: L. 39 × W. 30. 1 lemon tree, 2 orange trees, and 3 peach trees. The house of Hasan Kethüda on the one side and the house of Mustafa Çelebi on the other.

44. House of Haci Hasanzade Mustafa Çelebi, in ruin: L. 27 × W. 21. The house of İdris Ağa on the one side and the wall of the fortress on the other.

[TT880, p. 94]

45. Ten houses of Muslims close to the house of Haci Hasanoğlu Mustafa Çelebi, on the side of the small harbor and on the way to the bastion *(tabya):* L. 110 × W. 57. The fortress wall on the one side and the road on the other.

46. An orchard next to the gate of the workshop. L. 55 × W. 15. The fortress wall on the one side and the big street on the other.

47. The house of Haci Mustafa Ağa, in ruin: L. 35 × W. 15. The house of Kurd Ali on the one side and the street on the other.

48. The house of the *dizdar* Haci Kurd Ali Ağa, in ruin: L. 30 × W. 30. The street on the one side and the house of Haci Mustafa on the other.

49. The attached house of İbrahim Hoca and Deli Yusuf: L. 25 × W. 23. 2 lemon trees, 1 pomegranate. The Friday Mosque on the one side and the road on the other.

50. The house of Kurd Ali Ağa, in ruin: L. 26 × W. 21. The Friday Mosque on the one side and the street on the other.

51. The house of Deli Ahmed, in ruin: L. 21 × W. 18. The street on the one side and the house of Kurd Ali Ağa on the other.

52. Three ruined houses of Muslims, attached to the house of Deli Ahmed: L. 30 × W. 25. The house of Deli Ahmed on the one side and the house of Mehmed Ağa on the other.

53. The house of Kuparmazoğlu Mehmed Ağa, in ruin: L. 21 × W. 18. The house of Deli Ahmed on the one side and the street on the other.

54. On the way from the house of Uskufoğlu to the house of Mehmed, an area of empty houses: L. 65 × W. 50. Next to the wall of the fortress.

55. The house of Mehmed Uskufoğlu, in ruin: L. 30 × W. 20. The wall of the fortress on one side and the street on the other.

56. The houses of 5–6 Muslims on the way from the house of Kuparmazoğlu Mehmed to the fortress wall: L. 35 × W. 21. The street on the one side and the wall of the fortress on the other.

57. A church across from the gate of the lower tower *(kule):* L. 12 × W. 10.

58. The house of Mustafa Bey, in ruin: L. 15 × W. 14. The church on the one side and the house of Mehmed Ağa on the other.

59. The house of Kara Abdürrahman and attached to it the houses of 5–6 Muslims: L. 50 × W. 45. The church and the street on one side, and the gate of the lower *yalı* (waterside residence).

60. The house of Mutaciloğlu, in ruin: L. 31 × W. 22. The wall of the fortress on one side and the house of Kara Abdürrahman on the other.

61. The land of 10 ruined houses next to the small harbor: L. 135 × W. 100. The house of Keyvanoğlu on one side and the house of Cağaloğlu on the other.

62. The house of a Muslim next to the church: L. 15 × W. 12. The street on one side and the church on the other.

63. The house of Ahmed Kethüda, in ruin: L. 41 × W. 25. The Friday Mosque on one side and the road on the other.

64. The house of Usta Osman next to the house of Ahmed Kethüda: L. 24 × W. 15. The street on the one side and the Friday Mosque on the other.

65. The land of the house of Cağaloğlu: L. 12 × W. 9. The fortress on one side and the public square of the Friday Mosque on the other.

66. The house of Keyvanoğlu, in ruin: L. 15 × W. 12. The house of Cağaloğlu on one side and the church on the other.

67. The ruins of the house of Abdi: L. 25 × W. 20. The house of Keyvanoğlu on one side and the market *(çarşı)* on the other.

68. The land of the house of Osman Halife, in ruin: L. 40 × W. 25. The house of Keyvanoğlu on one side and the street on the other.

69. The land of 5 ruined houses next to the inner fortress *(içhisar)*, attached to the big bastion: L. 80 × W. 60. The gate of the fort on one side and the land of the church on the other.

70. The houses of Müfti Efendi, the walls in good shape but the roof in ruin: L. 25 × W. 20. The prayer hall *(nemazgah)* on one side and the Friday Mosque on the other.

71. The houses of Mustafa Bey, the walls in good shape, the roof in ruin: L. 20 × W. 18. The prayer hall on one side and the Friday Mosque on the other.

[TT880, p. 95]

72. The Friday Mosque known as the Friday Mosque of Bayezid: L. 21 × W. 21. The inner court: L. 25 × W. 9, and the primary school *(mekteb)*: L. 15 × W. 12. A water tank *(şatirvan)*:[67] 1.

67. A tank with taps in the side for ablution, usually attached to a mosque.

73. Another primary school, 1: L. 11 × W. 8.

74. The endowed *(vakf)* orchard attached to the Friday Mosque to the south: L. 35 × W. 25. 3 lemon trees, 1 almond tree, 1 apple tree, 1 orange tree.

75. The prayer square next to the Friday Mosque: L. 90 × W. 30.

76. The land of the *kadı*'s court *(mahkeme)*, in ruin: L. 21 × W. 16.

77. Primary school area, close to the inner fortress area: L. 15 × W. 13.

78. Inside the gate, the Janissary winter barracks *(kışla),* 5 rooms in it: L. 97 × W. 30.

79. The house of Hüseyin Reis and his brother, Fezli Kethüda, in ruin: L. 36 × W. 16. The house of Mustafa Bey on one side and the *hamam* on the other.

80. The house of Kahveci[coffee-seller]oğlu Hüseyin, in ruin: L. 17 × W. 15. The Friday Mosque on one side and the *hamam* on the other. The *dizdar* Hüseyin Çavuş of Anavarin claims this as his own property. It remains to be proven.

81. The house of Baba Alioğlu, in ruin: L. 19 × W. 12½. The Friday Mosque on one side.

82. Inside the fortress, in front of the gate, 2 shops of the *kethüda* attached: L. 12 × W. 9.

83. Area of more shops attached to these shops, in ruin: L. 15 × W. 10.

84. The house and shops of the *kundakçı* (incendiary/manufacturer of gun carriages) Bekir, the walls in good shape, the roof in ruin: L. 16 × W. 10.

85. The shop of Kurd Ali, in ruin: L. 10 × W. 8.

86. 2 shops of Kaztağli Mehmed Ağa, in ruin: L. 15 × W. 9.

87. The land of shops across from it, in ruin: 2, L. 12 × W. 6.

88. Again, 3 attached masonry shops: L. 18 × W. 10; the square in the back, L. 15 × W. 10, bounded by the cistern *(sarınc)* and the street.

89. Again, the land of 7 masonry coal shops, in ruin.

90. Again, across from them, 5 attached shops, in ruin: L. 25 × W. 8.

91. The house of Mustafa Çelebi, in the market, and the 2 shops underneath: L. 29 × W. 16.

92. 1 shop of Velioğlu Mustafa: L. 6 × W. 5. The house of Mustafa Çelebi on one side.

93. 1 shop of Baba Ali: L. 6 × W. 5.

94. The land of the houses of Muslihuddin Efendi, inside the gate:
    L. 15 × W. 13.

The Inner Fortress (İçhisar)
95. 3 attached masonry rooms of soldiers, in the direction of the
    varış: L. 25 × W. 11.

96. Again, in the same area, the empty land of ruined houses:
    L. 40 × W. 35.

97. The land of empty houses in the direction of the outer fortress:
    L. 79 × W. 37.

98. The land of a house, close to the big bastion: L. 11 × W. 7.

The Varış
The buildings in the *varış* of the fortress.
99. 4 attached Frankish shops: L. 20 × W. 7.

100. Across from them, on the road, the land of shops, in ruin:
     L. 10 × W. 10.

101. A shop under the road: L. 11 × W. 7. It formerly belonged to
     the Muslim Makrunoğlu.

102. 2 shops under the road, with rooms above: L. 14 × W. 12.

103. Again, on the road, the attached top rooms built by Estefan,
     the Frank: 3. One has a shop below: L. 35 × W. 25. Two have a
     stable below. Another room, with a room above and a storeroom
     underneath: L. 12 × W. 8. A kitchen attached to it: L. 11 × W. 9.
     The market and the *zimmi* (non-Muslim) Yudi on the other.

104. Attached to it, the house of Budur, with a room above and a
     storeroom underneath, 2 rooms: L. 31 × W. 25. The market on
     one side and the house of Estefan on the other. The owner is in
     captivity in the fortress of Modon.

[TT880, p. 96]

105. Inside the market, on the road, 2 newly built rooms: L. 25 ×
     W. 15. 2 shops underneath. A lower room next to it: L. 10 ×
     W. 8. A courtyard: L. 14 × W. 10. The house of the *tüfenkçi*
     (musket-seller) *zimmi* Zakarya/Zakhariye on the one side and
     the house of Yani Varvaris/Varvarin, *zimmi,* and the market on
     the other.

106. The house of Sivrikuzoğlu Mehmed Ağa, in the market; a
     room on top: L. 15 × W. 10. A storeroom and shop below. The
     courtyard around it: L. 71 × W. 55. The house of *zimmi* Zakarya/
     Zakhariye on one side and the market on the other.

107. Below the road, an oil press, on top of a room in the market,
     in ruin but the stones remain: L. 25 × W. 12. It was in the
     possession of Sivrikuzoğlu Kurd Ali Ağa.

108. The house of the *babucı* (shoemaker) Zaman, below the market, in ruin. The land: L. 30 × W. 15. The house of Kurd Ali Ağa on one side and the market on the other.

109. The house of Kırlı Kapucı Mustafa Çelebi, in ruin. The land: L. 27 × W. 19. The houses of *babucı* Ramazan on one side and Zakhari *zimmi* on the other.

110. Attached to it, the house of Arnavud Receb, in ruin. The land: L. 28 × W. 17. Surrounded by the houses of Kapucı Mustafa and *babucı* Zakhari.

111. The house of two Muslims, attached to the house of Receb, in ruin. The land: L. 30 × W. 25. 6 fig trees, 2 pear trees. Surrounded by the house of Yani and *boyacı* (dyer) Zakhir.

112. The house of Firuzoğlu Mustafa, in ruin. The land: L. 45 × W. 37. 2 lemon trees, 2 fig trees, 2 almond trees. The house of Manuli Kaltaban on one side and the house of Curci on the other.

113. The area of 10 houses and shops on the road in the area that lies between the gate of the fortress and the *varış:* L. 145 × W. 120.

114. 10 more houses on the road in the area that lies between the gate of the fortress and the *varış:* L. 150 × W. 132.

115. The orchard of Çabuk Ömer Ağa on top of the *varış:* L. 100 × W. 95. Bounded by the aqueduct on the one side and the valley with the stream on the other.

116. The orchard of Şaban Bey, in ruin: L. 110 × W. 90. The harbor on one side and the hill on the other.

117. The orchard of Muslihuddin Ağa, in ruin: L. 120 × W. 100. 5 lemon trees. The public road on one side and the sea on the other.

118. The orchard of Deli Mustafa behind the fortress, in ruin: L. 15 × W. 12. The wall of the fortress on one side and the sea on the other.

The Reaya *in the* Varış

119. Petru son of Danas
    1 house; 30 sheep

120. Yanağu Kukuri son of Yurğake
    1 house

121. Papa Yurki son of Çayalidi
    1 house

122. Yanağu, dragoman *(tercüman),* son of Angelu Polu
    1 house; 30 sheep

123. Marku his son

124. Mikali son of Varduke
    1 house

125. Nikula son of Angelu Polu
    1 house

126. Kostantin Tunkar son of Tunkar
    1 house

127. Marinu son of Yurki
    1 house

128. Ğanlu son of Soğancı[68]
    1 house

129. Manuli son of Lindi
    1 house

130. Hiristu son of Aku
    1 house

131. Yani son of Hurinu
    1 house

132. Yani son of Zengin
    1 house

133. Panu son of Çuka
    1 house

134. Nikula son of Vanduke
    1 house

135. Nikula son of ~~Vanduke~~ Kurzbale
    1 house

136. Yani Kikri son of Yurğake
    1 house

137. Nikula son of Kundiyurğa
    1 house

138. Yanağu Yanağupulu son of Yanağu
    1 house

139. Andiria son of Marku
    1 house

140. Yani son of Tanak
    1 house

141. Panayud son of Tanak
    1 house

142. Manuli Kaltaban son of Anuştaş
    1 house

68. "Son of Soğancı" may mean "son of *the soğancı* (onion-seller)."

143. Curci Monti son of Monti
    1 house

144. Koca Angeli, dragoman, son of Angeli
    1 house

145. Zekhiriye son of Tüfenkçi[69]
    1 house

146. Zakhiri son of Vafir
    1 house

147. Yurğake son of Yorğu
    1 house

148. Dimitri son of Dimu
    1 house

Revenue: one-seventh of the grain
Tithes (1/7 of grain) and other dues:
Total: [empty]

30 people

The revenues are to be listed when taxes are imposed—taxes such as market dues *(bac-i bazaar)*, the dues of the chief inspector of the market *(ihtisabiyye)*, a citation fee *(ihzariyye)*, an inheritance fee *(beytülmal)*, market dues on sheep, and dues at the slaughterhouse *(başhane, serhane)*.

[*TT8080, p. 97*]

2[70]/500. To be written with the *mazraᶜa* of Yufiri.

36. ÇİFTLİK OF KURD BEY
Mîrî. Formerly a *timar.* A dependency of Anavarin.

3 attached lower rooms, roof in ruin, walls standing: L. 35 × W. 12.
7 attached lower rooms, roof in ruin, walls standing: L. 50 × W. 15.
8 attached lower rooms: L. 52 × W. 11.
1 lower room, roof in ruin, walls standing: L. 11 × W. 7.
1 lower room, roof in ruin, walls standing: L. 9 × W. 6.
1 lower room, roof in ruin, walls standing: L. 15 × W. 9.

Orchard of 6 dönüms
24 lemon trees; 2 orange trees; 12 apple trees; 3 peach trees; 10 fig trees; 6 mulberry trees; 6 pear trees; 2 walnut trees; 3 vine trellises[71]

Orchard of 1 dönüm
9 apple trees; 3 peach trees

Orchard of 1 dönüm
4 apple trees; 1 vine trellis; 1 fig tree

69. "Son of Tüfenkçi" may mean "son of *the tüfenkçi* (musket-seller)."

70. The number "2" is crossed out.

71. The same item *(asma)* is listed at Huri (12), Zaimzade (29), and Ağurliçe (42). Here, as at Huri and Ağurliçe, it is not listed under *Revenue.*

Vineyard of 10 dönüm*s*
1 fig tree; 1 peach tree

The *tarla*s of this *çiftlik* require only 15 pairs of oxen to plow 900
    *dönüm*s. There are 2 mills, in ruin. Full year, when in operation.

There is an olive orchard of 1½ *dönüm*s.

Revenue: one-seventh of the grain
Wheat: [empty]
Barley: [empty]
Fodder: [empty]
Millet: [empty]
Broad beans: [empty]
Lentils: [empty]
Tithe of figs: 12 trees
Tithe of lemons and oranges: 24 trees
Tithe of peaches: 7 trees
Tithe of apples: 21 trees
Tax on mulberries: 6 trees
Tithe of pears: 6 trees
Tithe of walnuts: 2 trees
Tax on vineyards: 10 *dönüm*s
Tax on wastelands: [empty]
Tax on mills: 2 mills, in ruin
Tax on land deeds: [empty]
Crime tax from fines: [empty]

The total tithes have not been set apart.

Bounded by Talyan, Tavarne, Vavalari, Tupçin, and İstikamne

3/500
37. *ÇİFTLİK* OF TUPÇİN
Mirî. Formerly a *timar* of men.[72] A dependency of Anavarin.

Lower room, ruined on top, but with a wall remaining: L. 15 ×
    W. 11.

2 fig trees
1 mill, in ruin, full year when it was in operation
1 mill, also full year
12 mulberry trees

*Tarla*s of 120 *dönüm*s require 3 pairs of oxen. They are cultivated
    by the *reaya* of Kurd Bey.

Revenue: one-seventh of the grain and other taxes

The *çiftlik* is bounded by Kurd Bey, the road to Pile, the *mazraᶜa*
    of Tursun, and Kurd Tağı.

The revenues should be combined with those of the *mazraᶜa* of
    Tursun. It is a plain.[73]

72. By "*timar* of men," the scribe
apparently means that the property had
been a "military" *timar*, in the possession of Janissaries.
73. Written vertically at the left
margin.

1/500. It should be registered with the *çiftlik* of Tupçin.

38. *MAZRA^cA* OF TURSUN ~~NEAR THE~~. IT IS NEAR THE *ÇIFTLIK* OF TUPÇIN

Miri. A dependency of Anavarin.

*Tarla*s: 5 *dönüm*s

Mulberries: 2 trees
Pear tree: 1 tree
2 mills, 1 damaged. 1 is working; both are full year when in operation.

Revenue: one-seventh of the grain and other taxes

The *çiftlik* is bounded by Tupçin, Pila,[74] the *tarla* of Elyas Ağa, and the big valley with the stream.

6/400

39. *ÇIFTLIK* OF LEFKU OR TAVARNE

Miri. A plain. Formerly a *timar* of men. A dependency of Anavarin.

1 tower, in ruin: L. 12 × W. 9.
1 olive tree
1 mulberry tree
1 pear tree

*Tarla*s of 200 *dönüm*s
These *tarla*s require 6 pairs of oxen to plow 100 Istanbul *kile*s of seed.

Revenue: one-seventh of the grain

The *çiftlik* is bounded by Usti Biğadi, Kunduri, the public road, and Seri Putamu Valley. It used to be cultivated by Hunduruz. Now it is empty.

It is cultivated by the *reaya* of the *çiftlik* of Osman.[75]

1/500

40. *MAZRA^cA* OF OTHER YUFIRI. ANOTHER NAME IS RUM BAĞLARI

Miri. Formerly a *timar*. A dependency of Anavarin.

*Tarla*s of 45 *dönüm*s
These *tarla*s require 1 pair of oxen.

Revenue: one-seventh of the grain and other taxes

Bounded by the *tarla* of Alafine, the *tarla* of Rustem Ağa, the boundaries of Karunihuri, and the *tarla* of Hasan Ağa *çiftlik*. It used to be cultivated by the *reaya* of Hasan Ağa *çiftlik*. It is empty now.

74. Here "Pila" is definitely written with a terminal "a."

75. This annotation was added later in a different hand.

[TT880, p. 98]

1/500. It should be written with Anavarin-i cedid.

41. *MAZRA^A* KNOWN AS USTA MUSLİ NEAR ANAVARİN-İ CEDİD

Mîrî. A dependency of Anavarin.

> *Tarla*s of 30 *dönüm*s
> They require 1 *çift* of oxen.

> *Revenue:* one-seventh of the grain and other taxes
> In possession of the people of the *varış*

> Bounded by the arches of the aqueduct *(su kemerler)*, the mountains, the channel of the aqueduct *(su handak)*, and the public road

12/500. Should be written in Arkadiye. A plain. Should be written as a *karye*.

42. *ÇİFTLİK* OF AĞURLİÇE

Previously in possession of a certain Mustafa Ağa. *Mîrî.* Previously a *timar* of men. A dependency of Anavarin.

> 1 house. Top room; lower storeroom: L. 15 × W. 7. × H. 7.
> Another lower room: L. 13 × W. 6.
> Another lower room: L. 12 × W. 6.
> Oil press: L. 20 × W. 7.
> 1 damaged mill, full year when in operation.

> 16 fig trees
> 7 mulberry trees
> 12 pear trees
> 5 apple trees
> 10 almond trees
> 16 pomegranate trees
> 2 walnut trees
> Vineyard: 80 *dönüm*s
> Olives: 510 roots

> *Tarla*s require 10 pairs of oxen: 320 *dönüm*s.
> 1 pair of oxen are required to sow 15 *kile*s of seeds.

> *Sharecroppers:*
> 1. Yorğu son of İstimad
>   1 *çift* of land; 1 pig; 1 house; 1 pear tree; 3 mulberry trees; 7 fig trees; 3 lemon trees; and 2 pomegranate trees
> 2. Nikula son of Yurğake
>   1 *çift* of land; 1 pig; 1 house; 2 fig trees; 1 pear tree
> 3. Yani son of Kiryazi
>   1 house; 1 *çift* of land; 1 pig
> 4. Mihali his brother
>   1 house; 2 fig trees; 1 lemon tree; 2 mulberry trees
> 5. Yanağu son of Anuştaş
>   1 house

6. Panayud son of İstaşnu

   1 *çift* of land; 1 house; 1 pig; 1 lemon tree; 3 mulberry trees;
   6 fig trees; 3 pomegranate trees

7. Yani his son

8. Dimitri son of İstaşnu

   2 fig trees; 2 mulberry trees; 1 apple tree; 2 pomegranate trees;
   1 house

9. Kuzma son of Panayud

   1 *çift* of land; 50 sheep; 1 pig; 1 house; 3 fig trees; 2 pear trees;
   8 beehives; 2 pomegranate trees; 2 vine trellises

10. Yorğu his son

11. Yani son of Duke

    1 *çift* of land; 25 sheep; 5 fig trees; 1 house; 2 pomegranate trees;
    1 lemon tree; 2 apple trees; 2 beehives

12. Anuştaş his son

13. Nikula son of İstamu

    ½ *çift* of land; 10 beehives; 1 house; 1 pig; 2 lemon trees;
    6 fig trees; 4 pomegranate trees

14. Kostantin his son

15. Kostantin son of Nikula

    1 *çift* of land; 30 sheep; 1 pig; 1 house; 5 fig trees; 1 pear tree;
    4 mulberry trees; 1 lemon tree

16. Yani his brother

17. Kalenuri his son

    1 *çift* of land; 100 sheep; 1 pig; 1 house; 1 lemon tree; 3 mulberry
    trees; 3 fig trees

18. Manuli son of Yani

19. Yanağu his brother

20. Dimitri son of Panayud

    1 *çift* of land; 1 pig; 1 house; 2 mills; 4 beehives

21. Tirandafilu his brother

22. Liftari his brother

23. Yorğu Virazu son of Tanaş

    2 fig trees; 1 house

24. Yorğu son of Nikula

    1 house; 1 pig; 3 pear trees; 4 fig trees; 2 beehives; 1 lemon tree

25. Tanaş son of Ayustu

    1 *çift* of land; 1 pig; 2 lemon trees; 3 fig trees; 2 mulberry trees;
    1 house

26. İstaşni son of Futuni

    1 house; 2 lemon trees

27. Tanaş son of Hurun

    ½ *çift* of land; 50 sheep; 1 house; 1 pig; 3 fig trees; 1 lemon tree;
    1 walnut tree

28. İstatni son of Dimu

    1 *çift* of land; 1 house; 1 pig; 1 lemon tree; 2 mulberry trees;
    3 fig trees

29. Dimitri son of İstamu

    1 house; 2 fig trees; 2 pomegranate trees

30. Kostantin his son

31. Vasil his son
32. Yani his son

Before the conquest, the sharecroppers acquired permission to
   build a house from those in possession of the *çiftlik,* and they
   also established an orchard in front of the house. They do not
   possess anything else.

Revenue: one-seventh of the grain
Head tax: 32 persons
Wheat: 12 *çift*s
Barley: [empty]
Fodder: [empty]
Millet: [empty]
Broad beans: [empty]
Lentils: [empty]
Tithe of olives: 510 roots
Tax on vineyards: 160 *dönüm*s, of which 80 belong to the *reaya*[76]
Tithe of figs: 74 trees, of which 58 belong to the *reaya*
Tax on mulberries: 30 trees, of which 23 belong to the *reaya*
Tithe of pears: 20 trees, of which 8 belong to the *reaya*
Tithe of apples: 13 trees, of which 8 belong to the *reaya*
Tithe of almonds: 15 trees, of which 5 belong to the *reaya*
Tithe of pomegranates: 33 trees, of which 17 belong to the *reaya*
Tithe of walnuts: 4 trees, of which 2 belong to the *reaya*
Tithe of beehives: 26 beehives
Sheep tax: 255 head
Tithe of kitchen gardens: [empty]
Tax on oil presses: 1 press
Tax on mills: 1 mill, in ruin
Innovative tax on pigs and piglets: 11 head[77]
Tax on wastelands: [empty]
Tax on marriage: [empty]
Tax on land deeds: [empty]
Crime tax from fines: [empty]

The *tarla*s of this *çiftlik* require 10 pairs of oxen. But they used to
   cultivate the *tarla*s of another *çiftlik.*

The total tithes have not been set apart.

[TT880, p. 99]

20[78]/350. Should be written as a *karye.* Should be listed in Arkadiye.
43. ÇİFTLİK OF MUZUSTE
Previously in possession of Mustafa Çelebi. *Mîrî.* Previously a *timar* of
men. A plain. A dependency of Anavarin.

4 attached lower rooms: L. 40 × W. 7. 5 big barrels inside.
Another lower room: L. 17 × W. 8.
Upper tower and lower storage room: L. 8 × W. 6.
2 attached rooms: L. 16 × W. 9.
Another attached room: L. 8 × W. 6.

76. The text here and below literally
reads: "Tax on vineyards: 80 belonging
to the *reaya* + 80 = 160."
   77. Inserted between lines 3 and 4
of the *Revenue* list near the left margin.
   78. The number "20" has been
erased.

2 attached lower rooms: L. 20 × W. 9.
Courtyard in front: L. 30 × W. 25.
Lower room: L. 12 × W. 8.

53 olive roots
4 mulberry trees
8 almond trees
25 fig trees
31 pear trees
9 apple trees
3 apricot trees

Vineyard: 90 *dönüm*s

Sharecroppers:
1. Panayud the son of Huruni
    1 *çift* of land; 1 pig
2. Yakumi his brother
    ½ *çift* of land; 1 pig
3. Anuştaş his brother
4. İstatni son of Panayud
    1 *çift* of land; 50 sheep; 1 pig
5. Kuste his brother
6. Dimitri the son of Lağuri
    1 *çift* of land; 20 sheep; 1 pig; 15 beehives
7. Dimitri the son of Kakuni
    ½ *çift* of land
8. Yani his son
9. Lamiru the son of Yani
    1 *çift* of land; 1 pig
10. Adamir his brother
11. Dimitri his brother
12. Yani the son of Yorğu
13. Nikula the son of İlya
    ½ *çift* of land; 1 pig
14. İlya Kunari the son of İstimad
    1 pig
15. İstatni the son of Ğuliani
    1 pig
16. Yorğu İstahtu the son of Dimu
    ½ *çift* of land; 25 sheep; 1 pig
17. İstimatlu the son of Yani
    1 pig
18. Dimu İstahtuta the son of Yorğu
19. Panayud İskidia son of Nikule
    ½ *çift* of land; 1 pig
20. Kalenuri his brother

These *reaya* are sharecroppers of this *çiftlik*. They do not have the
    same rights in others.[79]

The *tarla*s of this *çiftlik* require only 20 pairs of oxen. 1 pair of oxen
    plows 15 Istanbul *kile*s of seed.

79. I.e., they do not sharecrop elsewhere.

Revenue: one-seventh of the grain

Head tax: 20 persons

Wheat: 6½ *çift*s

Barley: [empty]

Fodder: [empty]

Millet: [empty]

Broad beans: [empty]

Lentils: [empty]

Tithe of olives: 53 roots

Tithe of figs: 25 trees

Tax on vineyards: 90 *dönüm*s

Tithe of almonds: 8 trees

Tithe of pears: 31 trees

Tithe of apples: 9 trees

Tithe of apricots: 3 trees

Tithe of kitchen gardens: [empty]

Tax on mulberries: 4 trees

Sheep tax: 95 head

Innovative tax on pigs and piglets: 16 head

Tax on wastelands: [empty]

Tax on marriage: [empty]

Tax on land deeds: [empty]

Crime tax from fines: [empty]

The total tithes have not been set apart.

This *çiftlik* is bounded by the ditch *(handak)*[80] of Fulke, İsbiliaz, Uste Birnar, the ditch of Ağurliçe *çiftlik,* and the ditch of Burğu/Pirğu located in Limuniaz.

Near Anavarin. ~~It is cultivated by the *reaya* of Fulke in Arkadiye.~~
2/400
44. *Mazra^a* of Ayanu
It has become *miri.* It is close to Fulke. Dependency of Anavarin. 2 pairs of oxen are required. Previously it was in the hands of Muslims.

Revenue: one-seventh of the grain and other taxes

It is bounded by Usti Biğadi, Ustu Ayuyani, Ustu Şika, and the ditch of Ğarğalian.

Should be written in Arkadiye.[81]

4.5/500. *Miri.* A *çiftlik.* Should be written in Arkadiye.
45. *Mazra^a* of Tristena
Close to Muzuste. Used to be in the hands of Muslims. *Miri.* Dependency of Anavarin.

Vineyard: 30 *dönüm*s

Olives: 25 roots

80. It seems this term may have a topographic origin, probably referring to steeply defined ravines; see also Ayanu (44) below.

81. Annotation in the left margin.

*Tarla*s of this *mazra*ᶜ*a* require 6 pairs of oxen.

Length and width 40 paces (*adım*s).[82] Oil is Istanbul.[83] 80/100[84] *dönüm*s of land are defined as 1 *çift*, and that is how it is trusted to be by the *reaya*.

The *tarla*s used to be cultivated by the monks of Ayu Yurki monastery.

Revenue: one-seventh of the grain and other taxes

Bounded by Vavalari, Vivir Binari, the *tarla*s of Alafine, and the *tarla*s of the *çiftlik* of Hasan Ağa

[*TT880, p. 100*]

11[85]/350. Should be in Arkadiye.

46. *KARYE* OF İSKARMİNKE[86]

Used to be a *timar* of men. It is in the mountains.[87]

1. Dimu son of Kuste
   1 *çift* of land; 25 sheep; 1 pig; 1 house; vineyard of 4 *dönüm*s; 10 fig trees
2. Yanağu son of Andiria
   25 sheep; 1 house; 1 pig; 2 fig trees
3. Yani son of Tanaş
   1 *çift* of land; 100 sheep; 5 *dönüm*s of vineyard; 6 fig trees; 2 pigs; 1 house
4. Yanağu his son
5. İstimad son of Tanaş
   1 house
6. Pindazi son of Yorğu
   1 *çift* of land; 50 sheep; 2 pigs; 3 *dönüm*s of vineyard; 1 fig tree; 1 house
7. Yani son of Buduva/Tuduva/Yuduva
   ½ *çift* of land; 80 sheep; 1 pig; 1 house
8. Yorğu son of Duke
   ½ *çift* of land; 3 *dönüm*s of vineyard; 1 pig; 1 house
9. Yanağu son of Anuştaş
   1 *çift* of land; 60 sheep; 4 *dönüm*s of vineyard; 4 fig trees; 1 pig; 3 beehives; 1 house
10. Tanaş son of Yorğu
    ½ *çift* of land; 20 sheep; 2 *dönüm*s of vineyard; 1 pig; 1 house
11. Nikula son of Anuştaş
    ½ *çift* of land; 50 sheep; [illegible] *dönüm*s of vineyard; 1 fig tree; 1 pig; 1 house
12. Huruni son of Panayud
    ½ *çift* of land; 50 sheep; 1 pig; 1 house
13. Yani son of Yorğu
    ½ *çift* of land; 3 *dönüm*s of vineyard; 20 sheep; 1 pig; 1 house
14. Yani son of Dimitri
    ½ *çift* of land; 1 pig; 1 house

82. This annotation seems to define the area of the *dönüm*, also defined as 40 × 40 paces in the *kanunname* translated at the beginning of this chapter.

83. Presumably the Istanbul *kile* is meant.

84. The number "100" is written below the number "80."

85. The scribe here first wrote the number 7, then struck it out and wrote the number 11 below it.

86. Only four entries in TT880 (46–49) were initially registered as *karye*s. None of these is said to be *miri*. Two entries (42, 43) originally recorded as *çiftlik*s and marked with the letter "m" for *miri* were later changed to *karye*s.

87. Literally, "It is mountain."

15. Tanaş his brother
    ½ *çift* of land; 1 pig; 1 house
16. Yorğu son of Hiristufilu
    20 sheep; 1 pig; 1 house
17. Dimu son of Andiria
    7 pigs

4 *dönüm*s in the possession of Mihalu from the village of Kavalari
2 *dönüm*s in the possession of Yorğu from the village of Kavalari

Property of the Venetians that formerly belonged to Osman Ağazade
5 attached lower rooms: L. 28 × W. 9.
Upper tower; lower barn: L. 7 × W. 6.
Lower room attached to it: L. 6 × W. 5.
Olives: 25 roots
Walnuts: 6 trees
Figs: 10 trees
Mulberries: 18 trees
*Tarla*s of 240 *dönüm*s
These *tarla*s require 3 pairs of oxen, which sow 45 Istanbul *kile*s
    of seed.

Bounded by Kuli Karye, Mustafa Mandrasi, the orchard of Şake
    Mules/Kules, Ayu Yani, Seyid Yarağne, İstakatu, and Vardalu

Revenue: one-seventh of the grain
Head tax: 17 persons
Wheat: 8 *çift*s
Barley: [empty]
Fodder: [empty]
Millet: [empty]
Chick peas: [empty]
Lentils: [empty]
Tithe of olives: 25 roots
Tithe of figs: 34 trees (24 + 10)
Tithe of walnuts: 12 trees (6 + 6)
Tax on vineyards: 33 *dönüm*s
Tax on mulberries: 18 trees
Tithe of kitchen gardens: [empty]
Sheep tax: 50[88] head
Tithe of beehives: 3 beehives[89]
Innovative tax on pigs and piglets: 23 head
Tax on acorns *(palamud):* [empty]
Tax on wastelands: [empty]
Tax on marriage: [empty]
Tax on land deeds: [empty]
Crime tax from fines: [empty]

The total tithes have not been set apart.

88. Note the major discrepancy between this number and the total number of sheep listed as being in the possession of "individuals": 500.

89. The entry is inserted between lines 2 and 3 of the *Revenue* list, toward the left margin.

2/500
47. *KARYE* OF MİNİAKİ OR İBSİLİ RAKE
Was a *timar* of men. It is in the mountains.[90] 10 *çift*s of land.
A dependency of Anavarin.

It should be written in Arkadiye.

1. Yanağu son of Yani
   1 *çift* of land; 80 sheep; 1 pig; 5 *dönüm*s of vineyard; 6 pear trees
2. İlya his brother
   1 *çift* of land; 75 sheep; 5 *dönüm*s of vineyard

Revenue: one-seventh of the grain and other taxes

3/500. Arkadiye.
48. *KARYE* OF İSTİLİANU
Previously was a *timar*. It is in the mountains.[91] 15 *çift*s of land, of which 3 belonged to the *reaya*.

1. Kostantin son of Nikula
   1 *çift* of land; 8 *dönüm*s of vineyard; 8 olive roots; 1 fig tree;
   50 sheep; 2 pigs; 10 beehives; 1 house
2. Nikule son of Yani
   1 *çift* of land; 6 *dönüm*s of vineyard; 6 beehives; 1 fig tree;
   50 sheep; 2 pigs; 1 house
3. İstaşnu his brother
4. Yanağu son of Ayumerinu
   5 olive roots; 20 sheep; 2 fig trees; 1 house
5. Biraşkiva son of Ayustu
   ½ *çift* of land; 2 *dönüm*s of vineyard; 1 beehive; 1 fig tree; 6 olive
   roots; 1 house
6. Yani son of İstimad
   ½ *çift* of land; 2 *dönüm*s of vineyard; 25 sheep; 1 pig; 1 house

Revenue: one-seventh of the grain
Head tax: 6 persons
Wheat: 3 *çift*s
Barley: [empty]
Fodder: [empty]
Millet: [empty]
Tithe of olives: 19 roots
Tax on vineyards: 18 *dönüm*s
Tithe of figs: 5 trees
Tithe of beehives: 17 beehives
Sheep tax: 125 head
Innovative tax on pigs and piglets: 5 head
Tithe of kitchen gardens: [empty]
Tax on wastelands: [empty]
Tax on marriage: [empty]
Tax on land deeds: [empty]
Crime tax from fines: [empty]

The total tithes have not been set apart.

90. Literally, "It is mountain."
91. Literally, "It is mountain."

The villages of İskarminke, Miniaki, and İstilianu are on the side of the mountain. It is medium-quality (land).

1 *kile* of wheat becomes 5; 1 *kile* of barley becomes 6.
1 *çift* of oxen can only sow 6 Istanbul *kile*s of wheat, 6 *kile*s of barley, and 3 *kile*s of fodder.

[TT880, p. 101]

12.5[92]/450. Should be in Arkadiye.

49. *KARYE OF VİRVİÇE*

Was a *timar* of men. The middle of the [?].[93] A dependency of Anavarin. It is in a plain.[94] It is medium-quality (land).

1. Papa Panayud son of İstimatlu
   1 *çift* of land; 1 pig; 2 *dönüm*s of vineyard; 1 house
2. Mihali son of Yurğake
   1 house
3. Papa Hiristufilu son of Yani
   ½ *çift* of land; 2 *dönüm*s of vineyard; 1 mulberry tree; 1 house
4. Mihali his son
5. Papa İstimatlu son of Anduni
   ½ *çift* of land; 3 *dönüm*s of vineyard; 2 olive roots; 1 pig; 1 house
6. Tanaş son of Ayustu
   1 *çift* of land; 15 sheep; 2 *dönüm*s of vineyard; 2 olive roots; 2 mulberry trees; 1 pig; 1 house
7. Hirsuviri his son
8. Petru son of Yorğu
   ½ *çift* of land; 10 sheep; 2 *dönüm*s of vineyard; 2 olive roots; 2 pigs; 1 house
9. Ayustu his son
10. Yanağu son of İstimad
    1 *çift* of land; 8 sheep; 4 *dönüm*s of vineyard; 2 olive roots; 1 mulberry tree; 2 pigs; 1 house
11. Yurğake son of Valinar
    ½ *çift* of land; 10 sheep; 3 *dönüm*s of vineyard; 1 house
12. Nikula his son
13. Kostantin son of Tudurake
    ½ *çift* of land; 1 pig; 4 *dönüm*s of vineyard; 3 mulberry trees; 1 olive root; 1 house; 2 mills
14. Tanaş his son
15. İlya son of İstimatlu
    ½ *çift* of land; 50 sheep; 5 *dönüm*s of vineyard; 1 olive root; 1 house
16. İstaşnu his son
17. İstaşnu son of Anuştaş
    ½ *çift* of land; 1 pig; 2 *dönüm*s of vineyard; 2 olive roots; 1 house
18. Dimu his brother

92. The figure is unclear and could read "13.5."
93. Possibly, "The middle of the forest *(orman)*."
94. Literally, "It is plain."

19. Kanalu son of Nikula
    1 *çift* of land; 1 pig; 5 *dönüm*s of vineyard; 1 mulberry tree; 1 house
20. Kostantin son of İstimatlu
    ½ *çift* of land; 40 sheep; 3 *dönüm*s of vineyard; 3 olive roots;
    2 pigs; 1 house
21. İstimatlu his son
22. Yurğake son of İstilud
    ½ *çift* of land; 40 sheep; 3 *dönüm*s of vineyard; 3 olive roots;
    1 fig tree; 1 house
23. Tuduri his brother
24. Yanaki son of Yorğu
    ½ *çift* of land; 3 *dönüm*s of vineyard; 3 pigs; 1 house
25. Dimitri son of İstaşnu
    ½ *çift* of land; 3 *dönüm*s of vineyard; 1 house
26. Anaştu his brother
27. Adamir son of İlya
    ½ *çift* of land; 10 sheep; 5 *dönüm*s of vineyard; 1 olive root;
    1 house
28. Tuduri his brother
29. Anuştaş son of Yani
    ½ *çift* of land; 2 *dönüm*s of vineyard; 1 mulberry tree; 1 house
30. İstaşnu son of Asastu
    ½ *çift* of land; 4 *dönüm*s of vineyard; 15 sheep; 3 olive roots;
    1 house
31. Yorğu son of Dimitri
    ½ *çift* of land; 50 sheep; 3 *dönüm*s of vineyard; 1 house
32. Yurğake his son
33. Zefir son of Tudurake
    ½ *çift* of land; 2 *dönüm*s of vineyard; 2 olive roots; 1 house
34. Tudurake his son
35. Dimitraki son of Panayud
    ½ *çift* of land; 40 sheep; 2 *dönüm*s of vineyard; 1 house
36. Kostantin his brother
37. Anuştaş son of Yorğu
    ½ *çift* of land; 25 sheep; 3 *dönüm*s of vineyard; 1 house
38. Dimu his brother
39. Panayud son of Katlu
    4 *dönüm*s of vineyard; 1 house
40. Hiristu son of Arnavid
    1 house
41. Tanaş son of Arnavid
    1 house
42. Kostantin his brother
43. Aleksandiri son of Kuste
    1 house
44. Nikula son of Mihali
    ½ *çift* of land; 30 sheep; 1 pig; 5 *dönüm*s of vineyard; 3 olive roots;
    3 mulberry trees; 2 mills, 1 damaged, the other operating all year;
    1 house

45. Mihali his son
46. Yanağu son of Anduni
    1 house; 1 pig
47. Dimitri his son

Revenue: one-seventh of the grain
Head tax: 47 persons
Wheat: 13½ *çift*s
Barley: [empty]
Millet: [empty]
Fodder: [empty]
Broad beans: [empty]
Tithe of flax: 90 *lidre*s[95]
Tax on vineyards: 46 *dönüm*s
Tithe of olives: 27 roots
Tax on mulberries: 11 trees
Sheep tax: 343 head
Innovative tax on pigs and piglets: 17 head
Tithe of cotton: 60 *lidre*s
Tax on mills: 3 mills. All three are operating all year.
Tax on wastelands: [empty]
Tax on marriage: [empty]
Tax on land deeds: [empty]
Crime tax from fines: [empty]

The total tithes have not been set apart.

In accordance with the imperial order, these servants were assigned to survey the *kaza*s of Arkadiye and of Anavarin-i atik and Anavarin-i cedid, whether the property of Muslims or Venetians or the usufruct of the *reaya*, including villages (*karye*s), *çiftliks, mazraᶜas,* vineyards, and trees. And all of this was registered with the hand of your servant, Seyyid Mehmed Hatemi, who accompanied us. This is our survey that was carried out in accordance with the imperial order and is presented to the registrar.

20 *Muharrem* A.H. 1128/15 January A.D. 1716
Your servant,
Registrar Hüseyn

SEAL (Hüseyin)

95. In every instance elsewhere, flax is measured in *vukiyye*s.

CHAPTER 3

A Reconstruction of the Human Landscape of the *Kaza* of Anavarín

by John Bennet and Jack L. Davis

The purpose of this chapter is to analyze and reconstruct the geography of the *kaza* of Anavarin that is recorded in the part of the text of TT880 that has been translated in Chapter 2 (Fig. 2.1). We examine the names of the 49 principal entries registered for the *kaza* of Anavarin (see Table 3.1 below, pp. 149–150) for the purpose of producing a map of settlements and other agricultural properties that existed in the region in 1716. This has been a painstaking process and requires a full presentation, since it forms an essential underpinning for all subsequent interpretation of TT880. Only when the locations of the places mentioned in this document had been established was it possible for us to examine evidence for economic and social variation in land use and the distribution of population within the *kaza* of Anavarin. To the best of our knowledge, ours is the most detailed analysis of the toponymic structure of any Ottoman *defter* for Greece yet published, and as such it may, we hope, serve as a model for others who might want to undertake similar studies of other parts of Ottoman Greece.[1]

THE HUMAN GEOGRAPHY OF PYLOS WITHOUT TT880

The human geography of the Pylos area at the beginning of the 18th century is imperfectly known from contemporary Greek and Western European records. The first comprehensive map of this part of the Peloponnese was created for the French expeditionary force to the Morea and published in 1835 in the fifth volume of the *Expédition scientifique de Morée*.[2] Any cadastral surveys completed during the Venetian occupation of the Morea (1685–1715) have apparently not survived for the *territorio* of Navarino (i.e., Ottoman Anavarin), although one for the *territorio* of Navarino

1. Similar discussions have been published by Balta (1989, pp. 115–136), Doorn (1989), Forsén and Karavieri (2003), and Lowry (2002, pp. 63–68), although the documents they have studied address only villages (*karye*s) and uninhabited agricultural lands

(*mazra'a*s), not boundaries of properties in toponymic detail.

2. *Atlas*, pls. III.3 and III.5. For a discussion of the Expédition's mapping program, see Peytier 1971 and Saïtas 1999.

was sent to Venice when Antonio Zeno was *provveditore generale* of the Morea (1690–1694).[3]

Most of the cadasters in the Venetian archives were composed during the administration of Francesco Grimani, Venetian governor of the Morea from 1698 to 1701. Two types are represented in the archives: the *catastico ordinario,* a general summary of property in a *territorio* with maps of the extent of its settlements; and the *catastico particolare,* a comprehensive catalogue with accompanying maps of all fields, indications of their owners, and specifications of the legal basis for their ownership (e.g., through pre-existing deed or grant from the state). Documents of the former type[4] survive for Nafplion, Vostitsa (modern Aigion), Fanari (southern Eleia), Kalamata, and Argos, while documents of the second kind exist only for Vostitsa,[5] parts of Tripolitsa (modern Tripolis), and Romania (Nafplion). No trace of cadastral surveys submitted prior to Grimani's governorship has yet been found in the archives of Venice.[6] On the other hand, published engravings from the 17th century, as well as individual Venetian[7] and Frankish documents, can on occasion provide clues to the locations of specific toponyms recorded in TT880. Where relevant, we introduce these sources to discussions of the locations of particular toponyms later in this chapter.

We have, however, located an unpublished map of the *territorii* of Navarino and Modon produced during the Venetian occupation and now housed in the War Archive of the Austrian State Archive.[8] This map, prepared by Francesco de Fabretti and probably dating to around 1700, covers the two districts in four sheets (each 0.58 × 0.75 m) at a scale of 1:39,000. In addition to the two forts ("Navarin Vechio" and "Nouo"), the map indicates villages *(villa),* sometimes with the additional abbreviation "d\ufffd" *(diserta,* "abandoned"), plus the boundaries of their lands, marked by red lines highlighted in yellow. Topography (relief and forest) is suggested by shading in brown, while many rivers (labeled *fiume*) and valleys *(valle, valleta)* are indicated (see Fig. 3.7 below). In general, since it gives the boundaries of each village, this map seems to offer a level of information intermediate between that of the *catastici* and larger-scale maps of entire provinces.[9] This is not the place to provide a detailed commentary on this map, but we have, based on other sources, incorporated specific observations relevant to the entries below when they have added to or changed the picture.[10]

3. See Dokos and Panagopoulos 1993, p. xxxiii; Davies 2004, p. 88.

4. See Dokos and Panagopoulos 1993, pp. lvii–lix; Katsiardi-Hering 1993, pp. 289–290.

5. Published completely in Dokos and Panagopoulos 1993. See also Wagstaff, Sloane, and Chrysochoou 2001–2002.

6. See Dokos and Panagopoulos 1993, p. lvii.

7. Davies 2004.

8. Cat. no. B.III.a.124. We thank Malcolm Wagstaff for drawing our attention to the publication of a reference to this map, and the director of the War Archive, Hofrat Dr. Christoph Tepperberg, and his staff, for permission to cite and reproduce it here and for providing negatives from which our figures were produced. Katsiardi-Hering (1993) gives a full account of the history of this group of maps, together with a descriptive catalogue;

see also Wagstaff and Chrysochoou-Stavridou 1998. This map is no. 6 in Katsiardi-Hering's catalogue (1993, p. 302).

9. Katsiardi-Hering 1993, pp. 289–291.

10. Where we refer to a specific feature on the map, we have arbitrarily labeled the sheets A = northwest sheet; B = northeast sheet; C = southwest sheet; D = southeast sheet.

Figure 3.1. Excerpt from a map of the area of the Bay of Anavarin (Navarino). *Atlas,* pl. III.5

Only Sauerwein has attempted to reconstruct the total settlement system of the Pylos region as it existed in the 18th century, as part of a much larger venture to map place-names for the entire Morea.[11] His study was based on an analysis of lists of names of settlements published by Father Pietro Antonio Pacifico in his *Breve descrizzione corographica del Peloponneso o Morea.*[12] Sauerwein relied heavily on the *Atlas* of the *Expédition scientifique de Morée* as his major source of information about the locations of these settlements (Fig. 3.1). Both editions of Pacifico's work contain lists, and the source of his information is acknowledged in the second as Giusto Alberghetti, "superintendent of the Cadaster of the Morea," perhaps the compiler of the census mandated by Francesco Grimani in 1700.

11. Sauerwein 1969.
12. Pacifico 1700, 1704.

But a number of difficulties arise in using the *Atlas* in the manner in which Sauerwein did. First, the *Atlas* is not comprehensive. Second, names were often greatly distorted by the Venetians, and their equivalent Greek forms can be difficult to recognize. Third, some 18th-century settlements were no longer occupied at the time the French team collected its data. Some had been deserted by the Venetian period, even though they appear on Venetian censuses. Finally, toponyms not in the *Atlas* may also be missing from modern maps, especially because many of those of non-Greek origin have been "purified" since the establishment of the modern Greek state, through the substitution of official Greek names for those of blatantly non-Greek origin used in Ottoman times.[13] Despite such problems, Sauerwein was able to identify more than 80 percent of the names included on Pacifico's lists.

THE CHALLENGES AND OPPORTUNITIES PRESENTED BY TT880

TT880 presented an even greater challenge for us than the mapping of Pacifico's toponyms did for Sauerwein, to a large extent because Greek names can be grossly distorted as heard by a Turkish speaker.[14] In addition, many uncertainties in spelling are introduced because the scribes who composed TT880 used the *siyakat* script, wherein the diacritical dots distinguishing one Arabic letter from another are often intentionally omitted.[15] But problems with transliteration are by no means the only ones that need to be confronted. TT880 includes properties of the sort described in Ottoman documents as *mazraᶜa*s, a form of unsettled agricultural estate (see below). Balta has observed that "placing the *mezraa*s on the map is also a painstaking task although when the indication *der kurb-i* . . . (in the village proximity) appears following the registered village," it provides us with the approximate broader geographical setting. The note *der kurb-i* "aids us in our task but rarely do we find information [about *mazraᶜa*s] in the existing literature or any clues in the work of early cartographers."[16]

Compared with the Ottoman documents examined by Balta, Lowry, and others (see n. 1 above), TT880 is much richer in minor toponyms. Not only are settlements and unsettled agricultural properties described, but even the location of arable fields (*tarla*s) may be specified. We foresaw great difficulties in locating minor toponyms in the Pylos area because Balta, in her comprehensive study of two Ottoman *defter*s from Euboia, had been able to identify only about 30 percent of the *mazraᶜa*s, and most that she could locate had become villages and were still in existence.[17]

13. For discussion of the issue of name changes, see also Balta 1989, p. 184; Politis 1912–1913, 1915; Kyriakidis 1926.

14. Balta (1989, pp. 119–120) and Lowry (2002, p. 181) note some of the systematic changes produced by the transformation of Greek words into Turkish. For the process by which we imagine TT880 was compiled, see below, Chapter 4.

15. Faroqhi 1999, pp. 72–73; Fekete 1955.

16. Balta 1992, p. 63.

17. Balta 1989, pp. 115–129.

4. ALAFİNE *(çiftlik)*

The name Alafina is at present given to a ridge near the modern village of Tragana (1:50,000, Filiatra, E182, N260), to the stream that borders it (Alafinorema [Αλαφινόρεμα]), and to another ridge (Αλαφινόραχη) nearer the town of Hora. This location makes sense in terms of the boundaries of the *çiftlik* that can be located: the "valley with a stream" is likely to be that which is now called Alafinorema; Küçük Bisacki must be the *çiftlik* of Küçük Pisaski (14). Balinmiyuz seems to be another corruption of Palaiomylos, presumably in reference to an old water mill nearby. Other boundaries—Diyuli, Diyuli Yariye, and İstelidsire—cannot be identified. Fields (*tarla*s) worked by those resident at this *çiftlik* seem to be nearby and are located with reference to other *çiftlik*s recorded in TT880. One, at Pilalutaluni (Palaioaloni [Παλαιοαλώνι]), is bounded by Hasan Ağa (5) and a valley with a stream, probably the modern Selas River. Another is next to a "big bridge," probably one that crossed this same river,[26] and is defined with reference to Rustem Ağa (6) and Purnari (Pournari[a] [Πουρνάρι(α)] = evergreen oak[s]);[27] a place called Pournaria is located near the ridge of Alafina, in the territory of modern Ambelofyto (Ağurliçe [42]). A third field is next to Has *çiftlik* (9) and a place called Putme, clearly "Potamos" and probably another reference to the Selas River. A final field is next to Other Yufiri (40) and the public road, probably the coastal road running north from Anavarin to Arkadiye (modern Kyparissia). A few olive trees are located at Likuvun (Λυκοβούνι), a place-name associated elsewhere in the document with Kukunare (22) some distance to the southeast. In this particular instance, perhaps the Lykovouni to the east of Hora (1:50,000, Filiatra, E249, N225) is intended.

5. HASAN AĞA *(çiftlik)*

Hasan Ağa (Fig. 3.6) is not marked on either the 1:5,000 or the 1:50,000 map, but the name is locally applied to a knoll at the northern edge of the valley of the Selas River near Tragana (1:50,000, Filiatra, E184, N271).[28] Its boundaries suggest a rather extensive territory bordered by the "great valley with the river," presumably the Selas River, and the sea, several kilometers to the west. It is striking that, on the Venetian 1700 map (Fig. 3.7), Hasan Ağa (written as "Casanaga"), together with the "villages" of Alafine (4, "Lafina"), Rustem Ağa (6, "Rustamagá"), Huri (12, "Curu"), Küçük Pisaski (14, "Psaschi picilo"), and Büyük Pisaski (15, "Psaschi grande"), share a common boundary that follows a river (the modern Selas, formerly Romanos) to the sea. Of these, Alafine (4), Rustem Ağa (6), and Hasan Ağa (5) in TT880 are said to be "attached," sharing the same *tarla*s, a situation that appears to be reflected in the Venetian boundaries also. Rustem Ağa *çiftlik* (6) is nearby, on the lower Englianos ridge. Bey Konaki, literally "the mansion of the *bey*," cannot be precisely located, although the only direction not covered by the other boundaries is north. Perhaps this refers to the main house of the *çiftlik*.

26. Perhaps this is the bridge referred to in the name of the *mazraʿa* of Other Yufiri (40): see below.

27. Cf. Georgacas and McDonald 1967, 015.6628 (Πουρνάρι) and 015.6629 (Πουρνάρια).

28. See Alcock 1998; Davis et al. 1997, pp. 481–482; Bennet, Davis, and Zarinebaf-Shahr 2000, pp. 365–366.

Figure 3.6. Hasan Ağa from near
modern Tragana

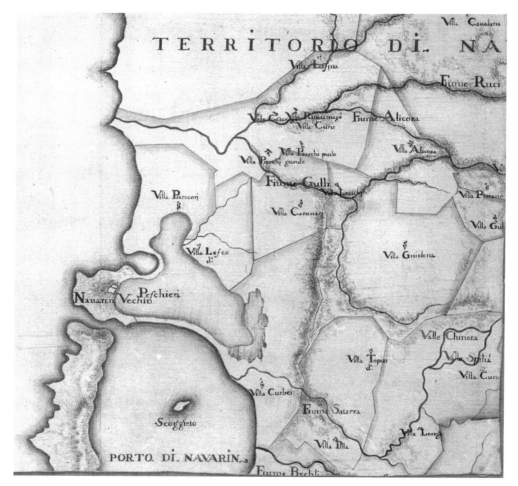

Figure 3.7. Excerpt from an unpublished Venetian map of the territories
of Modon and Navarino, ca. 1700.
War Archive of the Austrian State Archive,
cat. no. B.III.a.124, A, by permission

6. RUSTEM AĞA *(çiftlik)*

Rustem Ağa does not appear on the 1:5,000 or 1:50,000 maps, nor was it collected by Georgacas and McDonald, causing us initial problems in identifying its location. The published map in the *Atlas* places this *çiftlik,* marked "deserted" *(ruine),* southeast of Osman Ağa (15), immediately south of a valley leading inland to Iklaina, clearly that now known as the Xerolangado (Fig. 3.1). The closest modern village to that location is that of Elaiofyto (earlier called Sgrapa, a name that does not appear in TT880 or in Venetian cadasters, or Gouvalogara).[29] If Rustem Ağa had been near the site of modern Elaiofyto, it is surprising that it was not said to share boundaries with İklina (23) or Kukunare (22). Rustem Ağa instead is said to be "attached" to Hasan Ağa (5) and Alafine (4) and may be presumed to be very near these other properties, as is the case elsewhere where properties are said to be "attached." It is also clear that specific fields registered in this *çiftlik* are located in the same general area as Hasan Ağa (5), Alafine (4), and Osman Ağa (15): Narincir (perhaps Νεράντζι?) next to Huri (12) and Bisaci (Küçük Pisaski [14]); Famirlerun next to the big valley, presumably that of the Selas River; Tirankambu (Tranokambos [Τρανόκαμπος]) next to Alafine (4); Aliğulivad (-livadi: Alekoulivadi? [Αλέκου λιβάδι?]) next to Alafine; Arkudis (Arkouda [του Αρκούδα?[30]) next to Huri and Bisaci; Akşirulakad (Xerolangades [Ξερολαγκάδες],[31] but Xerolangado [Ξερολάγκαδο] on the 1:50,000 Pylos map) next to fields of Osman Ağa (15); Makrikirak (Makriarahi? [Μακριά Ράχη?], but not attested in this area) and Osman Ağa (15); Velanidia (Βελανίδια) next to the valley and Bisacki (probably Küçük Pisaski [14]); Kuri (probably Huri [12]) next to the valley and the road; Rumenu (probably in the general area of the modern village of Romanou [Ρωμανού]) next to Alafine (4) and the sea; and at Rumike next to fields of Osman Ağa and Has (9).[32] All of these fields and places appear to be in the area of the lower reaches and mouth of the Selas River, near modern Koryfasio, and from a Venetian text it is clear that the Englianos ridge also lay within this *çiftlik:* "Engliono confin di Rustan Aga," that is, within the boundaries of Rustan Aga.[33] In fact, this location is confirmed by the 1700 Venetian map, where "Rustamagá" appears immediately east of "Casanaga" (Hasan Ağa [5]; Fig. 3.7),[34] and by an unpublished draft map, one of a series on which the published large-scale map in the *Atlas* of the Expédition scientifique was based.[35] Finally, a Venetian document of 1698[36] recording church property mentions a church of Ayios Athanasios at Rustem Ağa, and there is a church with this dedication at the end of the Englianos ridge, where we believe

29. Biris 2002, pp. 116–117.

30. Georgacas and McDonald 1967, 216.680, but not in this part of Messenia.

31. See Georgacas and McDonald 1967, 72 = 108.5727.

32. Local tradition has it that the village of Romanou itself was founded after the Greek Revolution, in the 19th century: see Bory de Saint-Vincent

1836, pp. 162–164, where the Selas River is called the Romanou River. Leake, too, marks the Romanos River on his map of Messenia: Leake 1830, pl. 5. Neither author mentions a village.

33. ASV, Archivio Grimani ai Servi, b.28, f.839r.

34. B.III.a.124, A.

35. We thank Philippos Mazarakis-

Ainian of the National Historical Museum of Greece for allowing us to study these maps (acc. no. 6334). For a study of the drafts and their relation to the final *Atlas* sheets, see Saïtas 1999. The relevant map is reproduced by Biris (2002, p. 10), although the scale of reproduction there makes reading the name difficult.

36. Dokos 1971–1976, p. 136.

Figure 3.8. Romanou and Petrohori from the road between Yialova and Elaiofyto

Rustem Ağa lay.[37] It is possible that the error in the *Atlas* arose because the village was deserted at the time it was mapped, although the first Greek census of 1830 records one resident family.

7. PETREHURİ *(mazraʿa)*

The registered boundaries of the modern village of Petrohori (Πετροχώρι, 1:50,000, Pylos, E270, N265 [all eastings on the Pylos map sheet are negative numbers; we do not write the minus signs]) correspond well to those of the modern *koinotis* (community) of Romanou (to which the village of Petrohori belongs; Fig. 3.8): İsbilia (η Σπηλιά; probably the Cave of Nestor at Palaionavarino, although we have been informed that the Tragana tholos tombs were also called "caves" before their excavation); the road (the coastal road from Anavarin to Arkadiye?); İstuputamu (*sto Potamo* [στο Ποταμό]), probably the Selas River near the modern village of Romanou, although the *Atlas* of the Expédition scientifique also depicts a stream flowing into the Osmanaga Lagoon from the north, roughly bisecting the plain between Petrohori and Lefku (39); the sea; and Has (9). Petrehuri was unsettled, but was worked by residents of nearby Hasan Ağa *çiftlik* (5). Its yields were calculated with those of Rum Bağ (8).

8. RUM BAĞ OR LEFKU *(mazraʿa)*

There was once a settlement called Lefkos on the plain north of the Osmanaga Lagoon, but this toponym has now completely vanished. Gell mentions the "little villages of Petrachorio and Leuka,"[38] and Bory de Saint-Vincent mentions a place called Leukos.[39] The *Atlas* published by the Expédition scientifique and the 1700 Venetian map locate Leukos immediately north of Osmanaga Lagoon (Figs. 3.1, 3.7),[40] halfway between the modern asphalt road and Petrohori, in the area labeled Barakou (Μπαράκου) on the 1:50,000 map (Pylos sheet). Leukos there was probably what TT880 calls the *çiftlik* of Lefku or Tavarne (39), while the small *mazraʿa* of Rum Bağ (presumably meaning "Greek vineyard") or Lefku here under consideration seems to have been located closer to Petrehuri, in the direction of the Selas River and the modern village of Romanou. It was bounded by Rustem Ağa (6), located at the southwest end of the Englianos ridge, the sea, Has (9), İstuputamu (see above, Petrehuri [7]), and the mountains (possibly the ridge between Petrehuri and Voidokoilia Bay).

37. In Chapter 4, we suggest that this *çiftlik* should be identified with remains of a specific settlement discovered in the course of archaeological survey.

38. Gell 1823, p. 61.

39. Bory de Saint-Vincent 1836; Bennet, Davis, and Zarinebaf-Shahr 2000, pp. 362–363.

40. B.III.a.124, A: "Villa Lefco dᵃ."

9. HAS *(çiftlik)*

Has *çiftlik* was near the Selas River, somewhere in the area between the modern villages of Tragana, Romanou, and Koryfasio. Alafine (4) has a field next to Has that is bordered by Putme (perhaps the Selas River); Rustem Ağa (6) has a field near Has and fields of Osman Ağa (15); Huri (12) has a field that is bordered by Has and Bisaci (Küçük Pisaski [14]?); and Has is a border of Petrehuri (7) and of Rum Bağ or Lefku (8).[41] There are a few clues as to the placement of localities named as boundaries of the *çiftlik*. Thanasis P. Koulafetis of Romanou has informed us that "on the same height of the river [namely, as the location Other Yufiri (40)] and on its north side the vicinity is called 'Hani.'"[42] Although this could be the Kaniruni recorded as a boundary of Has, the word Kaniruni is more likely to conceal the name of the *mazra'a* of Karunihuri (11), which, in that case, would have lain to the east of it. Kati Usta Baruli could be a garbling of the phrase *kato sta Voroulia* (κάτω στα Βορούλια), with reference to a well-known place on the outskirts of the modern village of Tragana.[43] Ağirlia is clearly a transliteration of the Greek Agrilia (Αγριλιά), an Albanian place-name common in Messenia with the literal meaning "wild olive," or "oleaster."[44] The "boundary of Petrehur" must conceal the suffix -*hori* (village) and refers to Petrehuri (7), with which Has shares a boundary. The public road may be that linking Anavarin to Arkadiye.

10. AZAKE *(çiftlik)*

Azake seems to be an Ottoman representation of Greek Lezaki (Λεζάκι), a name that appears in the Venetian census of 1689 and in auction figures for the Venetian tithe in 1701 and 1704 as "Lesachi."[45] The name Lezaki appears on the 1:50,000 map sheet Filiatra, E205, N277. The specified boundaries support such an identification and suggest that Azake was situated to the east of modern Koryfasio. It was bordered by Küçük Bisaci (Küçük Pisaski [14]), Huri (12), Ali Hoca (1), and Osman Ağa (15). It is to be registered with the *çiftlik* of Muçaçu (34) and was presumably near it. The fact that one of the boundaries of Muçaçu was "Lezake" appears to clinch the identification of Azake and Lezaki.

11. KARUNİHURİ *(mazra'a)*

Karunihuri must be equivalent to modern Karvounohori (Καρβουνοχώρι), a toponym not recorded on the 1:50,000 or the 1:5,000 maps, but well known locally and collected by Georgacas and McDonald.[46] The *mazra'a*

41. It seems worth considering that Has should be identified with the ridge, about a kilometer south of the modern village of Koryfasio, which is today called Beylerbey (τοῦ Μπελέρμπεη; see Georgacas and McDonald 1967, 108.5153). A *hass* was the benefice of a *beylerbey* (e.g., Faroqhi 1999, p. 86; Adanır 1998, p. 278), and we also note the existence of the place-name *stou*

Haratsari (of the tax collector) nearby (see discussion below under Huri [12]). It seems unlikely that the name Beylerbey could have been applied to this location after Ottoman times.

42. T. P. Koulafetis of Romanou, pers. comm.

43. Georgacas and McDonald 1967, 242.1112.

44. Georgacas and McDonald 1967,

0215, attested in the vicinity of Mouzousta (130), Pyrgaki (204), and Floka (252). We wonder if this place-name refers to the location of the 500 wild olives mentioned under Has in TT880.

45. Panayiotopoulos 1987, p. 226; Davies 2004, p. 81, table 3.

46. Georgacas and McDonald 1967, 108.2656.

Figure 3.9. Church of Ayios Yioryios at Karvounohori

was bounded by Osman Ağa (15), Seri Putamu, Ayu Yurki, İstinayurki, and Likuvuni. Seri Putamu is obviously a transliteration of the Greek Xeropotamos (Ξεροπόταμος) and may well be the equivalent of Xerolagkado (Ξερολάγκαδο,[47] literally "dry gorge/valley"; 1:50,000, Pylos, E250, N270). Ayu Yurki (Ayios Yioryis [Αγιος Γιώργης]) and İstinayurki (στον Αϊ Γιώργη) must refer to a church or churches of Ayios Yioryios; a church in the place called Karvounohori today is, in fact, dedicated to this saint (1:50,000, Pylos, E246, N268; Fig. 3.9). Likuvuni is clearly equivalent to Lykovouni (Λυκοβούνι), literally "Wolf Mountain" in Greek (1:50,000, Pylos, E210, N250), but this ridge lies somewhat farther south than one might expect. Given the appearance of Lykovouni as a boundary for this *mazra'a*, it is worth entertaining the possibility that it lay near modern Elaiofyto, a village we have been unable to equate with any Ottoman-period property (see above, Rustem Ağa [6]). However, Elaiofyto, known until 1956 as Sgrapa, appears only to have moved to its current location in 1845.[48] Formerly it lay to the southwest, near a church of the Panayia overlooking the Yialova plain, and was also known as "Gouvalogara," according to Biris.[49] A "Gouvalovoros" appears at this location in the Expédition's *Atlas* (Fig. 3.1).[50] The equation of Karunihuri with a location this far south seems unlikely, and the Venetian 1700 map, although its topographic detail is not complete, places "Villa Carunari" below (i.e., west of) the line of hills that bounds the plain surrounding the Osmanaga Lagoon (Fig. 3.7).[51] The two churches of Ayios Yioryios might be accounted for by the one whose location is noted above and a second, larger one that appears south-southwest of Elaiofyto (1:50,000, Pylos, E232, N253). Karunihuri would therefore lie northwest of Lykovouni, which appears to have formed the northern boundary of Tupçin *çiftlik* (37; see below).

12. HURI *(çiftlik)*

A hill northeast of modern Pisaski is today called *tou Horou to hani* (του Χορού το χάνι; Fig. 3.10), and it seems to be the location of the Huri *çiftlik*.[52] No boundaries are specified in TT880, but toponyms mentioned

47. See Georgacas and McDonald 1967, 108.5727, and Rustem Ağa (6) above.
48. Biris 2002, p. 117.
49. Biris 2002, p. 116.
50. The earlier 1:50,000 draft map has a place-name Valovara at this location, presumably corrected for the final version.
51. B.III.a.124, A.
52. See McDonald and Hope Simpson 1961, pp. 238–239; also Georgacas and McDonald 1967, 192.8542a, where the same place is called *Horou to Hani* (Χορού το Χάνι).

Figure 3.10. Lower Englianos ridge
area from near modern Tragana

in connection with fields attached to Huri all seem to be in the general
area of Osman Ağa (15), Küçük Pisaski (14), Karunihuri (11), and Ali
Hoca (1). The revenues of Karunihuri and Huri are to be combined, a fact
that also suggests the two properties were near each other. A field in İstilake
(*sti Laka* [στη Λάκα]) is bordered by a valley with a stream (the Selas
River) and Beruli (Boroulia [Βορούλια], a border of Has *çiftlik* [9]); a field
in İstukufru is bordered by Bisaci (Küçük Pisaski [14]) and Has *çiftlik;* a
field in Usta Vilanide (*sta Velanidia* [στα Βελανίδια]) is bordered by Osman
Ağa (15) and Ser Putamu (Xerolangado),[53] also a boundary of Karunihuri
(11) and the location of fields belonging to Rustem Ağa (6) and to Küçük
Pisaski (14); and a field in Ustu Hirisari/Stohroyasari, probably a garbling
of *stou Haratsari* (στου Χαρατσάρη), an area south of the Selas River near
Osman Ağa (15), is bordered by a field of Hasan Ağa (5) and the road.
Other fields are defined with reference to Osman Ağa, Karunihuri (11),
Lezake (Azake [10]), and the road to Ali Hoca ([1], i.e., the road passing
Lezaki that links the modern villages of Koryfasio and Iklaina).

13. ANAVARİN-İ ATİK *(kale)*

Anavarin-i atik is the fortress today known as Palaiokastro or Palaionavarino
(1:50,000, Pylos, E276, N249; Fig. 3.11). There is a detailed discussion of
the fortress in Appendix II. Various properties are associated with this
entry, including a *çiftlik* of Budran[54] that is also mentioned as a border of
Osman Ağa (15). Residents of the fortress are said to work this *çiftlik,* but
their names are not recorded. Perhaps Ottoman administrators intended
to resettle the fortress at a later date. Other properties include a pasture at
Büyük Göl, literally "Big Pond," presumably a reference to Osmanaga
Lagoon (called "Lake" on modern Greek maps); it lies immediately east of
the fortress. A village called Kilursarin "used to cut the pasture." This name

53. Labeled "Fiume Gulli" on the
1700 Venetian map (B.III.a.124, A; see
Fig. 3.7); see below, Ğuli (24).

54. We cannot locate this name any-
where in the vicinity of the fort itself,
but wonder if it conceals the name
"Bourbon." The fort was for a time
owned by Marie de Bourbon: see Appendix II. Biris (2002, p. 116) mentions
a local tradition that the church of the
Virgin at old Sgrapa/Gouvalogara overlooking the lagoon was built by Marie
de Bourbon between 1381 and 1402.

Sphakteria

Sykia Channel

Anavarin-i atik

Divari

Osmanaga Lagoon

is not mentioned elsewhere in TT880 or in any published Venetian source, and it cannot be identified with any obvious Greek toponym in the vicinity, although the ending is presumably the Greek -*ari* (-άρι). Monthly revenues from Talyan are, however, clear. These must refer to the fisheries (Turkish *dalyan*s) in Osmanaga Lagoon: the toponym Daliani (Νταλιάνι) has been preserved locally, and fisheries still exist,[55] while the 1700 Venetian map has the label "Peschieri" immediately east of Palaionavarino ("Navarin Vechio") in the lagoon (Fig. 3.7).[56] Talyan is also one of the borders of Kurd Bey *çiftlik* (36). Sphakteria is the only island that could be described as "across from the fort."

14. Küçük Pisaski (*çiftlik*)

Küçük (Little) Pisaski is the village that today is called Pisaki (1:50,000, Pylos, E193, N273), and even in 1716, it seems that "Pisaski" could be employed interchangeably with "Küçük Pisaski." Küçük Pisaski needed to be used only to distinguish this *çiftlik* from that of Büyük (Big) Pisaski, otherwise known as Osman Ağa (15). The name Osman Ağa, rather than Büyük Pisaski, was regularly used when specifying a boundary: see, for example, the register of fields attached to Rustem Ağa (6). Venetian censuses normally use the same distinction of *piccolo* and *grande* Pisaschi, the latter alternately referred to as Suman Agà.[57] The most distant fields attached to Küçük Pisaski include a *tarla* in Pulatnu (Platne [2]) and another near Karunihuri (11) that is said to be bordered by the fortress of Ustu İklina (*stin Iklaina* [στην Ικλαινα]) and Akşilukirayi. The fortress must be the Frankish fortress at İklina (23):[58] its remains (Fig. 3.12) are today covered by the modern church of Ayios Ioannis and the adjacent plateia. Akşilukirayi may be a garbling of the toponym Psilirahi (Ψηλή Ράχη; often spelled Schili- in Venetian sources),[59] and there is a Psilirahi about two kilometers southwest of Elaiofyto. Other toponyms include Seri Putamu (mentioned also in connection with Lefku [39], Karunihuri [11], and Huri [12]); Osman Ağa (15); Vlanidiye (Velanidia [Βελανίδια]), mentioned in reference to fields of Rustem Ağa (6) and Huri (12); Yufır, perhaps the *mazraʿa* of Other Yufiri (40); İspitse, probably a garbling of Pispitsa (16); and İstilake (*sti Laka* [στη Λάκα]), also mentioned in association with Huri (12).

Figure 3.11. Osmanaga Lagoon and Anavarin-i atik from the road between Yialova and Elaiofyto

55. See Baltas 1997, p. 128. On the word and its possible ultimate derivation from Greek, see Kahane, Kahane, and Tietze 1958, pp. 477–481, no. 729.

56. B.III.a.124, A.

57. Panayiotopoulos 1987, pp. 226, 262. The 1700 Venetian map observes the same distinction (B.III.a.124, A): "Villa Psaschi picilo" and "Villa Psaschi grande" (see Fig. 3.7).

58. See Hodgetts and Lock 1996, p. 82.

59. E.g., property number 47 (Miniaki or İbsili Rake), which appears in the 1700 Venetian census as "Schilirachi": see discussion below, under Miniaki (47).

THE HUMAN LANDSCAPE OF THE *KAZA* OF ANAVARİN

Figure 3.12. Remains of medieval fortifications at Iklaina

15. OSMAN AĞA OR BÜYÜK PİSASKİ *(çiftlik)*

This is the modern town of Koryfasio (1:50,000, Filiatra, E190, N278), until recently commonly known as Osman Ağa (Fig. 3.10). The toponym Büyük Pisaski seems completely lost. All the fields (*tarla*s) associated with Büyük Pisaski are said to lie in the area known as Tavarne (39). The deserted *çiftlik* of Tavarne is in turn said to be cultivated by the residents of Osman Ağa. Tavarne appears to lie near the lagoon, north of the Bay of Navarino, and the cultivation of fields there may explain why this lagoon has come to be known as Osmanaga Lagoon, although it is some distance from the village of Osman Ağa (cf. Lefku/Tavarne [39], below). The borders of Büyük Pisaski can be fixed with some precision. Budran presumably lies west-southwest, in the direction of Palaionavarino (see Anavarin-i atik [13], above). Seri Putamu (Karunihuri [11]) seems to be the Xerolangado River, southeast of Büyük Pisaski near Beylerbey. Vlanidiye appears to be near Küçük Pisaski (see Rustem Ağa [6]), on the Englianos ridge, and Azake (10) lies east of Büyük Pisaski, along the road to Iklaina.

16. Pispitsa (çiftlik)

Ottoman Pispitsa is the modern village of Myrsinohori, formerly Pispi-sia or Pispisa (Πισπίσια or στου Πίσπισα, 1:50,000, Filiatra, E230, N252; Fig. 3.13). The Putamu Valley here is presumably the valley that separates Pispisia from the uplands around modern Hora and lands cultivated by the *karye* of Kavalari (registered in Arkadiye). Another large valley, Μαύρη Λίμνη[60] (1:50,000, Filiatra, E215, N260), separates Pispisia from the settle-ment of Platanos. The "valley across from Platne" is obviously that valley. We assume that Munadundiyeri conceals Monodendri (Μονοδέντρι), and that the first element of İskilukranes is *psilo-* (ψηλο-), although neither can be identified with toponyms in the vicinity of Myrsinohori.

17. Nase or Memi Ağa (mazra⁽ᶜ⁾a)

Nasa is a locality on the ridge that runs between the modern villages of Myrsinohori (Pispisa) and Metamorfosi (Skarminga) (1:50,000, Filiatra, E245, N245), where the place is called Nasia (Νάσια) and the valley im-mediately south of it is Nasorema (Νασόρεμα). In the *Atlas* of the Expé-dition, it appears in this location as "Nassa" (Fig. 3.1). This area is today within the community borders of Pispisa, and in TT880 it is said to be "within the boundaries of Pispitsa."

18. Rotsi or Denmusarin (mazra⁽ᶜ⁾a)

It is clear that this *mazra⁽ᶜ⁾a* is near Nase (17), because their revenues are combined. The name Routsi (Ρούτση) is well known today, as is the church of Panayia Routsi (Παναγία Ρούτση, 1:50,000, Filiatra, E238, N242). The area of Routsi is located to the northeast of Pispisa. This area is today within the community borders of Pispisa, and in TT880 it is said to be "in the vicinity of Pispitsa."

Figure 3.13. Modern villages of Myrsinohori (far right) and Meta-morfosi (center); the properties Nase (17) and Rotsi (18) lie on the ridge connecting the two.

60. Georgacas and McDonald 1967, 194.4534.

Figure 3.14. Modern villages of
Glyfada, Platanos, and Myrsinohori

19. Papla or Mustafa Ağa (*çiftlik*)

The modern village still known as Papoulia was once called Ano (Upper) Papoulia to distinguish it from a second Papoulia, today known as Glyfada (1:50,000, Meligalas [Μελιγαλάς], E194, N265 [all eastings and northings on the Meligalas map sheet are negative numbers; we do not write the minus signs]; Fig. 3.14).[61] The location of only one boundary is clear: that of Luteru, which must be a transliteration of *Loutro,* "Bath" (Λουτρό), a place about 1.5 kilometers west-southwest of Papoulia (1:50,000, Filiatra, E235, N270). Yalelulunuryu is garbled but seems to preserve the prefix *palaio-* (Παλαιο-), perhaps Palionero (Παλιονερό).[62] Buhalu appears to reflect Bouhali (Μπουχάλη).[63] Both lie in the vicinity of Papoulia, but they cannot be identified on either map. Martilaf may just conceal Triandafyllies (Τριανταφυλλιές), a place-name that lies just to the east of modern Papoulia (1:50,000, Meligalas, E175, N265).

20. Other Papla or Ağaku (*çiftlik*)

Papla or Ağaku is the village of Glyfada, previously known as Kato Papoulia (1:50,000, Meligalas, E190, N275). Borders include Pulatnu, clearly Platne (2), and Papla, clearly Papla or Mustafa Ağa (19). The suffix *-lake* (-λακκα, meaning "a level plot of land") is clearly a part of the toponym Çupurulake.

21. Kirmiti or Sefer Hoca Çiftlik (*mazraᶜa*)

Kirmiti or Sefer Hoca is the modern village of Kremmydia (1:50,000, Koroni [Κορώνη], E165, N268 [all eastings on the Koroni map sheet are negative numbers; we do not write the minus signs]; Fig. 3.15). In the 19th century the village may have been farther northeast, at the foot of Mt. Manglavas (where "Palaiokremmydia" can be found on the 1:50,000 map sheet Meligalas, E160, N276). This *mazraᶜa* lay at the boundary of

61. Interestingly, neither Papoulia is indicated on the 1700 Venetian map, but boundaries are indicated for a region to the east of Iklaina, into which the Papoulias would presumably have been inserted: B.III.a.124, A, B.

62. Georgacas and McDonald 1967, 179.5989.

63. Georgacas and McDonald 1967, 179.5379. In TT80, p. 824 (1512–1520), there is an entry for the *karye* of Platano Buhali.

Figure 3.15. Area of Kremmydia
from Profitis Ilias above Handrinou

the *kaza* of Anavarin and was cultivated by residents of Furiçi, a village in
Modon (Methoni). The name Furiçi (Φουρτζή) was officially changed
to Velanidies (Βελανιδιές) in 1927 and to Velanidia (Βελανιδιά) in 1940
(1:50,000, Koroni, E155, N265). Under the Venetians, both Furiçi and
Kirmiti were in the *territorio* of Modon. Serukambu is a rendering of Xero-
kambos (Ξερόκαμπος, 1:50,000, Koroni, E190, N251). Likuri also seems
to be mentioned as a boundary of Kukunare or Muslihuddin Efendi *çiftlik*
(22), where there is reference to the Likurni Mountains. We have not been
able to document the existence of this toponym in Greek sources, but the
most prominent mountain in the area is Manglavas. While traveling south
from Gargaliani to Pylos early in the 19th century, Pouqueville refers to a
Mt. "Lyraki," which dominates the area of Osman Ağa (15) and Hasan
Ağa (5); this may be a version of the place-name Likuri.[64] We have not
been able to determine when Manglavas came into regular usage, but it is
the name applied to the mountain in the *Atlas* of the Expédition scientifique
(in the form "Maglada"). Ustunu Rake may contain the suffix -*rahi* (-ραχη),
"ridge," but perhaps more likely conceals *sto Neraki* (στο Νεράκι): Neraki
is a place-name in the vicinity of both Ano and Kato Kremmydia according to Georgacas and McDonald.[65] Usku Kunuri appears to be a garbling
of Kukunare (22). In the period 1512–1520 Kremmydia was classed as a
karye, and 8 males were registered there.

22. KUKUNARE OR MUSLİHUDDİN EFENDİ ÇİFTLİK (*çiftlik*)

Kukunare or Muslihuddin Efendi is clearly the modern village of Koukounara (1:50,000, Koroni, E193, N245; Figs. 3.15, 3.16). As a boundary,
this *çiftlik* shares the Likurni Mountains with Kirmiti (21). Usti Kineta is
a version of the Greek *sti Kineta* (στη Κινέτα), itself from Albanian *kënetë*,
"marsh" or "swamp," and the Venetian 1700 map shows a "Valle Chineta"
to the northwest of Koukounara.[66] Yalihur/Palihur represents Greek Palaiohori (Παλαιοχώρι) and there is, in fact, a location called Palaiohoria

64. Pouqueville 1826–1827, vol. 6,
p. 26. Gell, too (1817, p. 52), refers to a
"hill called Lirachi" in his narrative of
travel through the area: see Bennet, Davis, and Zarinebaf-Shahr 2000, p. 364.

65. Georgacas and McDonald 1967,
23.5469 (Ano Kremmydia), 97.5469
(Kato Kremmydia).

66. B.III.a.124, A; see Fig. 3.7.

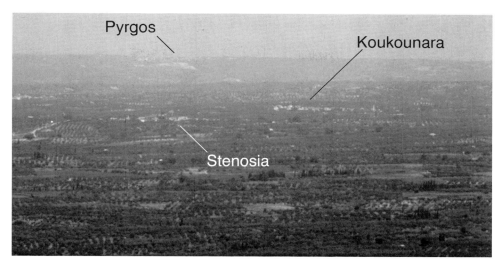

Figure 3.16. Area of Koukounara from Profitis Ilias above Handrinou

(Παλαιοχώρια), "Old Villages," two kilometers west of Koukounara (1:50,000, Pylos, E205, N232).[67] Rumiani Valley presumably refers to the Gouvalari (Γουβαλάρη) Valley (colloquially *to Potami tou Arapi* [το Ποτάμι του Αράπη], "The River of the Black"), which runs east of Koukounara (1:50,000, Koroni, E190, N240).

23. İKLİNA OR KURD AĞA ÇİFTLİK *(çiftlik)*

İklina or Kurd Ağa is the modern village of Iklaina (1:50,000, Pylos, E218, N273; Fig. 3.12). Revenues are combined with the *mazra'a* of Ğuli (24), which is nearby. Borders include Balyamilu, a garbling of Palaiomylos (Παλαιόμυλος, "Old Mill"). About 1.5 kilometers west of Iklaina is a place that is today called Μύλος Καλύβα, "Mill Shack" (1:50,000, Pylos, E230, N275). Ustane Yuri must represent the phrase *ston Aï Yioryi* (στον Αϊ Γιώργη); there is a church of Ayios Yioryios about two kilometers southwest of Iklaina (1:50,000, Pylos, E232, N254), which may also be a boundary of Karunihuri (11). Hamulus may be Greek Hamilos (Χαμηλός). Another possibility appears in the compound name of a ridge north of Pyla, Kamilorahi [Καμηλόραχη][68] (1:50,000, Pylos, E215, N222), but this place seems too far away.

24. ĞULİ OR MEHMED AĞA ÇİFTLİK *(mazra'a)*

The *mazra'a* of Ğuli or Mehmed Ağa was northeast of the village of Iklaina on a ridge currently called του Γουλή τη ράχη, near the toponym Panayia on both the 1:5,000 and the 1:50,000 Filiatra map sheet (E232, N278 on the latter). "Gugli" appears in Venetian tithe-auction records of 1701 and 1704,[69] and "Villa Guli" appears on the 1700 Venetian map to the east-northeast of Iklaina.[70] Borders include Platne (2), here written Pilatnu, and İklina (23). Usulu Tirak may render the phrase *sto Loutraki* (στο Λουτράκι), with reference to the border of Papla (19) called Λουτρό. Kifuri (see also Muçaçu [34], below) may be Kivouri (Κιβούρι), but it cannot be located.[71]

67. See McDonald and Hope Simpson 1969, p. 150.

68. Georgacas and McDonald (1967, 202.2495) write Kambylorahi (Καμπυλόραχη).

69. Davies 2004, p. 81, table 3.

70. B.III.a.124, A (right edge).

71. Cf. Georgacas and McDonald 1967, 2979, not in this part of Messenia.

Figure 3.17. Xerias (Beşli) Valley,
showing the Beşli-Yialova-Kanonia
area from Miden

25. RUDİYE OR KURD ALİ AĞA ÇİFTLİK *(mazraᶜa)*

Rudiye must be Rodia (Ροδιά, 1:50,000, Pylos, E227, N196; Fig. 3.17),
on the south side of the Xerias River valley, just north of Miden where the
road to Yialova meets the main road from modern Pylos to Handrinou.
The area is called Ayios Vasilios on the 1:5,000 and 1:50,000 maps. It is
clear that this *mazraᶜa* is near Anavarin since it is cultivated by the *reaya* of
the *varış* of Anavarin-i cedid. Other than the sea, none of the borders can
be located, although İstisile might be *stis Elies* (στις Ελιές).

26. MELİS OR DERVİŞ KETHÜDA ÇİFTLİK *(mazraᶜa)*

Melis must be Melissi (Μελίσσι), a location immediately north of the main
road from Pylos to Kalamata, in low hills at the south side of the Xerias
Valley, about one kilometer from the coast. The revenues of Melis and Rudiye
are combined. "Mellissi e Rudhia" also appear as a single entry in Venetian
tithe-auction records of 1701 and 1704,[72] and "Villa Meglisi dᵃ" appears at
this location on the 1700 Venetian map.[73] Melis is, however, in the possession of Pile (31), which we take to mean that it was being farmed by the
reaya of Pile, as is explicitly noted in other entries. Zurbe is Zorbas and lies
to the east (1:50,000, Pylos, E210, N205). Kumariçe presumably is Kama-
ritsa (Καμαρίτσα) and refers to arches in the aqueduct that led to Navarino
from the spring of Koube.[74] Ustu Ayvarniçe/Ayurniçe is presumably *stin
Avarnitsa* (στην Αβαρνίτσα; cf. Avarniçe [30] below), but Ustu Birniçe remains obscure.

27. YUFİRİ OR BEŞLİ *(mazraᶜa)*

The modern Xerias River (see Fig. 3.17, which shows the lower part of the
Xerias Valley) was called the Pesili River by early Western European travelers, a name that must derive from a Turkish toponym Beşli, or "fivefold,"
doubtless a reference to the many rivulets that here flow into the Bay of
Navarino.[75] This *mazraᶜa* must have been located north of Rudiye since it
is in the possession of Kurd Bey *çiftlik* (36). Yufiri is obviously named for

72. Davies 2004, p. 81, table 3.
73. B.III.a.124, C.
74. Bennet, Davis, and Zarinebaf-
Shahr 2000, pp. 352, 358–359.
75. Bennet, Davis, and Zarinebaf-
Shahr 2000, p. 357. On the 1700 Venetian map, it appears, on the bottom
edge of the northwest sheet, as "Fiume
Bechli": B.III.a.124, A (see Fig. 3.7).

Figure 3.18. Modern villages of Stenosia, Shinolakka, Balodimeïka, and Pyla, from Profitis Ilias above Handrinou

the bridge, Yiofyri (Γιοφύρι), that crosses the major branch of the river.[76] Apart from "the public road" (presumably that running north along the eastern shore of the bay from Anavarin to Arkadiye), the borders of the *mazraʿa* all appear to render Greek words: İsbili, Spilia (Σπηλιά); İstaluniye, st'Alonia (στ' Αλώνια); and Ustu Namu, *ston Ammo* (στον Αμμο).

28. ELYAS AĞA *(çiftlik)*

Elyas Ağa is the modern village of Stenosia (Στενωσιά; 1:50,000, Pylos, E195, N227; Fig. 3.18), formerly called Lezaga (Λέζαγα), spelled by the Venetians "Lesaga" or "Lesega" (Fig. 3.7). Like Kirmiti (21), Elyas Ağa was in the possession of Kufurci (a version of Fourtzi [Φουρτζή], written elsewhere [see above, Kirmiti (21)] as Furiçi). Andirinu *çiftlik* (certainly Handrinou [Χανδρινού]) is included as a border, but is not listed in the *kaza* of Anavarin in TT880; under the Venetians it had been in the district of Modon. Modern Stenosia lies between two valleys that meet immediately to its west: that of the Gouvalari (Γουβαλάρη, 1:50,000, Koroni, E190, N240; see also above, Kukunare [22]), to the northwest, and a second, to the southeast, marked Tourkoporos (Τουρκόπορος), farther upstream from Stenosia, near Handrinou (1:50,000, Koroni, E160, N237). It is, therefore, not surprising to find two of its boundaries marked by valleys. The "valley with the stream" is likely to be the one that is southeast of the village. The Tursun Valley is probably that of the Gouvalari River, marked on contemporary maps Drosouni (Δροσούνι) in its lower reaches (1:50,000, Pylos, E205, N225) and, when nearing Yialova, the Yiannouzaga (Γιαννούζαγα, 1:50,000, Pylos, E230, N227).[77] Although Tursun is an Ottoman personal name (see below, Tursun [38]), we wonder if Drosouni has resulted from a reanalyzed Tursun, or vice versa. The identification is apparently confirmed by the fact that the same valley also forms a boundary of Pile (31, see below); by this point, both valleys have merged. Paliamilu must be Palaiomylos (Παλαιόμυλος), and there are indeed prominent ruins of a water mill in the valley between Stenosia and Balodimeïka (Fig. 3.19).

76. Bory de Saint-Vincent (1836, p. 137) describes two bridges as he traverses this area en route north from Navarino (cf. Fig. 3.1), while a 1:50,000 draft sheet of the *Atlas* marks a stone bridge over the river, which is there referred to as the "Kumbey" River.

77. On the 1700 Venetian map this river is labeled "Fiume Satirra" (B.III.a.124, A; see Fig. 3.7).

Figure 3.19. Old mill race at Palaiomylos, Balodimeïka

29. ZAİMZADE *(çiftlik)*

Zaimzade is the current village of Balodimeïka (Fig. 3.18).[78] The village
appears to have been deserted in the early 19th century and refounded
after Greek independence by members of the Balodimas clan, a family
name that is still locally dominant. This Zaimzade is the same place as the
village of Zaimoglou/Zaimogli that appears in Venetian censuses as a possession of Navarino; it has been confused with a village of the same name
in the territory of Koroni.[79] The revenues of the village were combined
with those of Avarniçe (30). Borders of the *çiftlik* include the name Demus,
perhaps the Greek male name Dimos (Δῆμος).[80] Ayu Nikula is a church of
Ayios Nikolaos, also a border of Pile (31) nearby. Neither Mankariarike
nor İstinkayu can be located, although they may correspond to Manga-
niariko (Μαγγανιάρικο)[81] and *ston Kambo* (στον Κάμπο), respectively.

30. AVARNİÇE *(mazraʿa)* OR HACİ HASAN *(çiftlik)*

Avarniçe or Haci Hasan is to be identified with remains of a deserted village at Avarnitsa (Αβαρνίτσα,[82] 1:5,000, 72555, E19200, N20100; Fig. 3.20).
The *mazraʿa* is said to be in the possession of a place whose name can be

78. Bory de Saint-Vincent 1836,
p. 191; Blouet 1831–1838, vol. 1,
pp. 5–7; *Atlas,* pl. III.5. The village appears, as "Saimogli," on the Venetian
1700 map: B.III.a.124, C (top edge).

79. Sauerwein 1969, map; cf. Panayiotopoulos 1987, p. 168. That village,
formerly Zaimogli (Ζαΐμογλη), is now
known as Drosia (Δροσιά): Georgacas
and McDonald 1967, 69.1968.

80. We wonder if the presence of
this name in the vicinity suggests a
possible link with the village's modern

name, Balodimeïka (Μπαλοδημέϊκα;
Georgacas and McDonald 1967,
163.5042), of which it forms the second element. The first element might
be "Balis" (Μπαλής), from the Venetian status-term *bailo,* attested as an
element in Greek personal names
(Boutouras 1912, p. 110). Since *zaïm*
is also a status term in Ottoman Turkish, and the Ottoman village name
means "son of the *zaïm,*" there may
just be a link through family name
and title between the two (seemingly

unrelated) names Zaimzade and
Balodimeïka.

81. Cf. Georgacas and McDonald
1967, 4278, but not in this part of
Messenia. The place-name appears to
include the word *mangano* (μάγγανο),
or stream-driven "press," the nearest of
which would be in the valley between
modern Balodimeïka and Stenosia.

82. See McDonald and Hope Simpson 1961, p. 233; 1969, pp. 150–151. It
appears on the 1700 Venetian map as
"Avarigniza dᵃ": B.III.a.124, C, D.

Figure 3.20. Avarnitsa area and
upper Xerias (Beşli) Valley

transliterated as *P-s-p-e-ts-e/a.* On linguistic grounds alone this could be
Pispitsa (16), but that village seems too distant.[83] Uste Yufiri appears to be
a transliteration of *sto Yiofyri* (στο Γιοφύρι), probably with reference to a
Venetian bridge near Avarnitsa mentioned by Bory de Saint-Vincent[84]
(1:50,000, Koroni, E188, N195) and indicated in the *Atlas* of the Expédition
(Fig. 3.1). Ustune Yurki must be *ston Aï Yioryi* (στον Αϊ Γιώργη, 1:50,000,
Koroni, E182, N215). Murafia might just be a garbled version of Horafia
(Χωράφια). In 1512–1520, Avarniçe was registered as a *karye* but was
"empty of cultivators."

31. Pİle *(çiftlik)*

Pile is the modern village of Pyla (1:50,000, Pylos, E209, N217; Fig. 3.21).
Ustna Nikula must be *sto Aï Nikola* (στο Αϊ Νικόλα), also a border of nearby
Zaimzade (29). The Tursun Valley also bounds Elyas Ağa (28); and there
is a Tursun *mazraʿa* (38) near Tupçin (37). Beşli and Yufiri probably refer
to the Yufiri or Beşli *mazraʿa* (27) and may imply that Pile's lands extended
into the Xerias Valley. Tirukalyun might reflect Trohalia (Τροχαλιά).[85]

83. In Venetian tithe-auction
registers, Candinou (if this represents
Handrinou, which is near Avarniçe) is
listed with Pispisa (Davies 2004, p. 81,
table 3: "Pispissa con il luoco Candinu"
[1701; 1704]). Other combined
locations in these registers are usually
closer, however: e.g., Mellissi e Rudhia
(1701; 1704) and Musustà e Tristena
(1701; 1704; cf. below, Muzuste [43]
and Tristena [45]): Davies 2004, p. 81,

table 3). In light of this fact, it is worth
noting that Georgacas and McDonald
(1967, 46 = 179.3212) list a "Kontinou"
(Κοντινού) near Vlahopoulo and Papoulia, much closer to Pispisia (modern
Myrsinohori). The Expédition scientifique lists a "Kontinou" in the eparchy
(district) of Navarin (with zero population) in its census (Puillon de Boblaye
and Virlet 1833–1834, p. 85), presumably the same as Pouqueville's "Koudi-

nou" in the same *canton:* Pouqueville
1826–1827, vol. 4, p. 73, with "24
families" (probably individuals: cf.
Bennet, Davis, and Zarinebaf-Shahr
2000, p. 352, n. 25).
84. Bory de Saint-Vincent 1836,
p. 213.
85. Cf. Georgacas and McDonald
1967, 7960, but not in this part of
Messenia.

Figure 3.21. Portion of the Xerias (Beşli) Valley, showing the location of Pyla

32. ARKADİANU OR THE MÜFTİ ÇİFTLİK *(mazraʿa)*

Both this *mazraʿa* and that of Deli Ahmed Çiftlik (33) are very near the fortress of Anavarin-i cedid and appear to be adjacent to each other, as they are said to be attached and a boundary of Deli Ahmed is "the boundaries of Arkadianu." Arkadianu seems to be closer to the sea, because it is bordered by it and Deli Ahmed is not. We have not been successful in locating either place more precisely. Of the borders, only Mesinmure or Mesihure is clearly identifiable, as the village of Mesohori (Μεσοχώρι, 1:50,000, Pylos, E220, N140). The village is said to possess the *mazraʿa* but is not in the *kaza* of Anavarin; under the Venetians, it lay in the district of Modon. Viğle/Vifle is likely to be Vigla (Βίγλα), possibly that to the north of modern Pylos;[86] the mountains presumably refer to the uplands southeast of modern Pylos. Arkadianu is likely to be "Arcadina di Lazaretto," recorded in the Venetian census of 1700.[87] It should then have been near the part of the harbor (the *lazaretto*) where inbound ships were quarantined.[88] If so, we imagine the territory of Arkadianu stretching southwest from Vigla in the northeast toward the Pylos–Methoni road, where it met the territory of Deli Ahmed (33).

33. DELİ AHMED ÇİFTLİK *(mazraʿa)*

Deli Ahmed Çiftlik cannot be precisely located (see Arkadianu [32]), but it must have been somewhere along the road to Modon (Methoni [Μεθώνη]). The name is attested in a Venetian tithe register of 1698 as Delacmeti, where it is coupled "con li terreni di Miuti [Minti?], e Usta Musulogli." Can Miuti be a garbling for Müfti (32)? In any case, Deli Ahmed is also linked to Usta Musli (41) in a Venetian document of 1701 and may be presumed to be nearby: "Delachmeti, con li terreni di Muscugli."[89]

34. MUÇAÇU OR MUSLİHUDDİN ÇİFTLİK *(çiftlik)*

This *çiftlik* is not listed in geographical order and must have been located somewhere between Osman Ağa (15) and İklina (23), as it is to be recorded with Azake (10) and is in the possession of the *çiftlik* of Küçük Yasaci (i.e., Küçük Pisaski [14]). We have not, however, identified this

86. Bennet, Davis, and Zarinebaf-Shahr 2000, p. 359.
87. Panayiotopoulos 1987, p. 262.
88. Although on a Venetian map prepared for Grimani (Andrews 1953, pl. XI, "F"), "Lazareta" is labeled as a structure near the plateia of modern Pylos—north, rather than south, of the fortress of Anavarin.
89. Davies 2004, p. 81, table 3; ASV, Archivio Grimani ai Servi, b.28, f.1255r.

toponym in that area.[90] The borders of the *çiftlik* include Lezake (Azake [10]), Ali Hoca (1), and Osman Ağa (15). Kifuri is also a border of Ğuli (24). The Putamu Valley mentioned here is likely to be that elsewhere called the Ser Putamu or Seri Putamu Valley (e.g., see above, Karunihuri [11] and Huri [12]).

35. ANAVARİN-İ CEDİD *(kale)*

The *kale* (fortress) of Anavarin-i cedid and its *varış* (suburb) are fully discussed in Appendixes III and IV.

36. KURD BEY *(çiftlik)*

A river or place called Kurbeh is frequently mentioned in travelers' accounts of the early 19th century, and it is clear from them that Kurbeh was located at or near modern Yialova.[91] Gell (traveling in 1804) reached the river Kurbeh 75 minutes after his departure from Navarino. Captain Smyth labeled the river at Yialova "Kurbeh" on a map of 1823 prepared for the British Admiralty, and it is also so designated on Leake's map of Messenia.[92] Three of the borders recorded in TT880 can be mapped with confidence. Talyan refers to the fisheries in Osman Ağa lagoon (Anavarin-i atik [13]); Tavarne is the *çiftlik* of Lefku or Tavarne (39); and Tupçin is an adjacent *çiftlik* (37) that must have lain somewhere between Yialova and Pile (31). İstikamne appears to be a transliteration of the Greek *sta kaminia* (στα καμίνια), literally "at the kilns." Vavalari is probably a surname (as represented at nearby Pile [31, item 10]).[93] In the period 1512–1520 Vavalari is listed, along with Pile, as a *mazraʿa* dependent on the original fort of Anavarin (see above, Chap. 1, Table 1.5).[94]

Venetian sources provide some insight into Kurd Bey's sad history. Curbei is mentioned in 1686, at the time of the Venetian conquest of Navarino, and is said to be near Koukounara,[95] while in 1693 Molin proposed it as the site for a biscuit factory.[96] But in 1698 it was raided by pirates, and 26 people were captured.[97] On April 1, 1700, the *provveditore* writes that the tenancy of Curbei had expired and was up for auction, but

90. Even though it does not help in locating the toponym, it is just possible that it appears in a Venetian tax record of 1704 as "Mischa Catto" (Davies 2004, p. 81, table 3), if this toponym does not refer to Aşağı Katu (3): see discussion above.

91. Bennet, Davis, and Zarinebaf-Shahr 2000, p. 361. A Venetian map published by Andrews (1953, pl. VII, "M") shows a "Villa corbei" at this location, as does the 1700 Venetian map (B.III.a.124, A; see Fig. 3.7, "Villa Curbei"). The following poem is written on an otherwise blank page in a notebook (dated 1952–1955) kept by the archaeologist Dimitris Theocharis when he was working at the Palace of

Nestor and the Cave of Nestor. It seems to be a song or poem that he heard and found of interest. The original is now in the Archives of the American School of Classical Studies at Athens: Εδώ το λένε Κούρμπει, το λεν' Παλιο-Ναβαρίνο. | Τρώνε τα ποντίκια ζωντανά και τα σκυλιά ψημένα | [και με μία σκύλου κεφαλή] σαράντα λημερνάνε. (Here they call it Kurbei, they call it Palaionavarino, | They eat their mice live and their dogs roasted, | And with just one dog's head forty can be fed.) The association of Kurd Bey and Palaionavarino suggests that they are near each other.

92. Leake 1830, pl. 5.

93. We wonder if there is any connection between this name and the place-names Gouvalari (Γουβαλάρι or Γουβαλάρη) or Babalorrema (Μπαμπαλόρρεμα), both in the vicinity of modern Koukounara (cf. Georgacas and McDonald 1967, 111.1659; 1:50,000 Koroni, E253, N175).

94. TT80, pp. 20–21.

95. Locatelli 1691, pp. 218, 222; also Stouraiti 2001, p. 96.

96. Molin 1693 [1896–1900], p. 438.

97. ASV, Archivio Grimani ai Servi, b.26, f.866r. The total recorded population was 68 in the Venetian census of 1689 (Panayiotopoulos 1987, p. 226); see Chapter 4.

no renter was found because of the desolate state of the place. Most of the workers had been enslaved, and the others had had to sell their animals to raise ransom money.[98] Marco Corner offered to rent the place and to bring in foreign families to cultivate the land. He received the property for eight years with an exemption from labor services if he did as promised. Figures in the Venetian census of 1700 attest a serious gender imbalance in the population, with twice as many adult men as women. In 1716 Kurd Bey was unoccupied.[99] But because this is so, the fact that Tupçin (37) is said to be cultivated by the *reaya* of Kurd Bey *çiftlik* can mean only that it has been customary that they cultivate it (but are no longer doing so) or that the *reaya* of Kurd Bey *çiftlik* continue to farm the land but are not living in the *çiftlik*. That the latter may be the case is suggested by the fact that individuals are living both in Zaimzade (29) and at Pile (31) who are said to hold land in Kurd Bey *çiftlik*.

37. Tupçin *(çiftlik)*

The name Tupçin is not preserved today, but it is attested in a Venetian tithe register as "Topici" and appears, as "Villa Topizi dᵃ," to the northeast of "Villa Curbei" on the 1700 Venetian map (Fig. 3.7).[100] The text of TT880 suggests its approximate location. The *çiftlik* was bordered by Kurd Bey (36), which appears to be at Yialova, and it is cultivated by the *reaya* of that place. It is near the *mazraᶜa* of Tursun (38), and it is near Kurd Tağı (Wolf Mountain), which is clearly a translation of the Greek name Lyko-vouni (Λυκοβούνι, 1:50,000, Pylos, E210, N250), elsewhere directly transliterated from the Greek as Likuvun/Likuvuni (see Alafine [4], Karunihuri [11]). The road to Pile (31) is also a border, and this we assume to be the track that runs along the north side of the Xerias Valley.[101] Today the ridge that lies immediately to the north of this road is called Kanonia (Κανόνια, "Cannons," 1:50,000, Pylos, E225, N223; Fig. 3.21), and it is tempting to see in this place-name a misunderstanding of the Turkish, since Turkish *top* is "cannon" and *topçu* is "cannoneer." However, the 1700 Venetian map is quite clear in placing Topizi north of the Yiannouzaga River, perhaps at or close to the location of the modern village of Shinolakka (1:50,000, Pylos, E215, N235), and this location fits with it sharing a boundary (Likuvuni) with Karunihuri (11) farther north.[102]

38. Tursun *(mazraᶜa)*

The *mazraᶜa* of Tursun is near Tupçin (37). Tursun itself is an Ottoman male proper name.[103] If the proposed location at or near the modern village of Shinolakka for Tupçin (37) is correct, then the *mazraᶜa* must have

98. ASV, Archivio Grimani ai Servi, b.49/135, f.84r.

99. Although on the 1700 Venetian map "Villa Curbei" is not annotated "dᵃ" (deserted) (see Fig. 3.7).

100. Davies 2004, p. 81, table 3; B.III.a.124, A.

101. Early in the 19th century, Bory de Saint-Vincent of the Expédition scientifique reached Pile by means of a road that followed the valley north of the Kanonia ridge, the modern Yiannouzaga, observing two waterfalls en route (Bory de Saint-Vincent 1836, pp. 175–179).

102. Note that this corrects our earlier suggestion (Bennet, Davis, and Zarinebaf-Shahr 2000, p. 361, n. 59).

103. E.g., Pulahu 1974, p. 347, with reference to the holder of a *timar*. But see discussion above under Elyas Ağa (28).

been located farther east. It was bounded by Tupçin, Pile (31), a field belonging to the *çiftlik* of Elyas Ağa (28), and a big valley with a stream, perhaps the valley that elsewhere is called the Tursun Valley (see above, Elyas Ağa [28] and Pile [31]).

39. LEFKU OR TAVARNE *(çiftlik)*

There is today an area called Taverna near a church of Ayios Nikolaos by the Pylos-Hora road, south of a gasoline station (currently British Petroleum; 1:50,000, Pylos, E251, N249). Rum Bağ or Lefku (8) presumably lay near this *çiftlik*, in the general direction of the modern village of Romanou. The toponym Taverna may be of considerable antiquity. In 1411 Venice negotiated to obtain the fort of Navarino (Palaiokastro): the border of the *casale* (hamlet) passed in front of a *taverna* belonging to the church of Niklina (Iklaina).[104] Did this *taverna* give its name to the area? We assume the name is preserved in the modern place-name Zvarna (Ζβάρνα, 1:50,000, Pylos, E255, N245). The *çiftlik* was bounded by Usti Biğadi, *sto Pigadi* (στο Πηγάδι, literally "at the well"); the public road, probably that running north from Anavarin-i cedid; and Seri Putamu, the Xerolangado River (see, e.g., Karunihuri [11], Huri [12]). The *çiftlik* is near Petrehuri (7) and, like it, in Venetian times had been cultivated by a Frank, Hunduruz. The boundary Kunduri presumably represents Koundouri (Κουντούρι),[105] a place-name deriving from the personal name Koundouris (Κουντούρης). Is this perhaps the name behind Hunduruz? At the time of the composition of TT880, the *çiftlik* was being cultivated by the *reaya* of Osman Ağa *çiftlik* (15).

40. OTHER YUFİRİ OR RUM BAĞLARI *(mazraᶜa)*

The Other Yufiri or Rum Bağlari derived its name, as did Yufiri or Beşli (27), from a bridge, in this instance one located in the area known as the Rum Gardens (elsewhere found in the singular as Rum Garden, Rum Bağ [8]). Venetian records refer to a "Gioffiri sta romeica," which is presumably this place.[106] The bridge is likely to be that which spans the Selas River on the road between Romanou and Tragana and is marked "Pt de Romanou" in the Expédition's *Atlas* (Fig. 3.1). Parts of an Ottoman-style bridge are preserved beneath the modern construction (Fig. 3.22), and two arches are visible on its north side. Thanasis Koulafetis of Romanou provided additional information: "On the basis of information provided by two elders, one from Tragana, the other from Romanou, I believe that we can conclude with certainty that the toponym Yiofyri is located a little to the west of the modern bridge (at a distance of about 200 m). The location was known by this name until a few decades ago."[107] The fact that Venetian tithe-auction records of 1701 and 1704 mention "Lefco e Giofiri"[108] suggests that this *mazraᶜa* lay in the direction of Lefku or Tavarne (39) and Rum Bağ or Lefku (8). It was bordered by the property of other *çiftlik*s near the Selas River: a field of Alafine (4), a field of Rustem Ağa (6), Karunihuri (11), and a field of Hasan Ağa (5). It used to be cultivated by the *reaya* of Hasan Ağa *çiftlik*.

104. See Hodgetts 1974, p. 476; Hodgetts and Lock 1996, p. 82.

105. Cf. Georgacas and McDonald 1967, 3481, but not in this part of Messenia.

106. National Library of Greece, Archivio Nani, b.3939, f.577r–578r.

107. Pers. comm.

108. Davies 2004, p. 81, table 3.

Figure 3.22. Arch of an old bridge
over the Selas River near Romanou

41. Usta Musli *(mazraᶜa)*

Usta Musli is said to be near Anavarin-i cedid and to be in the possession
of the people of its *varış*. Its boundaries include the arches of the aqueduct
that supplied the fortress, perhaps the particularly well-preserved arches
east of the *kale,* where the aqueduct from Goumbe joins that from Palaionero (App. III). Two Venetian documents link it to Deli Ahmed (33). The
mazraᶜa appears to have been named after an Ottoman officer with the
rank of *usta,* a lesser officer of the Janissaries.

42. Aǧurliçe *(çiftlik,* but should be registered as *karye)*

Aǧurliçe is the modern town of Ambelofyto, formerly called Agorelitsa
(Αγορέλιτσα, 1:50,000, Filiatra, E200, N218). No borders are recorded.
Notes in headings assign this *çiftlik* and the remainder of those listed in
the document in the northern parts of the *kaza* of Anavarin to that of
Arkadiye (i.e., Muzuste [43], Ayanu [44], Tristena [45], İskarminke [46],
Miniaki or İbsili Rake [47], İstilianu [48], and Virviçe [49]).

43. Muzuste *(çiftlik,* but should be registered as *karye)*

Muzuste is the modern village of Lefki, formerly called Mouzousta (Μουζούστα, 1:50,000, Filiatra, E175, N228).[109] Its borders include a *handak*
(ditch or channel) attributed to three separate places: Fulke, Aǧurliçe (42),
and Burǧu, probably to be read as Pirǧu. Fulke clearly is the village of
Floka, north of Muzuste (1:50,000, Filiatra, E180, N194), which is registered in Arkadiye; Aǧurliçe (42) is its nearest neighbor to the south. If the
reading Pirǧu is correct, then the most likely equivalent is the modern village officially named Pyrgos (Πύργος), but locally referred to as Pyrgaki
(Πυργάκι).[110] We know of no aqueduct that has existed in the area (in
contrast to the vicinity of Anavarin-i cedid; see Usta Musli [41]) and suggest that the term is being used to describe the prominent steep-sided

109. On the 1700 Venetian map
(B.III.a.124, A), the eastern boundary
of "Villa Mususta" is a prominent
valley, labeled "Valle Liuosta," perhaps
from nearby Ligoudista (an old name
for modern Hora; see Chap. 4).

110. If Burǧu is correct, then it here
seems to render the Italian *borgo* and
may in this context refer to the nearby
large town of Gargaliani in Arkadiye.

ravines that run down from each of the villages mentioned.[111] İsbiliaz is a transliteration of Spilaies (Σπηλιές); there is a location known by this name to the south of Mouzousta, beyond a place called Palaiohori. Uste Birnar may be a garbled rendering of *sta Pournaria* (στα Πουρνάρια), and the same name describes a place southwest of Ambelofyto (Ağurliçe [42]), in the general direction of Muzuste; it also was a border of a field at Alafine (4). Limuniaz may be a transliteration of the Greek Λεμονιές (*Lemonies*, "Lemon Trees"); today there is a place called Lemonia (singular in number) midway between Mouzousta and Floka, within the territory of Mouzousta.

Figure 3.23. Church of Ayios Ioannis on the eastern outskirts of Gargaliani

44. AYANU *(mazraᶜa)*

Ayanu is a transliteration of the Greek *Aï Yianni* (Αï Γιάννη). The *mazraᶜa* is said to be near Fulke (Floka). There is, in fact, a church of Ayios Ioannis between Floka and Gargaliani (1:50,000, Filiatra, E168, N202; Fig. 3.23), near the main asphalt road to Gargaliani. Immediately north of the central plateia of Mouzousta there is a low ridge, the southern slope of which is also called Ayios Yiannis, although no church exists there today. But that location seems too close to Muzuste to be identified with the *mazraᶜa* of Ayanu. Usti Biğadi is clearly *sto Pigadi* (στο Πηγάδι); in the territory of Gargaliani there is a place called Pigadia on the side of the hill of Ayios Ilias that faces Muzuste. Ustu Ayuyani must refer to the church of Aï Yianni itself. Ustu Şika may be a garbled form of *sti Tsouka* (στη Τσούκα), Albanian for "hill," a toponym that is found in two places in the vicinity: about a kilometer west-southwest of Muzuste (1:50,000, Filiatra, E165, N235), and about 1.5 kilometers southwest of the village of Pyrgaki (1:50,000, Filiatra, E185, N208). The ditch *(handak)* of Ğarğalian is probably the same as the ditch of Burğu/Pirğu that is a border for Muzuste (43), although the discussion above under that entry should be taken into account.

45. TRİSTENA *(mazraᶜa)*

The name as written in Ottoman Turkish does not indicate internal vowels and consists only of the consonants T-r-s-t-n-a. Today the place is locally known as Drestena (Ντρέστενα or Ντρέσταινα) and is situated on

111. An alternative suggestion was offered by H. Forbes (pers. comm.): "In my experience, *handaki* tends to mean something, anything, a bit deeper than an *avlaki*. And furrows are often used on Methana to delineate boundaries on plots, especially in places like a *lakka*, a broad flat field, where there is no obvious terrace wall to act as an obvious division."

a ridge (1:50,000, Filiatra, E175, N238) immediately north of Palaiohori and less than a kilometer south of the modern village of Mouzousta (Muzuste [43]).[112] The area is more commonly called Halasmata (Ruins) and is not labeled on any standard map. Auction figures for the Venetian tithe in 1701 and 1704 note a location called Musustà e Tristena.[113] The fields of Tristena used to be cultivated by monks from a monastery of Ayu Yurki, clearly Ayios Yioryis (Αγιος Γιώργης). There is a church of Ayios Yioryios on a knoll 300–400 meters northeast of Drestena (1:50,000, Filiatra, E178, N235), but no monastery. It is clear from a Venetian source that the monastery intended was that of Ayios Yioryios at Sapriki (modern Metaxada) in Arkadia, whose monks had cultivated land in this area in the late 17th century.[114] Borders include the fields of Alafine (4) and of Hasan Ağa (5). Vavalari could be a reference to the large settlement of Kavalaria (Καβαλαριά), near modern Hora and registered in Arkadiye (1:50,000, Filiatra, E215, N232). Another candidate is the locality Kavelarioti (Καβελαριώτη) near Ambelofyto (Ağurliçe [42]).[115]

46. İSKARMİNKE *(karye)*

İskarminke is the modern village of Metamorfosi (formerly Skarminga, 1:50,000, Meligalas, E180, N209; Fig. 3.24).[116] The premodern settlement seems to have been centered on the church of Ayia Sotira.[117] Residents of the village of Kavalari (here the village near modern Hora must be meant) own land here. The second part of Kuli Karye is perhaps a translation of the Greek *horio* (χωριό), "village." Mustafa Mandrasi ("Mustafa's sheepfold" or "cheese dairy") takes the Greek word for "pen" or "sheepfold" (also used in Turkish to describe a "cheese dairy"), *mandra* (μάντρα), and attaches a Turkish grammatical ending. The alternate name for Papla (19) was Mustafa Ağa, and this village lies only four kilometers to the south-southwest. İstakatu probably is a simple transliteration of the Greek phrase *sta kato* (στα κάτω), meaning "lower regions." There is a church of Ayios Yiannis (Ayu Yani) a few hundred meters to the northwest of Ayia Sotira (Fig. 3.24).

47. MİNİAKİ OR İBSİLİ RAKE *(karye)*

Miniaki or İbsili Rake (Psili Rahi [Ψηλή Ράχη]) is the village of Maniaki (Fig. 3.25). The village was called "Schilirachi" in the Venetian census of 1700. No borders are listed. The name Magnachi appears in the Venetian tithe register, and the village is named Magnaci on the 1700 Venetian map, bounded on its east and south by the lands of Vlahopoulo.[118]

112. On the 1700 Venetian map (B.III.a.124, A) "Villa Trestena d⁹" is south and slightly west of Mouzousta, within an extensive territory stretching to the coast and south as far as "Villa Lafina" (Fig. 3.7), Alafine (4).

113. Davies 2004, p. 81, table 3.

114. Dokos 1971–1976, p. 124. See also a Venetian document dated to 1704 that mentions the Monastery of "San Zorzi sto Vuno sii Agias," which held property in Tristena and Saprichi as well as surrounding villages (National Library of Greece, Archivio Nani, b.3939, f.460r).

115. See Georgacas and McDonald 1967, 15.2206.

116. Davis et al. 1997, pp. 477–480.

117. The 1700 Venetian map locates Villa Scarmingà here, too (B.III.a.124, B; see Fig. 3.27 below), east of a prominent valley, labeled "Fiume S⁴ Veneranda," running north to "Villa Saprichi" (modern Metaxada). The naming of this valley Santa Veneranda (= Greek Ayia Paraskevi) is somewhat puzzling, as the prominent peak of Aigaleon, along whose eastern edge it flows, is Ayia Kyriaki.

118. Davies 2004, p. 68, table 1; B.III.a.124, B.

Figure 3.24. Modern village of
Metamorfosi (Skarminga) from
Amygdalitsa

Figure 3.25. Modern village of
Maniaki

Figure 3.26. Modern village of Stylianos

48. İstilianu *(karye)*

İstilianu is the village of Stylianos (Στυλιανός; Fig. 3.26). It is not clear what is meant by the phrase "the villages of İskarminke, Miniaki, and İstilianu are on the side of the mountain," because they are certainly not on the side of the same mountain today. However, the 1700 Venetian map[119] clearly shows "Villa Stilianu" on the east bank of the Santa Veneranda River (Fig. 3.27; see İskarminke [46]), as it is in the Expédition's *Atlas.* Assuming this is not simply an error, we can place the three on the slopes of the Amygdalitsa-Velanidies ridge (1:50,000, Meligalas, E185, N185). No borders are listed.

49. Virviçe *(karye)*

Virviçe, formerly Vervitsa, is modern Petralona just north of the Neda River. Gell visited it and, as the scribe of TT880 also seems to have done, described it as "in the forest."[120] Although this village is far from any other village in Anavarin, the identification must be correct. Leake observed that "the district of Neokastro contains only twenty villages, none of which are large, except Vervitza, and this is not situated in the περίχωρα or vicinity, but in Arcadia, not far from the temple of Phigaleia."[121]

The population recorded for Vervitsa in TT880 agrees with information from Venetian cadasters. In 1689 the population of Vervizza was 119, with a total of 54 men. In 1700 the village was home to 42 families (the place-name was spelled Vernitsa, but this is clearly a mistake). As late as 1830 this village could be listed with settlements in the district of Anavarin,[122] but it is listed neither in Arkadia nor in Anavarin by the Expédition scientifique.

119. B.III.a.124, B.
120. Gell 1823, p. 114.
121. Leake 1830, p. 400.
122. See, e.g., Loukatos 1984.

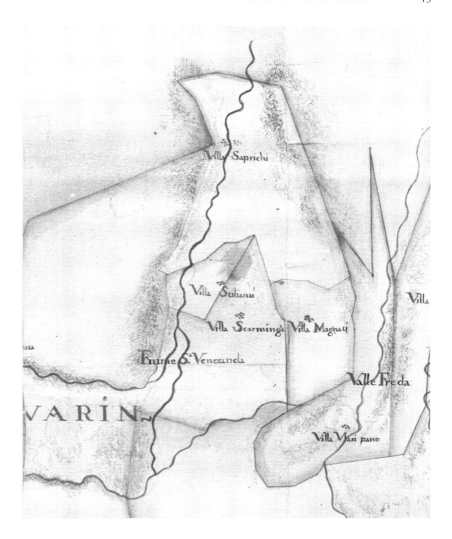

**Figure 3.27. Excerpt from an unpub-
lished Venetian map of the territories
of Modon and Navarino, ca. 1700.**
War Archive of the Austrian State Archive,
cat. no. B.III.a.124, B, by permission

THE TOPONYMY OF TT880

The degree to which the compiler of TT880 has engaged with the local
toponymy of the region is striking, confirming the fact that the *defter* must
have been assembled on the basis of firsthand experience in the region.[123]
The inclusion of boundaries for almost all properties has resulted in a strik-
ingly full repertoire of local place-names, although, as we note in the discussion above, by no means can all be readily identified with a Greek version or, if so, located on the ground.

Place-names are of three types: local names for settlements or topographic features (by far the majority), Turkish translations of local place-
names, and Turkish vocabulary items describing physical features. Taking
these in reverse order, the compiler regularly uses a road (often described
as "public road"), a valley, or the sea to denote a boundary of a property. In
such instances, he naturally uses his own language. Less often, he will
translate a local term into Turkish. Thus, in two instances, we have in
Ottoman transcription the Greek place-name Lykovouni (Λυχοβούνι)

123. See Kiel 1997, p. 317.

(4, Likuvun; 11, Likuvuni), but in the case of Tupçin *çiftlik* (37), it appears as Kurd Tağı, or "Wolf Mountain," a literal translation of Lykovouni. The *mazraᶜa* of Other Yufiri or Rum Bağlari (40) presents a similar situation, as its second name is Turkish for "Vineyards of the Greeks."[124] A slightly different example appears to be the *mazraᶜa* of Aşağı Katu (3), where both elements seem to have the same meaning, "lower," the first being Turkish, the second Greek. Tupçin *çiftlik* (37) itself may provide an example of "interference" between the two languages, although it now seems unlikely to us that this property was located on the ridge currently called Kanonia (Κανόνια).[125] Although it might seem that, in rendering the Venetian Lesaga as Elyas Ağa (28), the scribe has reinterpreted the second element as the common Turkish title "Ağa," he was probably, in fact, restoring its original name, since Venetian records describe Lesaga as a *seguolatio,* i.e., a *çiftlik.*[126]

The largest group of place-names by far is that pertaining to local settlements or topographic features, many still attested in the contemporary landscape.[127] While it is not surprising that the compiler simply transcribed local names with no obviously descriptive element, we consider it worth noting that he made no attempt to render into his own language such obviously descriptive elements as "cave" (İsbilia [7]; Σπηλιά), "well" (Usti Biğadi [39, 44]; στο Πηγάδι), or "bridge" (Yufiri [27, 31, 40]; Γιοφύρι). The small number of instances in which he did translate, noted immediately above, perhaps suggest that he was working with a Greek-speaking interpreter, a *tercüman.* The example of Aşağı Katu (3) is particularly suggestive in this regard.

Leaving aside the forms of the place-names used, we are also struck by the nature of those place-names used to mark the boundaries of the various properties in TT880. Except in the relatively few cases where another property is given as a boundary, most of the place-names (where we can determine their location) refer to obvious topographic elements (valleys, ravines, hills, ridges, peaks) or fixed human-made markers (roads, structures, bridges, areas of agricultural land, vineyards). The level of detail included in the boundary descriptions of the properties in TT880 seems to us unusual for an Ottoman *defter,* even one compiled immediately after a reconquest. Such detail is absent, for example, from the sections of TT80 (dated 1512–1520) relevant to our area, nor is it pres-

124. See, too, the *mazraᶜa* of Rum Bağ or Lefku (8).

125. It is just possible that the clue lies in an earlier Ottoman *defter,* TT80, p. 820, which lists a *timar* at a location called Pirğu Kukunare, distinct from Kukunare itself. This *timar* is in the possession of three Ottoman military personnel, each said to be an "artilleryman" *(topçu).* The specific location of Pirğu Kukunare cannot be determined, but modern Kanonia is not that far from Koukounara.

126. Davies 2004, p. 99. That such a reanalysis is possible is suggested by the modern folk etymology, common in the region, of the place-name Skarminga (Σκάρμιγγα) as Skarmin Ağa.

127. In researching the locations of place-names for this project, we were struck by the persistence of such local toponyms in the contemporary communities. We also found it interesting, when asking about the locations of such toponyms, that maps were never used to provide the answers; rather, we were either given verbal descriptions, they were pointed out from an appropriate vantage point, or, frequently, we were shown the spot itself. This point, we feel, highlights well the differing concepts of space between modern Western researchers and contemporary local inhabitants. The maps included in the Venetian cadastral documents represent the 18th-century equivalent of the modern, map-based view. To the best of our knowledge, such maps were alien to Ottoman traditions of land registry (see, e.g., Karamustafa 1992), although there is a rich tradition of Ottoman map-making, particularly in the context of navigation, as exemplified by the work of Piri Reis (see, e.g., Soucek 1996).

ent in the *defter*s dealing with Eğriboz (Euboia), dating to 1474 and 1507–1528, published by Balta.[128] We have not, however, consulted the *defter*s compiled in the wake of the conquest of Crete in 1669, quite close to the date of TT880.[129]

The level of detail, and indeed, the style of description recalls the near-contemporary Venetian cadasters drawn up for parts of the Morea in the wake of the late-17th-century reconquest. These documents, too, carefully draw boundaries around each property, using topographic markers or the boundaries of adjacent properties. Equally, they sometimes distinguish the status of properties: village *(villa)*, *çiftlik (seguolatio)*, *metohi (metochi)*.[130] Unfortunately, as noted above, neither the summary *(catastico ordinario)* nor the detailed cadaster *(catastico particolare)* survives for our region,[131] so specific comparison is impossible. For the sake of more general comparison, we quote an entry from the territory of Fanari, transcribed by Topping:

> The village of Agoulinítsa [consists of] arable fields in the plain, pasture lands in wooded hills and in a forest called Sendoúki, a fishery, and a vineyard. Its limits on the east are: the village of Volántza at the ravine of Bousalá, the mountain of Chondroliyiá, the source of Áyios Yeóryios, Yiftókastro, and a *luro* which falls into the Alfiós river; on the north, the river Alfiós and district of Gastoúni; on the west, the sea; on the south, the ruined village of Zagouroúni, the village of Aloupochóri at the point Bósi, a boundary stone placed above the fishery, the ruined village of Zagouroúni and the said boundary stone and Longofrázeri, *Licori*, Paliálona, Goúmas' vineyard, and the ravine of Bousalá.[132]

Such are the similarities that we wonder if the Venetian record-gathering might have influenced Ottoman administrators. We assume that the Ottoman compiler did not make use of Venetian *catastici* for the region, but the information may have been "prepackaged" in a certain format by local inhabitants who had dealt with the Venetians. Clearly the Ottoman administrators would have made use of earlier Ottoman documents, as the *kanunname,* discussed in Chapter 2, implies, and as is suggested by a few references within TT880 to property identified as formerly in Turkish hands. These earlier Ottoman documents may have contained the toponymic information presented in TT880, but it has not yet been possible to identify such sources at the level of detail presented in TT880, if indeed they exist.

SYSTEMATIC EQUIVALENCES OF OTTOMAN NAMES

Because of the rich repertoire of place-names (and non-Muslim personal names: Concordance I) presented by TT880, we include here a short discussion of systematic equivalences between the Ottoman versions and their probable original forms.[133] Note, however, that the ambiguities of the script as written on TT880 (especially the inconsistent use of diacritical dots to distinguish letters of similar form), and the difficulty of reading what are

128. Balta 1989, 1992.

129. Referred to, but not described in detail, in Greene 2000, p. 23, n. 38.

130. Usually referring to land belonging to a monastery, but not in the vicinity of the monastery itself.

131. Dokos and Panagopoulos 1993, p. lvii.

132. Topping 1972, p. 78. Many similar examples can be found in Dokos and Panagopoulos 1993, pp. 4–40.

133. For a similar discussion, see Balta 1989, pp. 115–129, and Lowry 2002, p. 181.

in many cases minuscule marks, mean that definitive identification of the actual pronunciation of any place-name or personal name in the Anavarin region cannot be reliably achieved. We nevertheless hope that the following discussion might prove useful to other scholars.

As Balta has noted,[134] Turkish does not permit initial consonant clusters. As a result, a prothetic vowel normally precedes such clusters: initial *sk-* (σκ-), *st-* (στ-), and *ps-* (ψ-) have *i-* inserted. Thus:

Skarminga	İskarminke (46)
Stylianou	İstilianu (48)
Psili Rahi	İbsili Rake[135] (47)

This feature is particularly noticeable in the frequent toponymic elements *sti(n)* (στη[ν]), *sto(n)* (στο[ν]), *sta* (στα), *stou* (στου), "at the place [of]," which are rendered as İsti-, İstu-, or Ustu-. Thus:

İstilake (12, 14)	*sti Lakka* (στη Λάκκα)
İstuputamu (7, 8)	*sto Potamo* (στο Ποταμό)
Ustu Ayuyani (44)	*sto(n) Aï Yianni* (στο[ν] Αϊ Γιάννη)

The prothetic vowel is also present frequently in personal names (Concordance I), such as İstimad (5.5.1, etc.), Stamatis (Σταμάτης).

This example also illustrates another point: the frequent loss of a final syllable, particularly after a Greek stress-accented syllable. From personal names, we have Panayud (2.3.1, etc.), Panayiotis (Παναγιώτης). We also have the place-name Melis (26), Melissi (Μελίσσι).

The exact value of vowels is less easy to determine, given the ambiguities of the script, but Ottoman *waw* is consistently used for Greek *o* or *ou*:[136]

Lefku (8, 39)	Lefkos (Λεύκος)[137]
Furiçi (21, 28)	Fourtzi (Φουρτζή)
Huri (12)	Hori (Χώρι), also represented in the compounds Petrehuri (7) and Karunihuri (11)

The above also illustrates the normal equivalence of Ottoman *h* with Greek *chi* (χ).

Consonant clusters are sometimes divided by vowels, for example:

Furiçi (21)	Fourtzi (Φουρτζή)

In general, Ottoman *ç* renders Greek *ts* (τσ), and *c* renders *tz* (τζ). Thus:

Ağurliçe (42)	Agorelitsa (Αγορέλιτσα)
Avarniçe (30)	Avarnitsa (Αβαρνίτσα)
Kufurci (28)	Kufourtzi (Κουφουρτζή)
Narincir (6)	Nerantzi (Νεράντζι)

Of course, this is the way modern Greek renders Turkish *c* too, as in Ali Hoca (1) = Alihotza (Αληχότζα). Finally, Greek *sigma* frequently appears as *z*, probably reflecting its actual pronunciation in these particular cases. Thus:

Vidizmadun (1)	Vythismata (Βυθίσματα)[138]
Limuniaz (43)	Lemonies (Λεμονιές)

134. Balta 1989, p. 120.

135. Although this might reflect Ypsili Rahi (Υψηλή Ράχη); note, too, the voicing of *-ps-* to *-bs-*. In Venetian censuses (see, e.g., Panayiotopoulos 1987, p. 262), this place is referred to as "Schilirachi," showing a transformation of *p-s-* (ψ) to *k-s-* (ξ), and metathesis of the *k-s-* element to *s-k-*.

136. We have transliterated it consistently as *u*, although in many instances the original sound must have been an *o*. See also Concordance I.

137. This is of interest, as it implies that there is no connection between this 18th- and 19th-century place-name and the modern village of Lefki (Λεύκη), formerly called Mouzousta (Μουζούστα), our Muzuste (43).

138. Note also that the fricative *theta* is rendered by the voiced stop *d* here, and a final *-n* is added. The addition of a consonant to end a word ending in a vowel in Greek is worth noting, as in the case of Narincir above, if it is definitely Nerantzi (Νεράντζι).

TABLE 3.1. NAMES OF *ÇIFTLIK*S, *MAZRA^CA*S, *KARYE*S, AND *KALE*S IN TT880 AND THEIR GREEK NAMES

Ottoman Name	Status	Greek Name	Current Name	Transliteration of Greek
1. Ali Hoca	Ç	Αληχότζα		Alihotza
2. Platne	Ç	Πλάτανος		Platanos
3. Aşağı Katu	M			
4. Alafine	Ç	Αλαφίνα		Alafina
5. Hasan Ağa	Ç	Χασάναγα		Hasanaga
6. Rustem Ağa	Ç			
7. Petrehuri	M	Πετροχώρι		Petrohori
8. Rum Bağ or Lefku	M	Λεύκος		Lefkos
9. Has	Ç			
10. Azake	Ç	Λεζάκι		Lezaki
11. Karunihuri	M	Καρβουνοχώρι		Karvounohori
12. Huri	Ç	του Χορού το χάνι		tou Horou to hani
13. Anavarin-i atik	*Kale*		Παλαιόκαστρο	Palaiokastro
			Παλαιοναβαρίνο	Palaionavarino
Budran	Ç			
Büyük Göl				
Kilursarin				
Talyan		Νταλιάνι		Daliani
14. Küçük Pisaski	Ç	Πισάσκι		Pisaski
15. Osman Ağa or Büyük Pisaski	Ç	Οσμάναγα	Κορυφάσιο	Osmanaga or Koryfasio
16. Pispitsa	Ç	στου Πίσπισα,	Μυρσινοχώρι	stou Pispisa or Pispisia,
		Πισπίσια		or Myrsinohori
17. Nase or Memi Ağa	M/Ç	Νάσα		Nasa
18. Rotsi or Denmusarin	M/Ç	Ρούτση		Routsi
19. Papla or Mustafa Ağa	Ç	Ανω Παπούλια	Παπούλια	Ano Papoulia
20. Other Papla or Ağaku	Ç	Κάτω Παπούλια	Γλυφάδα	Kato Papoulia or Glyfada
21. Kirmiti or Sefer Hoca	M/Ç	Κρεμμύδια		Kremmydia
22. Kukunare or Muslihuddin Efendi	Ç	Κουκουνάρα		Koukounara
23. İklina or Kurd Ağa	Ç	Ικλαινα		Iklaina
24. Ğuli or Mehmed Ağa	M/Ç	του Γουλή τη ράχη		tou Gouli ti rahi
25. Rudiye or Kurd Ali Ağa	M/Ç	Ροδιά		Rodia
26. Melis or Derviş Kethüda	M/Ç	Μελίσσι		Melissi
27. Yufiri or Beşli	M	Γιοφύρι		Yiofyri
28. Elyas Ağa	Ç	Λέζαγα	Στενωσιά	Lezaga or Stenosia
29. Zaimzade	Ç		Μπαλοδημέϊκα	Balodimeïka
30. Avarniçe or Haci Hasan	M/Ç	Αβαρνίτσα	Αβαρνίτζα	Avarnitsa
31. Pile	Ç	Πύλα		Pyla
32. Arkadianu or Müfti	M/Ç			
33. Deli Ahmed	M/Ç			
34. Muçaçu or Muslihuddin	Ç			
35. Anavarin-i cedid	*Kale*		Νιόκαστρο	Niokastro
Varış			Πύλος	Pylos
36. Kurd Bey	Ç		Γιάλοβα	Yialova
37. Tupçin	Ç	Κανόνια		Kanonia
38. Tursun	M	Δροσούνι		
39. Lefku or Tavarne	Ç	Ταβέρνα		Taverna
40. Other Yufiri or Rum Bağları	M	Γιοφύρι		Yiofyri
41. Usta Musli	M			

TABLE 3.1 *(cont.)*. NAMES OF *ÇİFTLİK*S, *MAZRAᶜA*S, *KARYE*S, AND *KALE*S IN TT880
AND THEIR GREEK NAMES

Ottoman Name	Status	Greek Name	Current Name	Transliteration of Greek
42. Ağurliçe	Ç̶/K	Αγορέλιτσα	Αμπελόφυτο	Agorelitsa or Ambelofyto
43. Muzuste	Ç̶/K	Μουζούστα	Λεύκη	Mouzousta or Lefki
44. Ayanu	M	Αϊ Γιάννης		Aï Yiannis
45. Tristena	M̶/Ç	Ντρέστενα		Drestena
46. İskarminke	K	Σκάρμιγγα	Μεταμόρφωση	Skarminga or Metamorfosi
47. Miniaki or İbsili Rake	K	Μανιάκι-Ψηλή Ράχη	Μανιάκι	Maniaki or Psili Rahi
48. İstilianu	K	Στυλιανού	Στυλιανός	Stylianou or Stylianos
49. Virviçe	K	Βερβίτσα	Πετράλωνα	Vervitsa or Petralona

Key: Ç = *Çiftlik;* M = *Mazraᶜa;* K = *Karye;* M/Ç = *Mazraᶜa or [x] Çiftlik;* Ç̶/K = *Çiftlik,* but should be written as *Karye,* according to the
document; M̶/Ç = *Mazraᶜa,* but should be written as *Çiftlik,* according to the document.
Note: "Greek Name" is the Greek equivalent of the name as it appears in the document, where we have been able to verify it in Greek
sources (see discussion in this chapter). "Current Name" is the official name of the village in contemporary usage. In many instances, the
names of settlements commonly employed in medieval and early modern times were changed in the 19th and 20th centuries, and the
official "Current Name" of a settlement is now different, although its older name may still be more commonly employed by its residents.

PROLEGOMENON TO CHAPTER 4

The preceding discussion is a necessary step in the analysis of a document
such as TT880 if the information contained in it is to be fully exploited for
the sake of economic and social history. This analysis has enabled us to
construct a detailed map of the Ottoman district of Anavarin, one that in
the following chapter permits us to examine variations within the district
in the nature of agriculture and in the distribution of population. Such
analysis has resulted in the recognition of patterns of land use that have
hitherto been undocumented and probably could not have been recovered
by any other means. These patterns in turn facilitate deductions about the
nature of Ottoman administration in this district that should be of considerable significance for historians of the Ottoman empire and of early modern Greece.

CHAPTER 4

An Analysis of the Ottoman Cadastral Survey of Anavarin, 1716

by Jack L. Davis, John Bennet, and Fariba Zarinebaf

In this chapter our emphasis is on the district of Anavarin, rather than the entirety of the Morea. We focus on one particular point in time, A.D. 1716, the date of the composition of TT880, but inspection of earlier and later historical sources allows us to add a diachronic and comparative dimension to our analyses, and assists in determining the extent to which the patterns recorded in TT880 reflect conditions typical of the entire period of Ottoman rule, or are the result of the preceding Venetian occupation. In Chapter 3, the principal places recorded in the cadastral survey of Anavarin are mapped with considerable success. This accomplishment now permits us, in the first section of this chapter, to extract data from that document (as translated in Chap. 2) in order to discuss the distribution of population and variability in the nature of agriculture in the district of Anavarin. In the second section we demonstrate how our understanding of the text of TT880 can also be improved by adducing archaeological evidence.

TOWARD A HISTORICAL AND ECONOMIC GEOGRAPHY OF EARLY MODERN ANAVARİN

> At 11.20 I arrive, by a bad paved causeway, at the skala of Neó-kastro [Anavarin-i cedid], and lodge in the house of Kyr Ghiórghio Ikonomópulo, who has all the trade of Neókastro in his hands, and is agent for some of the European nations. His house and maga-zines, which stand on the water side three or four hundred yards below the fort, very naturally excite the cupidity of the poor Turks of the town, who are starving by the effects of their pride and idleness. He tells me that their demands upon him are so frequent, that he finds himself under the necessity of abandoning Navarín to settle in some place, where, not being the only Greek of property, he may be less exposed to extortion.[1]

The preceding quotation from Colonel William Martin Leake, one of the most observant of Western travelers to Greece, offers a perspective on the settlement at Anavarin-i cedid as it existed at the beginning of the

1. Leake 1830, p. 399. On Leake's work in general, see Wagstaff 2001a.

19th century, a time of relative stability prior to the outbreak of the Greek
Revolution. Leake's narrative and many others published by Western travelers described the *kale* of Anavarin and its surroundings approximately a
century after the district had been recovered by the Ottomans in 1715.
Such Western accounts, along with the Ottoman sources discussed in
Chapter 1, Venetian archives from the period 1688–1715, French consular
reports of the 18th century, Greek governmental documents for the period
of the emergent Greek state, and the publications of the French Expédition
scientifique de Morée, provide raw material for a preliminary economic
and social geography of Anavarin in the Second Ottoman period.

Several general conclusions emerge from the evidence we shall present
here. First, it seems that the district of Anavarin, including its coastal areas, was far from desolate in the 18th and early 19th centuries, even though
accounts of some Western travelers may suggest otherwise.[2] It would appear, moreover, that the long-term picture of settlement in Anavarin
throughout the 18th and early 19th centuries was one of stability in the
size of its non-Muslim population. The Greek Revolution (1821–1828),
however, drastically depopulated the district of both its Greek and its
Muslim residents.

Second, it is clear that Anavarin, although not one of the major commercial centers of 18th-century Greece, had already in 1716 been integrated into larger regional economies. It is obvious from TT880 that some
of the crops were marketed there at the beginning of the 18th century and
that attention was paid to both subsistence and commercial agriculture. It
is also apparent that in 1716 the district of Anavarin was capable of supporting a much larger population than it actually did. Comments on agricultural affairs included in TT880 paint a picture of underutilization of its
agricultural resources.[3]

These results of our analyses should be of considerable interest to
Ottomanists and to historians and archaeologists specializing in the study
of post-Byzantine Greece. We think we have succeeded in demonstrating
how much can be learned by examining microregional variability in settlement and land use within a relatively small area of the Ottoman empire. It
would, of course, be a mistake to generalize from the conclusions we reach
in this chapter to the Morea as a whole, much less to the Balkan peninsula,
and we hope that others might be encouraged through the example of our
work to test our results by embarking on similar studies. A historical and
economic geography for the entire Ottoman Morea might ultimately result from such a collaborative effort.

The population of Anavarin is considered in the following section of
this chapter. It has been possible for us to estimate the number of inhabitants in the district and to compare the size of its population in 1716 to
population levels both during the Venetian domination of 1685–1715 and
in the period that immediately preceded and followed the outbreak of the
Greek Revolution in 1821. It has also been possible to examine the spatial
as well as the temporal dynamics of population increase and decrease, because the geography of Anavarin is now clearly understood for the first time.

Next we reconstruct the overall agricultural system described by TT880
and examine spatial variability in agricultural practice within the district
of Anavarin in 1716. Comparison of these data with detailed agricultural

2. On this point, see Bennet, Davis,
and Zarinebaf-Shahr 2000.

3. This state of affairs was adum-
brated in Chapter 1.

statistics compiled in the early 20th century suggests that local agriculture in 1716 provided subsistence support for the *reaya* who worked the land and for the Ottoman military personnel who served in the garrison at Anavarin-i cedid, and also had the potential to generate a substantial surplus for export.

THE POPULATION OF ANAVARİN

THE NON-MUSLIM POPULATION OF ANAVARİN IN 1716

The information contained in TT880 is of particular interest in that it has the potential to allow us to reconstruct population levels in 1716 for the non-Muslim inhabitants of Anavarin. Although TT880 does not contain an actual census of the entire population of Anavarin, it does report that 281 non-Muslim men over the age of puberty were liable to pay the head tax called *ispence* in each *çiftlik* and *karye,* and in the *varış* of Anavarin.[4] From this figure, the total number of non-Muslim individuals likely to have been living in the district can be estimated (Fig. 4.1:b, Table 4.1).

The use of information extracted from a document like TT880 to measure population makes it important to understand the methods employed, and the purposes intended, in its composition. These have been lucidly described by Machiel Kiel:

A census commission headed by a Census Master *(Emin)* and a Scribe travelled throughout the land, visiting all localities in existence. They were assisted by the Ottoman Judge *(Kadi)* of the district in question and by the members of the Ottoman cavalry, the *sipahi*s, who lived in or near the village(s) allotted to them. The *Kadi* had to bring copies of the local records, the villagers were summoned to show their documents and to give verbally an exposé about the manner in which the taxes were hitherto collected. The entire village population, headed by the priests and the village notables, had to appear before the commission and all married men and the unmarried boys from 13 years upward were written down with their name and patronym, and if they had one also with their family name. Because everybody was registered according to their family adherence it is easy to see who was the brother of who and how many sons a father had. This is very important information for reconstructing the family size and based on that the approximate total population of the settlement. Widows, mostly heads of an incomplete family, were also registered. As a rule every Christian house(hold) paid 25 *akçe*s as the fixed sum called *Ispence,* a tax with a local Balkan background.[5]

The census recorded in TT880 seems to have differed somewhat from that described by Kiel. For example, in TT880, widows are not directly recorded, and the marital status of men is not explicitly observed.[6] Filial and fraternal relationships are not noted except in those cases where unmarried sons and brothers appear not yet to have formed their own households and seem still to live with their father or brother as members

4. Only non-Muslims paid *ispence.* On the character of this tax, see Chapter 1.

5. Kiel 1997, p. 317; cf. İnalcık 1954, pp. 110–111.

6. The property of two women is, however, listed in a single instance: see Zaimzade (29), entry 22.

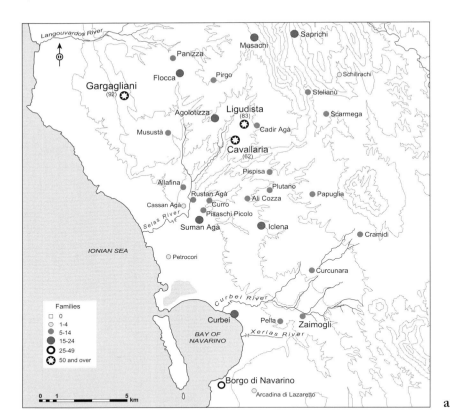

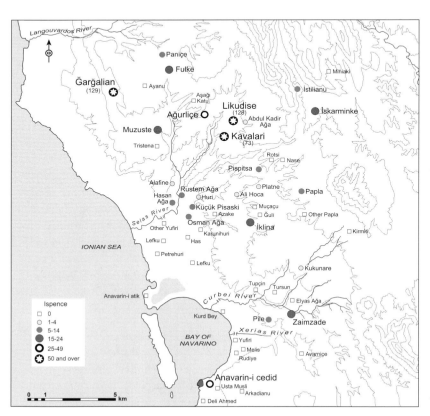

Figure 4.1. Distribution of the population according to *(a)* the Grimani census (1700); *(b)* TT880 (1716); *(c)* Pouqueville (1815); and *(d)* the Expédition scientifique de Morée (1829). Place-names appear in original orthography.
R. J. Robertson, after Bennet, Davis, and Zarinebaf-Shahr 2000, figs. 13–16

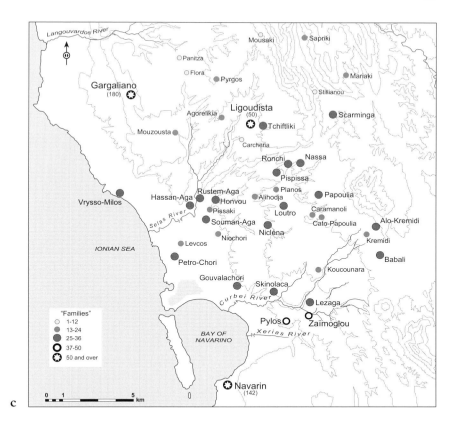

c

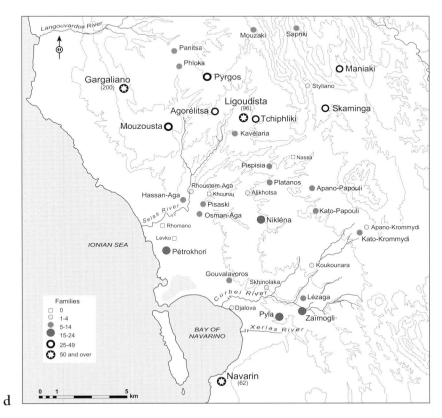

d

TABLE 4.1. POPULATION OF SETTLEMENTS LISTED IN TT880, 1689–1716

Settlement	1689 (a)	(b)	(c)	(d)	(e)	Settlement	(f)	(g)	(h)	(i)
Ali Coza	16	10	13	2	41	Alli Cozza (23)	6	18	2	2
Apanù Papugli	2	0	3	2	7	Papuglia (22)	8	5	2	1
Agorelizza	19	15	19	8	61	Agolotizza (1)	21	22	9	4
						Arcadina di Lazaretto (14)	3	3	3	2
Borgo di Navarin	33	15	36	17	101	Borgo di Navarino	30	18	16	10
						Città	29	10	12	6
Curbei	23	13	20	12	68	Curbei (24)	19	17	3	8
Cremidi	14	6	13	4	37	Cramidi (27)	6	8	2	4
Cuccunara	6	1	8	5	20	Curcunara (25)	6	4	3	2
Catù Papugli	10	3	8	4	25					
Cassanaga	12	4	14	7	37	Cassan Agà (3)	2	3	0	1
Curù	13	3	12	6	34	Curro (15)	12	12	2	7
Carvunoghori	10	1	6	2	19					
Cadir Agà	9	7	9	4	29	Cadir Agà (8)	12	19	3	5
Cavalaria	37	20	44	19	120	Cavallaria (12)	62	59	31	15
Floca	21	2	20	7	50	Flocca (5)	18	17	8	6
Guli	2	2	2	0	6					
Lesaga	8	8	7	0	23					
Lesachi	3	3	2	2	10					
Lafina	11	12	12	4	39	Allafina (20)	5	11	2	1
Ligudista	68	40	65	28	201	Ligudista (4)	83	95	35	28
Mususta	18	13	14	13	58	Musustà (2)	14	17	5	3
Niclena	19	9	19	11	58	Iclena (28)	15	7	3	5
						Petrocori (11)	4	4	1	0
Pila	15	7	16	7	45	Pella (13)	7	7	2	0
Platano	6	1	4	2	13	Plutano (10)	7	2	1	2
Pissaschi piccolo	12	9	14	9	44	Pisaschi picolo (21)	9	10	4	1
Pissaschi grande	24	5	21	4	54	Suman Agà (18)	17	15	4	9
Pispissa	14	4	13	13	44	Pispisa (6)	12	20	6	5
						Rustan Agà (9)	7	6	4	2
Saimogli	10	5	9	4	28	Zaimogli (16)	12	10	2	6
Saprichi	30	19	22	13	84	Saprichi (under Arcadia no. 13)	22	27	16	6
						Schilirachi (7)	3	3	2	0
						Scarmega (19)	10	12	5	6
Stiglianù	4	2	4	3	13	Stelianù (17)	6	8	3	2
Valta	12	11	13	8	44	Valta (under Arcadia no. 8)	8	11	4	5
Vervizza (under Arcadia no. 81)	54	18	37	10	119	Vernizza (under Arcadia no. 72)	42	27	10	12
Totals	535	268	499	230	1,532		517	507	205	166

Key: *(a)* Men; *(b)* Boys; *(c)* Women; *(d)* Girls; *(e)* Total
(f) Familes; Males of age: *(g)* 1–16; *(h)* 16–30; *(i)* 30–40; *(j)* 40–50; *(k)* 50–60; *(l)* Elderly
Females of age: *(m)* 1–16; *(n)* 16–30; *(o)* 30–40; *(p)* 40–50; *(q)* Elderly
(r) Total males and females
(s) Number of sons; *(t)* Total males paying *ispence;* *(u)* Estimated population (using a multiplier of four; see Erder 1975).

Note: All Venetian data are from Panayiotopoulos 1987, pp. 226–227, 250–251, 262. Names of settlements in the census of 1689 were listed in alphabetical order by Corner, who reported the results of the 1689 census. The original order of names recorded in the censuses of 1700 (reported by Grimani) and 1716 (TT880) is indicated by the number in parentheses that follows them.

1700									Settlement	1716			
(j)	(k)	(l)	(m)	(n)	(o)	(p)	(q)	(r)		(s)	(t)	(u)	±
1	3	0	7	1	3	3	0	40	Ali Hoca (1)	1	4	16	-24
4	1	2	13	3	4	2	1	38	Papla (19)	3	10	40	+2
5	1	6	14	4	6	3	7	81	Ağurliçe (42)	8	32	128	+47
0	0	0	1	2	0	1	0	12	Arkadianu (32)	0	0	0	-12
4	4	5	18	7	13	6	6	107	Anavarin/varış (35)	1	30	120	+13
7	1	1	6	5	7	8	4	67	Anavarin/kale (35)				
4	3	1	8	1	2	4	3	54	Kurd Bey (36)	0	0	0	-54
1	0	2	8	5	0	2	1	33	Kirmiti (21)	0	0	0	-33
0	1	2	9	2	1	1	3	28	Kukunare (22)	0	3	12	-16
									Other Papla (20)	0	0	0	-25
0	0	1	0	1	0	0	1	7	Hasan Ağa (5)	0	9	36	+29
0	1	1	8	4	3	1	3	42	Huri (12)	0	2	8	-34
									Karunihuri (11)	0	0	0	-19
1	1	3	6	2	1	2	3	46	(in Arkadiye)*				
10	8	10	61	27	10	8	15	254	(in Arkadiye)*				
3	4	4	17	6	5	4	5	79	(in Arkadiye)*				
									Ğuli (24)	0	0	0	-6
									Elyas Ağa (28)	0	0	0	-23
									Azake (10)	0	0	0	-10
2	1	0	3	0	4	0	1	25	Alafine (4)	0	3	12	-13
17	12	20	77	43	22	12	24	385	(in Arkadiye)*				
3	2	3	8	5	3	1	5	55	Muzuste (43)	1	20	80	+25
2	1	8	4	8	3	3	2	46‡	İklina (23)	0	15	60	+14
0	2	2	4	0	1	2	2	18	Petrehuri (7)	0	0	0	-18
2	0	1	8	2	2	3	1	28	Pile (31)	0	13	52	+24
0	2	1	2	2	0	2	2	16	Platne (2)	0	3	12	-4
2	3	1	8	2	1	3	2	37	Küçük Pisaski (14)	2	13	52	+15
2	1	1	17	9	2	2	0	62	Osman Ağa (15)	2	12	48	-14
3	0	5	10	4	4	4	4	65	Pispitsa (16)	1	12	48	-17
2	1	1	6	0	2	3	1	28	Rustem Ağa (6)	0	7	28	0
4	0	2	7	4	6	0	3	44	Zaimzade (29)	7	21	84	+40
4	0	4	23	11	3	8	3	105	(in Arkadiye)*				
1	2	0	4	2	0	1	1	16	Miniaki (47)	0	2	8	-8
1	1	3	14	4	3	1	4	54	İskarminke (46)	1	17	68	+14
1	0	1	9	5	2	0	3	34	İstilianu (48)	0	6	24	-10
1	1	1	17	2	5	1	—	48	(in Arkadiye)*				
12	4	8	37	15	16	10	6	157	Virviçe (49)	11	47	188	+31
99	61	100	434	188	134	101	116	2,111		38	281	1,124	
									Net gain/loss				-86

The symbol "±" indicates the increase or decrease in population between the 1700 Venetian figure (or 1689, if no 1700 figure is given) and TT880. These figures are only approximations. Note that if a multiplier of three were used (Erder 1975), population estimates for 1716 would be substantially lower, but if the percentage of the population under 15 years of age was notably greater than assumed in Erder's model, they would be higher.

* In TT880, this place is registered as belonging to the *kaza* of Arkadiye, rather than the *kaza* of Anavarin; see Fig. 2.1.

‡ The actual total figure given in Panayiotopoulos 1987, p. 262, is 42, possibly an error in his source documents, not consulted directly by us.

of an extended family. As a consequence, it is more difficult to reconstruct family sizes. Nonetheless, it is possible to deduce from the text a considerable amount of information concerning the structure of households.

In 38 instances it is clear that non-Muslim men recorded in the format "[x] his son" are dependent members of an extended household. In nearly every case in which this formula is used, the individual lacks property (that is, no land, livestock, beehives, trees, vines, or houses are listed as being in his possession). For example, in the *çiftlik* of Ağurliçe (42) and in the *karye* of Virviçe (49), where houses are listed with other property of the *reaya*, only a single man described as a son ever possesses a house.[7] These 38 men represent about 13.5 percent of the 281 men who pay *ispence*. This figure is approximately the same as the proportion of unmarried men (about 12%) that in 1461 were listed for Corinth as unmarried in an Ottoman cadaster.[8] It is also within the range of the percentages of unmarried men in villages of Boiotia in the 15th and 16th centuries.[9] The percentage of unmarried males in TT880 seems, however, relatively low when compared to the range represented in some other Ottoman *defter*s.[10]

In 29 other instances, non-Muslim men are described according to the formula "[x] his brother," and it also seems unlikely that many, if any, of these individuals are heads of independent households. At least some of these men were probably living with their brothers in instances in which their father was deceased, particularly when the father's name is not represented among the names of the *reaya* registered in the *çiftlik* or *karye*. Only four brothers (about 15%) have property (two are said to have houses). Only one (Ağurliçe [42], entry 16) might have a son. The scarcity of property in the hands of "brothers" and "sons" is all the more remarkable because, if the individuals without property are excluded, more than 95 percent of the other 218 men who pay *ispence* have some goods in their possession.

TT880 itself provides no information concerning the size of an average family. Figures collected for the district of Anavarin in the Venetian census of 1700 yield an average family size of four people.[11] A little more than a century after TT880 was composed, the French Expédition scientifique de Morée estimated the average size of a family in the Peloponnese at 4.75 people.[12] One way to approach the estimation of a total popu-

---

7. In the *çiftlik* of Küçük Pisaski (14), where the *reaya* are said to have a house each, one may assume that the scribe is referring only to married couples.

8. In TT10; see Beldiceanu and Beldiceanu-Steinherr 1986, p. 41.

9. See Kiel 1997, tables I and III; the figure there vacillates between 10 and 20 percent.

10. E.g., the proportion varies between 3 and 48 percent in certain Anatolian districts. Cook (1972, pp. 25–27) suggests that a low percentage of bachelors is characteristic of a rapidly growing population. See also Erder and

Faroqhi 1979 on interpreting fluctuations in numbers of bachelors in Ottoman *defter*s.

11. Based on 445 families and a total population of 1,797 for the district; see Panayiotopoulos 1987, pp. 203–206, 262. These totals do not precisely match those in Table 4.1 because of slight differences in the boundaries of the Ottoman district of Anavarin and the Venetian *territorio* of Navarino. Wagstaff (2001b) similarly argues for the appropriateness of a mean family size of four individuals in ca. 1700; see also Venetian data published by Ranke (1957, p. 177).

12. Puillon de Boblaye and Virlet 1833–1834, p. 85. There was a range of 4.18–5.54 individuals per family in the 11 districts *(eparchies)* where such information was available. Data were presented to the Expédition scientifique (Puillon de Boblaye and Virlet 1833–1834, pp. 58–65) by Count Ioannis Antoniou Kapodistrias, president of Greece, through the good offices of General Antoine-Vergile Schneider, commander of the French army in the Morea, and were based on statistics that had been collected in 1828–1829.

lation for the district in 1716 is to multiply the 218 non-Muslim men who pay *ispence* and who possess property by an estimated family size of 4–4.75 individuals, yielding a total population estimate of 872–1,036 individuals. To this figure should be added an unspecified number of households headed by widows.[13]

The total population of the district can also be estimated from standard life tables.[14] A total of 281 males pay *ispence* and therefore are at the age of maturity or older. The percentage of the male population *under* the age of maturity may be estimated at about 36 percent of the total population (158 boys) by employing the Model West, mortality level 4 and growth rate 5.[15] The total male population would be about 439 individuals. Multiplying this figure by 0.83 (an estimated ratio of males to females) suggests that the number of women and girls in the district would have been on the order of 364 and would yield a grand total of 803 individuals of all ages in Anavarin.[16]

THE MUSLIM POPULATION OF ANAVARİN IN 1716

The discussion in the previous section provides only an estimate of the size of the non-Muslim population of the district. An estimate of its total population is possible only if ranges for the size of the Muslim population can also be determined, as it is obvious (see Apps. II, III, and Chap. 2 [Anavarin-i atik (13) and Anavarin-i cedid (35)]) that a substantial number of Turks lived in Anavarin at the time that the area was captured by Venice. This Muslim population (mostly military) had been concentrated in the forts of Anavarin-i atik and Anavarin-i cedid. It is also clear from sources other than TT880 that at least some members of the Ottoman military and the bureaucracy had already returned to Anavarin in 1716 (see Chap. 1).[17]

In contrast, there is no evidence in TT880 for Muslim *reaya* in the countryside of Anavarin or in the fortresses of Anavarin-i atik and Anavarin-i cedid. The only personal tax assessed against residents of the *karye*s

13. Lowry (2002, p. 51) estimates that such households in Limnos in the 15th and 16th centuries constituted 7 percent of the total. Malliaris (2001, p. 210) notes that 28 percent of Chiot households in Modon in 1699 were headed by widows.

14. Coale and Demeney 1966.

15. See Hansen 1986, pp. 9–13. It is this model that Hansen suggests is most appropriate for estimating the structure of ancient Greek populations. Here we use figures for the percentage of the male population under 15, rather than 13, years of age, as does Erder (1975).

16. On the estimation of ratios between sexes, see Erder 1975, p. 296,

fig. 1. Empirical data from Venetian sources suggest, however, that the assumption of Model West 4 may not be entirely valid for Anavarin. In 1700, the average percentage of boys in the male population of the Morea as a whole was 39.9 percent, and for Anavarin the figure was 45 percent; see Panayiotopoulos 1987, pp. 202, 262. The figure of 45 percent would yield a total population estimate for Anavarin of 935. Erder has proposed a slightly different model (Model East 3) for estimating populations based on Ottoman *defter*s (one that is also perhaps inappropriate for Anavarin). Accordingly, only about 31 percent of the male population would be under 15 years of

age. If we follow Erder's suggestion and derive a population estimate for Anavarin by multiplying the number of taxpaying individuals by 3–4, the resulting total population estimate for the district is 843–1,124, nearly the same range as that reached by multiplying our estimate for the number of heads of household in the district by Venetian and French estimates of average household size.

17. The *kanunname* translated in Chapter 2, however, anticipates that other Muslims were yet to return. Because Muslim administrators and soldiers and their families were exempt from paying taxes, their names were not listed in *defter*s such as TT880.

or *çiftlik*s recorded in TT880 is the *ispence*. No individual is recorded as paying the *çift resmi*, a personal tax that was regularly imposed on Muslim cultivators instead of the *ispence*.[18] Nor does it seem likely that Muslim *reaya* were systematically omitted and recorded elsewhere, because the stated purpose of TT880 was to list all property in the district, not just that of non-Muslims, and this goal was achieved.[19] Muslim property in *çiftlik*s and in *karye*s was registered and described in detail. In *çiftlik*s, property in the possession of the holder of the *çiftlik* was recorded at the start of each entry. In contrast, for *karye*s and for the *kale* of Anavarin-i cedid, individual pieces of property of Muslims were listed under their names. For example, this was the case at İskarminke (46), where houses, fields, and trees had belonged to Osman Ağazade, possibly a Janissary *ağa* who lived in the countryside.

We have a few clues as to the number of Muslim military and administrative personnel that would have been normal in Anavarin. There had been a few hundred Turks present in Anavarin-i atik in 1686 at the time of its surrender to Venice,[20] apparently only a fraction of them under arms.[21] In the 17th century there may have been a similar number of Turks resident in the fortress. Evliya Çelebi recorded 80 houses in the outer citadel and 5 in the middle citadel (see App. I, [310], [266b/20] and [266b/25]).[22] He also described the strength of the Janissaries stationed here, but without including a count of them: "The young stalwarts of this castle are a finer, more effective, braver and more celebrated body of men than the imperial forces *(kul)* in the castle of New Navarino below. The castle detachment consists of garrison personnel, but is a levy of poor men" ([311], [267a/5]).

Immediately prior to the Venetian conquest, the fortress does not, however, seem normally to have been well maintained or well populated. Randolph observed in the 1670s that "the Walls are very much out of repair, great parts being fallen down; there are very few Inhabitants in it."[23] Although in TT880 the defenses and structures in Anavarin-i atik are all

18. On land taxes paid by Muslim *reaya*, see the *kanunname* translated in Chapter 2, paragraphs 2 and 5.

19. We have considered the possibility that Muslims may have been residing in those *çiftlik*s in the district where no Christian population is recorded. This does not seem likely, inasmuch as several of these *çiftlik*s are specifically said to be cultivated by the residents of other settlements (e.g., Petrehuri [7]). See also below in this chapter.

20. Venetian documents from 1689 list the number of good and destroyed houses; see Davies 2004, p. 69. The description of Anavarin-i atik in TT880 refers to the condition in which this fortress was found after it was retaken

by the Ottomans. Twenty-six houses were registered as *miri* in the outer citadel and six in the inner citadel. Although Venice appears to have given up the idea of defending the fortress (Andrews 1953, pp. 41–42), 24 soldiers and 2 sergeants were stationed there in 1703; see Davies 2004, p. 69.

21. Locatelli 1691, p. 212 ("Che occupata con prestezza si fecero uscir i Turchi dalla Fortezza con le loro famiglie, ch'erano poco più di trecento custoditi a Lidi de Mare"); Foscarini 1696, p. 263 ("Sortirono 400 Turchi, e lasciarono 43 pezzi di bronzo"); Anonymous 1687, p. 65 ("500. animi trà quali più di cento huomini d'armi"); Anonymous 1689, p. 67 (400 "men," 100 "soldiers" among them); Garzoni 1720, vol. 1,

p. 155 ("cento venti uomini atti all'arme, il rimanente femmine, e neri in tutti quattrocento uscirono del ricinto"); Stouraiti 2001, p. 54 ("il popolo che la constituiva ascendea in tutto a 450 persone in circa, de quali però duecento erano a sostenere il peso dell'armi").

The Venetians left 160 infantry to hold the fort (Coronelli 1686, p. 69). See also Rycaut 1700, pp. 223–224, concerning the evacuation of Ottoman forces; and Schwencke 1854, p. 74, regarding the strength of the Venetian garrison.

22. In the 16th century, the numbers of Janissaries and *sipahi*s at Anavarin-i atik varied greatly (see Chap. 1, p. 20).

23. Randolph 1689, pp. 5–6.

registered for the state, no houses are said to be the possession of a specific Muslim owner. Such treatment is very different from that found in the entry for Anavarin-i cedid, where only the property of individual Muslims is described, not the fortress *(kale)* itself.

In contrast to Anavarin-i atik, it is clear from the text of TT880 that Anavarin-i cedid was substantially populated when it was taken by Venice in 1686, a few days after Anavarin-i atik fell. At the time of Anavarin-i cedid's surrender, Venice had evacuated 3,000 Turks from it.[24] Within the fortress, nearly 100 separate pieces of property were recorded in 1716 as having been in Muslim hands, and it seems clear that in normal circumstances a garrison of substantial size would have maintained residence there.[25] The fortress was intentionally ruined when it was abandoned by Venice in 1715, and this devastation is reflected in the text of TT880.[26]

One of the fullest accounts of Anavarin-i cedid in the decades immediately preceding the Greek Revolution is that of Sir William Gell, who helps us to understand the function of such a *kale:*

> The town within the walls is like those in this part of the world, encumbered with the fallen ruins of former habitations. These have been generally constructed by the Turks, since the expulsion of the Venetians; for it appears that till the long continued habit of possession had induced the Mahometans to live upon and cultivate their estates in the country, and the power of the Venetian republic had been consumed by a protracted peace, which is the inevitable ruin to that form of government, a law was enforced which compelled every Turk to have a habitation in some one of the fortresses of the country. I imagine that they were bound to maintain these residences, and to keep in them a constant supply of such provisions as were best suited to the purpose. Every Turk ought, upon this supposition, to owe personal service to some fortress in his neighbourhood, and in fact nominally belongs to the garrison. The houses have fallen into decay, and the provisions had long ceased to be prepared, as there seemed no necessity for them. I should even doubt if the property in many of the castles could be ascertained, as the habitations present generally an indiscriminate mass of ruins; they were originally erected in haste, and being often cemented with mud instead of mortar, the rains of autumn, penetrating between the outer and inner faces of the walls, swell the earth, and soon effect the ruin of the whole structure.[27]

24. Andrews 1953, p. 49; Foscarini 1696, p. 267 ("Uscirono dalla Piazza tre mille persone, e tra queste più de mille atti all'armi"); Anonymous 1687, p. 70 ("4 milla persone in circa, tra quali mille d'armi"); Anonymous 1689, p. 73 (1,000 "soldiers," 2,000 "other Turks"); Garzoni 1720, vol.1, p. 160 ("Tre mila si numerarono le persone, de'quali un terzo almeno abile al peso dell'armi");

Stouraiti 2001, p. 58 ("Turchi, consistenti in 700 soldati in tutto di presidio e 3,000 cittadini"). Finlay (1877, vol. 5, p. 180) says that 3,000 Turks surrendered, 1,500 of them soldiers. According to Coronelli (1686, pp. 72, 77), a Greek messenger sent by the Turkish garrison to seek reinforcements reported more than a thousand "bons hommes" inside the fortress, and on

its surrender an equal number were evacuated, among a total of 3,000 "infidels." See also Rycaut 1700, p. 225; Schwencke 1854, p. 82.

25. When *timar*s were allocated in 1716, it appears, however, that there were only 64 *sipahi*s in Anavarin; see Chapter 1, p. 42.

26. Brue 1870, p. 42.

27. Gell 1823, pp. 19–20.

From this passage it might be expected that all or most members of the Ottoman military and bureaucracy would have maintained a residence at Anavarin-i cedid. The number of houses in the *kale* of Anavarin-i cedid may, therefore, provide us with a maximum estimate for the number of Muslim soldiers and administrators in the district as a whole, whether their primary place of residence was in the fortress or in the countryside. A Venetian inventory recorded a total of 198 houses in the fortress, and this figure can, with the addition perhaps of a modest garrison for Anavarin-i atik, be accepted as a very approximate indication of the maximum number of tax-exempt Turkish households that may have been present in the district.[28]

POPULATION TRENDS IN ANAVARİN, 1685–1821

From the preceding discussion we may conclude that the Christian population of Anavarin in 1716 must have consisted of 1,000 individuals, more or less, whereas the Muslim population in the early 18th century is unlikely to have amounted to many more than 200 families. It is clear that the Venetian conquest of the Morea had a major impact on the Muslim population: many or most Muslims fled, whereas some converted to Christianity.[29] In contrast, the Christian population appears to have remained more or less at the same level throughout the Venetian occupation.[30]

Furthermore, the reconquest of the Morea by the Ottomans in 1715 does not appear to have resulted in a substantial decrease in the size of the Christian population of Anavarin. There was no fighting in the district. Venice simply destroyed and abandoned the fortress of Anavarin-i cedid in the face of the advancing Ottoman army.[31] Certain Latins must have fled, and the Venetian retreat must have resulted in the evacuation of some families from the district, along with the garrison, including those who had held the Frankish (that is, Venetian) property recorded in TT880 both in the *varış* of Anavarin and in the countryside, and those immigrants from Chios and elsewhere who had held Venetian grants of land in

28. See Davies 2004, p. 70, and below, Appendix III. Evliya Çelebi speaks of 600 houses in the outer citadel and 33 in the inner, with 200 houses in the suburb, mostly Greek. This account is obviously not consistent with the text of TT880 or Venetian sources, and Evliya may be intentionally inflating his figures. Exaggeration is a feature of his text: see Jameson, Runnels, and van Andel 1994, pp. 607–611, in which the trustworthiness of his descriptions—particularly of his measurements and quantities—for the southern Argolid are evaluated. See also Faroqhi 1999, pp. 160–161. More generally, see Kiel 1973, pp. 353–354, on the need to

check, wherever possible, Evliya's information against independent historical and topographical sources. On the other hand it does seem that, from time to time, greater numbers of soldiers were assigned to Anavarin. In 1613, 352 *sipahi*s and Janissaries were stationed there; see Chapter 1, p. 20.

29. See Dokos and Panagopoulos 1993, p. 113; Davies 2004, p. 105. The Venetians reported 4,000 Muslim converts in 1690. Several are documented in the district of Anavarin. We do not know what happened to these individuals after the Ottoman reconquest, and in only a single instance does TT880 point to the presence of a Christian

who has converted to Islam; see Concordance I.

30. Venetian censuses provide detailed data very close in time to that of TT880 and invite direct comparison with it on a settlement-by-settlement basis (see Table 4.1, Fig. 4.1:a). See Panayiotopoulos 1987, pp. 225–230 for the Corner census of 1689, and pp. 231–289 for the Grimani census of 1700. Wagstaff (1993) offers a brief study of settlement and population in the entire Morea, drawing on the Grimani census data. See also Lambros 1885 and Corner 1691 [1885–1889] regarding the nature of the Corner census.

31. Brue 1870, pp. 41–42.

the district. But, in contrast to other parts of the Morea, such as Anabolu (Nafplion),[32] the number of Venetians living in the district of Anavarin was not great.[33]

The distribution of the Christian population within the district did change under Venetian rule, however. Individual settlements, including several in highland valleys, appear to have lost population between 1700 and 1716. The overall picture suggests that areas north of the Bay of Navarino in particular were underpopulated.[34] There were dramatic decreases in the sizes of settlements at Ali Hoca (1), Kukunare (22), Other Papla (20), Huri (12), Alafine (4), Osman Ağa (15), and Pispitsa (16). Communities at Arkadianu (32), Kurd Bey (36), Kirmiti (21), Karunihuri (11), Ğuli (24), Elyas Ağa (28), Azake (10), and Petrehuri (7) were completely abandoned.[35] Incentives intended to encourage Christian settlement in the lowlands do not seem to have enjoyed much success. Venetian administrators found it difficult to encourage families to move to Anavarin-i cedid, even from nearby parts of Arkadiye.[36]

The district of Anavarin at the end of the Venetian occupation of the Morea was as a whole thinly populated (Table 4.1, Fig. 4.1:a, b), particularly in comparison to the later 19th and early 20th centuries. For example, in 1920, the population of areas that had been within the borders of Anavarin numbered more than 6,000 individuals (Table 4.2), excluding the modern town of Pylos.[37]

In 1716 the largest Christian communities in the Pylos area lay in Arkadiye, just outside the borders of Anavarin. These included Ğarğalian, and three villages collectively known as Hores: Likudise, Abdul Kadir Ağa, and Kavalari.[38] Hores and Ğarğalian in the 17th and 18th centuries were much bigger than the *varış* of Orthodox households clustered outside the gate of the fortress of Anavarin-i cedid. The combined population of the three constituent villages of Hores as recorded in the 1828 census mandated by Count Ioannis Antoniou Kapodistrias was 153 families.[39] Following Greek independence, all three villages were officially known as Ligoudista until 1927, when the name of the community was changed to Hora.

32. Dokos 1975.

33. This conclusion is supported by the fact that our estimates of the non-Muslim population in 1716 are close to totals in the Grimani census of 1700, where 1,194 individuals were recorded in settlements that belonged to the district of Anavarin in 1716.

34. Locatelli (1691, p. 216) refers to the burning of villages by the Ottoman commander north of the Bay of Navarino during the Venetian conquest of the region.

35. Robbery and piracy must have been a threat to lowland communities. In the case of Kurd Bey (36) (Curbei),

we know that in 1698 it was raided by Turks, who took 26 captives. In 1700 robbers also attacked Osman Ağa (15); see Davies 2004, p. 75.

36. I.e., from Likudise (Ligoudista) and Kavalari (Kavalaria), which were in the *territorio* of Navarino at the time. Davies (2004) discusses these incentives. Under Venetian rule, settlement of immigrants from Chios and elsewhere in these villages, which the Ottomans assigned to Arkadiye, was substantially greater than in the district of Anavarin. See also Bennet, Davis, and Zarinebaf-Shahr 2000, p. 375.

37. The modern town of Pylos was founded after the Greek Revolution, near the fortress of Anavarin-i cedid; see Bennet, Davis, and Zarinebaf-Shahr 2000, p. 354.

38. It is our intention to publish elsewhere a commentary on the parts of TT880 that describe these villages. Under the Venetians they had belonged to Anavarin/Navarino.

39. The results of this census were published by the Expédition scientifique. See Puillon de Boblaye and Virlet 1833–1834, p. 85; Frangakis-Syrett and Wagstaff 1992, pp. 439–440.

TABLE 4.2. POPULATION OF THE AREA OF THE *KAZA* OF ANAVARİN (EXCLUDING MODERN PYLOS), 1920–1981

Settlement	1920	1928	1940	1951	1961	1971	1981
Αμπελόφυτον (Ambelofyton)	531	595	702	724	783	570	427
Γλυφάδα (Glyfada)	286	320	396	356	343	314	242
Ικλαινα (Iklaina)	360	450	567	573	559	459	352
Κορυφάσιον (Koryfasion)	636	849	911	843	926	779	689
Κουκκουνάρα (Koukkounara)	288	299	363	340	324	246	196
Κρεμμύδια (Kremmydia)	768	1,010	1,117	1,156	974	854	757
Λεύκη (Lefki)	293	354	383	326	300	232	211
Μανιάκιον (Maniakion)	290	294	280	251	182	100	60
Μεταμόρφωσις (Metamorfosis)	335	317	358	378	401	360	316
Μεταξάδα (Metaxada)	322	315	329	349	279	196	150
Μπαλοδημαίικα (Balodimaiika)	64	80	81	120	101	67	48
Μυρσινοχώριον (Myrsinohorion)	311	323	351	356	311	217	141
Παπούλια (Papoulia)	192	214	243	238	238	168	125
Πετροχώριον (Petrohorion)	173	202	189	191	169	111	93
Πισάσκιον (Pisaskion)	115	133	142	164	126	48	34
Πλάτανος (Platanos)	127	141	191	185	228	191	152
Πύλα (Pyla)	178	209	276	321	281	217	159
Ρωμανός (Romanos)	214	236	298	269	289	279	270
Στενωσιά (Stenosia)	227	247	388	463	487	376	442
Τουλούπα Χάνι (Touloupa Hani)	—	—	—	—	43	23	26
Τραγάνα (Tragana)	119	121	129	127	136	94	88
Total	5,829	6,709	7,694	7,730	7,480	5,901	4,978

Source: Data from Houliarakis 1988.

Likudise in 1716 was a large town (128 households), comparable in size to Ğarğalian (see below).[40] Before 1685 it had been a *ze*ᶜ*amet* of Kasim Pashazade. TT880 describes its Greek residents and their property. Houses, olive groves, gardens, and orchards formerly owned by Turks or Venetians and in the possession of Greeks are also noted. The toponym Abdul Kadir Ağa has been entirely lost, but it is clear from the text of TT880 that this must be the real name of an area near the church of Ayios Yioryios in Hora that is called Tsifliki today. In TT880 Abdul Kadir Ağa is said to be joined to Likudise, and no *ispence* figure is given for it, although four sharecroppers *(ortakçıyan)* are registered as living there.[41] Kavalari remains only as a toponym (Kavalaria) that is applied to an area around the church of Ayios Nikolaos, about 600 meters south of the limits of the modern town of Hora. There are today only a few houses there, but in 1716 it had been a large village (73 households).[42] The houses and gar-

40. TT880, pp. 30–34.

41. TT880, p. 34. The name Abdul Kadir Ağa also occurs in Venetian records (as Cadir Agà), and it appears that the name did not go out of use until sometime later in the 18th century, perhaps because residents of the villages of Likudise and Kavalari (both classified as *karye*s) were accustomed to refer to that part of their larger community that held a different status simply as "the *çiftlik*." This is how the settlement was recorded in 1815 by Pouqueville (1826–1827, vol. 6, p. 73; see Fig. 4.1:c, "Tchiftliki"), and in 1829, by the Expédition scientifique (Puillon de Boblaye and Virlet 1833–1834, p. 85; see Fig. 4.1:d, "Tchiph-liki"). The village of Paniçe (Panitza), northwest of Hora and northeast of Gargaliani, is recorded immediately after Likudise and Abdul Kadir Ağa.

42. TT880, pp. 38–40; see S. Gerstel in Davis et al. 1997, pp. 480–481, on archaeological remains at the site.

dens had formerly been owned by Turks but were occupied by Greeks. One Albanian resided there.[43]

Ǧarǧalian (Gargaliani) lies at the northern edge of the area investigated by PRAP. In 1716 it was approximately the size of Likudise (129 households).[44] Prior to the Venetian occupation of the Morea it had been a *timar* of the commander *(dizdar)* of the fortress of Anavarin-i cedid.

For the remainder of the 18th century and the early 19th century we are almost entirely dependent on Western travelers to Anavarin for snippets of information about its population.[45] These are, however, fairly consistent in the information they provide. They permit the fortunes of the district to be traced along general lines and allow us to conclude that the pattern of settlement in the district and its population were relatively stable until the Greek Revolution.[46] Warfare in the later 18th century, however, resulted in massive perturbations that gravely affected Muslims and non-Muslims alike and ultimately led, during the Greek Revolution, to the total elimination of the Turkish population of Anavarin.

Again, the only direct evidence for the size of the Muslim population depends on estimates of the number of Turks in the garrisons of the district. No substantial Muslim population appears to have lived at Anavarin-i atik.[47] The fortress did, however, continue to serve a military function, and from time to time it was manned.[48] By the early 19th century, nearly the entire Muslim population of the district appears to have been based at Anavarin-i cedid. A significant source of information about its size is an account by Pouqueville. He writes: "Le canton de Navarin . . . compte entre les murs de capitale moderne six cents Turcs, et cent trente Grecs qui habitent le varochi. Cette population, calculée avec celle de trente-six villages relevant de la jurisdiction de Navarin, donne un total de seize cent treize individus justiciables de son *cadi*."[49] These figures (600 Turks and 130 Greeks resident in Anavarin-i cedid itself) seem plausible, and, since Pouqueville was held prisoner in the fortress after his capture by pirates

43. Kavalari appears slightly later in TT880 than Likudise, and its entry is followed by the small villages of Potamia and Papayurki, the latter probably the location known as *tou Papayiori* (του Παπαγιώρη) in the territory of the village of Ano Voutaina near Potamia; see Georgacas and McDonald 1967, 19.6150; Dokos 1971–1976, p. 134. Both places are far away, but elsewhere in TT880, Kavalari is also clearly associated with settlements to the northeast: e.g., two residents of Kavalari are said to own property in İskarminke (46), modern Metamorfosi).

44. TT880, pp. 22–30. More generally concerning the history of Gargaliani, see Lyritzis 2000.

45. Houliarakis 1973, otherwise an important source regarding Greek population dynamics, is of little use to us.

On pl. 2 (p. 27), Houliarakis reports a population for the Pylia (i.e., the district of Pylos) at the time of the Greek Revolution of 6,688 Christians and 7,343 Ottomans. But for him, the Pylia represents the subprefecture *(eparchia)* of the Greek state (including the constituent municipalities *[demoi]* of Pylion, Kollonidon, Koronaion, Methonis, and Voufrasou) and is equivalent to the entirety of the Ottoman districts of Anavarin, Modon, and Koron, as well as parts of Arkadiye and Andrusa. On the administrative structure of the early Greek state, see Mansolas 1867, p. 28.

46. Bennet, Davis, and Zarinebaf-Shahr 2000, p. 370.

47. By the time Gell visited in 1804, the fortress was abandoned (Gell 1823, pp. 25–28).

48. Bellin implies that it was not entirely deserted when he saw it several decades earlier than Gell (Bellin 1771, cited in Bory de Saint-Vincent 1836, p. 51), and Bory de Saint-Vincent in 1829 speculated that parts of the fortress had been cultivated in the period preceding the Greek Revolution, since he observed traces of recently abandoned gardens on the lower slopes of the citadel. But, at the same time, he assumed that the upper citadel had been in a state of neglect since the 17th century. In 1770 the Russians found it without a garrison. The Ottomans retook it without a shot (Rulhière 1807, pp. 456, 471–472; Bory de Saint-Vincent 1836, p. 129; Baltas 1990, p. 146).

49. Pouqueville 1820–1821, vol. 5, p. 123.

in 1800, his estimates should be reliable.[50] As phrased above, they imply a total for the entire *kaza* of 1,613 individuals, of which 600 were Turks.

Pouqueville is also an invaluable source for the non-Muslim population of the district, since we have been unsuccessful in locating an Ottoman *defter* dating to the period 1716–1821. In the second edition (1826–1827) of his *Voyage dans la Grèce,* Pouqueville published figures for many Ottoman districts that he says were derived from an Ottoman *cadastre* of 1815.[51] For Anavarin (Table 4.3, Fig. 4.1:c), these figures differ significantly from those presented in the first edition, and the relevant passage from the second edition is worth quoting: "Le canton de Navarin ... compte entre les murs de sa capitale moderne six cents Turcs, et cent trente Grecs qui habitent le varochi ou faubourg. Cette population, calculée avec celle de trente-six villages, donne un total de cinq mille quatre-vingt-quinze individus pour toute l'étendue de son canton."[52]

The original figure Pouqueville was given is clearly 1,019 families, and he has arrived at the figure of 5,095 individuals simply by multiplying by five.[53] There are reasons to doubt the accuracy of these figures, however.[54] In the first place, the text implies that the total of 5,095 individuals should still include 600 Turkish and 130 Greek individuals resident at Navarin. The table in the second edition merely lists 142 Greek *families* resident at Navarin, with an unspecified number of Turkish families.[55] Use of Pouqueville's multiplication factor of five means that 142 families would represent 710 individuals, considerably more than the 130 Greek individuals mentioned in the text in both editions. It would seem likely, therefore, that this figure of 142 might in fact denote Greek "individuals," not families. But if we assume the remaining figures do actually record families, not individuals, then there are further problems.

Elsewhere, in both editions, Pouqueville reports 447 non-Muslims as paying a poll tax *(cizye)* in the *kaza* of Anavarin in 1816.[56] This figure is not in agreement with the total figures he publishes in 1826–1827, because the number of those liable to the *cizye* ought to approximate the number of heads of non-Muslim households, and therefore families.[57]

50. On Pouqueville's captivity, see Lair 1902 and 1904. Leake's estimate, also at the beginning of the 19th century, was somewhat greater: 300 Muslim families (Leake 1830, p. 400). When the Ottoman garrison first capitulated in 1821, 200 Turkish men, women, and children, who had sheltered in the fortress, were allowed to die of hunger, in contravention of the agreed terms of surrender (Blouet 1831–1838, vol. 1, p. 2). In 1828, but in a state of war, the French general Maison found 400 Arabs, 70 Turkish cannoneers, and 60 Peloponnesian Turks, a total of 530 men in all, inside the fortress; see Bessan 1835, p. 54; Duheaume 1833, p. 28.

51. Pouqueville 1826–1827, vol. 6, p. 73.

52. Pouqueville 1826–1827, vol. 6, pp. 72–73.

53. A factor he uses throughout the work in computing the population of individuals from the figures he was given. Pouqueville also provides *cadastres,* quoting the same source, for the districts of Arkadiye, Koron, and Modon (1826–1827, vol. 6, pp. 19–20, 61–62, and 69, respectively). The figures for Koron are, however, explicitly labeled "habitants," not "familles."

54. Problems in using Pouqueville's statistics are discussed in Bennet, Davis, and Zarinebaf-Shahr 2000, p. 352, n. 25, p. 376.

55. In Pouqueville's table, the entry for Turks appears above that for Greeks; next to the entry for Turks are marks resembling "ditto" marks. We interpret these to mean "no data," not to indicate that the figure of 142 includes both Turkish and Greek families.

56. Pouqueville 1820–1821, vol. 5, pp. 15–16; 1826–1827, vol. 6, p. 222 (there referred to as "caratch").

57. The figure of 447 is also well in excess of the 281 non-Muslims who were recorded as paying *ispence,* similarly levied on adult males (see discussion above), in TT880 in 1716. If taken literally, it would imply a 59 percent increase in the non-Muslim adult male population between 1716 and 1816.

TABLE 4.3. POPULATION OF THE DISTRICT OF NAVARINO ACCORDING TO TT880, POUQUEVILLE, AND THE EXPÉDITION SCIENTIFIQUE DE MORÉE

TT880 (1716)		Pouqueville (1815)		Expédition scientifique (1829)	
Place-name	Population	Place-name	Population	Place-name	Population
Ağurliçe (42)	32	Agorelikia	18	Agorélitsa	28
Alafine (4)	3	—	—	—	—
Ali Hoca (1)	4	Alihodja	24	Alikhotsa	3
Anavarin (13)	30	Navarin	142	Navarin	62
—	—	Alo Kremidi	25	Apano-Krommydi	4
—	—	Babali	28	—	—
—	—	Caramanoli	21	—	—
Elyas Ağa (28)	0	Lezaga	25	Lézaga	9
—	—	Gouvalachori	15	Gouvalavoros	8
Hasan Ağa (5)	9	Hassan-Aga	28	Hassan-Aga	5
Huri (12)	2	Honvou	25	Khourou	0
İklina (23)	15	Nicléna	32	Nikléna	17
İskarminke (48)	17	Scarminga	28	Skaminga	28
İstilianu (48)	6	Stillianou	12	Styliano	4
—	—	Calivia	20	—	—
Kirmiti (21)	0	Kremidi	19	Kato-Krommydi	7
Küçük Pisaski (14)	13	Pissaki	22	Pisaski	9
—	—	Koudinou	24	Kondinou	0
Kukunare (22)	3	Koucounara	14	Koukounara	3
Lefku (39)	0	Levcos	17	Levko	0
—	—	Loutro	27	—	—
—	—	Micréna	18	—	—
Miniaki (47)	2	Mariaki	16	Maniaki	27
—	—	—	—	Misdras	0
Muzuste (43)	20	Mouzousta	22	Mouzousta	27
Nase (17)	0	Nassa	26	Nassa	0
—	—	Niochori	16	—	—
Osman Ağa (15)	12	Souman-Aga	29	Osman-Aga	7
Other Papla (20)	0	Cato-Papoulia	23	Kato-Papouli	8
Papla (19)	10	Papoulia	30	Apano-Papouli	8
Petrehuri (7)	0	Petro-Chori	26	Pétrokhori	15
Pile (31)	13	Pylos	40	Pyla	20
Pispitsa (16)	12	Pispissa	30	Pispisia	12
Platne (2)	3	Planos	23	Platanos	5
—	—	—	—	Rhomano	0
Rotsi (18)	0	Ronchi	25	—	—
Rustem Ağa (6)	7	Rustem-Aga	32	Rhoustem-Aga	1
—	—	Skinolaca	29	Skhinolaka and Djalova	4
Virviçe (49)	47	—	—	—	—
—	—	Vrysso-Milos	30	—	—
Zaimzade (29)	21	Zaïmoglou	38	Zaïmogli	15
Totals	281		1,019		336

Sources: TT880 (individuals paying *ispence*); Pouqueville 1826–1827, vol. 6, p. 73 (individual non-Muslims); Puillon de Boblaye and Virlet 1833–1834, pp. 65–66, 85 (families).
Note: Spellings of place-names, if present, are given for all three sources. Only if a place is named, and it is explicitly said to have been unoccupied, is its population indicated as "0" here.

Pouqueville's figure for families is 1,019, however, well over twice the number of *cizye* "billets" assessed. Equally, 447 *cizye* payments implies a total population five times larger (2,235), but still well below Pouqueville's own estimate of 5,095 individuals. Pouqueville himself believed that the *cizye* numbers had been inflated to maximize income, implying an actual non-Muslim adult male population smaller than 447, which would increase the difference still further between adult males and family numbers. On the other hand, Kiel has suggested that *cizye* registers systematically omitted as many as 25 percent of the men liable to pay the tax,[58] which, if we accept the factor, would imply a total figure of 560 males liable to the tax in the region, still well below the number of families recorded in Pouqueville's second edition. There seems, therefore, to be no simple way to relate Pouqueville's *cizye* figures to his population figures, and apparently one cannot be used to verify the other.[59] The discrepancy is somewhat surprising since, if Pouqueville's tables are derived from official Ottoman sources, they are likely to have been records of taxes paid by individuals rather than total population statistics, which were not collected by the Ottoman state until the late 19th century.[60] It is worth noting, however, that his figures offer discrepancies for the districts of Arkadiye, Koron, and Modon, too.[61] A possible explanation, both for the inaccuracies and for the "missing data" in relation to Muslim population levels, is that Pouqueville's source was the local "Christian administration," that is, the Church.[62]

Another way of checking the figures for Anavarin is to compare the changes in population there between 1700 and 1829 with those in the districts of Arkadiye and Modon. According to the Grimani census of 1700, the total population of Navarino (excluding those settlements later listed under Arkadiye) was 288 families; in 1829 it was 336, an increase of nearly 17 percent. That of Arkadiye (including those areas listed under Anavarin in 1700, but *later* under Arkadiye) was 2,000 families in 1700; in 1829 it was 3,354, an increase of 68 percent. For Modon, the equivalent figures are 654 (1700) and 763 (1829), an increase of 17 percent. If we take Pouqueville's 1815 figures at face value, they are: Navarin 1,019, a 250 percent increase from 1700, with a drastic drop to the 1829 figure;[63] Modon 1,637 (150%), again with a large drop by 1829; and Arcadia 3,021 (51%), with a further modest increase by 1829. These figures imply that the figures for both Navarin and Modon are overestimates.

We could regard the figures as total population figures, already "corrected" before they were given to Pouqueville, which he then further (and erroneously) "corrected" by his factor of five. Some support for this theory is provided by the fact that his table for Koron is labeled "habitants grecs."[64] But the possibility should be entertained that they are, in fact, a mixture, with the figures for the number of families within Anavarin-i cedid itself perhaps correct. Detailed comparison on a settlement-by-settlement basis (Table 4.3) shows a similar pattern of anomalously high numbers in 1815, except in those settlements classified as *karye*s, where the pattern resembles more closely that of the district of Arkadiye. It may be that the figures collected by Pouqueville differed depending on the status of the property, with *çiftlik*s representing total populations, but *karye*s comprising heads-of-household only. Since, in contrast with the situation in Arkadiye, the

58. Kiel 1997, p. 320.

59. Sakellariou 1939, pp. 277–278, in discussing the use of *cizye* figures to estimate population in the 19th-century Morea, notes this discrepancy as well.

60. Faroqhi 1999, p. 88.

61. The ratios of non-Muslim family numbers to *cizye* numbers in those districts are as follows: 3,021 to 3,971 (Arkadiye), 490 to 1,201 (Koron), and 1,297 (minimum) to 756 (Modon). The ratio for Arkadiye seems the most plausible.

62. Panayiotopoulos (1987, p. 212) makes this suggestion in relation to his study of the *kaza* of Karytaina. He further notes that the figures for individual villages are unreliable and that the greatest value of Pouqueville's tables is in giving the names of villages and their number.

63. We should also bear in mind that the *ispence* figure for 1716 in TT880 suggests 218 heads of family liable to pay (see discussion above), a figure reasonably close to that in the Venetian census.

64. Pouqueville 1826–1827, vol. 6, pp. 61–62.

area of Anavarin was dominated by *çiftlik*s, the overall population estimates for the latter are skewed. At the very least, it would seem likely that, if only in the case of his figures for Navarin, Pouqueville's figures cannot clearly be regarded as consistent in the distinction between families and individuals.[65]

We devote such an extended discussion to Pouqueville's figures because they represent the only potentially reliable and global figures we have between 1716 and the Expédition scientifique's statistics of 1829.[66] In theory, they offer the possibility of determining whether populations had remained static between 1716 and the eve of the Greek Revolution, and whether levels then were higher or lower than they were in its immediate aftermath. The above discussion suggests that, although the figure for individuals given in Pouqueville's second edition must be a considerable overestimate, the figure of 1,019 can be regarded as only an absolute minimum number of individuals.

The fact that that figure is suspiciously close to the total population given in the first edition, minus the 600 Turks said to be resident at Anavarin-i cedid itself, might suggest a source for the error: Pouqueville simply confused individuals and families. The Christian population of 130 individuals in the *varış* of Anavarin recorded in his first edition is also plausible and is not significantly greater than the figure recorded in TT880.[67] Subtraction of the number of Christians in the *varış* (130) and the number of Turks in the *kale* (600) from Pouqueville's total population of 1,613 yields a non-Muslim population of about 900 individuals resident in the villages of the district. Such a figure is of the same order of magnitude as estimates (1) deduced from TT880, (2) from the 1700 Venetian census (1,112 individuals, correcting for boundary changes), and (3) from the actual population given in Pouqueville's second edition, perhaps a minimum number of individuals, suggesting that the long-term picture of population in the district of Anavarin in the period 1716–1815 was one of stability, or perhaps modest increase.[68]

At the same time, it is clear from other sources that substantial short-term fluctuations in both the Muslim and the non-Muslim population of the district did occur during this time. In 1770 the district of Anavarin was a focus of warfare when Russian troops promoted a general rebellion of the Greeks against the Ottomans. A Russian legion was based at Arkadiye

65. Because of the uncertainties outlined here, and because it encompasses properties listed by Pouqueville in both Navarin and Arcadia, we have retained the label "families" in Fig. 4.1:c, but the patterns presented there should be regarded with caution.

66. A discrepancy also exists between Pouqueville's figures and those recorded in a French report, entitled "Considérations sur la Morée," that was probably written in 1786 (Belia 1978, p. 285); for a full discussion and presentation of this document, see Anoyatis-

Pele 1987. Its anonymous author reported that Anavarin contained 38 villages and that its population amounted to 3,000 individuals, giving equivalent figures for Arkadiye of 40 villages and 6,000 individuals, and for Modon 43 villages and 4,000 individuals. Pouqueville's individual population figures are 5,095 (Anavarin), 15,105 (Arkadiye), and 8,185 (Modon).

67. See Bennet, Davis, and Zarinebaf-Shahr 2000, p. 352, n. 25, p. 376.

68. If we assume, for the sake of argument, that Pouqueville's figure of

142 does equal families resident in Anavarin-i cedid and that the figures for *karye*s are for families, too, then we arrive at a total of 226 families (142, plus 18 [Agorelikia], 28 [Skarminga], 16 [Mariaki], and 22 [Mouzousta]; cf. Table 4.3), or 1,130 individuals, plus 793 individuals on the remaining properties, giving a total of 1,923. This exceeds the 1829 population (1,596; see Table 4.4 below) by over 20 percent, and would represent an increase of 73 percent over the maximum population calculated for 1700.

(Kyparissia), Anavarin-i cedid itself had been captured by April 1770, and the Russian fleet was headquartered there. Many thousands of civilian Turks were murdered in the towns and villages of the Morea during this rebellion, and some 4,000–5,000 Greek fugitives were abandoned in late May 1770 on the island of Sphakteria, after Anavarin-i cedid was deserted by Alexis Orlov and the Ottomans regained control.[69]

Although devastating to the region, the Russian-led rebellion does not appear to have resulted in a significant long-term reduction in either the Muslim or the non-Muslim population of Anavarin. The Greek Revolution, on the other hand, had more drastic consequences. Parts of Anavarin were totally depopulated when İbrahim Pasha of Egypt, in response to an invitation from the Sublime Porte (i.e., the Ottoman government), made Anavarin-i cedid his principal base between 1825 and 1828 and from it attempted to recapture the Morea.[70] Much of the countryside was pillaged, and a significant part of the non-Muslim population fled to safety in the British protectorate of the Ionian islands. Some Greeks who remained suffered greatly, and the *varış* of Anavarin-i cedid itself was entirely deserted by non-Muslims.[71]

The non-Muslim population recovered rapidly from this blow (Table 4.4, Fig. 4.1:d). A census compiled by the French Expédition scientifique de Morée had already in 1829 recorded 336 families.[72] These figures are based on statistics provided by the Greek government of Kapodistrias, and differ only slightly from them.[73] The French emphasized that their figures, even at the time of publication, required substantial emendation: "Cette éparchie . . . était presque entièrement dépeuplée en 1828. Mais déjà en 1830, Navarin, qui ne figure au catalogue que pour 62 familles, en avait plus de 300."[74]

Other statistics collected by the Greek government support those of the French and suggest that the population of the district was rapidly increasing. In February of 1830, Konstantinos Ramfos, the Greek provisional commander of the fort of Neokastro (Anavarin-i cedid), reported

69. See Chapter 1 concerning this revolt (the so-called Orlov rebellion) and both Turkish and Greek casualties. See also Finlay 1877, vol. 5, pp. 249–262; Dakin 1972, p. 17; Bory de Saint-Vincent 1836, pp. 123, 129; Rulhière 1807, pp. 454–472. On Ottoman military movements in Trifylia and the recapture of Anavarin-i cedid, see Gregoriadis 1934, pp. 64–67. The French mercantile house of Jean-Louis Éméric lost 1,660 *grosia* (*kuruşes*) at Anavarin-i cedid as a result of predations by Greek insurrectionists (Kremmydas 1972, p. 92). Twenty thousand Greeks from the Morea are said to have fled to the Venetian (Ionian) islands (Rulhière 1807, p. 472).

70. Woodhouse 1965, pp. 21–22; Bessan 1835. İbrahim Pasha and his father, Mehmet Ali of Egypt, were generally defiant of the Porte and planned, after capturing the Morea, to use it as a base for dominating trade in the eastern Mediterranean. On their campaigns in the Morea, see Sayyid Marsot 1984, pp. 206–208; Sabry 1930, chap. 2; Kotsonis 1999.

71. See Bennet, Davis, and Zarinebaf-Shahr 2000, pp. 354–355 and 360–363, regarding the effects of İbrahim Pasha's presence on settlements in Anavarin.

72. Puillon de Boblaye and Virlet 1833–1834, p. 85.

73. See Kapodistrias 1987, pp. 172–173, table 17. The total of 336 families is the same as that reported by the Expédition scientifique, and the names and number of settlements are the same. There are very slight differences in the figures for three places: Kato Kremmydia (eight families), Ano Kremmydia (seven families), and Ano Papouli (four families).

74. By "Navarin," the French mean the new town that had grown up around the small port north of the fortress of Anavarin-i cedid. Kapodistrias also recognized that the data required revision already in 1831, owing to an influx of population to larger cities. Certain other figures also seemed to the Expédition scientifique to be suspect, perhaps the result of intentional undercounting of individuals in an attempt to evade taxation. Firsthand observations by members of the Expédition scientifique can be employed to some extent to correct such biases, albeit in an anecdotal manner.

TABLE 4.4. POPULATION OF THE DISTRICT OF NAVARINO, 1829

Settlement	Families	Individuals (4.75/Family)*	Individuals (4.0/Family)**	Increase/Decrease since 1716
Navarin	62	295	248	+128
Pyla	20	95	80	+28
Zaïmogli	15	71	60	-24
Lézaga	9	43	36	+36
Gouvalavoros	8	38	32	+32
Skhinolaka and Djalova	4	19	16	+16
Nikléna	17	81	68	+48
Kato-Krommydi	7	33	28	+28
Apano-Krommydi	4	19	16	+16
Kato-Papouli	8	38	32	-8
Apano-Papouli	8	38	32	+32
Platanos	5	24	20	+8
Koukounara	3	14	12	0
Alikhotsa	3	14	12	-4
Skaminga	28	133	112	+44
Maniaki	27	128	108	+100
Styliano	4	19	16	-8
Pispisia	12	57	48	0
Agorélitsa	28	133	112	-16
Mouzousta	27	128	108	+28
Pétrokhori	15	71	60	+60
Pisaski	9	43	36	-16
Souman-Aga	7	33	28	-20
Hassan-Aga	5	24	20	-16
Rhoustem-Aga	1	5	4	-24
Misdras	0	0	0	?
Nassa	0	0	0	?
Kondinou	0	0	0	?
Rhomano	0	0	0	0
Khourou	0	0	0	-8
Levko	0	0	0	0
Total	336	1,596	1,344	+460

Sources: Data from TT880 and Puillon de Boblaye and Virlet 1833–1834, pp. 65–66, 85.
Note: Increases and decreases are calculated using a multiplier of four for the *ispence* figures in TT880, and an estimate of a family size of 4.0 individuals for the figures from Puillon de Boblaye and Virlet 1833–1834. On the approximate nature of the estimates for 1716, see the notes to Table 4.1.
*Assumes family size averaging 4.75 individuals.
**Assumes family size averaging 4.0 individuals.

2,739 individuals in the district, or about 575 families, if one calculates using the ratio of 4.75 individuals per family employed by the Expédition scientifique.[75]

The overall distribution of non-Muslim settlement in the district during this period was in the long term not greatly changed prior to the establishment of the modern Greek state. Of all settlements recorded in TT880, only Alafine (4) and Huri (12) were completely depopulated by 1829 (Table 4.3, Fig. 4.1.b, d). Reduction in the non-Muslim population appears to have been most severe in the lowlands around Osman Ağa and near Anavarin-i cedid, including Alafine (4), Ali Hoca (1), Osman Ağa

75. Loukatos 1984, p. 219, n. 1.

(15), Küçük Pisaski (14), Hasan Ağa (5), Rustem Ağa (6), Zaimzade (29), and Huri (12), areas that are known to have been targeted by the rampaging Egyptian troops of İbrahim Pasha.[76] The number of villages (37, including Navarino itself) that Pouqueville assigns to Anavarin is considerably higher than the 21 that were occupied in the time of TT880 (Table 4.3) and is the same as the number reported in his second edition; his list does not differ appreciably from the list of 31 toponyms (including deserted settlements) published by the Expédition scientifique (Table 4.3, Fig. 4.1:c, d).[77] Where it is possible to determine the location of the additional settlements, they seem to represent expansion from existing villages: Babali probably lay near Koukounara; whereas Caramanoli, Koudinou, Loutro, and Micréna were located near the Papoulias.[78] New settlements were founded at Gouvalachori (attested as Gouvalovoros or Sgrapa) and at Shinolakka, both near modern Yialova; at Romanou; and at Vrysomylos, near modern Vromoneri, below Gargaliani.[79]

In contrast, between 1821 and 1828 the entire Muslim population of the district departed or was eliminated. In 1821 many Turks from Kyparissia had taken refuge in the fortress of Anavarin-i cedid, along with Turks from Anavarin. Greek besiegers agreed in articles of capitulation that the Turks would be transported to safety in either Egypt or Tunis, but an altercation occurred in the course of the evacuation and the resulting melée ended in a general massacre. Men, women, and children were slaughtered or left to die on an islet in the harbor.[80] Although Anavarin was recaptured by the Ottomans in 1825, in the fall of 1828 the evacuation of the army of İbrahim Pasha by the French general Nicolas-Joseph Maison removed the last Turks from Anavarin. These and similar events that occurred elsewhere during the Greek Revolution resulted in the massacre or emigration of virtually the entire Turkish population of the Morea and paved the way for the ethnic homogenization of the area under the aegis of the modern Greek state.[81]

76. Bory de Saint-Vincent (1836, pp. 179, 158–159, 191) describes Zaimzade, Pile, and Lefku as completely deserted as a result of İbrahim's campaign. More generally, with regard to the campaigns of İbrahim in the area of Anavarin, see Kotsonis 1999, esp. chaps. 3 and 4.

77. See Pouqueville 1826–1827, vol. 6, p. 73; Puillon de Boblaye and Virlet 1833–1834, p. 85.

78. For Babali, cf. Chapter 3, p. 137, n. 93, s.v. Kurd Bey (36). Karamanoli (i.e., Caramanoli) is the former name for modern Glyfada (Georgacas and McDonald 1967, 91/179.2606; and see Chap. 3, p. 129, s.v. Other Papla [20], apparently distinct, in Pouqueville's source, from Cato-Papoulia). For Kondinou (Georgacas and McDonald 1967, 46/179.3212), see Chapter 3, p. 135, n. 83, s.v. Avarniçe (30); for Loutro, see Chapter 3, p. 129, s.v. Papla (19);

and for Micréna, see Georgacas and McDonald 1967, 91.4803 (Μίκραινα), in the vicinity of Karamanoli.

79. For Gouvalovoros, see Chapter 3, p. 124, s.v. Karunihuri (11); for Shinolakka, Chapter 3, p. 138, s.v. Tupçin (37); for Romanou, Chapter 3, pp. 121, 122, 139, s.vv. Rustem Ağa (6), Rum Bağ (8), and Other Yufiri (40); for Vrysomylos, Georgacas and McDonald 1967, 51/52.1221β (Βρυσόμυλος). It is probable that Pouqueville's Niochori represents Karunihuri (11), and the Calivia may refer to wooden structures near the harbor of Anavarin-i cedid.

80. Gordon 1832, pp. 230–231; Frantzis 1839, pp. 399–400; Finlay 1971, pp. 214–215. Baltas (1990, p. 148) says that 500 armed men and 234 women, children, and elderly surrendered. See also Gregoriadis 1934, pp. 100–104, where the details of the surrender are discussed and original

documents describing it are reproduced. Firsthand descriptions of the siege and the surrender of the Turkish garrison are described in official reports addressed to the Greek Parliament that are published in Anonymous 1857, pp. 445–448.

81. See Finlay 1877, vol. 6, pp. 139–140, 152. Finlay reported that during the period between March 28 and April 22, 1821, alone, an estimated 10,000–15,000 Muslims were slaughtered in every part of the Morea, and that 3,000 farmhouses were destroyed to make it impossible for those who had fled to fortresses to return to the countryside. Finlay records many other exterminations of Muslims during the Greek rebellion. Perhaps as many as 20,000 or more Muslims were killed by Greek revolutionaries. The evidence is summarized in McCarthy 1995, pp. 10–12.

THE ECONOMY OF THE DISTRICT OF ANAVARİN

Anavarin, although not one of the major commercial centers of 18th-century Greece, was integrated into a broader Mediterranean economy, and it is clear from TT880 that some of the crops grown there were marketed already at the beginning of the 18th century.[82] The text of TT880 also suggests which crops were sources of cash, as market values are supplied for certain products, although olives are the only agricultural product specifically said to have been exported.[83] At the beginning of the 19th century, additional cash crops can be added to the list: Pouqueville notes grain, vermilion, maize, cheese, wool, silk, tobacco leaves, oil, and goat hides.[84] Leake includes some of these products: "Six or seven hundred barrels of oil in good years, some vermilion, tobacco, and goat-skins."[85] It is worth noting that several export crops recorded a century later by Pouqueville or Leake (including silk, maize, and tobacco) are not attested in TT880.[86] Nor does rice appear, although it is mentioned by Gell.[87]

In addition to marketed products, travelers describe mercantile activities like those mentioned at the beginning of this chapter. According to Leake, at the beginning of the 19th century, trade was controlled by a single Greek archon, Yioryios Ikonomopoulos. Both Leake and Gell were entertained in his house during their visits to Anavarin. Greeks also served as consuls and consular agents for various foreign powers. Castellan mentions a Greek consul of France at Anavarin.[88] Gell met there an English consular agent from Arkadiye (Kyparissia), a Ragusan consul based at Modon, and a doctor with French sympathies who was in the pay of Russia.[89]

82. See also Bennet, Davis, and Zarinebaf-Shahr 2000, pp. 353, 376, on the participation of the residents of the *varış* of Anavarin-i cedid in external trade in the 18th century. Under the Venetians, export (except to Venice) was largely forbidden until 1704, although the free sale and export of grain from one's own property had been allowed in the territory of Navarino after 1699; see also Davies 2004, p. 82. In 1716 the total of customs dues collected at the port of Anavarin-i cedid was lower than at other major ports of the Morea; see Chapter 1. For Patras (Balye Badre) as a major port in the region in the 18th and 19th centuries, see, e.g., Wagstaff and Frangakis-Syrett 1992; Frangakis-Syrett and Wagstaff 1996.

83. It is safe to assume that *palamud* (acorns; *velanidia* in Greek) were also harvested as a source of revenue; see Chapter 2, İskarminke (46). It may be of relevance that the ridge overlooking the village of İskarminke (now called

Metamorfosi) bears the toponym Velanidies (Βελανιδιές, oak trees). Later in the 18th century (ca. 1786), an anonymous French report recorded local production in Anavarin (apparently not specifically for export) of 1,000 *kile*s of wheat, 1,500 *kile*s of maize, 100 *kile*s of barley, 1,500 barrels of olive oil, and 500 *okka*s of wax; see Belia 1978, p. 285.

84. Pouqueville 1820–1821, vol. 5, p. 41; Leake glosses vermilion as the Greek πρινοκόκκι, i.e., cochineal, an insect, when dried, employed in the production of scarlet dye. Pouqueville says: "Je suivrai, dans cette partie de ma narration, qui ne comprend que les produits livrés au commerce intérieur et extérieur" (1820–1821, vol. 5, p. 24).

85. Leake 1830, p. 401.

86. Although there is a reference to a silk workshop in TT880 at Osman Ağa (15), and we are told elsewhere that silk had in the past been produced, none is listed as "revenue." Maize is first present in a pollen core from nearby Osmanaga Lagoon, in a layer of the

18th century according to radiocarbon dating (Zangger et al. 1997, p. 595). Venetian documents mention tithes of maize in the districts of Modon and Anavarin (Navarino), but not specifically in the latter; see Davies 2004, p. 80.

87. Gell 1817, p. 51. See Bennet, Davis, and Zarinebaf-Shahr 2000, p. 361.

88. Castellan 1808, p. 98.

89. Gell 1823, pp. 6, 11, 12. French consular sources provide information about earlier mercantile activities at Anavarin (Kremmydas 1972): Anavarin-i cedid was one of the busiest ports in the Morea in the 18th century (pp. 27, 30); French vice-consuls represented French interests there (pp. 42–43, 52, 68), including those of a mercantile house (pp. 92, 276–278); the district exported substantial quantities of grain (especially between 1726 and 1749) and wax (pp. 191–195), but a Greek merchant, Hristos Mermigkas, went bankrupt there in 1754 (pp. 300–301).

Mazra*c*as, Çiftliks, and Karyes

Because Anavarin had a predominantly agricultural base, it is necessary to examine in detail the rural infrastructure and means of agricultural production that existed in the district in 1716 if we are to understand how the local economy functioned. Three types of agricultural property are registered in TT880: *mazra*c*as*, *çiftliks*, and *karyes* (Fig. 3.2).

In general Ottoman usage, a *mazra*c*a* is a piece of agricultural property that possesses attributes needed to support a settlement, but is abandoned.[90] *Mazra*c*a* "means in general arable land, a field; as used in the Ottoman survey registers, it designates a periodic settlement or a deserted village and its fields.... Usually a *mazra*c*a* has fixed boundaries. A *mazra*c*a* might have gained over time a few families of settlers, but would still be registered as a *mazra*c*a*.... Every *mazra*c*a* is referred to by a specific name which often reveals its origin or first possessor."[91]

Nineteen of the 49 properties registered in the district of Anavarin were classified as *mazra*c*as*. No buildings were recorded at any except the *mazra*c*a* of Rudiye (25), where there was a "tower in ruin." In no *mazra*c*a* are there listed *reaya* who pay *ispence;* all presumably were uninhabited or abandoned. The *reaya* of neighboring villages cultivated the lands of most (12 of 19).[92] The yields or revenues of *mazra*c*as* were in some instances combined with those of nearby properties for a purpose related to the collection and assignment of revenue from them, as they had been for tithe auctions under Venetian rule.[93] Both properties need not have been in the possession of the same cultivators. For example, a note in the margin indicates that the revenues of Rudiye (25) and Melis (26) should be combined, but the former is a possession of Anavarin-i cedid (35) and the latter belongs to Pile (31).

In instances where the produce of a *mazra*c*a* is combined with that of another property (e.g., Rum Bağ [8], Karunihuri [11], Rotsi [18], and Tursun [38]), it seems reasonable to assume that its lands were cultivated, even if the identity of its cultivators is not recorded in TT880. It is not, however, clear that all *mazra*c*as* were cultivated. The fields of Tristena (45) "used to be cultivated by the monks of Ayu Yurki monastery," but we are not told who, if anyone, is currently farming them. Nor are we informed that anyone is currently cultivating Ayanu (44), because the annotation to that effect was struck through on the document. One *mazra*c*a* (Other Yufiri [40]) certainly is not being worked, as we are specifically told that it used to be cultivated by the *reaya* of Hasan Ağa (5), but "is empty now." And some of the land of Ğuli (24) is said to be uncultivated.

Nine *mazra*c*as* had become *çiftliks* at some time before TT880 but were not inhabited in 1716. Most of these properties have two names: first

90. See also Chapter 1.

91. *EI²*, vol. 6, pp. 959–961.

92. The *reaya* of Ğarğalian cultivated Aşağı Katu (3); the *reaya* of Hasan Ağa (5), Petrehuri (7); the *reaya* of Furiçi in Modon, Kirmiti (21); the *reaya* of İklina (23), Ğuli (24); the *reaya* of Anavarin-i cedid (35), Rudiye (25),

Arkadianu (32), Deli Ahmed (33), and Usta Musli (41); the *reaya* of Pile (31), Melis (26); the *reaya* of Kurd Bey (36), Yufiri (27); the *reaya* of an unreadable name (Pispitse/Pisitse), Avarniçe (30); and the *reaya* of Fulke in Arkadiye had cultivated Ayanu (44).

93. Davies 2004, p. 81, table 3.

a traditional local non-Turkish name, then usually an Ottoman personal male name, plus the term *çiftlik*.[94]

Twenty-four of the 49 properties in Anavarin were registered only with the classification of *çiftlik*. Sixteen of these were settled in 1716, and the majority of the non-Muslim population of the district lived in them (179 of those who paid *ispence*, about 64%).[95] The number of men registered in one *çiftlik* ranges from 2 to 32 (2–21 after the conversion of Ağurliçe [42] to a *karye*). Eight *çiftlik*s were uninhabited.[96]

*Çiftlik*s in the lowlands north of the Bay of Navarino and in the vicinity of Anavarin-i cedid were particularly likely to be uninhabited.[97] We have already seen in this chapter that some of the depopulation of this area occurred while Anavarin was under Venetian rule. The text of TT880 also hints that there had been a decline in the extent of arable cultivation in the district. Although in 1716 the lowlands around the Bay of Navarino were cultivated by farmers based in the villages that ringed the coastal plain, comments on agricultural affairs in TT880 point to an underutilization of resources there and elsewhere.[98] Such a state of affairs may in part be a result of the immediate effects of the war between Venice and the Ottomans in 1685.

This situation may also have been aggravated by the Venetian retreat in 1715, since arable land at Petrehuri (7) and Lefku or Tavarne (39) had been cultivated by a "Frank," and there was Venetian property at İskarminke (46). But in other instances, *çiftlik*s may have been deserted already. For example, Avarniçe or Haci Hasan *çiftlik* (30), even though registered as a *karye* in 1512–1520 (TT80), was abandoned by 1689. Similarly, although in TT880 it is said that at Hasan Ağa (5), "6 pairs of oxen were used when the *çiftlik* was in good condition. Now only 3 pairs suffice," this land may have been underutilized already at the beginning of the Venetian occupation, as the same number of oxen (i.e., three pairs) are recorded for Hasan Ağa in Venetian documents.

Individuals (*nefer*s) resident on *çiftlik*s are always described as *ortakçıyan* (sharecroppers). The first part of the entry for each *çiftlik* consists of a description of goods not in the possession of the sharecroppers, that is, state property that the holder of the *çiftlik* controlled. Real property is

94. These include Nase or Memi Ağa (17), Kirmiti or Sefer Hoca (21), Ğuli or Mehmed Ağa (24), Rudiye or Kurd Ali Ağa (25), Melis or Derviş Kethüda (26), Avarniçe or Haci Hasan (30), Arkadianu or Müfti (32), and Deli Ahmed (33). At least two of these properties, Ğuli and Deli Ahmed, were explicitly called *seguolatii* (i.e., *çiftlik*s) by the Venetians: Davies 2004, p. 99, and ASV, Archivio Grimani ai Servi, b.28, f.859r; b.52/152, f.256r. See also Panayiotopoulos 1987, p. 226, for the appearance of Ğuli in the 1689 census. The name Denmusarin (18) is of uncertain origin. Nase or Memi Ağa (17) and Rotsi or Denmusarin (18) are

near Pispitsa (16); Ğuli or Mehmed Ağa (24) is near İklina (23); the others are very near Anavarin-i cedid. Another *mazraᶜa*, Tristena (45), was reclassified as a *çiftlik* by the addition of a note in its heading after the composition of TT880.

95. Two of the 24 *çiftlik*s—Ağurliçe (42), with 32 adult men, and Muzuste (43), with 20—were later registered as *karye*s, reducing the percentage of *ispence*-paying men residing on *çiftlik*s to 45 percent. Addition of the 9 *mazraᶜa*s that had become *çiftlik*s yields a total of 33 *çiftlik*s in the district.

96. Has (9); Azake (10); Budran, listed under the *kale* of Anavarin-i atik

(13); Other Papla or Ağaku (20); Muçaçu or Muslihuddin (34); Kurd Bey (36); Tupçin (37); Lefku or Tavarne (39).

97. Has (9); Budran, listed under the *kale* of Anavarin-i atik (13); Kurd Bey (36); Tupçin (37); and Lefku or Tavarne (39).

98. Rustem Ağa (6) "used to require 10 pairs of oxen for plowing when under Muslim rule. Now some parts are uncultivated, and the *çiftlik* only requires 6 pairs of oxen." At Kukunare (22), Ğuli (24), and Elyas Ağa (28), some areas are uncultivated. Muçaçu (34) "has turned into a forest and wilderness," and at Has (9), 500 olive trees are uncultivated.

listed first, structures (houses and towers) and their dimensions as well as furniture. A list of presses and mills follows, sometimes with comments on their condition or with indications that the mills are in use seasonally or all year long. The size of vineyards (*bağ*s) and orchards (*bağçe*s) are recorded in *dönüm*s,[99] whereas fruit trees and olive trees are counted individually. Arable fields (*tarla*s) are also sometimes recorded in *dönüm*s or, more commonly, in *çift*s.[100] We are not told who the current owners of *çiftlik*s are, although the names of the *çiftlik*s themselves imply Turkish ownership at some point in the past, possibly because the Turkish owners were not physically present at the time of the survey.

The second part of each entry consists of a list of the non-Muslim male residents of the *çiftlik,* and a census of grain fields (always measured in *çift*s), real estate, livestock, and beehives in their possession. Finally, TT880 records revenue *(hasil)* from the landholding, not in cash but in the form of a list of taxable items. From this list it was presumably possible to calculate the amount of tax owed on each item.[101] It is explicitly stated in each entry that the tithe of grain is one-seventh. Mistakes, generally minor, were sometimes made in summing property to be listed as revenue.[102] It appears that the revenue was not collected in 1716 in order to facilitate recovery in the wake of the Ottoman reconquest.

It seems clear that all property within the *çiftlik,* except arable land, was calculated as revenue, whether the specific items belonged to the sharecroppers or not. The entry for Ağurliçe (42) is of particular importance in understanding how this was done. There the scribe wrote: "Before the conquest, the sharecroppers acquired permission to build a house from

99. The *dönüm* of Ottoman times is etymologically related to the Greek *stremma* (στρέμμα). Both words are derived from a verb "to turn" and refer to the back-and-forth motion of plowing a field. See also Lowry 2002, pp. 107–108, where a definition of the *dönüm* as 40 × 40 *arşun*s is accepted as a calque for the Byzantine *stremma* of 40 × 40 paces. The text of TT880 (Tristena [45]) seems also to define the *dönüm* as 40 × 40 paces (*adım*s), whereas the *kanunname* clearly defines it as 40 × 40 steps (*hatve*s). In this volume we calculate the size of the *dönüm* as 919.3 m² (1,600 square *arşun*s = [of 0.758 × 0.758 m]), not as 939.3 m², the figure used by Lowry (following Redhouse 1890, p. 928). See also İnalcık 1997, p. xxxviii, and more generally concerning Ottoman measures, İnalcık 1983 and Berov 1975.

100. A *çift* was a flexible unit of land measurement that referred hypothetically to the amount of land area that could be plowed by a *çift* (pair) of oxen in an agricultural season. It is the etymological equivalent of the Venetian

para di bo and Greek ζευγάριον. Although the size of a *çift* might vary drastically from one place to another according to local agricultural conditions and traditions (see below), it was necessary for administrators and farmers alike to reach some agreement regarding the notional average size of a *çift* in an area being registered for taxation. See Berov 1975, p. 24, regarding the customary Ottoman lack of precision in measuring land, other than gardens and vines, prior to the middle of the 19th century.

101. This practice differs considerably from that known from earlier *defter*s, including the 1512–1520 survey of this same district (TT80), in which the total amount of tax in *akçe*s is listed rather than the total quantities of taxable goods. Cf. also Balta 1989, 1997, pp. 86–96 (a register for Santorini dated 1731); and Lowry 2002 (a register for Limnos in 1490), where revenue is listed in cash.

102. E.g., in the *çiftlik* of Platne (2), almond trees are listed in an orchard, but do not appear in the list of revenue.

There are said to be 7 *dönüm*s of vineyard, but 15 *dönüm*s are listed as revenue. In some entries, oranges are listed separately, in others they are lumped together with lemons. At Rustem Ağa (6), 2 pigs are recorded as property of the *ortakçıyan,* but none is listed as revenue. For Has (9) and Azake (10), the actual amounts for revenue were omitted altogether, although blank entries for commodities were listed. There are 2 mulberry trees in the orchard of Küçük Pisaski (14), but 3 listed as revenue. At Papla (19), counts of olives, pears, and apples do not agree. At İklina (23), oranges and lemons are omitted from the revenue. At Elyas Ağa (28), 3 orange trees become 2. At Zaimzade (29), the sharecroppers own 64 beehives, but only 62 are listed. At Pile (31), 1 pig is not listed. Total revenues at Kurd Bey (36) do not agree for lemons and oranges or for walnuts. At Ağurliçe (42), 13 pigs are miscounted as 11. At Muzuste (43), the *reaya* have 11 pigs, but 16 are listed; on the other hand, they have 15 beehives, none of which is listed.

those in possession of the *çiftlik,* and they also established an orchard in front of the house."[103] This is the house and orchard that are listed at the beginning of the register for Ağurliçe. In the calculation of revenue at the end of the register, the trees in this orchard are distinguished from those that belong to sharecroppers. Here as elsewhere, the types of property owned by *reaya* are very limited: vineyards, olive trees, presses, and mills are invariably the property of the *çiftlik* holders, not the *reaya.*[104] Other types of property (e.g., beehives) may or may not belong to the sharecroppers. Ağurliçe is the only *çiftlik* for which sharecroppers are listed as owners of property other than houses, livestock, and beehives.[105] Also only at Ağurliçe are vineyards (80 *dönüm*s) explicitly said to belong to the sharecroppers in general. Other trees and vine trellises are listed under the names of individuals.

Houses of non-Muslims in *çiftlik*s are explicitly listed as property of individual sharecroppers only at Ağurliçe (42). At Küçük Pisaski (14) it is simply stated that "all these *reaya* have a house each," whereas for other *çiftlik*s, houses are not noted at all.[106] The small number of buildings recorded as state property and as belonging to the holder of the *çiftlik* in most cases would, however, have been insufficient to house the sharecroppers and their families who were resident in the *çiftlik.* It therefore seems safe to assume that the *reaya* had houses even where they are not listed. And it follows that only taxable property of the *reaya* in *çiftlik*s needed to be included in the *defter.*

Initially only four settlements in the district of Anavarin were described as *karye*s.[107] Three of these—İskarminke (46), Miniaki (47), and İstilianu (48)—were in the northeastern corner of the district, in uplands at some distance from the coastal plains around the Bay of Navarino. The fourth, Virviçe (49), was far to the north, in the valley of the Neda River.[108] Later, Ağurliçe (42) and Muzuste (43) were also registered as *karye*s, as indicated in the headings of TT880. Annotations also indicate that all *karye*s and the *mazra°a*s near them were later moved to Arkadiye, leaving *çiftlik*s and the *varış* of Anavarin-i cedid as the only non-Muslim settlements in the district of Anavarin.

103. The conquest here appears to refer to the Venetian conquest in 1686.

104. These distinctions are also reflected in statistics collected by the government of Kapodistrias (Kapodistrias 1987, pp. 172–173), systematically gathered soon after the Greek Revolution. Property is divided into private and national. For the former, vines, olive trees, herd animals, farming animals, and transport animals are listed. National property includes dry cultivated land, marshy land, rocky land, vines, domesticated olive trees, wild olive trees, fig trees, and other trees. There, almost all vines and olive trees are registered as state, rather than private, property, as they consisted of former Turkish possessions that had been nationalized by the Greek state (see McGrew 1985 for general discussion of the origin of the national lands in Greece and their subsequent disposition).

105. For the district of Navarino, the Kapodistrian census, conducted a century later, recorded private vines (71 *stremmata*) and olive trees (146) only at Ağurliçe (42). For Ağurliçe, TT880 lists 80 *dönüm*s of vines, 98 fruit trees, and 23 mulberry trees in the hands of the *reaya,* but no olive trees.

106. For Osman Ağa (15), 10 houses are simply listed. These may be those of the *reaya,* but this is not explicitly stated.

107. The word *karye* is used, other than in headings, only infrequently, and seemingly in a less technical sense: e.g., Kirmiti (21) is cultivated by the *reaya* of the *karye* of Furiçi (although we do not know Furiçi's official status, as it lay in the district of Modon), and two sharecroppers at Pile (31) farm land in the *karye* of Kurd Bey (36), which is registered as a *çiftlik* in TT880.

108. No Virviçe data appear on the maps in this chapter; the place is located far to the north, in Arkadia, but was attached administratively to Anavarin by the Turks for reasons we do not understand. See Chapter 3 for a discussion of the location of Virviçe.

The format of entries for *karye*s differs from that of *çiftlik*s in significant ways. Each entry begins with a list of residents of the village and of their property, and the *reaya* are not identified as *ortakçıyan*. *Karye*s are also the only entries that are not said in their headings to be *mîrî*, suggesting that such revenue was employed differently from that from *çiftlik*s. Property that was not in the hands of the *reaya* is always specified as such. For example, at İskarminke (46), "property of the Venetians that formerly belonged to Osman Ağazade" is listed under a separate heading. This heading *was* marked with an "m" for *mîrî*.[109] All property was included in revenue totals, whether it belonged to the *reaya* or to Turks. The exception is arable land, where, as for *çiftlik*s, only that over which the *reaya* held usufruct is listed.[110]

In the case of *çiftlik*s, the state retained its rights to assign as *timar*s tithes on agricultural production and income from the *ispence*.[111] Because for *karye*s only the income from properties of individual Turks or Venetians was designated as *mîrî*, at the time TT880 was written there is no indication that other income from the *karye*s had yet been assigned to a beneficiary.[112] Many properties are said previously to have been "*timar*s" or "*timar*s of men." They are located in all parts of Anavarin and include *karye*s, *çiftlik*s, and *mazra'a*s.[113] But when the *timar* system was reinstituted in 1716, only income from *çiftlik*s was distributed.[114]

The Agricultural Products of Anavarin

The size and spatial distribution of crops cultivated in Anavarin can be deduced from information in the text of TT880. Discussion here will concentrate on those agricultural products that are likely to have offered a significant source of revenue from surplus production. It is important to note that TT880, like other Ottoman *defter*s, is not a complete inventory of agricultural products. Beef cattle, draft oxen, donkeys, horses, and mules are not listed.[115] Also, in TT880, unlike in other *defter*s, the only grain registered is wheat. Entries for barley, millet, and oats were

109. The annotator who added fractions to the manuscript (see below) seems to have been confused in the case of İskarminke, first counting the number of *çift*s that belonged to the *reaya*, then striking out this figure and substituting the sum of *çift*s that belonged to the *reaya* and the three *çift*s that had been in Venetian possession. See also p. 105, n. 85.

110. In Miniaki (47), 8 *çift*s of land do not belong to the *reaya*, and in İstilianu (48), 12 *çift*s do not.

111. See Chapter 1 concerning *timar* lists compiled in 1716 subsequent to the reconquest of the Morea. See also the *kanunname* in Chapter 2 (paragraph 7), where it is clear that Muslim property is to be registered as *mîrî*, and

is to be held in escrow *(mevkuf)* by the state on behalf of individual Muslim property holders who have not yet returned to the Morea. On the classification of property as *mîrî*, see further İslamoğlu 2000, pp. 16–19, 27–28, 31.

112. One possibility is that these *karye*s ultimately would have been assigned to pay the expenses of the provincial administration and then would have been classified as *hass*es. It is also important to note that the situation described in TT880 was temporary. As Turks returned, they would have been assigned *çiftlik*s and *timar*s. See Chapter 1, where the return of the Ottoman population is discussed further.

113. *Karye*s include İskarminke (46), Miniaki (47), İstilianu (48), and Virviçe

(49). *Çiftlik*s include Has (9), Azake (10), Huri (12), Pispitsa (16), Papla (19), Other Papla (20), Kukunare (22), Elyas Ağa (28), Zaimzade (29), Kurd Bey (36), Tupçin (37), Lefku (39), Ağurliçe (42), and Muzuste (43). Two *mazra'a*s also formerly were *timar*s: Kirmiti (21) and Other Yufiri (40).

114. See Chapter 1 with regard to the villages in Anavarin from which income was assigned.

115. Lowry (2002, p. 117) notes: "So essential was [the yoke of cattle] to the Ottoman peasant that it was never taxed separately from the land." Horses, mules, and donkeys were clearly present on Limnos, but were not listed as taxed there either.

left blank, even though market values and sowing rates are given for these crops.[116]

TT880 also contains significant information about the prices of crops grown in the district. Much that has previously been published about market values in Ottoman Greece is anecdotal or is not specific to a particular time or place. The latter issue is especially problematic because prices of agricultural goods fluctuate wildly from one season to the next. Only rarely do we gain insight into such characteristics of the market from the accounts of travelers.[117] The average prices reported by consuls and other more informed individuals (Table 4.5), however, suggest that the prices for wheat recorded in TT880 (40–50 *akçes*/*kile*) were normal in markets in the Morea in the early 18th century. Such prices are quite close to those recorded by French consuls in Patras.

VINES

The Turkish word *bağ* (vineyard or garden) is used in TT880 to describe vineyards. In several instances it is explicitly stated that a given area of *bağ*, measured in *dönüm*s, will produce a weight of grapes that varies between 200 and 300 *vukiyye*s (256–384 kg).[118] Productivity on this order (278–418 kg per metric *stremma* of 1,000 m²) falls within ranges previously reported for preindustrialized agriculture in Greece. Allbaugh's figures for Crete suggest a range between 3,600 and 5,000 kilograms of grapes per hectare (i.e., 360–500 kg per *stremma*).[119] Van Wersch gives similar figures for Messenia: 350–700 kilograms of grapes per *stremma*.[120]

Just over a thousand *dönüm*s of vineyards are recorded in the district of Anavarin in 1716, far less than the amount of land that was devoted to this purpose in 1911 (Figs. 4.2, 4.3, Table 4.6), when 32 metric *stremmata* were in cultivation for table grapes, 3,342 for wine grapes, 13,761 for currants, and 260 for sultanas. There is no indication in TT880 as to the specific use of grapes that were grown.[121] Vine cultivation was practiced in 1716 in most parts of the district in 1716, except in the immediate vicinity

116. Venetian documents record wine, oil, wool, cheese, silk, kermes, wax, honey, wheat and other cereals as produced in the district. Venetian tithe auctions mention wheat, barley, oats, and millet, as well as maize, vegetables, oil, silk, and cotton. Duties on wine were of special importance; see Davies 2004, p. 84.

117. An important exception is the journal of Brue, interpreter of the French Embassy at the Porte at the time of the Ottoman reconquest of the Morea. He described how the prices of produce in the Morea rose dramatically in the late spring and summer of 1715 (see Table 4.5). As a foreigner, Brue also discovered that it was difficult to ensure that he would pay a fair market price (see Brue 1870,

p. 98, n. 1): "Quelque exhorbitant que paraisse le prix de l'orge, ainsi que je le passe icy et ci aprez, c'est pourtant un fait constant que les Turcs l'ont acheté à des prix bien plus considérables, ainsi qu'on peut s'en informer d'eux-mêmes, et que j'aurois esté obligé de l'acheter à ces-mêmes prix sans le secours de M. Mauro Cordato, premier interprète de la Porte, qui faisoit venir de l'orge des villages de la Morée au camp, et qui m'en fournissoit sur le même pied qu'il l'achettoit dans le tems qu'un yem ou mesure d'orge pour un cheval coûtoit quarante sols et au delà."

118. See İklina (23): "1 *dönüm* of vineyard produces 200 *vukiyye*s of grapes"; Ali Hoca (1), "1 vineyard of 1 *dönüm* produces 250 *vukiyye*s of . . .

grapes"; and Rustem Ağa (6), "vineyard: 1 *dönüm* produces 300 *vukiyye*s of . . . grapes."

119. Allbaugh 1953, p. 280, table M24.

120. Van Wersch 1972, p. 179.

121. There is no evidence in TT880 that any of these grapes were processed as raisins or currants, despite the flourishing export industry in these products in the Morea in the later 18th and 19th centuries. On the currant trade in the Morea, see Sutton in Wright et al. 1990, pp. 599–600; Wagstaff and Frangakis-Syrett 1992, p. 82. With regard to the processing of grapes, it is worth noting that the *kanunname* of 1716 translated at the beginning of Chapter 2 mentions dried grapes.

TABLE 4.5. PRICES RECORDED IN TT880 COMPARED WITH THOSE REPORTED IN ROUGHLY CONTEMPORARY SOURCES

Source	Price	Standardized Price	Date	Place
WHEAT				
Brue	4.0–20.0 *paras/yem*	48–240 *akçes/kile*	1715	Morea
Mantran		50–80 *akçes/kile*	17th century[a]	Istanbul
TT880	40.0–50.0 *akçes/kile*		1716	Anavarin
Kremmydas	0.7 *para/okka*	46 *akçes/kile*	1708	Balye Badre (Patras)
Kremmydas	1.1 *paras/okka*	73 *akçes/kile*	1709	Balye Badre
Kremmydas	0.5 *para/okka*	33 *akçes/kile*	1717	Balye Badre
Svoronos	2.0 *piastres/kile*	60 *akçes*	Sept. 1713	Selânik (Thessaloniki)
Svoronos	4.0 *piastres/kile*	120 *akçes*	Dec. 1713	Selânik
Svoronos	9.0 *piastres/kile*	270 *akçes*	May 1714	Selânik
Svoronos	3.0 *piastres/kile*[b]	120 *akçes*	1719	Selânik
BARLEY				
Mantran		20–30 *akçes*	17th century[c]	Istanbul
TT880		30 *akçes*	1716	Anavarin
COTTON				
Svoronos		35 *akçes/okka*	1717	Selânik
Frangakis-Syrett	48.0 *livres/quintal*[d]	49 *akçes/okka*	1715	İzmir
Frangakis-Syrett	34.0 *livres/quintal*	34 *akçes/okka*	1716	İzmir
Frangakis-Syrett	36.0 *livres/quintal*	36 *akçes/okka*	1717	İzmir
TT880	9.0–10.0 *akçes/lidre*[e]	27–30 *akçes/okka*	1716	Anavarin
OIL				
TT880	10.0 *akçes/vukiyye*[f]	10 *akçes/okka*	1716	Anavarin
Kremmydas	12.3 *paras/okka*	37 *akçes/okka*	1718	Marseilles
Kremmydas	11.1 *paras/okka*	33 *akçes/okka*	1719	Marseilles

Sources: Brue 1870; Frangakis-Syrett 1992, p. 318, table 9; Kremmydas 1972, p. 210, table xxvi; Mantran 1962, pp. 165, 273; Svoronos 1956, p. 78, table 1. Frangakis-Syrett reports prices for cotton for all years 1700–1789, drawn from the Archives de la Chambre de Commerce de Marseilles. It is unclear if the prices refer to market value in İzmir or in Marseilles. Kremmydas gives relevant comparanda extracted from French consular reports. In the case of oil, prices are taken from charts compiled by the directorate of commerce at Marseilles and reflect the value of the oil in the markets of Marseilles (see Kremmydas 1972, p. 213, table xxvii). Data are not available from consular reports for markets of the Morea, where oil was doubtless much less expensive. In the case of wheat, the difference between prices in the Morea and in Marseilles varied between three and five times the base value of the crop. Prices in Svoronos 1956, p. 78, table 1, were extracted from consular reports and reflect average conditions in the markets of Selânik.

[a] Averaging 60 akçes in the last quarter of the 17th century.

[b] The *kile* here is the *kile* of Selânik, which varied in weight between 80 and 84 *okka*s, i.e., equivalent to about 4 *kile*s of Istanbul, the unit of measure employed for grain in TT880; see Svoronos 1956, pp. 87, 383.

[c] Averaging 25 *akçe*s.

[d] Three *livres tournois* = 1 *kuruş*; 1 *quintal* = 100 pounds of 498.5 g.

[e] Prices are given as 3 *paras* (i.e., 9 *akçe*s) per *lidre* and 10 *akçe*s per *lidre* of 133 *dirhem*s; 1 *okka* = 400 *dirhem*s. There are ca. 3 *lidre*s in an *okka*. See also İnalcık 1983, where the *lidre* is described as equivalent to 100 *dirhem*s.

[f] A *vukiyye* is equivalent to an *okka*.

TABLE 4.6. RAW PRODUCTION FIGURES FOR PRODUCTS MAPPED IN FIGURES 4.2–4.9

Property Number	Vines, 1716 (in Dönüms)	Vines for Wine, 1911 (in Stremmata)	Olives, 1716 (in Trees)	Olives, 1911 (in Stremmata)	Mulberry, 1716 (in Trees)	Cotton, 1716 (in Lidres)*	Flax, 1716 (in Vukiyyes)*
1	32	—	400	—	5	50	10
2	15	70	50	—	25	—	—
3	—	—	—	—	—	—	—
4	1	—	474	—	—	—	5
5	—	—	395	—	—	—	15
[Tragana]**	—	87	—	36	—	—	—
6	10	—	465	—	9	—	—
7	4	20	—	15	—	—	—
8	—	—	—	—	—	—	—
[Romanou]**	—	30	—	20	—	—	—
9	100	—	1,500	—	40	—	—
10	5	—	166	—	2	—	—
11	—	—	—	—	—	—	—
12	12	—	210	—	—	—	—
13	—	—	—	—	—	—	—
14	35	—	1,000	—	3	—	25
15	300	500	1,903	3,000	2,100	100	40
16	—	131	350	—	25	—	20
17	—	—	53	—	—	—	—
18	—	—	—	—	—	—	—
19	25	135	139	300	6	30 vukiyyes	—
20	—	—	30	—	2	—	—
21	—	195	2	116	—	—	—
22	—	200	50	100	12	15 vukiyyes	—
23	40	100	400	10	40	60	25
24	7	—	50	—	4	—	—
25	—	—	—	—	—	—	—
26	—	—	—	—	—	—	—
27	—	—	—	—	—	—	—
28	—	10	1	—	11	—	—
29	—	30	—	—	6	30	—
30	—	—	—	—	—	—	—
31	20	100	139	200	4	100	40
32	—	—	—	—	—	—	—
33	—	—	—	—	—	—	—
34	—	—	—	—	5	—	—
35	—	50	—	200	1	—	—
36	10	10	—	—	6	—	—
37	—	100	—	50	12	—	—
[Sgrappa]**	—	80	—	100	—	—	—
38	—	—	—	—	2	—	—
39	—	—	1	—	1	—	—
40	—	—	—	—	—	—	—
41	—	—	—	—	—	—	—
42	160	559	510	273	30	—	—
43	90	264	53	71	4	—	—
44	—	—	—	—	—	—	—
45	30	—	25	—	—	—	—
46	33	154	25	236	18	—	—
47	—	99	—	—	—	—	—
48	18	50	19	—	—	—	—
49	46	—	27	—	11	60	30 lidres
Totals	993	2,974	8,437	4,727	2,384	535	190

Source: Data for 1911 are drawn from Ἐθνικὴ Στατιστικὴ Ὑπηρεσία τῆς Ἑλλάδος 1911.
* Except where indicated.
** Place-names in brackets are not mentioned in TT880. They are here listed following the settlement registered in TT880 to which they are closest geographically.

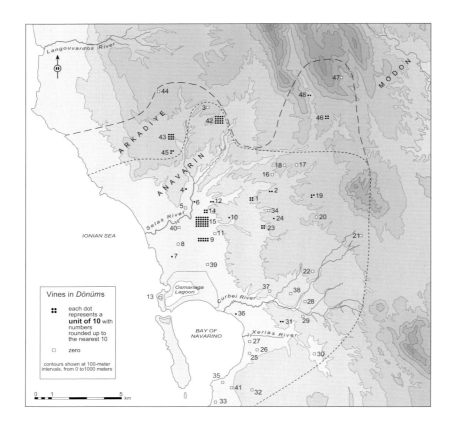

Figure 4.2. Distribution of vines according to TT880. D. K. Harlan and R. J. Robertson

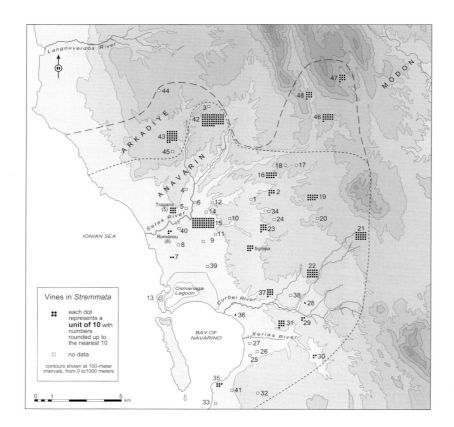

Figure 4.3. Distribution of vines in 1911. D. K. Harlan and R. J. Robertson

of the *kale* of Anavarin-i cedid, although many individual settlements had no vineyards. In most settlements, the *reaya* were cultivating between one-third of a *dönüm* and eight *dönüm*s of vineyards per person.

Only Osman Ağa (15) stands out as exceptional in this picture of small-scale production. Farmers there were cultivating an average of about 30 *dönüm*s per individual (300 *dönüm*s in all). This is a level of production so extraordinarily high that it would have demanded additional labor.[122] The description of the nearby Has *çiftlik* (9) as having 100 *dönüm*s of vineyard suggests that there was an emphasis on viticulture elsewhere in the area of Osman Ağa.[123]

On the basis of Allbaugh's figures for Crete,[124] it can be estimated that about 97 kilograms of grapes were consumed per individual per annum. One *dönüm* of vineyard is thus likely to have provided, or nearly so, for the immediate needs of a family. Any settlement producing in excess of this sum would have had a surplus, but only at Osman Ağa (15) could that have been substantial: namely, the product of more than 280 *dönüm*s (i.e., between 56,000 and 84,000 *vukiyye*s), valued at an equivalent number of *akçe*s. In the district as a whole, as many as 725 *dönüm*s may have produced a product in excess of the needs of the *reaya,* with a value of roughly 145,000–220,000 *akçe*s.

OLIVE TREES

There is no evidence that sharecroppers on *çiftlik*s in Anavarin owned olive trees, and only a few examples are listed as property of the *reaya* in *karye*s. In all instances, the scribe has recorded the total number of "roots" (*dib*s) of olive trees.[125] More than 8,500 domestic trees are recorded in

122. H. Forbes comments (pers. comm.):

So 300 *dönüm*s would necessitate 900 man-days. There's a limited time in which the digging can be done, between the time the winter weather starts to improve and the time the vine buds start to break. . . . On Methana I doubt that there is more than a two-week window when digging can comfortably be done. . . . Even if vine-digging were worked differently and workers had a month to spend on it, 30 men would still be needed working flat out for a month. . . . Again the vintage leaves only a very limited time for harvesting the grapes. . . . Where would they draw the population to harvest something like 30 ha of grapes over the course of a few days, not to mention transport of the produce? . . . Aschenbrenner's data suggest 6 person days per stremma for harvest and transport.

For 300 *dönüm*s, that's some 1650 person days! . . . The amount of produce involved is vast. Since grapes do not keep and do not travel well, in what form were they sold/exported? If it was all made into wine, the '15 big earthenware jars' listed in the defter are not going to hold it all. . . . In addition, who is making the wine? The treading etc. is also time-consuming: there would need to be a work force separate from the harvesters to make the moustos and put it into barrels, *vel sim.* Or was it made into *petimezi* (syrup)?

123. The significance of the area of Osman Ağa for viticulture is reflected also in a Venetian document, where the most important area for vines appears to have been "Cassi"; 486 of 592 *zappade* of vines there were being worked in 1700 (Davies 2004, p. 107). At Osman Ağa itself, an additional 140 *zappade* are recorded. The actual numbers of vines recorded in TT880 as associ-

ated with Has ([9]: 100 *dönüm*s) and the adjacent *çiftlik* of Osman Ağa ([15]: 300 *dönüm*s) give a total in the two places that is 400 *dönüm*s (ca. 37 ha). It is possible that the extent of vines recorded by Venice is similar to that registered in TT880 (ca. 34 ha) if the Venetians were thinking of a *zappada* equivalent to 470 m², one-quarter of a large Venetian *stremma* of 1880 m² (see Davies 2004, p. 114, table 8, concerning the variable size of the *stremma*), or one-half of an Ottoman *dönüm* (Balta 1993, p. 53).

124. Allbaugh 1953, p. 384, table M28 (75.49 oke = 96.6 kg); cf. Wagstaff and Augustson 1982, p. 125, table 10.23, there reported as 75 kg instead of 75 okkas.

125. The word "roots" (*rizes* [ρίζες]) is also commonly used in Greek to describe olive trees, since one process by which olive orchards are propagated has involved grafting twigs of domestic trees to the roots of wild trees; see Foxhall 1990, chap. 4.

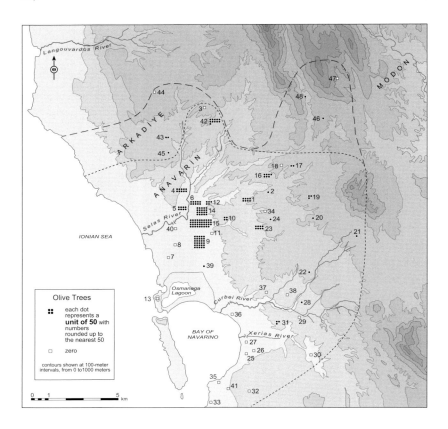

Figure 4.4. Distribution of olive trees according to TT880. D. K. Harlan and R. J. Robertson

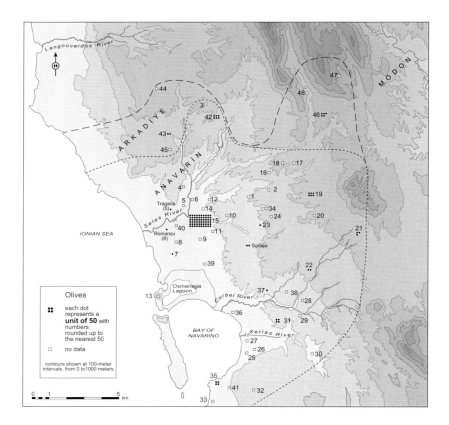

Figure 4.5. Distribution of olives in 1911. D. K. Harlan and R. J. Robertson

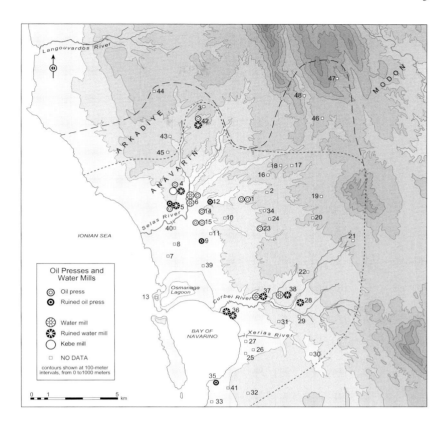

Figure 4.6. Distribution of oil presses and water mills according to TT880. R. J. Robertson

Anavarin. Another 500 wild trees are registered at Has (9).[126] But, as for vines, the olive trees enumerated in TT880 (Fig. 4.4, Table 4.6) are only a small fraction of the number cultivated in the same area in the early 20th century. In 1911 some 6,500 metric *stremmata* were planted in olive trees (Fig. 4.5), namely 52,000–65,000 trees. In 1716, some olives were cultivated virtually everywhere in Anavarin, but production was concentrated in the area between İklina (23) and modern Tragana, and was centered at Osman Ağa (15), where 1,903 trees were registered.[127] The same area was the center of olive production in 1911. This area of Anavarin also contained almost all of the oil presses attested in TT880 (Fig. 4.6).[128] All the

126. H. Forbes remarks (pers. comm.): "It is just possible that these are real wild olives awaiting grafting with domesticated scions. However, since the olive press is identified as being in ruin, it is more likely that these trees have been abandoned and left untended. Without regular pruning, abandoned olive trees put out suckers from the base of the wild tree below the graft, which slowly 'bleeds' plant nutrients away from the domesticated part of the tree until the domesticated part has died off and the whole tree has reverted to wild anyway. Hence wild and uncultivated could be the same thing."

127. Forbes remarks (pers. comm.): "If there are over 1900 olive trees, that means that each household must pick ca. 160 trees in an 'on' year. At 4 trees picked per family per day, which is highly optimistic if they are decent sized trees, this will take 40 days for each family. . . . If families have a *çift* of 40–50 *dönüm*s of arable land to cultivate as well, most of that will be sown in winter crops (barley, wheat, broad beans). . . . These winter crops are sown at about the same time as the olive harvest. . . . Certainly in terms of what I have seen for family farms on Methana, there is seriously far too much work implied in the *çiftlik* holdings for

12 normal families to fit into the time available."

128. Ali Hoca (1), Hasan Ağa (5), and Osman Ağa (15) each had two presses, although one is said to be "in ruin" at Hasan Ağa. Alafine (4), Rustem Ağa (6), Has (9) [in ruin], Huri (12) [in ruin], Küçük Pisaski (14), İklina (23), and Ağurliçe (42) each had one press. The only other olive press attested in the document, also said to be "in ruin," is in the *varış* of Anavarin-i cedid (35, item 107). Pispitsa (16), with 350 roots, a higher total than Huri's 210, is unusual in not having a press listed in TT880.

extant (i.e., nonruined) olive presses were clearly housed in structures, since dimensions are given for them, as they are for other structures in *çiftliks*.[129]

Information pertaining to recent olive cultivation in the Morea, gathered by Hamish Forbes and adjusted by Lin Foxhall, is particularly helpful in interpreting statements in TT880:

> The olive oil production statistics from Kranidhi, Southern Argolid, Greece which cover the 20 year period from 1960 to 1980 vividly show the variability in yield. These figures were collected from oil pressing establishments for statistical purposes, not for taxation, but they are nonetheless likely to be under-reported since they came from their recorded accounts. They suggest an average yield of around 2.6 kg oil per tree per olive harvest *(elaiona)* for the decade 1961–70, and 3.4 kg oil per tree per *elaiona* for the decade 1971–80. Ghiannakaris' statistics on olive production from Khalkis over a much shorter period (1976–1979) give an average annual return of around 780 kg fruit per ha = 1560 kg fruit per *elaiona*. At a fruit:oil ratio of 4–5:1, and allowing around 80–100 trees per ha this puts average oil production per *elaiona* at between 3.12 and 4.8 kg oil per tree.[130]

At first glance, it might appear that the productivity of olive trees in Anavarin in 1716 and in Messenia in the 20th century was substantially greater than in the southern Argolid in the 20th century. Aschenbrenner reported the following yields of oil (not fruit) per tree for a heavy harvest year in Messenia: large mature tree: 50 kilograms; medium (30–40 year) tree: 15–20 kilograms; small (15–30 year) tree: 7–15 kilograms.[131] The yields of olives and oil per tree reported in TT880 fall at the low end of Aschenbrenner's range. In two instances (Ali Hoca [1] and İklina [23]), a tree is said to yield 30 *vukiyye*s (38.4 kg) of olives; in one case (Rustem Ağa [6]), the figure is double that, 60 *vukiyye*s (76.8 kg) of olives per tree. Trees at Ali Hoca and İklina would thus have yielded 5.12 kilograms of oil, with those at Rustem Ağa producing double that amount, that is, 10.24 kilograms per tree.

Forbes suggests that the figures in TT880 are reasonable, if notional, estimates of the highest yield that a tree could produce. On the other hand, some of Aschenbrenner's statistics appear problematic to him:

> Different olive trees are bound to be of different sizes and different productivities. When you are working on a tree-by-tree basis, year in

129. Their locations on stream systems confirm that another type of mill (*asyab* without a modifier) is a water mill, although in this period *asyab* with a modifier could be applied to other types of mills or presses. See Chapter 2, p. 56, n. 17, where *asyab-i revğan* is used to describe an olive press; Balta 1997, pp. 86–96, where "windmills" on Santorini are called *asyab-i badi;* and Lowry 2002, p. 118, where "windmills" are *asiyab-i yelleri* and water mills are

asyab-i abi. The water mills at Alafine (4), Hasan Ağa (5), Rustem Ağa (6), and Ağurliçe (42) exploit the streams running toward the Osmanaga Lagoon north and south of the Englianos ridge. Rustem Ağa had one that was active and one in ruin, while those at Alafine, Hasan Ağa, and Ağurliçe were in ruin. At Alafine, there was a second mill, for felt *(kebe)*, probably a fulling mill. A second group of mills was associated with the valley systems entering the

Bay of Navarino near modern Yialova: Elyas Ağa (28), one, in ruin; Tupçin (37), one in ruin, one functioning; Tursun (38), one in ruin, one functioning; and Kurd Bey (36), two in ruin. The only other mills, a group of three functioning, are at Virviçe (49) in the Neda Valley.

130. Foxhall 1990, chap. 4.

131. Aschenbrenner 1972, p. 54, table 4-2.

and year out, you learn their potential productivities. What interests me is the fact that trees from two *çiftlik*s are given the same productivity figure and those from the third are given exactly double that—reality is unlikely to have been that simple. This makes me think that the figures are highly notional.

The recurring appearance of units of 30 also makes me suspicious: it seems to me that these are probably notional figures representing something else.[132] Another possibility is that 30 *vukiyye*s of olives is a notional time measurement, like a *merokamato* (wage) of vines—i.e., the number of vines that could be dug in a day. These notional time measurements for vines and land area turn up in cadasters from the time of the second Venetian occupation. I have to say, however, that I do not know of any example of the use of a notional time measurement to measure potential olive productivity.

An alternative explanation is that these fruit yield figures represent thinking in terms of how much oil could be produced. In the Southern Argolid, although it was quite difficult to get an idea of potential yields, I was sometimes quoted notional yield per tree figures in kilograms of oil, not fruit. The figures for yield in TT880 are all based on a basic unit of 7.5—which just happens to be the standard figure for the weight of fruit producing 1 *vukiyye* of oil. The most likely explanation for these figures in my view is that they represent some idea of the yield of oil, even though the yield of fruit is basically what is quoted.

I do not in any case think that the yields described are average yields. Greek farmers of my acquaintance tend to give maximum possible figures—the most that a tree or plot could give under the best possible conditions. This practice evidently goes back a long way—Pouqueville at one point gives yields of different varieties of wheat that he has been told about, using maxima. This information was plainly as he received it from informants. I have written about this problem of what farmers are actually working with when they mention yields.[133] Olive yields quoted are presumably for the alternate "on" years, not averaged out over both years of the olive production cycle.

Are the trees recorded in TT880 and those described by Aschenbrenner really that much more productive than others in Greece? Trees belonging to two of these *çiftlik*s produce a maximum of 30 *okades*[134] of fruit (4 *okades* of olive oil) and one produces a maximum of 60 *okades* of fruit (8 *okades*) oil. In the Southern Argolid the largest trees are claimed to produce some 100 kg of fruit. Taken at face value this is 78 *okades*, but since many of the elders who talked to me may have been thinking *oka* but saying *kilo*, 100 *okades* may be closer to what they meant. At a 4:1 or 5:1 extraction ratio (the current ratio in the area) this gives 20–25 *okades* of oil. Extrapolating from Aschenbrenner's oil per *stremma* figures for 1969 (evidently an "on" year) and trees per *stremma*, I get an average oil per tree range of 10–13 kg of oil.[135] On the other hand, Van Wersch gives oil yield per tree in 1961–63 as 3.0 kg, on average, with a range 2.5–15 kg.[136] The idea of 50 kg oil per tree is outside my experience.[137]

132. We were told in 1998 in an interview in the village of Mouzousta (Lefki) that a *kouveli* of 15 *okades* (for this term see n. 134 below) had been employed locally as a measure before the adoption of the metric system. This may well be the basic unit of measurement that lies behind the totals reported in TT880.

133. Forbes 1992, p. 100.

134. *Oka* (pl. *okades*) is a pre-metric Greek weight, equivalent to the Ottoman *okka*, and equal to 1.28 kg.

135. See Aschenbrenner 1972, table 4-2.

136. Van Wersch 1972, p. 179.

137. Pers. comm. We excerpt H. Forbes's remarks here with his permission.

TT880 is consistent in reporting a fruit-to-oil ratio for olives of 15 *vukiyye*s to 2 *vukiyye*s, that is, a ratio of 7.5:1, less efficient than modern olive-pressing. Forbes again comments: "I am fascinated by the poor extraction ratio of olives to oil—7.5:1 versus 4:1–6:1 in Aschenbrenner. This supports my argument that one reason for the low level of olive growing in, for example, the Southern Argolid before the 19th century was the inefficiency of olive presses."[138]

The amount of oil produced within the district apparently was in excess of the needs of local producers and consumers, not least because TT880 itself suggests that half of the olive crop was exported.[139] Trees in Anavarin in heavy harvests yielded sufficient olives to result in 4–8 *vukiyye*s (5.12–10.24 kg) of oil, 2–4 *vukiyye*s (2.56–5.12 kg) of which were retained locally. The 8,500 trees recorded in TT880 would thus have produced between 43,520 and 87,040 kilograms of oil in "on" years, and much less in "off" years. Since only half of the crop would have been available for local consumption (by ca. 1,124 persons [Table 4.1]), it is hard to avoid the conclusion that local oil consumption was on the low side, in comparison with estimates that have been made for other times and places.[140] In "on" years, 21,760–43,520 kilograms of exported oil would have had a market value of nearly 217,600–435,200 *akçe*s (at the price of 10 *akçe*s per *vukiyye* recorded in TT880).[141]

Cloth

Nearly 2,400 mulberry trees are registered in TT880 (Fig. 4.7, Table 4.6), 90 percent of them in the territory of Osman Ağa (15), where 1,500 trees planted in an orchard of 95 *dönüm*s are joined by another 600 trees. At this settlement there was also a silk manufactory *(ipekhane)*, a unique item in the district of Anavarin, and a reference to three *mengene*, a word that can be used to describe a silk press.[142] However, in the list of revenue for Osman Ağa, all the trees are described as *fiddan* (saplings), suggesting a fledgling rather than a well-established industry.[143] No silk is recorded here as revenue, but this is the only place in TT880 where cocoons appear to be listed. Small quantities of silk were presumably produced elsewhere, but at

138. Brumfield (2000, pp. 60–69) comments on the introduction of the more efficient screw press onto Crete in the 18th century. Presumably the presses used in Anavarin at the time were not of this type.

139. See, e.g., Ali Hoca (1), Rustem Ağa (6), and İklina (23).

140. E.g., the suggestion that oil consumption on Methana would have been 25–35 kg per person per year, or 50 kg per person per year. See Foxhall 1990, chap. 4; Forbes 1982, p. 177; and Forbes 2000, p. 66, where it is noted that most of the annualized olive oil per person figures for the Venetian period fall well short of this.

141. Cash obtained from the sale of olive oil was being used in the middle of the 18th century to pay the expenses of fortresses of the Morea; see Chapter 1.

142. The *kanunname* refers to the tax on silk presses: see p. 52. *Mengene* can be used to describe other devices for exerting pressure as well, such as a screw press for extracting juice from grapes; see Redhouse 1890, pp. 2,013–2,014, and cf. Redhouse 1987.

143. In the list of property preceding the list of revenue, only 1,500 of the 2,100 are described as *fiddan*. The *kanunname* also envisions trade in mulberry leaves in the Morea.

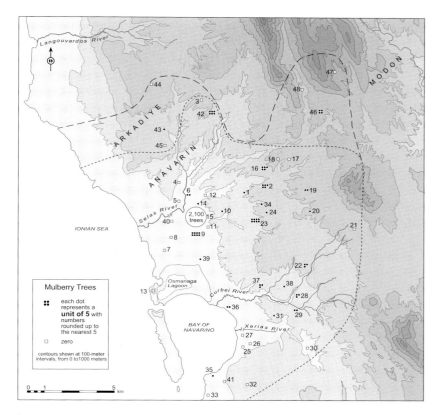

Figure 4.7. Distribution of mulberry trees according to TT880.
D. K. Harlan and R. J. Robertson

İklina (23) it is specifically noted: "Silk also used to be produced in this *çiftlik*, but they have not made silk for a few years."

Production of cotton appears to have been restricted to eight settlements (Fig. 4.8, Table 4.6). Total production (ca. 535 *lidre*s) at these places is measured both in a *lidre* of 133 *dirhem*s and in a *vukiyye* of 400 *dirhem*s. The value of the total crop would have been about 5,000 *akçe*s if sold at the prices recorded in TT880.[144] In 1911, no cotton was recorded in Anavarin.

In TT880 small quantities of flax are recorded at nine settlements (Fig. 4.9, Table 4.6). The largest amounts are at Pile (31), Osman Ağa (15), and Virviçe (49). Production is reported in *vukiyye*s in all cases except one (Virviçe), where the *lidre* is the unit of measurement. If *lidre* is not a scribal mistake, the total production of flax in the district was about 190 *vukiyye*s or 243 kilograms. In 1911, about 80 *stremmata* of flax were under cultivation in areas that once belonged to Anavarin, all in villages in the uplands or mountains: Agorelitza (Ağurliçe [42]), Mouzousta (Muzuste [43]), Veristia (Virviçe [49]), (Floka (Fulke), and Sapriki (see Fig. 2.1).[145] Farmers have cultivated flax elsewhere since World War II, for example, at Hora and Koryfasio (Osman Ağa [15]), and machines for breaking flax can still be seen in these villages.[146]

144. See Ali Hoca (1): "1 *lidre* of medium-quality cotton costs only 10 *akçe*s, and 1 *tarla* of 1 house produces only 10 *lidre*s of cotton"; Rustem Ağa (6): "This *çiftlik* also produces cotton. 1 *tarla* of 1 house produces 15 *lidre*s of cotton. 1 medium-quality *lidre* of cotton is 10 *akçe*s. Every *lidre* is 133 *dirhem*s"; and İklina (23): "The *tarla* of 1 household would normally produce 8 *lidre*s of cotton. A *lidre* of medium-quality cotton sells for 3 *para*s."

145. Of these villages, only Ağurliçe (42) and Muzuste (43) were listed in Anavarin in TT880.

146. On recent flax production in the area, see Halstead 2001, p. 46.

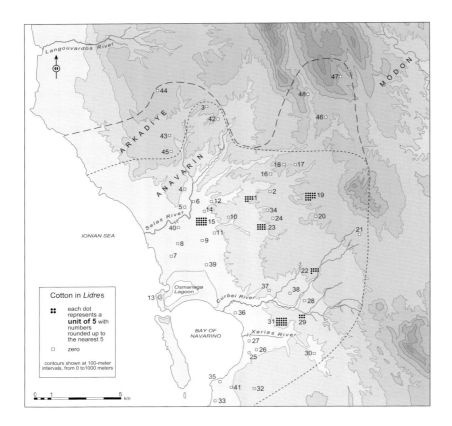

Figure 4.8. Distribution of cotton according to TT880. D. K. Harlan and R. J. Robertson

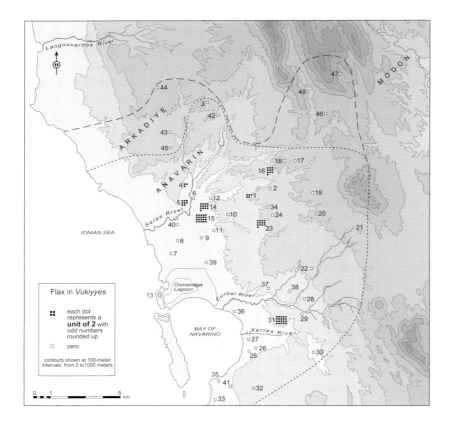

Figure 4.9. Distribution of flax according to TT880. D. K. Harlan and R. J. Robertson

ARABLE LAND

Tarlas, Çifts, *and* Dönüms

Two units are employed to measure quantities of arable land: the *dönüm*, a standardized Ottoman surface measure equivalent to 919.3 square meters, and the *çift*, a highly variable surface measurement based on an estimate of the amount of land that could be cultivated annually with a single team of oxen.[147] *Çiftlik*s and *karye*s registered in TT880 contain two categories of arable land, fields in the possession of the *reaya* and fields that belonged to the state or were in the possession of *çiftlik* holders. Only those over which the *reaya* held usufruct are included in the list of revenue generated by each property, and these are invariably registered under the heading "Wheat" *(hınta)*.

The division between *reaya* and state land is especially clear in the case of İstilianu (48): "Previously was a *timar*. It is in the mountains. 15 *çift*s of land, of which 3 belonged to the *reaya*." Only the three *çift*s of land belonging to the *reaya* are listed under revenue. Although it is not explicitly stated, it is obvious that a similar division obtained at other *karye*s.[148]

The same distinctions are found in *çiftlik*s. In the *çiftlik* of Kukunare (22), for example, *tarla*s (i.e., arable fields) of 550 *dönüm*s are registered, but only two *çift*s of wheat are in the possession of the sharecroppers. In the *çiftlik* of Muzuste (43) the situation is similar. "The *tarla*s of this *çiftlik* require only 20 pairs of oxen," but just 6½ *çift*s are registered as in the possession of the *reaya*.[149] And at Kurd Bey (36), although extensive *tarla*s and other revenues are recorded, no wheat is listed as revenue, since the *çiftlik* is unpopulated.[150]

*Tarla*s in *çiftlik*s were normally measured in *dönüm*s, a more tightly defined measure than the flexible *çift*. This precision may reflect a desire by *çiftlik* owners to protect themselves from encroachments by the *reaya*.[151] The individual holdings of the *reaya* are almost always recorded in *çift*s, as is land in *karye*s that is not in their possession.[152]

The size of a *çift* varied wildly, and a search for precision can lead to frustration. The Venetians discovered this during their occupation of the

147. On the *dönüm*, see n. 99 above.

148. Miniaki (47), e.g., is said to have 10 *çift*s of land, but only 2 are registered as property of the *reaya*. Two hundred forty *dönüm*s of *tarla*s at İskarminke (46), once the property of Osman Ağazade, are distinguished from arable land in possession of the *reaya* of the *karye* and are not listed as revenue. S. Davies comments (pers. comm.): "It is remarkable that the only instance in which land is recorded in *dönüm*s in a *karye* is at İskarminke where we know that the Venetians distributed Turkish property and where the Ottoman measures match exactly the Venetian. The Venetians did not reassign property in İstilianu and Mini-

aki and there it is all recorded in *çift*s. Does this suggest that the only reason *tarla*s are recorded in *dönüm*s elsewhere is because the Venetians had already measured them in *stremmata*?" Such an interpretation would fit with the apparent similarity in recording properties between Venetian *catastici* and TT880 (see Chap. 3).

149. S. Davies notes (pers. comm.), however, that there is no public land registered, unlike in entries for other *çiftlik*s. She suggests that "20 is a mistake, particularly as the scribe erased the 20 in the fraction," and she asks: "Given the phrase: 'These *reaya* are sharecroppers in this *çiftlik*. They do not have the same rights in others,'

could this imply that the land mentioned here is all technically public, rather than private?" Venetian records record 6 *para di bo* for this *çiftlik*, a figure that elsewhere seems to represent the total arable land belonging to the estate rather than to its sharecroppers.

150. Land held in an uninhabited *çiftlik* by sharecroppers living elsewhere is registered as wheat at their place of residence (e.g., see Pile [31]).

151. Mutafcieva 1970, pp. 110–116; cf. Davies's suggestion above, n. 148.

152. Exceptions are found at İskarminke (46), where there is recorded in *dönüm*s the property of two individuals who live at Kavalari; see n. 43 above.

Morea when they attempted to impose order on metrological chaos by establishing a fixed size for it. Confusion arose over one matter in particular. Did a *çift* refer to the amount of land actually plowed by a team of oxen, or did it also include land that had been left fallow? Some owners attempted to claim title to 120 *stremmata* by arguing that 60 were cultivated each year and 60 were left fallow.[153]

It is generally accepted that in the most fertile areas of the Ottoman empire, a *çift* was equivalent to 60 *dönüm*s; in moderately fertile soils, 80–90 *dönüm*s; and in unproductive soils, 100–150 *dönüm*s.[154] The size range of a *çift* specific to the district of Anavarin can be deduced from the document itself, although measurements of parcels of land in *dönüm*s sometimes are clearly formulaic. In 18 of 32 instances where *tarla*s are measured in *dönüm*s, sizes are multiples of a basic unit of 40, a value that can also be calculated mathematically in cases where we are told how large an area could be plowed by a yoke of oxen. Most other sizes are divisible by either 45 or 50.

For the majority of properties recorded in TT880, the scribe has recorded the size of arable fields (*tarla*s) belonging to the *çiftlik* in *dönüm*s and the number of yoke of oxen needed to plow them. From these data it is possible to calculate notional sizes of a *çift*: 23–80 *dönüm*s per yoke (mean 44.5 *dönüm*s per yoke, median 40 *dönüm*s per yoke). Changes in the size of the *çift* may reflect real variability in the fertility of land and in the heaviness of the soil.[155] A persistent value is 40 *dönüm*s per yoke; farmers appear to be thinking in *çift*s.[156]

153. Dokos and Panagopoulos 1993, pp. xxxix–xlvii.

154. Mutafcieva 1970, p. 85. The *kanunname* translated in Chapter 2, paragraph 5, provides for the Morea a slightly different range, 80, 100–120, and 150, presumably reflecting the absence of the most fertile types of land there.

155. H. Forbes has commented (pers. comm.): "Your range of 23–80 *dönüm*s per yoke may in part be explained by whether or not one or two ploughings were necessary: presumably the low figures indicate areas with heavy soils." He also notes that Ağurliçe (42) has one of the highest figures for seed density and one of the lowest yoke-to-*dönüm* ratios, features that both suggest heavy soils.

156. In the following list, *çiftlik*s, *mazra'a*s, and *karye*s are ranked from lowest to highest value:

Küçük Pisaski (14). Separately listed parcels of land total 185 *dönüm*s; 8 pairs of oxen; 23 *dönüm*s per yoke

Huri (12). 85 *dönüm*s; individual fields (one said to be "attached") totaling 84 *dönüm*s are registered; 3 pairs of oxen; 28 *dönüm*s per yoke

Platne (2). 120 *dönüm*s; 4 pairs of oxen; 30 *dönüm*s per yoke

Usta Musli (41). 30 *dönüm*s; 1 pair of oxen; 30 *dönüm*s per yoke

Ağurliçe (42). 320 *dönüm*s; 10 pairs of oxen; 32 *dönüm*s per yoke

Lefku (39). 200 *dönüm*s; 6 pairs of oxen; 33 *dönüm*s per yoke

Rudiye (25). 75 *dönüm*s; 2 pairs of oxen; 37 *dönüm*s per yoke

Muçaçu (34). 150 *dönüm*s; 4 pairs of oxen; 37 *dönüm*s per yoke

Aşağı Katu (3). 80 *dönüm*s; 2 pairs of oxen; 40 *dönüm*s per yoke

Azake (10). 80 *dönüm*s; 2 pairs of oxen; 40 *dönüm*s per yoke

Ğuli (24). 40 *dönüm*s; 1 pair of oxen; 40 *dönüm*s per yoke

Melis (26). 80 *dönüm*s; 2 pairs of oxen; 40 *dönüm*s per yoke

Yufiri (27). 80 *dönüm*s; 2 pairs of oxen; 40 *dönüm*s per yoke

Avarniçe (30). 80 *dönüm*s; 2 pairs of oxen; 40 *dönüm*s per yoke

Arkadianu (32). 80 *dönüm*s; 2 pairs of oxen; 40 *dönüm*s per yoke

Tupçin (37). 120 *dönüm*s; 3 pairs of oxen; 40 *dönüm*s per yoke

Pile (31). 250 *dönüm*s; 6 pairs of oxen; 42 *dönüm*s per yoke

Deli Ahmed (33). 90 *dönüm*s; 2 pairs of oxen; 45 *dönüm*s per yoke

Other Yufiri (40). 45 *dönüm*s; 1 pair of oxen; 45 *dönüm*s per yoke

Ali Hoca (1). 300 *dönüm*s; 6 pairs of oxen; 50 *dönüm*s per yoke

Petrehuri (7). 200 *dönüm*s; 4 pairs of oxen; 50 *dönüm*s per yoke

Rum Bağ (8). 50 *dönüm*s; 1 pair of oxen; 50 *dönüm*s per yoke

Budran (13). 500 *dönüm*s; 10 pairs of oxen; 50 *dönüm*s per yoke

Hasan Ağa (5). 160 *dönüm*s; 3 pairs of oxen; 53 *dönüm*s per yoke

Kukunare (22). 550 *dönüm*s; 10 pairs of oxen; 55 *dönüm*s per yoke

Kirmiti (21). 170 *dönüm*s; 3 pairs of oxen; 57 *dönüm*s per yoke

Karunihuri (11). 350 *dönüm*s; 6 pairs of oxen; 58 *dönüm*s per yoke

In three instances, the number of *dönüm*s being plowed is significantly lower than the average.[157] At Has (9), 10 *dönüm*s are plowed by a single pair of oxen. At Rustem Ağa (6), "attached" fields totaling approximately 100 *dönüm*s are listed under a general heading "Attached *tarla*s of 100 *dönüm*s." Six pairs of oxen seem too many for *tarla*s of this size, and the scribe may have meant to say that the *tarla*s within the *çiftlik* require six yoke of oxen, while there were an additional 100 *dönüm*s in other places. The situation at Alafine (4) finds no such convenient explanation. Ten yoke of oxen plow *tarla*s of 153 *dönüm*s that are divided in two categories: in the first group, locations are not specified; in the second, they are.[158] Is this simply a scribal mistake, or does the answer lie in the fact that Alafine is said to be "attached" to the *çiftlik*s of Hasan Ağa and Rustem Ağa, and so the oxen are "shared" over a much larger area?[159]

For a few *çiftlik*s and *mazra'a*s, less detail was recorded. In eight cases, only the number of yoke of oxen required was noted, and presumably it would have been possible to estimate the approximate size of the property from this information.[160] In three instances, the scribe wrote down the number of yoke of oxen and the amount of seed that each pair could plow.[161] For two entries, only the size of *tarla*s is recorded.[162] Only for Virviçe (49) is there no explicit or implicit reference to *tarla*s, yokes of oxen, or sowing rates, perhaps because the scribe could not determine such details "on the ground" at a distant property while he was gathering data within the territory proper of Anavarin.

All of the evidence that can be extracted from TT880 suggests that most farmers imagined that 40 *dönüm*s of land could be sown by a team of oxen, although the range (23–80 *dönüm*s) is much broader. A calculated average of approximately 40 *dönüm*s is about half the size of the *çift* that is given in TT880 as a unit of land measurement: for example, at Tristena (45), "80/100 *dönüm*s of land are defined as 1 *çift*." It must be that farmers included fallow land when employing a *çift* as a unit of measurement, but only calculated the area of land in cultivation at any one time when estimating the number of yoke of oxen needed for plowing.[163]

Kurd Bey (36). 900 *dönüm*s; 15 pairs of oxen; 60 *dönüm*s per yoke

Other Papla (20). 350 *dönüm*s; 5 pairs of oxen; 70 *dönüm*s per yoke

İskarminke (46). 240 *dönüm*s; 3 pairs of oxen; 80 *dönüm*s per yoke

157. These three examples have been omitted from the preceding calculations.

158. Olive trees in Alafine are registered in a similar way.

159. We owe this possible explanation to S. Davies, who writes (pers. comm.): "Looking at yokes of oxen, the figures for Rustem Ağa and Alafine are odd. However, the entry for Rustem Ağa says that: 'the *çiftlik*s of Alafine, Hasan Ağa, and Rustem Ağa are attached and share the same taxes and *tarla*s.' If the ten yoke of oxen had earlier applied to Rustem Ağa and Alafine collectively, the ratio would be much better. It seems to me likely that the ten yoke for Alafine are the same ten yoke as had been listed for Rustem Ağa. Venetian records list seven yoke for Rustem Ağa and one for Alafine, which seem to me more realistic."

160. These include Pispitsa (16), Nase (17), Rotsi (18), İklina (23), Elyas Ağa (28), Zaimzade (29), Ayanu (44), and Tristena (45). In three instances (Pispitsa, Elyas Ağa, and Zaimzade) the land is explicitly designated as "medium quality," and this is implicit too for Nase and Rotsi, both described as "in the vicinity of Pispitsa."

161. Papla (19), where 1 pair can plow 12 *kile*s of seed; Kirmiti (21), where 1 pair can plow 10 *kile*s of wheat; and Muzuste (43), where 1 pair can plow 15 *kile*s.

162. Osman Ağa (15), where only *tarla*s outside the *çiftlik* are listed, and Tursun (38).

163. It may be noted, however, that crop-rotation systems other than two-part could be imagined at this time. A report submitted by Domenico Gritti (Topping 1974, p. 317) describes a three-part rotation system: (1) chief grains (wheat, barley, oats, rye, and flax), (2) lesser grains (millet, maize, and cotton), and (3) fallow.

The Extent of Arable Cultivation in Anavarin

The amount of arable land in cultivation in Anavarin appears to have been about 1,500 hectares (about 400 in possession of the *reaya*, and an additional 1,065 ha also worked by them; see below), distributed between *çiftlik*s, *mazraʿa*s, and *karye*s, an average of 6.72 hectares per family.[164] This is a substantial total, a bit more even than in 1911, when about 1,300 hectares, excluding fallow, were planted in wheat (800 ha), barley (107.8 ha), oats (159.9 ha), and rye (228.7 ha). As already noted, TT880 records wheat only grown on the land of the *reaya*, but market prices and sowing rates are given for other grains. Though the *reaya* may have chosen to plant wheat on their own possessions because of its higher market value, significant parts of the remaining arable land in the district must have been devoted to barley, millet, and oats.

There are 109 *çift*s of arable land registered as being in possession of the *reaya*. If it can be assumed that 40 *dönüm*s were being cultivated in each *çift* (see above), this much land would have been the equivalent of 400 hectares under cultivation.[165] The soils of Anavarin were not particularly fertile in comparison to the Greek national average, but they were comparable to, or somewhat better than, those of the southern Argolid. With regard to the southern Argolid, Jameson, Runnels, and van Andel have written: "Sowing rates as well as expected yields are an indication of the quality of the land. In the Fournoi valley today the sowing rate for wheat of 150 kg per ha is that of Thessaly early in this century . . . for Greece as a whole ca. 1875, the sowing rate was 190–290 on better land, 120–140 on poor land. But Fournoi has the best soils in the Southern Argolid. In the southern zone, the Halias, we have been told that 100 kg is sown for good land, 70 kg for poor."[166]

The quantity of seed grain required to sow a field in Anavarin varied considerably. In Budran *çiftlik* (Anavarin-i atik [13]), 10 pairs of oxen sow 100 *kile*s of seed in 500 *dönüm*s (2,800 kg of seed in 46 ha)—that is, approximately 60 kilograms of seed per hectare, a low sowing rate even in comparison to the southern Argolid.[167] In other *çiftlik*s, sowing rates were as high as 160 kilograms of seed per hectare, implying that the quality of land was also higher.[168]

164. Employing the figure of 218 non-Muslim probable heads of household, as calculated earlier in this chapter. Such an average compares favorably to that calculated by Forbes for the southern Argolid in 1700 on the basis of statistics contained in a Venetian *catastico particolare*. See Forbes 2000b, pp. 49–50, 49, table 3.2, p. 62.

165. The calculation is (109 *çift*s × 40 *dönüm*s × 919 m² per *dönüm*) ÷ 10,000 m².

166. Jameson, Runnels, and van Andel 1994, p. 267.

167. The *kile* employed in TT880 seems always to be the standard Istan-

bul *kile*, equivalent to 16 *okka*s of barley (ca. 20.5 kg) or 22 *okka*s (ca. 28 kg) of wheat; we here follow Wagstaff and Augustson 1982, p. 126, table 10.25. Hinz 1955 gives slightly different figures for the *kile*, corresponding to 25.656 kg of wheat and 22.25 kg of barley.

168. The following is a ranked list of productivity rates including only those *çiftlik*s, *mazraʿa*s, and *karye*s for which data are available:

İskarminke (46). 3 pairs of oxen together sow 45 *kile*s in 240 *dönüm*s (1,260 kg in 22 ha; ca. 57 kg/ha)

Pile (31). 6 pairs of oxen sow 12 *kile*s of seed each in 250 *dönüm*s (2,016 kg in 23 ha; ca. 88 kg/ha)

Muçaçu (34). 4 pairs of oxen sow 12 *kile*s of seed each in 150 *dönüm*s (1,344 kg in 14 ha; 96 kg/ha)

Ali Hoca (1). 6 pairs of oxen sow 100 *kile*s of seed in 300 *dönüm*s (2,800 kg in 28 ha; 100 kg/ha)

Rudiye (25). 2 pairs of oxen sow 15 *kile*s of seed each in 75 *dönüm*s (840 kg in 7 ha; 120 kg/ha)

Platne (2). 4 pairs of oxen sow 50 *kile*s of seed in 120 *dönüm*s

TABLE 4.7. PRODUCTIVITY OF ARABLE CROPS RECORDED IN TT880

Property	Wheat			Barley			Millet			Fodder			Unspecified Grain		
	S	Y	R	S	Y	R	S	Y	R	S	Y	R	S	Y	R
Budran çiftlik (13)	1	4	1:4	1	5	1:5	1	10	1:10	1	5	1:5	—	—	—
İklina çiftlik (23)	6	30	1:5	6	36	1:6	1	15	1:15	5	30	1:6	—	—	—
Pile çiftlik (31)	1	7	1:7	—	—	—	—	—	—	—	—	—	—	—	—
Muçaçu çiftlik (34)	—	—	—	—	—	—	—	—	—	—	—	—	1	5	1:5
İstilianu karye (48)	1	5	1:5	1	6	1:6	—	—	—	—	—	—	—	—	—

Key: S = Seed planted *(kile);* Y = Yield *(kile);* R = Ratio of S:Y

The estimated yields given in TT880 (Table 4.7) seem to be realistic. Although in areas of exceptional fertility and in good years, much higher yields of grain, particularly barley, were reported in some parts of early modern Greece (e.g., 1:10, 1:25), ratios of seed to yield on the order of 1:5 or 1:6 are far more likely.[169] Sowing rates of 60–160 kilograms per hectare and yields of 1:6 could, given the availability of sufficient labor, have produced between 144,000 and 384,000 kilograms of grain per annum.[170] At an average consumption rate of 128 kilograms per person, even the lower estimate would have provided for the needs of the non-Muslim population of Anavarin.[171] In addition to *çift*s in possession of the *reaya*, about 1,065.5 hectares of additional arable land were available for cultivation in Anavarin.[172] After a sufficient quantity was retained to provide for the requirements of the local Muslim population and for seed for subsequent plantings, much of the produce from this land must have been available for export, and thus had the potential to generate a substantial cash income for the district.

The Meaning of Annotated Fractions in TT880

As noted in Chapter 2, a fraction in the form "*x* number of *çift*s from a total of *y* çifts" was written in the hand of an annotator above the heading of each entry in the cadaster for Anavarin. We here suggest that these otherwise enigmatic additions to the manuscript provide evidence that in the course of the 18th century, the *reaya* came to control more land than they had in 1716. The meaning of the fractions is not explained in TT880 and can only be deduced from the document itself.

It seems to us likely that the fractions were added because the properties were being assembled into groups of particular values for some purpose

(1,400 kg in 11 ha; ca. 127 kg/ha)

Ağurliçe (42). 10 pairs of oxen could sow 15 *kile*s of seed each in 320 *dönüm*s (4,200 kg in 29.5 ha; ca. 142 kg/ha)

Lefku (39). 6 pairs of oxen could plow 100 *kile*s of seed in 200 *dönüm*s (2,800 kg in 18.5 ha; ca. 151 kg/ha)

Aşağı Katu (3). 2 pairs of oxen sow

40 *kile*s of seed in 80 *dönüm*s (1,120 kg in 7 ha; 160 kg/ha)

169. For the higher rates, see Leake 1835, p. 79; Wagstaff and Augustson 1982, p. 128. More generally, see Davis 1991, p. 168; Jameson, Runnels, and van Andel 1994, p. 267. Millet is the only crop in TT880 with a markedly higher ratio than the others.

170. The calculation is 400 ha × 60–160 kg × 6.

171. See the discussion of consumption rates in Davis 1991, p. 166.

172. A total of 1,365 *dönüm*s and 12 *çift*s of arable land registered in *mazraʿa*s; 2,400 *dönüm*s and 6 *çift*s in uninhabited *çiftlik*s; 3,705 *dönüm*s and 57 *çift*s in inhabited *çiftlik*s; and 240 *dönüm*s and 22 *çift*s in *karye*s. We assume a value of 40 *dönüm*s per *çift* in these calculations.

relating to taxation, perhaps for sale as tax farms, or in anticipation that groups would be assigned as benefices to members of the Ottoman elite. The denominators of the fractions contain only four unique numbers: 350 (twice), 450 (once), 400 (11 times), and 500 (34 times).[173] The word *çift* in this context does not appear to refer to actual pairs of oxen, since numerators can be expressed as half-*çift*s. Entries with the same denominator are not spatially segregated from those with different denominators, but most in the lowlands of Anavarin have denominators of 500, and most with denominators of 400 are farther from the sea. Entries with a denominator of 500 represent a total of 107½ *çift*s; with a denominator of 400, 56½ *çift*s; with a denominator of 450, 12½ *çift*s; and with a denominator of 350, 15½ *çift*s.

The numerators in each place do not correspond to the size of the *tarla*s that belong to the state or to *çiftlik* holders. Nor are they equivalent to the number of yokes of oxen required to plow *tarla*s that belong to them.[174] The numerators do, however, relate in a general way to the number of *çift*s of land that the *reaya* possess, and in several instances the correspondence is too close to be coincidental.[175] In half of the cases, there is not a perfect correspondence between figures in numerators and *çift*s in the possession of *reaya*, but the divergences are usually very minor.[176] In most instances, the numerator of the fraction is greater than the number of *çift*s of the *reaya* recorded in the principal text of TT880.

We believe that the most likely explanation is that the fractions were added some years after 1716, at a time when the number of *çift*s in the hands of the *reaya* had changed. The fractions would thus represent an emendation made to the text, in order to update the document. The total number of *çift*s (192) in possession of the *reaya*, as would be indicated by the fractions, is much greater than the number first recorded (109), implying that the *reaya* had acquired inheritable rights over a much larger area of arable land. Moreover, the fact that fractions were recorded for unoccupied *çiftlik*s and *mazra'a*s suggests that at least some of the land associated with these properties was not sharecropped and had been acquired by the *reaya*.

LIVESTOCK

Among livestock, only sheep, goats, pigs, and beehives are listed as revenue, all in the hands of the *reaya*.[177] Nearly 4,000 head of sheep and goats are recorded (Table 4.8, Fig. 4.10), with the largest numbers (200+) on inland and upland properties. These are in the possession of 97 of the 281 non-Muslims who pay *ispence*. The number of sheep per owner can be

173. In one case the fraction is not legible (Rum Bağ [8]).

174. In the case of Muzuste (43), the annotator does seem first to have written the number of yokes as the numerator, but he then erased the figure.

175. In these instances the numbers are exceptionally large, and two contain fractions: Pispitsa (16), 9 *çift*s; İklina (23), 7 *çift*s; Zaimzade (29), 10½ *çift*s; Ağurliçe (42), 12 *çift*s; and Virviçe (49), possibly 13½ *çift*s.

176. E.g., at Ali Hoca (1), the numerator is 2, whereas the *reaya* have 2½ *çift*s in their possession.

177. See Redhouse 1890, p. 152, with regard to the word *ağnam* meaning sheep and goats collectively (and cf. Redhouse 1987). Balta (1993, p. 52) has, in fact, translated the Turkish *adet-i ağnam* (sheep tax) as the Greek φόρος προβάτων, i.e., "tax on herded animals, both sheep and goats."

TABLE 4.8. LIVESTOCK RECORDED IN TT880

Property	Sheep	Owners	Sheep/ Owner	Pigs	Owners	Pigs/ Owner	Population (İspence)	Sheep Owners/ Population (approx. %)	Pig Owners/ Population (approx. %)
Ali Hoca (1)	120	2	60.0	2	1	2.0	4	50	25
Platne (2)	155	3	51.7	16	3	5.3	3	100	100
Alafine (4)	110	2	55.0	0	0	—	3	67	0
Hasan Ağa (5)	10	1	10.0	5	4	1.3	9	11	44
Rustem Ağa (6)	50	1	50.0	2	1	2.0	7	14	14
Huri (12)	80	2	40.0	1	1	1.0	2	100	50
Küçük Pisaski (14)	85	3	28.3	3	3	1.0	13	23	23
Osman Ağa (15)	55	2	27.5	0	0	—	12	17	0
Pispitsa (16)	245	9	27.2	5	2	2.5	12	75	17
Papla (19)	330	6	55.0	6	4	1.5	10	60	40
Kukunare (22)	30	1	30.0	6	3	2.0	3	33	100
İklina (23)	555	11	50.5	15	6	2.5	15	73	40
Zaimzade (29)	430	10	43.0	12	7	1.7	21	48	33
Pile (31)	160	4	40.0	1	1	1.0	13	31	8
Anavarin-i cedid varış (35)	60	2	30.0	0	0	—	30	7	0
Ağurliçe (42)	255	5	51.0	13	13	1.0	32	16	41
Muzuste (43)	95	3	31.7	16	11	1.5	20	15	55
İskarminke (46)	540	11	49.1	23	15	1.5	17	65	88
Miniaki (47)	155	2	77.5	1	1	1.0	2	100	50
İstilianu (48)	125	4	31.3	5	3	1.7	6	67	50
Virviçe (49)*	343	13	26.4	17	12	1.4	47	28	26
Total	3,988	97		149	91		281		
Mean	190		41.0	7		1.8	13.4	47.6	38.3

* None of the Virviçe data appears on any of the maps in this chapter; see n. 108 above.

quite large, even when averaged across an entire settlement (as high as 55 at Alafine [4], but is only 10 at Hasan Ağa [5]). Such averages mask, however, some probable specialization in pastoral activity. At Platne (2), Pispitsa (16), and Papla (19), one owner has 100 of the property's sheep, and at İklina (23) one person owns 200, whereas at Zaimzade (29) and İskarminke (46), for example, numbers are more evenly spread. Similarly, only one resident (of 7) owns sheep at Rustem Ağa (6); only two residents (of 12) at Osman Ağa (15); and only 13 residents (of 47) at Virviçe (49).

There are 149 pigs registered in the possession of 91 individuals (Table 4.8, Fig. 4.11). The majority have 1 or 2 pigs at most (mean 1.8), which is what one might expect for a household—browsing animals with the potential for providing meat. At Platne (2), however, two individuals have larger numbers (one has 7 pigs, the other has 8), perhaps suggesting specialization. One of these is also the owner of 100 sheep.

There are 231 beehives registered in the possession of at least 14 individuals (Fig. 4.12). Like sheep, goats, and pigs, beehives are most common in areas away from the coastal lowlands, with the highest number by some margin at Zaimzade (29).

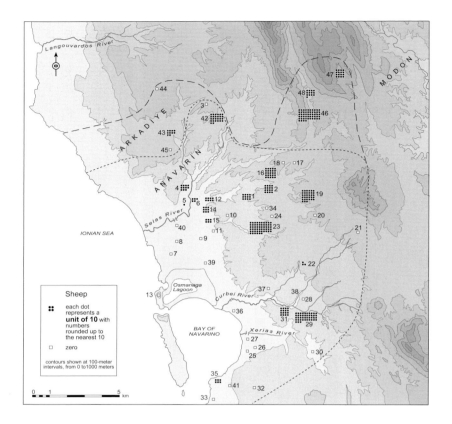

Figure 4.10. Distribution of sheep according to TT880. R. J. Robertson

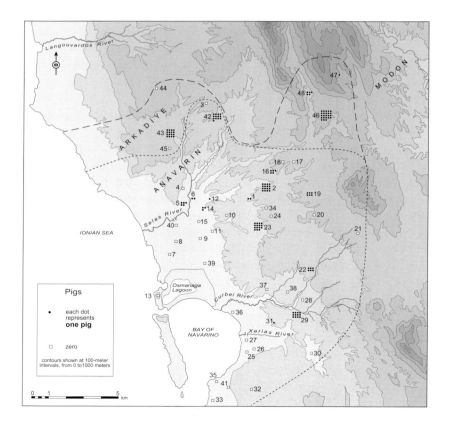

Figure 4.11. Distribution of pigs according to TT880. R. J. Robertson

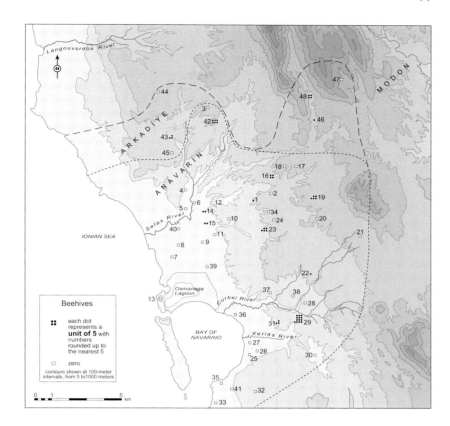

Figure 4.12. Distribution of beehives according to TT880. R. J. Robertson

TOWARD AN ARCHAEOLOGY OF PYLOS FOR THE EARLY MODERN PERIOD

As noted above in the Introduction, for various reasons it is not our mission here to analyze fully the archaeological data that has resulted from fieldwork supported by PRAP. This evidence has already been summarized elsewhere and will later be described in greater detail.[178] Here we intend only to emphasize the important contribution that examination of the material remains of the PRAP study area can make to an understanding of Ottoman cadastral surveys such as TT880.

There are remarkably few standing remains in the area that are demonstrably older than 1821. At Anavarin-i cedid, which is today the modern town of Pylos, only the fort and parts of the aqueduct that supplied it with water survive. The history of these structures is fully discussed in Appendixes III and IV. No other settlements in the district appear to have been fortified in the Second Ottoman period. A fortress was built at Iklaina in the Frankish period (Fig. 3.12), but there is no evidence that it continued to serve a defensive function after it was acquired by Venice in 1423,[179] even though the remains appear to have been visible in 1716, as they are today, because a "fortress of Ustu İklina" served as a boundary of a *tarla* in the possession of the *çiftlik* of Küçük Pisaski (14).

Few ecclesiastical structures can be dated, at least in their current form, to the Ottoman period, although it is clear from a Venetian inventory of religious property dating to 1698 that many did exist.[180] Several of the

178. See the preliminary report of S. Gerstel in Davis et al. 1997, pp. 474–482; also Davies 2004, p. 108.

179. For the Frankish fort, see Bon 1969, pp. 431–432, which collects the textual references; also Topping 1972, pocket map 5-8. For its acquisition by Venice, see Hodgetts and Lock 1996, p. 82; Hodgetts 1974, p. 476.

180. Dokos 1971–1976.

churches recorded were located within the area covered by TT880: for example, at Ğarğalian, Kavalari, Pispitsa (16), Rustem Ağa (6), Ağurliçe (42), Muzuste (43), Likudise, and İskarminke (46). We have not attempted systematically to study the physical remains of all these churches, where they might still exist, and only a few have been the target of special studies.[181]

Domestic structures are even rarer, even in the largest communities within the area studied.[182] Ottoman Hora has not fared well. Lolos discusses no standing architectural remains that are older than the middle of the 19th century.[183] The situation at Gargaliani is not much better. Lyritzis illustrated the now-demolished ruins of a towered mansion of the Ottoman period, and parts of another tower are incorporated into a modern house.[184] There are caves in cliffs facing the sea at the west edge of the town, in an area known as *tou Bala* (του Μπάλα). Systematic survey by PRAP on the slopes below these caves produced finds of the early modern period, and it is clear that there were churches in them in the centuries preceding 1821.[185] In the one village (Maryeli) where we have systematically studied prereinforced concrete constructions, none of the standing houses appears to predate the Greek Revolution.[186]

There are also few preserved remains of public infrastructure dating from the Ottoman period in the area of Anavarin. Although TT880 appears to mention *handak*s (channels or ditches) near Ğarğalian, Burğu or Pirğu, and Ağurliçe (42), it is unclear whether the word refers to an aqueduct channel. In fact, a more plausible interpretation is that it refers to the distinctive steep ravines emanating from these locations.[187] Indeed, only parts of the aqueduct systems that supplied the fortresses of Anavarin-i cedid and Anavarin-i atik still stand.[188] Two arches of an earlier bridge of Ottoman style are preserved beneath the modern concrete over the Selas River where the road from modern Romanou to Tragana crosses it (Fig. 3.22).[189] No obvious traces of old bridges remain over the Xerias (Beşli) or Yialova (Yiannouzaga, Kurbeh) rivers, even though they are referred to by early-19th-century travelers and are preserved in the name of the *mazraʿa* of Yufiri or Beşli (27).[190] Remains of premodern roads of Ottoman type (sing., *kaldırım;* Greek *kalderimi*) are also relatively rare, in part probably because building stone is not plentiful in much of the area. On the outskirts of modern Pylos, at Miden, traces of a *kaldırım* lead down into the Xerias Valley (Fig. 4.13).[191]

181. Exceptions include Ayia Sotira at Metamorfosi (İskarminke) and Ayios Nikolaos at Kavalaria (Kavalari): S. Gerstel in Davis et al. 1997, pp. 477–482.

182. For a systematic study of surviving medieval and early modern architecture in the northwestern Peloponnese, see Cooper 2002.

183. Lolos 1998.

184. Lyritzis 2000, pp. 51, 383–384, 441; see also Bory de Saint-Vincent's (1836, pp. 171–172) description of a towered house in Gargaliani in 1829.

185. Reference is made to churches in the caves in the Venetian inventory published by Dokos (1971–1976, p. 133), and one cave-church was examined by PRAP (POSI M5: Gargaliani *Analipsi*). See also Lyritzis 1987, pp. 104, 109.

186. Lee 2001, pp. 73–75.

187. See the discussion in Chapter 3 regarding Muzuste (43) and Ayanu (44).

188. For fuller discussion, see Appendixes II and III, respectively. Arches of the aqueduct at Anavarin-i cedid are

mentioned in TT880 as a boundary for the *mazraʿa*s of Usta Musli (41) and, apparently, Melis (26).

189. It is far from certain, however, that these remains are entirely of Ottoman date, since Bory de Saint-Vincent (1836, p. 164) mentions a destroyed bridge over the "Romanou river" in approximately this location.

190. E.g., Bory de Saint-Vincent 1836, p. 137; Chapter 2 above, Yufiri (27).

191. Bennet, Davis, and Zarinebaf-Shahr 2000, pp. 357–358, fig. 3.

Figure 4.13. *(above) Kaldırım* near Miden; *(below)* section near Miden, leading down toward the Xerias (Beşli) Valley

Because there are virtually no standing remains of domestic structures in the large towns of modern Pylos, Gargaliani, and Hora, the potential for archaeological studies in these places without excavation seems extremely limited. Elsewhere prospects are better, particularly in the case of Ottoman-period settlements recorded in TT880 that are no longer the focus of occupation. There are several outstanding examples in our study area, including the large village of Kavalari, the smaller village of İskarminke ([46] Metamorfosi), and the hamlet of Hasan Ağa (5).

Figure 4.14. Ayios Nikolaos at Kavalaria

The settlement at Kavalari lies on the outskirts of modern Hora, on the Englianos ridge, in the direction of the Palace of Nestor (Fig. 2.1). In the course of systematic survey in 1992, we recognized the remains of a large community here.[192] A church of Ayios Nikolaos (Fig. 4.14) stands in the center of the site and is dated by an inscription above its door to 1709. Artifacts are densely concentrated around the church in an area approximately 7 hectares in extent, and a site on the nearby slope of Kalianesi seems to have served as a cemetery for the community.[193] As noted above, the settlement had 73 *ispence*-payers in 1716.

The Venetian inventory of church property already mentioned allows us to suggest a definition for this community's hinterland, as it lists the ecclesiastical structures that belonged to it in 1698.[194] These include churches dedicated to Ayia Eleni, Ipapanti, Ayios Yioryios, Ayios Panteleimon, Panayia, Ayia Kyriaki, Ayios Athanasios, Ayios Nikolaos, and two more churches of the Panayia. Although only in the aforementioned case of Ayios Nikolaos (and perhaps Ayios Athanasios) is it clear that visible remains date as far back as the Venetian period, the locations of most of these churches can be fixed because modern churches preserve the name of the saint to whom they were dedicated. These churches give a rather good impression of the perceived limits of the village's territory at this time, but not necessarily of its occupied area. Ayios Athanasios (Fig. 4.15) is 300 meters northeast of Ayios Nikolaos, across the road to Myrsinihori. Ayia Eleni (Fig. 4.16) stands west of the road from Hora to the Palace of Nestor, about 350 meters west-northwest of Ayios Nikolaos. Ayios Panteleimon is nearly one kilometer south-southwest of Ayios Nikolaos, after a big turn in the road on the way to the Palace of Nestor, while Ipapanti and Ayios Yioryios are nearly as distant from Ayios Nikolaos to the southwest. It thus appears that the agricultural catchment of Kavalari reached nearly as far as the Palace of Nestor, an extent that is borne out by the boundaries drawn on the 1700 Venetian map (cf. Fig. 3.7, top right).

İskarminke (46) is another settlement of substantial size, considerable remains of which were documented by systematic survey in the area immediately northeast of the village of Metamorfosi (formerly Skarminga; Fig. 3.24).[195] At the center of the site is a large spring and the Church of

192. S. Gerstel in Davis et al. 1997, pp. 480–481.

193. S. Gerstel in Davis et al. 1997, p. 481. The toponym Kalianesi, in the form "Kilaneş," appears as the location of a vineyard *(bağ)* under Kavalari in TT880, p. 39.

194. Dokos 1971–1976, p. 136.

195. See S. Gerstel in Davis et al. 1997, p. 481.

Figure 4.15. Ayios Athanasios at Kavalaria

Figure 4.16. Ayia Eleni at Kavalaria

the Transfiguration (Ayia Sotira). Other constructions, probably of Ottoman date, survive at the western edge of the site, at a place called Loutra
(Λουτρά), where modern inhabitants of Metamorfosi believe there was a
Turkish bath. Segments of stone-paved roads (*kaldırım*s) lead eastward
from this site toward the modern hamlet of Touloupa Hani and, northeast
over the hill of Velanidies, toward the village of Maniaki (Miniaki [47] in
TT880).

The hamlet of Hasan Ağa (5) was considerably smaller than either
Kavalari or İskarminke (46), but it was easily identified through archaeological survey on the basis of surface remains on the summit and slopes of
a knoll east of the modern village of Tragana (Fig. 3.6).[196] Remains of
collapsed buildings occupy its summit, and there are house compounds at
the foot of the hill. An early-20th-century tower-style house may imitate
earlier towered types.

Any of the above locations offers archaeologists the possibility of com-
paring in some detail the extent and nature of surface with subsurface
archaeological remains, since each was systematically surveyed in the course
of field-walking sponsored by PRAP. Many of the other properties in-
ventoried in TT880, though not intensively surveyed, are also promising

196. S. Gerstel in Davis et al. 1997,
p. 481; Alcock 1998; Bennet, Davis,
and Zarinebaf-Shahr 2000, pp. 365–
366, fig. 9.

targets for archaeological investigation.[197] For the present, however, we prefer to emphasize the contribution that archaeological fieldwork on a regional scale has made to our understanding of documents such as TT880.

We have been remarkably successful in locating almost all of the *karye*s, *çiftlik*s, and *mazra*ᶜas registered in TT880. In some cases their precise situation, though previously unknown, can be determined from surface archaeological remains. For example, at Ali Hoca (1) there is a mound of collapsed stone and tile (Fig. 3.4), whereas at Tristena ([45], Greek Drestena), there are plentiful fragments of tile and pottery.

Archaeological evidence has, in addition, the potential to allow us to solve more complex cartographic problems with the text of a document such as TT880. The location of the *çiftlik* of Rustem Ağa (6) is a good example. The name Rustem Ağa is not in contemporary usage. It is not attested in the inventory of toponyms compiled by Georgacas and McDonald, but it does appear, as "Rhoustemaga rᵉ," in the Expédition scientifique's *Atlas,* which places it a little inland, as if tucked into a small bowl on the south side of a ravine leading up to Iklaina, which lies on its north side. It is given the map symbol for "ruines helléniques."

The *Atlas* of the Expédition scientifique is generally accurate and initially led us to identify Rustem Ağa with the closest modern village to this location, namely Elaiofyto. This identification seemed to us to be confirmed by the Venetian document of 1698 listing church properties in the Anavarin (Navarino) and Arkadiye (Arkadia) regions; it mentions a church of Ayios Athanasios at Rustem Ağa.[198] The church in modern Elaiofyto is, in fact, dedicated to this saint.

However, there are difficulties with this apparently unproblematic association. First, although Elaiofyto has changed its name (more recently than most places in the region—it was officially known by its old name at least until 1939),[199] its older name is Sgrapa (Σγράπα), not Rustem Ağa. This is not necessarily a problem, because if the settlement had been ruined and abandoned, it might have been renamed Sgrapa when resettled after 1830 to avoid the Turkish associations borne by Rustem Ağa. Indeed, we have an example of such a change in the modern village of Balodimeïka, which must be the *çiftlik* of Zaimzade (29), which appears both in TT880 and in the Expédition scientifique's *Atlas* (as "Zaimoglou").

Second, and much more damning, however, the entry for Rustem Ağa (6) in TT880 suggests very strongly that it is close to the *çiftlik*s of Alafine (4) and Hasan Ağa (5), both of whose locations we know, as noted above. It is said to be "attached" to these *çiftlik*s: "Alafine, Hasan Ağa, and Rustem Ağa are attached and share the same taxes and *tarla*s." Its boundaries are given as the *çiftlik*s (not toponyms, but estates) of Hasan Ağa (5), Huri (12), Alafine (4), and Osman Ağa (15). Further, it has *tarla*s (among other places) next to Huri (12) and Küçük Pisaski (14), next to Alafine, and next to Osman Ağa's *tarla*s. The evidence of TT880 seems to suggest, therefore, a location northwest of Osman Ağa to be bounded by Alafine, Hasan Ağa, Osman Ağa, and Huri.[200] Clearly none of this evidence is compatible with a location of Rustem Ağa at Elaiofyto/Sgrapa.

This apparent inconsistency between TT880 and the *Atlas* of the Expédition scientifique can be resolved by drawing on archaeological evi-

197. Notably Ali Hoca (1); see discussion in Chapter 3.
198. Dokos 1971–1976, p. 136.
199. According to Georgacas and McDonald 1967, 218.7010, the name was changed in 1956.
200. Interestingly, Küçük Pisaski (14) is not a boundary.

201. POSI B6. See Davis et al. 1997, p. 393, fig. 2, for the location of the site.

202. The census of the Expédition scientifique gives one family at Rhoustemaga in 1829, despite the map symbol. "Hasanaga," by contrast, has five families recorded in the same census table; see Puillon de Boblaye and Virlet 1833–1834, p. 85. A mistake in locating Rustem Ağa seems quite plausible, since the maps of the *Atlas* (at 1:200,000 scale) were copied from maps at 1:50,000 scale by cartographers unfamiliar with the area; see Saïtas 1999, p. 107.

203. ASV, Archivio Grimani ai Servi, b.28, f.839r.

204. See Chapter 3, Rustem Ağa (6), for further discussion of these sources.

205. Puillon de Boblaye and Virlet 1833–1834, p. 85. Pouqueville may list the settlement in his *cadastre,* if we accept his "Neochori" as a corruption of "Karunihuri": Pouqueville 1826–1827, vol. 6, p. 73.

206. See Chapter 3, Karunihuri (11), for further discussion.

207. Biris 2002, pp. 116–117.

dence. In the course of archaeological survey, PRAP defined a modest early modern site at the end of the Kato Englianos ridge, overlooking the valley between the ridge and Osman Ağa ([15], modern Koryfasio).[201] A few ruined structures are visible there today, plus a church dedicated to Ayios Athanasios, right next to the modern road. The road running inland past the church leads up into the flood plain of the ravine that extends south of the Englianos ridge, off which (to the south) lay Osman Ağa (15), Küçük Pisaski (14), and Huri (12). This location offers a good fit with the position of Rustem Ağa (6) implied by TT880, and we might note that the number of *ortakçıyan* (sharecroppers) at Rustem Ağa is not huge (seven individuals), implying a relatively small *çiftlik*—not even as large, for example, as Hasan Ağa, which lay on the other side of the valley to the west, and is said to have had nine *ortakçıyan*.

Therefore we might be able to explain the Expédition scientifique's error, as the topographic situation of our site is somewhat similar to that of the location indicated for "Rhoustemaga" on their map—not far inland on one of the many ravines leading down from the Aigaleon/Manglavas ranges. Taken together with the fact that Rhoustemaga is listed as a *ruine,* this observation might mean that the dot on the map of the Expédition was simply misplaced.[202] Moreover, a general location of Rustem Ağa as lying at the end of the Englianos ridge has now been confirmed by subsequent research. First, there has recently been discovered among Venetian documents pertaining to the district of Navarino (Anavarin) a reference to land at "Engliono" said to be "within the boundaries" *(confin)* of "Rustan aga."[203] Clear confirmation of the identity of this archaeological site with the *çiftlik* of Rustem Ağa was also offered by the examination of the previously unpublished Venetian map of about 1700 (Fig. 3.7) and examination of earlier drafts of the maps produced for the Expédition scientifique's *Atlas.*[204]

These discoveries, however, left us with the untidy situation of not being able to locate an Ottoman-period settlement at Elaiofyto/Sgrapa, making it the only village in the area without an obvious predecessor in the Second Ottoman period. We did wonder if the *mazraʿa* of Karunihuri (11) might be located here, given its stated boundaries in TT880: Osman Ağa *çiftlik,* Seri Putamu, Ayu Yurki, İstinayurki, and Likuvuni. In the Venetian period, Carvunoghori appears initially (1689) to have been settled, with a small population (19 individuals), but it is not included in the Grimani (1700) census (Table 4.1). In TT880 Karunihuri (11) is a *mazraʿa,* and it does not appear among the Expédition scientifique's toponyms, as a settlement either populated or deserted.[205] The 1700 Venetian map seems clearly to locate this property below and west of the ridge marking the edge of the high ground on which modern Elaiofyto sits, however.[206]

The explanation for the absence of Sgrapa among earlier Venetian or Ottoman sources seems, in fact, to be that it was established at its current location only in 1845. Previously, the village had been located in the vicinity of a church of the Panayia on the edge of the uplands overlooking modern Yialova, approximately two kilometers southwest of its current location. The village was also known as "Gouvalogara" and, according to Biris, was first inhabited in 1835, when the church was rebuilt after İbrahim Pasha's depredations.[207] Biris's account is supported by the evidence of the

Expédition's *Atlas*, which indicates a settlement named "Gouvalovoros" (surely too close to Biris's form to be coincidental) in this location (Fig. 3.1). Moreover, an earlier 1:50,000 draft map has the place-name "Valovara" at this same spot, its orthography presumably adjusted for the final version. However, the date of settlement predates that given by Biris, since both Pouqueville and the Expédition list populations at "Gouvalachori" (1815) and "Gouvalovoros" (1829), respectively.[208] Yet another version of the name appears in an 1830 census: "Vouvoulogoroi."[209]

The variability of this place-name in our sources and its location at a point on the edge of the upland immediately northeast of modern Yialova make us wonder if it can be equated with the "Vavalari" that occurs in TT880 in three places: as a boundary of Kurd Bey *çiftlik* (36), as a family name[210] at Pile (31, item 10), and as a boundary of Tristena (45). In the Ottoman sources, the existence in the 1512–1520 *defter* of a *mazraᶜa* of Vavalari, one of two dependent on Anavarin-i atik, the other being Pile, is also striking.[211] It seems that the old location of Biris's "Gouvalogara" was that of a church of the Panayia dating back to the period 1381–1402, repeatedly destroyed and rebuilt before being moved in 1835.[212] This would not be inconsistent with the location of a *mazraᶜa* in the 16th century and would be entirely consistent with a boundary of Kurd Bey in the 18th. The association with Pile in the 16th-century *defter* and the proximity of the two locations are suggestive of how Vavalari might appear as a family name at Pile in 1716.[213]

The apparent variation between names beginning with Va- and those beginning with Gou- might be explained by a conflation of the name of a river system—the Gouvalari Rema (Γουβαλάρη P.)—that runs from near Koukounara and feeds into the Yiannouzaga/Yialova River (1:50,000, Koroni, E190, N240).[214] The two forms may have become confused because the river formed a link between coastal and inland settlements.[215] It seems very probable that the location of "old Sgrapa/Gouvalogara" is that of Vavalari, a boundary of Kurd Bey in the early 18th century and a *mazraᶜa* in the early 16th.

Why are the preceding arguments important? A minor point of interest is that our proposed solution for the location of Rustem Ağa came initially from the analysis of archaeological and textual information, not

208. Pouqueville 1826–1827, vol. 6, p. 73 (15 "families," with the provisos mentioned already above); Puillon de Boblaye and Virlet 1833–1834, p. 85 (8 families).

209. Loukatos 1984, pp. 211–212 n. 1.

210. Although we consider it unlikely, we raise the possibility that the scribe has here automatically written "Tanaş son of Vavalari" when the information given was "Thanasis from Vavalari."

211. TT80, pp. 20–21.

212. Biris 2002, p. 116.

213. Less easy to explain is its association with Tristena, which lies some distance to the north. It may simply be a homophonous place-name, but a possible explanation is that the scribe wrote Vavalari in error instead of Kavalari, which would probably have been the next property over to the east of Tristena (see Fig. 2.1). The way in which the word is written is, however, consistent with Vavalari, and such an explanation remains tentative.

214. Georgacas and McDonald (1967, 111.1659) also list a place-name Gouvalari (Γουβαλάρι) in the vicinity

of Koukounara. A little farther up the same river system, toward modern Kremmydia and Velanidia, the name Babalorema (Μπαμπαλόρεμα) appears (1:50,000, Koroni, E175, N255), close to where a 19th-century settlement labeled "Barbali rᵉ" is shown on the Expédition's *Atlas* (Fig. 3.1).

215. It is worth noting in this connection that the Expédition lists the population of coastal Yialova (Gialova/ Djalova) and inland Shinolakka (Skhinolaka) together: Puillon de Boblaye and Virlet 1833–1834, p. 85.

from a map, although it was subsequently confirmed by map data, and maps have been enormously useful to us in many other cases. More significant, however, is the fact that without both PRAP's fieldwork and our study of TT880 and other documents, Rustem Ağa would not have been definitively located, and, equally, the status of our site would have remained enigmatic. Documentary evidence now suggests that this site was occupied before, during, and after the Venetian occupation, right up until the early 19th century. In relation to the wider question of Rustem Ağa's location and its possible relevance to the location of Elaiofyto/Sgrapa, our further research has uncovered a settlement (Sgrapa/Gouvalovoros) established after 1716, perhaps part of a pattern of expansion around more established settlements. Unfortunately, without population data for the remainder of the 18th century, we cannot define when this settlement was established, merely that it had come into existence before Pouqueville's figures dating from 1815.

There is also a broader implication of the foregoing in relation to the period of TT880. Rustem Ağa is among a small number of *çiftlik*s listed in TT880 that bear Turkish names in Venetian census records of 1689 and 1700. There, and in TT880, they are known only (or predominantly) by the Turkish owner's name. In contrast, the majority of the *çiftlik*s and *mazra*ᶜ*a*s in TT880 either have local "village" names (e.g., Platne [2] or Pispitsa [16]) or have double names of the pattern "[village name] or *çiftlik* of [Turkish personal name]," such as "*çiftlik* of Papla or *çiftlik* of Mustafa Ağa" (19). The location of those *çiftlik*s with single Turkish names is significant: they dominate the lower reaches of the major valleys leading into the Bay of Navarino, or are very close to Anavarin-i cedid itself (Figs. 2.1, 3.2). This suggests that already in the First Ottoman period, there had been a concerted effort by the Ottoman local elite to exploit areas with extensive lowland agricultural land. Had we located Rustem Ağa (6) at Elaiofyto, this pattern would have been obscured or disrupted.

By the time of the Venetian censuses, these settlements had come to be known only by their Ottoman names.[216] Even though we cannot define exactly when prior to the Venetian conquest these properties became *çiftlik*s, already in the 16th century a *çiftlik* is attested (Table 1.1). Other *çiftlik*s, still known by village names, might have been developed not long before the Venetian occupation. Where the alternative form "*çiftlik* of [x]" appears in TT880, we imagine that this might reflect the ownership immediately prior to the Venetian occupation.

There is possible support for this idea in the fact that some of the names of Ottoman individuals attested as *çiftlik* owners also appear among those individuals whose property is listed in Anavarin-i cedid (35). The property of over 70 Ottoman individuals is recorded at Anavarin-i cedid. Twelve entries in TT880 bear the alternative form "*çiftlik* of [x]."[217] Of these 12 names, 6 or 7 show an exact correspondence with names of

216. See also Chapter 1, and Bennet, Davis, and Zarinebaf-Shahr 2000, pp. 374–375, regarding the dates at which *çiftlik*s were established in Anavarin. See also Davies 2004, pp. 98–104,

for a discussion of these issues.

217. This assumes that Denmusarin (18) and Ağaku (20) are, in fact, proper names.

property holders in the fort.[218] This situation contrasts with that of the nine properties that are listed solely with Ottoman names.[219] Of these, only two, Deli Ahmed ([33], and see Anavarin-i cedid [35], item 51) and Osman Ağa ([15], and see Anavarin-i cedid [35], item 17), share names with property owners in Anavarin-i cedid.

Another group of properties may have been named only a generation earlier. There is a property in Anavarin-i cedid owned by the son of Usta Musli (Usta Muslioğlu: Anavarin-i cedid [35], item 2), suggesting, if Usta Musli is the same individual, a generation's difference between the naming of the *mazra'a* of Usta Musli and the register of property within Anavarin-i cedid. A similar situation may also apply to Osman Ağa, whose son (Osman Ağazade) is said to have owned property taken over by the Venetians at İskarminke (46), although there is an Osman Ağa listed among the property owners in the fort (Anavarin-i cedid [35], items 16–18, 21). Another possible equivalence is the Haci Hasan listed as the father of Mustafa Çelebi (Anavarin-i cedid [35], item 1 or 44) and Mustafa (Anavarin-i cedid [35], item 8). Might this be the Hasan of Hasan Ağa *çiftlik* (5)?

EPILOGUE

In concluding this chapter, we would like to suggest that the following contributions have been made. First, it has proven to be possible, on the basis of the information contained in TT880, to propose a probable reconstruction for the level of population in the district of Anavarin at the beginning of the 18th century, and for the agricultural and settlement system that formed the basis of the local economy at that time. A detailed understanding of local geography within the district, gained as a result of the arguments set forth in Chapter 3, has also allowed us to examine patterns in the density of settlement and in the location of agricultural activities within the district and to suggest, in some instances, specific historical, social, and economic explanations for such variability. At the same time, the availability of earlier and later texts (published and unpublished) and archaeological evidence has permitted us both to evaluate the quality and completeness of the data contained in TT880, and to construct the framework for something like a continuous population and economic history for Anavarin during the last century of Ottoman rule. Such conclusions will doubtless be of interest to demographers and agricultural historians of early modern Greece.

In the past, general histories of the Peloponnese or of Greece under Ottoman domination have had little material at their disposal for the compilation of a continuous political narrative for the 15th to early 19th cen-

---

218. Mustafa Ağa (19): Anavarin-i cedid (35), item 29 or 47; Muslihuddin Efendi (22 and 34): Anavarin-i cedid (35), item 94; Mehmed Ağa (24): Anavarin-i cedid (35), item 26, 53, 86, or 106; Kurd Ali Ağa (25): Anavarin-i cedid (35), item 48, 50, or 107; Müfti (32): Anavarin-i cedid (35), item 70.

We can also note that Ağurliçe (42) is said to have been owned previously by Mustafa Ağa (cf. Anavarin-i cedid [35], item 29 or 47), and Muzuste (43) by Mustafa Çelebi (cf. Anavarin-i cedid [35], item 1 or 44). Similarly, elsewhere in TT880 (p. 34), the *çiftlik* of Abdul Kadir Ağa, within the modern

village of Hora, shares the name of a property owner in Anavarin-i cedid ([35], item 16).

219. Ali Hoca (1), Hasan Ağa (5), Rustem Ağa (6), Osman Ağa (15), Elyas Ağa (28), Zaimzade (29), Deli Ahmed (33), Kurd Bey (36), and Usta Musli (41).

turies, let alone for the composition of a social or economic history. The structure of narratives has to a large extent been dictated by the availability (or unavailability) of Western sources, whether political histories such as those published in Venice during its occupation of the Morea, or the reports of Western consuls, or accounts of Western travelers. Historians have understandably responded by focusing on those periods for which documentation is most plentiful, and the result has been an extremely patchy (both chronologically and regionally) view of Ottoman Greece.

The absence of information is a long-standing problem. Volume 5 of Finlay's monumental history of Greece was able to devote only some 60 pages to the period from 1453 to 1684, but about 60 pages each to the period of Venetian occupation from 1684 to 1718 and to the last century of Ottoman rule.[220] Topping's valuable discussion of the post-Classical documentary history of the Pylos area also has little to say about the First Turkish Occupation (1460–1685)—hardly more than a page.[221] Although pioneering in its subject matter, Sakellariou's book-length treatment of the Peloponnese in the Second Ottoman period relies almost exclusively on Western sources or Ottoman data quoted secondhand in those sources.[222] Specific information about particular parts of Greece has rarely been available except when places such as Pylos appeared on the stage of international politics.[223]

For the district of Anavarin, this has meant that a standard regional history of the area, such as that published by Mihail in 1888, leaps quickly across the centuries of the Turkish "yoke" in just 20 pages—from the initial Ottoman conquest to the aftermath of Lepanto to the Venetian capture of the Morea to the Orlov rebellion to the fall of Anavarin-i cedid to Greek forces in 1821.[224] More recent histories (and guidebooks) of Pylos follow these same patterns.

In this chapter we hope to have demonstrated amply that recourse to the Ottoman sources offers historians golden opportunities to fill the gaps in knowledge with systematically collected information that is relevant for writing social and economic, as well as political, history. At the same time, because the Ottoman documents supply such a wealth of locally detailed information, there is also the chance to restore to Greek communities, such as those in the Pylos area, a sense of the history of their own local areas that has, in most cases, been lost entirely. A history can be returned to these "people without history."

Finally, we would suggest that the compilation of a richly documented local social and economic history based on the exposition and analysis of Ottoman sources (of which this chapter might serve as a component) is of much more than parochial interest. Such regional histories clearly have the potential to shed light on much larger issues that are of concern to historians of the Ottoman empire, indeed to historians of the Mediterranean in general.

220. Finlay 1877, vol. 5, pp. 55–120, 165–229, 230–299.

221. Topping 1972, pp. 70–71. Topping later (p. 80) refers to work then in progress by John Petropoulos on the Ottoman documents for the period, but, to the best of our knowledge, this research has not been published.

222. Sakellariou 1939.

223. We are, of course, aware of important research, some of it published, some of it in progress, that is bringing the rich Ottoman data to bear on other areas of Greece: see the discussion in the Introduction.

224. Mihail 1888.

CHAPTER 5

CONCLUSIONS

by Fariba Zarinebaf, Jack L. Davis, and John Bennet

The historiography of the Balkans and Greece during the Ottoman period remains an underdeveloped field and until lately has been based largely on the accounts of Western travelers or on a limited number of local documents. But this picture is slowly changing, as more local and foreign scholars are turning to the rich Ottoman archives in the hope that they will bring balance to the often ideologically charged scholarship of this neglected period of history. Both Western and Greek scholars have already utilized Ottoman sources for reconstructing a history of some parts of Greece during the Ottoman period.[1]

Our own efforts should be viewed in that context. They represent an attempt to determine the extent of catalogued Ottoman archival material in Istanbul that might be of use in writing a history of the Morea from the second half of the 15th century to the 19th. For practical purposes, given the scale of the endeavor, and because of the specific focus of the archaeological investigations of the Pylos Regional Archaeological Project, the geographical and historical focus of this volume has been the district of Anavarin during the 18th century. But in Chapter 1, Zarinebaf has set this local, and some might say parochial, study within a much broader historical context. In so doing, she has taken into consideration the bulk of catalogued Ottoman archival material from the Başbakanlık Archives in Istanbul, Ottoman contemporary chronicles, and, where relevant, the accounts of Western travelers. She has also situated her findings within the context of Ottoman historiography.

Our collaboration has yielded several significant results that should, we think, be of considerable interest to historians, as well as to archaeologists. First, we have come to question the received wisdom that Ottoman conquest and rule necessarily resulted in a demographic decline and the flight of local Greek peasantry.[2] For the Pylos district, at least, there appears to have been stability in the demography of the non-Muslim population during the period we have examined, except during the wars between Venice and the Ottoman empire in the second half of the 17th century and the beginning of the 18th. Following the Ottoman reconquest of the Morea in 1715, the Christian population of the district was maintained at Venetian levels, while more land appears to have been brought under cultivation.

1. One excellent recent review of such research is Adanır 1998.

2. Specifically, we feel that the "height zonation hypothesis" critiqued by Frangakis-Syrett and Wagstaff (Frangakis and Wagstaff 1987; Frangakis-Syrett and Wagstaff 1992) can be shown to be oversimplified when examined at the microlevel, as we have done: see Bennet, Davis, and Zarinebaf-Shahr 2000, pp. 345, 374–377. For another view on the same question, see now Forbes 2000a.

In no small part, it has been our close attention to the topography and the toponymy of the district of Anavarin that has permitted us to set our conclusions on a firm foundation, through identification of spatial variation not only in densities of population, but also in types of settlement and varieties of crops grown within the district. Such exhaustive (but, we hope, appropriately detailed) analysis has laid the groundwork for future archaeological fieldwork, not only by identifying locations for excavation, but also by providing a cartography and geography of Ottoman Anavarin, with which the evidence of material culture may be integrated. It has also suggested how archaeological evidence can be employed to improve our understanding of the text itself. Perhaps it is of even greater significance that such a close examination of the district has enabled us to study mechanisms of agricultural production within the region from an emic perspective, rather than as a generalized mass of summary statistics to which Ottoman *defter*s have so often been reduced.

Examination of cadastral surveys for the districts of Modon and Anavarin has also shown that settlement by Muslims was limited except in the largest villages and towns. Moreover, in the Morea as a whole, the Turkish military administrative class, as well as *timar*-holding *sipahi*s, appear to have been concentrated in a dozen or so fortress towns and at Tripoliçe, the capital of the province, in relative isolation from the local Greek inhabitants that formed the vast majority of the rural population. Islamic court records and Church records are likely to reveal more about the nature of interaction between the Turkish ruling class and the Greek *reaya*.[3]

During the Ottoman-Venetian wars of the late 17th century, Peloponnesian Turks fled to Chios, Anatolia, and elsewhere, and some returned after the Ottoman reconquest of the Morea in 1716. As we have seen, the Ottoman administration encouraged the return of the former Turkish residents who had survived and provided them with incentives to establish a claim to their land based on old Ottoman registers in Istanbul. It is clear from TT880 that some of their land had been acquired by Venetian settlers and Greek peasants between 1699 and 1715.

In 1716, one striking effort of the Turkish administration that was clearly intended to reestablish Turkish control of the district was the apparent restoration of the *timar* system. The *timar* system had formed the backbone of the Ottoman administrative system in the Morea from the second half of the 15th century to the late 17th.[4] It was based on the assignment, on a rotating basis, of rural and urban revenues to members of the Ottoman provincial administration and cavalry (*sipahi*s). Several *sipahi*s would collect a share of their *timar* from a given village for a limited number of years (usually one or two). This system ensured the collection of revenue by the Ottoman cavalry, guaranteed local security, and, at the same time, prevented the development of hereditary assignments and provincial power bases.

This system of benefices began to change with the transformation of the Ottoman military technology that made the traditional cavalry system of defense outdated, and with the expansion of tax-farming, particularly in the late 17th century. Growing fiscal needs in the face of an expanding military and civil bureaucracy and in response to wartime emergency

3. Ottoman Islamic court records (*sicil*s) appear not to be widely preserved for the Morea for the 18th century (M. Kiel, pers. comm.). But see Faroqhi 1997, p. 602, with reference to 17th-century documents from Patras. Relevant local church records remain to be located and studied by others. For a recent exploration of interaction between Ottoman elite and Greeks on Ottoman Crete, see now Greene 2000. More generally concerning sources for the Ottoman history of Greece, see Balta 1997, pp. 259–275.

4. See, e.g., Kunt 1983.

expenditures required the state to farm out the collection of rural and urban revenues to the highest bidders, usually members of the royal household and central administration or Janissary *ağa*s. Most tax-farmers were Muslim Turks, resident in Istanbul, who generally subcontracted their responsibilities to local notables and merchants and to Ottoman provincial officers.

Driven by the profit motive and encouraged by the introduction of life-term tax-farms in the mid-1690s, tax-farmers took the liberty of collecting a range of illegal taxes from peasants. Many had also consolidated their holdings in the form of *çiftlik*s already in the 17th century. Most of these *çiftlik* holders and local subcontractors were members of the Ottoman military class, for example Janissary *ağa*s and former *sipahi*s. Contrary to the views of many scholars, however, it is clear from TT880 that these *çiftlik*s had not been universally consolidated by the 18th century into large commercial estates oriented toward the export of cash crops. In 1716, most of the *çiftlik*s in the district of Anavarin remained small, and only a few Greek sharecroppers were resident in them, although the holdings of some *çiftlik*s, such as Osman Ağa (15), imply the seasonal presence of a substantially larger labor force.

The gradual incorporation of the Ottoman empire into the world economy[5] encouraged a transformation of its traditional economy and a change in structure of the classical peasant family unit of production *(çifthane)* in the Aegean and in the Balkans. Istanbul was no longer the sole or principal importer of foodstuffs from the Morea and elsewhere. In addition to the Mediterranean commercial republics such as Venice, Western European states such as England and France became very active participants in the international trade of the Morea. In response, there was a Balkan-wide tendency for *çiftlik*s located on the coast to replace village farms. These might produce subsistence crops, including grains, as well as cash crops such as olive oil, wine, dried fruits, and cotton. As yet, however, little evidence has been extracted from TT880 that any such transformation had occurred in the Pylos district at the beginning of the 18th century.[6]

In 1716, the *çiftlik*s as well as the *karye*s of the district appear to have remained devoted to a diversified agriculture based on subsistence crops, even though this system was capable of producing a substantial surplus under the right conditions and *çiftlik*s were concentrated in lowlands near the sea and the fortress of Anavarin-i cedid. In 1716, an average sharecropper in a *çiftlik* in the district of Anavarin often owned his own arable land (½–1 *çift*) and might have had a few sheep and pigs, fruit trees, and beehives. But he did not own the means of production (plow, oxen, and mills) and had to pay taxes and share produce with the state as well as the holder of the *çiftlik*. He also did not enjoy the protection of a *timar*-holder, who was under the supervision of Istanbul and could lose his assignment if he violated rules.[7]

Such conditions set the stage for abuse. Istanbul had very little control over the actions of tax-farmers. Moreover, in the course of the 18th century, the burden of taxation in the Morea became substantial, as attested by the increase in the number of petitions that peasants filed with the state

5. See, e.g., Abou El-Haj 1991; İslamoğlu-Inan 1987; Kasaba 1988.

6. Except perhaps in the case of Osman Ağa *çiftlik* (15), where production beyond subsistence level of olives, vines, and silk appears to have been anticipated by 1716.

7. *Çiftlik*s of this sort, not principally oriented toward monocropping and production for export, were, in fact, characteristic of most of southern Greece (McGrew 1985, pp. 30–31).

against tax-farmers. Fiscal abuse of this sort by tax-farmers, as well as by Turkish and Greek officials, may have helped to precipitate the local uprisings of the late 18th and early 19th centuries. Certainly banditry also played a role.[8] Furthermore, a growing presence in the Morea of Western European, Levantine, and Russian merchants who cooperated with Ottoman (Greek) subjects under the shelter of national trade privileges (Capitulations) granted by the Turkish government served to shift the loyalty of many of the sultan's Christian subjects from the Sublime Porte to Saint Petersburg, London, and Paris.

In the subtle changes to the local economy of the district of Anavarin attested in TT880, we have witnessed only the beginning of major imperial and commercial rivalries that would continue throughout the 18th and 19th centuries in the Mediterranean and the Balkan world, and that would ultimately pay considerable dividends both to local actors in the Morea (by the creation of the modern Greek state) and to the Western European powers, as they profited from the decline of Ottoman power in the Mediterranean.

8. See, e.g., Alexander 1985b; Gallant 1988, 1999.

Evlİya Çelebİ's Account
of Anavarİn

by Pierre A. MacKay

The following passages are excerpted from the *Seyahatname* of Evliya Çelebi, translated from the personal manuscript (either autograph or directly edited by Evliya himself).[1] The manuscript is MS Istanbul, Topkapı Sarayı, Bağdat Köşkü 308. Folio and line references, separated by a solidus and enclosed in square brackets, are inserted in the text at five-line intervals and refer to Evliya's actual text; page references to the Türk Tarih Encümeni edition of 1928, also enclosed in square brackets, have been inserted as well.

An account of the construction of that lofty elevation which is the castle of Anavarin-i atik [266b/10]

It is called this because . . . it was built by the *Bundukani*[2] Venetians, and in the year 906, it was taken by Sultan Bayezid Khan from the Venetians, who turned over the keys and surrendered it on terms. They knew that they would not be able to resist the onslaught of the sovereign, for he brought back the memory of how the Conqueror in former days had taken such fortresses as Corinth. Therefore, they made terms to surrender this castle that no longer gave them security. God's truth, however, [310] this lofty castle is not one to be taken by the effort of battle. If it had had water and provisions, we should have been burdened with a seven-year siege, for it is an unequalled castle, reaching up to the Milky Way in heaven. [266b/15] According to the cadastral register of Sultan Bayezid

1. *Note from Zarinebaf, Bennet, and Davis:* This appendix constitutes the first English translation of Evliya Çelebi's travels in the Pylos area, and its text is here reproduced as it was provided to us by Pierre MacKay, who employs a transliteration system that differs somewhat from what is used elsewhere in this book. The entire account of Evliya Çelebi's journey in the Morea has been published in Greek (Loupis 1999a) and in Turkish (Kahraman, Dağli, and Dankoff 2003). Brief comments con-

cerning Evliya's career may be useful for non-Ottomanists: he was an Ottoman courtier who devoted his career to travel; his journeys were mainly restricted to the boundaries of the Ottoman empire, and he described them in the 10 volumes of a travelogue called *Seyahatname*, a mixture of personal observations and the imaginary. Evliya visited Anavarin in the summer of 1668; the date of the *Seyahatname* is ca. 1680. For further discussion of Evliya's career and travels, see Bruinessen

and Boeschoten 1988; Dankoff 1991, pp. 3–20; Dankoff and Kreiser 1992; and Faroqhi 1999, esp. pp. 160–161. For difficulties in establishing the text of the *Seyahatname* see, e.g., Dankoff 2000; MacKay 1975.

2. *Bunduq*—or *Bunduk*—is an Arabic reshaping of the name of Venice, apparently deriving from the Greek Βενετικός. *Bundukani* is a standard adjectival form from this noun. Evliya treats *Bundukani* and *Venedigi* as separate, complementary terms.

Khan, this castle is part of the Governorate of Morea and is free
from all special imposts. The fortress is a lofty castle, strongly built
like the castle of Kahkaha Mountain [a prison castle on a peak
somewhere in the Caucasus Mountains], on the peak of a steep
yellow rock that reaches up to the clouds in the sky. It resembles
the castle of Van in Kurdistan, but the sea beats up against the
rock of this castle on all four sides and surrounds it completely.
Only on the east is there the sandy road that makes a mainland
castle of it, and there is also another narrow sandy road in the
middle of the harbor. Except for these two points, there is the sea
on all four sides, so that the castle cannot be reached from any side.
From the harbor below to the castle above is three thousand steps
up an almost perpendicular rocky slope. On that side [266b/20]
there is a firm, strong, iron-gated lofty portal facing east, and
inside that gate is what they call the lower castle. It contains eighty
small, cramped, tile-roofed masonry houses, with no gardens or
orchards, but each of them has a splendid view. The mosque of
Sultan Bayezid is here, a serviceable but abbreviated mosque of
old-fashioned construction. There are *in toto* five shops, but there
is no inn, bath, upper or lower school, nor any trace of gardens or
orchards, for this is a waterless island.

They bring up water from a well down below in the sandy area
by the harbor that has previously been mentioned, and it is transported by donkeys, which are a remarkable sight. These water-
bringing donkeys are loaded up with water jars in the castle, and
when they have descended to the well, the men there below fill up
the jars with water and [266b/25] send the donkeys back up to the
castle. When the donkeys arrive with the water in front of a house,
they sing the opening bars of the old donkey song, in the time-
honored traditional mode, and the householder, knowing by this
that the donkey has arrived with water, takes it from the animal and
sends him back down again. The intelligence of these donkeys has
given rise to a saying in the Governorate of Morea, as when they
address a servant, saying, "I'll have the donkeys of Anavarin teach
you some sense." In this way, then, with the aid of donkeys, they get
their water up to the castle on this high summit, and there is a
cistern provided in every residence.

From this lower castle that I have just been describing, a road
made of white stone goes up steeply into the middle castle. This has
a small, but strong, iron gate, and five [266b/30] houses, and there is
also a huge cistern into which all the blessed rain is directed to flow
by means of gutters and drain channels. In order that not a single
drop of rainwater shall be wasted, even from the streets, the public
roads are made of clean stone, and arranged so as to flow into and
fill the cistern. There are no dogs in this middle castle, since they
might affect the water. In this middle castle [311] there are a few
mulberry trees by the houses, and the Castle Commandant lives
here. Farther in from the middle castle is a simple, small, inner
citadel, but its walls are partially in ruins, and except for one more
cistern, there is no trace of any building, because it would exhaust
any of Adam's sons to go up into this inner citadel.

Along the eastern side of the castle, there are no walls, neither for the lower nor for the upper castle, but for all that it is still a mighty [267a] fortress, since there is a high, smooth cliff, ten minarets in height, along this side. Here not even the birds that fly in the air can find a place for their claws to grip, for the rock is slick and polished. Only a few falcons, eagles, vultures, and kites perch there and make their miserable nests. As God is my refuge, a man dare not look down at this point. To the east, all the plains, mountains, and cultivated orchard lands are seen laid out at one's feet, while on the south and west, the whole Mediterranean Sea shows up like a little lake. That tells you how [267a/5] high this castle is. There are twenty-three large cannon in the castle that look out toward the mouth of the harbor, and these lofty cannon can fire all the way across to the point of Anavarin-i cedid down below.

The young stalwarts of this castle are a finer, more effective, braver, and more celebrated body of men than the imperial forces [kuls] in the castle of Anavarin-i cedid below. The castle detachment consists of garrison personnel, but is a levy of poor men.

At the time of the conquest, this castle was attached to the jurisdiction of Modon, and it is even now counted as one of the districts of Modon under a judge-substitute. After the conquest, Sultan Bayezid is said to have constructed a sturdy long wall up from the sea to a side of the castle, but this has fallen into ruin in several places. Opposite the aforementioned long wall there is a long, dark-colored [267a/10] little island running from southeast [q]³ to west in the long dimension. This is rather like a small detached mountain. Between the castle rock and the little island is a close, narrow channel with only a fathom of water at the inner end, but galleys can pass through it by keeping to the side away from the island. If a young man throws a stone from one side of this channel to the other, he will make his mark, for the island is that close. As you go down to the shore by the harbor, there is a huge arched structure that is supposed to have brought water in from the rocks and mountains to this castle of Anavarin, but it has fallen into ruin in many places with the passage of time, and because they have not rebuilt it, the water no longer flows.

Praise of the great harbor of Anavarin

In the tongue of the Italian Franks, it is called "Porto Giunco," [267a/15] which means a bed of spiky bulrushes. In very truth, in the shallows all around this harbor, they grow bright green bulrushes and weave fine plaited mats, like the rush mats of Egypt. It is nine

3. To a pious Muslim, the *qibla* (the precise direction toward the Kaaba in Mecca) is more important than any other compass heading. Muslim doctrine requires that it be unique and exact for each location, but in practice there may be several *qibla*s attested by the mosques in a single town. In most of Greece, the *qibla* will be a bit south of southeast. Evliya Çelebi tends to use the term *qibla* for any direction between due east and due south. For a modern, non-Muslim reader, this practice would be confusing. I have therefore converted most of Evliya's *qibla* references to conventional compass directions, using knowledge of the site where possible. When the abbreviation *[q]* follows such directions, it indicates that what Evliya wrote was *qibla*.

miles from this harbor to Modon, and the course out of Modon
to this harbor is toward the northwest. This is a huge natural
[312] harbor, in which five hundred galleys, galleons, and *bargias*[4]
can be accommodated. At the south entrance, there are two rocks
positioned like gates, and all the cannon face this strait. This is a
huge harbor, safe from the winds from all eight wind-directions,
so large that three great rivers empty into it. Their names are
noted above.[5] When too large a number of [267a/20] big ships
arrives in the harbor, there is a small island in the middle, and
ships can make their hawsers fast to this island and cast anchor
out in any direction at all, whatever happens to be appropriate
for the wind direction, for this is a fine, well-ordered, and safe
harbor.

In the year . . . , at the beginning of what they were calling
the Malta campaign, the naval commander Yusuf Pasha brought
the whole Ottoman navy, with its seven hundred ships, into this
harbor, and the entire Ottoman navy was berthed and watered
here. The old galleys were left behind, and all provisions and
supplies were transferred to other ships by the soldiers. Then,
one evening, our forces left the harbor, and began with an instan-
taneous conquest of the castle of Ayioi Theodoroi on the island
of Crete. After this, having surrounded the castle of Hanea and
pounded it for [267a/25] . . . days, we took that, too. The point
of these remarks is that this harbor of Anavarin is a safe anchorage,
capable of containing the entire Ottoman fleet.

From here we went on for one hour along the shore of the
harbor in a southeasterly *[q]* direction, through productive fields,
and crossed the . . .[6] river on horseback. And so we came to
Anavarin-i cedid.

A written account of the low-lying castle of Anavarin-i cedid

This is a fine castle built by the hand of Kılıç Ali Pasha in the year
977, during the reign of Sultan Murad Khan the third. It is administered by a *voyvode* as part of the Governorate of Morea, and is a
district of the jurisdiction of Modon. There is a chief Mufti, a
Marshal (of the descendants of the Prophet), a Local Commander
([Sipâh] Kâhya Yeri), a Captain of Janissaries, and a Castle Commandant with . . . personnel. There is an Inspector of Commerce,
a Collector of Transit Dues, a Commissioner of Tribute Taxes, a
chief Architect, a City Intendant, and twelve garrison officers with
the rank of *Ağa* as [267a/30] well.

The reason for the building of Anavarin-i cedid

It is this. The harbor is so huge that it can be entered by two
different channels, and the cannon of the above-mentioned castle
of Anavarin-i atik could not protect it, because the cannon balls
overshot the range and went past their mark. Therefore, they built
this castle at the harbor mouth, down close to sea level, and they
certainly hit their own target, for this is a celebrated and sturdy
rampart, a mighty fortress of Islam, and a strongly built edifice at

4. For *bargia*, see Kahane, Kahane,
and Tietze 1958, s.v. no. 80, barça. A
bargia is a heavy warship, larger and
deeper than a galley, in use from the
15th century to the 17th. Evliya is
showing off his vocabulary; he may
not have much sense of the difference
between a *bargia* and a galley.

5. The names, unfortunately, are *not*
listed above.

6. The name is left blank by Evliya
in anticipation of adding it to the text
later.

the mouth of the harbor, which makes that harbor safe and secure. It is a handsome fortress [313] with the sea to both east and west of it. There is a fine lower fortress built in the elongated form of an almond-shaped money-counting board on a long, rocky point right at the mouth of the harbor. The circumference of this castle, [267b] paced out on top of the walls, is three thousand eight hundred paces. There is no moat on the landward side since the castle is on a rock. There are two gates. One, which is down by the sea, is the harbor gate, and looks north; the other is on the landward side and opens southeastward *[q]*. This is the great gate to the outer suburb. When you go into this gate, the inner citadel is on the left side. It is a six-sided castle, a hexagon like Solomon's seal, after the manner of Uyvar castle. Each angle forms a sturdy bastion, and thus there are six such bastions. The whole fine citadel is a strong rampart built entirely of brick and stone, [267b/5] and every stone has been cut to shape. On top of each corner bastion there is a lead-roofed guard-chamber built of masonry, and the decorative lead domes of these give a very attractive appearance to the castle. On each bastion are two large pieces of artillery, and these top-quality cannon are all aimed at the harbor. At the embrasures around the battlements, there are hundreds of iron *Şahi* guns [muzzle-loading cannons] and other small-shot pieces. The circumference of the citadel, taken by itself, is fully a thousand paces, and these are good long paces. There are thirty-three inhabited houses, with tile roofs, but no gardens, and a gateway opening to the north. Over the space between the inner and outer faces of this gateway, there is a great domed chamber that serves as the council room for the officers and men of the garrison, and here all the watchmen and sentries remain day and night, [267b/10] fully armed and ready to take their watch in turn. The walls of this citadel are solid masonry, a full thirty feet thick, and their height is a full 15 meters (20 *arşın*s).

Praise of the lower, outer castle

The circumference of this castle is three thousand eight hundred paces. Including the masonry structures just accounted for in the inner castle, there are altogether six hundred accommodations of masonry construction. These are prosperous residences, roofed all over with tiles. There is in the castle a mosque of Sultan Murad Khan the third, son of Selim Khan, and this is a fine mosque with a lead-roofed masonry cupola and an elegantly constructed minaret. It is not in the marketplace, however, but on an elevated location in the middle of the city. There is a fountain and pool in the courtyard. Over the entrance door of this luminous mosque is the following date:

> In praise of God this mosque was built
> Nor [267b/15] did the Lord of right, may He be exalted, leave it destitute.
> Pilgrims to it have said the date of this shrine,
> "Excellent. The best of health and prosperity."
> In the year 1016.

After this there is the Ferhad Ağa mosque in the marketplace,
which has a tile roof and an elegant and decorative minaret.
[314] One enters it by a flight of ten stone steps, for this is a
house of worship built high up on a platform, with shops set in
vaulted masonry chambers below. The inscription over the
entrance door of this mosque is:

> Ferhad Ağa of the people of religion built this,
> A dedication to God for pious folk to worship in.
> To the best of His slaves, mosques within the fortress
>   were a care,
> And the date is "in the establishment of a mosque for the
>   Muslims."
> In the year [A.H. 1014].

In addition to this mosque there are . . . neighborhood mosques as
well. There is one upper school for scholars, and one [267b/20]
children's primary school, which is one of the benefactions of Sultan
Murad the third. There is one dervish chapel, one commercial inn,
[*in margin:* "one bath, which is Çigale Pasha's,"] and eighty-five
shops. In most streets there are many fountains of running water,
which is led in from outside, and at the head of each street there is
a fountain. The city is embellished with trees and vines so that the
sun does not beat into the fine marketplace at all, and all the city
notables sit here, playing backgammon, chess, various kinds of
draughts, and other board games, for this is an isolated place.

The costumes of the heroes

Old or young, great or small, they all wear Algerian costume and
stroll bravely about. The old men wear turbans wound on a fez
[267b/25] or various sorts of cloth skullcap. They wear three knives
all tucked in at the same place on the waist, and short black riding
boots on their feet. The young men wear white knee breeches,
European shoes, and crimson fezzes. They wear their shirt-fronts
open down the breast, leave their arms bare, and stroll around with
a sash about their waists. I did not see what sort of clothes the ladies
wear, because here, a woman never comes out of doors until after
she is dead. These are people with an intense and punctilious sense
of personal honor, Godly men, full of zeal for the maintenance of
moral propriety.

All the people from Tripoli, Tunis, and Algiers come here every
year with their ships, and drop anchor in this harbor, bringing every
sort of merchandise, as well as black African [315] slaves. This is
because ships making a run for it from the western lands pull up
their steeds at this [267b/30] station and cast anchor here, for this
castle of Anavarin stands with its chest bared toward the west. Ships
coming from Algiers run north before a southwest wind for a full
thousand miles to arrive at this Anavarin, and the business of these
people is continually with the Algerians.

Since the air and water are good, the populace is healthy. The water is the result of a great benefaction by Sultan Murad Khan the fourth, the conqueror of Baghdad. His naval commander and surgeon-barber, Hasan Pasha, spent a hundred thousand silver groats as a dedication to God, and brought to this city and its people a generous abundance of water from a place a day's journey away, like Ferhad cutting through rocks and through mountains as great as Behistun. Truly it is a great benefaction. The place where this water comes in, at the back of the castle, is all gardens and orchards, where [268a] lemons, bitter oranges, citrons, pomegranates, figs, and other fruits are grown. There are also many olive and cypress trees. On the other side of the road that runs in front of the castle gate, in the garden behind the shop of Cerah Ali Çelebi, there is a coffee tree, which produces beyond measure every year. If you wonder about the appearance of this tree, it is rather like the evergreen oak that grows throughout all Greek lands, a small, low-growing tree. It is just like the trees that grow in Yemen, but because the evil eye might fasten on it, [268a/5] he does not show it to anyone. During wintry days he covers it with felt, and keeps a brazier burning inside the felt. It is a very amusing tree to visit.

Among their praiseworthy manufactures here is a cloth like Chios dimity, so light that it is almost invisible. Indeed, this cloth is even clearer than Chian dimity and more resembles the cloth of Ahmedabad. It is sent as gifts to every land. Also, they work flints for the firelocks of muskets here, and these are widely renowned. Neither in Algiers, nor in Plevle (Taşlice) of Herzogovina, do they make firelock flints such as these.

An account of the outer suburb

Outside the castle to the southeast *[q]*, on a wide, level plateau, there are two hundred houses, all with gardens like the gardens of Irem, two-story masonry structures roofed with tile. Most of these houses are Greek, and there are no Armenians or [268a/10] Jews. There is one neighborhood mosque, one inn for voyagers, and fifteen shops for merchants, but no bath nor any other public benefaction. There is, however, one inhabited cloister of poor devotees of God that ought to be visited.

I made a further tour of this castle and said goodbye to all the valiant and heroic warriors. As a father and son part shedding tears, so we shed tears as we parted from one another. Then I went southeastward *[q]* following the seashore, and passing sometimes through orchards and olive groves, and sometimes through stony places, came in three hours to Modon. [316] [268a/15]

THE FORTRESS OF ANAVARİN-İ ATİK

by Aaron D. Wolpert

Ne cessando il vento nella premura, che teneva Sua Eccellenza di proseguire il camino, convenne farlo con sudorose fatiche delle Ciurme, giungendo nel primo giorno delle feste dello Spirito Santo in poca distanza da Navarino Vecchio, nel mentre erano alquanto lontane in Mare le Galeazze, e Navi, à quali stavano unite quelle del Convoglio Priuli, come si seppe à Vassilicò, vi fù spedito sdruscito Legno per farle venire alla spiaggia di Vrexomilo, lontano due miglia in circa da detto Navarino; ove si sbarcorono mille Cavalli, e dodeci mila, e trentatrè Fanti, essendovene sopra le Navi, ch'erano nell'Arcipelago altri mille, e cinquecento trentatrè, e spinto immediate da Sua Eccellenza Bergantino con Bandiera bianca sotto detta Piazza à chiederla à quell'Agà, con comminatione, che negandola sarebbe colla forza stata destrutta.[1]

The hurried Ottoman surrender on June 2, 1686, signaled the demise of Anavarin-i atik as a defensive installation.[2] When Otto Vilhelm von Königsmark and his Venetian troops captured the dilapidated fortress, it was exposed as strategically redundant. The citadel guarding the southern end of the Bay of Navarino—Anavarin-i cedid—was by this time firmly entrenched as the center of Ottoman defenses for Anavarin and its environs. An undermanned Anavarin-i atik was a weak target for hostile forces, and Königsmark attacked the older fortress only in the course of a campaign against the better-defended Anavarin-i cedid. That the soldiers guarding Anavarin-i atik numbered only about 100 (though they possessed some 35 cannons and 29 mortars)[3] and capitulated without firing a shot suggests

1. Locatelli 1691, p. 210.
2. Today the fortress is commonly known as Palaionavarino or Palaiokastro. Other names employed for it in the 17th, 18th, and 19th centuries included Abarmus, Abarinus, Albarinos, Albaxinus, Avarinos, Coryphasium, Ivérin, Nelea, Port de Jonc, Porto Giunco, Pylos, Zonklon, and Zunchio

(see Evliya Çelebi in Appendix I; Bellin 1771; and Bory de Saint-Vincent 1836, p. 128). For the etymology of Avarinos/Abarinus/Navarino, see Miller 1921, pp. 107–109. With regard to the surrender of Anavarin-i atik, see further Stouraiti 2001, pp. 40, 53–54; Marasso and Stouraiti 2001, pp. 30, 50–51, 58; Garzoni 1720, vol. 1, pp. 153–155.

3. Locatelli 1691, p. 212. In 1572, only 10 men were under the command of the *dizdar*, whereas in 1574, 33 men had been ordered to be transferred from the garrison there to the fortress of Manya (Mani); see Appendix IV. On the size of the garrison, see also Chapter 4.

that Ottoman commanders considered Anavarin-i cedid *the* bulwark defending the bay sheltered behind the island of Sphakteria.

The purpose of this appendix is to examine in detail the text of TT880 with regard to its description of the fortress of Anavarin-i atik in 1716, after the fortress had once again fallen into Ottoman hands.[4] In particular, the physical remains of the fortress, as illustrated on early maps, and as preserved in the accounts of Venetian administrators and early modern travelers (both Ottoman and Western), are compared with the information noted by the scribe of TT880. It has been possible not only to spatially reference his account and to verify its essential accuracy, but also to gain some understanding of why Anavarin-i atik and Anavarin-i cedid are described so differently in the document. Brief examinations of the strategic significance and the evolution of Anavarin-i atik as a military installation provide a geographical and historical context for the discussion that follows.

THE STRATEGIC SIGNIFICANCE OF ANAVARİN-İ ATİK

The fortress of Anavarin-i atik, at ancient Koryphasion, sits on a towering rock formation (over 200 m high) that erupts sharply from the sea, shielding an expansive lagoon that stretches inland to the east (Figs. II.1, II.2).[5] The formation extends about half a mile from north to south along the coast and includes the island of Sphakteria (Fig. II.3), which is separated from the mainland only by the narrow Sykia Channel.

The fortress commands not only the northern end of the Bay of Navarino, but also a picturesque kidney-shaped cove to the north called Voidokoilia (Fig. II.4).[6] The cliffs that rise over the lagoon are unassailable, a rocky face is turned toward the sea, and steep and difficult paths lead to the fortress (Fig. II.5).[7] Such an imposing presence impressed medieval travelers and early modern visitors, who often insisted on the defensive capacity of the fortress, even as they commented on its depleted garrisons and ramshackle defenses: "To the West end of the Harbour stands Old Navareene (formerly called Pylus) on a high Hill very steep; the walls are very much out of repair, great part being fallen down; there are very few Inhabitants in it. It might be made impregnable, no hills being near it. I cannot say whether they have any Guns in it."[8]

4. Anavarin-i atik is entry 13 in TT880; see Chapter 2.

5. See Zangger et al. 1997, pp. 556–559, for the geological history of the area.

6. The sheltered beach there evoked images of the Homeric "sandy Pylos" for the members of the Expédition scientifique (Blouet 1831–1838, vol. 1, pp. 4–7), who disputed Pouqueville's (1826–1827, vol. 6, p. 72) assertion that the Palace of Nestor had been located near the modern village of Pyla.

7. A narrow spit separating the lagoon from the bay affords the most direct access to the southern end of the fortress, where a paved road led to the main gate. Modern tracks ascend from the Voidokoilia beach to the north end of the fortress, where there is no gate.

8. Randolph 1689, pp. 5–6. See also the approximately contemporary account of Evliya Çelebi [267a–a/5] (App. I).

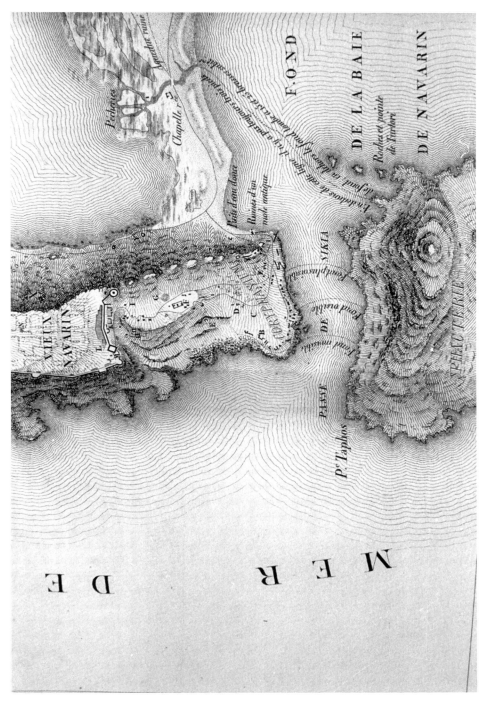

Figure II.1. Excerpt from a map of the area of Anavarin-i atik (1835). *Atlas, pl.* X

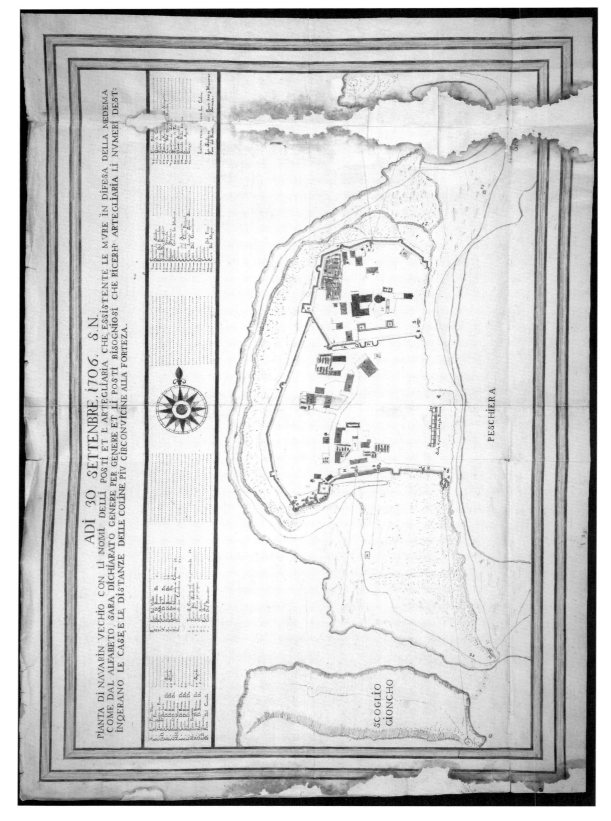

Figure II.2. Venetian plan of Anavarin-i atik, possibly part of Provveditore Generale Francesco Grimani's original collection and dated to 1706.
Courtesy of the Gennadius Library, American School of Classical Studies at Athens

Figure II.3. Southern end of Anavarin-i atik with the Bay of Navarino and Sphakteria in the distance

Figure II.4. Voidokoilia and the Osmanaga Lagoon from the inner fortress at Anavarin-i atik

Figure II.5. Anavarin-i atik from the north; Cave of Nestor (center) with the rear of the inner fortress above

During the three decades of Venetian occupation (1686–1715), *prov-*
veditori generali inspected the site and listed it among the most defensible
fortresses in the Morea, with Francesco Grimani calling for major renova-
tions.[9] Two other Venetian administrators, Giacomo Corner and Antonio
Molin, considered its advantages and disadvantages as follows:

> A prospetto d'esso vi sorge la fortezza di Navarino Vecchio molto
> più stimabile per li riguardi della sua situatione col benefitio di cui
> resta così sottratta all'offese che poco cura le regole dell'arte per
> fortificarsi. Si drizza su la sommità d'un sasso distaccato dal con-
> tinente, a cui due sole strade, che possono agevolmente tagliarsi,
> v' aprono ristretto accesso, nè in alto so ritrovarla peccante, che alla
> porta, ove si riduce tutto il debole, rimediabile però col travaglio di
> qualche operatione, di cui n'è il sito capace.[10]

> La Fortezza di Navarin vecchio situata dirimpetto il nuovo Nava-
> rino, con la sola separatione che gli rifferisce la lunghezza del Porto,
> gode il benefitio di valida difesa sopra l'eminenza d'alpestre diruppo,
> non però essente dalle sue imperfetioni e naturali diffetti.[11]

Miller notes that despite such optimism, the fortress was facing imminent
demolition even as the last Venetian garrison was ejected in 1715.[12] And
there is little evidence for Venetian modifications in the years 1686–1715.
Nor did the Turks subsequently renovate the crumbling citadel, although
it was not yet entirely deserted.[13] Immediately following the Ottoman retreat from the Morea in 1828, members of the Expédition scientifique de
Morée could not ignore the ruined condition of Anavarin-i atik. Their
commentaries read more like archaeological reports than like the travelers'
accounts of the preceding centuries.[14]

Bory de Saint-Vincent provides a detailed description of the "port"
facilities and the Turkish graves scattered along the road ascending the citadel. For the "méconnaissables" ruins, "tout ce qui reste d'une cité dont la
population acheva de se disperser," he laments that all the carpentry, doors,
windows, and so on have disappeared, along with any trace of marble façades
or even any cut stone, such that the cultural life of Anavarin-i atik cannot be
reconstructed, "si les arts y furent jamais cultivés."[15] Nor did he recognize
among the ruins chapels, churches, or convents—in short, "choses cede-
pendant qui sembleraient devoir être inhérentes aux cités du moyen âge."[16]
What he found instead were unidentified vestiges, a small cylindrical tower
with a tree growing in the center, vaults and cellars, a stairway, a large lime-

9. Grimani 1701 [1896–1900],
p. 484. Throughout its occupation of
the Morea, the Venetian administration
wrestled with the question of which
fortresses to maintain and which to
demolish, a particularly pressing question because the manpower available
to secure its dominion was rapidly
depleted. See Pinzelli 2000 and, specifically with reference to the fortresses
on the Bay of Navarino, p. 392, n. 36,
pp. 399, 401, 405–409, 413, 421, 425;

also Stouraiti 2001, pp. 86, 95.
    10. Corner 1691 [1885–1889],
p. 308.
    11. Molin 1693 [1896–1900],
p. 438.
    12. Miller 1921, p. 424; see also An-
drews 1953, p. 42.
    13. See Chapter 4, p. 165.
    14. Blouet (1831–1838, vol. 1, p. 5)
turned his attention toward the prehistory of the region: "Maintenant que
l'existence d'une ville antique nous est

démontrée dans les lieux que nous
avons parcourus, et que nous avons
retrouvé sur le mont Coryphasium
l'aspect de la Pylos inaccessible et
sablonneuse décrite ainsi par Homère,
notre conviction intime nous porterait
à affirmer que nous avons découvert
la ville de Nestor."
    15. Bory de Saint-Vincent 1836,
p. 150.
    16. Bory de Saint-Vincent 1836,
p. 151.

Figure II.6. Anavarin-i atik from the east

stone block for an olive press, and a cistern that still held water gathered from a side trough.

There are a number of good reasons why Anavarin-i atik, because of practical shortcomings, failed to live up to the expectations invoked by its imposing topography (Fig. II.6) and was of relatively little use to the Ottomans. Artillery placed there commanded the harbor of Anavarin only imperfectly (Fig. II.7), and defending the main southern entrance to the Bay of Anavarin was a major concern for Ottoman strategists.[17] Evliya Çelebi, pointing out the strategic significance that this expansive "safe anchorage" held for the Ottoman fleet, recorded that Yusuf Pasha in 1669 assembled some 700 ships there for an attack on Crete.[18] Anavarin-i atik guarded the narrow passage north of the island of Sphakteria, yet the Sykia Channel (see Fig. II.8) was closed with scuttled ships shortly after the Battle of Lepanto in 1571 in response to skirmishes that threatened Ottoman control of the bay.[19]

17. Evliya Çelebi asserts that the 23 large cannons in the fortress could reach Anavarin-i cedid, but that they were not effective in covering the southern channel because they "overshot the range": Appendix I, [267a/30]. Paruta (1658, p. 185) maintains the same for the bay: "It not being [possible] to be injured by shot from the Castell, which is seated very high, and far off." Kevin Andrews (1953, p. 42) is more specific: "Old Navarino's guns were ineffective inside the Bay, where enemy ships could withdraw out of range." Andrews counts only five guns "of any appreciable size" on Grimani's plan of 1706 (Fig. II.2; Andrews 1953, pl. X), with the implication that the citadel no longer served as a significant artillery installation for controlling harbor access. The drawing, reproduced

here as Fig. II.2, is not marked by the coat of arms that adorns other plans commissioned by Grimani, but because the plan was produced in the first year of Grimani's governorship, Andrews (1953, p. 9) thinks it possible that it was included in Grimani's original collection.

18. Appendix I, [267a/15–a/30]. Paruta (1658, p. 185) notes that "the Haven of Navarino is very spacious, very convenient for water, and for other accommodations and also a safe receptacle for any Fleet."

19. With regard to incidents at Anavarin in the wake of Lepanto, see Paruta 1658, pp. 182–189. For the blocking of the Sykia Channel in 1576, see Appendix IV, Document 29. See also Randolph 1689, pp. 5–6: "Formerly there were two Entrances into the Har-

bour, but in the Year 1571 when the Christians obtained the great Victory over the Turks before the Gulph of Lepanto, the Turks having several Ships, and Gallies in the Harbour, and fearing the Christians would come in and destroy them, stopped up the Entrance to the West of the Island (so as only small Boats can now pass); and built a very strong castle to the eastward called New Navareene." Don Juan of Austria followed his victory at Lepanto with unsuccessful assaults on Modon and Anavarin-i atik. Ottoman reinforcements supporting Anavarin-i atik harassed Spanish and Italian troops for three days from positions outside the fortress walls, after which the besieging force abandoned the attack for lack of supplies.

Figure II.7. Sphakteria from the outer fortress at Anavarin-i atik

The Ottomans soon afterward constructed Anavarin-i cedid on the headland west of the modern town of Pylos. Southern emplacements at Anavarin-i cedid more effectively covered what was the only practical entrance to the harbor after 1576, the wide channel south of Sphakteria. Not only did Anavarin-i atik inadequately control access to the strategic harbor, it was also ill equipped to manage the seaborne commercial traffic that passed through the bay. Political geography mattered as well, since the incorporation of the fortress into the administrative jurisdiction of Modon in 1439 (an arrangement that was preserved following the Ottoman conquest) removed the fortress from its function as a Frankish border outpost, the very circumstance that had motivated its construction in the 13th century.[20]

Inadequate command of local maritime affairs was not the only disadvantage of Anavarin-i atik as an effective defensive fortress; water-supply problems and rather inhospitable immediate environs handicapped the installation as well. The former in particular was a significant obstacle to effective defense of Anavarin-i atik in the event of siege.[21] Evliya Çelebi characterizes Anavarin-i atik as a "waterless island" and highlights extraordinary efforts devoted to water collection and conservation. According to his account, daily demand was satisfied by a group of

20. Bory de Saint-Vincent (1836, pp. 128–129) states that "Pylos ou le vieux Navarin fut la seul ville réellement importante de toute cette côte jusqu'au quatorzième ou au quinzième siècle. Il est probable que Néokastron ou le nouveau Navarin l'absorba seulement après la conquête de Morosini, et quand le petite passe du nord entre Sphactérie et Coryphasium se trouva insuffisante pour les grands navires devenus d'un usage plus général: il pourrait se faire même que le détroit en ait été dégradé par les hommes." He follows here the earlier observa-

tions recorded in Bellin 1771: "Au fond du port, (et) du côté du nord, est le vieux Navarin, ville fort ancienne, nommée Zunchio, connue aussi sous le noms de Pylus et de Coryphasium, bâtie sur une hauteur escarpée qui n'est que roche, dont la pente va se perdre à la mer. Cette ville est en assez mauvais état aujourd'hui, il y a derrière elle un étang assez considérable qui communique avec le fond du port par un canal fort étroit; ce qui rend les environs fort malsain; il y a un passage fort mauvais entre le cap sur lequel le ville est bâti, et la

pointe du nord de l'île (Sphactérie); aussi n'est-il d'aucun usage si ce n'est pour quelques bateaux du pays. Le nouveau Navarins est mieux fortifié et plus peuplé que le vieux. Le fort qui est au dessus de la ville fut bâti par les Turcs en 1752." This passage is quoted in Bory de Saint-Vincent 1836, pp. 50–51, with some minor alterations to Bellin's text.

21. Buchon (1843, pp. 459–463) points out the practical features that really mattered at Anavarin-i atik—cisterns.

Figure II.8. Sykia Channel from the northwest

donkeys trained to descend a path leading to a well[22] "down below in the sandy area by the harbor," where handlers would fill the water jars for transport back up to the citadel. Evliya claims that the donkeys returned the jars to the townspeople, stopping in front of houses and braying their arrival.[23]

Residences were outfitted with private cisterns, and immense public tanks were conspicuous structures that rarely failed to attract the attention of later visitors.[24] Evliya also records a strictly controlled water-recycling program, where for the inner castle there was a cistern "into which all the blessed rain is directed to flow by means of gutters and drain channels. In order that not a single drop of rainwater shall be wasted, even from the streets, the public roads are made of clean stone, and arranged so as to flow into and fill the cistern."[25] No dogs were permitted inside the inner circuit in an effort to keep the collected runoff clean.

Sections of the two aqueducts that served Anavarin-i cedid still stand, and it is possible to reconstruct their courses from springs to that fortress.[26] In contrast, an aqueduct running along the sandy spit separating the Bay of Anavarin from the Osmanaga Lagoon was, according to Evliya Çelebi, dilapidated even in the later 17th century.[27] A map drawn by François Levasseur shows short sections of it that ran no farther east than the Yialova River. He extends the aqueduct well inland in a vague easterly direction, but the inaccurate coastline and riverine network depicted on that map make it impossible to reconstruct the course of the aqueduct with confidence.[28]

22. Baltas (1987, p. 106; 1990, p. 106) identifies a "Roman well" at number 6 on his plan 2, at the southwestern edge of Osmanaga Lagoon. Feature "33" on Grimani's 1706 map (Figure II.2, Andrews 1953, pl. X) is a "Pozo con Aqua" on the beach south of Voidokoilia.

23. Appendix I, [266b/20–b/30].

24. E.g., Bory de Saint-Vincent 1836, p. 151; Buchon 1843, pp. 459–463.

25. Appendix I, [266b/30].

26. See Appendix III.

27. Appendix I, [267a/10]. Schwencke (1854, p. 73) comments on the lack of drinking water being a problem both for Anavarin-i atik and

for Anavarin-i cedid, as aqueducts were easily cut by an enemy.

28. Andrews 1953, pl. VIII. A depiction of the aqueduct on a map by Vincenzo Coronelli (Coronelli [1708], pl. 31; cf. Biblioteca Nationale Marciana di Venezia 203.d.201) suggests that it continued into the valley of the Xerias River.

Figure II.9. Foundations east of
Anavarin-i atik

Bory de Saint-Vincent's expedition encountered the aqueduct somewhere along the road running the length of the north end of the bay[29] and
followed the overgrown remains through the scrub to a terminus "aux bords
fangeux d'un chenal, qui met en communication la baie avec l'étang."[30]
The double-arched bridge spanning the canal and a ruined square church—
"la plus grande des constructions de ce genre que j'eusse encore vues,"[31]—
nearby (Fig. II.9), are almost certainly the same landmarks Blouet notes in
locating the aqueduct: "Après avoir traversé un ruisseau sur lequel est un
petit pont ruiné, près d'une chapelle aussi en ruines, et les restes d'un petit
aqueduc, on rencontre quelques chaumières. . . . Une chapelle ruinée, et
tout près, un petit canal qui communique du lac à la rade; sur le canal, un
petit pont en ruines, de deux arches, et très-près un petit aqueduc."[32] A
still-existing segment of this aqueduct, recently described by Baltas, has
a channel "20 εκατοστά του μέτρου και προστατεύεται μ'ένα ελαφρώς
τοξοτό σκέπαστρο. Το υλικό κατασκευής είναι θρύμματα κεράμου με
αμμοκονίασμα ως συνδεκτικό υλικό."[33]

THE HISTORY OF THE POST-CLASSICAL
FORTRESS

Post-classical construction commenced at Anavarin-i atik in the 13th century, following the Latin capture of Constantinople, at the direction of
the Flemish Saint Omer family, lords of Frankish Thebes.[34] Nicholas II
extended Saint Omer authority southward to Anavarin by marrying the
widow of Prince William de Villehardouin, and then ordered a castle erected
at "Avarinos" for his nephew, Nicholas III. Though the younger Nicholas
survived the Catalan slaughter of Frankish nobles at Kephissos in 1311,

29. Perhaps at the "ruins of medieval
aqueduct" marked at no. 22 on plan 2,
Baltas 1987, p. 106; 1990, p. 106.

30. Bory de Saint-Vincent 1836,
p. 141.

31. Bory de Saint-Vincent 1836,
p. 142.

32. Blouet 1831–1838, vol. 1, p. 6.

33. Baltas 1990, p. 105: "20 cm
wide, and it is protected by a slightly

arched cover. The construction material
consists of broken tile bound together
with mortar."

34. See Andrews 1953, pp. 40–42.

the fortress at "Port de Jonc" (i.e., Anavarin-i atik) fell into Genoese hands in the mid-14th century and served as a base for raids on Venetian colonies in Messenia.[35]

Marie de Bourbon occupied the citadel in the course of a dispute over succession in the principality, defending it against the combined forces of the barons of Achaea, the archbishop of Patras, and her brother-in-law Philip, the self-styled "Prince of Achaea."[36] After her abortive campaign against Patras, in which Carlo Zeno broke the siege and drove the attackers back within the walls of Anavarin-i atik, only the intervention of Amadeo VI of Savoy defused a rapidly escalating conflict. By 1381 the Navarrese Grand Company had annexed the fortress as protection for its headquarters in Andrusa, a venture that worried the Venetian governors at Modon and Koron because of the threat posed should the harbor return to Genoese control.

An initial Venetian offer to purchase the fortress and its hinterland from the Navarrese was declined, but the Genoese baron of Achaea, Centurione II Zaccaria, did sell the fortress to Venice in 1423, when his principality came under increasing pressure from Greeks and the Italian adventurer Oliverio Franco. Venice was still more concerned about protecting its commercial interests in the Morea: "The lack of settled government, and of any proper police, practically ruined [Venetian] traffic in the Malmsey wine. . . . In 1417 [Venice] had garrisoned Navarino, just in time to prevent its occupation by the Genoese," and actually in advance of the official purchase from Zaccaria in 1423.[37] Several other castles were acquired in succeeding years, and Navarino was assigned to the jurisdiction of Modon in 1439.

Anavarin stood as a stronghold of Christendom even after the initial Ottoman conquest of the Morea. Mehmed II affirmed Venetian control in 1460,[38] but the citadel was targeted by Sultan Bayezid II as he swept through the Venetian colonies a generation later. An assault on the fortress failed a year or two before the turn of the 16th century, but Ottoman forces returned in 1500 from a more advantageous strategic position. Repelled by Venetian defenders at Nafplion, Bayezid II successfully besieged Modon and moved on to Anavarin.[39] When Ottoman forces arrived announcing the fall of Modon, the commandant of Anavarin surrendered immediately, despite abundant provisions and a 3,000-man garrison; commandant Carlo Contarini was subsequently beheaded for cowardice.[40] Not long afterward, a Greek ensign known as Demetrios, an unnamed Albanian, and 50 Venetian soldiers stormed the fortress, only to abandon it and its inhabitants again without a fight when Ottoman cavalry and galleys

35. Miller 1908, pp. 300–301.
36. Zakythinos 1953, pp. 109–110.
37. Miller 1908, p. 385. With regard to the significance to Venice of Anavarin-i atik, the Genoese and Navarrese presence there, and negotiations for its acquisition, see further Hodgetts 1974, pp. 477–478; Gertwagen 2000, p. 125, p. 249, n. 20; and Chrysostomides

1996, p. 54, no. 25, p. 55, no. 26, p. 68, no. 32, pp. 73 and 77, no. 33, pp. 225–228, nos. 117 and 118, p. 336, no. 168, and p. 587, no. 314.
38. Miller 1908, p. 449; 1921, pp. 105–106.
39. Coronelli 1687a, p. 53.
40. On this episode see also Sagredo 1679, pp. 113–114.

returned in force.[41] As we have seen, defending the castle was difficult irrespective of the commandant's temerity. Though the fortifications were adequate and the defensive topography sublime, a series of commanders was unwilling to commit to long sieges.

Figure II.10. Venetian east *(left)* **and south** *(right)* **views of Anavarin-i atik, a late and undated insertion into Provveditore Generale Francesco Grimani's collection.** Courtesy of the Gennadius Library, American School of Classical Studies at Athens

THE ACCOUNT OF TT880

Standing structures in Anavarin-i atik were still recognizable in the 17th century, when an Ottoman garrison was stationed in the citadel, preserving some sense of building functions. Evliya Çelebi's account[42] corroborates the information recorded in TT880 better than any other narrative, despite a tendency toward breathless embellishment, because it recounts conditions inside the fortress shortly before the Venetian conquest of 1686. That narrative assistance is important for deciphering what information TT880 provides about Anavarin-i atik. The plans and views drawn for Grimani and for the Expédition scientifique are invaluable as well, as are the later descriptions of the fortifications composed by Bory de Saint-Vincent and Andrews.[43]

TT880 does not refer to the road that winds up the southern end of the citadel (Figs. II.10, II.11). The text also ignores a curtain wall that protected the lowest part of the fortress on its landward (southeast) side.

41. Coronelli 1687a, pp. 53–55. An uncle of Piri Reis was responsible for its recapture; see Loupis 1999b, p. 312. Thirty years later, the Ottomans at Anavarin-i atik continued to be harassed by Franks, this time by Spaniards based at Koroni (Laiglesia 1905, pp. 23, 43–44). The Ottoman version of events differs slightly from the

Italian in suggesting that Anavarin had already been taken when Modon was captured. See also Ökte 1988, p. 661.

42. See Appendix I. In the Biblioteca Nazionale Marciana di Venezia there are additional unpublished Venetian plans of the fortresses of the Morea (see Steriotou 2003 for a complete catalogue; those relevant to

Anavarin-i atik and Anavarin-i cedid include nos. 62–68).

43. Andrews 1953 reproduces the relevant plans from the Grimani collection (pls. VII, VIII, IX, X). For descriptions of the fortifications, see Bory de Saint-Vincent 1836, pp. 148–154; Andrews 1953, pp. 42–48.

Figure II.11. Southern approach to the outer fortress

Already in the 17th century, that wall had "fallen into ruin in several places"[44] and was identified as *Mura Anticha* on the plan drawn for Grimani (Fig. II.2, feature 31).[45] Evliya Çelebi assigns the construction of the wall to Sultan Bayezid, but does not mention the tower connected to it.[46] TT880 also makes no mention of the graves and gardens scattered outside the main gate of the outer fortress and noted in passing by Bory de Saint-Vincent.[47] Instead, its account begins with the "stone-built walls" of Anavarin-i atik.

The length of all walls is given in the metrical unit *ziraʾ*.[48] Both the outer and inner fortresses are said to be 454 *ziraʾ*s. Approximate measurements drawn from the scale plan of Anavarin-i atik published by the Expédition scientifique (Fig. II.12)[49] suggest that the outer and inner fortifications were indeed of nearly equal length, about 350–360 m each.[50] For the outer circuit are listed:

The walls on the side of the gate: 165 *ziraʾ*s, 30 *ziraʾ*s of these in ruin
The right side: 132 *ziraʾ*s
The left side: 157 *ziraʾ*s

44. Appendix I, [267a/5].
45. Also Andrews 1953, pl. X.
46. Bory de Saint-Vincent 1836, p. 149; Andrews 1953, p. 42.
47. A Turkish cemetery is marked on the Grimani plan, Fig. II, feature 30; also Andrews 1953, pl. X.
48. Equivalent to 0.758 m.
49. Blouet 1831–1838, vol. 1, pl. VI, fig. II.
50. This conclusion presumes that those who composed the description in TT880 considered the "few stretches of low, thin parapet" along the eastern side of the inner fortress to be a continuous wall. Andrews (1953, p. 48) insists that

"the inner circuit is in the form of a horseshoe, with its eastern flank unwalled," yet it is clear enough that according to several earlier accounts it was thought that the fortifications surmounting the eastern precipice constituted a wall of the inner fortress. Three of the four maps from the Grimani collection that Andrews 1953 reproduces (pls. VII–IX) depict a fortification wall along the eastern side of the inner fortress and no corresponding wall for the outer fortress. The plan prepared for the Expédition scientifique (Blouet 1831–1838, vol. 1, pl. VI) also clearly shows the course of this wall.

In contrast, Evliya Çelebi claims that there were no walls on the eastern side of the castle, "since there is a high, smooth cliff, ten minarets in height, along this side. Here not even the birds that fly in the air can find a place for their claws to grip, for the rock is slick and polished," except for "a few falcons, eagles, vultures, and kites." But to take his testimony at face value would be unwise. There is some reason to suspect that Çelebi never investigated the upper fortress closely, as it would "exhaust any of Adam's sons to go up into this inner citadel" (App. I, [266b/30–67a]).

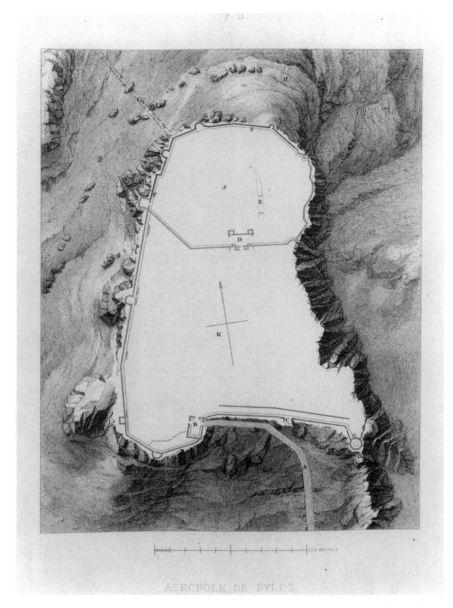

ACROPOLE DE PYLOS.

The inner fortress is divided into four sections:

> The walls next to the gate: 105 *zira*ʾs, of which 30 are in ruin
> The left wall: 175 *zira*ʾs
> The right wall: 84 *zira*ʾs
> The west wall: 90 *zira*ʾs[51]

The ascertainment of what is meant by "right" and "left" is of immediate significance. The scribe probably marked off sections of the circuit wall according to the placement of towers and in recognition of sharp directional changes, and it should be possible to match those divisions with dimensions estimated from the plan published by the Expédition scientifique. Because the entries for the inner and outer fortresses begin

Figure II.12. Scale drawing of Anavarin-i atik. Blouet 1831–1838, vol. 1, pl. VI, fig. II

51. For the walls "on the side of" and "next to" the inner and outer gates, the scribe records exactly 30 *zira*ʾs dilapidated for both the inner and the outer fortifications. One senses here a certain amount of formulaic composition, an impression reinforced by the fact that for the inner circuit, the "right" and "west" walls are nearly the same length.

Figure II.13. Portion of the western circuit of the outer fortress, from the southeast

with the fortifications in the vicinity of the gates, left and right must also take the gates as a central reference point.

For the outer fortress, it follows that the 157 *zira³*s for the "left side" must describe the long western fortifications that run north to the wall of the inner circuit, between "G" and the numeral "1" = "i" (Figs. II.2, II.12, II.13; capital letters and numbers refer to those on Grimani's plan in Fig. II.2).[52] The "walls on the side of the gate" would then mean those immediately east and west of the main gate (A) of the outer fortress and would include the round tower (G) at the southwestern corner of the enceinte (compound) and the main gate itself (Figs. II.14, II.15). The 132 *zira³*s on the right side would refer to that section of the fortification farther east of the main gate, including tower M (Fig. II.16) at the southeastern corner of the enceinte.

It seems likely that the scribe composed the description of the walls of the outer fortress while walking along the main road that leads through the main gate (A) and then continued to the inner fortress. It is for this reason that he records the southern curtain wall near the gate before describing the western wall of the outer fortress.

In addition to the segments of the curtain wall of the outer fortress, TT880 describes the conspicuous square bastion (C) built around the gate (Fig. II.15) at the start of the 16th century.[53] The locations of two smaller bastions placed at the left and right "corners" of the gate are uncertain. TT880 positions them close to the gate itself but does not associate them with the curtain wall. Two rectangular structures drawn at oblique angles just inside the gate on Grimani's plan may represent these bastions.

For the inner fortress, there are no real difficulties in matching the description in TT880 to the physical remains. The "walls next to the gate" clearly refer to the straight sections of walls on either side of the gate to the inner fortress (Q). These run on an east–west axis between the round towers (R) and (2).[54] Andrews, following the plan submitted to Grimani in 1706, places the gate just west of a prominent double bastion.[55] TT880 registers "two bastions attached to the left of the gate."

52. Also on pl. X in Andrews 1953.

53. Andrews 1953, p. 44, and pl. X, "C." In TT880 this structure is the "bastion above the gate." On Grimani's plan it is the same: "Tore sopra la Porta."

54. The plan in Blouet 1831–1838, vol. 1, pl. VI, shows neither tower.

55. Andrews 1953, pl. X. On the plan in Blouet 1831–1838, vol. 1 (pl. VI), the gate is drawn between the two towers. Andrews (1953, p. 47) also mentions the remains of a vaulted passage piercing the wall between them.

Figure II.14 *(left)*. Southwestern corner of the outer fortress, from the east

Figure II.15 *(below)*. Gate to the outer fortress, from the east

Figure II.16. Southeastern extension of the outer fortifications, from the southwest

In the next line of TT880 there is listed a ruined "bastion at the left corner of the wall" that must be the round tower (2) that stood near the juncture of the inner and outer enceintes (Z).[56] For someone viewing the inner fortress from a position just outside its gate, this tower would be in the "left corner." The "west wall" of the inner fortress should be that section of the wall that extends from the round tower (2) to the prominent inset in the western curtain wall of the outer circuit wall.[57] The "left wall" starts at that inset and reaches around to the north, east, and finally south to the edge of the eastern precipice, approximately to the point where the fortification wall ends on the map drawn for Grimani. The irregular remains of walls on the eastern side of the fortress would then be those of the "right wall."

Insufficient detail is recorded in TT880 to reconstruct the route of the scribe through the ruins, and there is no reason to think that he was much concerned with the spatial arrangement of the features inside the fortress.[58] Houses in the outer fortress are almost ignored, with 26 described only as having ruined roofs but structurally sound. In contrast, Evliya Çelebi counts in the "lower castle . . . eighty small, cramped, tile-roofed masonry houses, with no gardens or orchards."[59] The mosque likewise has a ruined roof but intact walls, according to TT880. Çelebi provides slightly more detail: "The mosque of Sultan Bayezid is here, a serviceable but abbreviated mosque of old-fashioned construction."[60] The only building in the Grimani drawing large enough for the 23 × 17 *zira*ᵓs assigned to the mosque is the Latin church of the Spirito Santo (17) just south of the gate to the inner fortress on that plan.[61] The long and narrow building (20) that is represented immediately southwest of it must be the "harem in front of it" in TT880, and its presence on Grimani's plan appears to clinch the identification of the mosque. Grimani's plan also places a cistern (19) northwest of the building that may be assumed to be the mosque, but it does not match the dimensions noted in TT880 (18 × 11 *zira*ᵓs).

56. Also on pl. X in Andrews 1953.

57. This feature is marked on all the maps in the Grimani collection as well as on the map published for the Expédition scientifique.

58. This situation contrasts with the description of Anavarin-i cedid, where it is possible to suggest the path followed by the scribe; see Appendix III.

59. Appendix I, [266b/20].

60. Appendix I, [266b/20].

61. The mosque had apparently been reconsecrated by the Venetians in the name of the Spirito Santo, during the festival of which the fortress was captured; see Locatelli 1691, p. 210.

Two cisterns are listed following the description of the defenses of the inner fortress.[62] There are only six "half-ruined" houses in the inner fortress, and Evliya Çelebi's account also suggests that there were fewer here than in the outer fortress. One of the houses must have been the *Casa del Ajutante* (15),[63] which TT880 does not specifically mention. The "church in good shape" appears on Grimani's plan as a building with an apse (13), near the eastern precipice. The guardpost to the left of the gate is not clearly identifiable on the Venetian plan, since any possible structures are too large for the building measuring 5×5 *zira*'s listed in TT880.

That the survey in TT880 records no more buildings does not necessarily imply neglect on the part of the Ottoman administrators—there was not much else to catalogue.[64] Evliya Çelebi claims that "there are *in toto* five shops, but there is no inn, bath, upper or lower school, nor any trace of gardens or orchards, for this is a waterless island."[65] The structures inside the fortress were mostly ruined in any case. The sparse description of Anavarin-i atik in TT880 makes sense when framed within a historical sequence that suggests a waning Ottoman presence and interest in the fortress. This emptiness is reinforced by the fact that the Budran *çiftlik* associated with Anavarin-i atik was totally uninhabited, and no *reaya* are listed as living in the fortress itself.

62. Three major cisterns are marked on Grimani's plan and may be the same as the three described in TT880.

63. Also on pl. X of Andrews 1953.

64. A Venetian source from 1689 recorded 8 good houses in the "castle" and 12 destroyed, with 12 good houses in the "fortress," 70 destroyed, and 8 good shops; see Davies 2004, p. 69, n. 38; and ASV, Senato, Provveditori di Terra e da Mar, b.860, f.217r.

65. Appendix I, [266b/20].

THE FORTRESS OF ANAVARİN-İ CEDİD

by John Bennet, Jack L. Davis, and Deborah K. Harlan

Il n'y existe pas plus de traces romaines ou byzantines: le peu de débris qu'on y voit, datent, à ce qu'il paraît, de la dernière occupation par les Vénetiens; ce sont quelques écussons d'armoiries, encastrés dans certains murs, ou tout au plus des mots à demi effacés, griffonnés sur un portail, où l'on dit qu'ils indiquaient l'entrée d'un pauvre hòpital. La ville est construite sur une pente assez rapide, exposée au couchant et un peu plus longue que large. Il ne règne point de fossés autour de ses murailles, celles-ci s'élèvent sur des roches tellement dures, qu'il eût été difficile d'en creuser, et qu'il serait impossible d'y ouvrir des tranchées pour l'attaque. C'est principalement avec la grosse artillerie des flottes qu'on en pourrait détruire les ouvrages. . . . Parmi les décombres de Navarin encaissés entre ses remparts demeurés seuls debout, on pouvait reconnaître que les rues y furent tortueuses, mal percées, étroites et souvent disposées en escalier, particulièrement vers l'orient, aux alentours de la citadelle: on y reconnaissait aussi les emplacements de quelques jardins, que couvraient des mauves, l'ortie pilulifère, le souci commun, des chardons et des amas d'ordures.[1]

Thus the prominent French naturalist and leader of the Expédition scientifique de Morée, Jean Baptiste Geneviève Marcellin Bory de Saint-Vincent, described the sad condition of the fortress of Anavarin-i cedid in his own day (1829), and the paltry remains of the Venetian occupation little more than a century after the collapse of the "Regno di Morea" (Fig. III.1).

ANAVARİN-İ CEDİD IN TEXTS AND FIGURES

In the summer of 1715, the army of the Ottoman grand vizier, Damad Ali Pasha, marched through the Peloponnese into Messenia. Its ultimate objective was the conquest of the Venetian strongholds of Modon and Koron, but its more immediate goal was the fortress of Anavarin-i cedid.[2] On the night of August 10 (Gregorian), this expeditionary force had camped "dans une plaine auprez d'un ruisseau qu'on appelle Handrino, à une lieue et demy de Navarin, que les Vénetiens avoient ruiné et abandonné."

1. Bory de Saint-Vincent 1836, p. 128.

2. See Chapter 1 for a discussion of the circumstances of these events. On the recapture of the Morea, see also Pinzelli 2000, pp. 426–427.

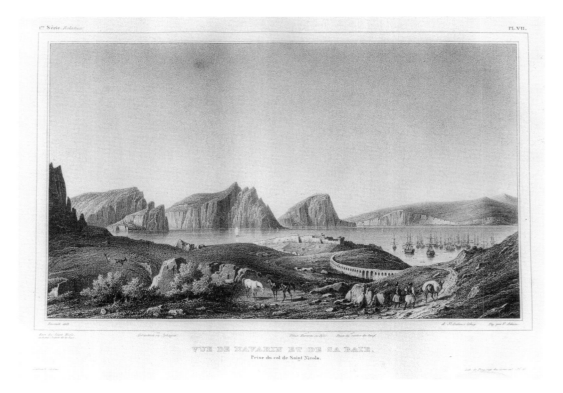

Figure III.1. View of Anavarin-i cedid and the Bay of Navarino, ca. 1829. *Atlas*, pl. VII

Because Anavarin-i cedid had been destroyed and deserted by the Venetians, however, the Ottoman army was diverted to Modon.[3] The fortress thus fell without a shot, but suffered considerable damage at the hands of its own garrison.

The extent of the destruction effected by the Venetians becomes clear even from a cursory examination of the text of TT880.[4] As might be expected, virtually all residential structures are described as being in ruin (nos. 43, 45, 49, 56, 62, 64, and 65 are exceptions), given that hardly more than six months had passed between the Venetian departure and the registration in Istanbul of this *mufassal defter*. It seems possible, however, that some reconstruction of public structures had already occurred in the six months between the reconquest and the composition of TT880. The *hamam* of the *Beylik* (no. 28), a church (no. 57), the Friday Mosque of Bayezid (no. 72), a primary school (no. 73), the prayer square next to the Friday Mosque (no. 75), and the Janissary winter barracks (no. 78) are not explicitly said to be damaged. Several shops also appear intact (nos. 88, 91–93). The Friday Mosque and the other church may have es-

3. Brue 1870, pp. 41–42. With regard to these events, see also Hammer-Purgstall 1842, p. 356; Iorga 1913, pp. 190–191. Hammer-Purgstall says that the army was camped at a place called "Begoghli," four leagues equidistant from Koron, Modon, and Anavarin, and that Anavarin had been deserted by the Venetians. Iorga pub-

lishes a firsthand Roumanian account of the expedition (attributed to Constantinos Dioikitis) that often provides more detail than Brue's. In this account, the Ottoman army camps at the *clairière de Kourt-bey* on July 30, 1715 (Julian), here clearly the spring of Goumbe, because the water is said to emerge from a basin with a stone vault

and then is led by a stone aqueduct to Anavarin-i cedid, after a journey of more than two hours.

4. As translated in Chapter 2. Numbered pieces of property discussed in this appendix refer to items in Chapter 2, entry 35, the *kale* of Anavarin-i cedid.

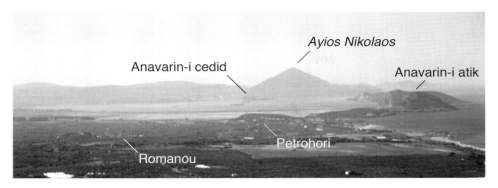

Figure III.2. Panorama showing the entire Bay of Navarino and the locations of both fortresses, Anavarin-i atik and Anavarin-i cedid

caped destruction because they were places of worship for the Venetians (see below).

It would perhaps be unwise to attribute all of the devastation to the Venetian retreat, since this was not the first occasion on which the fortress had experienced the impact of war. Only 30 years earlier, on June 18, 1686, Venice was poised to capture Anavarin-i cedid from its Ottoman garrison when, "on the night of the capitulation certain fires, which had been started by the bombardment, caused the explosion of a powder store in one of the bastions of the hexagonal fort."[5] The explosion led subsequently to the reconstruction of one corner of the *içhisar* (the inner redoubt of the fortress), and its use by Venice as an arsenal.[6]

Anavarin-i cedid was just over a century old when it was captured by Venice. The fortress had been built on sloping ground near the southern entrance to the harbor of Anavarin soon after the battle of Lepanto in 1571, and as a direct consequence of that particular conflict between the Holy League and the Ottoman empire (Fig. III.2).[7] At the same time the Sykia Channel, between the island of Sphakteria and the fortress of Anavarin-i atik (Fig. 3.11), was blocked by the deliberate sinking of ships in it.[8]

Otherwise, very little is known from Western sources about the history of the fortifications of Anavarin-i cedid. Kevin Andrews in his *Castles of the Morea* thought it likely that the western sea fort, labeled "forte Stᵃ Barba." (Santa Barbara) on Venetian plans, was the first part of

5. Andrews 1953, p. 49; also Locatelli 1691, pp. 224–225; Coronelli 1686, p. 77. With regard to damage inflicted on Anavarin-i cedid in the course of the Venetian siege, including a fire in the Friday Mosque, see Rycaut 1700, p. 225; Schwencke 1854, pp. 81–82. See further Stouraiti 2001, pp. 41, 57–58; Marasso and Stouraiti 2001, pp. 30, 50–51, 58; Garzoni 1720, vol. 1, pp. 159–160.

6. Andrews 1953, pp. 53–54.

7. Bory de Saint-Vincent's description of the physical geography of the fortress portrays its situation well. There has been disagreement about

the date of its construction. Evliya Çelebi (see App. I, [267a/25]) says that Neokastro was built by Kılıç Ali Pasha in A.H. 977 (A.D. 1569–1570), before the Battle of Lepanto. It is, however, clear from Ottoman archival sources that it was built after 1573 (see App. IV). See also Bory de Saint-Vincent's views on the date of Neokastro (1836, p. 51) and his evaluation of an earlier discussion by Bellin (1771), who believed it was built in 1752 by Turks. Beauvau (1615, p. 19), on the other hand, had written that Anavarin has "deux chasteaux, qui le deffendét l'un est le vieux *Navarin,* sur une haulte

montaigne, qui fut assiegé de la S. Ligue, en l'an 1572. & tient une autre entrée du port, que depuis ce temps là a esté bouché en telle sorte, qu'a present il n y seauroit passer qu'une petite barque à la fois. Mais sur la grande entrée, plusieurs grand vaisseaux peuvent passer de front. Les *Turcs* y ont faict un lieu fort d'un chasteau, et d'une petite ville de guerre." Oddly, Blouet (1831–1838, vol. 1, p. 2) of the *Expédition scientifique* mistakenly dates the construction of the fortress to the Venetian occupation.

8. See Appendixes II and IV regarding the blocking of this channel.

Figure III.3. Spring at Goumbe near Handrinou. *Atlas*, pl. XII

the installation to be built.[9] It is clear that the Venetians envisioned a strengthening of the fortress in a manner described in a plan prepared by the French engineer François Levasseur for Francesco Grimani, active in the Morea as *provveditore generale dell'armi* in the Morea (1699–1701) and as governor (1706–1708), but only a small part of this project was completed.[10]

We are even less well informed by Western sources about the history of buildings within the fortress and about the system of aqueducts that supplied the inhabitants with water. We do know, however, that water was conveyed to the citadel from two distinct locations. One is about four kilometers to the southeast, at a location that is today known as Palaionero (Old Water); the other is fed from the spring of Goumbe (Γκουμπέ), about nine kilometers to the northeast, near the town of Handrinou (Fig. III.3).[11] Channels of the two aqueducts converge at a place called Kamares (within the southeastern section of the modern town of Pylos, next to the road to Modon), where a series of well-preserved arches indicate where the aqueduct fed the water into an underground channel that debouched into cisterns within the citadel (Fig. III.4).[12] Haralambos A. Baltas, a local teacher and antiquarian, provides the fullest discussion of the aqueducts in his guidebook to the Pylos area. He has concluded that the section of the aqueduct that carried water from Palaionero was the first to be built, and

9. Andrews 1953, p. 53. Ottoman sources (see App. IV) clarify this matter: the bastion was built only slightly before the adjacent curtain wall.
10. Andrews 1953, p. 56.

11. The spring remains, but any surviving Ottoman constructions are entirely hidden beneath modern concrete.
12. See Navari 1991, p. 50, where a proof plate of a lithograph of this

section of the aqueduct, based on an 1841 sketch by E. M. Grosvenor, is published. See also Westminster 1842, facing p. 194; Castellan 1808, facing p. 77.

Figure III.4. Remains of the aqueduct at Anavarin-i cedid

that the longer segment from Handrinou was built in the Second Otto-man period, after the reconquest of Anavarin in 1716.[13]

Baltas adduces evidence from a map prepared for Grimani and pub-lished by Andrews: on it seems to be indicated only the segment of the aqueduct at Kamares and its course toward Palaionero.[14] Two other Vene-tian maps tell a different story, however, and Baltas's reconstruction of events must be rejected. An unpublished plan in the Grimani Archive, entitled "Plan de la ville et de citadelle de Navarin," clearly shows the course of the Handrinou aqueduct, thus demonstrating that the structure was in existence before 1686.[15] Similarly, a general map of the Bay of Ana-varin, although inaccurate in its depiction of coastlines, unmistakably in-dicates the courses of *three* aqueducts: one brings water to Anavarin-i atik; two conduct it to Anavarin-i cedid, the northernmost from the direction of Handrinou, the other from Palaionero.[16]

The text of Evliya Çelebi supports the dating of the aqueduct from Handrinou to the 17th century: he writes that the aqueduct serving Ana-varin-i cedid was a benefaction in the time of Murad IV (1623–1640) and brought water from a place a day's journey away. Only one aqueduct is mentioned. Evliya is certainly exaggerating the distance, but his descrip-tion is more likely to allude to the spring at Goumbe, which is consider-ably farther from Anavarin-i cedid than was Palaionero.[17]

13. See Baltas 1987, pp. 65–69. This opinion is contrary to local tradition, which declares the Goumbe segment to be the oldest and that from Palaionero to have been built by Venice in 1686. There are traces of a tower at the spring of Palaionero, and the Goumbe segment was repaired by the French and served the community of Pylos until 1907. See also Baltas 1987, p. 67, on the entrance of the aqueduct into the fortress.

14. Andrews 1953, pl. XI.

15. ASV, Grimani ai Servi, b.57, fasc. 172, E/D. This map shows the placement of cannons in a siege of the fortress and seems to have been pre-pared in anticipation of a Venetian

assault. We are grateful to S. Davies for bringing it to our attention.

16. Andrews 1953, pl. VIII; this drawing bears the signature of Levas-seur, who produced other drawings of Anavarin, including that on pl. XII; that on Andrews's pl. XI bears the arms of Grimani and was drawn by the Ger-man Beler; that on his pl. XIII, top, which shows the actual arcades of the aqueduct at Kamares, is unsigned.

17. See Appendix I, [267b/30–268a]. Blouet (1831–1838, vol. 1, pp. 6–7) describes a journey to and from the source at Goumbe; the return to Ana-varin took 2 hours and 12 minutes. Bory de Saint-Vincent (1836, pp. 191–

193) similarly followed the course of the aqueduct to its source at "Kourbeh." See also Leake 1830, pp. 398–399; Castellan 1808, pp. 83–84 and the illustration opposite p. 77. Castellan notices dilapidated remains of the aqueduct many miles from the citadel. As he approaches the fortress, he de-scribes the arcades of Kamares and an old quarry. See also the account of the Ottoman conquest of the Morea in 1715, where it is clear that a stone aqueduct carried water from Goumbe to Anavarin-i cedid (Iorga 1913, p. 190); the water is said to have arrived at the fortress with sufficient force to drive a small mill.

Sir W. Gell del. J.M.Baynes Litho.   Printed by C. Hullmandel

NAVARINO.

There are even smaller scraps of information regarding the interior of the citadel. Permission for entry needed to be arranged in advance, and some travelers were too impatient to bear the inevitable wait.[18] Certainly by the beginning of the 19th century, the entire fortress was already in a deplorable state. Pouqueville wrote that "Navarin ne se compose maintenant que de quatre bastions délabrés, garnis de canons en fer et sans affuts, ce qui n'empêche pas qu'elle ne soit comptée au nombres des villes de guerre, ayant ses janissaires, ses cannonniers et ses bombardiers, qui avaient de mon temps pour général et commandant d'armes un boulanger et un barbier tenant four et boutiques au bazar."[19] Gell visited the fortress at about the same time and painted a similar, dismal picture (Figs. III.5, III.6).[20]

Leake offered a more personalized narrative. From his account, it seems that, if Anavarin-i cedid had ever fully recovered from the Venetian retreat, it had suffered additional ravages during the Greek revolt (the so-called Orlov rebellion) sponsored by Catherine the Great of Russia in 1770.[21]

Edris Bey the commandant, whom I visit today in the fortress, is a young Stambuli, or Constantinopolitan, who, having spent the greater part of the property left him by his father, one of the chief kapidjis [i.e., head of the palace doorkeepers (kapucı s), a high-ranking Ottoman office] of the Sultan, was glad to sacrifice the remainder in obtaining this government, though, with all his efforts, its profits are so small, that he is often under the necessity of having recourse to Kyr Ghiorghio. There are about 300 Turkish families in the fortress, most of them in a wretched state of poverty. . . . The fortress consists of a low wall without any ditch, flanked by small bastions. On the side towards the sea, where it

Figure III.5. William Gell's rendering of Anavarin-i cedid, 1804.
Gell 1823, facing p. 26

18. See, e.g., Castellan 1808, p. 83.
19. Pouqueville 1826–1827, vol. 6, pp. 70–71.
20. See Chapter 4, p. 161.
21. On these events, see Chapter 1, p. 46, and Chapter 4, pp. 169–170.

Figure III.6. Current view of Anavarin-i cedid from the approximate position from which views by Gell (Fig. III.5) and by the Expédition scientifique de Morée (Fig. III.1) were drawn

ought to be the strongest, it has received only a miserable patching since it was battered by the Russians from the island [Sphakteria], in the year 1770.[22]

Although Leake's account is in disagreement with several nearly contemporary texts as to the number of Muslim families in the fortress, it is clear that, in the 18th and early 19th centuries, there was a substantial number of Turks resident at Anavarin-i cedid.[23] Differences in estimates of population, if not merely the result of misinformation, may reflect ad hoc fluctuations in the size of the Ottoman garrison. In times of war, additional troops would naturally have been stationed in the fortress, and Turks from outside the district took refuge there.[24] The text of TT880, along with a Venetian inventory, suggests that only a couple of hundred Turkish families resided at Anavarin-i cedid on the eve of the Venetian conquest (see below), although it is clear from Ottoman sources that initially it was envisioned that 700 houses would be built for the garrison (see App. IV).

Ottoman Anvarin-i cedid consisted of two distinct parts: the fortress proper *(kale)* and an outer suburb *(varış)* to the east.[25] The fortress consists of two components. A small hexagonal inner redoubt *(içhisar)* was built on the highest ground (Fig. III.7). At its northwest side, a gate leads

22. Leake 1830, pp. 399–400. Kyr Ghiorghio is Yioryios Oikonomopoulos, a properous Greek merchant in the village; see Bennet, Davis, and Zarinebaf-Shahr 2000, pp. 352–353. Anavarin briefly became a Russian base in the spring of 1770; see Dakin 1972, p. 17; Rulhière 1807, pp. 454–472.

23. See Chapter 4, pp. 165–166, where evidence pertaining to the Mus-

lim population of the fortress is fully discussed.

24. Such factors may explain why 3,000 Turks were evacuated by Venice in 1686 (Andrews 1953, p. 49; Coronelli 1686, p. 77; Rycaut 1700, p. 225; Schwencke 1854, p. 82).

25. Neither area was included in the new city of Pylos founded after the Greek Revolution. The first actual

plan of that community, drawn by an architect, dates to 1831 and was executed for Kapodistrias. By this time, the settlement had been established in its modern location on the slopes of a gorge leading inland from the harbor (see Baltas 1997, p. 13, fig. 3, for a view of this feature); see also Kyriazis 1976, p. 323.

Figure III.7. Eastern wall of the
içhisar and dry moat

Figure III.8. Main (northeastern)
entrance to Anavarin-i cedid

Figure III.9. *Kaldırım* in the area of the *varış* of Anavarin-i cedid

into the substantially larger outer fortress.[26] The road linking Anavarin with Modon led from the main gate of the outer fortress (Fig. III.8) through the suburb (Fig. III.9) and past the arcaded section of the aqueduct at Kamares. A second "Harbor Gate" opened toward a small harbor, Mandraki (Italian *Mandracchio*),[27] where the Turkish customs house was located (Fig. III.10).[28] From there, a road continued north to Balye Badre (Patras).

26. Evliya Çelebi's geography (see App. I) is correct: the landward gate of the fortress opens to the northeast and the outer suburb; as one enters the fortress, the inner redoubt (six-sided, with six bastions) lies to the left. His estimates of the size of the walls and of the individual parts of the fortress are, however, much exaggerated. Whereas he says that the walls of the fortress are 3,800 paces in circumference, they actually measure 1,055 m. He says that the *içhisar* is 1,000 "good long paces" (*adıms*) in circumference, but the actual measurement is 415 m. Evliya's estimates of the width

(30 *ayaks* or "feet") and height (20 *arşıns* or 15 m) of the fortification walls of the fortress also seem similarly exaggerated, since the walls are really only about 9 m high and 1.2–1.4 m wide (see Andrews 1953, pp. 49–50), and Ottoman documents (see App. IV) ordered that they would be only 10 *zira*'s (7.5 m) high and 3 *zira*'s (2.28 m) wide. Foscarini (1696, pp. 264–265) estimated that the whole exterior circuit was no more than 225 geometric paces; his would be a relatively accurate measure only if the maximum width of the lower fortress is meant, rather than its circumference.

27. On the term see Kahane, Kahane, and Tietze 1958, pp. 542–543, s.v. no. 808, μανδράκι (mandraki).

28. The customs house is indicated on the map included in Mangeart 1850, Mandracchio is labeled on pl. VIII in Andrews 1953, and both gates are mentioned by Evliya Çelebi and are depicted on pl. XIII, top, of Andrews 1953. Plates XI and XIII, top, in Andrews 1953 show the courses of roads. That leading from the fountain at the port to the citadel had been paved, at least by the time of the Greek Revolution: see Blouet 1831–1838, vol. 1, p. 2.

Figure III.10. Harbor Gate of Anavarin-i cedid

Figure III.11. Lower fortress from the *içhisar*

Figure III.12. Friday Mosque

Few buildings in the *kale* are specifically mentioned by Western visitors. The most prominent was the Friday Mosque, today converted into an Orthodox church and dedicated to the Transfiguration of Christ *(Metamorphosis)* (Figs. III.11–III.14).[29] The same building (no. 72) in TT880 is called the Friday Mosque of Bayezid.[30] It is clear that this precise structure existed at the time of the Venetian conquest in 1686, and that it was then immediately dedicated as a Catholic church. Construction of the Friday Mosque and of a *mescid* in the *kale* was authorized in 1577 by Murad III (see App. IV). Evliya Çelebi calls it the Mosque of Murad III, but dates its construction to A.H. 1016 (A.D. 1607–1608), later than the rule of Murad III (1574–1595): he says that he is quoting an inscription on the building.[31] Evliya's description of the location of the mosque is correct, because he says that it stands in an elevated location in the middle of the city and has a courtyard; the courtyard in turn had a fountain and pool.

Evliya describes other mosques in the fortress, including a Ferhad Ağa Mosque, which he locates in the marketplace and dates to A.H. 1014 (A.D. 1605–1606); neighborhood mosques (including one in the *varış*); and a dervish chapel. A Venetian military drawing illustrates buildings in the interior of the fortress, but depicts only a single minaret and mosque at its center.[32] But drawings prepared to illustrate texts of the various editions

29. Bory de Saint-Vincent (1836, p. 127) described its condition at the time of the *Expédition scientifique*: "Ce temple, si souvent, et tour à tour, turc, catholique ou grec, devint, lors de l'arrivée de l'expédition libératrice, un magasin militaire. . . . Ce monument consiste en cinq arcades moresques, formant un disgracieux portique au devant de quatre gros murs, avec une sorte de dôme très-lourd: il est de peu d'importance et de fort mauvais goût." See Davis 1998, p. 259, fig. 119, for the illustration of this building prepared by the Expédition scientifique; also Blouet

1831–1838, vol. 1, pl. 4. Blouet (1831–1838, vol. 1, p. 2) mentions the reuse of the mosque as a grain warehouse.

30. In TT880 the mosque, its inner court, and a primary school all represent one entry. The area that they occupy is 846 square *zira*'s (486 m²), almost precisely the size of the Church of the Transfiguration of Christ as it exists today.

31. One possible explanation for the discrepancy in date between Evliya's account (App. I, [267b/10–b/20]) and that of TT880 is that a *vakf* (of which this mosque was a part) may

have been established during the reign of Murad III, pursuant to Document 35 (1577) presented in Appendix IV. This *vakf* may have subsumed a mosque built earlier by Bayezid II (1481–1512) at Anavarin-i atik. The Venetians dedicated the Friday Mosque to San Vito on the day the fortress fell to them (Coronelli 1686, p. 78; Locatelli 1691, p. 225; Bory de Saint-Vincent 1836, p. 127).

32. Andrews 1953, pl. XIII, top; for Evliya, Appendix I, [267b/10–b/20].

Figure III.13. Gate to the courtyard
of the Friday Mosque

Figure III.14. Porch of the Friday
Mosque

Figure III.15. Sketch of the eastern part of the interior of the fortress of Anavarin-i cedid in 1829, looking northeast. Baccuet drawing no. 23, courtesy of the Gennadius Library, American School of Classical Studies at Athens

of Coronelli's works, some published before and others after the Venetian conquest, show two minarets.[33] Late in the Second Ottoman period, Castellan and Gell also illustrate two mosques.[34]

Actual firsthand accounts of the state of the fortress at the time of its capture by the French in 1828 also provide glimpses of its interior. Mangeart offers valuable insights into its geography: "La ville a deux portes. En entrant par celle du nord-est, je vis, dans la seconde rue à gauche, les restes des cahutes qui formaient le bazar. Vers le bas de la ville est située la maison qu'occupait le bey, gouverneur de la place. La grande mosquée n'est guère remarquable aujourd'hui que par les fragments de colonnes de marbre qui soutenaient la façade; les rues sont toutes étroites, hautes et basses, à cause de l'inégalité du sol qui incline à l'ouest."[35] This account serves to locate the market of the fortress between the Friday Mosque and the inner redoubt of the fortress. It also seems to place the house of the governor of the fortress in the area between the mosque and the bastion of Santa Barbara.[36]

33. Navari 1995, pp. 516–519, and figs. 17–20.

34. See Castellan 1808, fig. 19; Gell 1823, fig. facing p. 26. The intent in 1577 was to build two mosques, a *mescid* in the citadel and a Friday Mosque outside. The *mescid* was destroyed when the Russians attacked the fortress in 1770. See Appendix IV.

35. Mangeart 1850, p. 354. This is one of the few Western descriptions of the interior of the *kale* of any date. Quinet (Aeschimann and Tucoo-Chala 1984, p. 13) describes only the devastation and a single minaret: "Les murs de Navarin, avec leurs meurtrières, leurs petites portes sombres et les décombres entassés, ressemblaient à un cimetière de campagne dont les tombes auraient été ouvertes et labourées. Au sommet, le blanc minaret d'une mosquée écroulée et couchée sous un palmier, figurait un pacha assis à mi-côte, qui regarde de là sur la mer et sur les îles."

36. See Blouet 1831–1838, vol. 1, p. 2, and n. 38 below.

Figure III.16 *(opposite, above).* **Sketch of the western part of the interior of the fortress of Anavarin-i cedid in 1829, looking west.** Baccuet drawing no. 24, courtesy of the Gennadius Library, American School of Classical Studies at Athens

Figure III.17 *(opposite, below).* **Sketch of the shantytown rebuilt on the site of modern Pylos in 1829, looking southwest.** Baccuet drawing no. 49, courtesy of the Gennadius Library, American School of Classical Studies at Athens

Figure III.18 *(right).* **Area of ruined houses in the lower fortress, with the** *içhisar* **behind**

Figure III.19. **Gate to the seaward bastion of Santa Barbara**

The minaret of the Friday Mosque had been removed by the time the Expédition scientifique arrived.[37] There exist, however, two drawings by Prosper Baccuet, published here for the first time as Figures III.15 and III.16, prepared for the Expédition scientifique and now in the Gennadius Library of the American School of Classical Studies at Athens. These depict in detail the interior of the outer fortress, and only a single mosque is illustrated. A third drawing (Fig. III.17) is probably the earliest surviving depiction of modern Pylos, a mere shantytown rebuilt after the evacuation of İbrahim.[38]

37. Baccuet drawings, nos. 23, 24, and 49 in the Gennadius Library, American School of Classical Studies at Athens; cf. Bennet, Davis, and Zarinebaf-Shahr 2000, pp. 354–355. We thank Alexis Malliaris and Haris Kalligas for facilitating our examination of the drawings, and the latter for permission to publish them.

38. The house of the *bey,* to which Mangeart refers as lying "toward the bottom of the town" (see above, p. 253), does not appear to be the *sérail* (palace) of İbrahim that Blouet mentions (1831–1838, vol. 1, p. 2), as is clear from Baccuet's drawing no. 24 (Fig. III.16), which depicts "Navarin vu de [i.e., 'seen from'] la maison qui fut le Sérail d'Ibrahim." The French, according to Blouet's account, had restored certain better-preserved structures for the use of their officers: the palace of İbrahim was being employed as headquarters for the "payeur de l'armée et à l'administration de la poste."

Figure III.20. Main east–west street in the lower fortress

Figure III.21. Side street in the lower fortress

Figure III.22. Ottoman fountain in the lower fortress, between the Friday Mosque and the *içhisar*

Figure III.23. Remains of a *hamam* in the lower fortress

39. Bory de Saint-Vincent 1836, p. 134, discusses the provision of water to the fortress, in particular the numerous cisterns that would store rainwater in the event of a siege. Both aqueducts are visible in one of the drawings prepared by Baccuet for the Expédition scientifique (no. 49; see Fig. III.17).

The preceding sources, although exiguous, together with inspection of remains still visible, permit certain fundamental elements of the fortress and suburb of Anavarin-i cedid to be mapped. The placement of its two gates is clear, as is the location of the redoubt (Fig. III.18), the lower fortress, the walls and towers (Fig. III.19), and the streets (Figs. III.20, III.21). The positions of the Friday Mosque and the market can be fixed. The residence of the Ottoman commander was near the seaward bastions. The main reservoir of the fortress lay in the upper part of the town, near the point at which the aqueduct entered it.[39] A fountain house of Ottoman construction is still extant not far from the entrance to the *içhisar* (Fig. III.22). Finally, the remnants of a building immediately southwest of the Church of the Transfiguration of Christ clearly belonged to an Ottoman bathhouse, or *hamam* (Fig. III.23).

THE FORTRESS OF ANAVARİN-İ CEDİD
IN TT880

The purpose of the catalogue of property in TT880 is clear. Immediately after the reconquest of the Morea, Sultan Ahmed III had issued a direct order that Turks who had been expelled from the Morea should be restored to their homes and property.[40] On January 15, 1716, a Greek who was visiting Patras (Balye Badre) wrote:

> I was an inhabitant of Gastouni at the time of Venetian rule. Now I am established with my family in Ioannina, my homeland. Twenty-eight days ago I was in Patras on business and there was a *tahrirci* [an official charged with compiling a written survey of a province] or commissioner there, who was making the cadaster of all the properties. He is in charge of that part where the majority of the inhabitants are Jews of Larissa. In each district there is a *tahrirci* who is registering the properties; but they are not issuing a property deed . . . to anyone of those who used to possess them. From Roumeli the Turks are arriving who used to live in the Kingdom and they are taking back all their houses and fields.[41]

Anavarin-i cedid is described in three different parts in TT880. The first and most extensive part includes only those remains that were located in the lower fortress (items 1–94). A separate brief part (items 95–98) addresses the *içhisar*. The third describes the *variş*. All measurements of buildings are assumed to be in *zira²*'s.[42]

The first 71 entries in the catalogue appear to follow one another in roughly geographical order, and to have been recorded as the scribe made his way around the lower citadel in a counter-clockwise direction (Fig. III.24). From the main gate of the fortress he walked downhill toward the Harbor Gate and, after inventorying properties in that area, proceeded to the bastion that the Venetians called Santa Maria.[43] From there he continued toward the seaward bastion of Santa Barbara, examining the area west of the mosque. Finally, he described the mosque and property in its vicinity before continuing eastward to the *içhisar*. It is difficult or impossible, however, to locate individual structures with any precision. This document was not intended to be a plat registry, and the scribe is inconsistent in the number of boundaries that he specifies for each parcel of land. It is also clear that several items were not recorded in geographical order.

40. See Chapter 1. The proclamation ordering the return of the Peloponnesian Turks is published in a Greek translation in Mavropoulos 1920, document 50, pp. 66–67, which we render here in English: "Since it is at present necessary that all the locally born Turks return with their wives, children, and relatives to their hearths, my command is that, in accordance with my Imperial favor and grace, they should quit the places in which they have been established, and there should

be returned to them their property and the lands which of old they had in their possession, with the provision that they have in hand their titles of possession and that they prove by reliable witnesses and in front of the religious court, with participation of the *serasker* of the Morea, their authority over these possessions."

41. In the so-called Codex Mertzios and quoted in Topping 1976, p. 101. This eyewitness account was coincidentally written on the very day that

TT880 was being registered in Istanbul.

42. The *zira²* is equivalent to 0.758 m. Only in entry 13 (Anavarin-i atik) in TT880 (see Chap. 2) is the measurement employed for structures specified to be the *zira²*. The *zira²* is not explicitly said to be the unit used for the buildings at Anavarin-i cedid.

43. Andrews 1953, p. 51; on p. 244, regarding pl. XII, however, Andrews transcribes the legend as "S Marco."

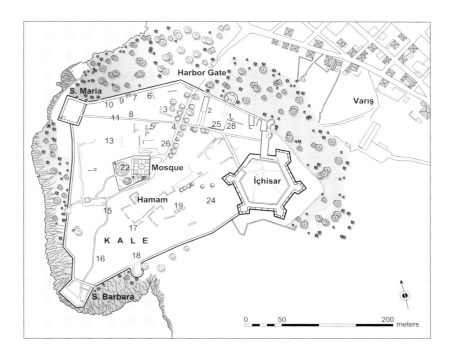

Figure III.24. Plan of Anavarin-i cedid showing the principal existing monuments and groups of structures described in TT880. R. J. Robertson, after Karpodini-Dimitriadi 1990, p. 193, fig. 156

Below we have divided the properties listed for the lower fortress into 28 subgroups of parcels that seem to form homogeneous units, because their boundaries refer either to each other or to monuments—such as the Friday Mosque—whose locations are known.[44] These groups serve no purpose other than to allow us to fix the approximate locations of the properties in each group. This makes it possible to be more precise about the geography of the fortress, and we hope that this information may have value in the future in guiding the archaeological researches of others, and in aiding in the interpretation of the results of their excavations.

Group 1. 850 square meters
Nos. 1–5. These lie between the "gate of the fort" and the Harbor Gate. The Janissary barracks are nearby (see Group no. 2).

Group 2. 1,150 square meters
Nos. 6–9. Items are located with reference to the Harbor Gate, to a "big street," and to each other. The "big street" seems to run southwest from the Harbor Gate and then west to the bastion of Santa Maria, as no. 9 is located between the street and the Harbor Gate. No parcel in the group is bordered by the fortification wall.

Group 3. 11,500 square meters
Nos. 10–22. The first entries are located near the Harbor Gate and near the fortification wall. No. 10 is bordered by no. 9 in Group 1, which in turn is bordered by the Harbor Gate. The "big road" or "big street" is again a boundary for several houses. The group includes two very large areas of ruined houses (nos. 12, 13), one of which (no. 12) was adjacent to the fortification wall; they seem to have been located north of the "big road." The scribe walked in a circle, ending where he began near the Harbor Gate (no. 22). A workshop was in this area.

44. The area covered by each group is calculated in square meters by summing the sizes of all of its buildings. The approximate location of each group where it can be determined is indicated in Fig. III.24.

The structures in this group must have covered much of the area between the Harbor Gate and the Friday Mosque.

Group 4. 2,015 square meters

Nos. 23–28. Descriptions of borders of houses in this group include many references to parcels in Groups 2 and 3. The owner of two houses (nos. 23, 24) also owns a house in Group 2 (no. 7) and Group 3 (no. 20). The "big road" or "big street" is frequently used as a boundary, but neither the wall of the fortress, nor the Harbor Gate, nor the mosque is mentioned. It seems most likely that these houses lay south of the road, opposite those in Group 3.

Group 5. 740 square meters

Nos. 29–31. Houses in this group share boundaries with parcels in Groups 3 and 4: no. 29 and no. 30 with no. 26, no. 30 with no. 15, and no. 31 with no. 16. Only no. 31 is bordered by the "big road." The parcels are likely to have been located west of those in Group 4, but still south of the road.

Group 6. 165 square meters

No. 32. With this group the scribe seems to have shifted north of the road, as this house is bordered by the fortification wall.

Group 7. 630 square meters

Nos. 33–35. The scribe stays on the north side of the road. No. 33 is bordered by the wall of the fortress.

Group 8. 400 square meters

Nos. 36–37. Both houses border the "big road." No. 36 borders no. 35 in Group 7.

Group 9. 185 square meters

No. 38 is located between the road and the wall of the fortress and probably lay between parcels in Groups 8 and 11.

Group 10. 475 square meters

No. 39 is located between the road and the wall of the fortress and probably lay between parcels in Groups 8 and 11.

Group 11. 105 square meters

No. 40 is said to be attached to no. 39 and must also be north of the road.

Group 12. 675 square meters

No. 41 is not explicitly linked to any other parcel, unless the name Hacioğlu is meant to refer to Haci Hasanzade Mustafa Çelebi in Group 13 (no. 44).

Group 13. 4,865 square meters

Nos. 42–45. There are references to the fortification wall and to the road. Houses (no. 45) that are said to be "on the way to the bastion *(tabya)*" are on the side of the small harbor, thus making it clear that the bastion of Santa Maria is meant. This group, like Group 3, is large, and its parcels must have covered most of the area between the Friday Mosque and the bastion of Santa Maria.

Group 14. 475 square meters

No. 46. An orchard rather than a house. This entry seems to be an afterthought and does not occur in geographical order, as it is bordered by the workshop mentioned among the parcels of Group 3.

Group 15. 4,965 square meters

Nos. 47–56. Parcel nos. 49 and 50 border the Friday Mosque, and nos. 54–56 are bordered by the fortification wall. One of the houses in the group (no. 53) is also bordered by the church (no. 57) in Group 16. Group 15 is another large group and must have covered most of the area between the mosque and the bastion of Santa Barbara.

Group 16. 1,875 square meters

Nos. 57–60. Parcels are located with reference to the church (no. 57) or to each other. The church is said to be across from the "gate of the lower tower," which must be the sea bastion that the Venetians knew as Santa Barbara. One house (no. 60) is near the wall of the fortress. Reference to a "lower *yalı*" (waterside residence) recalls the palace in the lower town mentioned by Mangeart; this structure is used as a boundary for no. 59 but is not catalogued.

Group 17. 7,765 square meters

No. 61. This enormous area of ruined houses is bordered by nos. 65 and 66 in Group 19; one of those (no. 66) is in turn bordered by the church. The houses would therefore seem to be closer to the sea bastion than to the market. In saying that this area is "next to the small harbor," the scribe presumably means that the ruined houses lie on the northwest side of the area that he was describing at that moment.

Group 18. 100 square meters

No. 62. The house is said to be next to the church.

Group 19. 1,825 square meters

Nos. 63–68. Parcels are defined with reference to the mosque, the wall of the fortress, and the market, and therefore must lie to the south of the mosque, in the area between the market and the lower sea bastion.

Group 20. 2,760 square meters

No. 69. The description of this parcel is puzzling. What big bastion is meant? The property would seem to be located near the main gate of the fortress. If so, the church land that borders it is not that of the church catalogued as parcel no. 57, and this item is entirely out of geographical order.

Group 21. 475 square meters

Nos. 70–71. Both properties are located with reference to the Friday Mosque.

Group 22. 5,700 square meters

Nos. 72–75. The locations of both the Friday Mosque and, by extension, the other items located with reference to it, are

indisputable. The mosque together with the prayer square
covered a much larger area than does the church and its courtyard at present.

Group 23. 195 square meters

No. 76. The *kadı*'s court cannot be located with reference to
any other structure.

Group 24. 110 square meters

No. 77. The primary school can be located only with reference
to the *içhisar*.

Group 25. 1,675 square meters

No. 78. It is clear that the Janissary barracks were near the main
gate to the fortress because they are described as a boundary for
item no. 2 in Group 1.

Group 26. 615 square meters

Nos. 79–81. Three houses are located with reference to the
mosque and a *hamam*. It is clear that this *hamam* was near the
mosque but on the opposite side of it from the *hamam* that is
still preserved today.

Group 27. 1,010 square meters

Nos. 82–93. This group includes structures in the market
(çarşı). All are shops, or houses and shops combined. Few
boundaries are specified, but no. 82, the first item in the series,
is said to be "in front of the gate." No. 91 is explicitly said to
be "in the market." There is a cistern in the market (no. 88).
A location near the gate to the *içhisar* is probable and would
also agree with Mangeart's description of the location of the
market at the time of the French occupation.

Group 28. 112 square meters

No. 94. The parcel is said only to be "inside the gate." It was
probably near the market.

In the area of the lower fortress, 52 houses are said to be owned by a
single person.[45] These properties range from 108 to 1,170 square *zira²*s in
size; the mean is about 495 square *zira²*s.[46] There are seven properties that
are listed separately, but without specified owners. The houses of these
anonymous Muslims are considerably smaller than the others and range in
size from 168 to 276 square *zira²*s, with a mean of 212 square *zira²*s.[47] In
addition, there are several large areas that are simply described as regions in
which ruined houses existed. Thirty-four houses (250–1,350 square *zira²*s
in size) are specifically mentioned as existing in these areas, and there would
be space for as many as 70 additional houses, were they no bigger than the
smallest houses that are explicitly recorded for this area (i.e., 250 square
*zira²*s).

The only nonresidential structures that are intermixed with private
houses are the *hamam* (no. 28) and a church (no. 57).[48] Most buildings
with public functions are listed in sequence (Groups 22–25 [nos. 72–78]).
These include the Friday Mosque, primary schools, an endowed orchard,
a prayer square, a *kadı*'s court, and the Janissary barracks. It is clear that the
mosque and the barracks were not near each other and that they were

45. In only one instance (no. 24) are
"harem houses" distinguished from a
selamlık (no. 20). Orchards are sometimes listed with houses (e.g., no. 8),
sometimes separately.

46. With a standard deviation of
267.5.

47. With a standard deviation of
47.5.

48. A workshop and a market *(çarşı)*
are mentioned as boundaries but are
not catalogued by the scribe, nor is a
"lower *yalı*."

recorded together only because they were nonresidential properties. The catalogue concludes with other nonresidential properties, mostly shops, that are likely to have been located in the market of the fortress (nos. 82–94). These structures are numerous (about 30) and are all very small, ranging from 30 to 150 square *zira*'s (about 70 square *zira*'s on average). Only in two instances is a shop attached to a house; in one case (no. 91) the structure had two stories, with residential quarters above.

More than 160 residential structures thus appear to have existed in the lower fortress.[49] There was additional space for houses in the *içhisar*, but only "the land of" a single house is recorded separately (no. 98); it is small, only 77 square *zira*'s. Three "masonry rooms of soldiers" (no. 95), as a group, are only slightly larger, around 90 square *zira*'s each. Perhaps as many as 50 more houses of these sizes could have existed in areas of ruined houses that are recorded in the *içhisar*.[50]

The total number of residential structures belonging to Muslims, along with shops and public buildings, must have nearly filled the area within the walls. It therefore seems clear that TT880 preserves a nearly complete inventory of property in the fortress. The actual calculated area of the lower fortress is about 52,500 square meters, excluding the few structures mentioned as boundaries, but for which no dimensions are recorded. The total area of the structures enumerated in TT880 is 91,894 square *zira*'s, equivalent to 52,799 square meters. Property recorded in the *içhisar* is 2,688 square meters in extent, whereas its actual calculated area is 3,270 square meters.[51]

THE *VARIŞ*

The manner in which property in the *varış* is recorded also clearly reflects the goal of Sultan Ahmed III to return Ottoman property to its rightful owners. The scribe's intention was to identify Turkish possessions and to confirm their owners in them: for example, shops, houses, and orchards (nos. 101, 102, 106–112, 115–118). Unlike the fortress, where all real estate is recorded as being in Muslim hands, the suburb was divided between Muslim and non-Muslim interests. For the *reaya*, houses and livestock are, for the most part, only summarily noted. Detailed descriptions are included only for houses (nos. 103, 104) and shops (nos. 99, 103) that were confiscated from Venetians or from others who have been arrested (one man is imprisoned at Modon; see no. 104), or for items of unclear ownership (nos. 100, 102, 105, 113, 114). These items are to become property of the state *(miri)*.

49. Such numbers are of the same order of magnitude as the Turkish property recorded by the Venetians in 1689: 97 good and 88 destroyed houses in the outer fortress, along with 24 good shops; see Davies 2004, p. 70; and ASV, Senato, Provveditori di Terra e da Mar, b.860, f.217r.

50. The Venetian survey suggests, however, that there were actually far fewer. It listed only 10 good and 3 destroyed houses in the inner fortress.

51. These 200 or so houses are far fewer, and were considerably larger, than the 700 houses proposed in 1577 (Document 34 in App. IV). It

is, moreover, difficult to imagine how 700 houses, even of such a small size (12 × 16 *zira*'s), would have fit into the area within the walls of Anavarin-i cedid, since they would have required an area of ca. 134,400 square *zira*'s (ca. 77,220 m²).

The *varış* of Anavarin-i cedid consisted of shops and houses that lined the road leading to Modon, as is clear from Venetian maps; reference in TT880 is made to structures "below the road," "under the road," and "on the road."[52] A few buildings had two stories (e.g., nos. 102–106), as might be expected from the account of Evliya Çelebi.[53] Living rooms were on the top floor; shops or storage spaces were below. The total area covered by the structures listed in TT880 is 48,334 square *zira*ʾs or 27,777 square meters, half the size of the occupied area in the lower fortress.

The entire *varış* is likely to have been much larger, as the area of non-Muslim houses is not recorded. At least 30 houses were still in possession of Christian owners, and several had been owned by Franks. Ottoman owners are specified for fewer than 10 houses, but more than 20 others are recorded and had also probably been in Muslim hands.[54] The borders of Muslim properties are defined with reference to houses of non-Muslims, who in several cases are explicitly said to be *zimmi* (non-Muslims). Most of these individuals may have still been living in the community. In the case of Manuli Kaltaban this is clear, because he is included on the list of *reaya* that concludes the description of Anavarin-i cedid.[55]

52. The unpublished plan, labeled "Plan de la ville et de citadelle de Navarin" (see above, p. 245), shows a suburb of considerable size, the road to Modon passing through it, with a space between it and the gate to the citadel. This same plan illustrates several large prominent orchards in the vicinity of the fortress. Are these the same as those listed at the end of entry 35 in TT880, nos. 115–118? In addition to the main buildings in the *varış*, there are depicted a few structures in the area between the fortress and what is now the modern plateia of Pylos; cf. Andrews 1953, pl. XIII, top. A recently published account of the Venetian conquest (Liata 1998, p. 89) describes the ruins of habitations in 1686 as being closer to the sea than the current *varış*, suggesting that that suburb perhaps shifted its location at some

unspecified time: "Havera un borgo nella parte del porto Mà derocato, ne tiene un altro dalla parte del Mare che era et è hoggidi habitato da Greci, che non si può Credere." A map included opposite p. 62 in an anonymous Venetian chronicle (Anonymous 1687), although it greatly distorts local topography, attaches the label "Borgi Abrugiati" to an area near Anavarin-i cedid, suggesting that the suburb of the fortress had been burned in the course of the Venetian-Ottoman struggles of 1686. See also the drawing by Coronelli (1687b, pl. 7; cf. Biblioteca Nationale Marciana di Venezia 16.d.287) that situates a "Borgo Distrutto" outside the main gate to the citadel.

53. See Appendix I, [268a/5–a/10].

54. The Venetian survey listed 16 good and 51 destroyed Muslim houses, with 2 good shops in the suburb, num-

bers considerably in excess of those recorded in TT880.

55. It is possible that the house of Curci, mentioned as a boundary for no. 112, is that of Curci Monti, no. 143. The fact that he is listed next to Manuli Kaltaban, no. 142, suggests that there may also be some geographical order to the list of names of the *reaya* (nos. 119–148). The musket-seller Zakarya/Zakhariye, whose house is recorded as a boundary for no. 105, may also be the same as Zekhiriye, no. 145, although the name is spelled differently and in the latter case he is said to be the son of the musket-seller, not the musket-seller himself. *Boyacı* Zakhir, no. 111, could also be the same as Zakhiri, no. 146. Yani Varvaris/Varvarin, no. 105, could be any of three men with this Christian name who appear on the list of *reaya*.

CONSTRUCTION OF THE OTTOMAN CASTLE OF ANAVARİN-İ CEDİD

ACCORDING TO ORDERS OF THE IMPERIAL COUNCIL AS PRESERVED IN THE *MÜHIMME DEFTER*S 19–31: FROM 2 *SAFER* A.H. 980 TO 10 *RECEB* A.H. 985 (JUNE 1572–NOVEMBER 1577)

by Machiel Kiel

The prime minister's Ottoman archives in Istanbul (BBA) contain not only a mass of information on population and production at village level, but also much on administrative and financial affairs, as well as on local political problems.[1] A large part of the correspondence between the Imperial Council *(Divân)* and the governmental organs in the provinces is preserved in the "registers of important matters" (*mühimme defter*s [MD]), of which over 263 volumes have been preserved, starting in 1558 and ending in 1906.[2] As each volume contains between 1,200 and 1,600 copies of letters, it easy to imagine what a treasure trove for the historian this collection is.[3] Alas, only seven volumes have been published. From others dealing with the years 1553–1610, typewritten catalogues have been assembled that contain short extracts of each letter, written in modern Turkish script. The rest of their text remains in the original, written in an often difficult type of Ottoman shorthand called *divânî kırması*, in which ligatures are made but, according to the strict rules of the Arabic orthography, should not be, and in which the so-essential diacritical marks (dots) are often lacking. Turkish researchers in particular have developed the bad habit of working only on the basis of the transcripts. Besides missing much of the flavor of the original document, they miss much information.[4]

The *mühimme defter*s were not kept in strict systematic or chronological order but apparently were arranged in the way that the scribe found letters on his desk. Sometimes they were copied twice, or were repeated at short time intervals. For the most part, it is written at the top of each letter—or order—who was to carry it to its destination via the imperial post system, when it was given to that person, and the date that it was written. For the following presentation, we have gone through all of the

---

1. The source materials for this contribution were collected during several working campaigns in the Turkish archives sponsored by the Netherlands Organization for the Advancement of Scientific Research (ZWO/NWO), The Hague, and the Deutsche Forschungs-gemeinschaft (DFG), Bonn. For the conversion from Hicra/Hegira dates to A.D. dates, the conversion system of the University of Zürich (www.oriold.unizh.ch/static/hegira.html) is used.

2. See also the discussion of these documents in Chapter 1.

3. For a succinct description of the *mühimme defter*s, see Elezović's pioneering work (1950, pp. 571–574). See also Binark's foreword to the publication of MD3 (Başbakanlık Archives 1993, pp. xxxiii–lvii), and Veinstein and Qaᶜidi 1992 (very analytical).

4. A good example is the short study in Turkish by Tanyeli (1996) concerning Anavarin, which is exclusively based on the abstracts in Latin characters.

original letters pertaining to the construction of the Anavarin castle that we were able to find (here Documents 1–40). The style of writing is often repetitive and cumbersome for the modern reader. The sultan, the source of all authority, speaks for himself, that is, in the first person. In cases where the provincial authorities had submitted a request or report, this is repeated briefly. Then, if the request or report is granted or accepted, it is reproduced almost word for word, with an order to act accordingly. If it is a direct order, then the style is more straightforward. In this short contribution, we have chosen to present some of the letters in their entirety in an English translation faithful to the original language and wording, together with the Ottoman text and a transliteration at the end of the chapter, and to give the content of most other letters in a much abbreviated version.

The *mühimme defter*s contain a great deal of information concerning the construction of the castle of Pylos/Anavarin-i cedid, one of the largest and best-preserved works of Ottoman fortification in Greece.[5] There follows here a presentation of the content of the 40 letters, ranging in date from June 1572 to November 1577 and concerning Anavarin. We largely refrain from comments, as the texts speak for themselves.

Document 1, the first letter that could be found, dates from 2 *Safer* 980 (June 14, 1572).[6] It is an answer to a letter from the fortress commander *(dizdar)* of Anavarin-i atik, stating that the important harbor of Anavarin has to be protected. The *dizdar* has under his command only 10 men and has asked for 10 additional gunners and 20 more soldiers. This request was granted.

Document 2, the second order concerning Anavarin, is dated 21 *Zilkade* 980 (March 6, 1573).[7] An order for the "repair" of Anavarin-i atik is given to the *bey* of the Morea and to the inspector of the work, the *kadı* of Patras. A secretary *(katip)* had to be appointed to control and write down all necessary expenditures for construction. This secretary must have been Katip Abdülnebi, who had the usufruct of a *timar* with a revenue of 10,000 silver pieces *(akçe*s).[8] He was part of the census *(tahrir)* commission of the Morea, and he was known for his integrity, piety, and expertise. No penny was to be spent aside from the sums written down in the register of the construction.

It is clear that in the interval of nine months between Documents 1 and 2 there must have been other orders, in response to proposals from the military officials on the spot, that dealt with the actual decision to build a castle at the southern entrance to the Bay of Navarino. These orders, or correspondence, must have been in volume 20, but that volume is "missing." It is also clear that the long interval between the Battle of Lepanto (October 7, 1571) and the start of the construction resulted from the need to pay attention to the other projects that were undertaken immediately after that catastrophic defeat. One of these was the reconstruction of the "Mora Kastelli" (or "Kestel-i Mora" [Rion]) near Patras, at the entrance to the Gulf of Corinth, covering Lepanto itself. Some of the building accounts of that fortress are preserved in the *mühimme defter*s. The administration also would have been very busy rebuilding the fleet. Be that as it may, our third preserved document, from *Şevvâl* 980 (February 1573),[9] contains a short order stating that the work at Anavarin-i cedid had to be started immediately.

5. For a description of the castle, with plans and photographs, and an outline of its history, see Andrews 1953, pp. 49–57; Weithmann 1991; and Appendix III in this volume.

6. MD19, p. 113, order 246.

7. MD21, p. 206, order 492.

8. This was a lot of money. In the mid-16th century, an *imam* earned 3–4 *akçe*s per day, a good carpenter or mason 6–7 *akçe*s. The secretary thus earned an annual salary five to nine times greater than an average *imam* or construction worker. For the value of the *akçe*, see Sahillioğlu 1989; see also Darling 1990.

9. MD22, p. 101, order 210.

The fourth order is from five months later, 6 *Rebiyülevvel* 981 (July 6, 1573).[10] It is addressed to the *kadı*s of the *sancak* of Eğriboz (Euripos, i.e., Chalkis, comprising the mainland of central Greece from Lamia to Cape Sounion and the great island of Negroponte (Euboia) itself). Masons and carpenters, it says, are necessary for the construction of the castle of Anavarin, which had been ordered to be built. They (the workmen) have to be sent there and must work for normal salaries. In addition, the *kadı*s are ordered to buy, at state expense, provisions for the workforce at Anavarin and to dispatch them to the building site.

In a letter from the beginning of September 1573 (Document 5),[11] the *bey* of the Morea reported to Istanbul that Venetian subjects from Corfu were coming to the Morea to do business. The Porte answered that this was to be permitted as there was now peace between the two states. The same page in the register contains two more letters that pertain directly to the castle. The complete texts of these two letters (Documents 6 and 7),[12] which are orders, are given here in English translation, along with their transliterations in the second part of this appendix:

Document 6, Given to Mustafa Çavuş, on the 11th of Cemaziyülevvel *[981] (September 8, 1573)*

Order to the *Bey* of the Morea:
For the necessities of the castle at the harbor of Anavarin, the construction of which has been ordered, three loads (*yük*s, altogether 300,000 *akçe*s) have been assigned from the local tax-farms (*mukataʿa*s). A noble order [concerning this matter] has been sent by the Department of Finances. The plan of the castle to be built has previously been dispatched with the messenger *(çavuş)* Hızır. I herewith order that as soon as it (the order) arrives you should not stand opposing each other and you should begin the construction of the castle before this season is over. You should let the money be brought from the inspector *(nazır)* of the mentioned tax-farms, and you should spend it for the necessities. You should lose no time and should have the castle constructed strong and solid according to the plan. A noble order has been sent to the admiral of the fleet (*kapudan* pasha)—may his good fortune increase—that he should leave behind [in Anavarin] the architect who is with him.
When the Imperial Fleet—if God is willing—returns victorious to that place, you should bring my noble order to my *kapudan* and ask for the architect, who is at his side, and you should employ him for the building of the castle together with the architect Şaban.

Document 7 (September 8, 1573)

Order to the Admiral of the Imperial Fleet:
When this year you arrive with my Imperial Fleet in Anavarin, it is necessary that the architect who designed [the plan of] the castle in Frankish style, the castle that has to be built by your men, should stay at the building site. Therefore I ordered that when you succeed—if God Almighty is willing—in returning with my Imperial Fleet and arrive at the aforesaid harbor, you should leave

10. MD22, p. 128, order 258.
11. MD22, p. 323, order 640.
12. MD22, p. 323, orders 641 and 642.

behind the aforesaid architect and impress on him that until the completion of the construction—conform to my noble order—he [the designer] should serve together with the architect Şaban and should build the castle, employing people accordingly.

In Document 8,[13] which immediately followed the previous order, the *bey* of the Morea wrote to Istanbul that he needed more money for the necessities of the construction of the castle, both for the building material and to pay and feed the work force. The money assigned (300,000 *akçe*s) had not been given to him in its entirety. He also wanted to know if the unskilled workers (*cerahor*s, who normally were subject to corvée for the state as part of their duties) had to be paid regular salaries. The Porte answered that it was not customary to pay *cerahor*s for their service to the state. The work was for the protection of the land and therefore had to be done without payment. The word used to describe the manner of their service—*imece*—may possibly be of Greek origin;[14] it denotes "work done for the community by the whole village, by the efforts of the community" and reflects pre-Ottoman, Byzantine institutions. The *cerahor*s were ordered to work in shifts of several days' duration. The master builders and stonecutters, who were erecting the walls of the castle, had to be paid "in the usual way." The *bey* was warned especially not to squander money. He was instructed to bring to the Inspector of the State Finances of the Morea a special imperial order pertaining to the financial problem and to take the amount of money necessary for the construction, which should not suffer any delay.

The special imperial order just referred to (Document 9)[15] follows immediately upon Document 8. The *nazır* Mehmed had answered that he did not have enough money to pay the required sum. He now was ordered to take it from sums that had been assigned to other activities and to give it to the men of the *bey* of the Morea upon receiving a bill acknowledging the debt *(temessük)*.

A month later, in Document 10 from 8 *Cemaziyüleahir* (October 5, 1573),[16] the *kadı*s of the *sancak* of İnebahtı (Lepanto/Naupaktos) are instructed to recruit *cerahor*s from every village in their districts and to send them to Anavarin, to work on the construction of the castle. In the order is given the name of the *bey* of the Morea, Mehmed, who had reported to Istanbul that there was a need for extra workmen. The names of the *cerahor*s had to be listed in a special register, and the men would be asked to work in shifts of several days in a row.

The next order (Document 11), on the same page and of the same date, reminded the *kadı*s of the *sancak* of Eğriboz to buy at current market price "whatever cereals they could find" and to send them to Anavarin. The *bey* of the Morea, Mehmed, had been informed about this matter.

In Document 12, of 7 *Receb* 981 (November 2, 1573), the *nazır* of the *mukataᶜa* of the Morea is again encouraged to assert himself and to find the necessary money for the construction of the castle.[17]

On the same day, Document 13[18] was written and given to Mehmed Çavuş, messenger of the *bey* of the Morea, who had come to Istanbul with the letter of the *bey*. The *bey* had reported that the *cerahor*s were now working in shifts, conforming to the customary practice in the case of labor for the

13. MD22, p. 324, order 643.
14. See Eren 1999, pp. 189–190, for discussion, with references, of the etymology of *imece*.
15. MD22, p. 324, order 644.
16. MD23, p. 48, order 97.
17. MD23, p. 134, order 273.
18. MD23, p. 134, order 274.

benefit of the community. Money was not given to them. Stone, lime, and wood were required. Because the local subjects of the province were insufficient in number, the Yürüks (Turkish-speaking nomads or seminomads), from the district of Selânik (Thessaloniki), were now required to come to Anavarin by the early spring of the following year. The *bey* had also reported to Istanbul that the *kadıs* of İnebahtı/Lepanto and of Eğriboz (Euboia) had not yet sent the required provisions. The *bey* was ordered to organize ships and their crews, and to take the provisions after submitting a *temessük*.

Two months later, on 12 *Ramadan* 981 (January 5, 1574), the *bey* of the Morea had sent another letter to Istanbul (Document 14)[19] stating that provisions were needed for the master masons, carpenters, and others. In Document 15, from the same day and written on the same page on which the previous letter was,[20] the Porte now ordered the *sancakbey* of Eğriboz (no longer the *kadıs*) to send three ships with wheat and two with barley to Anavarin. He had to fetch the provisions and to pay the merchants at market price, to place a sufficient number of soldiers from the garrison in the ships for protection, and to make sure that the workmen were provided with victuals. The matter was of the utmost importance!

On March 15, 1574 (Document 16),[21] the *bey* of the Morea received a letter from Istanbul stating that the *kadı* of Corinth had reported that, during the recruitment of the *cerahors*, the poor subjects had been oppressed by the *timar*-holders, the members of the local Ottoman cavalry forces. This had to be forbidden, and trustworthy people had to be appointed (by the *bey*) to control the procedure. They had to take care that "not a single grain" was unlawfully taken from the poor subjects.

Toward the end of March 1574, the Porte was apparently getting nervous about the five ships with provisions from Eğriboz. Moreover, the *bey* had reported that the *kadıs* of Morea, İnebahtı, and Tirhala (Trikala) were also slow in fulfilling the order.[22] They now got furious letters from Istanbul. The old order was repeated, and more details were given that were lacking in the previous order, apparently because they were obvious (buy at market price, supply freight money for the ships, and enlist reliable soldiers to protect them). It was emphasized that the matter was of the utmost importance "because a multitude of people will come to this place [Anavarin]." As the building season was about to begin, the Porte was rightfully anxious to get the food to the building site in time.[23] In this context, it should be mentioned that in the rather unfertile Anavarin area, very little surplus grain could be found (Documents 17 and 18, from 29 *Zilkade* 981 [March 22, 1574]).

In the middle of February 1574, the Porte reacted to a recommendation of the *bey* of the Morea. The order was written weeks before our Document 18 but was copied in the *mühimme defter* much later (Document 19), on 14 *Zilhicce* 981 (April 6, 1574).[24] The *bey* reported that the subjects were working on the castle in exchange for freedom from (unpopular) service as oarsmen (*kürekçis*)in the fleet. He now suggested that in the whole of the Morea, the recruitment of Christian boys for military or palace service *(devşirme)*, which was due to take place at this time, should also be skipped because the men were working at the castle as *cerahors*

19. MD23, p. 225, order 476.
20. MD23, p. 225, order 477.
21. MD24, p. 26, order 79, 22 *Zilkade.*
22. MD24, p. 52, order 149.
23. The building season traditionally ran between Saint George's Day (Hızır İlyas Günü; April 23, old style) and Saint Demetrius's Day (Kasım Günü; October 26, old style), which was also the time armies could campaign; see Murphey 1999, p. 21.
24. MD24, p. 89, order 237.

(and had thereby fulfilled their duties toward the state). The recruitment officer *(yayabaşı),* who was already in the Morea, was ordered not to carry out a recruitment until the castle of Anavarin was completed. The letter was given to the man who had brought the *bey*'s letter to Istanbul and was now taking the answer home.

Document 20, on the same page, immediately following the answer to the *bey*, on 7 *Zilhicce* 981 (March 30, 1574), is the order to the *yayabaşı* and his recruitment crew.[25] It is short and straightforward.

Document 20 (March 30, 1574)

> Order to *Yayabaşı*, who, for the recruitment of Christian boys *(acemi oğlan*s), came to the Morea:
>
> Because at present the subjects of the aforesaid province do service in the construction of the castle of Anavarin, the recruitment of this year has been waived. I therefore order that, as soon as this letter arrives, you waive the recruitment of Christian boys until it reaches its completion because the subjects do service at the construction of the aforesaid castle. Beware of not acting on my noble order!

The Porte was evidently concerned not to strain the local Moreote population too much and to avoid disturbances. We may assume that the letter of the *bey* of the Morea to Istanbul contained serious warnings in this regard, but this cannot be verified.

Document 21, addressed to the *bey* of the Morea and to the *kadı* and the fortress commander *(dizdar)* of Anavarin, was written on the third day of *Muharrem* of the new year of 982 (April 25, 1574).[26] The *dizdar* of the Castle of Anavarin-i cedid, Mustafa, came to the Porte at Istanbul and reported that for iron, lead, and steel necessary for Anavarin-i cedid, a large amount of money would be needed. In the castle of Anavarin-i atik, many rusted and broken old iron guns were lying about. Lead and steel was also available. If the order was given to take a sufficient quantity from there and to use it for Anavarin-i cedid, it would be very profitable for the state treasury. The Porte decided to "cannibalize" the old castle, but only partly. It was ordered that the defective cannons, and the lead and steel in store should be given to the *dizdar* of the new castle, that the quantities taken should be recorded in a register, and that the register should be dispatched to Istanbul. It is evident from this order that the new castle was taking shape and was defendable. The Porte, however, did not want to give up the old castle totally.

The *dizdar* of Anavarin-i cedid had not come all the way to Istanbul to acquire a bit of scrap iron: he needed men. Document 22 from 11 *Muharrem* 982 (May 3, 1574)[27] to the *bey* of the Morea notifies the latter that the *dizdar* of the "newly built castle of Anavarin" had come to Istanbul and had stated that "the mentioned castle lies on a dangerous place. A big garrison is needed." He asked for the 33 men from the garrison of Anavarin-i atik, *azeb*s (light infantry) and *mustahfizân* (garrison soldiers), who had been ordered to go to the newly built castle of Mayna (Mani). They should be ordered back and employed at Anavarin-i cedid. The Porte was apparently convinced and ordered that the men should be deployed as *mustahfizân* at

25. MD24, p. 89, order 238.
26. MD24, p. 163, order 438.
27. MD24, p. 194, order 517.

places deemed most necessary. Obviously there had been a conflict between the *bey* and the new fortress commander. Men were needed everywhere after the defeat at Lepanto, and they were evidently a scarce article. The problem of getting men to defend the new castle was not to end with this order.

Another indication that the castle was near completion is Document 23 from 3 *Safer* 982 (May 25, 1574),[28] in which the *bey* of the Morea asks permission for the soldiers of the garrison of the new castle of Anavarin to "make gardens and vineyards on empty land around the castle that belongs to nobody, and to make it bear fruit." The *bey* was instructed that the site had to be inspected first, and that permission was granted on the condition that the gardens, etc., were not on the glacis of the fort, within reach of its guns. When this condition was met, the *bey* was to give the soldiers title deeds *(tapu)* in return for a small payment and was to note the amount of money thus collected in a register and dispatch it to the capital.

Two months after the furious letter from Istanbul about provisions, an order was given to the *kapudan* pasha (Document 24) on 3 *Safer* 982 (May 25, 1574).[29] He was told that the *bey* of Eğriboz, Karaca Ali, had reported that the three ships full of provisions of wheat for Anavarin had arrived. İbrahim Çavuş had reported this to him by letter. The two ships with barley were ready to start. There had been much obstruction locally. The Porte now ordered that ship's biscuit *(peksimet)* should be baked and sent to Anavarin. Hereupon the *bey* of Eğriboz replied that this was not possible because there was no more wheat on the island. The admiral was ordered that those found guilty of obstruction and deceit should be thrown into the galleys.

It seems that the local authorities on Euboia had great difficulty in scraping together the desired amount of cereals because the harvest of the previous year had been almost totally consumed, and the new crop was expected only months later.

From Document 25,[30] dated the same day as the previous one, it is clear that the citadel was finally almost completed. The *bey* of the Morea had sent a letter to the Porte stating that 70 *azeb*s from the castle of Modon were to be dispatched to the new castle of Mayna.[31] For the defense of the "Outer Castle" *(Taşra Kalᶜe),* however, 500–600 warlike men were needed. The Porte thereupon ordered him to send the mentioned 70 *azeb*s to Anavarin.

Half a year later, two letters largely settle the matter of the garrison: Documents 26 and 27, both from the first of *Şabân* 982 (November 16, 1574). The first order[32] commands the chief gunner of the imperial court (Dergâh-i Muᶜalla Topcıbaşısı) to send 60 gunners to the newly built castle of Anavarin and to replace them with others after the fulfillment of their term *(nöbet).* The next order, on the same page,[33] concludes that 100 men are insufficient as a garrison for the new castle of Anavarin. It has to have 200 men. Furthermore, a detachment *(bölük)* of 60 gunners and their commander shall be sent, and later 100 extra soldiers are to be sent to Anavarin. The *sancakbey* of the Morea must see that a register is made containing their names and must send it to the capital.

Document 28, from more than a year later, 21 *Şevvâl* 983 (January 23, 1576), is of such great interest for the history of the construction of the castle that the text is given here in its entirety, despite the clumsy and repetitive style in which it has been written:[34]

28. MD24, p. 274, order 735.
29. MD24, p. 276, order 740.
30. MD24, p. 290, order 790.
31. For this kind of soldier, see Bostan 1991; more generally, Murphey 1999.
32. MD26, p. 327, order 942.
33. MD26, p. 327, order 943.
34. MD27, p. 214, order 491.

Document 28, Given to the Adjutant of the (Chief) Architect on Şevvâl *21 of* 983 *(January 23, 1576)*

Order to the Governor of the Morea:

It was made known that a noble order was sent [with which] I have given instructions that the ordered curtain wall *(hisar peçe)* between the upper and the lower towers of the castle of Anavarin has been ordered. The height of the curtain wall should be ten cubits *(zira³s)* high and two cubits thick. Previously you have sent a letter [to us] and because you presented it this way that, essentially, if the curtain wall's height is ten cubits and its thickness two, this is too little. If the said curtain wall is three cubits thick and has on the inside pillars of two cubits, which at the top are connected with arches, and if every 400 cubits of the total length of 1,200 cubits a tower is built, then two towers have to be erected. Because more building material is needed to make this [wall] and two strong and solid towers in which it is possible to use heavy siege guns *(kolumborna)*,[35] I order herewith that you personally take care of it and let the curtain wall, the construction of which was ordered, be three cubits thick, and on the inside you should add pillars of two cubits thick, connected with arches. At every 400 cubits of the total length of 1,200 cubits, according to my order, you should erect a tower, which requires two towers in total. You should build two solid towers in which it is possible to use *kolomborna* guns. You should be cautious not to act—by mistake—against my noble order, and you should write down and dispatch to us what [materials] were procured and how far you came with [the construction work on] the fort. Furthermore, it is necessary that in the tower, which is being built down by the shore, heavy and far-reaching guns *(kolomborna* and *bacaluşka-top)* can be used [to fire] at sea level.[36] According to this, you should build it. For this matter an earlier noble order has [also] been sent; act accordingly.[37]

It is clear from this order that the idea of a curtain wall *(hisar peçe)* between the coastal batteries and the star-shaped citadel was conceived more than a year after the citadel was completed. The actual construction must have begun in April of 1576.

A month after the previous document, another important order was sent to the governor *(bey)* of the Morea (Document 29),[38] which is also given here in its entirety:

Document 29, Given to the Çavuş *of the Artillery on 24* Zilkade *983 (February 24, 1576)*

Order to the *Sancakbey* of the Morea, Mehmed Bey—may his honor increase:

The Artillery commander of the castle of Anavarin-i cedid has sent a report to my Threshold of Felicity stating that enemy ships come through the strait of Anavarin-i atik into the harbor [the Bay of Navarino]. It cannot be protected by [the guns of] Anavarin-i cedid and has to be filled in. I order therefore that you go yourselves to the strait of Anavarin-i atik and that according to the advice of

35. Italian: *colubrina*, "far-reaching guns," used on ships and on land; see Agoston 1994, pp. 41–42. See also Parry 1960, pp. 1,060–1,062; Nicolle 1983; Kahane, Kahane, and Tietze 1958, pp. 175–176, s.v. no. 210, Colubrina.

36. Italian, Portuguese, and Spanish: *basilisco*, a large and heavy siege gun; see Agoston 1994, pp. 37–40; Kahane, Kahane, and Tietze 1958, pp. 99–100, s.v. no. 81, Basilisco.

37. The original has here *fermân olunmuş idi* (a *fermân* had been issued), which we understand to be a mistake that occurred when the scribe shortened the original text to its essentials.

38. MD27, p. 240, order 558.

experts you fill it in such a way that the ships of the Unbelievers can no longer pass through. After having completed the work, you should submit to us a written report [about it].

In a letter (Document 30) of 15 *Ramadan* 983 (December 18, 1575),[39] the governor of the Morea, Mehmed Bey, informed the Porte that for the completion of the Outer Castle of Anavarin, more unskilled workers (*cerahor*s) and food for them were needed. The *kadı*s of the Morea were instructed to organize the work. In an order of 8 *Zilhicce* 983 (March 9, 1576), the Porte replied that it had received a letter from the *bey,* stating that the subjects of the Morea could no longer be expected to complete the Outer Castle. The Porte thereupon ordered some Yürüks from Selânik to come down to the Morea and to complete the work (Document 31).[40]

An undated order from about the end of 1576 (Document 32)[41] remarks that "the newly built castle on the harbor of Anavarin nears its completion." Those living in the castle had cattle and were trying to acquire pasture grounds. The Porte instructs the *bey* of the Morea to organize and register the matter.

On 25 *Muharrem* 985 (April 14, 1577), an order (Document 33) regulates the garrison of the now-complete fortification.[42] Men had to be taken from the garrisons of some smaller castles in the *sancak* of the Morea, and especially from the (large) garrison of the castle of Koron in the province of Mezistre (Mystras).

Five months later, on 10 *Receb* 985 (September 23, 1577), three interesting orders (Documents 34–36) illuminate the final stage of the construction of the new castle, six years after the disastrous Battle of Lepanto.[43]

Document 34, September 23, 1577

Order to the Governor of the Morea:
The architect of the castle which at present is built at the harbor of Anavarin, Şaban, came [to my *divân* and brought a message] from you. You informed [us] that it is possible to build within the walls of the aforementioned castle 700 houses, by using plots of 12 architect's cubits (*zira³*s) in width and 16 cubits in length. I order that the houses within the castle should be [built and] distributed as you proposed. Herewith I command that when [this order] arrives, the houses within the aforementioned castle should be built, according to my order and the decision of the aforementioned architect, and should be distributed to those who wish to settle there. When this is accomplished, you should make a register to which persons, of whatever origin, [the houses] were given and how many houses were actually distributed; you should write this down and inform [us].

Document 35, September 23, 1577

Order to the Governor of the Morea and to the Judge *(Kadı)* of Anavarin:
Yahya, previously the Judge of Modon, has sent a letter and has communicated that the fortress commander and the chief of the artillery and other military men of the castle, which has been built

39. MD29, p. 12, order 28.
40. MD27, p. 345, order 833.
41. MD29, order 58.
42. MD30, p. 24, orders 60 and 223.
43. MD31, p. 287, orders 636–638.

at the harbor of Anavarin, came [to him]. They said that it was
necessary to build in the citadel a *mescid* (small mosque) for the five
daily prayers, and outside it a mosque to perform the Friday Prayer,
and asked for [this] grace. I therefore command that at the expense
of my glorious imperial majesty, a noble Friday Mosque should be
built at the harbor of Anavarin. Herewith I order when [this
message] arrives, without delay you should take care that master
architects and masons are brought and that those who are suitable
should be employed to build a noble mosque [at the expense] of my
noble majesty in an appropriate form. You should take the money
for it from the revenue of the tax-farm *(iltizam)* of this area and
spend it. In case more is needed, you must write and report.

Document 36, September 23, 1577

Order to the Governor of the Morea:
    You have sent to my Threshold of Felicity the register of the
*kadı*s and reported that the castle, which has newly been built at
the harbor of Anavarin, has reached its completion. However, to
bring it to life and to make [people] dwell in it [it would be nec-
essary] to bring in Jews from the area. I command you [therefore]
that you should bring Jews from the aforementioned province
and from Patras and Lepanto in sufficient numbers, and that you
should send them to the aforesaid place. Herewith I order that
when this writ arrives, you should take Jews from the aforesaid
places and make them settle and report how many Jews [actually]
came and settled.

    It is not clear how, and if, this last order was carried out. The town of
Patras had a sizeable Jewish community. The census—and taxation—register TT376 from 1528/1530 mentions 252 Jewish households in that
town, with 568 Greek Christian households and 76 Muslim households,
in addition to the garrison of 80 men.[44] We at least know that Jews from
Lepanto were not sent. A note in the *mühimme defter* from 9 *Cemaziyülevvel*
986 (mid-July 1578)[45] mentions that the governor of the province of
İnebahtı/Lepanto and the fortress commander of the town of Lepanto
itself had written to the Porte that they wished to keep "their" Jews,
because during the Christian attack of October 1571, they had fought
bravely side by side with the Muslim defenders. The Jewish population of
Lepanto had at any rate been much smaller than that of Patras. The register TKGM 50 (Ankara), from 977 (1569–1570), records only 71 Jewish
households in the town, in comparison with 313 households of Muslims
and 241 of Christians.
    Even with the construction of the mosque and *mescid,* the work on the
new castle was not yet complete. Two entries in MD33, Documents 37
and 38 from the first day of *Ramadan* 985 (November 12, 1577), explain
this.[46] Document 37 reports that even after more than two years, the garrison of Anavarin still had no permanent lodgings. They appear to have
camped in tents. It was now ordered that carpenters and timber be brought
from the *kaza* of Arkadiye. The second order (Document 38), on the same
page, mentions that the *bey* of the Morea had sent a letter to the Porte,

44. See Kiel 1992b.
45. MD35, p. 135, order 343.
46. MD33, p. 65, orders 129, 130.

reporting that it was not possible to finish the castle of Anavarin because the subjects of the Morea had now worked four or five years at the construction of the castle and were exhausted. In the spring of the following year, they had to be replaced by *cerahor*s from the province of Lepanto, some from each *kaza,* and these had to work at the Anavarin castle. At the same time, Yürüks from Selânik were to be sent, guided by their chiefs, and a register had to be made of those who came.

Two orders (Documents 39 and 40) from two days earlier, 28 *Şabân* 985 (November 10, 1577), do show that the work in fact was almost done. They deal again with the gardens, orchards, and vineyards, the "fortress commander, his adjutant, the heads of the small detachment, and the soldiers themselves," and how to divide the property among themselves.[47]

Documents 37–40 are the last we could find about the construction of the castle. They give an intimate view of how the project was organized and who pulled the strings. They also illustrate the difficulty of constructing such a great work, and the strains it had put on the local population. But this story echoes those of the many hundreds of large and beautiful castles throughout Europe.

The castle of Anavarin served just over a century without any major complications. In 1686, during the long war with the Christian coalition of the "Holy League," the Ottomans lost it to the Venetians without a great fight. They recaptured it in 1715, also without major military actions. The real trial came in 1770, when Russian invaders under the command of the Orlov brothers, together with Greek insurgents, attacked the castle by land and sea and bombarded it severely.[48] Although an enormous explosion in the powder magazine of one of the bastions of the citadel destroyed a large part of the fortification, flattened the small mosque *(mescid)* and the school and shops near it, and badly damaged large stretches of the curtain walls, the castle held out. A detailed, 18-page report from 1186 (1772) related these events and gave the exact measurements of parts of the castle that had been destroyed and rebuilt. At the same time, it described which parts of the sultan's mosque were damaged or destroyed and had to be reconstructed. The full publication of this document must, however, be the subject of another study.

TRANSLITERATION OF SOME OF THE MOST IMPORTANT ORDERS

Document 6 (concerns: money, architects, and building plans)
MD22, p. 323, no. 641 (Fig. IV.1), 11 *Cemaziyülevvel* 981 (September 8, 1573)

Bu dahi[49] [given to Mustafa Çavuş]

1) Mora Beyine hüküm ki: halen Anavarin limanında binâsı fermân olunan kalᶜe mühimmatı içün mukataᶜatından üç yük akçe havale olunub
2) maliye tarafından emr-i şerif gönderilmişdi ve binâ olunacak kalᶜeniñ resmi mukaddema Hızır Çavuş ile irsal olunmuşdur buyurdum ki:

47. MD33, pp. 36–37.
48. Regarding this episode, see pp. 46-47, 169–170, above.
49. Note that these transliterations use a simplified version of the system used in *EI²*, not that used elsewhere for individual terms in this book. Specifically, *c* is used where *EI²* has *dj*; *ḳ* is not used; in Arabic words, long vowels are indicated as, e.g., *â;* and *ñ* is used for final *kef.*

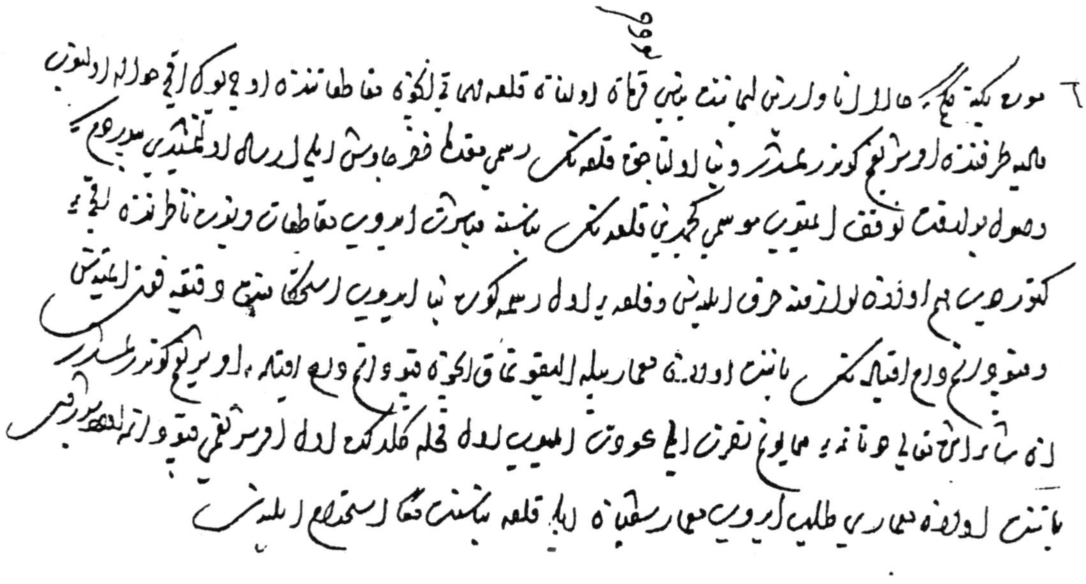

3) vusul buldukda tevakkuf etmeyüb mevsimi geçmeden kalᶜeniñ binâsına mübâşeret edüb mukataᶜat-i mezbure nazarından akçeyi

4) getürüb mühim olan levâzımına sarf eyleyesin ve kalᶜeyi ol resme göre binâ edüb istihkâmında dakika fevt etmeyesin

5) ve Kapudanım—dame ıkbâlehunun—yanında olan miᶜmâr bile alıkonmak içün Kapudanım—dame ıkbâlehuya—emr-i şerifim gönderilmişdir

6) inşa Allah teᶜala donanma-i humayun nusret ile avdet eyleyüb ol mahalle geldikde ol emr-i şerifimi Kapudanıma ulaşdırub

7) yanında olan miᶜmârı taleb edüb Miᶜmâr Şaᶜbân ile kalᶜe binâsında maᶜan istihdam eyleyesin.

Figure IV.1. Document 6, MD22, p. 323, no. 641

Document 7 (order to admiral of the fleet concerning architects and plans in "Frankish style")
 MD22, p. 323, no. 642 (Fig. IV.2), 11 *Cemaziyülevvel* 981 (September 8, 1573)

bu dahi

1) Kapudan Paşaᶜya hüküm ki: donanma-i hümayunumla bu yıl Anavarina

2) varduğuñuzde seniñ adamlarıñdan binâ olınacak kalᶜe

3) firenk üslubında maᶜen isim eyleyen miᶜmârıñ kalᶜe-i mezbûre binâsında

4) bile olmasında lâzım olmağın buyurdum ki: inşâallah-i taᶜâlâ donanma-i

5) hümayunumla ᶜavdet müyesser olub limân-ı mezbûre varıldıkda merkûm miᶜmâri

anda alıkoyub tenbih eyleyesin-ki emrim üzere kalᶜe-i mezbûre binâsı itmâme . . .

8) iyreşinçe Miᶜmâr Şaᶜbân ile maᶜen ol hizmet olub

9) kalᶜe-i gereği gibi istihdâm üzere binâ edesin.

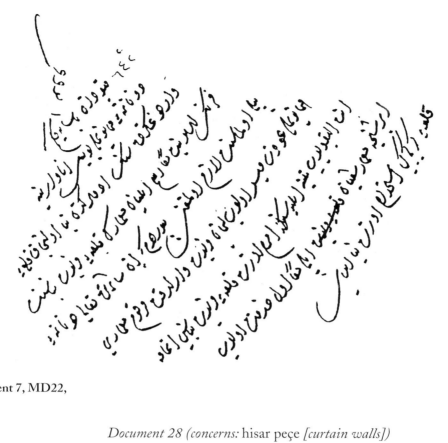

Figure IV.2. Document 7, MD22, p. 323, no. 642

Document 28 (concerns: hisar peçe *[curtain walls])*
MD27, p. 214, no. 491 (Fig. IV.3), 21 Şevvâl 983 (January 23, 1576)

1) Miᶜmar Kethüdasına verildi fi 21 [Şevvâl] sene 983.

2) Mora Beyine hüküm ki: binâsı fermân olunan

3) Anavarin kalᶜesınıñ yukaru kulleden aşağı kulleye varınca

4) hisar-peçe binâ olunmak emrim olan hisar-peçe divarınıñ kaddı on ziraᵓ

5) ve kalınlığı iki ziraᵓ olmak emrim olup hüküm-i şerif gönderildüği iᶜlâm olunub

6) bundan akdem sen mektup gönderüb ol vech-ile ᶜarz eyledügüñ ecilden fermân olunmuş idi fi nefsil-emr

7) hisar-peçe divarınıñ kaddı on arşün olunmak ᶜırżı iki arşün olmak azdır imdi zikr olunan hisar-peçe divarlarınıñ

8) kalınlığı üç arşün alup ve iki arşün dahi iç yüzünde ayaklar olup yukarusı kemer olmak ve biñ iki yüz arşün olan

9) tûlünün her dörtyüz arşün nihayet bulduğı yerde bir kulle bina olunmak ki ol takdîrce iki kulle bînâ olunmak lâzım olur kolumborna

10) yarakları istiᶜmâl olunmağa kâbil iki metîn ve mustahkem kulleler bînâ olunmak ziyâde mühimmâtdan olmağın buyurdum ki: biᶜz-zat mukayyed olup

11) bînâ olunmak fermân olunan hisâr-peçeniñ divarınıñ kalınlığın üç arşün eyleyüp iç yüzünde dahi

12) iki arşün ayaklar eyleyüp kemer etdiresin ve biñ iki yüz arşün tûlünün emrim üzere her dörtyüz arşün nihayet

Figure IV.3. Document 28, MD27, p. 214, no. 491

13) bulduğu mahallde birer kulle ki iki kulle olmak iktizâ eder, kolomborna istiᶜmâl olunmağa kâbil iki muhkem kulle binâ etdirüp

14) sehv ile emr-i şerifime muhalif iş olmakdan ziyâde ihtiyât eyleyesin ve bu vech-ile tedârik olunduğı ve kalᶜe ne mertebeye

15) varduğun yazup bildiresin; ve aşağıda binâ olunan kulleniñ suya beraber kolomborna

16) ve bacaluşka istiᶜmâl olunmağa kâbil olmak gerektir, aña göre binâ etdiresin,

17) bu bâbda sâbıka dahi emr-i şerifim gönderilmişdir

18) mûcebi ile amel eyleyesin.

Document 29 (to close the northern passage into the harbor)
MD27, p. 240, no. 558 (Fig. IV.4), 24 *Zilkade* 983 (February 24, 1576)

Topçılar Çavuşına verildi fî 24 Zuᶜl-Kade

1) Mora Sancağı Beyi Meḥmed—dame ᶜizzuhu—hüküm ki:

2) Eski Anavarin boğazında küffâr gemileri limana girüb

3) Yeñi Anavarinden korutmayı mumkün olmayub dolması lazımdır

4) deyü Yeñi Anavarin kalᶜesiniñ Topçıbaşı Ali ibn Kurt

5) Südde-i Saᶜadetime iᶜlâm etdükde

6) buyurdum ki: vardukda teᶜhir olmayub

7) Eski Anavariniñ boğazı ner bir tarikile Lakin biᶜz-zât

8) üzerine varub ehl-i vukûf müşaveresiyle bir vechle

9) dolduresınkı küffâr gemileri gelüb girmeye kadır olmaya

10) ve yine vech-i tedârik edüb doldurduğun itmane

11) erişdükden soñra yazub ᶜarz eyleyesin.

Figure IV.4. Document 29, MD27,
p. 240, no. 558

Document 34 (to make 700 houses inside the castle)
MD31, p. 287, no. 636 (Fig. IV.5), 10 *Receb* 985 (September 23, 1577)

1) Mora Beyine hüküm ki: hala Anavarin limanında binâ olunan
   kalᶜeniñ miᶜmârı olan Şabân gelüb kalᶜe-i mezbûreniñ
2) sur daḫilinde bennâ ziraᵓ ile ᶜarżı on iki ve ṭuli on altı ẕirᶜa olmak
   üzere . . . üzere
3) yedi yüz ḫâne yapmak mümkün olduğın bildirmişsiz arż etdügin
   üzere kalᶜe daḫilinde olan
4) evler tevzîᶜ olmasın emr edüb buyurdum ki: vardukda emrim
   mucibince kalᶜe-i mezbûre içinde olan
5) evler . . . olub sakın olmak üstâdımız miᶜmâr-i mezkûrûñ taᶜîn
   etdügi üzere
6) tevzîᶜ eyleyüb itmâmına erişdükde ne aṣl kimesne de verildüğin
   ve cümle nemikdar ḫâne olduğın
7) vechle verildükde defter edüb yazub bildirisiz.

Document 35 (to make a mescid *and a mosque in the castle at the expense
of the sultan)*
MD31, p. 287, no. 637 (Fig. IV.6), 10 *Receb* 985 (September 23, 1577)

fî 10 receb sene 985

1) Mora Beyine [ve] Anavarin kâżsine hüküm ki: sâbıka Modon
   kâżîsı olan Yaḫya mektub gönderüb Anavarin
2) limânında binâ olunan kalᶜesiniñ dizdârı, topçu başısı ve sâᶜir
   neferât gelüb İç Kalᶜede
3) evkât-i ḫamse içün bir mescid ve taşrasında cumᶜa namâzın kılına
   bir câmiᶜ ibnâ olunmak lazımdı
4) deyü ᶜinâyet rica etdükleri bildirmeğin cenâb-ı celâlet meᶜâbım
   ṭafafından Anavarin limanında câmiᶜ-i şerîf binâ
5) olunması emr edüb buyurdum ki: vardukda teᶜeḫḫür etmeyüb
   üstâd miᶜmârlar ve bennâlar götürüb

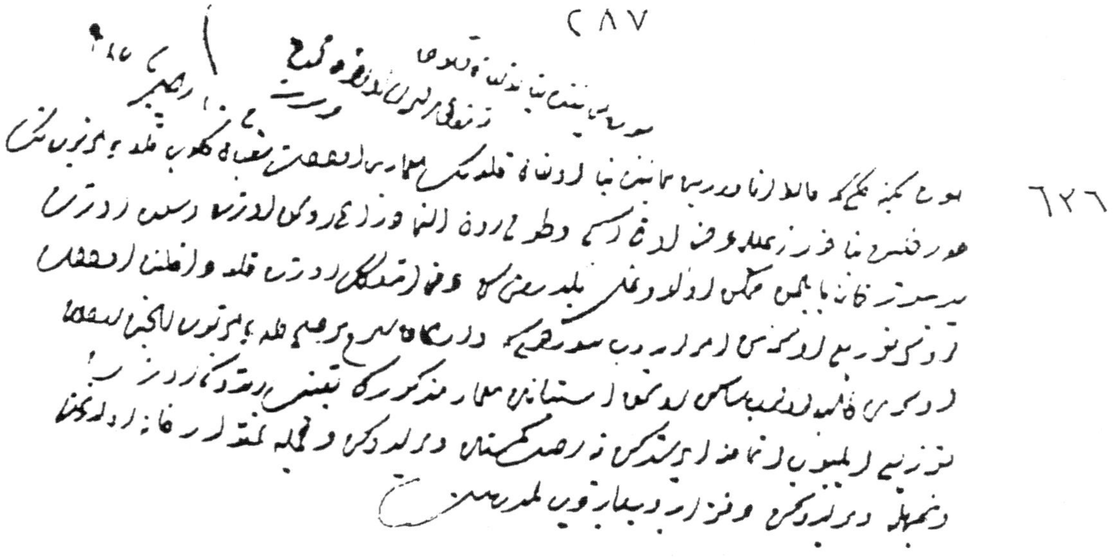

٦٣٦

Figure IV.5. Document 34, MD31,
p. 287, no. 636

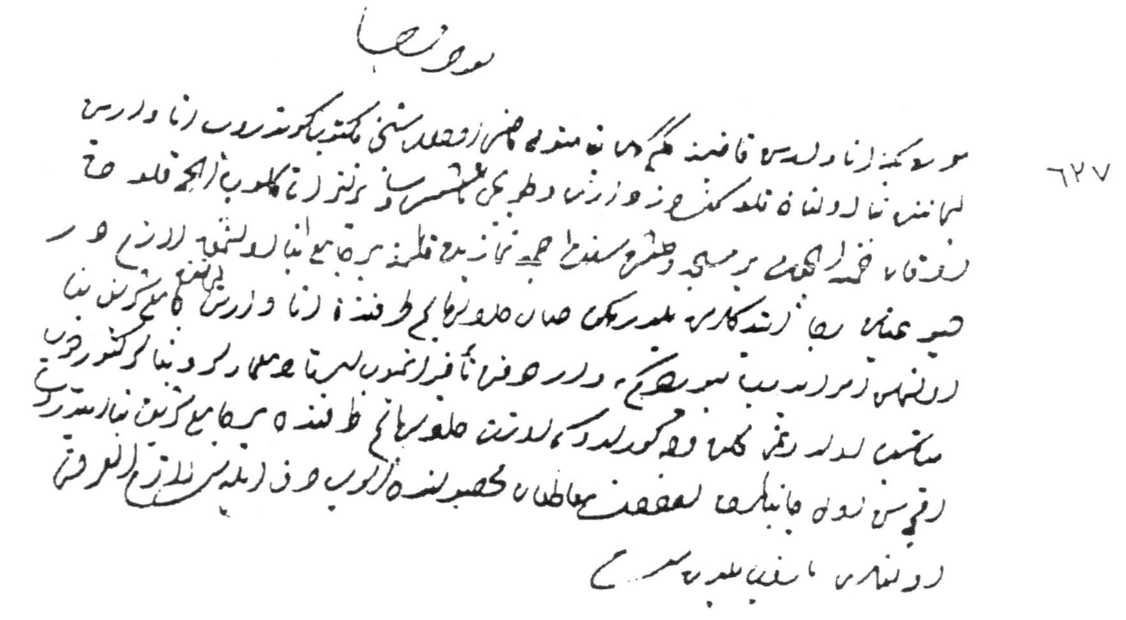

٦٣٧

Figure IV.6. Document 35, MD31,
p. 287, no. 637

6) münâsib olduğu gelene vech görüldüği üzere celâlet meᶜâbım
   ṭarafından bir câmiᶜ-i şerîf binâ etdürüb
7) akçesin ol câniblerde olan mukâtaᶜat maṣḥûlundan alub ṣarf
   eyleyesiz lazim ül-terakki
8) olanları yazub bildiresin.

Document 36 (to make Jews settle in New Anavarin)
   MD31, p. 287, no. 638 (Fig. IV.7), 10 *Receb* 985 (September 23, 1577)

1) Mora Beyine hüküm ki: südde-i saᶜâdetime kużât defterin
   gönderüb Anavar[in] limanında müceddeden binâ olunan
2) kalᶜe itmâme irişüb lakin içinde sâkin olub şenletmek için
   etrâfından Yahudi ṭaᶜifesi getürülmek
3) ḫuṣûṣun bildirmişsin. Livâ-yı mezbûrdan ve Balya Badraᶜdan ve
   İnebahtıᶜdan
4) kifâyet mikdarı Yahûdi ihrâc olunub maḥall-i mezbûre gönderesin
   emr edüb buyurdum-ki
5) varıldıkda emrim mûcibince ẕikr olunan yerlerden kifâyet
   mıkdârı Yahûdi iḫrâc eyleyüb kalᶜe-i mezbûrede
6) etdüresin ve ne mikdâr Yahudi gelüb sâkin olduğın yazub
   bildiresin.

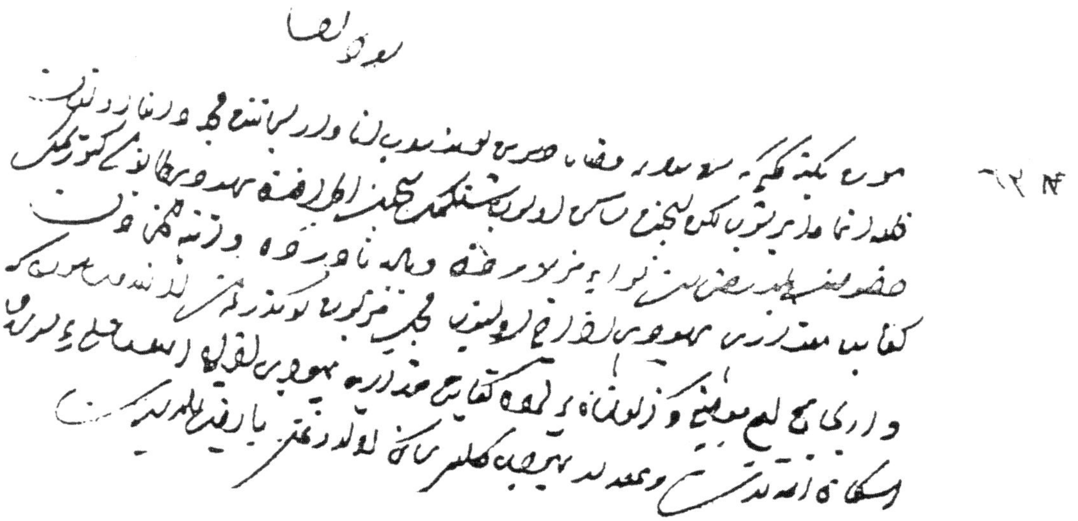

Figure IV.7. Document 36, MD31,
p. 287, no. 638

NAMES OF THE *REAYA* IN TT880

by Fariba Zarinebaf, Jack L. Davis, and John Bennet

The following concordance presents personal names of individuals recorded as taxpayers in the district of Anavarin. (Excluded are the names of Muslim property-holders in the fortress of Anavarin-i cedid; for these, see Concordance II.) Names are transliterated according to the usage of Ottoman Turkish and generally according to the standard conventions in *Redhouse*.[1] When a particular Greek name recorded can be recognized, it has been presented in the Greek alphabet in parentheses following the Ottoman form. Reference numbers allow the user to find the particular entry in the translation of TT880 in Chapter 2 (*çiftlik, karye,* or the *varış* of Anavarin) in which the name occurs. Thus 1.1.1 refers to the name of the first of the *reaya* listed for the *çiftlik* of Ali Hoca (Chap. 2, entry 1), while 46.5.2 refers to father's name of the fifth of the *reaya* recorded for the *karye* of İskarminke (Chap. 2, entry 46).[2]

COMMENTARY

The ethnicity of an individual is never specified in TT880, although in the case of the fortress of Anavarin-i cedid (35), some individuals are identified as Muslim or non-Muslim *(zimmi).*[3] Outside the fortress, given names suggest that almost all individuals are Greek and Orthodox. The name Abdi found at Pile (31.2.1) appears to be an exception. The name is clearly Turkish and is one commonly given to converts to Islam.[4] Here is a

1. The letter *o, waw* in Arabic/ Ottoman script, is transliterated as *u.* The Ottoman *siyakat* script often allows multiple transliterations, but we have not fully explicated these; and cf. Redhouse 1890, 1987.

2. In the few instances where a name occurs in an entry other than as the name of an individual or of his father (e.g., as an indication of a boundary of property), it is specified as in the example 35.112.3, where the

final "3" signifies this special use. Where the name is mentioned in an entry but not in the list of the *reaya,* this fact is indicated by referencing the name in the form 7.0.0, where "7" refers to the number of the entry in the translation of TT880 in Chapter 2.

3. Contrast earlier *defter*s for Greece, where villages are regularly specified as being Albanian or Orthodox (e.g., see Kiel 1997).

4. See Dokos and Panagopoulos

1993, p. 637, where it is noted that the land of a Turk named Avdi Magmuti has been confiscated. An Abdi also has property in the fortress of Anavarin-i cedid (35.67.1), and notice the Christian name of his father, Nikola. If this Adbi had converted to Christianity, he would have shed his Muslim name (e.g., Dokos and Panagopoulos 1993, p. 678, Giagni Turco fatto Cristian).

Christian who has converted, but he, like the other *reaya* at Pile, pays *ispence*, a tax normally levied only on non-Muslims.

The word "Albanian," in the form "Arnavid," appears only two times (49.40.2, 49.41.2), where men from the *karye* of Virviçe, both with Christian names, are said to be sons of Arnavid. Arnavid may be their surname, however.[5] Names of Albanian origin rarely appear (see below). Franks (Venetians or other Latins in this context) are also not often mentioned: the few attested names are not obviously Italian in origin. Hunduruz, a Frank, once farmed land in the *mazra'a* of Petrehuri (7.0.0) and a Hunduruz also did so in the *çiftlik* of Lefku or Tavarne (39.0.0);[6] Estefan had shops in the *varış* of Anavarin-i cedid (35.103.1, 35.104.3). A certain Budur, apparently a non-Muslim, had a house in the *varış* of Anavarin-i cedid (35.104.1) but was being held prisoner in the fort at Modon.

GIVEN NAMES

In *çiftlik*s, *karye*s, and in the *varış* of Anavarin-i cedid, virtually all personal names are Orthodox Christian in origin.[7] Most names are derived from the names of Christ, the Virgin Mary, prominent saints, or festivals of the Orthodox liturgical calendar: Anastasios (Anaştasni, Anaştu, Anuştaş), Andreas (Andiria, Andirğu), Athanasios (Danas, İstaşnu, İstaşni, Tanaş), Dimitrios (Dimitri, Dimitraki, Dimu), Emmanouil (Manialu, Manu, Manuli), Georyios (Curci, Yurğake, Yorğu, Yurki), Ilias (İlya), Ioannis (Yanağu, Yanaki, Yani), Konstantinos (Kostantin, Kuste), Lambros (Lamiru), Mihalis (Mihali, Mihalu, Mikali), Nikolaos (Nikula, Nikule), Panayiotis (Panayud, Panu), or Theodoros (Tudurake, Tuduri), expressed in either their full or abbreviated forms, frequently with diminutive terminations. The names Christos (Hiristu, Hilestu), Christofilos (Hiristufilu), and possibly Christoforos (Hirsuviri) are also represented. Other names derive from verbs expressing prayers: Stamatis (İstimad), Stamatelos (İstimatlu, İstamu).[8] Several names (e.g., Ilias) that are regularly found in TT880 were scarce or unattested in Peloponnesian documents of the 14th century; other names well represented in the 14th century (e.g., Paulos) are absent from TT880.[9]

Less common names include or appear to include:

Adamir (Αδάμης), Adamis[10]
Aleksandiri (Αλέξανδρος), Alexandros[11]
Aluviz (Αλεβίζος), derived from the Venetian name Alvise,[12] and
   also found in its adjectival form (Aluvizunlu), where -unlu

5. See Balta 1992, p. 115, for the use of Arvanid as a family name; also Dokos and Panagopoulos 1993, pp. 703, 704, s.vv. Albanos, Arvanitti. Arnavud is used once as a Muslim name (35.110).

6. Possibly the Greek name Χοντρός; see Dokos and Panagopoulos

1993, p. 709, s.v. Condro. But see also p. 139 above.

7. In many instances, however, the specific Greek forms that lie behind Ottoman transliterations are not immediately obvious, and a few may not, in fact, be Greek.

8. See Dokos and Panagopoulos

1993, p. 48, no. 128, Stamatelo.

9. See Topping 1969, p. 224.

10. See Dokos and Panagopoulos 1993, p. 703, s.v. Adhami; Boutouras 1912, p. 50.

11. Boutouras 1912, p. 35.

12. See Symeonidis 1992, p. 54.

seems to be a substitution of a Turkish adjectival ending for the
Greek -poulos ending

Angeli (Αγγέλης), Angelis[13]

Andruti (Ανδρούτσος)[14]

Ayustu (Αυγουστής)[15]

Duke (Δούκας, Doukas, a common name among Albanians)[16]

Futuni/Futni (Φωτινός), Fotinos[17]

Ğuliani, attested as a proper name, Gugliano, in Venetian documents[18]

Hurini/Hurinu/Hurun/Huruni (Χρόνης/Πολυχρόνης), Hronis[19]

İstahtu/İstahtuta/İstatni/İstatu (Στάθης/Ευστάθιος), Stathis[20]

İstifani (Στέφανος), Stefanos[21]

Kanalu/Kanlu (Κανέλος), Kanelos[22]

Kundilu, Kondilos? A surname?[23]

Kuzma (Κοσμάς), Kosmas[24]

Lazuru (Λάζαρος), Lazaros[25]

Liftari (Λευτέρης/Ελευθέριος), Lefteris[26]

Luke (Λουκάς), Loukas[27]

Marinu (Μαρίνος), Marinos[28]

Marku (Μάρκος), Markos

Mavurudi (Μαυρουδής), Mavrudis, probably deriving from the
name Mauros (Μαύρος), "Black"[29]

Petru (Πέτρος), Petros[30]

Pindazi (Πανταζής), Pantazis[31]

Puliduru (Πολύδωρος), Polydoros[32]

Şideri (Σιδέρης/Ισίδωρος), Sideris[33]

Tirandafilu (Τριαντάφυλλος), Triandafyllos[34]

Valinar (Βελισσάριος), Belissarios[35]

Vasil (Βασίλης), Vasilis[36]

Yakumi (Γιακουμής), Yiakoumis[37]

Zefir (Ζαφείρης), Zafeiris[38]

Zahir, Zahire, Zahiri, Zakhariye, Zakhir, Zehiriye, Zekhiriye
(Ζαχαρίας), Zaharias[39]

13. Boutouras 1912, p. 87.

14. Dokos and Panagopoulos 1993, p. 145, no. 26, Papa Andruzzo Cocla.

15. Boutouras 1912, p. 109.

16. Kiel 1997, p. 322.

17. Boutouras 1912, p. 99.

18. E.g., Dokos and Panagopoulos 1993, pp. 112, 115.

19. Dokos and Panagopoulos 1993, p. 157, no. 10, Crogni; Boutouras 1912, p. 168.

20. Dokos and Panagopoulos 1993, p. 47, no. 10, Stati; Boutouras 1912, p. 66.

21. Boutouras 1912, p. 82.

22. Dokos and Panagopoulos 1993, p. 535. The name may well be

preserved in the place-name Kanalos (Κάναλος) near Gargaliani: Georgacas and McDonald 1967, 52.2505.

23. Dokos and Panagopoulos 1993, p. 637, no. 33, Condillo Zorzi.

24. Boutouras 1912, p. 72.

25. Boutouras 1912, p. 75.

26. Boutouras 1912, p. 64.

27. Boutouras 1912, p. 75.

28. Boutouras 1912, p. 77.

29. See Boutaras 1912, p. 106. This name might also have functioned as a surname.

30. Boutouras 1912, p. 81.

31. Dokos and Panagopoulos 1993, p. 178, nos. 46 and 59, p. 193, Pandasi; Boutouras 1912, p. 167. This name

might also have functioned as a surname.

32. Boutouras 1912, p. 45.

33. Dokos and Panagopoulos 1993, p. 49, bottom, no. 36, Sidheri; Boutouras 1912, p. 71. This might also have functioned as a surname.

34. Boutouras 1912, p. 142.

35. Boutouras 1912, p. 102. The Turkish might be transliterated as Velisar.

36. Boutouras 1912, p. 59.

37. Dokos and Panagopoulos 1993, p. 50, no. 98, Giacomi; Boutouras 1912, p. 119.

38. Boutouras 1912, p. 144.

39. Boutouras 1912, p. 67.

FAMILY NAMES

Family names had already been used to qualify the given names of Greeks in Byzantine registers.[40] Surnames continued to exist and were routinely recorded in both Ottoman and Venetian cadasters.[41] Surnames were sometimes noted in an initial Ottoman census conducted when a Christian area was annexed from the Byzantines, after which scribes would regularly revert to the more usual Turkish practice of recording the name of the father.[42] In TT10, the Turkish register composed in the second half of the 15th century for parts of the Morea, Greeks could be identified either by the name of their father or by a surname.[43] This is the case also in TT25, composed for the island of Limnos in 1490.[44]

In almost all cases, the scribe of TT880 lists individuals as "[x] (given name) son of [y] (given name)." Only rarely does he deviate from this standard formula to record "[x] (given name, surname) son of [y] (given name)." Use of surnames seems to be more common in larger communities, namely, the *varış* of Anavarin-i cedid (35.120.1, 35.136.1, 35.142.1), or at Osman Ağa or Büyük Pisaski (15.2.1), Papla or Mustafa Ağa (19.1.1), İklina or Kurd Ağa (23.15.1), Muzuste (43.14.1, 43.16, 43.18.1), and Ağurliçe (42.23.1). In most instances, the given name of an individual with a surname is a very common name, and it seems possible that in these instances a surname or nickname was added so that homonymic *reaya* could be distinguished within these larger groups:

> Hilestu Avran son of Yilin; Avram is attested as a Greek family name.[45]
> Yurğu İstahtu son of Dimu, from the Greek given name Στάθης?[46]
> Dimu İstahtuta son of Yurğu, a corruption of the preceding name?
> Manuli Kaltaban son of Anuştaş, from the Turkish *kaltaban*, "pimp; dishonest or mean person"[47]
> Yanağu Kukuri son of Yurğake, the attested Greek family name Kakuri?[48]
> İlya Kunari son of İstimad, equivalent to the name Gunari (Γούναρης) in Ottoman and Venetian documents[49]

The same name occasionally appears both as a surname and as the father's name: Curci Monti son of Monti, Konstantin Tunkar son of Tunkar, and Yorğu Yurikan son of Yurikan. It is possible that in these cases, the name of [y] is actually the surname of [x], rather than the name of his father.[50]

In the Morea, Greek surnames were commonly formed by attaching -poulos (-πουλος), a diminutive suffix, to the given name of the father. This compound could then be fossilized in subsequent generations. There is one example in TT880 in which the scribe has written "Yanağu Yanağupulu, son of Yanağu" (35.138). If "Yanağupulu" here is a family name, the scribe may have misunderstood Greek usage to mean that Yanağu's own father's name was Yanağu.[51]

"Polu" is found twice elsewhere. Yanağu and Nikula are both said to be sons of "Angelu Polu" (35.122; 35.125), apparently with reference to the same father. Although Poulos (Πούλος) is attested (but not as a suffix)

40. See, e.g., Laiou-Thomadakis 1977, pp. 138–139.
41. See, e.g., Balta 1989 (15th century), 1992 (16th century); Dokos and Panagopoulos 1993 (17th century).
42. Lowry 1992, pp. 13–14.
43. Beldiceanu and Beldiceanu-Steinherr 1986, p. 42.
44. Lowry 2002, pp. 40–41, 180–181.
45. Assenova, Kacori, and Stojkov 1974, p. 71; see also Triandafyllidis 1982, p. 90.
46. For its use as a surname, see Dokos and Panagopoulos 1993, p. 722, s.v. Stathi.
47. The Greek family name Καλταμπάνης is attested; see Tombaïdis 1990, p. 83.
48. See Balta 1992, p. 119.
49. Balta 1992, p. 113; see also Dokos and Panagopoulos 1993, p. 713, s.v. Gunari.
50. See also the name Kundiyurğa (Κοντογιώργης), "Short-George," apparently a surname instead of the father's given name (35.137.2).
51. But it is also possible that the father had died before the baptism of his son and that they both had the same baptismal name.

in Ottoman cadasters from Euboia[52] and the Morea, in TT880 it is not likely to be a complete surname. Yanağu is a *tercüman*, or interpreter. The only other interpreter in the *variş* is Koca Angeli (35.144.1), who is said to be the "son of Angeli." Yanağu, the *tercüman*, was probably his son and is likely to have followed his father into this profession. Was his father's full name Angelos Angelopoulos?[53] There are other cases in TT880 where father and son have the same name, such as İstimad son of İstimad, and Hiristufilu son of Hiristufilu. Are these instances of posthumously baptized sons, or were the actual names of the individuals Stamatis Stamatopoulos and Hristofilos Hristofilopoulos?

There are instances in which the surname does not appear to be derived from the baptismal name of an ancestor. Several with Turkish roots may be nicknames. Examples include:

> Aksanu, which appears at Corinth in TT10: "Droit sur un moulin, pleine propriéte de Dimitri Aksano. . . ."[54]
> Çuka, perhaps Τσόκας, derived from the Turkish *çuka* or *çuha,* "(broad)cloth," and also a Turkish name for the island of Kythera (thus perhaps here meaning "from Kythera")[55]
> Kakuni, perhaps Κακούλης, a Greek family name derived from the Turkish *kâkül,* "curl"[56]
> Kiryazi, an attested Greek surname (Κυριαζής)[57]
> Lağuri, perhaps Λαγάρης, derived from the Turkish *lağar,* "skinny"[58]
> Vanduke/Varduke, attested elsewhere as an Albanian family name[59]
> Zengin, perhaps Greek Ζεγκίνης, derived from the Turkish *zengin,* "rich"[60]

There is at least one instance in which an individual's family name was recorded as [x] instead of his given name. The Venetian name Alvise appears in an adjectival form, Aluvizunlu, where -unlu may be understood to be a translation of the Greek -poulos ending.[61] The name Sakirli, if derived from the name Zahir with the Turkish adjectival termination -li, may represent a similar formation, equivalent to the Greek Ζαχαρόπουλος.

52. See, e.g., Balta 1992, p. 116.

53. The -poulos suffix was exchanged, apparently indiscriminately, with the genitive of a given name (with or without the article) in Venetian cadasters. The same man could be recorded in different parts of a document in different ways: e.g., Alessandro tou Dimu or Alessandro Dimopullo; Giogni or Gianopullo. See Dokos and Panagopoulos 1993, pp. 711, 713, s.vv. Dimu, Giogni.

54. Beldiceanu and Beldiceanu-Steinherr 1986, p. 44.

55. See Redhouse 1890, p. 738; cf. Redhouse 1987. Another possibility is that it is derived from the Turkish *çok,* "too much"; see Kalantzakos 1994,

p. 54; Triandafyllidis 1982, p. 75.

56. Kakuli is a possible transliteration of the Ottoman. For the name, cf. Tombaïdis 1990, p. 81; also Balta 1992, p. 134, s.v. Kaculo; Triandafyllidis 1982, p. 69.

57. Cf. Balta 1992, p. 139, Kirgazi; Triandafyllidis 1982, p. 14.

58. See Tombaïdis 1990, p. 107.

59. See Balta 1992, p. 121, Vunduka.

60. Tombaïdis 1990, p. 75. See Dokos and Panagopoulos 1993, p. 120, Panagiotti Sechina.

61. The name Alvisopoulos is attested in the Morea in the later 17th century; see Dokos and Panagopoulos 1993, p. 703, s.v. Alvisopulo.

PROFESSIONS

An individual could also be described with reference to a profession or his age. A small group of individuals appear to be priests: Papa Hiristufilu (49.3.1), Papa İstimatlu (49.5.1), Papa Panayud (49.1.1), Papa Yurğu (23.1.1), and Papa Yurki (35.121.1). Several other individuals may be monks, if the Turkish Kalenuri (15.6.2, 42.17.1, 43.20.1) and Kilayuri (29.10.1, 29.11.1) are equivalent to the Greek Καλόγερος.[62] But Kaloyeros also may be a surname or a nickname.[63] Secular professions are sometimes mentioned for individuals resident in the varış of Anavarin-i cedid, more commonly for Turks (see App. II) than for the reaya. Among non-Muslims are a tüfenkçi (musket-seller) named Zakarya/Zakhariye (35.105.3), a boyacı (dyer) named Zakhir (35.111.3), and Ğanlu, son of a soğancı, or onion-seller (35.128.1). It is unclear whether the designated individuals actually practiced these professions, if these were surnames inherited from an ancestor, or if they were nicknames. Zakarya/Zakhariye the tüfenkçi seems elsewhere to be "Zekhiriye son of the tüfenkçi" (35.145.1).

There are two interpreters (tercümans) in the varış of Anavarin-i cedid, apparently father and son (see above). Angeli (35.144.1), the elder of the pair, is explicitly called Koca, a translation of the Greek Γερο-, literally "old," a prefix commonly attached to Greek personal names as an expression of respect.[64] Elsewhere in TT880, this practice is attested by the Greek form "Yuri Nikula" (Γέρο-Νικόλας), and possibly also by the form "Yuriyan" (Γερογιάννης).[65]

CONCORDANCE OF NAMES OF THE *REAYA*

Abdi, 31.2.1
Adamir (Αδάμης), 1.2.1, 43.10.1, 49.27.1
Aksanu, 2.3.2
Aku (possibly Greek Ακης, a nickname for the diminutive of many Greek names), 35.130.2
Aleksandiri (Αλέξανδρος), 49.43.1
Aluviz (Αλεβίζος), 6.5.1
Aluvizunlu, 14.13.1
Anaştasni (Αναστάσιος), 29.22.2
Anaştu (Ανάστος), 49.26.1
Andirğu (Ανδρέας), 22.1.2
Andiria (Ανδρέας, Αντιριάς), 5.4.2, 15.1.1, 31.3.2, 35.139.1, 46.2.2, 46.17.2
Andruni, 29.15.1, 29.17.2
Andruti (Ανδρούτσος), 29.15.1, 29.17.2
Anduni (Αντώνης), 15.8.1, 49.5.2, 49.46.2
Anduni (Αντώνης) Bulinmirun, 15.8.1
Angeli (Αγγέλης), 35.144.1, 35.144.2
Angelu, 35.122.2, 35.125.2

62. The Ottoman might also be transliterated as Kaleyuri.

63. E.g., Dokos and Panagopoulos 1993, p. 706, s.vv. Callichireri/Callogera/Calogiera.

64. Kalantzakos 1994, p. 19; cf. Balta 1992, p. 137.

65. See Balta 1992, pp. 109, 140.

Angelu Polu, 35.122.2, 35.125.2
Anuştaş (Άναστάσιος), 5.6.2, 14.6.2, 19.5.2, 23.4.2, 23.14.2, 29.6.2,
    35.142.2, 42.5.2, 42.12.1, 43.3.1, 46.9.2, 46.11.2, 49.17.2,
    49.29.1, 49.37.1
Arnavid, 49.40.2, 49.41.2
Asastu, 49.30.2
Avran, 23.15.1
Ayumerinu, 48.4.2
Ayustu (Αύγουστής), 42.25.2, 48.5.2, 49.6.2, 49.9.1

Biraşkiva, 48.5.1
Budur, 35.104.1
Buduva, 46.7.2
Bulinmirun, 15.8.1, 15.8.2, 19.5.1

Curci (Τζίρτζης), 1.1.2, 35.112.3, 35.143.1
Curci Monti, 35.143.1

Çakuye, 14.9.2
Çayalidi, 35.121.2
Çuka, 35.133.2

Danas (Θανάσης), 35.119.2
Dimitraki (Δημητράκης), 49.35.1
Dimitri (Δημήτρης), 6.2.1, 6.4.1, 14.3.1, 14.12.1, 15.10.2, 16.6.2,
    22.3.2, 23.6.2, 23.13.2, 31.7.1, 35.148.1, 42.8.1, 42.20.1,
    42.29.1, 43.6.1, 43.7.1, 43.11.1, 46.14.2, 49.25.1, 49.31.2,
    49.47.1
Dimu (Δήμος), 2.1.1, 16.1.2, 16.3.1, 16.8.2, 16.9.2, 35.148.2,
    42.28.2, 43.16.2, 43.18.1, 46.1.1, 46.17.1, 49.18.1, 49.38.1
Dimu İstahtuta, 43.18.1
Duke (Δούκας), 42.11.2, 46.8.2

Estefan, 35.103.1, 35.104.3

Futni (Φωτινός), 5.6.1
Futuni (Φωτινός), 42.26.2

Ğanlu, 35.128.1
Ğuliani, 43.15.2

Hilestu (Χρήστος) Avran, 23.15.1
Hiristu (Χρήστος), 23.11.1, 35.130.1, 49.40.1
Hiristufilu (Χρηστόφιλος), 14.5.1, 14.5.2, 23.4.1, 29.14.2, 31.4.1,
    46.16.2, 49.3.1
Hirsuviri (Χρηστόφορος), 49.7.1
Hunduruz (Χοντρός), 7.0.0, 39.0.0
Hurini (Χρόνης), 23.2.1

Hurinu (Χρόνης), 35.131.2
Hurun (Χρόνης), 42.27.2
Huruni (Χρόνης), 43.1.2, 46.12.1

İlya (Ηλίας), 6.3.2, 15.2.1, 16.9.1, 19.1.1, 23.7.1, 29.8.1, 31.1.1,
     43.13.2, 43.14.1, 47.2.1, 49.15.1, 49.27.2
İlya Kunari, 43.14.1
İlya Mirevala, 19.1.1
İlya Panvilu, 15.2.1
İskabişnu, 19.9.1
İskidia, 43.19.1
İstabişnu, 19.9.1
İstahtu (Στάθης), 43.16.1
İstahtuta (Στάθης), 43.18.1
İstamu (Στάμος), 42.13.2, 42.29.2
İstanu, 15.9.2
İstaşni (Στασινός), 42.26.1
İstaşnu (Στασινός),[66] 42.6.2, 42.8.2, 43.8.2, 48.3.1, 49.16.1, 49.17.1,
     49.25.2, 49.30.1
İstatni (Στάθης), 6.2.2, 6.7.2, 19.2.1, 42.28.1, 43.4.1, 43.15.1
İstatu (Στάθης), 15.9.2
İstifani (Στέφανος), 15.11.2
İstilud, 49.22.2
İstimad (Σταμάτης), 5.5.1, 5.5.2, 31.9.2, 42.1.2, 43.14.2, 46.5.1,
     48.6.2, 49.10.2
İstimatlu (Σταματέλης), 12.2.1, 15.7.1, 16.5.1, 19.7.1, 43.17.1,
     49.1.2, 49.5.1, 49.15.2, 49.20.2, 49.21.1
İstiratni, 1.3.2

Kakuni, 43.7.2
Kalenuri (Καλόγερος), 15.6.2, 42.17.1, 43.20.1
Kaltaban, 35.112.2, 35.142.1
Kanalu (Κανέλος), 49.19.1
Kanlu (Κανέλος), 23.5.2
Katlu, 5.1.2, 49.39.2
Kikri, 35.136.1
Kilayuri, 29.10.1, 29.11.1
Kiryazi, 42.3.2
Koca (Γέρο-), 35.144.1
Koca (Γέρο-) Angeli (Αγγέλης), 35.144.1
Kostantin (Κωστάντης), 5.2.1, 14.10.2, 15.6.1, 16.11.2, 22.2.2,
     23.8.1, 31.8.1, 35.126.1, 42.14.1, 42.15.1, 42.30.1, 48.1.1,
     49.13.1, 49.20.1, 49.36.1, 49.42.1
Kostantin (Κωστάντης) Tunkar, 35.126.1
Kukuri, 35.120.1
Kunari, 43.14.1
Kundilu, 29.22.1
Kundiyurğa (Κοντογιώργης), 35.137.2
Kuntu, 29.13.1

66. See Boutouras 1912, p. 57.

Kurzbale, 35.135.2
Kuste (Κωστής), 2.1.2, 2.2.2, 23.13.1, 43.5.1, 46.1.2, 49.43.2
Kutnu, 14.7.1, 14.12.2, 16.6.1, 29.13.1
Kuzma (Κοσμάς), 42.9.1

Lağuri, 43.6.2
Lamiru (Λάμπρος), 6.1.1, 6.6.1, 14.10.1, 16.10.1, 22.2.1, 23.6.1,
    29.4.1, 29.12.1, 29.20.1, 43.9.1
Lazuru (Λάζαρος), 31.3.1
Liftari (Λευτέρης), 42.22.1
Lindi, 35.129.2
Luke (Λουκάς), 4.2.1

Manialu (Μανόλης), 31.11.2
Manu (Μάνος), 14.8.2
Manuli (Μανόλης), 35.112.3, 35.129.1, 35.142.1, 42.18.1
Manuli Kaltaban, 35.112.3, 35.142.1
Marinu (Μαρίνος), 35.127.1
Marku (Μάρκος), 35.123.1, 35.139.2
Mavurudi (Μαυρουδής), 23.3.2
Mihali (Μιχάλης), 1.1.1, 14.9.1, 23.1.2, 42.4.1, 49.2.1, 49.4.1,
    49.44.2, 49.45.1
Mihalu (Μιχάλης), 46.0.0
Mikali (Μιχάλης), 35.124.1
Minuli (Μανόλης), 29.3.1
Mirevala, 19.1.1
Miryan, 19.7.2, 19.9.2
Monti, 35.143.1, 35.143.2

Nekin, 29.19.2
Nikula (Νικόλας), 2.2.1, 4.1.1, 5.8.1, 5.9.2, 12.1.1, 12.2.2, 14.4.1,
    15.10.1, 16.11.1, 23.8.2, 29.5.1, 29.10.2, 29.11.2, 29.16.1,
    29.20.2, 31.2.2, 31.4.2, 31.6.1, 35.125.1, 35.134.1, 35.135.1,
    35.137.1, 42.2.1, 42.13.1, 42.15.2, 42.24.2, 43.13.1, 46.11.1,
    48.1.2, 49.12.1, 49.19.2, 49.44.1
Nikule (Νικόλας), 43.19.2, 48.2.1

Panayud (Παναγιώτης), 2.3.1, 4.2.2, 16.2.2, 16.7.2, 16.10.2, 23.12.2,
    29.1.2, 29.7.1, 31.1.2, 31.11.1, 35.141.1, 42.6.1, 42.9.2, 42.20.2,
    43.1.1, 43.4.2, 43.19.1, 46.12.2, 49.1.1, 49.35.2, 49.39.1
Panayud İskidia, 43.19.1
Panu (Πάνος), 35.133.1
Panvilu, 15.2.1
Papa Hiristufilu, 49.3.1
Papa İstimatlu, 49.5.1
Papa Panayud, 49.1.1
Papa Yurğu, 23.1.1
Papa Yurki, 35.121.1
Petru (Πέτρος), 14.2.1, 35.119.1, 49.8.1

Pindazi (Πανταζής), 19.8.1, 29.17.1, 46.6.1
Polu, 35.122.2, 35.125.2
Puliduru (Πολύδωρος), 4.3.1

Sakirli, 4.1.2
Soğancı, 35.128.2

Şideri (Σιδέρης), 29.7.2, 29.9.2

Tanak, 35.140.2, 35.141.2
Tanaş (Θανάσης), 1.2.2, 5.7.2, 6.3.1, 14.1.1, 15.4.1, 15.9.1, 16.5.2,
      16.8.1, 19.10.1, 31.10.1, 42.23.2, 42.25.1, 42.27.1, 46.3.2,
      46.5.2, 46.10.1, 46.15.1, 49.6.1, 49.14.1, 49.41.1
Tirandafilu (Τριαντάφυλλος), 23.10.1, 29.9.1, 42.21.1
Tudurake (Θοδωράκης), 49.13.2, 49.33.2, 49.34.1
Tuduri (Θοδωρής), 1.3.1, 23.7.2, 23.9.2, 23.10.2, 23.11.2, 29.2.1,
      49.23.1, 49.28.1
Tuduva, 46.7.2
Tunkar, 35.126.2

Vafır, 35.146.2
Valinar (Βελισσάριος), 49.11.2
Vanduke, 35.134.2, 35.135.2
Varduke, 35.124.2
Varvarin, 35.105.3
Varvaris, 35.105.3
Vasil (Βασίλης), 23.2.2, 42.31.1
Vavalari, 31.10.2
Velahuvirle, 19.3.1
Virazu, 42.23.1
Virku, 31.7.2

Yakumi (Γιαχουμής), 43.2.1
Yanağu (Γιαννάκος), 14.8.1, 15.1.2, 19.3.1, 22.3.1, 29.14.1, 29.18.1,
      31.13.1, 35.120.1, 35.122.1, 35.138.1, 35.138.2, 42.5.1, 42.19.1,
      46.2.1, 46.4.1, 46.9.1, 47.1.1, 48.4.1, 49.10.1, 49.46.1
Yanağu Kukuri, 35.120.1
Yanağupulu, 35.138.1
Yanağupulu Velahuvirle, 19.3.1
Yanağu Yanağupulu, 35.138.1
Yanaki (Γιαννάκης), 49.24.1
Yanani, 31.12.2
Yani (Γιάννης), 1.4.1, 5.3.1, 5.4.1, 5.7.1, 6.4.2, 14.3.2, 14.6.1,
      14.11.1, 14.11.2, 15.2.2, 15.3.1, 15.5.2, 15.11.1, 16.1.1, 16.4.1,
      16.12.1, 19.2.1, 19.4.2, 19.6.1, 19.8.2, 22.1.1, 23.3.1, 23.14.1,
      29.1.1, 29.19.1, 31.5.1, 35.105.3, 35.111.3, 35.131.1, 35.132.1,
      35.136.1, 35.140.1, 42.3.1, 42.7.1, 42.11.1, 42.16.1, 42.18.2,
      42.32.1, 43.8.1, 43.9.2, 43.12.1, 43.17.2, 46.3.1, 46.7.1, 46.13.1,
      46.14.1, 47.1.2, 48.2.2, 48.6.1, 49.3.2, 49.29.2

Yani Kikri, 35.136.1

Yani Varvarin, 35.105.3

Yani Varvaris, 35.105.3

Yilin, 23.15.2

Yorğu (Γιώργιος), 4.3.2, 5.1.1, 5.9.1, 6.1.2, 6.7.1, 15.7.2, 15.12.1,
    16.2.1, 16.7.1, 19.3.2, 19.4.1, 23.5.1, 23.9.1, 23.12.1, 29.6.1,
    29.18.2, 31.6.2, 31.8.2, 31.12.1, 31.13.2, 35.147.2, 42.1.1,
    42.10.1, 42.23.1, 42.24.1, 43.12.2, 43.16.1, 43.18.2, 46.6.2,
    46.8.1, 46.10.2, 46.13.2, 46.16.1, 46.0.0, 49.8.2, 49.24.2,
    49.31.1, 49.37.2

Yorğu İstahtu, 43.16.1

Yorğu Virazu, 42.23.1

Yorğu Yurikan, 15.12.1

Yudi, 35.103.3

Yuduva, 46.7.2

Yurğake (Γιωργάκης), 14.13.2, 29.15.2, 29.21.1, 35.120.2, 35.136.2,
    35.147.1, 42.2.2, 49.2.2, 49.11.1, 49.22.1, 49.32.1

Yurikan, 15.12.1, 15.12.2

Yuri Nikula (Γέρο-Νικόλας), 16.11.1

Yuriyan, 14.1.2

Yurki (Γιώργης), 15.5.1, 35.121.1, 35.127.2

Zahir (Ζαχαρίας), 29.4.2

Zahire (Ζαχαρίας), 29.22.3

Zahiri (Ζαχαρίας), 31.9.1

Zakarya (Ζαχαρίας), 35.105.3, 35.106.3

Zakhari (Ζαχαρίας), 35.109.3, 35.110.3

Zakhariye (Ζαχαρίας), 35.105.3, 35.106.3

Zakhir (Ζαχαρίας), 35.111.3

Zakhiri (Ζαχαρίας), 35.146.1

Zefir (Ζαφείρης), 49.33.1

Zekhiriye (Ζαχαρίας), 35.145.1

Zengin, 35.132.2

NAMES OF MUSLIMS IN THE FORTRESS OF ANAVARİN-İ CEDİD IN TT880

by Fariba Zarinebaf, Jack L. Davis, and John Bennet

In this concordance, numbers designate descriptions of principal property in the fortress and *varış* of Anavarin-i cedid (Chap. 2, entry 35) in the possession of the indexed individuals. The professions of individuals are more commonly noted for Turks than non-Muslims (see Concordance I). Military offices are specified, among them commanders of the fort, *dizdar* Ağa (35.21), *dizdar* Haci Kurd Ali Ağa (35.48), and *dizdar* Hüseyin Çavuş (35.80); guards Dustoğlu Mustafa Çavuş (35.9), Hasan Çavuş (35.11, 35.12), Bekir Çavuş (35.11), and Mustafa Çavuş (35.10); gatekeepers Kırlı Kapucı Mustafa Çelebi (35.109) and Kapucı Mustafa (35.110); and six stewards, Hasan Kethüda (35.43), Hasan Kethüdaoğlu (35.40), Hasan Kethüdaoğlu Mustafa (35.42), Ahmed Kethüda (35.63, 35.64), Fezli Kethüda (35.79), and a *kethüda* (35.82). There are also references to the barracks of Janissaries (35.2, 35.78).

A certain Muvali is a *şeyh*, or leader of a dervish community (35.25). Secular nonmilitary professions held by Turks include an *ayrancı* (yogurt-drink maker) Receb (35.33); a son of a coffee-seller, Kahvecioğlu Hüseyin (35.80); a *kundakçı* (manufacturer of gun carriages and incendiaries) Bekir (35.84); and two shoemakers, a *babucı* Zaman (35.108) and *babucı* Ramazan (35.109).[1] It seems possible that some of these names at least are nicknames and may not describe the actual profession of the individual described (see App. I).

1. Unless these are the same individual, recorded in two different ways by the scribe.

Abdi, 67
Abdulkadir Ağa, 16
Abdürrahman Ağa, 30
Abdürrahman (brother of), 32
Ahmed Kethüda, 63, 64
Ali Ağa, 41
Arnavud Receb, 110
Ataullah Efendi, 35, 36, 37
Ayrancı Receb, 33

Baba Ali, 93
Baba Alioğlu, 81

Babucı Ramazan, 109
Babucı Zaman, 108
Bekir Çavuş, 11
Bekir Hoca, 10

Cağaloğlu, 61, 65, 66

Çabuk Ömer Ağa, 115
Çaçe Hatun, 19

Deli Ahmed, 51, 52, 53
Deli İsmail, 3, 4

Deli Mustafa, 118
Deli Yusuf, 49
Dizdar Ağa, 21
Dizdar Haci Kurd Ali Ağa, 48
Dizdar Hüseyin Çavuş, 80
Dumbul Mustafa, 4, 5
Dustoğlu Mustafa Çavuş, 9

Fezli Kethüda, 79
Firuzoğlu Mustafa, 112

Haci Alioğlu, 39
Haci Bey, 19, 20, 22, 24, 25
Haci Hasanoğlu, 2
Haci Hasanoğlu Mustafa, 8
Haci Hasanoğlu Mustafa Çelebi, 1,
    45
Haci Hasanzade Mustafa Çelebi,
    44
Haci Mustafa, 48
Haci Mustafa Ağa, 47
Hacioğlu, 41
Halil Ağa, 14, 15, 16, 17, 30
Hasan Çavuş, 11, 12
Hasan Kethüda, 43
Hasan Kethüdaoğlu, 40
Hasan Kethüdaoğlu Mustafa, 42
Hüseyin Ağa, 36, 37
Hüseyin Hoca, 19
Hüseyin Reis, 79

İbrahim Hoca, 49
İdris Ağa, 20, 44

Kadir Ağa, 15, 17, 20, 23, 26, 31
Kahvecioğlu Hüseyin, 80
Kapucı Mustafa, 110
Kara Abdürrahman, 59, 60
Kaztağli Mehmed Ağa, 86
Kethüda, 82
Keyvanoğlu, 61, 66, 67, 68
Kırlı Kapucı Mustafa Çelebi, 109
Koca Firuz, 5
Kundakçı Bekir, 84
Kuparmazoğlu Mehmed, 56
Kuparmazoğlu Mehmed Ağa, 53

Kuparmazoğlu Mustafa Ağa, 29
Kurd Ali, 47, 85
Kurd Ali Ağa, 50, 51, 108
Kurd Ali Ağazade, 27, 28
Kurd Ali Ağazade Mehmed Ağa,
    26
Küçük Hüseyin Hoca, 18
Küçük İdris Ağa, 6, 7, 23

Makrunoğlu, 101
Mehmed, 54
Mehmed Ağa, 29, 30, 52, 58
Mehmed Uskufoğlu, 55
Musli Çelebizade Büyük İdris Ağa,
    43
Muslihuddin Ağa, 117
Muslihuddin Efendi, 94
Mustafa Ağa, 40
Mustafa Bey, 58, 71, 79
Mustafa Çavuş, 10
Mustafa Çelebi, 42, 43, 91, 92
Mutaciloğlu, 60
Müfti Efendi, 70

Osman Ağa, 16, 17, 18, 21
Osman Ağa (cousin of), 14
Osman Halife, 68

Ömer Ağa, cousin of Osman Ağa,
    14

Receb, 34, 111

Sakin Hoca, 7
Sivrikuzoğlu Kurd Ali Ağa, 107
Sivrikuzoğlu Mehmed Ağa, 106

Şaban Bey, 116
Şeyh Muvali, 25, 28

Uskufoğlu, 54
Usta Muslioğlu, 2, 3
Usta Osman, 64

Velioğlu Mustafa, 92

TOPONYMS IN TT880

by Jack L. Davis and Fariba Zarinebaf

The following concordance includes all names of places in the district of Anavarin that are mentioned in the cadaster included in TT880, except names of districts (Anavarin, Modon, Arkadiye) and the name of the fortress Anavarin-i cedid.[1] The toponyms are transliterated according to the usage of Ottoman Turkish.[2] Numbers following a place-name refer to entries in the text of TT880 in which that name occurs.

Ağaku, 20
Ağirlia, 9
Ağurliçe, 42, 43
Akşilukirayi, 14
Akşirulakad, 6
Alafine, 4, 6, 40, 45
Aliğulivad, 6
Ali Hoca, 1, 2, 4, 10, 12, 34
Anavarin-i atik, 13
Andirinu, 28
Antadiz, 12
Arkadianu, 32, 33
Arkadiyanu, 33
Arkudis, 6
Aşağı Katu, 3
Avarniçe, 29, 30
Ayanu, 44
Ayu Nikula, 29
Ayu Yani, 46
Ayu Yurki, 11, 45
Azake, 10, 15, 34

Balinmiyuz, 4
Balyamilu, 23
Beruli, 12
Beşli, 27, 31
Bey Konaki, 5

Bisaci, 6, 12
Bisacki, 6
Budran, 13, 15
Buhalu, 19
Burğu, 43
Büyük Göl, 13
Büyük Pisaski, 15

Çuçurine, 30
Çupurulake, 20
Çurukdun, 1
Çuruvne, 2

Deli Ahmed, 32, 33
Demus, 29
Denmusarin, 18
Derviş Kethüda, 26
Dirastu, 3
Diyuli, 4
Diyuli Yariye, 4

Elyas Ağa, 28, 38
Evluyol, 1

Famirlerun, 6
Fulke, 43, 44
Furiçi, 21

Ğarğalian, 3, 44
Ğuli, 23, 24

Haci Hasan, 30
Hamulus, 23
Has, 4, 6, 7, 8, 9, 12
Hasan Ağa, 4, 5, 6, 7, 12, 40, 45
Hiristududrile, 3
Huri, 6, 10, 11, 12

İbsili Rake, 47
İklina, 23, 24
İsbili, 27
İsbilia, 7
İsbiliaz, 43
İskarminke, 46, 48
İskilukranes, 16
İspitse, 14
İstakatu, 46
İstalulid, 26
İstaluniye, 27
İsta Platakia, 20
İstefani Rumi, 14
İstelidsire, 4
İstikamne, 36
İstilake, 12, 14
İstilianu, 48
İstinayurki, 11
İstinintambu, 14
İstinkayu, 29
İstirancuz, 12
İstisile, 25
İstru Lanka, 12
İstukufru, 12
İstuputamu, 7, 8

Kaniruni, 9
Karadimu, 3
Karunihuri, 11, 12, 14, 40
Kati Usta Baruli, 9
Kati Usta Baruvli, 9
Kavalari, 46
Kestusedile, 20
Kifuri, 24, 34
Kilursarin, 13
Kirmiti, 21
Kirunkur, 14
Klurun, 1

Kufurci, 28
Kukunare, 22
Kuli Karye, 46
Kumariçe, 26
Kunduri, 39
Kurd Ağa, 23
Kurd Ağa Bey, 27
Kurd Ali Ağa, 25
Kurd Bey, 27, 29, 31, 36, 37
Kurd Tağı, 37
Kuri, 6
Küçük Bisaci, 10, 34
Küçük Bisacki, 4
Küçük Pisaski, 14

Lefku, 8, 39
Lezake, 12, 34
Likuri, 21
Likurni Mountains, 22
Likuvun, 4
Likuvuni, 11
Limuniaz, 43
Luteru, 19

Makrikirak, 6
Mankariarike, 29
Martilaf, 19
Mavriliçne, 1
Mehmed Ağa, 24
Melis, 25, 26
Memi Ağa, 17
Mesinmure, 32
Miniaki, 47, 48
Mizin, 2
Muçaçu, 10, 34
Muğanbali, 23
Muğle, 25
Munadundiyeri, 16
Murafia, 30
Muslihuddin, 34
Muslihuddin Efendi, 22
Mustafa Ağa, 19
Mustafa Mandrasi, 46
Muzuste, 43, 45
Müfti, 32

Narincir, 6
Nase, 17, 18

Orman Mountains, 3
Osman, 39
Osman Ağa, 6, 10, 11, 12, 14, 15, 25, 34

Paliamilu, 28
Paliumlu, 2
Papla, 19, 20
Petrehur, 9
Petrehuri, 7, 8
Pila, 38
Pilalutaluni, 4
Pilatnu, 24
Pile, 26, 31, 37
Pirğu, 43
Pisitse, 2, 30
Pispitsa, 16, 17, 18
Pispitse, 30
Platne, 2, 16
Pulatnu, 14, 20
Purnari, 4
Putamu, 16, 34
Putme, 4

Rotsi, 18
Rudiye, 25
Rum Bağ, 7, 8
Rum Bağlari, 4, 40
Rumenu, 6
Rumiani, 22
Rumike, 6
Rustem Ağa, 4, 5, 6, 8, 14, 40

Sefer Hoca, 21
Ser(i) Putamu, 11, 12, 14, 15, 39
Serukambu, 21
Seyid Yarağne, 46
Stohroyasari, 12

Şake Kules, 46
Şake Mules, 46

Talyan, 13, 36
Tavarne, 15, 36, 39
Tirankambu, 6
Tirukalyun, 31
Tristena, 45

PROPERTIES LISTED IN TT880

by John Bennet

Name/Alternate name	Status	Pages in TT880	Pages in Chapter 2
1. Ali Hoca	*çiftlik*	78	56–58
2. Platne	*çiftlik*	78–79	58–59
3. Aşağı Katu	*mazra'a*	79	59
4. Alafine	*çiftlik*	79–80	60–61
5. Hasan Ağa	*çiftlik*	80	61–62
6. Rustem Ağa	*çiftlik*	80–81	62–64
7. Petrehuri	*mazra'a*	81	64
8. Rum Bağ/Lefku	*mazra'a*	81	65
9. Has	*çiftlik*	82	65–66
10. Azake	*çiftlik*	82	66
11. Karunihuri	*mazra'a*	82	66
12. Huri	*çiftlik*	82–83	67–68
13. Anavarin-i atik	*kale*	83–84	68–69
14. Küçük Pisaski	*çiftlik*	84–85	69–71
15. Osman Ağa/Büyük Pisaski	*çiftlik*	85	71–73
16. Pispitsa	*çiftlik*	86	73–75
17. Nase/Memi Ağa	*mazra'a* or *çiftlik*	86	75
18. Rotsi/Denmusarin	*mazra'a* or *çiftlik*	86	75
19. Papla/Mustafa Ağa	*çiftlik*	86–87	75–77
20. Other Papla/Ağaku	*çiftlik*	87	77
21. Kirmiti/Sefer Hoca	*mazra'a* or *çiftlik*	87	77–78
22. Kukunare/Muslihuddin Efendi	*çiftlik*	87–88	78–79
23. İklina/Kurd Ağa	*çiftlik*	88–89	79–81
24. Ğuli/Mehmed Ağa	*mazra'a* or *çiftlik*	89	81
25. Rudiye/Kurd Ali Ağa	*mazra'a* or *çiftlik*	89	82
26. Melis/Derviş Kethüda	*mazra'a* or *çiftlik*	89	82
27. Yufiri/Beşli	*mazra'a*	89	82
28. Elyas Ağa	*çiftlik*	90	82–83
29. Zaimzade	*çiftlik*	90	83–85
30. Avarniçe/Haci Hasan	*mazra'a* or *çiftlik*	91	85
31. Pile	*çiftlik*	91	85–86
32. Arkadianu/Müfti	*mazra'a* or *çiftlik*	91	87
33. Deli Ahmed	*mazra'a* or *çiftlik*	91	87
34. Muçaçu/Muslihuddin	*çiftlik*	92	87

Name/Alternate name	Status	Pages in TT880	Pages in Chapter 2
35. Anavarin-i cedid	*kale*	92–96	88–97
36. Kurd Bey	*çiftlik*	97	97–98
37. Tupçin	*çiftlik*	97	98
38. Tursun	*mazra'a*	97	99
39. Lefku/Tavarne	*çiftlik*	97	99
40. Other Yufiri/Rum Bağlari	*mazra'a*	97	99
41. Usta Musli	*mazra'a*	98	100
42. Ağurliçe	~~*çiftlik*~~/*karye*	98	100–102
43. Muzuste	~~*çiftlik*~~/*karye*	99	102–104
44. Ayanu	*mazra'a*	99	104
45. Tristena	~~*mazra'a*~~/*çiftlik*	99	104–105
46. İskarminke	*karye*	100	105–106
47. Miniaki/İbsili Rake	*karye*	100	107
48. İstilianu	*karye*	100	107–108
49. Virviçe	*karye*	101	108–110

References

Archival Sources

Archivio di Stato di Venezia (ASV), Venice
  Archivio Grimani ai Servi, b.26, f.866r; b.28, f.839r; b.28, f.859r; b.28, f.1255r;
    b.49/135, f.84r; b.57, fasc. 172, E/D
  Senato, Provveditori di Terra e da Mar, b.860, f.217r

Başbakanlık Arşivi (BBA), Istanbul
  *Baş Muhasebe Defter*s (DBŞM) 1750, 2055, 3998, 4175/A
  Cevdet Saray 1243, 1396, 1605
  *Maliyeden Müdevver Defter*s (MM) 561 (*per* Balta 2004)
  *Mora Ahkam Defter*s, vols. 1–21
  *Mühimme Defter*s (MD) 3, 4, 7, 12, 19, 21, 22, 23, 24, 26, 27, 29, 30, 31, 33, 35
  *Şikayet Defter*s (ŞD) 83, 102 (and for the entire 18th century)
  *Tapu Tahrir*s (TT) 10, 25, 80, 367, 376, 446, 509, 565, 605, 607, 777, 796, 825,
    876, 878, 880, 881, 884, 890

Gennadius Library (Γεννάδειος Βιβλιοθήκη), American School of Classical Studies
    at Athens, Athens
  Expédition scientifique de Morée, Prosper Baccuet drawings 23, 24, 49
  *Raccolta delli disegni della pianta de tutte le piazze del regno di Morea, e parte
    delli porti dello stesso*

National Historical Museum of Greece (Εθνικό Ιστορικό Μουσείο της Ελλάδος),
    Athens
  Accession no. 6334

National Library of Greece (Εθνική Βιβλιοθήκη της Ελλάδος), Athens
  Archivio Nani, b.3939, f.577r–578r; b.3939, f.460r

Tapu ve Kadastro Genel Müdürlüğü (TKGM), Ankara, 15, 50
  Tapu Kadastro (TK) 71 (*per* Barkan 1943)

Topkapı Sarayı, Istanbul
  Bağdat Köşkü 308, Evliya Çelebi, *Seyahatname*

War Archive of the Austrian State Archive (Österreichisches Staatsarchiv,
    Kriegsarchiv), Vienna
  Doi Territori Modon et Navarino divisa dal Color. Rosso. Scala di Passi Doi Milla,
    cat. no. B.III.a.124

PUBLISHED SCHOLARSHIP

Abou-El-Haj, R. A. 1991. *Formation of the Modern State: The Ottoman Empire, Sixteenth to Eighteenth Centuries,* Albany.

Adanır, F. 1998. "Ottoman Peasantries, c. 1360–1860," in *The Peasantries of Europe from the Fourteenth to the Eighteenth Centuries,* ed. T. Scott, London, pp. 268–310.

Aeschimann, W., and J. Tucoo-Chala, eds. 1984. *Edgar Quinet: La Grèce moderne et ses rapports avec l'Antiquité suivie du journal de voyage,* Paris.

Agoston, G. 1994. "Ottoman Artillery and European Technology in the 15th and 17th Centuries," *Acta orientalia academiae scientiarum hungaricae* 42, pp. 15–48.

Akdağ, M. 1995. *Türk halkının dirlik ve düzenlik kavgası: Celali isyanları,* Istanbul.

Alcock, S. E. 1998. "Hasanaga: A Glimpse into the Ottoman Countryside," in Davis 1998, pp. 262–266.

Alexander, J. C. 1978. "Δύο ὀθωμανικὰ κατάστιχα τοῦ Μοριᾶ, 1460–1463," in *Πρακτικὰ τοῦ Α΄ Συνεδρίου Μεσσηνιακῶν Σπουδῶν,* Athens, pp. 398–407.

———. 1985a. *Toward a History of Post-Byzantine Greece: The Ottoman* Kanunnames *for the Greek Lands, circa 1500–circa 1600,* Athens.

———. 1985b. *Brigandage and Public Order in the Morea, 1685–1806,* Athens.

———. 1998. "Φοροαπαλλαγὲς καὶ διάδοση κατασκευῆς τῆς μπαρούτης στὴν Πελοπόννησο τὸν 16ο αἰῶνα: Ὁ καζᾶς τῆς Καρύταινας καὶ ἡ περίπτωση τῆς Δημητσάνας," in *Πρακτικὰ τοῦ Ε΄ Διεθνοῦς Συνεδρίου Πελοποννησιακῶν Σπουδῶν (Ἄργος–Ναύπλιον. 6–10 Σεπτεμβρίου 1995)* 4, Athens, pp. 195–234.

Allbaugh, L. G. 1953. *Crete: A Case Study of an Underdeveloped Area,* Princeton.

Andrews, K. 1953. *Castles of the Morea* (Gennadeion Monographs 4), Princeton.

Anonymous. 1687. *Esatta notitia del Peloponneso, volgarmente penisola della Morea: divisa in otto provincie, descritte geograficamente, dove si legge l'origine de primi habitanti, con li nomi, che diedero alle provincie, città, & altro con sue istorie: & acquisti fatti dalla serenissima republica di Venetia, sall'anno 1684, sino al dì presente: adornato di quantità di figure in rame; consacrato al serenissimo prencipe Christiano Ernesto marchese di Brandemburgo . . .,* Venice.

———. 1689. *The History of the Venetian Conquests from the Year 1684 to This Present Year 1688,* London.

———. 1857. Ἀρχεῖα τῆς Ἑλληνικῆς Παλιγγενεσίας μέχρι τῆς ἐγκαταστάσεως τῆς Βασιλείας, Athens.

Anoyatis-Pelé, D. 1987. *Connaissance de la population et des productions de la Morée à travers un manuscript anonyme de la fin du XVIII siècle,* Athens.

Armstrong, P. 2002. "The Survey Area in the Byzantine and Ottoman Periods," in *Continuity and Change in a Greek Rural Landscape: The Laconia Survey* 1, ed. W. Cavanagh, J. Crouwel, R. W. V. Catling, and G. Shipley, London, pp. 339–402.

Artan, T. 1993. "From Charismatic Leadership to Collective Rule: Introducing Materials on the Wealth and Power of Ottoman Princesses in the Eighteenth Century," *Toplum ve ekonomi* 4, pp. 53–94.

Aschenbrenner, S. 1972. "A Contemporary Community," in McDonald and Rapp 1972, pp. 47–63.

Assenova, P., T. Kacori, and R. Stojkov. 1974. "Oikonymes et anthroponymes de Peloponnèse vers la moitié du XVe siècle," in *Actes du XIe Congrès international des sciences onomastiques, Sofia 28 VI–4 VII, 1972,* pp. 69–72.

Atlas = M. M. Puillon de Boblaye and T. Virlet, *Expédition scientifique de Morée: Section des sciences physiques* 5. *Atlas,* Paris 1835.

Babinger, F. 1978. *Mehmed the Conqueror and His Time,* ed. and trans. W. C. Hickman, Princeton.

Badekas, G. 1988. "Τα μετρικά συστήματα," in *Αρχαιολογία* 28, pp. 36–44.

Bakirtzis, C. 1989. *Βυζαντινὰ τσουκαλολάγηνα,* Athens.

Balta, E. 1989. *L'Eubée à la fin du XVe siècle: Économie et population, les registres de l'année 1474,* Athens.

————. 1992. *Rural and Urban Population in the* Sancak *of Euripos in the Early 16th Century* (Ἀρχείον Εὐβοϊκῶν Μελετῶν 29), Athens.

————. 1993. "Οἱ κανουνναμέδες τοῦ Μοριᾶ," *Ἴστωρ* 6, pp. 29–70.

————. 1997. *Problèmes et approches de l'histoire ottomane: Un itinéraire scientifique de Kayseri à Eğriboz*, Istanbul.

————. 1999. *Peuple et production: Pour une interprétation des sources ottomanes*, Istanbul.

————. 2004. "Settlement and Population in the Morea in 1645," *Osmanlı araştırmaları* 24, pp. 53–63.

Baltas, H. A. 1987. *Πύλος: Ναβαρίνο. Νιόκαστρο. Ἀνάκτορο Νέστορος. Τουριστικὸς ὁδηγὸς καὶ σύντομη ἱστορία*, Athens.

————. 1990. *Pylos: Navarino, Niokastro, the Palace of Nestor. Tourist Guide and Brief History*, Athens.

————. 1997. *Πύλος: Ναβαρίνο. Νιόκαστρο. Ἀνάκτορο Νέστορος. Τουριστικὸς ὁδηγὸς καὶ σύντομη ἱστορία*, 2nd ed., Athens.

Baram, U., and L. Carroll, eds. 2000. *A Historical Archaeology of the Ottoman Empire: Breaking New Ground*, New York.

Barkan, Ö. L. 1943. *XV ve XVI ıncı Asırlarda Osmanlı imparatorluğunda zirai ekonominin hukuki ve mali esasları* 1: *Kanunlar*, Istanbul.

————. 1953. "H. 933–934 (M. 1527–1528) Mali yılına ait bütçe örneği," *İktisat fakültesi mecmuası* (Istanbul University) 15, pp. 239–329.

————. 1957. "Essai sur les données statistiques de registres de recensement dans l'Empire ottoman aux XVᵉ et XVIᵉ siècles," in *École pratique des hautes études*, 6. section: *Les hommes et la terre* 11, Paris, pp. 343–417.

Barkey, K. 1994. *Bandits and Bureaucrats: The Ottoman Route to State Centralization*, Ithaca.

Başbakanlık Archives. 1993. *3 Numaralı mühimme defteri (966–968, 1558–1560)*, Ankara.

————. 1996. *12 Numaralı mühimme defteri (978–979/1570–1572)*, Ankara.

Beauvau, H. baron de. 1615. *Relation journaliere du voyage du Levant faict & descrit*, Nancy.

Beldiceanu, N., and I. Beldiceanu-Steinherr. 1980. "Recherches sur la Morée (1461–1512)," *Südost-Forschungen* 39, pp. 17–75.

————. 1986. "Corinthe et sa région d'après le registre TT 10," *Südost-Forschungen* 45, pp. 37–61.

Belia, E. D. 1978. "Εἰδήσεις περὶ Μεσσηνίας ἀπὸ γαλλικὸν ὑπόμνημα τοῦ 1786," in *Πρακτικὰ τοῦ Αʹ Συνεδρίου Μεσσηνιακῶν Σπουδῶν*, Athens, pp. 283–288.

Bellin, J. N. 1771. *Description géographique du golfe de Venise et de la Morée. Avec des remarques pour la navigation, & des cartes & plans des côtes, villes, ports & mouillages*, Paris.

Bennet, J., J. L. Davis, and F. Zarinebaf-Shahr. 2000. "Pylos Regional Archaeological Project, Part III: Sir William Gell's Itinerary in the Pylia and Regional Landscapes in the Morea in the Second Ottoman Period," *Hesperia* 69, pp. 343–380.

Berov, L. 1975. "Problèmes de la métrologie dans les territoires balkaniques à l'époque de la domination ottomane (XVᵉ–XIXᵉ ss.)," *ÉtBalk* 2, pp. 22–39.

Bessan, J. F. 1835. *Souvenirs de l'expédition de Morée en 1828, suivis d'un mémoire historique sur Athènes, avec le plan de cette ville*, Valognes.

Bintliff, J. 1999. "The Ottoman Era in the Context of Long-Term Settlement History: A Case-Study, The Archaeological Survey of the Valley of the Muses, Boeotia, Greece," in *Al-Majallah al-tarikhiyah al-ᶜArabiyah lil-dirasat al-ᶜUthmaniyah (Arab Historical Review for Ottoman Studies)* 19–20, pp. 203–229.

Biris, J. A. 2002. *A Road in the South, Chora, Pylos, Methoni: Nestor's Realm and the Mothon Stone, A Tourist and Historical Study*, Athens.

Birken, A. 1976. *Die Provinzen des osmanischen Reiches* (Beihefte zum Tübinger Atlas des vorderen Orients, ser. B, no. 13), Wiesbaden.

Blouet, A. 1831–1838. *Expédition scientifique de Morée, ordonnée par le gouvernement français: Architecture, sculptures, inscriptions, et vues du Peloponese, des Cyclades, et de l'Attique*, 3 vols., Paris.

Bon, A. 1969. *La Morée franque: Recherches historiques, topographiques et archéologiques sur la principauté d'Achaïe (1205–1430)*, Paris.

Bory de Saint-Vincent, M. 1836. *Expédition scientifique de Morée: Section des sciences physiques* 1. *Relation*, Paris.

Bostan, I. 1991. "Azeb," in *İslâm ansiklopedisi* 4, pp. 312–313.

Bourguet, M.-N., B. Lepetit, D. Nordman, and M. Sinarellis, eds. 1998. *L'invention scientifique de la Méditerranée: Egypte, Morée, Algérie*, Paris.

Bourguet, M.-N., D. Nordman, V. Panayotopoulos, and M. Sinarellis, eds. 1999. *Enquêtes en Méditerranée: Les expéditions françaises d'Égypte, de Morée et d'Algérie*, Athens.

Boutouras, A. H. 1912. *Τὰ νεοελληνικὰ κύρια ὀνόματα*, Athens.

Brue, B. 1870. *Journal de la campagne que le Grand Vezir Ali Pacha a faite en 1715 pour la conquête de la Morée*, Paris.

Bruinessen, M. van, and H. Boeschoten, eds. 1988. *Evliya Çelebi in Diyarbekir: The Relevant Section of the* Seyahatname, Leiden.

Brumfield, A. 2000. "Agriculture and Rural Settlement in Ottoman Crete, 1669–1898: A Modern Site Survey," in *A Historical Archaeology of the Ottoman Empire: Breaking New Ground*, ed. U. Baram and L. Caroll, New York, pp. 37–78.

Bryer, A., and H. Lowry, eds. 1986. *Continuity and Change in Late Byzantine and Early Ottoman Society*, Washington, D.C.

Buchon, J. A. 1843. *La Grèce continentale et la Morée: Voyage, séjour et études historiques en 1840 et 1841*, Paris.

Busch-Zantner, R. 1938. *Agrarverfassung, Gesellschaft, und Siedlung in Südosteuropa unter besonderer Berücksichtigung der Türkenzeit*, Leipzig.

Castellan, A. L. 1808. *Lettres sur la Morée*, Paris.

Charlesworth, A. 1983. *Atlas of Rural Protest in Britain, 1548–1900*, Philadelphia.

Chrysostomides, J. 1996. Monumenta Peloponnesiaca: *Documents for the History of the Peloponnese in the 14th and 15th Centuries*, Camberley, Surrey.

Çizakça, M. 1980. "A Short History of the Bursa Silk Industry (1500–1900)," *Journal of the Economic and Social History of the Orient* 23, pp. 142–152.

———. n.d. *Tax Farming and Resource Allocation in the Islamic Societies of the Past* (Boğaziçi University Research Papers 86–04), Istanbul.

Coale, A. J., and P. Demeney. 1966. *Regional Model Life Table and Stable Populations*, Princeton.

Cook, M. A. 1972. *Population Pressure on Rural Anatolia, 1450–1600*, London.

Cooper, F. 2002. *Houses of the Morea: Vernacular Architecture of the Northwest Peloponnesos (1205–1955)*, Athens.

Corner, G. 1691 [1885–1889]. "Relazione del n.u. Giacomo Corner ritornato dalla carica di provveditor general in Morea," pp. 293–317 in Ἡ περὶ Πελοποννήσου ἔκθεσις τοῦ Βενετοῦ Προνοητοῦ Κορνέρ (Δελτίον τῆς Ἱστορικῆς καὶ Ἐθνογραφικῆς Ἐταιρείας 2), ed. S. P. Lambros, Athens, pp. 282–317.

Coronelli, V. 1686. *Description géographique et historique de la Morée reconquise par les Venitiens, du royaume de Negrepont, et autres lieux circonvoisins: Enrichie de plusieurs plans, & vûës de places des mêmes païs*, pt. 1, Paris.

———. 1687a. *An Historical and Geographical Account of the Morea, Negropont, and the Maritime Places as Far as Thessalonica*, London.

———. 1687b. *Memorie istoriographiche delli regni della Morea e Negroponte . . . Conquiste nella Dalmazia*, Venice.

———. [1708]. *Teatro della guerra: Morea, Negroponte, & adiacenze*, Venice.

Cuno, K. M. 1992. *The Pasha's Peasants: Land, Society, and Economy in Lower Egypt, 1740–1858*, Cambridge.

Dakin, D. 1972. *The Unification of Greece, 1770–1923*, London.

Dankoff, R. 1991. *The Intimate Life of an Ottoman Statesman: Melek Ahmed Pasha (1588–1662)*, Albany.

———. 2000. "Establishing the Text of Evliya Çelebi's *Seyahatname*: A Critique of Recent Scholarship and Suggestions for the Future," *Archivum ottomanicum* 18, pp. 139–144.

Dankoff, R., and K. Kreiser. 1992. *Materialien zu Evliya Çelebi 2: A Guide to the* Seyahat-name *of Evliya Çelebi*, Wiesbaden.

Darling, L. T. 1990. "Ottoman Salary Registers as a Source for Economic and Social History," *Turkish Studies Association Bulletin* 14, pp. 13–33.

———. 1996. *Revenue-Raising and Legitimacy: Tax Collection and Finance Administration in the Ottoman Empire, 1560–1600*, Leiden.

Davies, S. 1994. "Tithe-Collection in the Venetian Peloponnese, 1696–1705," *BSA* 89, pp. 433–455.

———. 2004. "Pylos Regional Archaeological Project, Part VI: Administration and Settlement in Venetian Navarino," *Hesperia* 73, pp. 59–120.

Davis, J. L. 1991. "Contributions to a Mediterranean Rural Archeology: Historical Case Studies from the Ottoman Cyclades," *JMA* 4, pp. 131–216.

———. ed. 1998. *Sandy Pylos: An Archaeological History from Nestor to Navarino*, Austin.

Davis, J. L., S. E. Alcock, J. Bennet, Y. G. Lolos, and C. W. Shelmerdine. 1997. "The Pylos Regional Archaeological Project, Part I: Overview and the Archaeological Survey," *Hesperia* 66, pp. 391–494.

Dimitriades, V. 1986. "Ottoman Chalkidiki: An Area in Transition," in Bryer and Lowry 1986, pp. 39–50.

Dokos, K. 1971–1976. "Ἡ ἐν Πελοποννήσῳ ἐκκλησιαστικὴ περιουσία κατὰ τὴν περίοδον τῆς Β΄ Ἐνετοκρατίας," *Byzantinisch-neugriechische Jahrbücher* 21, pp. 43–168.

———. 1975. Ἡ Στερεὰ Ἑλλὰς κατὰ τὸν Ἐνετοτουρκικὸν πόλεμον, 1684–1699, καὶ ὁ Σαλόνων Φιλόθεος, Athens.

Dokos, K., and G. Panagopoulos. 1993. Τὸ βενετικὸ κτηματολόγιο τῆς Βοστίτσας, Athens.

Doorn, P. K. 1989. "Population and Settlements in Central Greece: Computer Analyses of Ottoman Registers in the Fifteenth and Sixteenth Centuries," in *History and Computing* 1.2, ed. P. Denley, S. Fogelvik, and C. Harvey, Manchester, pp. 193–208.

Duheaume, M. A. 1833. *Souvenirs de la Morée*, Paris.

*EI*² = *Encyclopedia of Islam*, 2nd ed., Leiden 1960–; CD ROM, Leiden 1999.

Elezović, G. 1950. "Documents tirés des archives turques de Constantinople," in *Iz carigradskih turskih arhiva mühimme defteri* (Srpska akademija nauka, zbornik za istočnjačku Istorijsku i Književnu Građu 2.1), Belgrade.

Erder, L. 1975. "The Measurement of Preindustrial Population Changes: The Ottoman Empire from the 15th to the 17th Century," *Middle Eastern Studies* 11, pp. 284–301.

Erder, L., and S. Faroqhi. 1979. "Population Rise and Fall in Anatolia, 1550–1620," *Middle Eastern Studies* 15, pp. 322–345.

Eren, H. 1999. *Türk dilinin etimolojik sözlüğü*, Ankara.

Ἐθνικὴ Στατιστικὴ Ὑπηρεσία τῆς Ἑλλαλάδος. 1911. Γεωργικὴ Στατιστικὴ τῆς Ἑλλάδος 1911, Athens.

Evliya Çelebi. 1928. *Seyahatname*, ed. A. Cevdet, Istanbul.

Faroqhi, S. 1991. "Wealth and Power in the Land of Olives: Economic and Political Activities of Muridzade Haci Mehmed Agha, Notable of Edremit," in Keyder and Tabak 1991, pp. 77–95.

———. 1997. "Social Life in Cities," in *An Economic and Social History of the Ottoman Empire* 1: *1300–1600*, ed. H. İnalcık, London, pp. 576–608.

———. 1999. *Approaching Ottoman History: An Introduction to the Sources*, Cambridge.

Faroqhi, S., B. McGowan, D. Quataert, and Ş. Pamuk. 1997. *An Economic and Social History of the Ottoman Empire* 2: *1600–1914*, London.

Fekete, L. 1955. *Die Siyaqat-Schrift in der türkischen Finanzverwaltung: Beitrag zur türkischen Paläographie mit 104 Tafeln*, Budapest.

Finlay, G. 1877. *A History of Greece from Its Conquest by the Romans to the Present Time, B.C. 146 to A.D. 1864* 5: *Greece under Ottoman and Venetian Domination, A.D. 1453–1821*; 6: *The Greek Revolution*, pt. 1, A.D. 1821–1827, Oxford.

———. 1971. *History of the Greek Revolution and the Reign of King Otto*, repr. London.

Forbes, H. A. 1982. *Strategies and Soils: Technology, Production, and Environment in the Peninsula of Methana, Greece*, Ann Arbor.

———. 1992. "The Ethnoarchaeological Approach to Ancient Greek Agriculture," in *Agriculture in Ancient Greece*, ed. B. Wells, Stockholm, pp. 87–101.

———. 2000a. "Security and Settlement in the Medieval and Post-Medieval Peloponnesos, Greece: 'Hard' History versus Oral History," *JMA* 13, pp. 204–224.

———. 2000b. "The Agrarian Economy of the *Ermionidha* around 1700: An Ethnohistorical Reconstruction," in *A Contingent Countryside: Settlement, Economy, and Land Use in the Southern Argolid Since 1700*, ed. S. B. Sutton, Stanford, pp. 41–70.

Forsén, B., and A. Karavieri. 2003. "The Roman–Early Modern Periods: Conclusion," in *The Asea Valley Survey: An Arcadian Mountain Valley from the Paleolithic Period until Modern Times*, ed. J. Forsén and B. Forsén, Stockholm, pp. 307–331.

Foscarini, M. 1696. *Historia della republica veneta*, Venice.

Foxhall, L. 1990. "Olive Cultivation within Greek and Roman Agriculture: The Ancient Economy Revisited" (diss. Univ. of Liverpool).

Frangakis, E., and M. Wagstaff. 1987. "Settlement Pattern Change in the Morea (Peloponnisos), c. A.D. 1700–1830," *Byzantine and Modern Greek Studies* 11, pp. 163–192.

Frangakis-Syrett, E. 1992. *The Commerce of Smyrna in the Eighteenth Century (1700–1820)*, Athens.

Frangakis-Syrett, E., and M. Wagstaff. 1992. "The Height Zonation of Population in the Morea, c. 1830," *BSA* 87, pp. 439–446.

———. 1996. "Patras and Its Hinterland: Cityport Development and Regional Change in 19th-Century Greece," in *Cityports, Coastal Zones, and Regional Change*, ed. B. Hoyle, Chichester, pp. 121–136.

Frantzis, A. 1839. Ἐπιτομὴ τῆς Ἱστορίας τῆς ἀναγεννηθείσης Ἑλλάδος, Athens.

Freeman-Grenville, G. S. P. 1995. *The Islamic and Christian Calendars, A.D. 622–2222 (A.H. 1–1650)*, Reading.

Gallant, T. W. 1988. "Greek Bandits: Lone Wolves or a Family Affair?"

Journal of Modern Greek Studies 6, pp. 269–290.

———. 1999. "Brigandage, Piracy, Capitalism, and State-Formation: Transnational Crime in an Historical World-Systems Perspective," in *States and Illegal Networks*, ed. J. Heyman and A. Smart, London, pp. 25–61.

Gandev, C. 1960. "L'apparition des rapports capitalistes dans l'économie rurale de la Bulgarie du nord-ouest au cours du XVIIIᵉ siècle," *Études historiques* 1, pp. 207–220.

Garzoni, P. 1720. *Istoria della repubblica di Venezia in tempo della Sacra Lega*, 2 vols., Venice.

Gell, W. 1817. *Itinerary of the Morea: Being a Description of the Routes of That Peninsula*, London.

———. 1823. *Narrative of a Journey in the Morea*, London.

Genç, M. 1975. "Osmanlı maliyesinde malikane sistemi," in *Türkiye iktisat tarihi*, ed. O. Okyar and Ü. Nalbantoğlu, Ankara, pp. 231–296.

Georgacas, D. J., and W. A. McDonald. 1967. *Place Names of Southwest Peloponnesus*, Athens.

Gerstel, S. E. J. 1998a. "Medieval Messenia," in Davis 1998, pp. 211–228.

———. 1998b. "The Estates of Niccolò Acciaiuoli," in Davis 1998, pp. 229–233.

Gertwagen, R. 2000. "Venetian Modon and Its Port: 1358–1500," in *Mediterranean Urban Culture, 1400–1700*, ed. A. Cowan, Exeter, pp. 125–148, 248–254.

Gordon, T. 1832. *History of the Greek Revolution* 1, Edinburgh.

Göyünç, N., and W.-D. Hütteroth. 1997. *Land an der Grenze: Osmanische Verwaltung im heutigen türkisch-syrisch-irakischen Grenzgebiet im 16. Jahrhundert*, Istanbul.

Greene, M. 1996. "An Islamic Experiment? Ottoman Land Policy on Crete," *Mediterranean Historical Review* 11, pp. 60–78.

———. 2000. *A Shared World: Christians and Muslims in the Early Modern Mediterranean*, Princeton.

Gregoriadis, A. 1934. Ἱστορικαὶ Ἀλήθειαι, Athens.

Grimani, F. 1701 [1896–1900]. "Relazione del nob. homo ser Francesco Grimani ritornato di provveditor

general dell'Armi in Morea,"
pp. 448–552 in "Ἐκθέσεις τῶν Βενετῶν Προνοητῶν τῆς Πελοποννήσου,"
Δελτίον τῆς Ἱστορικῆς καὶ Ἐθνογραφικῆς Ἑταιρείας 5, ed. S. P.
Lambros, Athens, pp. 425–567.

Grove, A. T., and O. Rackham. 2001.
*The Nature of Mediterranean Europe:
An Ecological History,* New Haven.

Grove, J. M. 1988. *The Little Ice Age,*
London.

———. 1990. "Climatic Reconstruction in the Eastern Mediterranean
with Particular Reference to Crete,"
Petromarula 1, pp. 16–20.

Grove, J. M., and A. Conterio. 1995.
"The Climate of Crete in the Six-
teenth and Seventeenth Centuries,"
Climatic Change 30, pp. 223–247.

Hahn, M. 1997. "Modern Greek, Turkish, and Venetian Periods: The Pottery and the Finds," in *The Greek-
Swedish Excavations at the Ayia Ai-
katerini Square, Kastelli, Khania,
1970–1987,* ed. E. Hallager and
B. P. Hallager, Stockholm, pp. 170–
196.

Halstead, P. 2001. "Mycenaean Wheat,
Flax, and Sheep: Palatial Intervention in Farming and Its Implica-
tions for Rural Society," in *Economy
and Politics in Mycenaean Palace
States,* (*PCPS* Suppl. 27), ed. J. T.
Killen and S. Voutsaki, Cambridge,
pp. 38–50.

Hammer-Purgstall, J. F. von. 1842.
*Histoire de l'empire ottomane depuis
son origine jusqu'à nos jours* 3, Paris.

Hansen, M. H. 1986. *Demography and
Democracy: The Number of Athenian
Citizens in the Fourth Century B.C.,*
Herning, Denmark.

Herzfeld, M. 1991. *A Place in History:
Social and Monumental Time in a
Cretan Town,* Princeton.

Hinz, W. 1955. *Islamische Masse und
Gewichte umgerechnet ins metrische
System,* Leiden.

Hodgetts, C. 1974. "The Colonies of
Coron and Modon under Venetian
Administration, 1204–1400" (diss.
London Univ.).

Hodgetts, C., and P. Lock. 1996. "Some
Village Fortifications in the Venetian Peloponnese," in *The Archaeology of Medieval Greece,* ed. P. Lock
and G. D. R. Sanders, Oxford,
pp. 77–90.

Hopf, C. 1873. *Chroniques gréco-
romanes,* Paris.

Houliarakis, M. 1973. Γεωγραφική,
διοικητική, καὶ πληθυσμιακὴ ἐξέ-
λιξις τῆς Ἑλλάδος 1, Athens.

———. 1988. Ἐξελίξεις τοῦ πληθυ-
σμοῦ τῶν ἀγροτικῶν περιοχῶν τῆς
Ἑλλάδος, 1920–1981, Athens.

Hütteroth, W.-D., and K. Abdulfattah.
1977. *Historical Geography of Palestine, Transjordan, and Southern Syria
in the Late 16th Century,* Erlangen.

İnalcık, H. 1954. "Ottoman Methods
of Conquest," *Studia islamica* 2,
pp. 103–129.

———. 1959. "Osmanlılarda Raiyyet
Rüsumu," *Belleten* 23, pp. 576–610.

———. 1972. "The Ottoman Decline
and Its Effects upon the *Reaya,*"
in *Aspects of the Balkans: Continuity
and Change,* ed. H. Birnbaum and
S. Vryonis, Paris, pp. 338–354.

———. 1973. *The Ottoman Empire:
The Classical Age, 1300–1600,* New
York.

———. 1977. "Centralization and
Decentralization in the Ottoman
Administration," in *Studies in
Eighteenth Century Islamic History,*
ed. T. Naff and R. Owen, Carbon-
dale, Ill., pp. 27–52.

———. 1980. "Military and Fiscal
Transformation in the Ottoman
Empire, 1600–1700," *Archivum
ottomanicum* 6, pp. 283–337.

———. 1982. "Rice Cultivation and
the Çeltükci-Reᶜâyâ System in the
Ottoman Empire," *Turcica* 14,
pp. 69–141.

———. 1983. "Introduction to Ottoman Metrology," *Turcica* 15,
pp. 311–348.

———. 1991a. "The Emergence of Big
Farms, *Çiftlik*s, State, Landlords,
and Tenants," in Keyder and Tabak
1991, pp. 17–34.

———. 1991b. "The Great Isthmus
Corridor Route at the Ottoman
Conquest," in *The Great Isthmus
Corridor Route: Explorations of the
Phokis-Doris Expedition,* ed. E. W.
Kase, Dubuque, Iowa, pp. 60–63.

———. 1997. *An Economic and Social
History of the Ottoman Empire* 1:
1300–1600, London.

İnalcık, H., and R. Murphey. 1978. *The
History of Mehmed the Conqueror by
Tursun Beg,* Minneapolis.

İnalcık, H., and F. Zarinebaf. In preparation. *Some Materials (Ruʾus Defteri) on the Ottoman Provincial Administration during the Seventeenth Century,* Istanbul.

Iorga, N. 1913. *Chronique de l'expédition des Turcs en Morée, 1715,* Bucharest.

İslâm ansiklopedisi = Türkiye diyanet vakfi İslâm ansiklopedisi, Istanbul 1988–.

İslamoğlu, H. 2000. "Property as a Contested Domain: A Reevaluation of the Ottoman Land Code of 1858," in *New Perspectives on Property and Land in the Middle East,* ed. R. Owen, Cambridge, Mass., pp. 3–61.

İslamoğlu-Inan, H., ed. 1987. *The Ottoman Empire and the World Economy,* Cambridge.

Issawi, C. 1980. *The Economic History of Turkey, 1800–1914,* Chicago.

Jameson, M. H., C. N. Runnels, and T. H. van Andel. 1994. *A Greek Countryside: The Southern Argolid from Prehistory to the Present Day,* Stanford.

Jelavich, B. 1983. *History of the Balkans, Eighteenth and Nineteenth Centuries,* Cambridge.

Kahane, H., R. Kahane, and A. Tietze. 1958. *The Lingua Franca in the Levant: Turkish Nautical Terms of Italian and Greek Origin,* Urbana.

Kahraman, S. A., and Y. Dağlı, eds. 2003. *Günümüz Türkçesiyle Evliya Çelebi* Seyahatnamesi: *Istanbul* 1, bk. 1, Istanbul.

Kahraman, S. A., Y. Dağlı, and R. Dankoff, eds. 2003. *Evliya Çelebi* Seyahatnamesi, vol. 8, Istanbul.

Kalantzakos, A. 1994. *Ονόματα, επώνυμα, παρατσούκλια,* Athens.

Kapodistrias, I. A. 1987. Ἀρχεῖον Ἰωάννου Καποδίστρια 7, Corfu.

Karamustafa, A. T. 1992. "Military, Administrative, and Scholarly Maps and Plans," in *The History of Cartography* 2.1: *Cartography in the Traditional Islamic and South Asian Societies,* ed. J. B. Harley and D. Woodward, Chicago, pp. 209–227.

Karpodini-Dimitriadi, E. 1990. *Κάστρα της Πελοποννήσου,* Athens.

Kasaba, R. 1988. *The Ottoman Empire and the World-Economy: The Nineteenth Century,* Albany.

Katsiardi-Hering, O. 1993. "Venezianische Karten als Grundlage der historischen Geographie des griechischen Siedlungsraumes (Ende 17. und 18. Jh.)," *Mitteilungen des Österreichischen Staatsarchivs* 43, pp. 281–316.

Keyder, Ç., and F. Tabak, eds. 1991. *Landholding and Commercial Agriculture in the Middle East,* Albany.

Kiel, M. 1973. "A Note on the Exact Date of the Construction of the White Tower of Thessaloniki," *Balkan Studies* 14, pp. 352–357.

———. 1992a. "Central Greece in the Süleymanic Age: Preliminary Notes on Population Growth, Economic Expansion, and Its Influence on the Spread of Greek Christian Culture," in *Soliman le Magnifique et son temps,* ed. G. Veinstein, Paris, pp. 399–424.

———. 1992b. "Balyabadra," in *İslâm ansiklopedisi* 5, pp. 42–43.

———. 1997. "The Rise and Decline of Turkish Boeotia, 15th–19th Century (Remarks on the Settlement Pattern, Demography, and Agricultural Production According to Unpublished Ottoman-Turkish Census and Taxation Records)," in *Recent Developments in the History and Archaeology of Central Greece: Proceedings of the 6th International Boeotian Conference (BAR-IS 666),* ed. J. L. Bintliff, Oxford, pp. 315–358.

———. 1999. "The Ottoman Imperial Registers: Central Greece and Northern Bulgaria in the 15th–19th Century, the Demographic Development of the Two Areas Compared," in *Reconstructing Past Population Trends in Mediterranean Europe (3000 B.C.–A.D. 1800),* ed. J. Bintliff and K. Sbonias, Oxford, pp. 195–218.

Kiel, M., and F. Sauerwein. 1994. *Ost-Lokris in türkischer und neugriechischer Zeit (1460–1981) (Passauer Mittelmeerstudien 6),* Passau.

Kostis, K. 1995. *Στὸν καιρὸ τῆς πανώλης,* Iraklion.

Kotsonis, K. 1999. Ὁ Ἰμπραὴμ στὴν Πελοπόννησο, Athens.

Koukkou, E. E. 1984. *Οἱ κοινοτικοὶ θεσμοὶ στὶς Κυκλάδες κατὰ τὴν Τουρκοκρατία,* Athens.

Kremmydas, V. 1972. *Τὸ ἐμπόριο τῆς Πελοποννήσου στὸ 18ο αἰῶνα (1715–1792),* Athens.

Kunt, M. 1983. *The Sultan's Servants: The Transformation of Ottoman Provincial Government, 1550–1650,* New York.

Kyriakidis, S. 1926. Ὁδηγίαι διὰ τὴν μετονομασίαν κοινοτήτων καὶ συνοικισμῶν ἐχόντων τουρκικὸν ὄνομα, Athens.

Kyriazis, P. 1976. Πρῶτοι Ἕλληνες τεχνικοὶ ἐπιστήμονες περιόδου ἀπελευθέρωσης, Athens.

Laiglesia, F. de. 1905. *Un establecimento español en Morea en 1532,* Madrid.

Laiou-Thomadakis, A. E. 1977. *Peasant Society in the Late Byzantine Empire: A Social and Demographic Study,* Princeton.

Lair, J. A. 1902. *La captivité de François Pouqueville en Morée (Publications diverses de l'Institut de France 23),* Paris.

———. 1904. *La captivité de François Pouqueville a Constantinople, 1800–1801 (9 prairial, an VII–16 ventôse, an IX),* Caen.

Lambros, S. P. 1885. "Ἀπογραφὴ τοῦ νομοῦ Μεθώνης ἐπὶ Βενετῶν," in Δελτίον τῆς Ἱστορικῆς καὶ Ἐθνογραφικῆς Ἑταιρείας 2, ed. S. P. Lambros, Athens, pp. 686–710.

Leake, W. M. 1830. *Travels in the Morea* 1, London.

———. 1835. *Travels in Northern Greece* 3, London.

Lee, W. 2001. "Pylos Regional Archaeological Project, Part IV: Change and the Human Landscape in a Modern Greek Village in Messenia," *Hesperia* 70, pp. 49–98.

Liata, E. 1998. *Με την Αρμάδα στο Μοριά, 1684–1687: Ανέκδοτο ημερολόγιο με σχέδια,* Athens.

Locatelli, A. 1691. *Racconto historico della veneta guerra in Levante diretta dall valore del principe Francesco Morosini, Capitan generale la terza volta per la serenissima republica di Venetia, contro l'impero ottomano* 1, Cologne.

Lolos, Y. G. 1998. *The Capital of Nestor and Its Environs: Sandy Pylos. Palace of Nestor, Museum of Chora, History, Monuments,* Athens.

Longnon, J., and P. Topping. 1969. *Documents sur le régime des terres dans la principauté de Morée, au XIVᵉ siècle,* Paris.

Loukatos, S. D. 1984. "Πολιτειογραφι-
κὰ Κορώνης, Μεθώνης καὶ Νεοκά-
στρου, 1830," in Πρακτικὰ τοῦ Β΄
Τοπικοῦ Συνεδρίου Μεσσηνιακῶν
Σπουδῶν (Κυπαρισσία, 27–29 Νοεμ-
βρίου 1982), Athens, pp. 209–231.

Loupis, D. 1999a. Εβλιά Τσελεμπί:
Οδοιπορικό στην Ελλάδα (1668–
1671)—Πελοπόννησος, Νησιά
Ιονίου, Κρήτη, Κυκλάδες, Νησιά
Ανατολικού Αιγαίου, Athens.

——. 1999b. Ο Πίρι Ρεΐς (1465–
1553) χαρτογραφεί το Αιγαίο:
Η οθωμανική χαρτογραφία και η
λίμνη του Αιγαίου, Athens.

Lowry, H. 1986. "The Island of Limnos: A Case Study on the Continuity of Byzantine Forms under Ottoman Rule," in Bryer and Lowry
1986, pp. 235–259.

——. 1992. Studies in Defterology:
Ottoman Society in the Fifteenth and
Sixteenth Centuries, Istanbul.

——. 2002. Fifteenth-Century Otto-
man Realities: Christian Peasant
Life on the Aegean Island of Limnos,
Istanbul.

Lyritzis, S. 1987. "Δευτέρα ἐτυμολογία
τοῦ τοπωνυμίου Γαργαλιάνοι,"
Πλάτων 38, pp. 102–123.

——. 2000. Γαργαλιάνοι: Ὁ τόπος
καὶ ἡ ἱστορία τοῦ (Μελετήματα),
Gargaliani.

MacKay, P. 1975. "The Manuscripts of
the Seyahatname of Evliya Çelebi,
Part I: The Archetype," Der Islam
52, pp. 278–298.

Majer, H. G. 1984. Das osmanische
Registerbuch der Beschwerden (Şikayet Defteri) vom Jahre 1675, Vienna.

Malliaris, A. M. 2001. "Ἡ συγκρότηση
τοῦ κοινωνικοῦ χώρου στὴ Β.Δ.
Πελοπόννησο τὴν περίοδο τῆς
Βενετικῆς Κυριαρχίας (1687–1715)"
(diss. Ionian Univ., Kerkyra).

Mangeart, J. 1850. Souvenirs de la
Morée, recueillis pendant le séjour des
Français dans le Péloponèse, Paris.

Mansolas, A. 1867. Πολιτειογραφι-
καὶ πληροφορίαι περὶ Ἑλλάδος,
Athens.

Mantran, R. 1962. Istanbul dans la
seconde moitié du XVIIᵉ siècle (Biblio-
thèque archéologique et historique
de l'Institut français d'archéologie
d'Istanbul 12), Paris.

Marasso, L., and A. Stouraiti, eds. 2001.
Immagini dal mito: La conquista

veneziana della Morea (1684–1699),
Venice.

Mavropoulos, H. B. 1920. Τουρκικὰ
ἔγγραφα ἀφορῶντα τὴν ἱστορίαν
τῆς Χίου, Athens.

Mazower, M. 2004. Salonica, a City of
Ghosts: Christians, Muslims, Jews,
1430–1950, New York.

McCarthy, J. 1995. Death and Exile:
The Ethnic Cleansing of Ottoman
Muslims, 1821–1922, Princeton.

McDonald, W. A., and R. Hope Simpson. 1961. "Prehistoric Habitation
in Southwestern Peloponnese," AJA
65, pp. 221–260.

——. 1969. "Further Explorations in
Southwestern Peloponnese," AJA 73,
pp. 123–177.

McDonald, W. A., and G. R. Rapp Jr.
1972. The Minnesota Messenia Expedition: Reconstructing a Bronze Age
Regional Environment, Minneapolis.

McGowan, B. 1981. The Economic Life
in Ottoman Europe: Taxation, Trade,
and the Struggle for Land, 1600–
1800, Cambridge.

McGrew, W. W. 1985. Land and
Revolution in Modern Greece, 1800–
1881: The Transition in the Tenure
and Exploitation of Land from Ottoman Rule to Independence, Kent, Ohio.

Mee, C., and H. Forbes. 1997. A Rough
and Rocky Place: The Landscape and
Settlement History of the Methana
Peninsula, Greece. Results of the
Methana Survey Project, Liverpool.

Mihail, A. P. 1888. Ἡ ἱστορία τῆς
πόλεως Πύλου, Athens.

Miller, W. 1908. The Latins in the
Levant, London.

——. 1921. Essays on the Latin
Orient, Cambridge.

Molin, A. 1693 [1896–1900]. "Relazione del nobil homo ser Antonio
Molin ritornato di provveditor
estraordinario di Morea," pp. 429–
447 in "Ἐκθέσεις τῶν Βενετῶν
Προνοητῶν τῆς Πελοποννήσου,"
Δελτίον τῆς Ἱστορικῆς καὶ Ἐθνογραφικῆς Ἑταιρείας 5, ed. S. P.
Lambros, Athens, pp. 425–567.

Moralı Süleyman Penah Efendi. 1942–
1943. "Mora ihtilalı tarihçesi veya
Penah Ef. Mecmuası, 1769," Türk
tarih vesikaları 2, no. 7, pp. 63–80;
no. 8, pp. 153–160; no. 9, pp. 228–
240; no. 10, pp. 309–320; no. 11,
pp. 385–400; no. 12, pp. 473–480.

Mostras, C. 1995. *Dictionnaire géographique de l'empire ottoman*, Istanbul.

Müneccimbaşı, A. D. [1974]. *Müneccimbaşı tarihi* 2, pt. 1, ed. İ. Erünsal, n.p.

Murphey, R. 1999. *Ottoman Warfare, 1500–1700*, New Brunswick.

Mutafcieva, V. 1970. "Περὶ τοῦ ζητήματος τῶν τσιφλικίων εἰς τὴν ὀθωμανικὴν αὐτοκρατορίαν κατὰ τὸν ΙΔʹ–ΙΖʹ αἰῶνα," *Δελτίον Σλαβικῆς Βιβλιογραφίας* 7, pp. 81–117.

Nagata, Y. 1976. *Some Documents on the Big Farms (Çiftliks) of the Notables in Western Anatolia*, Tokyo.

Navari, L. 1991. *From Willibald to Runciman: British Travellers in the Morea*, Monemvasia.

———. 1995. "Vincenzo Coronelli and the Iconography of the Venetian Conquest of the Morea: A Study in Illustrative Methods," *BSA* 90, pp. 505–519.

Nicolle, D. 1983. *Armies of the Ottoman Turks, 1300–1774*, London.

Nixon, L., S. Price, and J. Moody. 1998. "Settlement Patterns in Mediaeval and Post-Mediaeval Sphakia: Issues from the Archaeological and Historical Evidence," http://sphakia.classics.ox.ac.uk/bvtpaper.html (accessed Sept. 30, 2005).

Ökte, E. Z. 1988. *Kitab-i bahriye Piri Reis* 2, Istanbul.

Pacifico, P. A. 1700. *Breve descrizzione corographica del Peloponneso o Morea*, Venice.

———. 1704. *Breve descrizzione corographica del Peloponneso o Morea*, 2nd ed., Venice.

Pamuk, Ş. 2000. *A Monetary History of the Ottoman Empire*, Cambridge.

Panayiotopoulos, V. 1987. *Πληθυσμὸς καὶ οἰκισμοὶ τῆς Πελοποννήσου: 13ος–18ος αἰῶνας*, Athens.

Paolucci, R. 1990. *Le monete dei Dogi di Venezia*, London.

Parry, V. J. 1960. "Barut," in *EI*² 1, pp. 1060–1062.

Paruta, P. 1658. *Historia vinetiana*, pt. 2, trans. Henry, Earl of Monmouth, London.

Parveva, S. 2003. "Agrarian Land and Harvest in South-West Peloponnese in the Early 18th Century," *ÉtBalk* 38, pp. 83–123.

Peytier, E. 1971. *Liberated Greece and the Morea Scientific Expedition: The Peytier Album in the Stephen Vagliano Collection. Presented with an Introduction by Stelios A. Papadopoulos. Notes on the plates by Agapi A. Karakatsani*, Athens.

Pinzelli, E. G. L. 2000. "Les forteresses de Morée: Projets de restaurations et de démantèlements durant la seconde période vénitienne (1687–1715)," *Θησαυρίσματα* 30, pp. 379–427.

Pitcher, D. E. 1972. *A Historical Geography of the Ottoman Empire*, Leiden.

Polemis, D. I. 1981. *Ἱστορία τῆς Ἄνδρου*, Andros.

Politis, N. G. 1912–1913. "Τοπωνυμικά," *Λαογραφία* 4, pp. 575–500.

———. 1915. "Τοπωνυμικά," *Λαογραφία* 5, pp. 249–308, 522–552.

Pouqueville, F. C. H. L. 1820–1821. *Voyage dans la Grèce, comprenant la description ancienne et moderne de l'Épire, de l'Illyrie grecque, de la Macédoine cisaxienne, . . . avec des considérations sur l'archéologie, la numismatique, les moeurs, les arts, l'industrie et le commerce des habitants de ces provinces*, 5 vols., Paris.

———. 1826–1827. *Voyage dans la Grèce: Deuxième édition revue, corrigée et augmentée*, 6 vols., Paris.

Puillon de Boblaye, M. M., and T. Virlet. 1833–1834. *Expédition scientifique de Morée: Section des sciences physiques* 2. *Géographie et géologie*, Paris.

Pulahu, S. 1974. *Defteri i regjistrimit të sanxhakut të Shkodrës i vitit 1485*, Tirana.

Rackham, O., and J. Moody. 1996. *The Making of the Cretan Landscape*, Manchester.

Randolph, B. 1689. *The Present State of the Morea, Called Anciently Peloponnesus: Together with a Description of the City of Athens, Islands of Zant, Strafades, and Serigo. With the Maps of Morea and Greece, and Several Cities. Also a True Prospect of the Grand Serraglio, or Imperial Palace of Constantinople . . . Curiously Engraved on Copper*, 3rd ed., London.

Ranke, Leopold von. 1957. "Die Venezianer in Morea," in *Zur italienischen Geschichte (Leopold von Ranke, Historische Meisterwerke)*, ed. W. Andreas, Hamburg, pp. 127–177.

Raşid, M. 1930. *Tarih-i Raşid*, vols. 4, 6, Istanbul.

Redhouse, J. W. 1890. *A Turkish and English Lexicon Shewing in English the Significations of the Turkish Terms*, Constantinople.

———. 1987. *Turkish and English Lexicon, New Edition*, Beirut.

Rulhière, C. C. de. 1807. *Histoire de l'anarchie de Pologne, et du démembrement de cette république*, 4 vols., Paris.

Rycaut, P. 1700. *The History of the Turks: Beginning with the Year 1679. Being a Full Relation of the Last Troubles in Hungary, with the Sieges of Vienna, and Buda, and All the Several Battles both by Sea and Land, between the Christians and the Turks, until the End of the Year 1698, and 1699. In Which the Peace between the Turks, and the Confederate Christian Princes and States, Was Happily Concluded at Carlowitz in Hungary, by the Mediation of His Majesty of Great Britain, and the States General of the United Provinces. With the Effigies of the Emperors and Others of Note, Engraven at Large upon Copper, Which Compleats the Sixth and Last Edition of the History of the Turks*, London.

Sabry, M. 1930. *L'empire égyptien sous Mohamed-Ali et la question d'orient*, Paris.

Sagredo, G. 1679. *Memorie istoriche de monarchi ottomani*, Venice.

Sahillioğlu, H. 1989. "Akçe," in *İslâm ansiklopedisi* 2, pp. 224–227.

Saïtas, Y. 1999. "La documentation cartographique des trois péninsules méridionales du Péloponnèse élaborée par l'armée française (1829–1832)," in *Enquêtes en Méditerranée: Les expéditions françaises d'Égypte, de Morée et d'Algérie*, ed. M.-N. Bourguet, D. Nordman, V. Panayotopoulos, and M. Sinarellis, Athens, pp. 105–129.

Sakellariou, M. B. 1939. *Ἡ Πελοπόννησος κατὰ τὴν Δευτέραν Τουρκοκρατίαν (1715–1821)* (Texte und Forschungen zur byzantinisch-neugriechischen Philologie 33), Athens.

Salzmann, A. 1993. "An *Ancien Régime* Revisited: 'Privatization' and Political Economy in the Eighteenth-Century Ottoman Empire," *Politics and Society* 21, pp. 393–423.

———. 1995. "Measures of Empire: Tax Farmers and the Ottoman *Ancien Régime, 1695–1807*" (diss. Columbia Univ.).

Sarris, N. 1993. *Προεπαναστατικὴ Ἑλλάδα καὶ Ὀσμανικὸ Κράτος ἀπὸ τὸ χειρόγραφο τοῦ Σουλεϋμὰν Πενὰχ Ἐφέντη τοῦ Μοραΐτη (1785)*, Athens.

Sauerwein, F. 1969. "Das Siedlungsbild der Peloponnes um das Jahr 1700," *Erdkunde* 23, pp. 237–244.

Sayyid Marsot, A. L. el-. 1984. *Egypt in the Reign of Muhammad Ali*, Cambridge.

Schwencke, A. 1854. *Geschichte der hannoverschen Truppen in Griechenland, 1685–1689: Zugleich als Beitrag sur Geschichte der Türkenkriege*, Hannover.

Selânikî Mustafa Efendi. 1989. *Tarih-i Selânikî Mustafâ Efendi* 1: *1563–1595*, ed. M. İpşirli, Istanbul.

Soucek, S. 1996. *Piri Reis and Turkish Mapmaking after Columbus: The Khalili Portolan Atlas* (Studies in the Khalili Collection 2), 2nd ed., London.

Steriotou, I. 2003. "Ὁ πόλεμος τοῦ Μοριᾶ (1684–1697) καὶ ὁ κώδικας τῆς Μαρκιανῆς Βιβλιοθήκης τῆς Βενετίας," *Θησαυρίσματα* 33, pp. 241–283.

Stoianovich, T. 1953. "Land Tenure and Related Sectors of the Balkan Economy, 1600–1800," *Journal of Economic History* 13, pp. 398–411.

Stojkov, R. 1970. "La division administrative de l'eyalet de Roumélie pendant les années soixante du XVIIIᵉ siècle selon un registre turc-ottoman de 1668–1669," *Studia balcanica* 1, pp. 205–227.

Stouraiti, A. 2001. *Memorie di un ritorno: La guerra di Morea (1684–1699) nei manoscritti della Querini Stampalia*, Venice.

Sutton, S. B., ed. 2000. *A Contingent Countryside: Settlement, Economy, and Land Use in the Southern Argolid since 1700*, Stanford.

Svoronos, N. 1956. *Le commerce de Salonique au XVIIIᵉ siècle*, Paris.

Symeonidis, H. P. 1992. *Εἰσαγωγὴ στὴν ἑλληνικὴ ὀνοματολογία*, Thessaloniki.

Tabak, F. 1991. "Agrarian Fluctuations and Modes of Labor Control in the Western Arc of the Fertile Crescent, c. 1700–1850," in Keyder and Tabak 1991, pp. 135–155.

Tanyeli, G. 1996. "Bir osmanlı kalekentinin yapımı: Anavarin örneği," in *Prof. Doğan Kuban a Armağan*, ed. Z. Ahunbay, D. Mazlum, and K. Eyüpgiller, Istanbul, pp. 85–93.

Tombaïdis, D. 1990. Ελληνικά επώνυμα τουρκικής προέλευσης, Athens.

Topping, E. 1969. "Appendix I: Noms de personne," in *Documents sur le régime des terres dans la principauté de Morée, au XIVᵉ siècle*, ed. J. Longnon and P. Topping, Paris, pp. 221–231.

Topping, P. 1972. "The Post-Classical Documents," in McDonald and Rapp 1972, pp. 64–80.

———. 1974. "Domenico Gritti's Relation on the Organization of Venetian Morea, 1688–1691," in *Μνημόσυνον Σοφίας Ἀντωνιάδη*, Venice, pp. 310–328.

———. 1976. "Premodern Peloponnesus: The Land and the People under Venetian Rule," in *Regional Variation in Modern Greece and Cyprus: Toward a Perspective on the Ethnography of Greece*, ed. M. Dimen and E. Friedl, New York, pp. 92–108.

———. 1986. "Latins on Lemnos before and after 1453," in Bryer and Lowry 1986, pp. 225–232.

———. 2000. "The Southern Argolid from Byzantine to Ottoman Times," in *A Contingent Countryside: Settlement, Economy, and Land Use in the Southern Argolid Since 1700*, ed. S. B. Sutton, Stanford, pp. 25–40.

Triandafyllidis, M. 1982. *Τὰ οἰκογενειακὰ μᾶς ὀνόματα*, Thessaloniki.

Tucci, U. 1979. "L'avventura orientale del tallero veneziano nel xviii secolo," *Archivio veneto* 110, 5th series, no. 148, pp. 71–130.

Tulum, T., ed. 1993. *Mühimme defteri 90*, Istanbul.

Uluçay, G. 1980. *Padişahların kadınları ve kızları*, Ankara.

Uzunçarşılı, İ. H. 1956. *Osmanlı tarihi* 4, Ankara.

Vacalopoulos, A. E. 1967. *The Greek Nation, 1453–1669: The Cultural and Economic Background of Modern Greek Society,* trans. I. Moles and P. Moles, New Brunswick.

Van Wersch, H. J. 1972. "The Agricultural Economy," in McDonald and Rapp 1972, pp. 177–187.

Veinstein, G. 1991. "On the *Çiftlik* Debate," in Keyder and Tabak 1991, pp. 35–53.

Veinstein, G., and A. Qaʿidi. 1992. "Ordres originaux et *mühimme defteri,*" in *Mélanges offerts à Louis Bazin,* ed. J. L. Bacqué-Grammont and R. Dor, Paris, pp. 257–274.

Vionis, A. K. 2001. "Post-Roman Pottery Unearthed: Medieval Ceramics and Pottery Research in Greece," *Medieval Ceramics* 25, pp. 84–98.

Vroom, J. 1998. "Early Modern Archaeology in Central Greece: The Contrast of Artefact-Rich and Sherdless Sites," *JMA* 11, pp. 131–164.

———. 2003. *After Antiquity: Ceramics and Society in the Aegean from the Seventh to Twentieth Century A.C.: A Case Study from Boeotia, Central Greece,* Leiden.

Vryonis, S., Jr. 1986. *The Decline of Medieval Hellenism in Asia Minor and the Process of Islamization, from the Eleventh through the Fifteenth Century,* Berkeley.

Wagstaff, M. 1993. "Recent Research on the Settlement and Population of the Morea around 1700," *The Griffon,* ser. 3, no. 1, pp. 73–87.

———. 2001a. "Colonel Leake: Traveller and Scholar," in *Travellers in the Levant: Voyagers and Visionaries* (ASTENE Publications 2), ed.

S. Searight and M. Wagstaff, Durham, U.K., pp. 3–15.

———. 2001b. "Family Size in the Peloponnese (Southern Greece) in 1700," *Journal of Family History* 26, pp. 337–349.

Wagstaff, M., and S. V. Augustson. 1982. "Traditional Land Use," in *An Island Polity: The Archaeology of Exploitation in Melos,* ed. C. Renfrew and J. Wagstaff, Cambridge, pp. 106–133.

Wagstaff, M., and S. Chrysochoou-Stavridou. 1998. "Two Unpublished Maps of the Morea from the Second Venetian Period," in *Πρακτικὰ τοῦ Εʹ Διεθνοῦς Συνεδρίου Πελοποννησιακῶν Σπουδῶν (Ἄργος–Ναύπλιον. 6–10 Σεπτεμβρίου 1995)* 4, Athens, pp. 289–316.

Wagstaff, M., and E. Frangakis-Syrett. 1992. "The Port of Patras in the Second Ottoman Period: Economy, Demography, and Settlements c. 1700–1830," in *Les Balkans à l'époque ottomane* (Revue du monde musulman et de la méditerranée 66), ed. D. Panzac, Aix-en-Provence, pp. 79–94.

Wagstaff, M., L. Sloane, and S. Chrysochoou. 2001–2002. "The Town of Vostizza in A.D. 1700," *Πελοποννησιακά* 26, pp. 35–48.

Weithmann, M. 1991. "Osmanisch-türkische Baudenkmäler auf der Halbinsel Morea, Rhion (Castel Morea), und Pylos (Navarino)," *Münchner Zeitschrift für Balkankunde* 6–7, pp. 219–275.

Westminster, Elizabeth Mary Leveson-Gower Grosvenor, 2nd marchioness of. 1842. *Narrative of a Yacht Voyage in the Mediterranean, during 1840–41,* 2 vols., London.

Woodhouse, C. M. 1965. *The Battle of Navarino,* London.

Wright, D. G. 1999. "Bartolomeo Minio: Venetian Administration in 15th-Century Nauplion" (diss. Catholic Univ. of America).

Wright, J. C., J. F. Cherry, J. L. Davis, E. Mantzourani, S. B. Sutton, and R. F. Sutton Jr. 1990. "The Nemea Valley Archaeological Project: A Preliminary Report," *Hesperia* 59, pp. 579–659.

Zakythinos, D. A. 1953. *Le despotat grec de Morée,* Paris.

Zangger, E., M. Timpson, S. Yazvenko, F. Kuhnke, and J. Knauss. 1997. "The Pylos Regional Archaeological Project, Part II: Landscape Evolution and Site Preservation," *Hesperia* 66, pp. 549–641.

Zarinebaf, F. In preparation. *Murder on the Bosphorus: Sexual Violence and Crime in Eighteenth-Century Istanbul.*

Zarinebaf-Shahr, F. 1991. "Tabriz under Ottoman Rule, 1725–1730" (diss. Univ. of Chicago).

———. 1997. "*Qizilbash* Heresy and Rebellion in Ottoman Anatolia during the Sixteenth Century," *Anatolia Moderna/Yeni Anadolu* 7, pp. 1–15.

———. 1998. "Women and the Public Eye in Eighteenth Century Istanbul," in *Women in the Medieval Islamic World: Power, Patronage, and Piety,* ed. G. R. G. Hambly, New York, pp. 301–324.

———. 2000. "The Wealth of Ottoman Princesses during the Tulip Period," in *The Great Ottoman-Turkish Civilization* 2, ed. K. Çiçek, Ankara, pp. 696–701.

INDEX

RENEWALS 458-4574
DATE DUE

GAYLORD   PRINTED IN U.S.A.